9th Edition

Communication in Our Lives

Julia T. Wood
Lineberger Distinguished Professor of Humanities Emerita
Caroline H. and Thomas S. Royster Distinguished Professor of Graduate Education Emerita
The University of North Carolina at Chapel Hill

Rebecca C. Hains
Professor of Media and Communication
Salem State University, Salem, Massachusetts

Australia • Brazil • Canada • Mexico • Singapore • United Kingdom • United States

***Communication in Our Lives,* Ninth Edition**
Julia T. Wood, Rebecca C. Hains

SVP, Product: Cheryl Costantini

VP, Product: Thais Alencar

Portfolio Product Director: Colin Grover

Portfolio Product Manager: Cinthia Fabian

Product Assistant: Vivian Graham

Learning Designer: Hannah Ells

Content Managers: Joanna Post, Tangelique Williams-Grayer

Digital Project Manager: Allison Marion

Director, Product Marketing: Neena Bali

Product Marketing Manager: Danielle Dornbusch

Content Acquisition Analyst: Deanna Ettinger

Production Service: Lumina Datamatics Ltd.

Designer: Gaby McCracken

Cover Image Source: 184869906 / labsas / GettyImages

For product information and technology assistance, contact us at
Cengage Customer & Sales Support, 1-800-354-9706
or support.cengage.com.

For permission to use material from this text or product, submit all requests online at **www.copyright.com**.

Library of Congress Control Number: 2023903488

Student Edition:
ISBN: 978-0-357-65685-3

Loose-leaf Edition:
ISBN: 978-0-357-65691-4

Cengage
200 Pier 4 Boulevard
Boston, MA 02210
USA

Cengage is a leading provider of customized learning solutions. Our employees reside in nearly 40 different countries and serve digital learners in 165 countries around the world. Find your local representative at **www.cengage.com.**

To learn more about Cengage platforms and services, register or access your online learning solution, or purchase materials for your course, visit **www.cengage.com.**

Printed in the United States of America
Print Number: 01 Print Year: 2023

Brief Contents

Part I: Foundations of Communication

Part II: Contexts of Interaction

Part III: Public Communication

Contents

Part II: Contexts of Interaction

Part III: Public Communication

Preface

"When I was an undergraduate student, I discovered the field of communication. In my first communication course, I realized that communication was more central to my life than anything else I could study. That feeling grew stronger with each communication course I took during my undergraduate and graduate studies." – Julia T. Wood

Julia T. Wood wrote *Communication in Our Lives* to share with students her passion for communication and her belief that it is critically important in our everyday lives as professionals, citizens, and people in personal and social relationships. Since she published the book's first edition in 1996, her unique perspective and voice have made a difference to students in communication classrooms across the nation and around the world. I am honored to support Julia's visionary mission for this, the ninth edition of *Communication in Our Lives*.

Because Julia and I want this book to engage students, we've tried to make it as interesting and substantive as communication itself. We use a conversational style of writing, and all chapters include examples, reflections from students, and applications that invite students to engage material personally. To help students develop their practical competence as communicators, we emphasize concrete skills and hands-on exercises.

Distinguishing Features of *Communication in Our Lives*

Communication in Our Lives has two distinct conceptual emphases. In addition, it includes a number of pedagogical features designed to highlight the relevance of communication to students' everyday lives and experiences. Some of these features have been retained from the eighth edition, and some are new to this ninth edition.

Conceptual Emphases

Two conceptual goals guide this book: (a) to emphasize theories and research developed by scholars of communication and (b) to integrate coverage of diversity, equity, and inclusion as they relate to communication.

Emphasis on Communication Theory, Research, and Skills *Communication in Our Lives* highlights theories, research, and skills developed by scholars of communication. For example, Chapter 7 provides coverage of relational dialectics, a theory primarily developed by Leslie Baxter, a professor of communication at the University of Iowa. Chapter 11 relies on research by scholars of social media such as Sarah J. Jackson (2020) and her colleagues at Northeastern University to sharpen understanding of how various digital technologies are making our lives ever more connected. Chapters 12 through 16 draw on communication scholars' knowledge of effective public communication. For instance, James McCroskey and Jason Teven (1999) have shown that speakers who demonstrate goodwill toward listeners tend to have higher credibility than those who don't. We emphasize the work of communication scholars both because their research is valuable and because we want students to appreciate the intellectual richness of the communication field. Although we highlight the work of communication scholars, we also include relevant research conducted by scholars in fields such as sociology, health care, psychology, business, and anthropology.

Communication scholars have long recognized the profoundly ethical dimensions of human communication. We incorporate this tradition in communication scholarship by calling attention to ethical issues and choices in communication. In addition to identifying ethical aspects of communication in each chapter, we include questions related to ethics at the end of each chapter, signaled with an icon, that focus on ethics.

Integrated Attention to Diversity, Equity, and Inclusion We have woven discussion of diversity, equity, and inclusion into the basic framework of this book, with practical advice on how we can be more equitable and inclusive as communicators. Diversity, equity, and inclusion constitute a significant feature of contemporary life in the United States, and in this book, we respect the lived experiences of people of different ethnicities, ages, genders, physical and mental abilities, sexual orientations, socioeconomic classes, and religious and spiritual commitments.

Communication in Our Lives encourages students to appreciate social diversity as a fact of cultural life that has important implications for our communication with others. Because social diversity affects interaction in all contexts, we incorporate discussion of diverse cultures and communication practices into all chapters of this book. For example, in discussing personal identity in Chapter 3, we point out how social views of race, economic class, gender, and sexual orientation affect self-concept. In so doing, we attend to important ideas such as intersectionality, which Kimberlé Crenshaw developed to articulate how identity categories interact and can compound inequalities. In Chapters 12–16, we also note that effective speaking requires adapting to diverse audiences with varied experiences, backgrounds, and values.

In addition to weaving social diversity into all chapters, Chapter 10 is devoted exclusively to communication and culture. This chapter provides a sustained and focused exploration of the reciprocal relationship between culture and communication—inclusive of concepts new to this edition, such as cultural appropriation.

Changes in This Edition

Like communication, books are dynamic—they evolve over time. In revising this edition of *Communication in Our Lives*, I have attempted to retain the strengths of previous editions while also making changes in response to feedback. Before beginning work on this edition, I read feedback from hundreds of faculty members and students who used previous editions. Their suggestions and comments led me to make a number of changes in this new edition.

One significant change in this edition is **greater integration of digital media** as they affect all forms and contexts of communication. Chapter 11 focuses on media, attending to both mass media and digital media and the blurring of the boundaries between them. In addition, in preparing this edition, I expanded attention to digital media, integrating the role of digital media in communication within every chapter, rather than as a standalone section as in previous editions. The integration of digital media as part of communication in everyday life, rather than as a point of comparison separate to it, reflects today's students' lived experiences in a richly interconnected digital world. It also reflects the realities of the post-Covid-19 workplace for many professionals, who have increasingly needed to communicate with colleagues, supervisors, and clients remotely changing some parts of the equation for effective interpersonal and public communication.

Finally, this edition of *Communication in Our Lives* also reflects changes in scholarship. The current edition includes **more than 350 new references**—more than twice as many as in the eighth edition. Their recency and relevance enrich the textbook and signal my ongoing commitment to up-to-date scholarship and engaging new insights.

In making the above changes, I've been mindful of length. Rather than just adding new material to the former edition, I have weeded out dated material to make room for newer research and discussion of currently timely topics. As a result, this edition is the same length as its predecessor.

Pedagogical Features

In addition to the conceptually distinctive aspects of this book, several features are designed to make it interesting and valuable to students.

Julia and I adopt a *conversational style of writing* rather than the more distant and formal style often used by textbook authors. We share with students some of our experiences in communicating with others, and we invite them to think with us about important issues and difficult challenges surrounding communication in our everyday lives. The accessible, informal writing style encourages students to personally engage the ideas we present.

Student commentaries is another pedagogical feature. Every chapter is enriched by reflections written by students in my classes and other classes around the country who adopted previous editions of this book. The questions, thoughts, and concerns expressed by diverse students invite readers to reflect on their own experiences as communicators. I welcome ideas from students around the country, so students in your class may wish to send their insights to me at rebecca.hains@salemstate.edu for inclusion in future editions of this book.

Communication in Our Lives also includes pedagogical features that promote learning and skill development. Each chapter open with *learning objectives* so that students have a clear sense of how to focus their reading and studying. Within chapters, a *marginal glossary* and *marginal Review It! boxes* summarize key content. At the end of each chapter, exercises encourage students to apply concepts and develop skills discussed in the text. Many of these exercises end with a prompt to the book's online resources, which offer additional opportunities for skill application. Many chapters also include *Communication Highlights*, which call attention to interesting communication research and examples of communication issues in everyday life, and *Communication & Careers*, which focus on connections between communication and professional life.

The chapters conclude with the following features:

- A narrative *Chapter Summary* highlights the main themes throughout the chapter. This feature enables students to see whether what they retained from reading the chapter is consistent with the key content.
- *Experiencing Communication in Our Lives* encourages students to engage ideas actively. These brief scenarios and speeches appear at the end of each chapter to bring to life the ideas and principles presented. Rather than using generic case studies, we wrote the ones used in this book so that they would directly reflect chapter content and provide students with representative examples of communication theories and skills.
- Each chapter continues with a list of *Key Concepts* and then a series of *For Further Reflection and Discussion* questions that encourage students to reflect on and discuss the chapter's material. Each set of these questions includes at least one question that focuses on **ethics.**

Resources for Instructors

MindTap

Today's leading online learning platform, MindTap for Wood/Hains', *Communication in Our Lives*, 9th edition, gives you complete control of your course to craft a personalized, engaging learning experience that challenges students, builds confidence and elevates performance.

MindTap introduces students to core concepts from the beginning of your course using a simplified learning path that progresses from understanding to application and delivers access to eTextbooks, study tools, interactive media, auto-graded assessments and performance analytics.

Use MindTap for Wood/Hains', *Communication in Our Lives*, 9th edition as-is, or personalize it to meet your specific course needs. You can also easily integrate MindTap into your Learning Management System (LMS).

Cengage Infuse

Many instructors struggle with moving their courses online quickly and easily. Whether it's for a last-minute class or total change in course delivery, the ease with which you can organize your class and get yourself and your students acquainted with the materials is key. That's why we built Cengage Infuse, the first and only embedded course kit that lives inside your Learning Management system (LMS).

Cengage Infuse embeds your eTextbook, simple auto-graded comprehension checks and end of chapter quizzes right in your LMS—no need to learn a new technology. As an instructor, you can customize the content and personalize student feedback, or use it as is to complement your existing course materials. From course setup to course management and tracking student progress, you and your students never have to leave your LMS to access high-quality, pre-organized publisher content.

Cengage Infuse helps you get your course online in 15 minutes or less—and provides you with everything you need and nothing you don't—all within the LMS you already use.

Supplements

Instructor resources for this product are available online. Instructor assets include an Instructor's Manual, Educator's Guide, PowerPoint® slides, and a test bank powered by Cognero®. Sign up or sign in at www.cengage.com to search for and access this product and its online resources.

Acknowledgments

All books reflect the efforts of many people, and *Communication in Our Lives* is no exception. A number of people have helped this book evolve from an early vision to the final form you hold in your hands. I am grateful to my product manager, Cinthia Fabian, for her support and for her management of the team that worked on this book. I am also especially indebted to content managers, Joanna Post and Tangelique Williams-Grayer. They have been active partners in the project.

I am also grateful to the people who reviewed the previous editions of this book, who have been most generous in offering suggestions for improving the book, and to our external reviewers, who read the current edition manuscript with an eye to subject matter and to diversity, equity, and inclusion.

Julia has noted that she could not have written prior editions of this book without her undergraduate students, and I feel the same way about my students' importance to the revision process. My classroom experiences have helped me refine the ideas, activities, examples, and diverse sources that appear in this book. Invariably, my students teach me at least as much as I teach them, and they inspire me in countless ways. For that, I am deeply grateful.

Finally, I wish to thank my friends and family who are sources of personal support, insight, challenges, and experience. They help me to be a better writer, scholar, and advocate.

Rebecca C. Hains
March 2023
Salem, MA

About the Authors

Julia T. Wood joined the faculty at the University of North Carolina at Chapel Hill when she was 24. During her 37 years on the faculty, she taught classes and conducted research on personal relationships as well as gender, communication, and culture. She was named the Lineberger Distinguished Professor of Humanities and the Caroline H. and Thomas S. Royster Distinguished Professor of Graduate Education. In addition to publishing 25 books and 100 articles and book chapters, she has presented more than 100 papers at professional conferences and campuses around the country. Her accolades include 14 awards honoring her teaching and 16 awards recognizing her scholarship. She received her B.A. from North Carolina State University, her M.A. from the University of North Carolina at Chapel Hill, and her Ph.D. from The Pennsylvania State University.

Rebecca C. Hains is a professor at Salem State University in Salem, Massachusetts, in the Department of Media and Communication, where she teaches an array of media studies and experiential learning courses. She researches children's media culture from a critical/cultural studies perspective, taking an intersectional approach to exploring media representation, identity, and meaning-making. In addition to publishing 5 books and more than 20 scholarly articles and book chapters, she has given more than 50 presentations about her research at professional conferences and campuses. Amplifying her work's impact, she has served as a consultant for major children's brands and has been an expert commentator in national and international media, from news outlets to documentary films. Honors include a Fulbright award to Poland for 2023–2024; her appointment as a Faculty Fellow for Diversity, Equity and Inclusion at Salem State; and special selection by the White House Council on Women and Girls to join their White House Research Conference on Girls. She received her B.A. from Emmanuel College, her M.S. from Boston University, and her Ph.D. from Temple University.

Kollett/Shutterstock.com

Introduction

- A friend comes to you with a problem, and you want to show that you support them.
- A group you belong to is working on recycling programs for the campus, and you're frustrated by the group's inefficiency. You want to make meetings more productive.
- At the end of the term, the person you've been seeing will graduate and take a job in a city 1,000 miles away, and you wonder how to stay connected across the distance.
- You met an interesting person online. At first, you enjoyed interacting with them, but lately they've been texting you incessantly, and you feel they're intrusive.
- The major project in one of your courses is an oral research report, so your grade depends on your ability to present a good speech.

Situations like these illustrate the importance of communication in our lives. Unlike some of the subjects you study, communication is relevant to every aspect of your life. We communicate with ourselves when we work through ideas, psych ourselves up to meet challenges, and rehearse ways to approach someone about a difficult issue. We communicate with others to build and sustain personal relationships, to perform our jobs and advance our careers, to connect with friends and meet new people online, and to participate in social and civic activities. Every facet of life involves communication.

Although we communicate all the time, we don't always communicate effectively. People who have inadequate communication knowledge and skills are hampered in their efforts to achieve personal, professional, and social goals. On the other hand, people who communicate well have a keen advantage in accomplishing their objectives. This suggests that learning about communication and learning how to communicate are keys to effective living.

Communication in Our Lives is designed to help you understand how communication works in your personal, professional, and social life. To open the book, we'll describe the basic approach and special features of *Communication in Our Lives.*

Introduction to Julia Wood

As first author listed on this text, I'd like to take a moment to introduce myself. As an undergraduate, I enrolled in a course much like the one you're taking now. In that course, I discovered the field of communication, and my interest in it has endured and grown in the years since I took that class. Communication is the basis of cultural life, and it is a primary tool for personal, social, civic, and professional satisfaction and growth. It is a field that is both theoretically rich and exceptionally practical. I know of no discipline that offers more valuable insights, skills, and knowledge.

Because you will be reading this book, you should know something about the person who wrote it. I am a middle-class, Caucasian heterosexual woman. As is true for all of us, who I am affects what I know and how I think, act, interact, and write. My race, gender, social–economic class, and sexual orientation have given me certain kinds of insight and obscured others. As a woman, I understand discrimination based on sex because I've experienced it personally. I do not have personal knowledge of racial discrimination because Western culture confers privilege on European Americans. Being middle class has shielded me from personal experience with hunger, poverty, and class bias; and my heterosexuality has spared me from being a direct target of homophobic prejudice. Who you are also influences your experiences, knowledge, and ways of communicating.

Although identity limits our personal knowledge and experiences, it doesn't completely prevent insight into people and situations different from our own. From conversations with others and from reading, we can gain some understanding of people and circumstances different from our own. What we learn by studying and interacting with a range of people expands our appreciation of the richness and complexity of humanity. In addition, learning about people different from us enlarges our personal repertoire of communication skills and our appreciation of the range of ways to communicate.

Introduction to *Communication in Our Lives*

The aim of *Communication in Our Lives* is to introduce you to many forms and functions of communication in modern life. The title reflects our belief that communication is an important part of our everyday lives. Each chapter focuses on a specific kind of communication or a particular context in which we communicate.

Coverage

Because communication is a continuous part of life, we need to understand how it works—or doesn't—in a range of situations. Therefore, this book covers a broad spectrum of communication encounters, including communication with yourself, interaction with friends and romantic partners, work in groups and teams, interaction in organizations, mass and social media, interaction between and inclusion of people with diverse cultural backgrounds, and public speaking. The breadth of communication issues and skills presented in this book can be adapted to the interests and preferences of individual classes and instructors.

Students

Communication in Our Lives is written for anyone interested in human communication. If you are a communication major, this book and the course it accompanies will provide you with a firm foundation for more advanced study. If you are majoring in another discipline, this book and the course you are taking will give you a sound basic understanding of communication and opportunities to strengthen your skills as a communicator.

Learning should be a joy, not a chore. This book's style is informal and personal; for instance, as co-authors, we each refer to ourselves as *I* rather than *the author*, and we use contractions (*can't* and *you're* instead of the more formal *cannot* and *you are*), as we do in normal conversation. We also punctuate chapters with concrete examples and insights from students at campuses around the country.

Theory and Practice

Years ago, renowned scholar Kurt Lewin said, "There is nothing so practical as a good theory." His words remain true today. In this book, we've blended theory and practice so that each draws on and enriches the other. Effective practice is theoretically informed: It is based on knowledge of how and why the communication process works and what is likely to result from different kinds of communication. At the same time, effective theories have pragmatic value: They help us understand experiences and events in our everyday lives. Each chapter in this book is informed by the theories and research generated by scholars of communication.

Features

The following key features accent this edition:

Integrated Attention to Diversity, Equity, and Inclusion

Diversity, equity, and inclusion are woven into the fabric of this book. Awareness of diversity, equity, and inclusion—or "DEI" for short—is integral to how we communicate and think about communication; it is not an afterthought. We integrate DEI into the text in several ways. First, each chapter includes research on diverse people and highlights our commonalities and differences. Second, the photos we chose for this book include people of different races, ages, genders, body types, religions, and so forth. Likewise, each chapter includes examples from a range of people.

In addition to incorporating diversity into the book as a whole, in Chapter 10, we focus exclusively on communication and culture. There you will learn about cultures and social communities (distinct groups within a single society) and the ways cultural values and norms shape how we view and practice communication. Just as important, Chapter 10 will heighten your awareness of the power of communication to shape and change cultures, and learn about exploitative practices such as cultural appropriation. It will enhance your ability to participate effectively in a culturally diverse world.

To talk about social groups is to risk stereotyping. Throughout this book, we try to provide you with reliable information on social groups and their lived experiences while avoiding stereotyping. We rely on research by members of groups being discussed whenever that is available. We also use qualifying terms, such as *most* and *in general*, to remind us that there are exceptions to generalizations.

Student Commentaries

In our classes, our students teach us and each other by sharing their insights, experiences, and questions. Because we've witnessed how much students learn from one another, we've included reflections written by students at our universities and other campuses, sometimes adding questions for reflection or discussion immediately afterwards. As you read the student commentaries, you'll probably identify with some, disagree with others, and be puzzled by still others. Whether you agree, disagree, or are perplexed, we think you'll find that the student commentaries valuably expand the text by adding to the voices and views it represents. In the students' words, you will find much insight and much to spark thought and discussion in your classes and elsewhere. You may have insights about material covered in this book. If so, we invite you to send your commentaries to Rebecca Hains (Rebecca.Hains@salemstate.edu), so that she might include them in the next edition of this book.

Learning Aids

We've created three features to assist you in identifying and retaining key concepts and ideas as you read. First, each chapter opens with Learning Objectives, which you may use to guide how you read and study the chapter. Second, key terms are highlighted and defined in margins of chapters. Third, you will find Review It! boxes in the margins of the book. These summarize material you've read. By reviewing them, you increase your retention of content.

Communication and Careers

Most chapters include one or more "Communication and Careers" features. These highlight the connections between communication principles and practices and professional paths you may pursue. This feature will enlarge your understanding of the role of communication in shaping organizations, the importance of good communication in building and maintaining effective relationships with coworkers, clients, patients, and customers.

Communication Highlights

Most chapters also include several "Communication Highlights," which call your attention to especially interesting findings from communication research and news reports involving communication in everyday life. The "Communication Highlights" offer springboards for class discussions.

Experiencing Communication in Our Lives

Following each chapter is a case study, "Experiencing Communication in Our Lives." With each one, we invite you to think about how principles and skills we discuss in that chapter show up in everyday life. We ask a few questions about the case study that allow you to apply what you have learned in a chapter to analyzing real-life communication and developing strategies for improving interaction.

We hope you enjoy reading this book as much as we have enjoyed writing it. We also hope that this book and the class it accompanies will help you develop the skills needed for communication in your life. If so, then we all will have spent our time well.

Julia T. Wood
Rebecca C. Hains

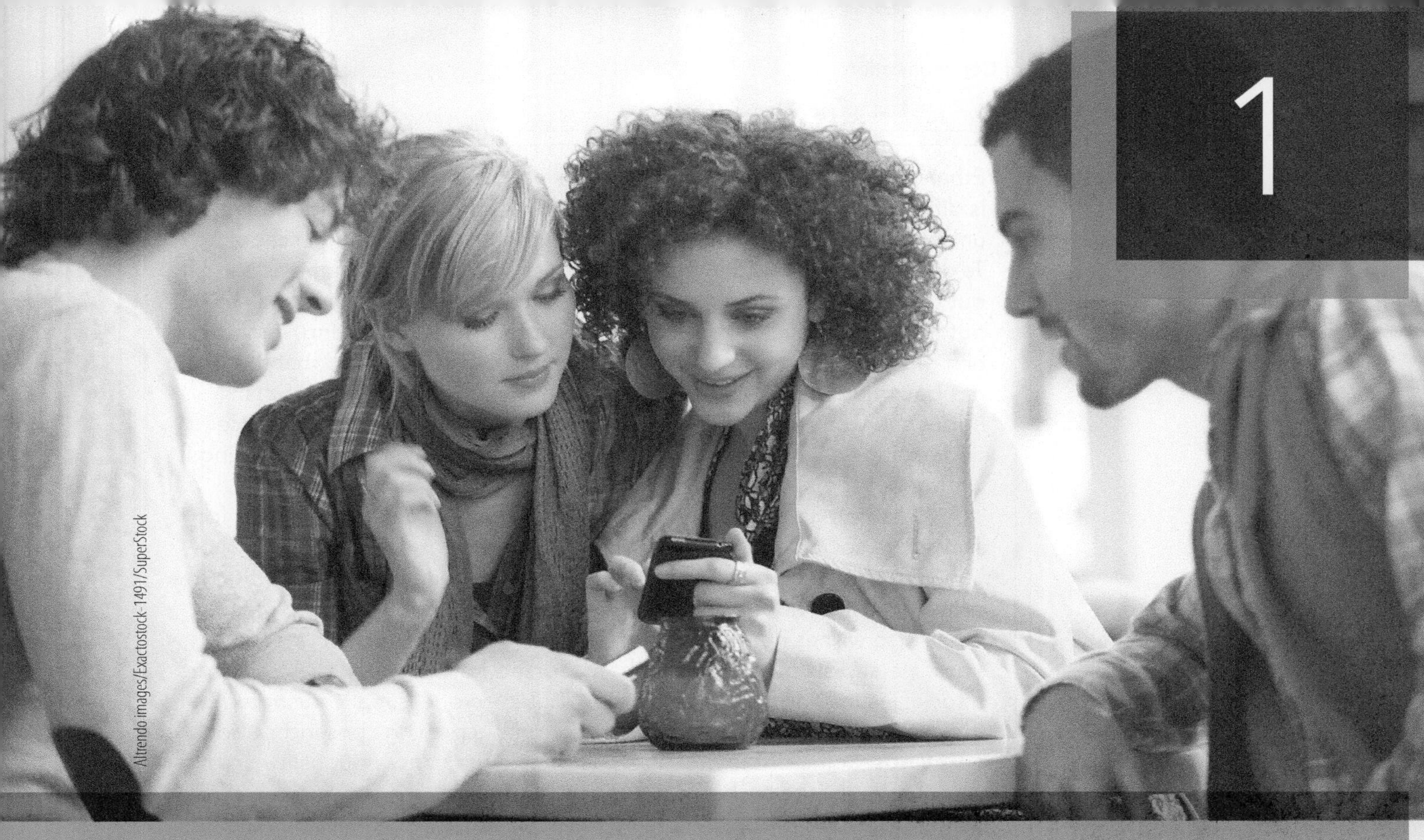

Altrendo images/Exactostock-1491/SuperStock

The World of Communication

> The way we communicate with others and with ourselves ultimately determines the quality of our lives.
>
> **Anthony Robbins**

How does communication affect your life the most?

Learning Objectives

After studying the topics in this chapter, you should be able to:

1. Describe the communication process.
2. Identify the types of human communication.
3. Explain the integration of human needs and communication.
3. Define communication in the context of human interaction.
5. Analyze the relationship between media, technology, and communication.

Ethan pockets his phone and shakes his head; staying in touch with Caleb is different now that they live 800 miles apart. Because they attend different universities, they have drifted away from each other since high school: Texting and playing video games together online isn't the same as hanging out together. Shrugging, he skims his news feed while getting ready to go out with Chloe. The top story is about another school shooting, reminding him of the active shooter drills he grew up with. He's worried that the world has become pretty violent. Turning his thoughts back to Chloe, Ethan hopes she won't want to talk about their relationship again tonight. He understands analyzing and discussing their relationship when something is wrong, but she also likes to talk about it when everything is fine.

While he's getting ready, Ethan thinks about his oral presentation for Thursday's sociology class. He has some good ideas, but he doesn't know how to turn them into an effective speech. He vaguely remembers that the professor talked about how to organize a speech, but he wasn't listening. Ethan also wishes he knew how to deal with a group that can't get on track. He and six other students have worked for three months to organize a social justice and equity association, but everyone is really frustrated by the campus climate, and they're having trouble gaining consensus about next steps. Some of the organizers dominate the conversations, while other voices seem not to be heard. His phone alerts him to a new message from a member of the group, who is worried that the others aren't as committed as they are to the project. Ethan decides to answer later and leaves to meet Chloe.

Like Ethan, most of us communicate continually in our daily lives. Effective communication is vital to friendships, romantic relationships, public speaking, participation in civic life, interviewing, classroom learning, and productive group work. Communication opportunities and demands fill our everyday lives.

Long after the college years, Ethan—and the rest of us—will rely on communication. You may need to talk with clients or patients, make progress reports, work on teams, and present proposals. You may represent your company at a press conference or team up with colleagues to develop company policies. You will have conflicts with coworkers, supervisors, and subordinates. Beyond your career, you'll communicate with family members, friends, neighbors, and civic and community groups.

Why Study Communication?

Communication is one of the most popular fields of undergraduate study. One reason for this popularity is that effective communication is important in all aspects of life. In 2015, the Pew Research Center reported that adults rank communication skills as number 1 for getting ahead in life—more important than writing, reading, math, science, and other skills (Goo, 2015). Recent studies continue to report that communication is widely regarded as a crucial skill in today's workplace and society (Parker & Rainie, 2020), with Georgetown University finding that communication is consistently the labor market's most in-demand competency (Georgetown, 2020), as shown in Figure 1.1.

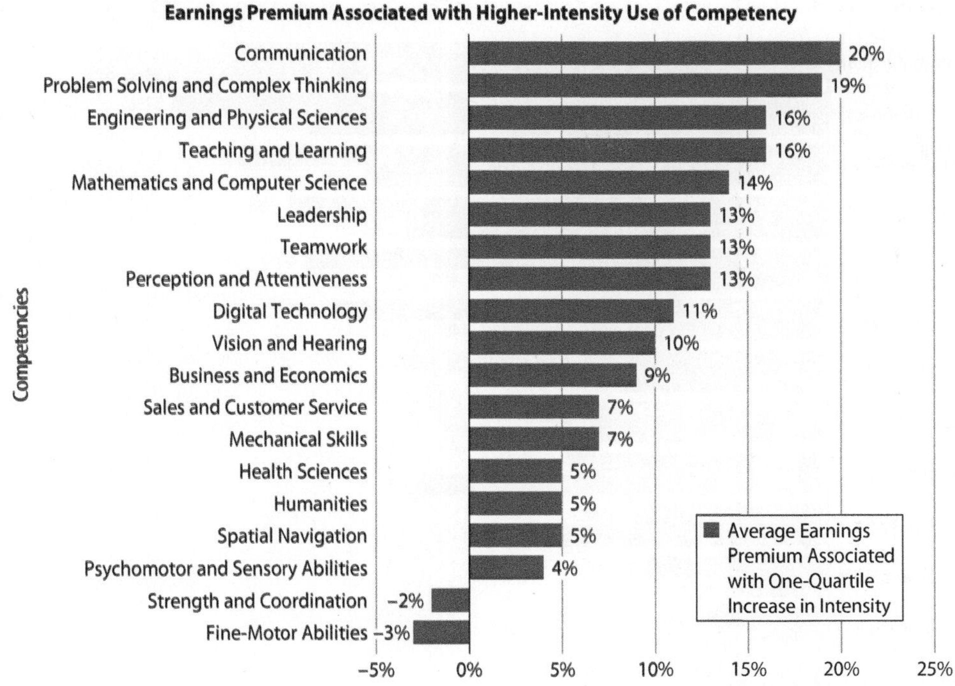

Figure 1.1
When people use communication skills intensely in their jobs, they tend to earn more than employees who intensely use other competencies. Jobs that require people to intensely use other competencies are associated with lower pay.

In fact, the Georgetown study noted that communication skills are so valuable that the more intensely employees use those skills, the higher their earnings tend to be. Figure 1.2 illustrates this finding.

Fortunately, communication skills can be learned, like all other skills, and even those who are already good communicators can become better. For example, some people have a natural aptitude for playing basketball. They become even more effective, however, if they study theories of offensive and defensive play and if they practice skills. Likewise, even if you communicate well now, learning about communication and practicing communication skills can make you more effective (Hargie, 2018).

Another reason to study communication is that theories and principles help us make sense of what happens in our lives, and they help us have personal impact. For instance, if Ethan learned about different gender communities, he might understand why Chloe enjoys talking about relationships, even when things are going well—as do many cisgendered heterosexual woman. If Ethan had better insight into the communication that sustains long-distance relationships, he might be able to enrich his friendship with Caleb—despite the miles between them. If he knew how to develop an agenda, he might be able to help his collaborators find common ground—and launch the student group they envision. Studying public speaking could help Ethan design a good presentation for his class report. Learning to listen better would help Ethan retain information like his professor's tips on organizing oral reports. Communication theory and skills would help Ethan maximize his effectiveness in all spheres of his life.

Communication in Our Lives will help you become a more confident and competent communicator. Part One clarifies how communication works (or doesn't work) and explains how the overall communication process is affected by perception, personal identity, language, listening, and nonverbal communication (meaning self-expression that happens without or in addition to words, such as

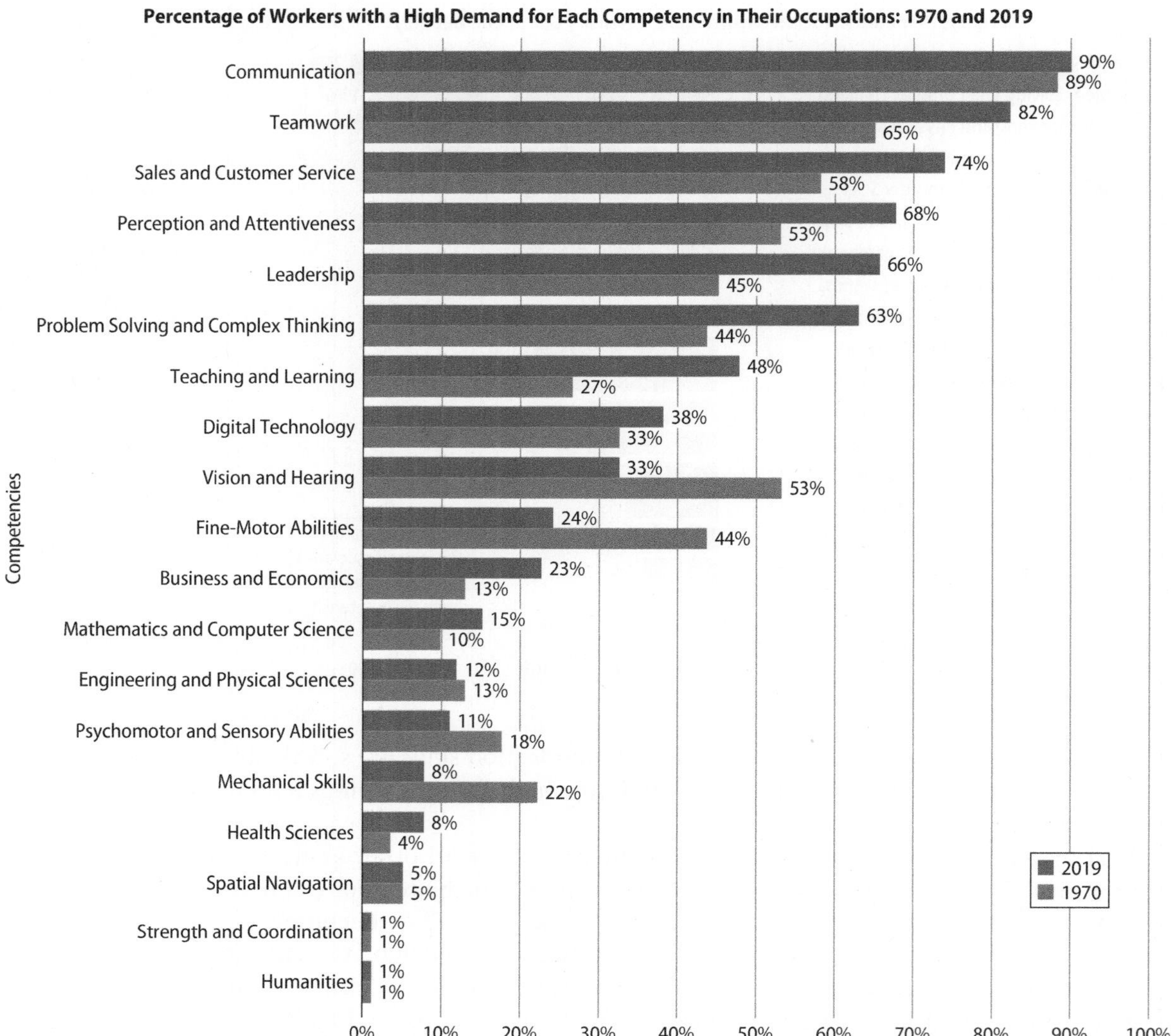

Figure 1.2
For decades, communication has been the most highly demanded workplace competency. In 1970, 89 percent of employees worked in occupations with a high demand for communication; by 2019, that percentage had reached 90 percent.

tone of voice and body language). In Part Two, we'll look at communication in five contexts: personal relationships, small groups, organizations, cultures, and mediated environments. Part Three focuses on public speaking.

This chapter lays a foundation for your study of communication. We'll first define communication. Next, we'll discuss the values of communication in many spheres of your life. Then we'll examine some models of communication to clarify how the process works. In the third section of the chapter, we'll describe the breadth of the communication field and careers for communication specialists.

Defining Communication

communication A systemic process in which people interact with and through symbols to create and interpret meanings.

Communication* is a systemic process in which people interact with and through symbols to create and interpret meanings. Let's elaborate the key parts of this definition.

*Boldfaced terms are defined in the margins and also in the glossary at the end of the book.

Communication is a **process**, which means it is ongoing and always in motion, moving ever forward and changing continually. It's hard to tell when communication starts and stops because what happened long before we talk with someone may influence interaction, and what occurs in a particular encounter may have repercussions in the future. We cannot freeze communication at any one moment.

process Something that is ongoing and continuously in motion, the beginnings and endings of which are difficult to identify. Communication is a process.

Communication is also systemic because it occurs within a **system** of interrelated parts that affect one another. In family communication, for instance, each member of the family is part of the system (Yoshimura & Galvin, 2017). In addition, the physical environment and the time of day are elements of the system that affect interaction. People interact differently in a formal living room and on a beach, and we may be more alert at certain times of day than at others. If a family has a history of listening sensitively and working out problems constructively, and then when one family member says, "There's something we need to talk about," the comment is unlikely to cause defensiveness. On the other hand, if the family has a record of nasty conflicts, then the same comment might arouse strong defensiveness. A lingering kiss might be an appropriate way to show affection in a private setting, but the same action would raise eyebrows in an office. To interpret communication, we have to consider the system in which it takes place.

system A group of interrelated elements that affect one another. Communication is systemic.

Our definition of communication also emphasizes **symbols**, which include all languages and many nonverbal behaviors, as well as art and music. Anything that abstractly signifies something else can be a symbol. We might symbolize love by giving a ring and saying "I love you" or by embracing. Later in this chapter, we'll have more to say about symbols. For now, just remember that human communication involves interaction with and through symbols.

symbol An arbitrary, ambiguous, and abstract representation of a phenomenon. Symbols are the basis of language, much nonverbal behavior, and human thought.

Finally, our definition focuses on meanings, which are the heart of communication. Meanings are the significance we bestow on phenomena—what they signify to us. Meanings are not in phenomena. Instead, meaning grows out of our interaction with symbols.

There are two levels of meaning in communication. The **content level of meaning** is the literal message. For example, if someone says to you, "Get out of here!" the content level of meaning is that you should leave the immediate area. The **relationship level of meaning** expresses the relationship between communicators. In our example, if the person who says, "Get out of here!" is a friend and is smiling, then you would probably interpret the relationship level of meaning as indicating that the person likes you and is kidding around—perhaps expressing good-natured disbelief or surprise at a story you just shared. On the other hand, if the person who says, "Get out of here!" is your supervisor, and they are responding to your request for a raise, then you might interpret the relationship level of meaning as indicating that your supervisor regards you as inferior and doesn't think your work merits a raise.

content level of meaning One of the two levels of meaning in communication. The content level of meaning is the literal, or denotative, information in a message.

relationship level of meaning One of the two levels of meaning in communication; expresses the relationship between communicators.

Values of Communication

From birth to death, communication shapes our personal, professional, civic, and social lives as well as the culture in which we live (Galvin, Braithwaite, & Bylund, 2015; Holt-Lunstad, Smith, & Layton, 2010; Salas & Frush, 2012). In order to advance a career, you'll need to know how to present your ideas effectively, build good relationships with colleagues, monitor your perceptions, manage conflicts constructively, and listen carefully. To have healthy, enduring relationships, you'll need to know how to listen well, communicate support, deal with conflicts, and understand communication styles that are different from your own. To be an engaged citizen, you'll need to express your points of view articulately, and you'll need to listen critically yet open-mindedly to others' ideas, respecting the lived experiences and cultural norms of people from backgrounds and communities different from your own.

Personal Identity and Health

George Herbert Mead (1934)* said that humans are "talked into" humanity. He meant that we gain personal identity as we communicate with others. In the earliest years of our lives, family members tell us who we are: "You're smart." "You're strong." "You're a clown." Later, we interact with teachers, friends, romantic partners, and coworkers who communicate how they perceive us. Thus, how we perceive ourselves reflects the views of us that others communicate.

The profound connection between identity and communication is dramatically evident in children who have been deprived of human contact. It would violate research ethics to conduct experiments depriving children of interaction with others, but on occasion, it has been possible to consider the cases of children who were isolated from others for long periods of time. Such case studies reveal that they lacked a healthy self-concept, and their mental and psychological development were severely hindered by lack of language (Shattuck, 1980).

A large body of research shows that communicating with others promotes health and reduces the risk of premature mortality, whereas social isolation can cause stress, disease, behavioral patterns, and early death (Holt-Lunstad, 2020; Smith & Pollak, 2021). Families that practice good communication are more cohesive and stable (Galvin & Braithwaite, 2015). College students who are in healthy, non-abusive, committed relationships tend to enjoy a greater sense of well-being (Gómez-López et al., 2019). Life-threatening medical problems are also affected by healthy interaction with others. Heart disease is more common among people who lack strong interpersonal relationships (Holt-Lunstad, 2020). Clearly, healthy interaction with others is important to our physical and mental well-being.

Communication skills are also essential to effective health care. Patients need to be able to communicate clearly with health care professionals to explain their concerns and symptoms—or have access to advocates like community health workers, who can communicate well with practitioners to help clarify the patients' needs. Moreover, doctors, nurses, dentists, and others involved in health care need to be able to communicate with patients from a wide range of backgrounds and identities. Practitioners who are skilled in listening and communicating in an understandable way can help decrease health care disparities and improve health equity among diverse groups of people (Ratanawongsa et al., 2021).

Relationship Values

Daniel Goleman, author of *Social Intelligence* (2007), says humans are "wired to connect" (p. 4). And communication is the primary way that we connect with others. Marriage counselors and researchers have long emphasized the importance of communication for healthy, enduring relationships (Farr et al., 2020;

*We are using the American Psychological Association's (APA) method of citation. For example, if you read "Mead (1934)," we are referencing a work by Mead that was written in 1934. If you read "Mead (1934, p. 10)" or "(Mead, 1934, p. 10)," we are referencing page 10 specifically of Mead's 1934 work. The full bibliographic citations for all works appear in the References section at the end of the book.

Gottman, 1994a, 1994b; Skipper et al., 2021). They point out that while all relationships encounter challenges and conflict, effective communication is a major distinction between relationships that endure and those that collapse.

Communication is important for more than solving problems or making disclosures. For most of us, everyday talks and nonverbal interactions are the very essence of relationships (Duck & McMahon, 2012; Goleman, 2011; Wood & Duck, 2006). Unremarkable, everyday interaction sustains intimacy more than the big moments, such as declarations of love. By sharing news about mutual acquaintances and discussing ordinary topics, partners keep up the steady pulse of their relationship (Duck, 2006; Schmidt & Uecker, 2007; Wood, 2006a). Although nonverbal communication can make a difference in text-based messages, such as private messages and instant messaging offered on various apps (Darics, 2017), a big challenge in long-distance relationships is not being able to share small talk.

Myca Last year, I did study abroad, and it was really hard to stay connected with my friends and family. I was in the Philippines so it was night here when it was day there—forget texting back and forth quickly. Plus, the Internet was spotty so sometimes I couldn't get on to share something cool that was happening in the moment. That was the hardest part—not being able to share the little things when they happened.

Question: Although Myca could text her friends and family while in the Philippines, her texts were out of sync with her friends. Have you ever found yourself out of sync with important or exciting group text threads—maybe while at work, in class, or in transit? How did you feel about it, and why?

Professional Values

Communication is among the most popular majors because communication skills are closely linked to professional success. Communication's importance is obvious in professions such as patient care, teaching, business, law, sales, and counseling, in which talking and listening are prominent.

In other fields, the importance of communication is less obvious but nonetheless present. Most employers list communication skills among the top qualities they seek in job candidates (Buffett, 2022; GMAC Research, 2020). Doctors who do not listen well are less effective in treating patients, and they're more likely to be sued than doctors who listen well (Levine, 2004; Milia, 2003). Poor communication is understood as a significant factor in the health care disparities that plague the United States, including higher death rates for Black infants and Black women in childbirth than their White counterparts (Butler & Sheriff, 2021). Communication has such a pivotal role in the quality and outcomes of health care that the Association of American Medical Colleges includes oral and written communication alike on its list of 15 core competencies for entering medical students (Association of American Medical Colleges, 2022).

In the workplace, poor communication means that errors and misunderstandings occur, messages must be repeated, productivity suffers, and—sometimes—people lose jobs. No matter what your career goals are, developing strong communication skills will enhance your professional success.

Cultural Values

Communication skills are important to our society's health. For a democracy to be effective, people must be able to express ideas and evaluate the ideas of others. One event typical of presidential election years is a debate between or among candidates. To make informed judgments, viewers need to think critically about which questions are prioritized and asked, and to listen critically to candidates' arguments and their responses to criticism and questions. We also need listening skills to grasp and evaluate opposing points of view on issues such as abortion, environmental policies, immigration, equity, and health care reform. To be a good community member, you need skills in expressing your point of view and responding to those of others.

Life in our era is characterized by increasing racial, ethnic, and cultural diversity. For example, in 2000, 64% of Americans identified as Caucasian (Milbank, 2014), but in the 2020 Census, that number declined to 61.6%—the first reported decline in the White population in United States history (Jones et al., 2021; The Learning Network, 2022). Furthermore, among people younger than age 18, a minority identified as White; the majority checked either Asian, Black, Hispanic, or multirace—a big change from 2010, when 65% of United States children were White (Tavernise & Gebeloff, 2021). This makes it more important than ever to learn how to communicate and interact with people whose backgrounds are different from our own with understanding and sensitivity—practices sometimes called **cultural competency** and/or **cultural humility** (Greene-Morton & Minkler, 2019; Khan, 2021).

cultural competency Being interculturally proficient, able to communicate effectively and appropriately with people of other cultural backgrounds.

cultural humility Being open-minded about cultural differences, approaching others in a humble and respectful manner with a willingness to learn and an awareness of one's own cultural biases.

In addition, approximately 4.6% of the students enrolled in United States colleges and universities are international students. Representing about 200 countries, their enrollment totaled 1,075,496 in the 2019–2020 academic year (Fwd. us, 2021). United States-born students benefit from the presence of peers from around the globe: exposure to students from a range of backgrounds has been noted as one of the best predictors of whether first-year college students return for a second year (Berrett, 2011).

Communication & Careers

Poor Communication = Preventable Death

Determining whether a hospitalized patient's death would have preventable with better medical care is challenging. Various studies estimate the number of preventable deaths in the United States to be 22,000 per year; 44,000–98,000 per year; and even 250,000 per year (Hathaway, 2020). On a global scale, estimates rise to as many as 5 million per year (Schreiber, 2018). But one thing is clear: Whatever the number, it's too high—and a percentage of those deaths, perhaps as many as one third, can be traced to poor communication among doctors, nurses, and other members of health care teams (Graham, 2018; Schreiber, 2018). This disturbing fact has made effective team work and oral and written communication a priority in training health care providers (Association of American Medical Colleges, 2022; Salas & Frush, 2012).

As a result, many medical schools now base admissions not only on academic record but also on communication competencies and the ability to collaborate with others. In addition, they require students to take courses in teamwork.

Ava There are so many people from different cultures on this campus that you can't get by without knowing how to communicate in a whole lot of ways. In my classes and my dorm, there are lots of Asian students and some Hispanic ones, and they communicate differently than people raised in the United States. If I don't learn about their communication styles, I can't get to know them or learn about what they think.

Ava is right. When she was a student in one of my courses, she and I talked several times about the concern she expresses in her commentary. Ava realized she needed to learn to interact with people who differ from her if she is to participate fully in today's world. She has learned a lot about communicating with diverse people, and no doubt she will learn more in the years ahead. Like Ava, you can improve your ability to communicate effectively with the variety of people who make up our society.

Communication, then, is important for personal, relationship, professional, and cultural reasons. Because communication is a cornerstone of human life, your choice to study it will serve you well. To understand what's involved in communication, let's now define the process.

Review It!

Values of Studying Communication:

- Personal
- Relationship
- Professional
- Cultural

Models of Communication

Over the years, scholars in communication have developed a number of models, which reflect increasingly sophisticated understandings of the communication process.

Linear Models

One of the first models (Laswell, 1948) described communication as a linear, or one-way, process in which one person acted on another person. This model

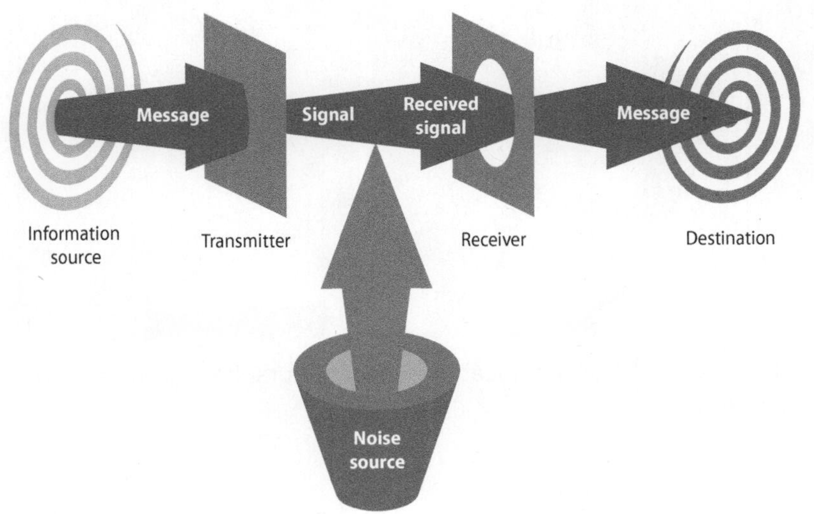

Figure 1.3
A Linear Model of Communication

Source: Adapted from Shannon, C., & Weaver, W. (1949). *The Mathematical Theory of Communication*. Urbana: University of Illinois Press.

consisted of five questions that described early views of how communication worked:

Who?
Says what?
In what channel?
To whom?
With what effect?

noise Anything that interferes with intended communication.

A year later, Shannon and Weaver (1949) advanced a model that included **noise**, which is anything that can interfere with the intended message. Figure 1.3 shows two versions of the Shannon and Weaver's model. Although linear models were useful starting points, they were too simple to capture the complexity of most kinds of human communication.

Interactive Models

The major shortcoming of linear models was that they portrayed communication as flowing in only one direction, from a sender to a receiver. This suggests that speakers only speak and never listen and that listeners only listen and never send messages.

feedback Response to a message; may be verbal, nonverbal, or both. In communication theory, the concept of feedback appeared first in interactive models of communication.

Realizing that receivers respond to senders and senders attend to receivers led communication theorists (Schramm, 1955) to adapt models to include **feedback**. Feedback may be verbal, nonverbal, or both, and it may be intentional or unintentional. Research has confirmed Schramm's insight that feedback is important.

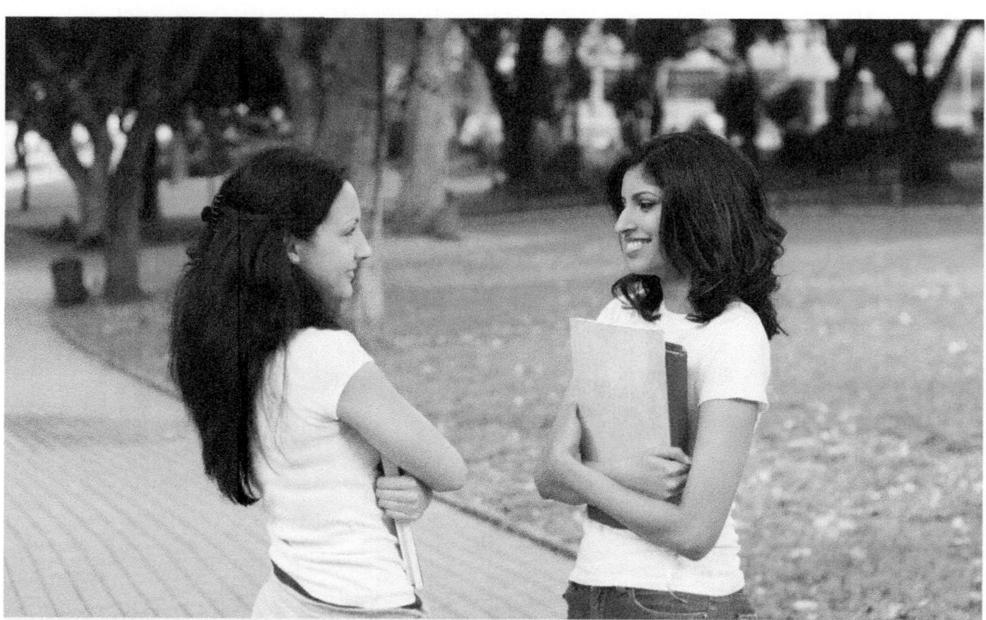

Verbal and nonverbal communication reflect cultural backgrounds and understandings.
michaeljung/shutterstock.com

Supervisors report that communication accuracy and on-the-job productivity rise when they encourage their subordinates to give feedback: ask questions, comment on supervisors' messages, and respond to supervisory communication (Deal & Kennedy, 1999).

The interactive model also shows that communicators create and interpret communication within their personal fields of experience. This recognizes communication as an interactive process in which both senders and receivers participate actively (Figure 1.4).

Figure 1.4
An Interactive Model of Communication
Source: Adapted from Schramm, W. (1955). *The Process and Effects of Mass Communication.* Urbana: University of Illinois Press.

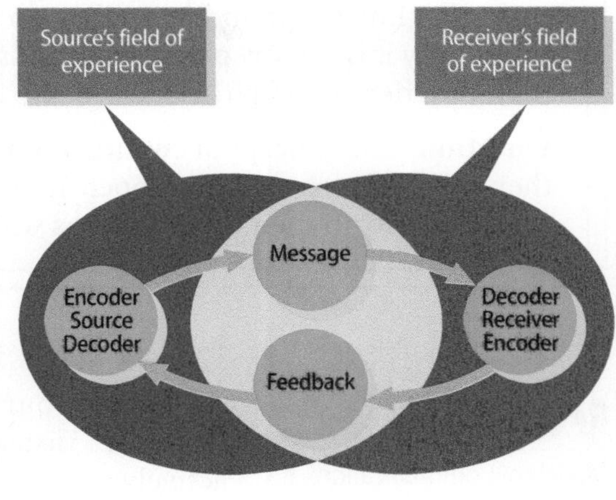

Transactional Models

A serious limitation of interactive models is that they don't acknowledge that everyone involved in communication both sends and receives messages, often simultaneously. While giving a press release, a speaker watches reporters to determine whether they seem interested; both the speaker and the reporters are "listening," and both are "speaking."

Interactive models also fail to capture the dynamism of communication. To do this, a model would need to show that communication changes over time as a result of what happens between people. For example, Ethan and Chloe communicated in more reserved and formal ways on their first date than after months of dating. What they talk about and how they talk have changed as a result of interacting. An accurate model would include the feature of time and would depict features of communication as dynamically varying rather than constant. Figure 1.5 is a transactional model of communication that highlights these features and others we have discussed.

The transactional model includes noise, which is anything that has the potential to interfere with the intended communication. This includes sounds like a lawn mower or people nearby talking on smartphones, as well as "noise" within communicators, such as fatigue and preoccupation. In addition, our model shows that communication is a continuous, constantly changing process.

The outer lines on our model emphasize that communication occurs within systems that themselves affect communication and meanings. Those systems include contexts that both communicators share (e.g., a common campus, town, and culture) as well as each person's personal systems (e.g., family, religious associations, and friends). Also notice that our model, unlike previous ones, portrays each person's field of experience and the shared field of experience between communicators as changing over time. As we encounter new people and grow personally, our field of experience expands.

Figure 1.5
A Transactional Model of Communication
Source: Adapted from Wood, J. T. (2010). *Interpersonal Communication: Everyday Encounters* (6th ed.). Belmont, CA: Wadsworth.

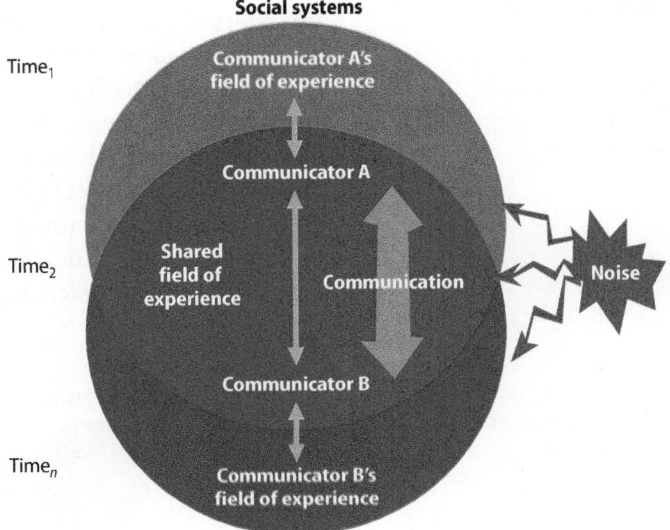

Nisha I lived in India until I was 14, and my family is still very Indian culturally. I am always surprised by how much United States college students disregard their parents' wishes. My parents insist that I marry an Indian so they do not want me to date Americans or other non-Indians. My friends say it is not my parents' business who I date. They don't care if their parents don't approve of their boyfriends and girlfriends.

Question: The concept of cultural humility suggests that people from different cultures benefit when they approach conversations open-mindedly, as co-learners. If Nisha's friends wished to practice cultural humility in their conversations with her, what could they have done differently?

Review It!

Models of Communication:
- Linear
- Interactive
- Transactional

Finally, our model doesn't label one person a "sender" and the other a "receiver." Instead, both people are defined as communicators who participate actively in the communication process. This means that, at a given moment in communication, you may be sending a message, receiving a message, or doing both at the same time (interpreting what someone says while nodding to show you are interested).

The Breadth of the Communication Field

The discipline of communication dates back more than 2,000 years to Aristotle, a famous Greek philosopher, who believed that effective public speaking was essential to citizens' participation in civic life (Borchers, 2006). The modern discipline includes seven major areas of research and teaching: interpersonal communication, group communication, organizational communication, public communication, health communication, mass communication, and intercultural communication.

Interpersonal Communication

interpersonal communication Communication between people, usually in close relationships such as friendship and romance.

Interpersonal communication deals with communication between people.

Interpersonal communication exists on a continuum from impersonal to highly personal. Refer to Figure 1.6. In impersonal communication, we ignore another person or treat another as an object. In the middle of the continuum is interaction with others within social roles. The most personal communication occurs in what philosopher Martin Buber (1970) called "I–Thou" relationships, in which each person treats the other as a unique and sacred person whom we know and interact with as a distinct individual. This makes a deep conversation with a friend more personal than a casual exchange with a sales clerk. Communication is the primary way

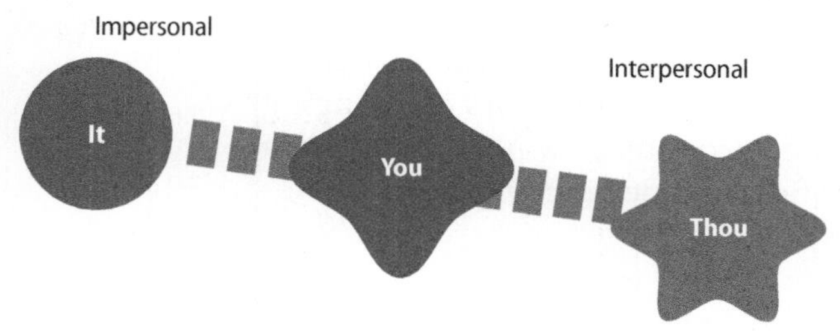

Figure 1.6 The Communication Continuum

people develop intimacy and refashion relationships to meet their changing needs and identities. Relationships in which both parties listen sensitively and talk with one another have the greatest chance of enduring.

Group Communication

Small-group communication, detailed in Chapters 10 and 11, is an important part of life. Whether you are participating in a social group, SGA committee, or work team, communication affects aspects of your group life. In group communication, leadership, member participation, agendas for decision making, and disruptive and constructive conflict all matter. For example, learning to communicate effectively in teams has become a criterion for success and advancement in careers.

Organizational Communication

Many organizational communication scholars study **organizational culture**, which focuses on understandings about identity and codes of thought and action shared by the members of an organization (Nicotera, Clinkscales, & Walker, 2002). From these understandings emerge rules for interaction and perspectives related to work. How we communicate in an organization can enhance professional success and impact morale, productivity, and commitment to organizations.

organizational culture Ways of thinking, acting, and understanding work that are shared by members of an organization and that reflect an organization's distinct identity.

Madison I've had a number of part-time jobs, and I've noticed one interesting gender difference in my bosses. Men who are in charge tend to tell staff what to do—not like in a mean way, but it's very firm, like "Get that done right away." Women bosses tend to ask, like, saying "Would you do this?" or "Could you get this to me?" The bottom line is the same: We know to do whatever the boss says. But it feels more inclusive when a boss asks you instead of telling you.

Health Communication

Health communication is a very broad area that includes patient–clinician interaction, communication on health care teams, organizational dynamics in health care settings, marketing and advocacy of healthy practices for individuals and communities, and policy making (Kreps, 2010; Schiavo, 2007). Whether in a doctor's office, in online spaces, or in apps and portals used to communicate with patients, the broad range of health communication is one reason that many people plan careers in this area.

Mass Communication and Digital Media

Communication scholars study mass communication media such as film, radio, newspapers, books, magazines, and television. Their research has given us insight into how the media work and how they represent and influence cultural values. For instance, the use of young, attractive models in ads perpetuates the cultural value placed on youth, and their presentation often reinforces unhealthy stereotypes about gender roles and beauty ideals (Kilbourne, 2010).

More recent work on digital media and social media has explored the fragmentation of media audiences (Roncallo-Dow & Arango-Forero, 2017; Webster & Ksiazek, 2012) and how tools such as social media, text messages and apps influence our thinking, working, and relating (Arikewuyo et al., 2020; Baum & Potter, 2019; Pekkala & van Zoonen, 2022; Sun et al., 2021). Our lives are intertwined with many communication technologies, allowing us to communicate quickly with one another despite physical separation, and giving us relatively more access to a much wider range of information and entertainment than was typically available a generation ago. These tools are decreasing the power of traditional mass media, as more people shift their screen time away from cable television and towards apps and streaming services.

Public Communication

Most of us have various opportunities to speak publically in life. When we join new groups, we may be asked to "say a few words about yourself." Others' first impressions of us will be based on our self-introductions.

Scholars of public communication focus on critical evaluation of speeches and on principles for speaking effectively. They also study principles of effective public speaking so we know a lot about what makes speakers seem credible to listeners and how credibility affects persuasion. Research has also enlightened us about the kinds of argument, methods of organizing ideas, and forms of proof that listeners find effective. Had Ethan studied this research, he could have gleaned useful guidelines for his oral report in class.

Review It!

Breadth of Field:

- Interpersonal
- Group
- Organizational
- Health
- Media
- Public
- Intercultural

Intercultural Communication

Intercultural communication is an increasingly important focus of research, teaching, and training. The United States has always been made up of many people with diverse cultural backgrounds and styles of communicating. Scholars of intercultural communication increase awareness of different cultures' communication practices and values, both *across* cultures—for example, the differences between a Saudi Arabian and a Canadian—and *within* cultures. For example, within the United States, there are distinct social communities based on race, gender, sexual orientation, and other factors. Intercultural communication scholars (Samovar, Porter, & McDaniel, 2011) have identified distinctive styles of communication used by women, men, Black people, White people, certain Native American nations, people with disabilities, and other groups. Learning about such intercultural communication differences is a great way to increase our cultural competency and cultural humility skills.

Meikko What I find most odd about Americans is their focus on themselves. Here, everyone wants to be an individual who is so strong and stands out from everyone else. In Japan, it is not like that. We see ourselves as parts of families and communities, not as individuals. Here *I* and *my* are the most common words, but they are not often said in Japan.

How satisfying do you find digital interaction systems such as Skype and FaceTime?
JOEL SARTORE/National Geographic Creative

Unifying Themes in the Field

After reading about the major branches of the modern field of communication, you might think that the field is a collection of separate, unrelated areas of interest. Actually, the field of communication is unified by a pervasive interest in symbols, meaning, critical thinking, and ethics.

Review It!

Unifying Themes:

- Symbols
- Meaning
- Critical Thinking
- Ethics

Symbols

Symbols are the basis of language, thinking, and much nonverbal behavior. A wedding band is a symbol of marriage in Western culture; your name is a symbol for you; and a smile is a symbol of friendliness. Because symbols are abstract, they allow us to lift experiences and ourselves out of the present concrete world in order to reflect on past experiences and imagine future ones. Because symbols let us represent ideas and feelings, we can share experiences with others, even if they have not had those experiences themselves.

Whether we are interested in social media or intrapersonal, interpersonal, group, public, or intercultural communication, symbols are central to what happens. Thus, symbols and the mental activities they enable are a unifying focus of study and teaching about all forms of communication.

Meaning

Closely related to interest in symbols is the communication field's pervasive concern with meaning. The human world is one of meaning. We don't simply exist, eat, drink, sleep, and go through motions. Instead, we imbue every aspect of our lives with significance or meaning. For example, we often layer food and eating with significance. Kosher products reflect commitment to Jewish heritage, ham is commonly associated with Easter, eggnog is a Christmas tradition, candles are part of Kwanzaa, and birthday cakes celebrate an individual.

To study communication, then, is to study how we use symbols to create meaning in our lives. Communication scholars regard romantic bonds, friendships, families, teams, organizations, and cultures as growing out of human communication.

Benita It's funny how important a word can be. Nick and I had been going out for a long time, and we really liked each other, but I didn't know if this was going to be long term. Then we said we loved each other, and that changed how we saw each other and the relationship. Just using the word *love* transformed who we are.

Critical Thinking

critical thinking Examining ideas reflectively and carefully to decide what you should believe, think, or do.

A third enduring concern in the communication field is **critical thinking**. To be competent communicators, we must examine ideas carefully to decide what to believe, think, and do in particular situations. Someone who thinks critically weighs ideas thoughtfully, considers evidence carefully, asks about alternative conclusions and courses of action, and connects principles and concepts across multiple contexts. Table 1.1 identifies key skills of critical thinking that affect communication competence.

Critical thinking is important in all aspects of our lives. The skills of critical thinking can enhance communication in friendships, romantic relationships, and family relationships. Critical thinking is also important to your success as a student. In class discussions and exams, you are asked to compare and contrast different policies or historical eras and to apply theories to particular situations—doing so requires critical thinking. Likewise, critical thinking is important in professional life. People who score low on measures of critical thinking are more likely to be unemployed than people who score highly (9.6% vs. 3.1%) (Berrett, 2012).

Ethics and Communication

A final theme that unifies research and teaching is ethical communication and interpretation of others' communication. Because all forms of communication involve ethical issues, this theme infuses all areas of the discipline. For instance, ethical dimensions of intrapersonal communication include the influence of stereotypes on our judgments of others. Ethical issues in the realm of interpersonal communication include honesty, compassion, and fairness in relationships. Pressures to conform that sometimes operate in groups are an ethical concern in

Table 1.1 **Critical Thinking Skills for Effective Communication**

- Identify assumptions behind statements, claims, and arguments.
- Distinguish between logical and illogical reasoning.
- Separate facts from inferences.
- Evaluate evidence to determine its reliability, relevance, and value.
- Connect new information and ideas to familiar knowledge; apply concepts learned in one context to other contexts; recognize when and where specific principles are and are not appropriate.
- Distinguish between personal experiences, attitudes, behaviors, and generalizations about human beings.
- Identify and consider alternative views on issues, solutions to problems, and courses of action.
- Define problems and questions clearly and precisely.
- Draw reasonable conclusions about the implications of information and argument for thought and action.
- Determine how to find answers to important questions by considering what needs to be known and what sources might provide relevant knowledge.

group communication. Ethical issues also surface in public communication. For example, speakers who misrepresent facts or deliberately lie are violating an ethical principle.

Another ethical issue relevant to a range of communication contexts concerns attitudes and actions that encourage or hinder freedom of speech: Are all members of organizations equally empowered to speak? What does it mean when audiences shout down a speaker with unpopular views? How does the balance of power between relationship partners affect each person's freedom to express

Communication Highlight

Thinking Critically About Language and Social Groups

It's especially important to think critically when using, listening to, or reading generalizations about social groups. The value of generalizations is that they allow us to recognize general patterns that can be useful starting points in understanding others. We can't learn about Koreans, Black people, White people, or Buddhists if we cannot use group labels such as *Korean* and *Black*. At the same time, generalizations do not necessarily apply to particular individuals. For instance, it is true that Koreans in general are more communal than native-born Americans, particularly Whites, in general, but a particular Korean may be very individualistic, and a particular native-born American may be very communal.

In this book, you will read many generalizations about various social groups. These generalizations are based on research, usually including research conducted by members of the social group being discussed. That doesn't mean that a generalization about men or Whites is true about all men or all Whites. You may well be a living exception to some of the generalizations about groups to which you belong.

To prevent ourselves from mistaking generalizations for absolute truths, it's important to use qualifying words such as *usually, in general, typically,* and *in most cases*. These remind us that there are exceptions to generalizations. As you read this book, notice how we qualify generalizations so we don't mistake them for universal truths. Notice also whether generalizations are appropriately qualified on television, in newspaper stories, in magazine articles, and in everyday conversations.

themselves? Because ethical issues infuse all forms of communication, we will discuss ethical themes in each chapter of this book. In the questions at the end of each chapter, the ethics icon will call your attention to a question focused on ethics of communication.

Careers in Communication

As we've detailed, communication skills are essential to success in most fields. In addition, people who major in communication are particularly sought after in a number of occupations.

Research

Communication research is a vital and growing field of work. A great deal of study is conducted by academics who combine teaching and research in faculty careers. In addition to academic research, communication specialists do media research on everything from message production to marketing. Companies want to know how people respond to different kinds of advertisements, logos, and labels for products. Before a new cereal or beer is named, various names are test marketed to test how customers will respond to different names. In addition, hospitals and other health care organizations need communication specialists to develop media campaigns for new products and services.

Education

Teachers are needed for communication curricula in secondary schools, junior colleges, colleges, universities, technical schools, and community colleges. The level at which a person is qualified to teach depends on how extensively they have studied communication. Generally, a bachelor's degree in communication education and certification by the board of education are required of teachers in elementary and secondary schools. A master's degree in communication qualifies a person to teach at community colleges, technical schools, and some junior colleges and colleges. The doctoral degree (Ph.D.) in communication is usually required for a career in university education, although some universities offer short-term positions to people with master's degrees. University faculty often teach in specialized areas of communication, such as interpersonal communication, media studies, organizational communication, intercultural communication, public relations, advertising, and journalism. Also, because communication is essential for doctors and businesspeople, increasing numbers of medical and business schools are creating permanent positions for communication specialists.

Media Production, Analysis, and Criticism

Careers in media and communication are very popular. Career paths include television production, news reporting, public relations, social media management, film production, and more. Written, visual, and spoken communication skills are essential in all of these roles. Likewise, because our society is media saturated, we rely on media critics to help us understand what media are doing. Are they representing information fairly? Are they biased? Are they offering messages that are healthy for us? Many media critics publish their critiques in book forms, in newspapers or magazines, and/or on social media. (As a media studies scholar and media critic myself, one of my favorite classes to teach is media criticism!)

Training and Consulting

Consulting welcomes people with backgrounds in communication. People with communication backgrounds often help organizations train employees in effective group communication skills, interview techniques, and group and team work. Some large hospitals and major corporations devote entire departments to training and development. Communication professionals also help government agencies and organizations develop work teams that interact effectively, train members of health care teams, help politicians improve their presentation styles and write their speeches, and more. In my own professional practice, when I'm not teaching or engaging in media criticism as a media studies scholar, I serve as a strategic nonprofit communication consultant, helping nonprofits communicate to prospective and past donors about their funding needs and recent accomplishments. Other communication consultants work with attorneys on jury selection and advise attorneys on courtroom communication strategies.

Human Relations and Management

Many communication specialists build careers in public relations, human resources, grievance management, negotiations, customer relations, and development and fund-raising. In each of these areas, communication skills are essential.

Communication degrees also open the door to career in management. The most important qualifications for management are the ability to interact with others and communicate effectively. Good managers are skilled in listening, expressing their ideas, building consensus, creating supportive work environments, and balancing task and interpersonal concerns in dealing with others.

Health Care and Health Communication

Communication is a central component of health care. Doctors and patients communicate interpersonally to discuss symptoms, diagnose illnesses, and agree upon treatment plans. Within and across hospitals and health care systems, practitioners and staff members need to communicate clearly with one another about emergent patient needs, new programs, best practices, and new initiatives. Medical and health care researchers need to be able to communicate clearly about their projects to secure grant funding and share their results with the public. And in the public health field, communicating clearly with diverse audiences about emergent health crises and safety measures helps keep the public safe.

Health communication is a field of study and professional practice. Health communication professionals are employed by medical and health care professionals, nonprofits, boards of health, biotechnology companies, and more. In these roles, they help such organizations communicate well with various audiences, internal and external—disseminating information, educating, and raising awareness.

People with strong communication skills have a range of career options.
Pressmaster/Shutterstock.com

Digital Media and Communication

Many of the values of communication discussed in this chapter are achieved using social media, which are now interwoven in many people's lives. For instance, we rely on social media to maintain personal relationships and sometimes to form relationships. We post updates and photos on social networking sites to let friends know what's happening in our lives and to learn what is happening in others' lives. We also use social media in careers. Many companies now request online submission of job applications. Once we have a job, we use digital media to establish and maintain professional ties. LinkedIn, for example, allows people to network professionally. Digital media also enlarge our ability to engage in civic life—online we can sign petitions for causes, blog about issues that matter to us, and read the blogs of others whose opinions we respect.

You might also consider what the definition of communication implies for interacting via social media. When we talk with people face to face, we are aware of their immediate physical context, which is not always the case with digital interaction. We may not know who else is present and what else is happening around a person we text. When the systems within which communication occurs are unknown to us, it's more difficult to interpret others. For instance, does a delayed response mean the person you texted is angry, is thinking over what you said, is talking with other people face to face, or is participating in a work meeting? Feedback is sometimes delayed when we interact via digital media. Also, because nonverbal communication in digital media is restricted, we may miss out on meaning, particularly on the relationship level.

Our definition also emphasizes process—changes in communication that happen over time. Think about how online and digital communication have evolved in just your lifetime. When email first became available to the general public, most people treated it much like letter writing: An email started with

"Dear" or "Hello" and ended with a closing such as "Thank you" or "Sincerely." As email became more popular and as all of us were flooded with email messages, the opening and closing courtesies largely disappeared. As email traffic continued to increase, abbreviations started being used: BRB (be right back), LOL (laughing out loud), and so forth. Texting and tweeting brought more innovation in use of symbols. Vowels are often dropped, single letters serve for some words (u for you, r for are), phrases, rather than complete sentences, are acceptable, and emoticons and emojis are used to convey feelings. The rules of grammar, syntax, and spelling have also been loosened by digital natives who assume the autocorrect function edits correctly.

You might also reflect on how digital media are integrated into the careers we discussed for people with strong backgrounds in communication. For instance, much research today is conducted online; human relations and management rely on digital communication to announce policies, update employees on issues, and even conduct meetings. Likewise, students majoring in journalism and public relations used to primarily focus on writing skills; now, reflecting changing expectations in these fields, they spend a lot of time learning digital and multimedia production skills, as well. In other words, few professions today do not involve digital media.

Chapter Summary

In this chapter, we took a first look at human communication. First, we defined communication, and then we discussed its value in our lives. Next, we considered a series of models, the most accurate of which is transactional. The transactional model emphasizes that communication is a systemic process in which people interact to create and share meanings.

Like most fields of study, communication has developed over the years. Today, communication scholars and teachers are interested in a range of communication activities. This broad range of areas is held together by abiding interests in symbolic activities, meanings, critical thinking, and ethics, which together form the foundation of personal, interpersonal, civic, and social life.

The central role of communication in our lives explains why it provides foundations for a range of careers. The final section of the chapter noted ways in which definitions and models of communication apply to digital media.

Experiencing Communication in Our Lives

Case Study: A Model Speech of Self-Introduction

Apply what you've learned in this chapter by analyzing the following case study, using the accompanying questions as a guide.

Hi. My name is Adam Currier, and I'm going to be introducing myself to you today. When I was first told that I had to introduce myself using a collage, I was afraid because I think collage, and I immediately think art, which is a subject that I have never been any good at.

So I was stuck on what I wanted to do for my collage to introduce myself. So when I'm stuck and when I need any kind of inspiration, I usually turn to my wall. And that's where I went—I turned to my wall. And when I look at my bedroom wall, I see quotes like "Be mindful of yourself and the world around you" and "Time is not a thing you have lost; it is not a thing you ever had." And I wondered why I had some of those quotes on my wall and other quotes like "We're not here to find a way to heaven. The way is heaven." And I started thinking about why I had these themes on my wall. And I realized that it was because of two major events that have happened in my life.

The first one was the theme that really got me thinking about pursuing the goals I wanted to pursue, even when other people told me that it wasn't possible. And that was my sophomore year of high school. I had decided that I wanted to take eight classes instead of the normal six. So instead of being at school from 8 a.m. to 3 p.m., I'd be there from 7 in the morning to 7 at night.

And the minute people heard that I was going to do this, everyone said it couldn't be done. My mom, my dad, the people who have been most supportive of me in my life, told me that I couldn't do it. And that I would wreck my grade point average, and I would end up not being able to get into a college that I wanted to go to. My friends, who have also supported me right by my parents, told me that I couldn't do it.

And I did it anyways. And I made it through without wrecking my GPA. I finished up with A's and B's just like I had all the years that I'd been in school. Realizing that even when no one was supporting me, I set my mind to a goal and achieved that goal; I realize that it's important to never let people tell you what you are capable of. If someone says you can't do that and it's something you really want to do, do it anyways.

The second theme on my wall was to enjoy every minute of life. And I was thinking about the main thing that made me think about that, and I realized that it was my grandfather. Every year since I ever remember, we've gone back to Iowa and spent a week of that summer just being with my dad's parents, my grandparents. And each year as I grew, I grew closer and closer to my grandfather. And it got to the point where I no longer just knew him as a relative, but I knew him as a human being.

Sitting outside on his porch one day, right before he died, he told me about his life and we were talking about what he had done—being in World War II, being a dentist, being a community leader—all the things that he had ever achieved in his life, and it all sounded so perfect. I said, "Grandfather, what do you regret most in your life?" And he said, "Adam, I regret not seeing more sunsets." A couple months later he passed on, and I realized that I didn't enjoy every single minute with him as much as I could have and I didn't have the time with him that I thought that I'd have.

So I look at my wall now and I see the quotes on it and I see the stories on it and the pictures on it, and I realize that everyone I've ever come into contact with, everyone I've ever met, everything I've ever done has all contributed to shaping the person I am, and my wall reflects the person that I am. So if I can pass on anything to you, I would hope that it would be to enjoy every minute of your life, and in that enjoyment never let people tell you what is possible, because only you know your potential. Thank you.

Questions for Analysis and Discussion

1. In his short speech, does Adam convey who he is?
2. Based on Adam's speech, what characteristics do you think describe him?
3. Does the closing of the speech reflect back to the opening?

Related Activity

Want to give your own self-introduction speech? Here's a basic blueprint:

Reflect on yourself and your life. Identify one interesting or unusual aspect of your identity or your life, and use that as the focus of your speech. Possible foci for your speech are experience of living in another country, the origin of an unusual name, a unique event in your life, or an interesting hobby or skill. Then, follow this structure for your speech:

I. My name is ______________________________

____

I want to tell you this about myself: __________

____

II. Describe the interesting or unusual aspects of yourself or your life. ______________

____

III. Conclude by restating your main idea. ______

____

Key Concepts

communication
content level of meaning
critical thinking
cultural competency
cultural humility
feedback
interpersonal communication
noise
organizational culture
process
relationship level of meaning
symbol
system

For Further Reflection and Discussion

1. Using each of the models discussed in this chapter, describe communication in your family. What does each model highlight and obscure? Which model best describes and explains communication in your family?
2. Interview a professional in the field you plan to enter to discover what kinds of communication skills they think are the most important for success. Which of those skills do you already have? Which skills do you need to develop or improve? How can you use this book and the course it accompanies to develop the skills you will need to be effective in your career?
3. Think critically about the impact of digital technologies of communication. In what ways do you think these technologies improve professional, personal, and social communication? In what ways may they be counterproductive?
4. How do social media affect your interactions? How are posts, tweets, and texts different from face-to-face interactions? Have you made any acquaintances or friends through social media? Did those relationships develop differently from ones formed through face-to-face contact? Do you feel differently about people you have never met and those you have met in person?
5. Two major professional organizations in the communication field are the National Communication Association (NCA) and the International Communication Association (ICA). They publish journals featuring the latest research and organize annual conferences where professors and graduate students gather to share their research. Take a moment to search for their web sites and look around. From their web pages, what can you tell about these organizations and the scope of the discipline they represent?

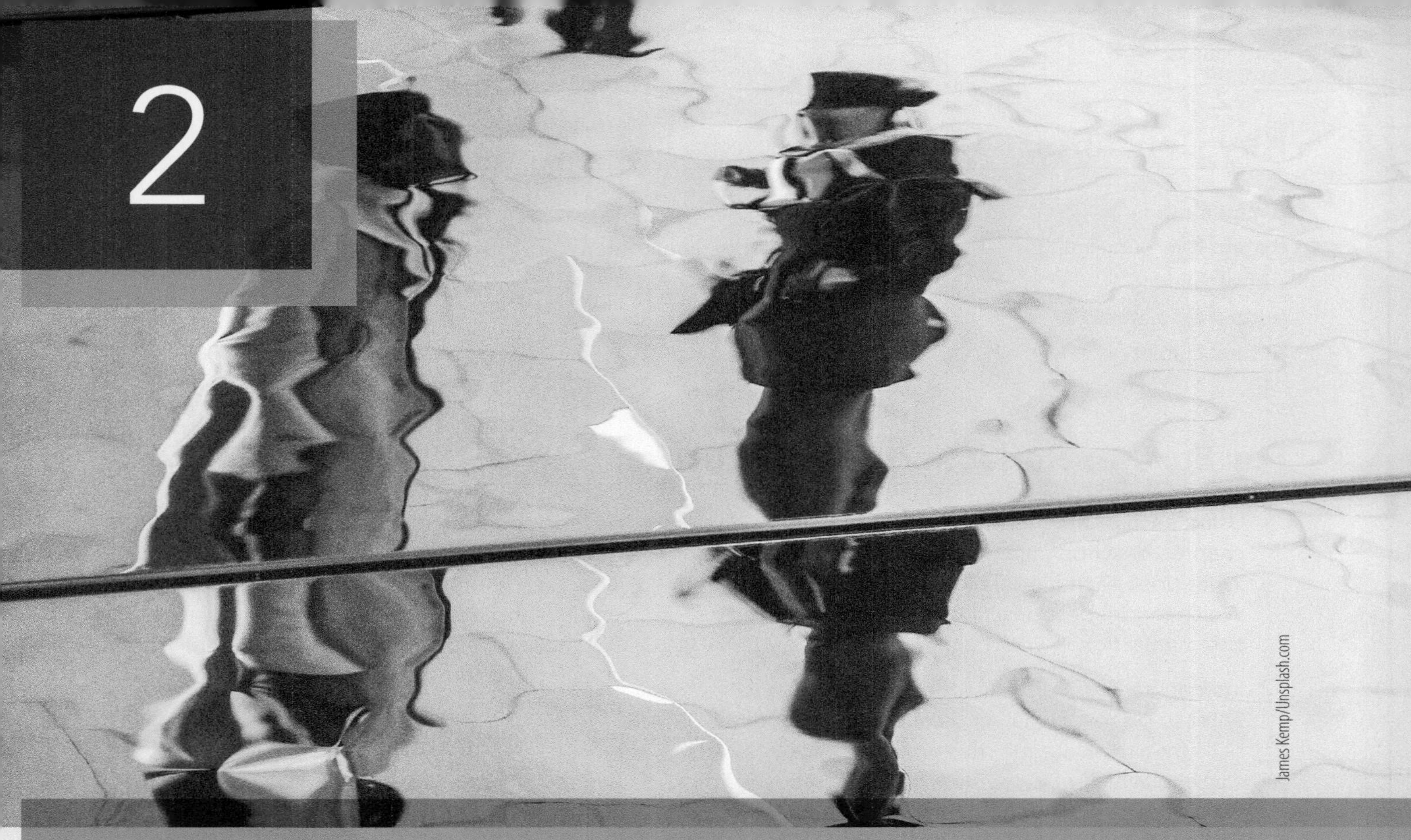

We see the world as "we" are, not as "it" is; because it is the "I" behind the "eye" that does the seeing.

Anaïs Nin

When the perceptions of you and a friend differ, how do you determine who is correct?

Perception and Communication

Learning Objectives

After studying the topics in this chapter, you should be able to:

1. Recognize that perception is made up of three steps in which we select, organize, and interpret information to create meaning.
2. List reasons that we notice certain information and ignore other.
3. Explain how, in the communication process, we interpret messages, assigning them meaning.
4. Describe how culture shapes our perceptions of ourselves and others.
5. Identify some strategies to improve the accuracy of your perceptions.

One December, as my family and I were about to board a cross-country flight, a TSA agent pulled me aside during a routine security check. The reason: In my family's carry-on bag, I had packed a Cupcake in a Jar, a specialty bakery item professionally packaged in a mason jar. It was an end-of-semester gift from a student, and it seemed like a perfect treat to share with my little boy during our long trip.

But what I saw as an in-flight snack, the TSA agent saw as a security risk: He told me he needed to confiscate it. Noting that the TSA website stated that pies and cakes were allowed through security, I asked what made it a security risk. The agent patiently explained that the frosting was a "gel-like substance" that "conformed to its container." This, in his opinion, made it unfit for travel in the aftermath of the infamous UK liquid bomb plot. His manager agreed, so he confiscated it.

Disappointed to lose such a fun dessert, I snapped a photo with the agent's permission, then sent it with some tongue-in-cheek commentary to the blog Boing. The idea of a cupcake being a security risk seemed so ludicrous that Boing published my photo and note, and the post went viral. The news media picked it up, calling me at home to request interviews; media outlets continued reporting on the story for several days. (It must have been a slow news week!) It seemed to be a great political unifier, with conservative and progressive commentators alike criticizing the TSA's decision.

A national discussion ensued: Was the TSA agent correct? Could the cupcake have been a bomb in disguise? Or was the TSA overreaching, confiscating items that they knew were perfectly ordinary? Was it "security theater," meant to give passengers and would-be terrorists a false sense of travel security in a post-9-11 world?"

The TSA agent's training led him to perceive dangers that I and the vast majority of commentators didn't perceive. The nicely packaged, unopened bakery item that most people regarded as a dessert, he saw as potential liquid bomb component. Our perceptions differed because we had different experiences and roles, which affected how we perceived everyday items in the context of a security checkpoint.

This chapter focuses on **perception**, which is the heart of communication. As we will see, perception is intricately intertwined with communication. Perception shapes how we communicate and how we interpret others' communication. In addition, communication influences our perceptions of people and situations. In the first part of this chapter, we elaborate the three-part process of perception. Next, we'll consider factors that affect our perceptions. Third, we will discuss perception in relation to digital media. Finally, we will explore ways to improve our abilities to perceive and communicate effectively.

Human Perception

perception The active process of selecting, organizing, and interpreting people, objects, events, situations, and activities.

Perception is the active process of selecting, organizing, and interpreting people, objects, events, situations, and activities. The first thing to notice about this definition is that perception is an active process. Phenomena do not have intrinsic meaning that we passively receive. Instead, we actively work to make sense of ourselves, others, situations, and other phenomena. To do so, we focus on only certain things, and then we organize and interpret what we have selectively noticed. What something means to us depends on which aspects of it we attend to and how we organize and interpret what we notice.

Perception consists of three processes: selecting, organizing, and interpreting. These processes are overlapping, so they blend into and influence one another. They are also interactive, so each affects the other two.

Selection

Stop and notice: Where are you right now, and what is it like there? Perhaps you're at home, in a library or classroom, or reading this at work or in a vehicle. Stop for a moment and notice what is going on around you right now. Is there music in the background? Are your surroundings warm or cold, messy or clean, large or small, light or dark? Can you smell anything? Is anyone else around? Do you hear other conversations or music? Can you hear muted sounds of activities beyond your immediate area? What about the words you're reading right now—what do you notice about them? Are you reading them in a book or on a screen? What kind? Is the type large, small, or easy to read? Do you like the colors used, the design of the text? Now think about what's happening inside you: Are you alert, sleepy, hungry, or comfortable? Do you have a headache or an itch anywhere?

You probably weren't conscious of most of these phenomena when you began reading the chapter. Instead, you focused on reading and understanding the material. You narrowed your attention to what you defined as important at that moment, and you were unaware of many other things going on around you. This is typical of how we live our lives. We can't attend to everything in our environment because there is simply far too much there, and most of it isn't relevant to us at any particular time.

Selective perception explains why it is dangerous to text while driving: When drivers text or use a speech-to-text system, their attention focuses on the messages and commands they are generating (Lowry, 2013). As a result, they are likely to stop scanning the road ahead, fail to check side and rear-view mirrors, and may not notice stop signs or pedestrians. Whether texting or giving voice commands, brain waves, eye movements, and reaction times demonstrate inattention to driving.

Which stimuli we notice depends on a number of factors. First, some qualities of external phenomena draw attention. For instance, we notice things that **STAND OUT** because they are immediate, relevant, or intense. We're more likely to hear a loud voice than a soft one and to notice a bright shirt than a drab one. Second, our perceptions are influenced by the acuity of our senses. For instance, if you have a good sense of smell, you're likely to be enticed by the smell of freshly baked bread. People who are visually impaired, blind, hearing-impaired, and/or deaf often develop greater sensitivity in their other senses.

Third, change or variation compels attention, which is why we may take for granted all the pleasant interactions with a friend and notice only the tense moments. Effective public speakers apply the principle that change compels notice to keep listeners focused on their speaking. For instance, they may raise or lower their voices or move to a different place to maintain listeners' attention.

We notice things that stand out or differ from their surroundings.
Hermes Rivera/Unsplash.com

Sometimes we deliberately call phenomena to our attention. Self-indication occurs when we point out certain things to ourselves. Right now you're learning to indicate to yourself that you perceive selectively, so in the future you will be more aware of the selectivity of your perceptions. People who want to eat healthy diets deliberately notice nutritional content of food items. Health care professionals notice aspects of appearance and behavior that are clues to a person's health.

What we select to notice is also influenced by who we are and what is going on inside us. Our motives and needs affect what we see and don't see. If you've just broken up with someone, you're more likely to notice attractive people than if you are in an established romantic relationship. People tend to perceive things they desire as more accessible than they really are. In one study, the researchers (Balcetis & Dunning, 2010) had people sit across the table from a full bottle of water and then had them either eat pretzels or drink water from a glass. The participants were then asked to estimate how close they were to the bottle of water. Consistently, the participants who were thirsty from eating pretzels perceived the water bottle as being closer than the other participants.

We are also more likely to perceive what we expect to perceive. This explains the phenomenon of the **self-fulfilling prophecy**, in which one acts in ways consistent with how one has learned to perceive oneself. Children who are told they are unlovable may perceive themselves that way and notice rejecting but not affirming communication from others. Research shows that lonely people tend to perceive themselves and others more negatively than nonlonely people (Gong & Nitikin, 2021). These negative judgments of self and others may cause those who feel lonely to make less effort to engage others. In turn, this leads to unsatisfying interactions and perhaps alienates others so loneliness continues or increases.

self-fulfilling prophecy An expectation or judgment of ourselves brought about by our own actions.

Lee Teng-Hui Before I came to school here, I was told that Americans are very pushy, loud, and selfish. For my first few months here, I saw that was true of Americans just as I had been told it would be. It took me longer to see also that Americans are friendly and helpful because I had not been taught to expect these qualities.

Organization

constructivism Theory that claims we organize and interpret experience by applying cognitive structures called schemata.

schemata (singular: *schema*) Cognitive structures we use to organize and interpret experiences. Four types of schemata are prototypes, personal constructs, stereotypes, and scripts.

prototype A knowledge structure that defines the clearest or most representative example of some category.

We don't simply string together randomly what we've noticed. Instead, we organize what we've selectively noticed to make it meaningful to us. The most useful theory for explaining how we organize what we've attended to is **constructivism**, the theory that we organize and interpret experience by applying cognitive structures called **schemata** (singular: *schema*). Originally developed by George Kelly in 1955, constructivism has been elaborated by scholars in communication and psychology. We use four kinds of cognitive schemata to make sense of phenomena: prototypes, personal constructs, stereotypes, and scripts (Burleson & Rack, 2008; Fehr, 1993; Hewes, 1995; Leschziner & Brett, 2021).

Prototypes A **prototype** is a knowledge structure that defines the best or most representative example of some category (Fehr, 1993). For example, you probably have prototypes of best teachers, friends, public speakers, and romantic partners. Each of these categories is exemplified by a person who is the ideal case; that's the prototype.

We use prototypes to define categories: Taylor is the ideal friend; Jayleen is the ideal romantic partner; Chance is the ideal work associate. We may then consider how close a particular phenomenon is to our prototype for that category. As Alicia's commentary points out, our prototypes can be faulty, leading us to fail to perceive someone as belonging in the appropriate category because they do not match our prototype for the category.

Amelia I was working with a male nurse. Every time he met a new patient, the patient would say, "Hi, doctor." Even when he told them he was a nurse, they treated him as a doctor. No one ever confused me with a doctor. Patients just assume that men in white are doctors and women in white are nurses.

Question: Amelia's story raises a good point about the prototypes many people have for nurses and doctors. Have you ever mistakenly assumed somebody's role to be different than what it was? Why might that have been?

personal construct A bipolar mental yardstick that allows us to measure people and situations along specific dimensions of judgment.

Personal Constructs **Personal constructs** are bipolar mental yardsticks that allow us to position people and situations along dimensions of judgment. Examples of personal constructs are intelligent–not intelligent, responsible–not responsible, kind–not kind, and attractive–not attractive. To size up a person, we measure them by personal constructs that we use to think about people. How intelligent, responsible, kind, and attractive is this person? Whereas prototypes help us decide into which broad category a person or situation fits, personal constructs let us make more detailed assessments of particular qualities of phenomena we have selectively perceived. Our personal constructs shape our perceptions because we define something only in terms of how it compares to the constructs we use. Thus, we may not notice qualities of people that are outside the constructs we use to perceive them.

Stereotypes **Stereotypes** are predictive generalizations about people and situations. Based on the category in which we place a phenomenon and how the phenomenon measures up to the personal constructs we apply, we predict what it will do. For instance, if you classify Meredith into the prototype of liberal, and you perceive her as compassionate, generous, and kind (personal constructs), you might predict that she is likely to support government-funded programs to help citizens from historically disadvantaged backgrounds.

stereotype A predictive generalization about people and situations.

Stereotypes may be accurate or inaccurate. They are generalizations, which are sometimes based on facts that are generally true of a group and sometimes on prejudice or assumptions. Even if we have accurate understandings of a group, generalizations may not apply to particular individuals in it. For example, although college students as a group are more liberal than the population as a whole, some college students are very conservative. A particular individual may not conform to what is typical of their group as a whole. Ethical communicators keep in mind that stereotypes are generalizations that can be both useful and misleading—as well as incredibly harmful, especially when applied towards members of marginalized communities.

> **Ashley** As a vegetarian, I find stereotypes about vegetarians really annoying. Because "meat" is seen as "masculine," there's this stereotype that being vegetarian is a feminine, frivolous thing. Like somehow it's weak and girly of me to care about animal rights—or that guys who are vegetarian aren't "manly." Then there are the stereotypes that vegetarians are picky and no fun to eat out with, or are loud and obnoxious and out to ruin everyone else's meals, like walking, talking PETA billboards. But to assume that these stereotypes are real is frustrating. Being vegetarian is a personal choice, and it's annoying when people seem surprised that I'm vegetarian because I fit none of these stereotypes.
>
> **Question:** Can you recall a time when you were surprised to learn that a person didn't fit a stereotype you had learned about a group they belong to? What did you do with this information? Do you think it changed how you thought about members of that group?

Scripts To organize what we notice, we also use **scripts**, which are guides to action. A script consists of a sequence of activities that define what we and others are expected to do in specific situations.

script One of four cognitive schemata. A script defines an expected or appropriate sequence of action in a particular setting.

Many of our daily activities are governed by scripts, although we're often unaware of them. You may have a script for greeting casual acquaintances: "Hey, how ya doing?" "Fine. See ya around." You may have scripts for texting friends or partners, perhaps connecting by sending memes you think they'll like. You may also have scripts for managing conflict, talking with professors, interacting with superiors on the job, dealing with clerks, and relaxing with friends. Christine Bachen and Eva Illouz (1996) studied 184 people to learn about their views of romance. They found that most people agree on the scripts for appropriate sequences of events for first dates and romantic dinners. Similarly, Sandra Metts (2006b) has identified consistent scripts for

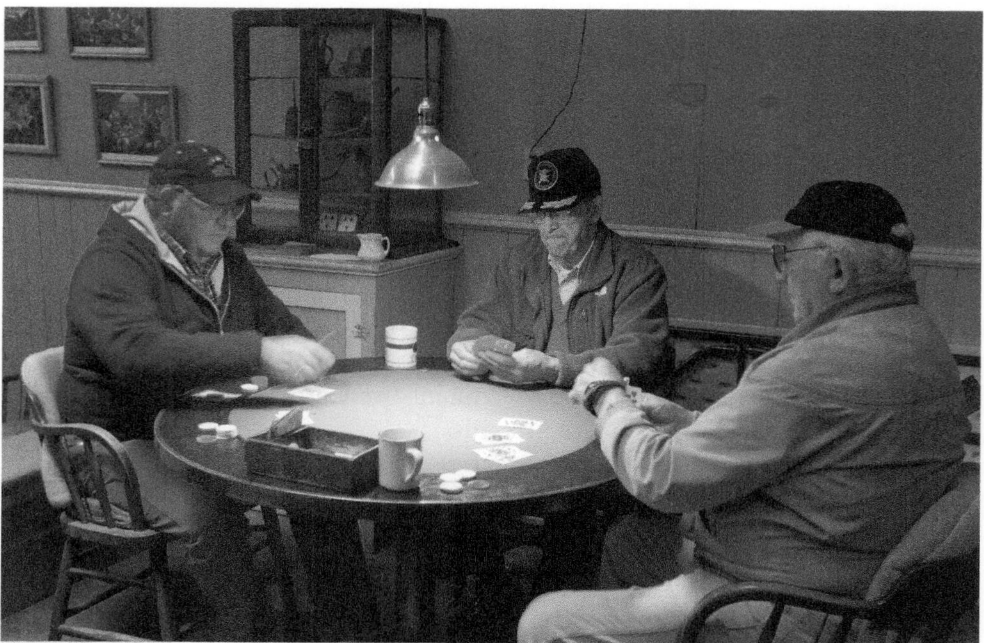

What stereotypes do you have of the men in this photograph?
Gary Crabbe/Enlightened Images/Alamy Stock Photo

heterosexual flirting—and Gray (2013) additionally found that an individual's gender identity influences their flirting style. Meanwhile, digital communication technology has opened up new scripts and patterns in cross-sex relationships, or relationships between people of differing genders or sexes. For example, couples are more likely to text one another in casual and early-stage relationships, with phone conversations becoming more appropriate as the couple grows closer (Larson, 2011).

Communication & Careers

Doctors' Stereotypes

In his book *How Doctors Think* (2007), Dr. Jerome Groopman points out that doctors' stereotypes may lead them to follow inappropriate scripts with patients. For instance, a doctor who perceives a patient as a homeless man might, based on that stereotype, diagnose the patient's stumbling as a symptom of intoxication and follow a script of letting the patient sober up rather than check for other causes of stumbling. If the doctor had perceived the patient as middle class, the doctor would be more likely to assume that stumbling indicated a medical problem and follow a script that included talking with the man and performing tests.

Likewise, research indicates that doctors' stereotypes about people's body types may lead them to follow inappropriate scripts. For instance, when treating patients with bodies they regard as much larger than average, many practitioners will assume the patients' medical complaints are caused by their weight. This prompts them to advise their patients to lose weight instead of providing actual medical care (Chrisler & Barney, 2017). Better training can help doctors become aware of biases such as fatphobia and sizeism, prompting them to follow scripts including asking more questions and ordering tests to secure an accurate diagnosis and treatment plan for their patients.

Prototypes, personal constructs, stereotypes, and scripts are cognitive schemata that we use to organize the phenomena to which we selectively attend. They help us make sense of what we notice and help us anticipate how we and others will act in particular situations. Our cognitive schemata are not entirely individualistic. Rather, they reflect our membership in a culture and in specific social groups. As we interact with others, we internalize their ways of classifying, measuring, and predicting interaction in various situations. Each of us has an ethical responsibility to assess social perspectives critically before relying on them to organize our perceptions and direct our activities.

Review It!

Cognitive Schemata:

- Prototypes
- Personal Constructs
- Stereotypes
- Scripts

Interpretation

To assign meaning, we must interpret what we have noticed and organized. **Interpretation** is the subjective process of explaining perceptions to assign meaning to them.

interpretation The subjective process of evaluating and explaining perceptions.

attribution A causal account that explains why a thing happened or why someone acted a certain way.

Attributions

Attributions are explanations of why things happen and why people act as they do (Fehr, 1993; Fehr & Russell, 1991; Heider, 1958; Kelley, 1967). It's good to remind ourselves that the attributions we make aren't necessarily correct—they are our subjective ways of assigning meaning.

Attributions have four dimensions (Table 2.1). The first is *locus,* which attributes what a person does to either internal factors ("There's something wrong with them.") or external factors ("The traffic jam frustrated them."). The second dimension is *stability,* which explains actions as resulting either from stable factors that won't change ("They're a Type A person.") or from temporary, unstable factors ("They're in a bad mood because they've just had a fight with their supervisor."). *Scope* (sometimes called *specificity*) is the third dimension, and it defines behavior as part of a global pattern ("They are a mean person.") or a specific instance ("They get angry when they're tired."). Finally, the dimension of *responsibility* attributes behaviors either to factors people can control ("They don't try to control their outbursts.") or to ones they cannot ("They have a chemical imbalance that makes them moody.").

A student who was reading this book for a class asked whether scope and stability are really distinct dimensions. This is a good question. Most global attributions are also stable. However, there are exceptions. For example, you might say that someone is always efficient at work but inefficient during leisure time. In this case, the attribution is stable and specific. If the person were efficient in all spheres of life, the attribution would be stable and global.

Investigations have shown that happy and unhappy couples have distinct attributional styles (Manusov & Harvey, 2001; Segrin, Hanzal, & Domschke, 2009; Tavris

Table 2.1 Dimensions of Interpersonal Attributions

Locus	Internal	External
Stability	Stable	Unstable
Scope	Global	Specific
Responsibility	Within personal control	Beyond personal control

& Aronson, 2007). Happy couples make relationship-enhancing attributions. They attribute nice things a partner does to internal, stable, and global reasons that the partner controls: "She paid extra to stream that new film because she is a good person who always does thoughtful things." They attribute unpleasant things a partner does to external, unstable, and specific factors and sometimes to influences beyond personal control: "He yelled at me because all the stress of the past few days made him irritable."

In contrast, unhappy couples make relationship-diminishing attributions. They explain nice actions as results of external, unstable, and specific factors: "She got the movie because she was looking to kill some time today." Negative actions are attributed to internal, stable, and global factors: "He yelled at me because he is an entitled jerk who always puts his own feelings first." Thus, we should be mindful of our attributions because they influence how we experience our relationships.

Review It!

Dimensions of Attributions:

- Locus
- Stability
- Scope
- Responsibility

self-serving bias The tendency to attribute our positive actions and successes to stable, global, internal influences that we control and to attribute negative actions and failures to unstable, specific, external influences beyond our control.

The Self-Serving Bias Research indicates that we tend to construct attributions that serve our personal interests (Hamachek, 1992; Hinton, 2016; Manusov & Spitzberg, 2008; Sypher, 1984). Thus, we are inclined to make internal, stable, and global attributions for our positive actions and successes. We're also likely to claim that good results come about because of our efforts. On the other hand, people tend to attribute negative actions and failures to external, unstable, and specific factors that are beyond personal control. In other words, we tend to attribute our misconduct and mistakes to outside forces that we can't help but attribute all the good we do to our personal qualities and effort. This **self-serving bias** can distort our perceptions, leading us to take excessive credit for what we do well and to abdicate responsibility for what we do poorly. Like many human tendencies, the self-serving bias is influenced by culture. For example, Western Caucasians are more likely to engage in the self-serving bias than people from many cultures, including Mexicans (Tropp & Wright, 2003), Native Americans (Fryberg & Markus, 2003), Chileans (Heine & Raineri, 2009), and some East Asians (Heine & Hamamura, 2007). Gender can also be associated with self-serving bias. For example, Voges et al. (2019) found that men tend to evaluate people's physical appearances with a self-serving bias, while women tend to be more fair-minded and less self-serving; and Ostafichuk and Sibley (2019) noted a link between self-bias and gender-bias in engineering students' peer evaluations.

MEG Last summer, I worked at a day-care center for 4- to 6-year-olds. Whenever a fight started and I broke it up, each child would say the other one made them fight or the other one started it or they couldn't help hitting. They were classic cases of self-serving bias.

Question: Self-serving bias is pervasive. If you follow politics, think back to some of the political debates or conversations you've heard. Can you think of an example when a politician took credit for something that they may not have fully deserved? Or can you think of a time when a politician tried to dodge responsibility for an issue that they may have had some responsibility for?

We've seen that perception involves three interrelated processes. The first of these, selection, allows us to notice certain things and ignore others. The second process is organization, in which we use prototypes, personal constructs, stereotypes, and scripts to order what we have selectively noticed. Finally, we engage in interpretation by using attributions to explain what we have noticed and organized. Although we discussed these processes separately, in reality they interact continually.

Influences on Perception

Review It!

Perception Processes:

- Selection
- Organization
- Interpretation

In opening this chapter, I mentioned an incident in which a TSA agent's perceptions differed from mine. His experience and training as a TSA agent led him to perceive a dessert item many people saw as harmless as a potential weapon component. Similarly, able-bodied people may not notice the lack of elevators or ramps in a building, but someone with a physical disability quickly perceives the building as inaccessible.

White students at predominantly White schools often don't notice that few people of color are in their classes, but to students who are not White, the overrepresentation of White people is obvious. Let's consider some reasons why people differ in how they perceive situations and other people.

Physiology

The most obvious reason perceptions vary is that people differ in sensory abilities and physiologies. Music that one person finds deafening is barely audible to another. On a given day on a college campus, students might wear everything from shorts and sandals to jackets, indicating that they have different sensitivities to cold. Some people have better vision than others, and still others are color blind.

Our physiological states also influence perception. If you are tired, stressed, or sick, you might perceive a comment from a coworker as critical of you, but the same comment wouldn't bother you if you felt good. If you interact with someone who is sick, you might attribute their irritability to temporary factors rather than to enduring personality.

Age also influences our perceptions. The older we get, the more complex is our perspective on life and people. Many people 18–22 years old consider it normal to pay over $3 for a gallon of gas, but to an 85-year-old person who recalls when gas cost less than 20 cents a gallon, paying $3 or more per gallon may seem high. The extent of discrimination still experienced by women and people from historically underserved communities understandably leads some young people to see inequities as unalterable. But to those who attended college when women weren't admitted on an equal basis with men, and almost all students of color attended minority

colleges, seeing substantial progress made during their lifetimes may lead them to perceive remaining inequities as changeable.

Culture

culture Beliefs, understandings, practices, and ways of interpreting experience that are shared by a number of people.

A **culture** consists of beliefs, values, understandings, practices, and ways of interpreting experience that are shared by a number of people. It is a set of taken-for-granted assumptions that form the pattern of our lives and guide how we perceive as well as how we think, feel, and act.

Consider a few aspects of modern Western culture that influence our perceptions. One characteristic of our culture is an emphasis on technology and its offspring, speed. We expect things to happen fast—almost instantly. We email or upload PDFs, jet across the country, send instant messages and texts, and microwave meals.

The United States of America is also a fiercely individualistic culture in which personal achievement and independence are rewarded. When children become adults, they often move away from their parents. Some other cultures are more communal, and identity is linked to family rather than being perceived as an individual quality. In communal cultures, children are looked after by the whole community instead of just their parents, and elders are given great respect and care.

The culture in which we live can even affect how we interpret visual stimuli. Look at Figure 2.1. Does line a or b seem longer to you? The lines are actually identical in length, but most Westerners perceive line b as longer. San Foragers of the Kalahari, however, perceive the two lines as equal in length. The reason for this difference in perception is that Westerners live in a world with carpentered corners, so we learn to see flat lines in three dimensions. People in less developed cultures are unaccustomed to carpentered corners so they tend not to perceive flat lines in three dimensions (Henrich & Norenzayan, 2010; Watters, 2013).

Scholars have explained that we are affected not only by the culture as a whole but also by our particular location within the culture (Cox et al., 2021; Gurung, 2020;

Figure 2.1
The Müller-Lyer Illusion

Communication in Everyday Life
DIVERSITY
Which Line Is Longer?

a b

Is line *a* or line *b* in the figure longer? The lines are known as the **Müller-Lyer illusion**. The lines are actually identical in length, but they don't appear so to some people. If you are a Westerner, it's likely that you perceive line *b* as longer. However, if you are a San Forager of the Kalahari, you are likely to perceive the lines as equal in length? Why the difference?

Researchers (Henrich & Norenzayan, 2010; Watters, 2013) have found that cultures shape not just our behaviors and values but also our perceptions. Westerners live in a world with lots of carpentered corners—squared corners in rooms and buildings—so they learn to perceive lines in three dimensions. People who live in less industrialized cultures see fewer carpentered corners, and their perceptions are not trained to see lines as three dimensional. Of more than a dozen cultures studied, Americans emerge as the most likely to perceive line *b* as longer.

Haraway, 1988; Harding, 1991; Gurung, 2020; Neitz, 2022; Wood, 2005). **Standpoint theory** claims that a culture includes a number of social communities that have different degrees of social status and privilege. Each social community distinctively shapes the perceptions, identities, and opportunities of its members. If a member of a social group gains political insight into the group's social location, then they can develop a standpoint. For example, a Muslim has the social location of Muslims. If that person learns about ways in which Western society discriminates against Muslims, the person may develop a Muslim standpoint. Without political awareness, however, a person cannot achieve a standpoint.

standpoint theory The theory that a culture includes a number of social groups that differently shape the knowledge, identities, and opportunities of members of those groups.

Asher I'll admit that when Krista and I had a child, I expected Krista to stay home and take care of her. Actually, we both did, and that worked fine for 3 months. Then Krista got cancer, and she was in the hospital for weeks and then in and out for nearly a year for treatments. Even when she was home, she didn't have the energy to take care of little Jennie. I had to take over a lot of the child care. Doing that really changed me in basic ways. I had to learn to tolerate being interrupted when I was working. I had to tune into what Jennie needed and learn to read her. Before that experience, I thought women had a maternal instinct. What I learned is, anyone can develop a parental sensitivity.

Gendered locations explain the difference between the amount of effort women and men, in general, invest in communication that maintains relationships. Socialized into the role of "relationship expert," women are often expected by others and themselves to take care of relationships (Wood, 1994d, 2007a, 2013).

Social and Professional Roles

Our perceptions are also shaped by social roles that others communicate to us. Messages that tell us that we are expected to fulfill particular roles, as well as the actual demands of those roles, affect how we perceive and communicate.

Speakers are more likely than audience members to notice the acoustics of presentation rooms. Teachers often perceive classes in terms of whether the students are interested, whether they have read material, and whether they engage in class discussion. On the other hand, many students perceive classes in terms of the number and difficulty of tests, whether papers are required, and whether the professor is interesting.

The careers people choose influence what they notice and how they think and act. Doctors are trained to be highly observant of physical symptoms, and they may detect a physical problem before a person knows that they have it. For example, some years ago at a social gathering, a friend of mine who is a doctor asked me how long I had had a herniated disk. Surprised, I told him I didn't have one. "You do," he insisted, and sure enough, a few weeks later a magnetic resonance imaging examination confirmed a ruptured disk in my back. His medical training enabled him to perceive subtle changes in my posture and walk that I hadn't noticed.

Cognitive Abilities

In addition to physiological, cultural, and social influences, perception is shaped by our cognitive abilities. How elaborately we think about situations and people, and the extent of our personal knowledge of others, affects how we select, organize, and interpret experiences.

cognitive complexity The number of constructs used, how abstract they are, and how elaborately they interact to create perceptions.

Cognitive Complexity

People differ in the number and types of knowledge schemata they use to organize and interpret people and situations. **Cognitive complexity** refers to the number of constructs used, how abstract they are, and how elaborately they interact to shape perceptions. Most children have fairly simple cognitive systems. They rely on few schemata, focus more on concrete categories (tall–not tall) than on abstract ones (introspective–not introspective), and often don't perceive relationships between different perceptions. For instance, infants may call every man Daddy because they haven't learned more complex ways to distinguish among men.

Adults also differ in cognitive complexity. If you perceive people only as nice or mean, you have a limited range for perceiving others. Similarly, people who focus exclusively on concrete data tend to have less sophisticated understandings than people who also perceive psychological data. For example, you might notice that a coworker is assertive, tells jokes, and contributes on task teams. These are concrete perceptions. At a more abstract, psychological level, you might infer that these concrete behaviors reflect a secure, self-confident personality. This is a more sophisticated cognition because it integrates three perceptions to develop an explanation of why the person acts as they do.

What if you later find out that the person is reserved in one-to-one conversations? Someone with low cognitive complexity would have difficulty integrating the new information into prior observations. Either the new information would be dismissed because it doesn't fit or the most recent information would alter the former perception, and the person would be redefined as shy. A more cognitively complex person would integrate all the information into a coherent account. Perhaps a cognitively complex thinker would conclude that the person is confident in social situations but less secure in more personal ones.

Cognitively complex people tend to be flexible in interpreting complicated phenomena and integrating new information into their thinking about people and situations. Less cognitively complex people are likely to ignore information that doesn't fit neatly with their impressions or to use it to replace the impressions they had formed (Delia, Clark, & Switzer, 1974). Either way, they fail to recognize some of the nuances and inconsistencies that are part of human life. The complexity of our cognitive systems affects the fullness and intricacy of our perceptions of people and interpersonal situations. Cognitively complex people also tend to communicate in more flexible and appropriate ways with a range of others. This probably results from their ability to recognize differences in people and to adapt their own communication accordingly.

person-centered perception The ability to perceive another as a unique and distinct individual apart from social roles and generalizations.

Person-Centered Perception

Person-centered perception reflects cognitive complexity because it entails abstract thinking and a broad range of schemata. Person-centered perception is the ability to perceive another as a unique and distinct individual. Our ability to perceive others as unique depends both on the general ability to make cognitive distinctions and on our knowledge of particular others. As we get to know individuals, we gain insight into how they differ from others in their groups ("Hunter's not like most political types on campus"; "Kai's more flexible than most managers."). The more we interact with one another and the greater variety of experiences we have together, the more insight we gain into

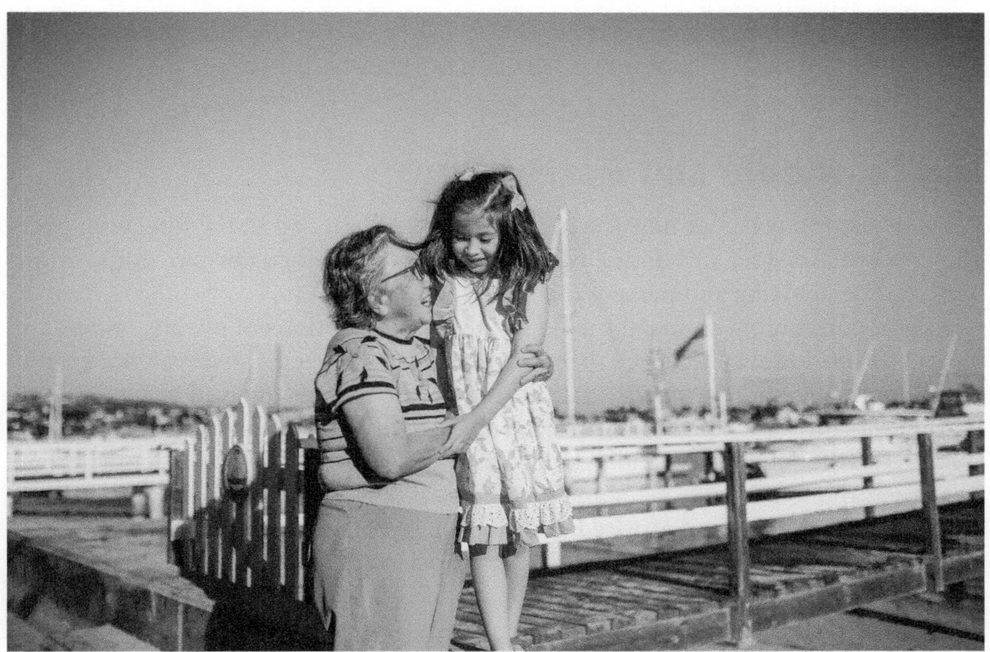

Was there an older person who took your perspective when you were a child?
Rodnae Productions/Pexels

other people. In long-term relationships, we fine-tune our perceptions throughout the life of relationships.

Person-centered perception is not the same as empathy. **Empathy** is the ability to feel with another person—to feel what they feel. Feeling with another is an emotional response. Because feelings are guided by our own experiences and emotions, it may be impossible to feel exactly and completely what another person feels. A more realistic goal is to try to recognize another's perspective and adapt your communication to how they perceive situations and people (Muehlhoff, 2006). With commitment and effort, we can learn a lot about how others see the world, even if that differs from how we see it.

empathy The ability to feel with another person or to feel what that person feels in a given situation.

When we take others' perspectives, we try to grasp what something means to them and how they perceive things. We can't really understand someone else's perspective when we're judging whether it is right or wrong, sensible or reckless. Instead, we have to let go of our own perspective and perceptions long enough to enter the thoughts and feelings of another person. Doing this allows us to understand issues from the other person's point of view so we can communicate more effectively (Servaty-Seib & Burleson, 2007). You might learn why your boss thinks something is important that you've been disregarding. You might find out how a friend interprets your behavior in ways inconsistent with what you intend to communicate.

At a later point in interaction, we may choose to express our own perspective or to disagree with another's views. This is appropriate and important in honest communication, but voicing our own views is not a substitute for the equally important skill of recognizing another's perspective. In sum, differences based on physiology, culture, membership in social groups, social roles, and cognitive abilities affect what we perceive and how we interpret others and experiences.

Review It!

Influences on Perception:

- Physiology
- Culture
- Roles
- Cognitive Abilities

Digital Media and Perception

We now want to consider how the ideas that we've discussed in the foregoing pages apply to social media and digital communication. We'll focus on two connections between social media and perception.

First, our choices of social media shape our perceptions of events, issues, and people. If you follow Tucker Carlson's tweets, you will get a conservative perspective on national and international issues and on the people involved in them. If you follow Alexandria Ocasio-Cortez's tweets, you will get a much more liberal perspective on the same issues and people. Carlson frequently disparages feminists: He has called the feminist movement "fake," stated he'd never let his daughter date a man who is feminist, and mocked accomplished women, such as those who serve in the military. In contrast, Ocasio-Cortez identifies as a feminist, speaks favorably about feminist issues, and is regarded as one of Gen Z feminism's most prominent figures. Carlson frequently demonizes immigration, stating that immigrants make the nation "poorer" and "dirtier" and are harming the United States and calling for greater restrictions; Ocasio-Cortez has expressed support for immigrants, calling for an end to the Department of Homeland Security (DHS) and Immigration and Customs Enforcement (ICE) and the detention centers in which immigrant families are separated. Your views on these issues and others are likely shaped by media sources and social media influencers you choose to follow.

Second, consider how membership in social communities affects what we say and post on social media. Try this experiment: Look at the social media content of people from various cultures. How often do their postings include boasting about individual accomplishments, which reflects Western but not Eastern values? Do people from communal and collectivist cultures post more photos of families and themselves with families than do people from individualist cultures? Now look at the profiles of people of various genders. Do certain posts about relationships, sports, fashion, and politics seem to come up more frequently among people who share a certain gender identity? If you find any trends, do you note whether they are consistent with research we've discussed about Western and non-Western cultural values and gendered social communities?

Guidelines for Effective Perception

To be a competent communicator, you need to realize how perception and communication affect each other. We'll elaborate on the connection between perception and communication and then discuss guidelines for enhancing communication competence.

Perceptions, Communication, and Abstraction

Words crystallize perceptions. When we name feelings and thoughts, we create precise ways to describe and think about them. But just as words crystallize experiences, they can also freeze thought. Once we label our perceptions, we may respond to our own labels rather than to actual phenomena.

Communication Highlight

Eyewitness Testimony: Fact or Fiction?

Many a defendant has been convicted because of eyewitness testimony. And many an *innocent* defendant has been convicted by eyewitness testimony: Eyewitness misidentifications account for about 69% of wrongful convictions in the United States (Innocence Project, 2018), making it a pervasive problem. In recent years, a number of convicted felons have been given new trials because DNA evidence could now be introduced. Nearly 75% of cases in which DNA exonerated a person serving time involved eye-witness testimony that the imprisoned person was the person who committed the crime (Beil, 2011).

The eyewitnesses in these situations aren't generally lying intentionally. Their perceptions are faulty. Factors like implicit bias and prejudice make eyewitness reports unreliable and make cross-racial misidentifications of Black people by White eyewitnesses commonplace (Chew, 2018; Vitriol et al., 2018). Researchers studying memory point out that most people perceive only a few details when an event happens. Later police questioning and line ups, coupled with repeating a false memory to themselves, make eyewitness very confident when they testify erroneously. For reasons such as these, the American Psychological Association (Azar, 2011) cautions courts and juries against relying too much on eyewitness testimony.

Consider this situation. You and five others form a study group, and a student named Olivia monopolizes the whole meeting with her questions and concerns. Leaving the meeting, one person says, "Gee, Olivia is so selfish and immature! I'll never work with her again." Another person responds, "She's not really selfish. She's insecure about her grades in this course, so she was emotionally spiraling in the meeting." Chances are these two people will perceive and treat Olivia differently depending on whether they label her selfish or insecure. The point is that the two people respond not to Olivia herself but to how they selectively perceive and label her.

Communication is based on a process of abstracting from complex stimuli. Our perceptions are not equivalent to the complex reality on which they are based because we can never fully describe or even apprehend total reality. This means that what we perceive is a step removed from stimuli because perceptions are always partial and subjective. We move a second step from stimuli when we label a perception. We move even further from stimuli when we respond not to behaviors or our perceptions of them but to the judgments we associate with the label we have imposed. This process can be illustrated as a ladder of abstraction, as shown in Figure 2.2 (Korzybski, 1948).

Thinking of communication as a process of abstracting suggests ways to enhance competence in interaction. Five guidelines help us avoid the problems abstraction may invite.

Recognize That All Perceptions Are Subjective Our perceptions are partial and subjective because each of us perceives from a unique perspective. A class you find exciting may put another student to sleep. Writing is a creative, enjoyable activity for some people and a tedious grind for others. A class on diversity that discusses racism in a frank way may be enlightening for a White student, but the content may risk triggering feelings of distress in Black students and other students of color who are no strangers to racial prejudice and hate speech. There is no truth or falsity to perceptions; they represent what things mean to individuals based on their individual social roles, cultural backgrounds, cognitive abilities, standpoints, and physiology. Effective communicators realize that perceptions are subjective and don't assume that their own perceptions are the only valid ones.

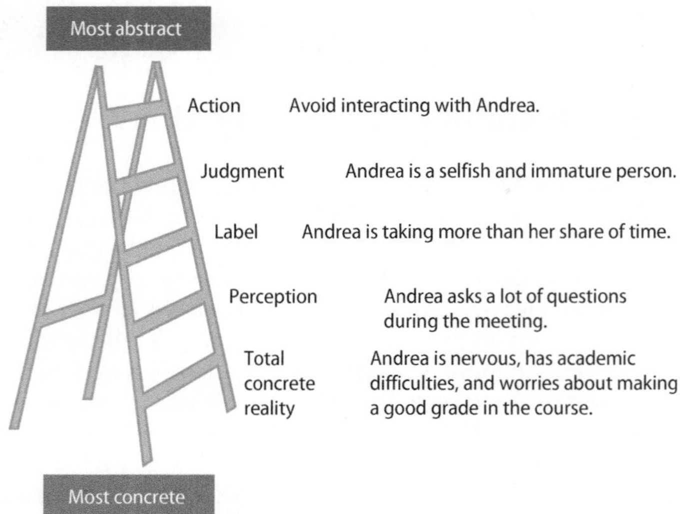
Most abstract
Action Avoid interacting with Andrea.
Judgment Andrea is a selfish and immature person.
Label Andrea is taking more than her share of time.
Perception Andrea asks a lot of questions during the meeting.
Total concrete reality Andrea is nervous, has academic difficulties, and worries about making a good grade in the course.
Most concrete

Figure 2.2 Perception, Communication, and Abstraction

mind reading Assuming that we understand what another person thinks or how another person perceives something.

Avoid Mind Reading One of the most common problems in communication is **mind reading**—assuming we understand what another person thinks or perceives. When we mind read, we act as if we know what's on another's mind, and this can get us into trouble. Marriage counselors identify mind reading as one of the behaviors that contributes to interpersonal tension (Gottman, 1993). According to communication scholar Fran Dickson (1995), one exception may be mind reading between spouses in long-lasting marriages. After living together for a long time, partners may have sufficient person perception to mind read with great accuracy.

For the most part, however, mind reading is more likely to harm than help communication. Doctors sometimes assume they know what patients think or feel and don't ask patients to express their perspectives (Chen, 2012). Mind reading invites problems when we say or think, "I know why you're upset" or "You don't care about me." We also mind read when we tell ourselves we know how somebody else will feel or react or what they'll do. The truth is we don't really know—we're only guessing. When we mind read, we impose our perceptions on others, which can lead to resentment and misunderstandings.

Check Perceptions with Others Because perceptions are subjective and mind reading is ineffective, we need to check our perceptions with others. Perception

Sawyer I learned my lesson about mind reading. A friend I'd known since childhood recently lost her mother to cancer. When I visited the friend, I said I was sorry for her sadness. She told me she wasn't sad at all; she said she was relieved. She had been sad to see her mother suffering so much. To her, death was a blessing.

Question: Over the course of your lifetime, you will likely have many conversations with people grieving losses. Lots of well-intended remarks, like "I'm sorry for your sadness," "I know just how you feel," or "This must be so difficult for you," can hint that mind reading is at play. Now, with this understanding, imagine you are encountering a friend or acquaintance who has recently experienced a death in their family. What kinds of things might you say to show compassion and support, while avoiding mind-reading language?

checking is an important communication skill because it helps people understand each other and their relationships. To check perceptions, you can follow these steps:

1. First, state what you have noticed. For example: "Lately you've seemed less attentive to me."
2. Check to see whether the other person perceives the same thing. "Do you feel you've been less attentive?"
3. Offer alternative explanations of your perceptions if desired or needed: "It might be that you're annoyed with me or that you're stressed out at work or that you're focused on other things."
4. Ask the other person to clarify how they perceive the behavior and the reasons for it. "What do you think is going on?"
5. If the other person doesn't share your perceptions, ask them to explain the behaviors on which your perception is based: "Why have you wanted to be together less often lately?"

It's important to speak tentatively when checking perceptions to minimize defensiveness and encourage open dialogue. Just let the other person know you've noticed something and would like them to clarify their perceptions of what is happening and what it means.

It's also a good idea to check perceptions directly with the other person. It is more difficult to reach a shared understanding with another person when we ask someone else to act as a go-between or when we ask others whether they agree with our perceptions of a third person.

Distinguish Between Facts and Inferences Competent communicators know the difference between facts and inferences. A fact is a statement based on observation or other data. An inference involves an interpretation that goes beyond

The self-serving bias can distort fans' perceptions of their team.
iStock.com/Urbazon

the facts. For example, one of my retired colleagues used to forget his belongings in our classrooms. I'd find his jacket, scarf, even his laptop left behind in the classroom he used last. (He even ran over his laptop with his car once!) These facts—which he was always had a great sense of humor about—might have caused bystanders to infer that he is thoughtless. But defining him as thoughtless is an inference that goes beyond the "fact" of his forgetfulness, which is equally well explained by preoccupation, general absentmindedness, or being so engaged in conversation with students as he left the classroom that he forgot to pick up his own things.

It's easy to confuse facts and inferences because we sometimes treat the latter as the former. When we say, "He is irresponsible," we make a statement that sounds factual, and we may then regard it that way ourselves. To avoid this tendency, substitute more tentative words for *is*. For instance, "Marcus's behaviors seem thoughtless" is more tentative than "Marcus is thoughtless." Tentative language helps us resist the tendency to treat inferences as facts.

Monitor the Self-Serving Bias The self-serving bias exemplifies humans' broad tendency to protect self-image (Tavris & Aronson, 2007). We want to be competent, good, smart, and right. If we make dumb decisions, we're inclined to deny or justify them. A primary means of doing this is to engage in the self-serving bias, which distorts our perceptions. Monitoring the self-serving bias also has implications for how we perceive others. Just as we tend to judge ourselves generously, we may also be inclined to judge others too harshly. Monitor your perceptions to see whether you attribute others' successes and admirable actions to external factors beyond their control and their shortcomings and blunders to internal factors they can (should) control. If you do this, substitute more generous explanations for others' behaviors, and notice how that affects your perceptions of them.

Perceiving accurately is a communication skill that can be developed. Following the five guidelines we have discussed will allow you to perceive more carefully and accurately.

Chapter Summary

In this chapter, we've explored human perception, which involves selecting, organizing, and interpreting experiences. These three processes are not separate in practice; they interact such that each one affects the others. What we selectively notice affects what we interpret and evaluate. In addition, our interpretations act as lenses that influence what we notice in the world around us. Selection, interpretation, and evaluation interact continuously in the process of perception.

Perception is shaped by many factors. Our physiological abilities and conditions affect what we notice and how astutely we recognize stimuli around us. In addition, our cultural backgrounds and social locations shape how we see and interact with the world. Social roles are another influence on perception. Thus, professional training and roles in families affect what we notice and how we organize and interpret it. Finally, perception is influenced by cognitive abilities, including cognitive complexity, person-centered perception, and perspective taking.

The factors that shape our perceptions affect our use of digital media. Our moods and cultural backgrounds, for example, influence the sites and blogs we visit and what we post in our own digital communication.

Thinking about communication as a process of abstracting helps us understand how perception works. We discussed five guidelines for avoiding the problems abstraction sometimes causes. First, realize that all perceptions are subjective, so there is no absolutely correct or best understanding of a situation or a person. Second, because people perceive differently, we should avoid mind reading or assuming we know what others perceive, think, and feel. Third, it's a good idea to check perceptions, which involves stating how you perceive something and asking how another person perceives it. A fourth guideline is to distinguish facts from inferences. Finally, avoiding the self-serving bias is important because it can lead us to perceive ourselves too charitably and others too harshly.

Experiencing Communication in Our Lives

Case Study: College Success

Apply what you've learned in this chapter by analyzing the following case study, using the accompanying questions as a guide.

Your friend Alex tells you about a problem they're having with their parents. According to Alex, their parents have unrealistic expectations. Alex tends to be an average student, earning Cs, a few Bs, and an occasional D—and Alex's parents are angry that their grades aren't better. Alex tells you that when they went home last month, their father said, "I'm not paying for you to go to school to party. I paid my own way and still made the Dean's List. How can you only have a C average? You have to study harder."

Now Alex says to you, "My parents are brilliant; they think college should be easy for me because it was for them. But, I'm not them. All my classes are hard. No matter how much I study, I'm not going to be an 'A' student—and spending less time with my friends won't magically put me on the Dean's List. How can I convince them that I'm already doing my best?"

Questions for Analysis and Discussion

1. Both Alex and their parents make attributions to explain Alex's grades. Describe the dimensions of Alex's attributions and those of their parents.
2. How might you assess the accuracy of Alex's attributions? What questions could you ask Alex to help you decide whether their perceptions are well founded or biased?
3. What constructs, prototypes, and scripts seem to operate in Alex's and their parents' thinking about college life?
4. What could you say to Alex to help them reach a shared perspective with their parents on Alex's academic work?

Key Concepts

attribution
cognitive complexity
constructivism
culture
empathy
interpretation
mind reading
perception
personal construct
person-centered perception
prototype
schemata
script
self-fulfilling prophecy
self-serving bias
standpoint theory
stereotype

For Further Reflection and Discussion

1. Identify an occasion when you engaged in the self-serving bias. Explain what you did, using the language of attributions.
2. Identify ethical issues involved in perceiving. What ethical choices do we make—perhaps unconsciously—as we selectively perceive, organize, and interpret others, particularly people whom we think are different from us in important ways?
3. Use the ladder of abstraction to analyze your perceptions and actions in a specific communication encounter. First, identify the concrete reality, what you perceived from the totality, the labels you assigned, and the resulting inferences and judgments. Second, return to the first level of perception and substitute different perceptions—other aspects of the total situation you might have perceived selectively. What labels, inferences, and judgments do the substitute perceptions invite? With others in the class, discuss the extent to which our perceptions and labels influence "reality."
4. Think about how cultural values such as efficiency and individualism affect communication in your workplace or a former workplace. What other strong aspects of United States culture impact the workplace?
5. As a service project, volunteer to work in a context that allows you to interact with people you have not spent time with. For example, if you have little experience with food insecurity, you might volunteer at a food pantry. Before you begin, make a list of schemata (i.e., prototypes, personal constructs, stereotypes, and scripts) you have about the people you would interact with. Afterwards, review your list of schemata. How accurate were they?

Comstock/Stockbyte/Getty Images

Go confidently in the direction of your dreams.

Henry David Thoreau

Communication and Personal Identity

Learning Objectives

After studying the topics in this chapter, you should be able to:

1. Explain how perception influences identity and communication.
2. Explain how culture and identity categories influence identity and communication.
3. Apply the guidelines in this chapter to set goals for improving your self-perceptions.

How do social media affect your self-esteem?

"Who are you?" asks Greta as an elderly man sits in a chair beside her.

"I am Sam, your husband," he replies taking her hand.

"Who am I?" she asks.

"You are Greta Williams," he says softly. "You taught school for many years, you loved to hike, and loved practical jokes. We have two daughters."

"Who liked jokes?" Greta asks.

Greta was also a star ballerina at age 5, a college student, and an amateur artist, but she isn't aware of any of these parts of her identity. On good days, she remembers fragments of her life. On bad days, like today, she has no memory of who she was for 70 years before she developed dementia.

Can you imagine not knowing who you are, what you loved doing, or who your partner is? Greta has lost a key anchor that most of us take for granted: her personal identity.

Like Greta, you've defined yourself in different ways over the years, and you'll redefine yourself further in the future. This reminds us that the self is not fixed firmly at one time and constant thereafter. Instead, the self is a process that evolves and changes throughout our lives. In this chapter, we explore how communication with others allows us to develop and refine personal identities. We begin by defining the self. Next, we consider how social media affects our identities. We conclude with guidelines for enhancing your identity.

What Is the Self?

self A multidimensional process in which the individual forms and acts from social perspectives that arise and evolve in communication with themselves.

The **self** is a process of internalizing and acting from social perspectives that we learn in the process of communication. At first, this may seem like a complicated way to define the self. As we will see, however, this definition directs our attention to some important insights into what is complicated: the human self.

The Self Arises in Communication with Others

The most basic insight into the self is that it isn't something we are born with. Instead, the self develops only as we communicate with others and participate in the social world. From the moment we are born, we interact with others. We learn how they see us, and we internalize many of their views of who we are and should be.

Communication with Family Members For most of us, family members are the first important influence on how we see ourselves (Bergen & Braithwaite, 2009). Parents and other family members communicate who we are and what we are worth. They rely primarily on three kinds of communication: *direct definition, identity scripts, and attachment styles.*

direct definition Communication that explicitly tells us who we are by specifically labeling us and reacting to our behaviors. Direct definition usually occurs first in families and then in interaction with peers and others.

Direct definition, as the term implies, is communication that explicitly tells us who we are by labeling us and our behaviors. For instance, parents might say, "You're my little girl" or "You're a big boy" and thus communicate to the child their sex. Having been assigned the label *boy* or *girl*, the child then pays attention to how others talk about boys and girls to figure out what it means to be a certain sex. Parents' own gender stereotypes typically are communicated to children, so daughters may also be told, "Be nice to your friends" and "Don't mess up your clothes." Sons, on the other hand, are more likely to be told, "Stick up for yourself" and "Don't cry." Children's media and consumer culture also reinforce these gender stereotypes by communicating that boys and girls enjoy different things (Hains, 2014; Hains and Hunting, 2018; Hains and Jennings, 2021). Through these messages, we pick up our parents' and society's gender expectations. Children who accept these expectations are generally praised, receiving positive reinforcement. But the pressures to conform are so intense that the **gender-nonconforming** children who resist them have a higher-than-average risk of receiving psychological abuse, physical abuse, bullying, and other forms of victimization from peers and adults alike (Roberts et al., 2013).

gender-nonconforming A person who does not conform to the gendered social norms and stereotypes associated with their sex.

Direct definition also takes place as family members respond to children's behaviors. If a child is praised for dusting furniture, being helpful is reinforced as part of the child's self-concept. Positive labels enhance our self-esteem: "You are smart," "You're great at baseball." Negative labels can damage children's self-esteem: "You're a troublemaker" and "You're stupid" are messages that can demolish a child's sense of self-worth.

Family members also use **identity scripts** to communicate who we are and should be. Psychologists define identity scripts as rules for how we are supposed to live and who we are supposed to be (Berne, 1964; Harris, 1969). Like the scripts for plays, identity scripts define our roles, how we are to play them, and basic elements in the plot we are supposed to have for our lives. Think back to your childhood to identify some of the principal scripts that operated in your family. Did you learn, "Always be prepared for emergencies," "We give back to our community," or "Live by God's word"? These are examples of identity scripts families teach us.

identity script A guide to action based on rules for living and identity. Initially communicated in families, identity scripts define our roles, how we are to play them, and basic elements in the plot of our lives.

Children seldom author, or even edit, initial identity scripts. In fact, children are generally not even conscious of learning identity scripts. As adults, however, we are no longer passive recipients of others' definitions. We have the capacity to review the identity scripts that were given to us and to challenge and change those that do not fit who we now choose to be.

attachment style Any of several patterns of attachment that result from particular parenting styles that teach children who they are, who others are, and how to approach relationships.

Finally, parents communicate who we are through **attachment styles.** These patterns of parenting teach us who we and others are and how to relate to others. From extensive studies of interaction between parents and children, John Bowlby (1973, 1988) developed the theory that we learn attachment styles in our relationships with our first caregivers—usually with parents. They communicate how they see us, others, and relationships. In turn, we are likely to internalize their views as our own. The first relationship is especially important because it can influence later relationships, such as romantic partnerships (Hermans et al., 2021). Four distinct attachment styles have been identified (Figure 3.1): secure, fearful, dismissive, and anxious/ambivalent.

A child is most likely to develop a *secure attachment style* when the primary caregiver interacts in a consistently attentive and loving way with the child. In response, the child develops a positive sense of self-worth ("I am lovable") and a positive view of others ("People are loving and can be trusted"). People with secure attachment styles tend to be outgoing, affectionate, and able to

Figure 3.1
Styles of Attachment

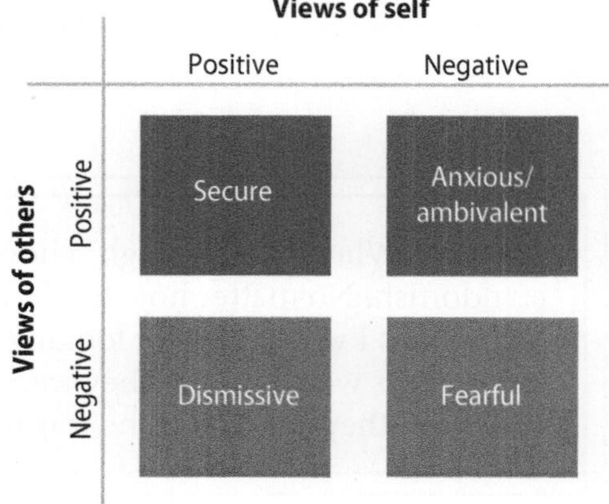

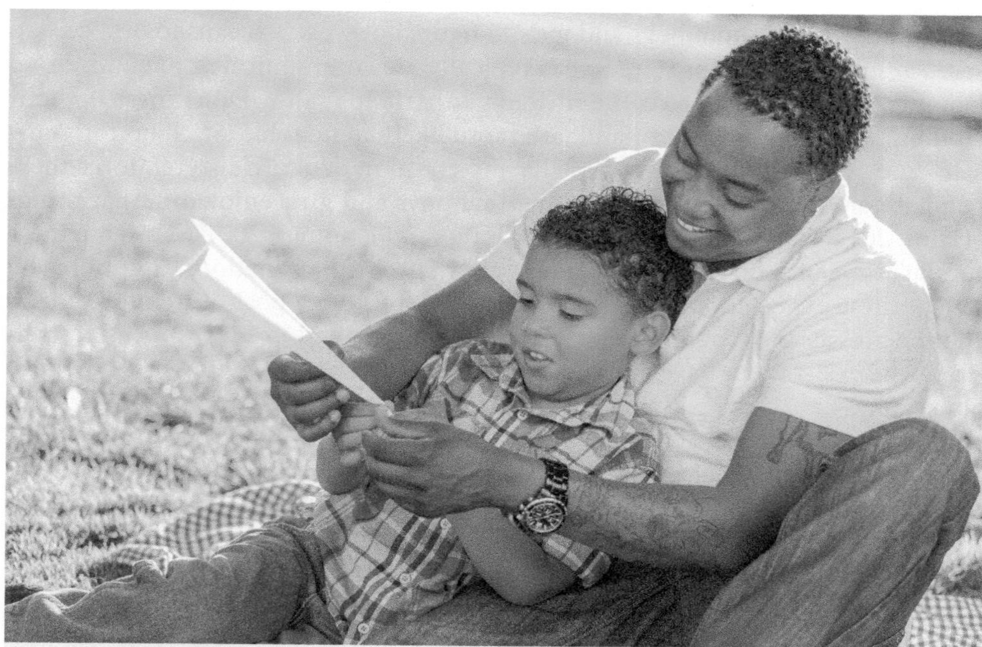

Parents' communication is a major influence on identity.
Andy Dean Photography/Shutterstock.com

handle the normal challenges and disappointments of close relationships without losing self-esteem. Securely attached individuals tend to have more secure relationships (Rowe & Carnelley, 2005) than less securely attached individuals (Candel & Turliuc, 2019).

Review It!

Attachment Styles:

- Secure
- Fearful
- Dismissive
- Anxious/ambivalent

A child may develop a *fearful attachment style* if the primary caregiver communicates in negative, rejecting, or abusive ways to the child. Children who are treated negatively often conclude that they are unlovable and others are rejecting. Although they may want close bonds with others, they fear that others will not love them and that they themselves are not lovable.

A caregiver who is disinterested, rejecting, or abusive may also lead a child to develop a *dismissive attachment style,* which often leads children to scorn others. People with dismissive attachment styles have a positive view of themselves and a low regard for others and relationships. This may lead them to regard relationships as unnecessary and undesirable.

Olivia When I was in high school, I babysat to make money. One little girl I watched was very standoffish. No matter how hard I tried to play with Liza and be friends, she kept her distance. But sometimes I would see her looking at me almost longingly like she wanted to play with me. When her parents were around, they were focused on work or each other. If Liza needed something or spoke up, they acted as if she was interrupting them.

Last is the *anxious/ambivalent attachment style,* which is the most complex of the four. Each of the other three styles results from a consistent pattern of treatment by a caregiver. However, the anxious/ambivalent style is fostered by *inconsistent* treatment from the caregiver. Sometimes the adult is loving and attentive, at other times indifferent or rejecting. The caregiver's communication is not only inconsistent but also unpredictable. They may respond positively to something a child does on Monday and react negatively to the same behavior on Tuesday. Naturally, this unpredictability creates anxiety in a child. Because children tend to assume that adults are right, they often believe they themselves are the source of any problem—that they are unlovable or deserve others' abuse. People who have high anxiety about attachments are likely to avoid or minimize attachments (Read et al., 2018).

Review It!

Parental Influences on Identity:

- Direct Definition
- Identity Scripts
- Attachment Styles

In adult life, people who have anxious/ambivalent attachment styles know that others can be loving and affirming, but they also know that others can hurt them and be unloving. Reflecting the pattern displayed by the caregiver, people with anxious/ambivalent attachment styles often are inconsistent themselves. One day they invite affection; the next day they deny needing closeness. Various studies have found that people with anxious/ambivalent attachment styles (Cole & Leets, 1999) and fearful styles (Dinkha et al., 2015) often form relationships with television characters. It may feel safer to be in relationships with television characters than with real people. Similarly, evidence suggests that people with negative attachment styles are more prone to intense use of social media to attempt to meet their emotional needs—sometimes in dysfunctional or addictive ways (D'Arienzo et al., 2019; Demircioğlu & Köse, 2021).

social comparison Comparing ourselves with others to form judgments of our own talents, abilities, qualities, and so forth.

Unless we consciously work to change the attachment styles we learned in our first close relationships, they tend to affect how we communicate in our adult relationships (Fraley, 2019). However, we can modify our attachment styles by challenging unconstructive views of us communicated in our early years and by forming relationships that foster secure connections today (Banse, 2004).

We measure our abilities against those of peers.
Edwin Verin/Shutterstock.com

Communication with Peers A second major influence on our self-concepts is communication with peers. From childhood playmates to work associates, friends, and romantic partners, we interact with peers throughout our lives. As we do, we gain further direct definitions that tell us how others see us. In turn, this affects how we see ourselves. As we interact with peers, we engage in **social comparison**, which involves comparing ourselves with others to gauge our talents, attractiveness, abilities, skills, and so forth (Stapel & Blanton, 2006). Social comparison is so common, it can influence our thoughts on everything from problem-solving to emotions to attitudes to our perceptions of others (Baldwin & Mussweiler, 2018, p. 72). We measure ourselves in relation to others in two ways. First, we compare ourselves with others to decide whether we are like them or different from them. Are we the same age, color, or religion? Do we have similar backgrounds and social and political beliefs?

Peers are particularly strong in commenting directly on conformity to expectations of gender, with males and females equally susceptible to peer pressure (McCoy et al., 2019)—though that pressure may take different forms. For example, some college-age men think drinking and sexual activity embody masculinity. Men who are not interested in drinking and hooking up may be ridiculed and excluded for not being "real men" (Cross, 2008; Kimmel, 2008). Women who don't wear popular brands of clothing or who weigh more than what is considered ideal may be belittled and excluded for being unfeminine (Adler, 2007; Barash, 2006). Due to perceived pressures like these, social media use can spur impulse purchases when we compare ourselves to content shared by people we perceive as superior or aspirational (Liu et al., 2019).

Isla I never cared a lot about clothes until I joined a sorority where the labels on your clothes are a measure of your worth. The girls compete with each other to dress the best and have the newest styles. When one of the sisters wears something out of style, she gets a lot of teasing, but really it's pressure on her to measure up to the sorority image. At first, I adopted my sisters' values, and I spent more money than I could afford on clothes. For a while I even quit making contributions at church so that I could have more money for clothes. When I finally realized I was becoming somebody I didn't like, I tried to change, but my sisters made me feel bad anytime I wasn't dressed well. Finally, I moved out rather than face that pressure all the time. It just wasn't a good place for me to be myself.

Question: Eliminating a source of peer pressure can be a difficult but ultimately healthy choice. Some, like Isla, will leave a peer group; others will get off of social media or switch to a different platform. Can you think of a time when social comparisons encouraged by peer pressure were a problem for you? What, if anything, were you able to do about it at the time? Is there anything you might do differently in a similar situation today?

In fact, social media are key sources for social comparison. We read others' updates and compare our accomplishments to theirs, our activities to theirs, our number of friends to theirs, and so on. On social networking sites, many, perhaps most, people emphasize what is positive in their lives and downplay or omit mention of what is not so positive (Krasnova, Wenninger, Widjaja, & Buxmann, 2013; Tierney, 2013). This suggests that we might be wise to be cautious in comparing ourselves to the selves others present online.

Assessing similarity and difference allows us to decide with whom we fit. Research has shown that people generally are most comfortable with others who are like them, so we tend to gravitate toward those we regard as similar (Chen et al., 2009; Filson, 2014; Morry et al., 2010). However, interacting only with people like us can impoverish our understandings of ourselves and the world.

We also use social comparison to measure ourselves in relation to others. Am I as good a goalie as Ella? Am I as smart as Tristan? We continuously refine our self-image by comparing ourselves to others on various criteria of judgment. This is normal and necessary if we are to develop realistic self-concepts. However, we should be wary of what psychologists call **upward comparison**, which is the tendency to compare ourselves to people who exceed us in what they have or can do (Tugend, 2011). While stretching to be better is desirable, it isn't constructive to judge our attractiveness in relation to that of movie stars and models or our athletic ability in relation to that of professional athletes. Nor is it helpful to compare our lives to those our friends and acquaintances curate for sharing on social media. Doing so can make us feel worse about ourselves (Burke et al., 2020).

upward comparison The tendency to compare the self to people who exceed us in what they have or can do.

Communication Highlight

Self-Help: A Healthier Self?

Do you love too much, too little, or the wrong people? Are you guilty of negative thinking? If so, there's a self-help book—or a dozen—for you. Don't want a book? No problem, buy self-help video and audio products, attend seminars, or hire a personal coach. You can join a support group with 12 steps or 7 principles. It's all part of the multibillion dollar self-help industry. And don't forget television programs such as *The Swan* (aired 2004), *Extreme Makeover* (aired 2002–2006), and *The Biggest Loser* (is being aired 2004–present), which also tell us to take charge of fixing ourselves with self-discipline perhaps along with multiple surgeries. Unfortunately, such shows capitalize on widespread judgments around larger bodies that can lead to eating disorders, depression, and avoidance of medical care due to the shaming and misdiagnosis that often occur. This means the advice offered by the self-help industry isn't always helpful or healthy.

Although the self-help industry is wildly popular today, it's not exactly new. The first self-help book was published in 1859 by Samuel Smiles. Titled *Self-Help* and appropriately self-published, Smiles' book opened by telling readers "Heaven helps those who help themselves." Within a year of publication, the book sold 20,000 copies, extraordinary for that era. Another early self-help author was Dale Carnegie. After a short stint as a salesman, Carnegie failed as an actor and wound up broke, unemployed, and living at the YMCA in New York. That's where he started teaching a public speaking course that formed the basis of *How to Win Friends and Influence People* (1936), which was a self-help manual for millions of readers.

The self-help category continues to be popular to this day, and bestselling self-help authors who use social media and traditional media to further their reach become household names. For example, Brené Brown is highly respected for her widely viewed Ted Talks and bestselling self-help books, including *The Gifts of Imperfection: Let Go of Who You Think You're Supposed to Be and Embrace Who You Are* (2010) and *Daring Greatly: How the Courage to be Vulnerable Transforms the Way We Live, Love, Parent, and Lead* (2012)—both #1 bestsellers boasting combined sales of more than 5 million copies in multiple languages. Likewise, Marie Kondo became an international phenomenon after publishing the best-selling *The Life-Changing Magic of Tidying Up: The Japanese Art of Decluttering and Organizing* (2014), followed by her own television show and additional well-received books. Her advice to ask whether objects "spark joy" is part of our common vocabulary, as is the term "Doing a Marie Kondo"—a popular synonym for decluttering one's physical or digital life.

Tommy Siegel/Cartoon Stock.com

Communication & Careers

Social Comparison in the Workplace

Performance reviews give professionals feedback on job performance. It's only natural to want to know not only how you are evaluated, but also how you compare to your peers. But what happens when you find out that your performance is regarded less well than that of coworkers? Research suggests that higher-ranking, higher-performing employees are more likely to respond to negative social comparisons by engaging in deception than other employees are (Edelman & Larkin, 2014). In an effort to maintain their standing, higher-status employees employ deceptive practices to make themselves look better. For example, higher-ranking professors downloaded their own publications to elevate the ranking of the publications.

Communication with Society A third influence on our identity is interaction with society in general. As we observe and interact with others and media and as we participate in institutions, we learn how society regards sex, gender, race, sexual orientation, ability, size, age, and socioeconomic class. We also learn broad cultural values.

Media are primary in teaching social perspectives. Whether we are watching blockbuster films, scrolling through social media, or reading the latest news, we are inundated with messages about which careers carry status, which clothes and hairstyles are cool, how people of various genders are supposed to look and act, and so forth. Media including TV, films, music videos, and pornography shape teens' views of sex and sexuality (Aubrey et al., 2021; Wood & Fixmer-Oraiz, 2017)—as well as their views on diverse matters ranging from politics (Anderson, 2020) to body image (Tamilselvi & Saranya, 2022) and body positivity (Maes & Vandenbosch, 2022).

The institutions that organize our society further communicate social perspectives by the values they uphold. For example, our judicial system reminds us that as a society we value laws and punish those who break them. The number of schools and the levels of education in America inform us that our society values learning. At the same time, institutions reflect prevailing social prejudices. For instance, we may be a lawful society, but not all laws are equitable, and wealthy defendants often can buy better "justice" than defendants from a lower socioeconomic status. Similarly, although we claim to offer equal educational opportunities to all, public schools are funded by property taxes. The United States has a long history of ***de jure* segregation**, or a confluence of laws and policies that cause Black people and White people to live in separate communities—not by chance or personal preference, but by design (Rothstein, 2017). One result is significantly different levels of per-pupil educational funding across the nation, with the most marginalized students receiving a public education that pales in comparison to that of their peers in Wealthy, predominantly White ZIP codes. Then, in college, students whose families have money and influence often can get into better schools than students whose families have fewer resources. These and other values are so thoroughly woven into the fabric of our culture that people who benefit from them give them little thought, assuming the status quo to be natural and right, with little effort or awareness of the pervasive injustices baked into the system.

***de jure* segregation**
A complex system of laws and government policies that cause White and Black people to live in separate communities.

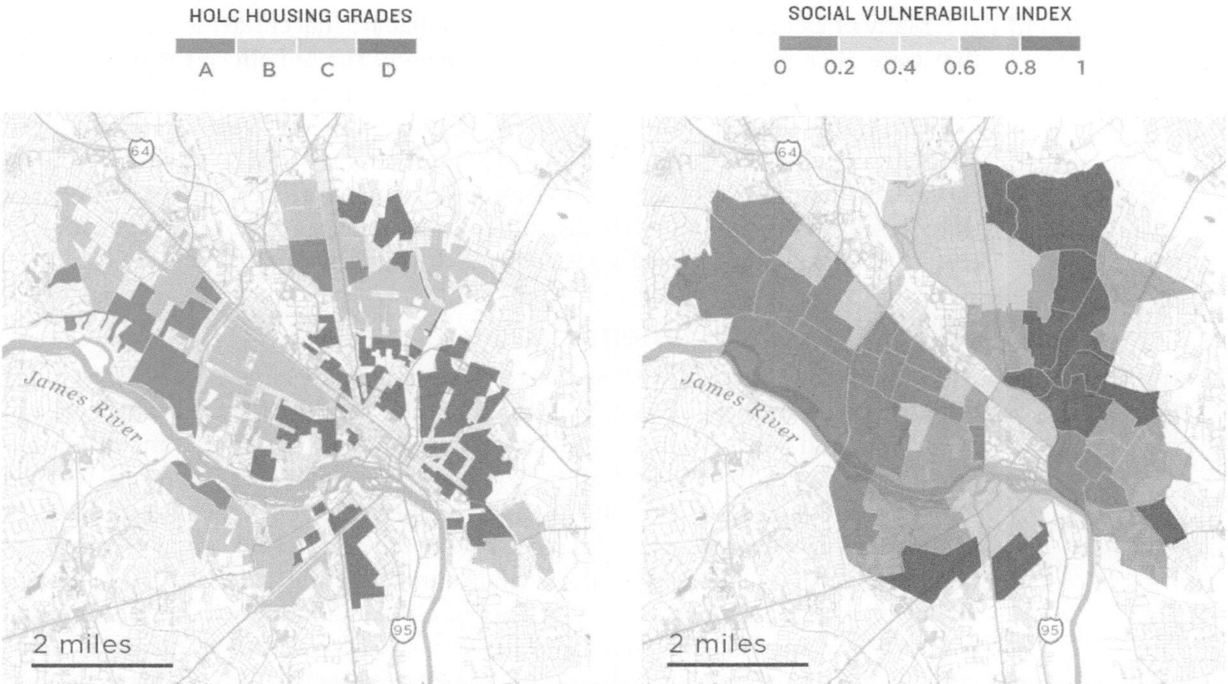

Redlining maps, used to enact and reinforce de jure segregation, communicated racist cultural values that assigned investment values on properties based specifically on the community's racial demographics. In these maps, the color red and a letter grade of "D," identified predominantly Black communities that banks used to deny loans to Black people.
Connie Hanzhang Jin/NPR

The Self-Fulfilling Prophecy One particularly powerful way in which communication shapes the self is the self-fulfilling prophecy, which we discussed in Chapter 2. Self-fulfilling prophecies operate when we act in ways that bring about expectations or judgments of ourselves. If you have done poorly in classes in which teachers didn't seem to respect you and have done well with teachers who thought you were smart, then you know what a self-fulfilling prophecy is. The prophecies that we act to fulfill usually are first communicated to us by others' direct definitions, identity scripts, and attachment styles. Because we often internalize others' perspectives, we may act to fulfill the labels.

Milo I can really identify with the self-fulfilling prophecy idea. In the second grade, my family moved from our farm to a city where my dad could find work. The first week of class in my new school, we had show and tell. When it was my turn, as soon as I started talking the other kids started laughing at me. I had been raised on a farm in the rural South, and the other kids were from the city. They thought I talked funny, and they made fun of my accent—called me "hillbilly" and "redneck." From then on, I avoided public speaking like the plague. I thought I couldn't speak to others. Last year, I finally took a course in public speaking, and I made a B. It took me a long time to challenge the label that I was a bad public speaker.

Question: It's easy for other people's judgments to become our own self-fulfilling prophecies. Fortunately, many schools today intentionally foster a culture of kindness, actively teaching children how to treat their peers in a healthy way—with positive rather than negative remarks. Can you think of a time when a friend, classmate, or teacher offered you a compliment or praise? Did it boost your confidence?

Many of us believe things about ourselves that are inaccurate. Sometimes labels that were once true aren't any longer, but we continue to believe them and act to fulfill them. In other cases, the labels were never valid, but we may believe them anyway. Unfortunately, children often are labeled "slow" or "stupid" when the real problem may be that they transferred from a school that was chronically underfunded, or that they have impaired vision or hearing or are too hungry to concentrate in school. By the time the true source of difficulty is discovered, the children may have already internalized a destructive self-fulfilling prophecy.

The Self Is Multidimensional

code-switching Switching between different styles of speech, mannerisms, and behaviors to fit within different contexts and social settings. Code-switching can also refer more specifically to when a person of color changes their self-presentation to make those around them more comfortable, particularly in predominantly white settings where the person's race or ethnicity is at risk of being negatively stereotyped.

Although we use the word *self* as if it referred to a single entity, the self has many dimensions. You have a physical self that includes your size, shape, skin, hair and eye colors, and so forth. In addition, you have a cognitive self that includes your intelligence, aptitudes, and education. You have an emotional self-concept. Are you interpersonally sensitive? Do you have a hot temper? Are you generally optimistic or pessimistic? You have a social self. Some people are extraverted, whereas others are more reserved. Our social selves also include our roles: child, student, worker, parent, volunteer, partner in a relationship. Each of us also has a moral self that is composed of ethical and spiritual principles we believe in and try to follow. As Carlyle points out, the different dimensions of ourselves sometimes seem at odds with one another.

This can be especially the case for people who need to engage in **code-switching**, or changing their behavior and appearance in various contexts or settings to make

Ezra On my own, like with friends or family, I'm pretty quiet—even shy, you could say. But my job requires me to be real outgoing and sociable. I tend bar, and people expect me to kid around and talk with them and stuff. Believe me, if I were as quiet with my customers as I am with my friends, my tips would drop to nothing.

Question: This anecdote illustrates that Ezra's self is multidimensional: quiet at home, and outgoing at work. Which self does Ezra seem to imply is their more authentic self, and why?

Ego boundaries develop as an infant distinguishes the self from the rest of the world.
iStock.com/Prostock-Studio

those around them more comfortable. For example, Harvard Business Review (2019) notes that Black people code switch when they are in locations where negative stereotypes of Black behavior are common, such as schools or the workplace, and that while it is a strategy for success, it takes a psychological toll. It would be healthier for these sites to be more inclusive, for example, by working to develop the cultural competence and cultural humility of the privileged group.

The Self Is a Process

The self develops over time; it is a process. A baby perceives no boundaries between its body and a nipple, a hand that tickles, or a breeze. As an infant has experiences and as others respond to them, the child gradually begins to develop **ego boundaries**, which define where the self stops and the rest of the world begins. This is the beginning of a self-concept: the realization that one is a separate entity.

ego boundaries A person's internal sense of where they stop and the rest of the world begins.

As infants begin to differentiate themselves from the rest of the world, the self starts to develop. Infants and young children listen to and observe others to define themselves and to become competent in the identities others assign to them (Kohlberg, 1958; Piaget, 1932/1965). For instance, children work to figure out what it takes to be nice, tough, and responsible, and they strive to become competent at embodying those qualities. The ways we define ourselves vary as we mature. Struggling to be a good mud-cake maker at age 4 gives way to striving for popularity in high school and to succeeding in professional and family roles later in life.

Of course, we all enter the world with certain abilities and limits, which constrain the possibilities of who we can be. Someone without the genes to be tall and coordinated, for instance, probably is not going to be a star forward in basketball. Beyond genetic limits, however, we have considerable freedom to create who we will be.

We Internalize and Act from Social Perspectives

We've already noted that in developing a self, we internalize many of the perspectives of others. Let's now look more closely at how we internalize both the perspectives of specific individuals who are significant in our lives and the general perspective of our society.

Particular Others We first encounter the perspectives of **particular others**. These are the viewpoints of specific people who are significant to us. Parents, siblings, and often day-care providers are particular others who are significant to most infants. In addition, we may be close to extended family members, grandparents, godparents, and others. Children from large, extended families often have a great many particular others who affect how they come to see themselves.

particular others One source of social perspectives that people use to define themselves and guide how they think, act, and feel. The perspectives of particular others are the viewpoints of people who are significant to the self.

Shennoa My grandmother was the biggest influence on me. I lived with her while my mama worked, and she taught me to take myself seriously. She's the one who told me I should go to college and plan a career so that I wouldn't have to depend on somebody else. She's the one who told me to stand up for myself and not let others tell me what to do or believe in. But she did more than just tell me to be a strong person. That's how she was, and I learned just by watching her. A lot of who I am is modeled on my grandmother.

Question: It sounds like Shennoa's grandmother served as a "looking-glass" to her during her youth. Can you think of a person who has been or currently is particularly important to you? What is a self-perception you have that reflects that person's communicated appraisal of you?

reflected appraisal Our perceptions of others' views of us.

The process of seeing ourselves through others' eyes is called **reflected appraisal**. It has also been called the "looking-glass self" because others are mirrors who reflect how they perceive us (Cooley, 1912). Reflected appraisals continue throughout our lives. When a teacher communicates that a student is smart, the student may come to see themselves that way. In professional life, coworkers and supervisors reflect their appraisals of us when they communicate that we're on the fast track, average, or unsuited to our position. The appraisals that others communicate shape how we see ourselves. In turn, how we see ourselves affects how we communicate. Thus, if you see yourself as an interesting conversationalist, you're likely to communicate that confidence when you talk with others.

perspective of the generalized other The collection of rules, roles, and attitudes endorsed by the whole social community in which we live.

cultural globalization The circulation of media (including film, television, the Internet, and social media) and commodities around the globe, accompanied by ideas and values—a process mainly driven by industrialized Western cultures.

privilege Unearned advantages and opportunities experienced by people who share a racial or gender identity perceived as being at the top of the social hierarchy.

The Generalized Other The second social perspective that influences how we see ourselves is called the **perspective of the generalized other**. The generalized other is the rules, roles, values, and attitudes endorsed by the specific culture in which we live (Mead, 1934).

Modern Western culture emphasizes race, sex, sexual orientation, gender, and economic class as central to personal identity. In contrast to the Western approach, Eastern cultures have tended to emphasize collective identity more than individual, personal identity (Facing History and Ourselves, 2014). That said, when people are exposed to **cultural globalization**—meaning exported media (often from the West) and commodities, along with the ideas and values they communicate—this exposure can cause some shifts in how emerging adults form their identities (Ozer et al., 2019).

Race. North American culture views race as a primary aspect of personal identity (González, Houston, & Chen, 2012). The White race has been **privileged**

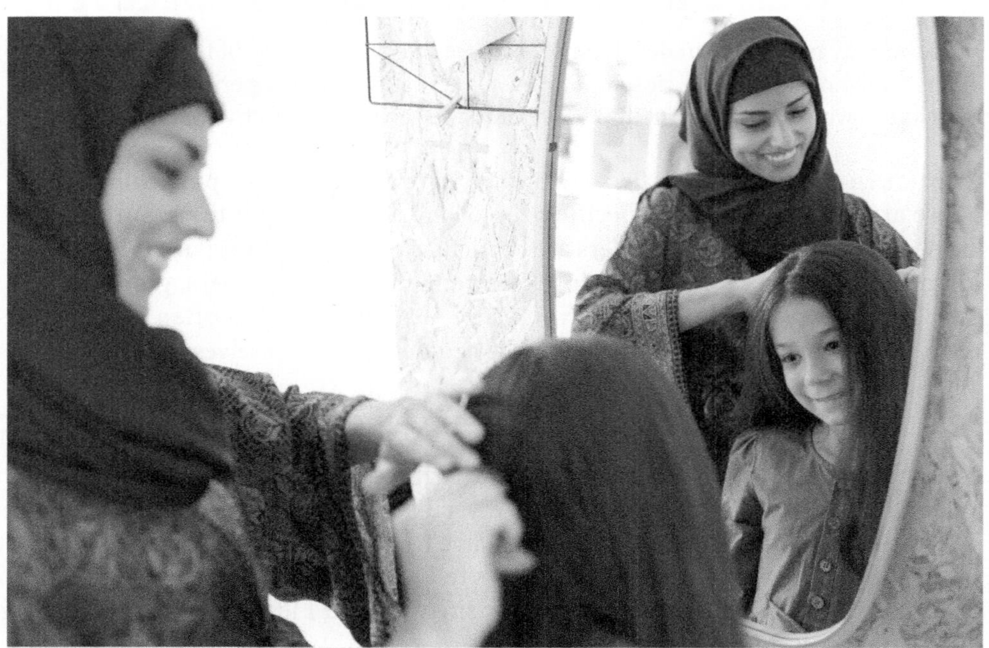

Who are the looking glasses through which you see yourself?
Leigh M. Wilco

throughout United States history. In this context, being "privileged" means enjoying advantages and opportunities that are not earned. Instead, as Peggy McIntosh famously explained this concept in her landmark 1989 essay, people who share an identity at the top of the social hierarchy (e.g., White people) benefit from these advantages and assets in an invisible way, often without even realizing it.

Racial privilege and identity have a long history in the United States. In the early years of this country, the majority of White lawmakers believed that White men had the right to enslave Black women, men, and children and to force them to work for no wages, in poor conditions, and in states of constant physical and psychological danger. Later, after slavery was made illegal, the White ruling class considered it natural that White men could vote but Black men could not. Thanks to the determined work of Black activists and their allies in the face of major resistance, this is no longer the case. Over time, it has become less socially acceptable to behave in overtly racist ways, and many once-common racist practices are now illegal. Even so, White men continue to dominate the upper levels of government, education, and business. People of color continue to fight overt and covert discrimination in many spheres of society and communicate to raise awareness of how historic racist practices continue to cause intergenerational harm today—information that is necessary for voters and political leaders to understand if we are to properly address these ongoing problems in our society.

WEN-SHU My family moved here when I was 9 years old. Because I look Asian, people make assumptions about me. They assume I am quiet (true), I am good at math (not true), and I defer to men and elders (true with regard to elders but not men). People also see all Asian people as the same, but Taiwanese are as different from mainland Chinese as French Caucasians are from United States Caucasians. The first thing people notice about me is my race, and they make too many assumptions about what it means.

Sex. Sex is also a key aspect of identity in Western culture, serving as a social structure (Risman, 2018). In the United States, historically, men—specifically, White men—have been seen as more valuable than women and more entitled to privileges such as education, voting rights, property ownership, and access to loans. In the 1800s, women weren't allowed to own property, attend college, or vote. Although there has been great progress in achieving equality between the sexes, in some respects women and men still are not considered equal or treated as such (Kaufman & Kimmel, 2011; Wood & Fixmer-Oraiz, 2017).

Western cultures also have long held strong ideas about sex roles. Girls and women are expected to be caring and cooperative, whereas boys and men are supposed to be independent and competitive. Consequently, women who are competitive and men who are gentle may receive social disapproval (Kimmel & Messner, 2012).

Sexual Orientation. At the same time, cultural communication also establishes sexual orientation as salient. Western culture's long-standing view has been that heterosexuality is normal and right. This bias is communicated both directly but also through privileges given to cisgendered heterosexuals but denied to gay men, lesbians, bisexuals, trans people, and gender-nonconforming people. Although in 2015, the Supreme Court ruled that all states must recognize same-sex marriage, society often still communicates that gender conformity is the norm. For example, toys continue to be marketed on the basis of gender stereotypes, with separate boys' and girls' toy aisles (Hains, 2015)—although this is beginning to change through a combination of corporate practice and legislation (Prang, 2021).

Likewise, most of us can find clothes that fit, but women's blouses are designed with cisgendered women's bodies in mind, and men's pants are designed with cisgendered men's hip-to-waist ratio in mind. But gender minorities may find it challenging to find apparel that both fits well and suits their desired gender expression (Italie, 2014).

gender binary Categorizing gender into two opposite forms: masculine and feminine, aligned with the male and female sexes.

Gender. Gender is also salient to cultural communication. Western cultures long associated gender with sex using a **gender binary**, in which men and women were viewed as being ideal if they had gender-stereotypical traits. For example, masculine gender stereotypes suggest the ideal man is tall and muscular, while feminine gender stereotypes suggest the ideal woman is slender or thin and not too tall.

Gender continuum Gender as an open-ended concept that can vary and include a person's gender identity, gender expression, conformity to gender roles, and anatomical or biological characteristics.

Western culture has been shifting, however, and moving towards acknowledging that gender is a continuum with diverse components. The components of a **gender continuum** may include a person's gender identity, their gender expression, their conformity to gender roles, and their anatomical or biological characteristics (Castleberry, 2019). Those whose identities fall outside stereotypical binary categories may face harassment, discrimination, and marginalization from prejudiced people, and researchers are working on ways to help more people overcome these prejudices (Cramwinckel et al., 2018). In the medical field, for example, it is now recognized that students and practitioners need to develop cultural competence with the gender continuum in order to provide quality care (Castleberry, 2019).

Likewise, many colleges and universities now include gender identity and expression in their nondiscrimination policies, have designated some bathrooms as available to everyone and enacted gender-neutral housing policies so that transgender students are not forced to live with people with whom they don't identify (Lazo, 2014; Tilsley, 2010).

Socioeconomic Class. Socioeconomic class is also central to the generalized other's perspective in Western culture (Acker, 2013; Kendall, 2011; Scott & Leonhardt, 2013). Socioeconomic class isn't just the amount of money a person

has. It's a basic part of how we understand our place in the world and how we think, feel, and act (Lawless, 2012). Socioeconomic class affects everything from the careers we pursue to the schools and lifestyles we see as possibilities for ourselves. Members of the middle and upper classes assume that they will attend college and enter good professions, whereas people from the working class may be directed toward vocational training regardless of their academic achievements. In such patterns, we see how the perspective of the generalized other shapes our identities and our concrete lives.

It's important to realize that social perspectives on race, sex, sexual orientation, gender, size, ability, and socioeconomic class interact with one another. The concept of **intersectionality**, developed by Kimberlé Crenshaw in 1989, is helpful in understanding these interactions. For example, race intersects with gender, so women of color often experience double oppression and devaluation in our culture. Class and sexual orientation also interact: Homophobia tends to be pronounced among people in the working class, so a lesbian or gay person in an underprivileged community may be socially ostracized. Socioeconomic class and gender are also interlinked; women are far more likely than men to live at the poverty level (Andersen & Collins, 2013; Kaufman & Kimmel, 2011). Intersections of race and class mean that minoritized members of the working class often are not treated as well as working-class Whites (Rothenberg, 2006).

Intersectionality The idea that identity categories such as race, sex, sexual orientation, gender, size, ability, and socioeconomic class overlap, which can compound inequalities.

Rochelle I got so mad in high school. I had a solid A average, and ever since I was 12 I had planned to go to college. But when the guidance counselor talked with me at the start of my senior year, she encouraged me to apply to a technical school that is near my home. When I said I thought my grades should get me into a good college, she did this double-take, like, "Your kind doesn't go to college." My parents both work in a mill and so do all my relatives, but does that mean that I can't have a different future? What really burned me was that a lot of girls who had average grades but came from "the right families" were told to apply to colleges.

Question: Although Rochelle has a strong self-concept and was able to defy her guidance counselor's expectations of her, the counselor's assumptions about Rochelle's future were nevertheless hurtful. Which identity categories do you think could have intersected to influence her guidance counselor's biased thinking? How could the guidance counselor have perceived and communicated differently to better fulfill her professional obligation to support Rochelle in her life goals and aspirations?

As we internalize the generalized other's perspective, we come to share many of the views and values of our society. Shared understandings are essential for collective life. If we all made up our own rules, there would be no common standards and collective life would be chaotic. Yet, shared understandings are not carved in stone: People sometimes work to change how their society operates. The changes we have seen in how Western culture defines and values people of different races, genders, and sexual orientations testify to the possibility of evolution in social perceptions. Each of us has an ethical responsibility to think critically about which social views to accept and use as guides for our own behaviors, attitudes, and values. This suggests a fourth proposition about the self.

Review It!

Western Culture's Identity Categories:

- Race
- Sex
- Sexual Orientation
- Gender
- Socioeconomic Class

Social Perspectives on the Self Are Changeable

The generalized other's perspectives are not fixed. Because they are constructed by members of a society, they can also be changed if enough members of a society challenge them.

Social perspectives are created in particular cultures at specific times. Unsurprisingly, they tend to reflect the views and values of those who are in power at that time. Yet power relations evolve over time and, when they do, social perspectives may also change.

settler colonialism A form of colonization in which colonizers settle an area, replacing Indigenous people and taking their land and resources.

In the 1600s, Europeans first colonized what is now the United States. The form of colonialism they practiced was what scholars call **settler colonialism**, in which the colonizers work to *replace* Indigenous people, taking their land and resources (Pulido, 2021). At the top of the European settlers' social hierarchy were White heterosexual men, especially those of means. Later, British North American colonists arranged with their trading partners to forcibly take Africans their homelands. The colonies' White ruling classes enslaved these people, subjecting them to chattel slavery and treating them as property, not people—assigning the enslaved people the lowest positions in the social hierarchy.

The laws and norms that developed in the early chapters of United States history privileged the interests of straight White men of means to such an extreme that chattel slavery was deemed socially acceptable. In addition to abusing Africans and their children, the White ruling class often marginalized and worked against the interests of Indigenous people, women, other people of color, people who were not heterosexual, people who were economically disadvantaged, people who were mentally or physically disabled, and people from new immigrant groups. They took many steps to prevent these other groups from equitable access to freedom and economic opportunities.

Social perspectives on same-sex relationships have changed over time.
Lifesize/Getty Images

Centuries later, the United States still has a social hierarchy, but it is less rigidly stratified. Laws and norms have become increasingly respectful of a range of sexes, races, sexual orientations, and gender identities. Women and people of color can vote; gay and trans people can marry; it is illegal to discriminate on the basis of sex, race, or sexual orientation; and nobody can own another human being. This is still a work in progress, of course, and we must continue to address many ongoing disparities in United States society and beyond. For example, the work of activists on social media have made racial, gender, disability, and larger body size justice movements widely known. Thanks to **hashtag activism**—such as #BlackLivesMatter, #SayHerName,#MeToo, #YesAllWomen, #SurvivorPrivilege, #CrimingWhileWhite, #OscarsSoWhite, #NoBodyIsDisposable, and #FatLiberation—we are raising our collective consciousness of these issues (Ashline, 2021; Jackson et al., 2020; #NoBodyIsDisposable, 2020).

hashtag activism When activists communicate on social media using hashtags to help direct attention to social justice matters.

But overall, the fundamental changes to date in how our society agrees to understand identities offer clear evidence that social perspectives can and do change. As they continue to evolve, each of us will probably modify views of others' identities and our own.

Social perspectives change in response to individual and collective efforts to weave new meanings into the fabric of common life. Feminist, Civil Rights, and Gay Rights movements have profoundly challenged and changed how identities are understood in the United States. Changes in how we view sex, gender, race, class, size, disability, and sexual orientation are negotiated in communication contexts ranging from one-to-one conversations to mass and social media. People likewise have conversations about raising the minimum wage and protecting warehouse employees from exploitation, and discuss what collective power we may have as consumers to vote with our dollars and help effect these changes. Boycotts of companies that do not reflect up-to-date inclusive values are common, with the boycotters readily communicating their reasoning in face-to-face and online exchanges. Each of us has an ethical responsibility to speak out against social perspectives that we perceive as wrong or harmful. By doing so, we participate in the ongoing process of refining social perspectives.

Guidelines for Enhancing the Self

So far, we've explained how the self develops in the process of communicating with others. Building on that knowledge, we'll now explore guidelines for encouraging personal growth.

Jessica My husband and I have really worked to share equally in our marriage. When we got married 8 years ago, we both believed women and men were equal and should have equal responsibilities for the home and family and equal power in making decisions that affect the family. But it's a lot harder to actually live that ideal than to believe in it. Both of us have struggled against our socialization that says I should cook and clean and take care of the kids and he should make big decisions about our lives.

Question: Jessica's situation is not uncommon. Although many couples believe in gender equality, research indicates that the division of household and child care labor is still significantly imbalanced in opposite-sex relationships (Barroso, 2021). Even in households where both partners have full-time jobs, the woman still does a disproportionate amount of the work. From a communication standpoint, what do you think couples could do to help minimize these imbalances?

Communication Highlight

Failure on the Way to Success

Who was Babe Ruth? If you know baseball history, you probably think of him as having hit 714 home runs. He did, but he also struck out 1,330 times. Superstar Michael Jordan was cut from his high school basketball team because he wasn't good enough. Early in his career, Walt Disney was fired from a newspaper job because his editor thought he had no good or creative ideas. The Beatles penned 59 songs before they had their first hit. Oprah Winfrey was fired from her job as an evening news reporter because her boss told her that her emotions made her "unfit for television news." Arianna Huffington's second book was rejected by 36 publishers before she found the right press for it. When Jay-Z couldn't find a record label to sign him, he created an indie label for his debut album and sold the CDs from his car.

Most people who succeed fail along the way; sometimes they fail many times. If Babe Ruth had let his strikeouts defeat him, he would never have been a champion batter. The same is true of most of us. Failures and defeats are inevitable. Letting them define who we are is not inevitable.

1. Make a Strong Commitment to Improve Yourself

First, make a firm commitment to personal growth. This isn't as easy as it might sound. A firm commitment involves more than saying, "I want to listen better" or "I want to be less judgmental." Changing ourselves takes ongoing effort and a determination not to let setbacks along the way derail us.

2. Gain Knowledge as a Basis for Personal Change

Several types of knowledge will help you spur changes in who you are. First, you need to understand how the self is formed. In this chapter, we've discussed the influence of particular others and the generalized other. You may not want to accept all the views and values you were taught.

Another important source of knowledge is other people. Perhaps you recall a time when you began a new job. If you were fortunate, you found a mentor who explained the ropes to you and gave you helpful feedback. In much the same way, others can also provide feedback on your progress in the process of change. In addition, others can serve as models. If you know someone you think is particularly skillful in supporting others, observe them carefully to identify concrete skills that you can tailor to suit your personal style.

3. Set Realistic Goals

Specific goals are more effective than vague goals. Self-improvement success requires taking concrete steps toward change. For instance, "I want to be better at intimate communication" is a vague objective. Instead, you could use this book to help you pinpoint concrete skills that facilitate healthy intimate communication, like the listening skills in Chapter 4.

Goals should also be realistic. If you are shy and want to be more extraverted, it is reasonable to try to speak up more often. On the other hand, it may not be reasonable to try to be the life of every party. A better method is to establish a series of small, incremental goals. You might focus first on improving one communication skill. When you're satisfied with your ability at that skill, you can work on another one.

Mike For a long time, I put myself down for not doing as well academically as a lot of my friends. They put mega-hours into studying and writing papers. I can't do that because I work 30 hours a week. Now I see that it's unfair to compare myself to them. When I compare myself to students who work as much as I do, my record is pretty good.

4. Self-Disclose When Appropriate

self-disclosure Revelation of information about ourselves that others are unlikely to discover on their own.

Self-disclosure is the revelation of information about ourselves that others are unlikely to discover on their own. We self-disclose when we share private information about ourselves—our hopes, fears, feelings, thoughts, and experiences. Although we don't reveal our private selves to everyone and don't do it often even with intimates, self-disclosure is an important kind of communication.

Self-disclosure has notable values. First, sharing personal feelings, thoughts, and experiences often enhances closeness between people (Hendrick & Hendrick, 1996, 2006; Samp & Palevitz, 2009; Stafford, 2009). By extension, when others understand our private selves, they may respond to us more sensitively, as unique individuals. Self-disclosing also tends to invite others to self-disclose, so we may learn more about them. Finally, self-disclosure can affect what we know about ourselves and how we feel about who we are. For example, if we reveal a weakness or an incident of which we're ashamed, and another person accepts the disclosure without judging us negatively, we may find it easier to accept ourselves. Self-disclosure involves risk—the risk that others will not accept private information or that they might use it against us. Appropriate self-disclosure minimizes these risks by proceeding slowly and establishing trust. Begin by revealing information that is personal but not highly intimate or able to damage you if exploited. Before disclosing further, observe how the other person responds to your communication and what they do with it. You might also pay attention to whether the other person reciprocates by disclosing personal information to you.

5. Accept That You Are in Process

Accepting yourself as you are now is a starting point for any change. The self that you are results from all the interactions and experiences in your life. You don't have to like or admire everything about yourself, but it is important to accept who you are today as a basis for moving forward.

Accepting yourself as being in process also implies that you realize you can change. Don't let yourself be hindered by defeating self-fulfilling prophecies or the fallacy of thinking that you can't change. You can change if you set realistic goals, make a genuine commitment, and then work for the changes you want.

6. Create a Supportive Context for Change

Just as it is easier to swim with the tide than against it, it is easier to change our views of ourselves when we have some support for our efforts. You can do a lot to create an environment that promotes your growth by choosing contexts and people who help you realize your goals. First, think about settings. If you want to become more extraverted, go to parties, not libraries. But libraries are a better context than parties if your goal is to improve academic performance.

Because how others view us affects how we see ourselves, you can create a supportive context by consciously choosing to be around people who believe in you and encourage your personal growth. Steer clear of people who put you down or say you can't change. In other words, people who reflect positive appraisals of us enhance our ability to improve who we are.

Others aren't the only ones whose communication affects our self-concepts. We also communicate with ourselves, and our own messages influence how we see ourselves. One of the most crippling kinds of self-talk we can engage in is **self-sabotage**—telling ourselves we are no good, we'll never learn something, there's no point in trying to change. We may be repeating others' judgments of us, or we may be inventing negative self-fulfilling prophecies. Either way, self-sabotage undermines belief in ourselves.

self-sabotage Self-talk that communicates that we're no good, we can't do something, we can't change, and so forth. Undermines belief in ourselves and motivation to change and grow.

Distinguished therapist Albert Ellis (1988) suggests you should challenge negative statements you make to yourself and replace them with constructive intrapersonal communication. Following Ellis' advice, the next time you hear yourself saying, "I can't do . . . ," challenge the self-defeating message, say out loud to yourself, "I can do it." Of course, you won't grow and improve if you listen only to praise, particularly if it is less than honest. Real friends can help us identify areas for growth without making us feel bad about ourselves.

In sum, to improve your self-concept, you should create contexts that support growth and change, and seek experiences and settings that foster belief in yourself and the changes you desire. Also, recognize uppers, downers, and vultures in yourself and others, and learn which people and which kinds of communication assist you in achieving your own goals for self-improvement.

Chapter Summary

In this chapter, we explored the self as a process that evolves as we communicate with others over the course of our lives. As we interact with others, we learn and internalize social perspectives, both those of particular others and those of the generalized other, or society as a whole. Reflected appraisals, direct definitions, and social comparisons are key communication processes that shape how we see ourselves and how we change over time. The perspective of the generalized other includes social views of key aspects of identity, including race, gender, and sexual orientation. However, these are arbitrary social constructions that we may challenge and resist once we are adults. When we resist social views and values that we consider unethical, we promote change in both society and ourselves.

The second section of this chapter identified ways that social media affect personal identity. We noted that social media expand the opportunities for direct definition, reflected appraisal and social comparisons, which can be beneficial and also destructive.

In the final section of the chapter, we focused on ways to enhance communication competence by improving self-concept. Guidelines include making a firm commitment to personal growth, gaining knowledge about desired changes and the skills they involve, setting realistic goals, accepting yourself as in process, and creating contexts that support the changes you seek. We can make amazing changes in who we are and how we feel about ourselves when we commit to doing so.

Experiencing Communication in Our Lives

Case Study: Parental Teachings

Apply what you've learned in this chapter by analyzing the following case study, using the accompanying questions as a guide.

Kate McDonald is in the neighborhood park with her two children, 7-year-old Emma and 5-year-old Jeremy. The three of them walk into the park and approach the swing set.

Kate: Jeremy, why don't you push Emma so she can swing? Emma, you hang on tight.

Jeremy begins pushing his sister, who squeals with delight. Jeremy gives an extra-hard push that lands him in the dirt in front of the swing set. Laughing, Emma jumps off, falling in the dirt beside her brother.

Kate: Come here, sweetie. You've got dirt all over your knees and your pretty new dress.

Kate brushes the dirt off Emma, who then runs over to the jungle gym set that Jeremy is now climbing. Kate smiles as she watches Jeremy climb fearlessly on the bars.

Kate: You're a brave little man, aren't you? How high can you go?

Encouraged by his mother, Jeremy climbs to the top bars and holds up a fist, screaming, "Look at me, Mom! I'm king of the hill! I climbed to the very top!"

Kate laughs and claps her hands to applaud him. Jealous of the attention Jeremy is getting, Emma runs over to the jungle gym and starts climbing. Kate calls out, "Careful, honey. Don't go any higher. You could fall and hurt yourself." When Emma ignores her mother and reaches for a higher bar, Kate walks over and pulls her off, saying, "Emma, I told you that is dangerous. Time to get down. Why don't you play on the swings some more?"

iStock.com/Henglein and Steets

Once Kate puts Emma on the ground, the girl walks over to the swings and begins swaying.

Questions for Analysis and Discussion

1. Identify examples of direct definition in this scenario. How does Kate define Emma and Jeremy?
2. Identify examples of reflected appraisal in this scenario. What appraisals of her son and daughter does Kate reflect to them?
3. What do Emma's and Jeremy's responses to Kate suggest about their acceptance of her views of them?
4. To what extent does Kate's communication with her children reflect conventional gender expectations in Western culture?

Key Concepts

attachment style
code switching
cultural globalization
***de jure* segregation**
direct definition
ego boundaries
gender binary
gender continuum
gender-nonconforming

hashtag activism
identity script
intersectionality
particular others
perspective of the generalized other
reflected appraisal
self
self-disclosure
self-sabotage
settler colonialism
social comparison
upward comparison

For Further Reflection and Discussion

1. Set one specific goal for personal growth as a communicator. Be sure to specify your goal in terms of clear behavioral changes and make it realistic. As you study different topics during the semester, apply what you learn to your personal goal.
2. What ethical issues do you perceive in the process of developing and continuously refining self-concepts, both your own and those of people around you? Is it as important to be ethical in communicating with yourself (self-talk, or intrapersonal communication) as in communicating with others?
3. How do people you get to know through social media affect your sense of who you are? Are they significant for you? Do they represent the generalized other to you? Do you find face-to-face and online communication are different or distinguishable in ways that matter to you, or not?
4. Recall examples of supervisors and coworkers' direct definitions of you or other employees. For example, were you defined as "a good worker" or "a quick learner"? Consider identity scripts that you were given in a particular workplace. What did others tell you about the company or workplace's identity and about how employees in this particular job were supposed to think and act?
5. How does what you learned in this chapter affect ethical choices about parenting? Reflect on the ethical implications of knowing that parents affect children's self-concepts by their choices of direct definitions, identity scripts, and attachment styles. What ethical responsibilities, if any, do parents have regarding their impact on children's self-concepts and self-esteem?

Listening Effectively

The best way to understand people is to listen to them.

Ralph Nichols

Learning Objectives

After studying the topics in this unit, you should be able to:

1. Describe the six steps in the listening process.
2. List major obstacles to effective listening, including the types of nonlistening.
3. Apply chapter guidelines to improve your listening skills.

In an average day, what percentage of your time are you listening?

"Do you have a minute to talk?" Summer asks her friend Natalie as she enters her dorm room.

"Sure," Natalie agrees without looking up from the text on her phone.

"I'm worried about what's happening between Drew and me," Summer begins. "He takes me for granted all the time. He never asks what I want to do or where I'd like to go. He just assumes I'll go along with whatever he wants."

"Yeah, I know that routine. Devin does it to me, too," Natalie says with exasperation as she looks up. "Last weekend, he insisted we go to this action movie that I had no interest in. But what I wanted didn't make a lot of difference to him."

"That's exactly what I'm talking about," Summer agrees. "I don't like it when Drew treats me that way."

"What I told Devin last weekend was that I'd had it, and from now on we decide together what we're doing, or we don't do it together," Natalie says forcefully. "We've had this talk before, but this time I think I really got through to him that I was serious."

"So are you saying that's what I should do with Drew?"

"Sure," Natalie says, mid-text. "Take it from me, subtlety won't work. Remember last year when I was dating Hunter? I tried to be subtle and hint that I'd like to be consulted about things. What I said to him went in one ear and out the other."

"But Drew's not like Devin or Hunter. I think he just doesn't understand how I feel when he makes all the decisions," Summer says.

"Well, I really don't think Devin's 'like that' either. He's just as good a guy as Drew," Natalie snaps.

"That's not what I meant," Summer says. "I just meant that I don't think I need to hit Drew over the head with a two-by-four."

"And I suppose you think Devin does need that?"

"I don't know. I'm just thinking that maybe our relationships are different," Summer says.

Poor listening is evident in Summer and Natalie's conversation. The first obstacle to effective listening is Natalie's preoccupation with her text messages. A second problem is Natalie's tendency to monopolize the conversation by focusing on her own problems and boyfriends instead of on Summer's concerns about the relationship with Drew. Third, Natalie listens defensively, taking offense when Summer suggests that their relationships may differ.

Usually, when we think about communication, we focus on talking. Yet talking is not the only part—or even the greatest part—of communication. Effective communication also involves listening. As obvious as this is, few of us devote as much energy to listening as we do to talking (Brady, 2015).

This chapter focuses on listening. First, we'll consider what's involved in listening, which is more than most of us realize. Next, we'll discuss obstacles to effective listening and how to minimize them. Third, we'll consider common forms of nonlistening. The fourth section of the chapter explores listening in the realm of digital communication. Finally, we discuss guidelines for improving listening effectiveness.

You spend more time listening—or trying to—than talking. Studies of people from college students to professionals indicate that the average person spends 45–75% of waking time listening to others who are speaking (Wolvin, 2009). If we don't listen effectively, we're communicating poorly most of the time.

In addition, most of us also listen to others on social media using a mix of our auditory and visual senses—listening to video and audio footage, in combination with the written word. Scholars call this type of listening **social listening**, which Stewart and Arnold (2017) define as "an active process of attending to, observing, interpreting, and responding to a variety of stimuli through mediated, electronic, and social channels" (p. 86).

social listening Actively attending to, observing, interpreting, and responding to auditory and visual digital content on social media.

When people don't listen well on the job—whether to coworkers or to their customers', clients', or constituents' social media posts—they may miss information that can affect their professional effectiveness and advancement or negatively impact their organization (Darling & Dannels, 2003; Gearhart & Maben, 2021; Landrum & Harrold, 2003; Pomputius, 2019). Skill in listening is also linked to resolving workplace conflicts. Doctors who don't listen fully to patients may misdiagnose or mistreat medical problems (Joshi, 2015; Scholz, 2005; Wen & Kosowsky, 2013). Ineffective listening in the classroom diminishes learning and performance on tests. In personal relationships, poor listening can hinder understanding of others, and listening ineffectively to public communication leaves us uninformed about civic issues.

The Listening Process

Although we often use the words *listening* and *hearing* as if they were synonyms, actually they're not. **Hearing** is a physiological activity that occurs when sound waves hit our eardrums. Hearing is passive; we don't have to invest any energy to hear. Listening, on the other hand, is an active process that requires effort, and the amount of effort people put into listening can vary (Francis & Love, 2019). Listening involves more than just hearing or receiving messages through sight, as when we notice nonverbal behaviors or when people with hearing impairments read lips or receive messages in American Sign Language (ASL).

hearing The physiological activity that occurs when sound waves hit our eardrums. Unlike listening, hearing is a passive process.

Listening is an active, complex process that includes being mindful, physically receiving messages, selecting and organizing information, interpreting communication, responding, and remembering. We engage in listening both interpersonally and in relation to the media, such as radio, TV, film, podcasts, and social media content. The complexity of listening is represented in the Chinese character for listening, which includes symbols for eyes, ears, and heart (Figure 4.1). As the character suggests, to listen effectively, we use not only our ears, but also our eyes and hearts.

listening A complex process that consists of being mindful, physically receiving messages, selecting and organizing information, interpreting, responding, and remembering.

Being Mindful

The first step in listening is deciding to be mindful. **Mindfulness** is being as fully engaged in the moment as possible. (I say "as engaged as possible" because various people, such as those with neurodiverse brains and those who have been impacted by trauma, may struggle to be "fully present.")

mindfulness Being as fully present as possible in the moment; the first step of listening and the foundation of all other steps.

To be mindful, focus on what is happening here and now. Keep your thoughts as focused as you can on what is happening in the present conversation. Don't think about what you did yesterday or about a friend you want to text, and don't think about your own feelings and issues. Instead, when you listen mindfully, tune in as fully as possible to another person or to the medium (note: "media" is a plural noun; "medium" is the singular form) you're engaged with. In an interpersonal setting,

Figure 4.1
The Chinese Character for Listening

when you listen mindfully, you try to understand the other person without imposing your own ideas, judgments, or feelings on the message. You may later express your thoughts and feelings, but when you listen as mindfully as possible, you attend to another as fully as you are able.

Mindfulness enhances interpersonal communication in two ways. First, attending mindfully to others increases our understanding of how they feel and think about what they are saying. Second, when we listen mindfully, others tend to express themselves in greater depth.

Being mindful is a personal commitment to attend fully and without diversion. No amount of skill will make you a good listener if you do not choose to attend mindfully. Thus, your own choice to be mindful or not is the foundation of how well you listen—or fail to.

Physically Receiving Messages

In addition to mindfulness, listening involves physically receiving messages. For many people, this happens through hearing. People who are hard of hearing, however, receive messages by reading sign language or physically sensing sound waves. Our ability to receive messages may decline when we are tired or ill. Physical reception of messages may also be impeded by background noises, such as blaring music, others talking nearby, or text message notifications.

Elle Hard-of-hearing people are capable of physically feeling sound waves, and we may in fact be more in tune to the physicality of sound waves than hearing people, because we've learned to rely on noticing these vibrations as an alternative to our ears. Sometimes I can feel loud trucks coming down the street when my hearing peers either can't or don't notice because they can hear them with their ears, for instance.

Communication Highlight

Chewing Causes Murder

How could chewing cause murder? Actually, it didn't, but a woman admitted that she felt like strangling her boyfriend whenever he chewed. The sound of his chewing enraged her. This woman is not a psychopath. Her problem is misophonia, which means "hatred of sound." Named in 2002, this is a condition in which particular sounds enrage or disgust a person. The most common sounds that trigger these responses are chewing, swallowing, lip smacking, breathing, typing, and pen clicking. Research suggests that misophonia usually begins in childhood (Palumbo et al., 2018) and may be caused by hyperconnectivity between the auditory system and the part of the brain that controls emotion (Lerner, 2015).

Selecting and Organizing Material

The third part of listening is selecting and organizing material. As we noted in Chapter 2, we don't perceive everything around us. Instead, we selectively attend to some messages and elements of our environments and disregard others. What we select to attend to depends on many factors, including our physiology, interests, cognitive structures, socialization, biases (conscious and unconscious), and expectations.

We can compensate for our tendencies to attend selectively by remembering that we are more likely to notice stimuli that are intense, loud, or unusual. Thus, we may overlook communicators who speak softly. If we're aware of this tendency, we can guard against it and choose to listen mindfully to communicators who are not especially dynamic.

Once we've selected what to notice, we organize what we've received. As you'll recall from Chapter 2, we use cognitive schemata to organize perceptions. When listening, we make decisions—usually not consciously—about how to organize what we hear: Does the communication fit the prototype of venting or problem solving or something else? We apply personal constructs to classify the message as rational or not rational, emotional or not emotional, and so forth. Based on how you construct what you are selectively attending to, you apply stereotypes to predict what the other person will do and expects you to do. Finally, based on the meanings you have constructed, you choose a script to follow in interaction.

When a friend is upset, you can reasonably predict that they may not want advice until they have first had a chance to express their feelings. On the other hand, when a coworker comes to you with a problem that must be solved quickly, you assume they might welcome practical advice. Your script for responding to a distraught friend in person might be to say, "Tell me more about what you're feeling"; or, if they've posted a video expressing distress on social media, after listening you might comment, "Want to talk?" With a colleague who is facing a deadline, you might adopt a more directive script and say, "Let's put our heads together and come up with a solution."

Interpreting Communication

The fourth part of listening is interpreting others' communication. When we interpret, we put together all that we have selected and organized to make sense of the overall situation. The most important principle in this process is to be person-centered, which means trying to take the other person's perspective. Certainly, you won't always agree with other people. However, if you want to listen well, you have an ethical responsibility to make an earnest effort to understand others' perspectives. To interpret someone with respect for their perspective is one of the greatest gifts we can give.

Maggie Don and I didn't understand each other's perspective, and we didn't even understand that we didn't understand. Once I told him I was really upset about a friend of mine who needed money for an emergency. Don told me she had no right to expect me to bail her out, but that had nothing to do with what I was feeling. He saw the situation in terms of what rights my friend had, but to me it was about feeling concerned for someone I like. Only after we got counseling did we learn to really listen to each other instead of listening through ourselves.

Review It!

Steps in Listening Process:

- Mindfulness
- Physical Reception
- Interpretation
- Response
- Remembering

Responding

Effective listening includes responding, which is communicating attention and interest as well as voicing our own views when that is appropriate. Skillful listeners give outward signs that they are interested and involved not only when others finish speaking but throughout interaction. Indicators of engagement include attentive posture, head nods, eye contact, and vocal responses such as "um hmm," "okay," and "go on." Or, while watching a live video stream on social media, effective social listening might involve posting real-time comments or reactions to help the speaker know you are not just listening, but are engaged. When we respond with interest, we communicate that we care about the other person and what they are saying. This is what makes listening such an active process.

Remembering

The final part of effective listening is remembering, or retaining what you have heard. We remember less than half of a message immediately after we hear it. As time goes by, retention decreases further; we recall only about 35% of most messages 8 hours after we hear them (Adler & Proctor, 2013). Because we forget about two-thirds of what we hear, it's important to make sure we hang onto the most important third. Later in this chapter, we'll discuss strategies for increasing retention.

Nick It's impossible to listen well in my apartment. Four of us live there, and at least two different devices are streaming music all the time. Also, Netflix is usually on, and there may be conversations or video calls, too. It's hard to talk to each other in the middle of all that noise. We're always asking each other to repeat something or skipping over whatever we don't hear. If we go out to a bar or something, the noise there is just as bad. Sometimes I think we don't really want to talk with each other, and all the distractions protect us from having to.

Question: Do you ever try to minimize distractions in your own living space? What steps do you take? Do your efforts make a difference?

Obstacles to Effective Listening

There are two broad types of obstacles to good listening: those external to us and those inside us.

External Obstacles

Although we can't always control external obstacles, knowing what situational factors hinder listening can help us guard against them or compensate for the interference they create.

Message Overload The sheer amount of communication in our lives makes it impossible to listen fully to all of it. When we're not talking face to face with someone, we're likely to be texting, watching TV, listening to podcasts, or streaming videos. We simply aren't able to listen mindfully to all of the things all of the time.

Message overload often occurs in academic settings. If you're taking four or five classes, you confront mountains of information. Message overload may also occur when communication takes place simultaneously in two channels. For instance, you might experience information overload if a professor presents information verbally while also clicking through PowerPoint slides with complex statistical data.

Message Complexity The more detailed and complicated ideas are, the harder it is to follow and retain them. Many jobs today are highly specialized so communication among coworkers and within organizations is complex (Beck, Qin, & Men, 2022). We need to guard against the tendency to tune out people who use technical terms, provide lots of detail, and use complex sentences.

Environmental Distractions Distractions in the environment can interfere with listening (Keizer, 2010). Perhaps you've been part of a crowd at a rally or a game. If so, you probably had trouble hearing the person next to you. Although most sounds aren't as overwhelming as the roar of crowds, there is always some noise in communication situations. Music, television in the background, side conversations in a class, or rings of smart phones can hinder communication.

Communication & Careers

New Epidemic: Distracted Doctors

Would you want your neurosurgeon making personal calls during an operation on your spine? Would you want a surgical nurse checking competitive air fares while attending an operation? Would you want the technician texting while operating a bypass machine? Would you be comfortable knowing doctors and nurses were shopping online while you were on the operating table? Welcome to what some call "distracted doctoring" (Richtel, 2011). All of these examples are based on observations of real doctors, nurses, and technicians in surgery.

Dr. Peter Papadakos is an anesthesiologist who directs critical care at the University of Rochester Medical Center. He says, "My gut feeling is lives are in danger" (Richtel, 2011, p. A4). Dr. Papadakos's concern is illustrated by a patient who was partially paralyzed during an operation in which his neurosurgeon made personal and business calls—at least 10 of them!

Good listeners try to reduce environmental distractions. It's considerate to turn off televisions, phones, and laptops if someone wants to talk with you. Researchers have found that mail alerts, IMs, and notifications of text messages undermine the ability to listen mindfully (Begley, 2009). In the example that opened this chapter, then, Natalie should have put her phone aside if she wanted to listen mindfully to Summer.

Review It!

External Obstacles to Listening:

- Message Overload
- Message Complexity
- Environmental Distractions

Internal Obstacles

In addition to external interferences, listening may be hindered by four psychological obstacles.

Preoccupation

When we are preoccupied with our own thoughts and concerns, we can't focus on what someone else is saying.

Andy I've been really stressed about finding a job. I've had lots of first interviews, but no callbacks and no offers. Even when I'm not interviewing—like when I'm with friends or in class—getting a job is in the back of my mind. It just stays there so that it's hard for me to really focus on anything else happening around me.

Prejudgments

Another obstacle to effective listening is prejudgment of others or their ideas. Sometimes we decide in advance that others have nothing to offer us, so we tune them out. If a coworker's ideas have not impressed you in the past, you might assume they will contribute nothing of value to a present conversation. The risk is that you might miss a good idea simply because you prejudged the other person. Research shows that, on average, doctors interrupt patients 11 seconds after patients have started explaining their medical situation or need—and that those who aren't interrupted speak an average of just 6 seconds (Phillips et al., 2019).

Attention to social media can interfere with mindful listening.
Rich Legg/E+/Getty Images

This is a problem: Hearing the patient's complete story is key to providing an accurate diagnosis as early as possible (Goranson, 2019). When doctors stop listening, they risk not getting information that could help them diagnose and treat patients. It's also important to keep an open mind when listening to communication regarding issues about which you already have opinions. You might miss important new information and perspectives if you don't put your prejudgments aside long enough to listen mindfully.

Another kind of prejudgment occurs when we assume we know what another feels, thinks, and is going to say, and we then assimilate their message into our preconceptions. This is a form of mind reading, which we discussed in Chapter 2.

Noah My parents need a course in listening! They are so quick to tell me what I think and feel, or should think and feel, that they never hear what I do feel or think. Last year I approached them with the idea of taking a year off from school. Before I could even explain why I wanted to do this, Dad was all over me about being responsible and getting ahead in a career. Mom jumped on me about looking for an easy out and not having the gumption to stick with my studies. The whole point was that I wanted to work as an intern to get some hands-on experience in media production, which is my major. It had nothing to do with wanting an easy out or not trying to get ahead, but they couldn't even hear me through their own ideas about what I felt.

Question: Noah's parents assumed they knew why he wanted to take a year off—a form of mind-reading. What might his parents have said or done if they wanted to truly understand his reasoning?

Lack of Effort Because active listening takes so much effort, we're not always able or willing to do it well. If you can't summon the effort to listen well, you might suggest postponing interaction until a time when you will be able to invest effort in listening. If you explain to the other that you want to defer communication because you really are interested and want to be able to listen well, they are likely to appreciate your honesty and commitment to listening.

Failure to Adjust to Diverse Communication Styles A final internal obstacle to effective listening is not recognizing and adjusting to different listening styles that reflect diverse communities and cultures (Samovar et al., 2015). The more we understand about different people's rules for listening, the more effectively we can signal our attention in ways they appreciate. For example, in the United States, it is generally considered polite to make frequent but not continuous eye contact in conversation. Yet in some United States subcultures and some cultures abroad, continuous eye contact is normative, while in others almost any eye contact is considered intrusive.

Within the United States, listening rules can differ based on membership in racial, gender, and other social communities. For example, men generally provide fewer verbal and nonverbal clues than women to indicate they are interested in what another person is saying. They may also respond primarily to the content level of meaning and less to the relationship level of meaning.

Men also tend to interrupt women more than they interrupt other men, though this dynamic improves in groups with more women present (Mendelberg et al., 2014). In formal presentations, women's talks are also interrupted more, and moderators are more likely to hold women to stricter time standards, denying them the extra time that men are often allowed to wrap up their speeches (Blair-Loy et al., 2017). Other gendered patterns in listening include men dominating a conversation (Afsahi, 2021) and patronizing women, explaining things to them they already know. Feminist author Rebecca Solnit (2008/2012) famously critiqued this tendency in an essay called "Men Explain Things to Me"—after which, she notes, young women soon dubbed the phenomenon "mansplaining." **Mansplaining** occurs both in person and on social media (Bridges, 2017; Koc-Michalska et al., 2019), and it is directed towards people of other genders and diverse sexualities.

mansplaining A slang term combining the words "man" and "explaining," used to criticize a communication style in which men fail to listen to people of other genders to discern what they already know before speaking.

If you understand these gender differences, you can adapt your listening style—whether face to face or during social listening—appropriately. You can even choose to be an ally to others who are interrupted, challenging the gendered inequalities in listening as you see them arise (Madsen et al., 2019)—just as you might if you noticed similar patterns occurring between people of different races, ages, abilities, or socioeconomic backgrounds.

Lavonda My boyfriend is the worst listener ever. Whenever I try to tell him about some problem I have, he becomes Mr. Answer Man. He tells me what to do or how to handle a situation. That doesn't do anything to help me with my feelings or even to let me know he hears what I'm feeling.

Question: What information about gender differences in listening might apply to Lavonda's situation with her boyfriend? Do you think understanding this information might help her in any way?

Review It!

Internal Obstacles to Listening:

- Preoccupation
- Prejudgment
- Lack of Effort
- Failure to Adjust to Diverse Communication Styles

We have seen that there are many obstacles to effective listening. Obstacles inherent in messages and situations include message overload, message complexity, and environmental distractions. In addition, there are four potential interferences inside us: preoccupation, prejudgment, lack of effort, and failure to recognize and adapt to diverse expectations of listening.

Forms of Nonlistening

Now that we've discussed obstacles to effective listening, let's consider some forms of nonlistening. As you read about these six types of nonlistening, they may seem familiar because you and others probably engage in them at times.

Pseudolistening

pseudolistening Pretending to listen.

Pseudolistening is pretending to listen. When we pseudolisten, we appear to be attentive, but really our minds are elsewhere. Superficial talk in social situations and boring lectures are two communication situations in which we may consciously choose to pseudolisten so that we seem polite even though we really aren't involved.

Souryana I do a lot of pseudolistening in classes where the teachers are boring. I pretend I'm taking notes on my laptop, but really I'm checking email or looking at what my favorite influencers are doing. Every now and then, I look up and nod at the teacher so I look like I'm listening.

Monopolizing

Monopolizing is hogging the stage by continually focusing communication on ourselves instead of the person talking. There are two primary forms of monopolizing. One is *conversational rerouting*, in which people shift the topic of talk to themselves. For example, if Harper tells Marla about a roommate problem, Marla might reroute the conversation by saying, "I know what you mean. My roommate is a real jerk." Then Marla goes off on an extended description of her own roommate problems.

monopolizing Continually focusing communication on oneself instead of on the person who is talking.

Another form of monopolizing is *diversionary interrupting*, which is interrupting in ways that disrupt the person speaking. Often, this occurs in combination with rerouting, so that a person interrupts and then directs the conversation to a new topic. In other cases, monopolizers fire questions that break up a speaker's concentration and impel the speaker to answer the questions before continuing. Both rerouting and diversionary interrupting are techniques for monopolizing a conversation. They are the antithesis of good listening.

It's important to realize that not all interruptions are monopolizing tactics. People with neurodiverse brains sometimes reroute conversations to talk about their own experiences as a way to connect with others. We also interrupt to show interest, voice support, and ask for elaboration. This type of interrupting usually takes the form of minimal communication such as "umm," "go on," and "really?" that shows interest in the person who is speaking.

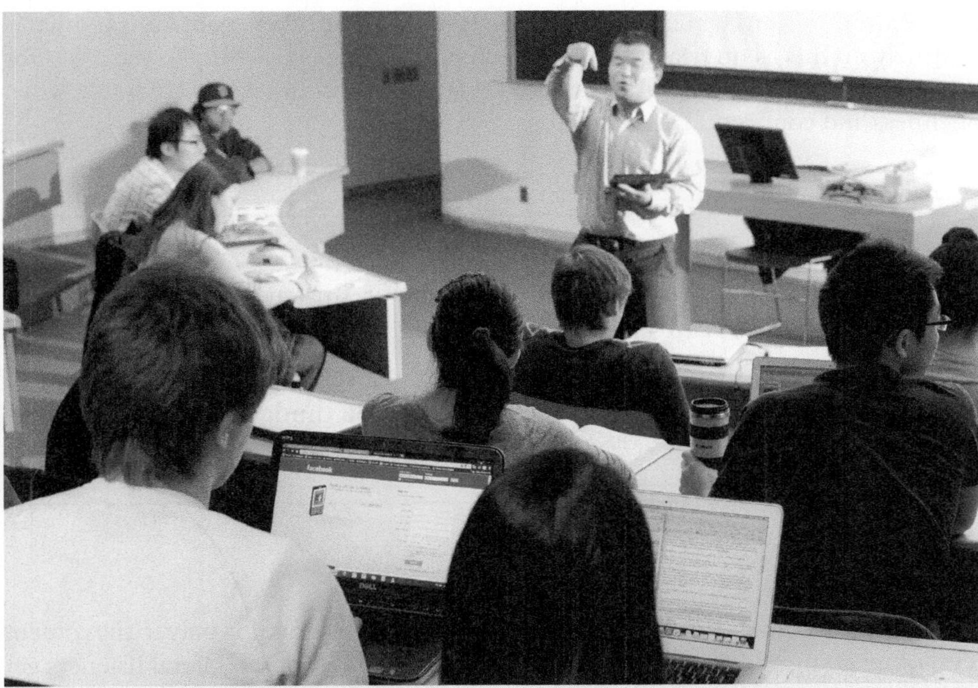

Do you ever pseudolisten in classes while also using digital media?
Aaron Harris/ZUMA Press/Newscom

Selective Listening

selective listening Focusing on only selected parts of communication. We listen selectively when we screen out parts of a message that don't interest us or with which we disagree and also when we rivet attention on parts of communication that do interest us or with which we agree.

Selective listening is focusing on only particular parts of messages. One form of selective listening is focusing only on aspects of communication that interest us or correspond with our values. Students often become highly attentive when teachers say, "This is important for the test." In the workplace, we may become more attentive when communication addresses topics such as raises, layoffs, and other matters that may affect us directly.

A second form of selective listening occurs when we reject communication that bores us or makes us uncomfortable. For instance, we may not listen when others praise accomplishments of public officials we don't like. Being mindful allows you to curb the tendency to tune out messages you find boring or uncomfortable.

Defensive Listening

defensive listening Perceiving personal attacks, criticisms, or hostility in communication when no offense is intended.

ambushing Listening carefully to attack a speaker.

Defensive listening involves perceiving personal attacks, criticisms, or hostility in communication when no offense is intended. When we listen defensively, we read unkind motives into whatever others say. Thus, an innocent remark such as "Have you finished your report yet?" may be perceived as suspicion that you aren't doing your work. Although defensive listening is often limited to particular moments, some people perceive insults and criticism in most communication (a global, stable attribution).

Review It!

Forms of Nonlistening:

- Pseudolistening
- Monopolizing
- Selective Listening
- Defensive Listening
- Ambushing
- Literal Listening

Ambushing

Ambushing is listening carefully for the purpose of attacking. Unlike the other kinds of nonlistening we've discussed, ambushing involves very careful listening, but it isn't motivated by interest in another. Instead, ambushers listen intently to gather ammunition, which they then use to attack a speaker. Political candidates routinely do this as do trial attorneys. Each person listens carefully to the other for the sole purpose of undercutting the adversary. Ambushing is not advisable when openness and connection are wanted.

Eric One of the brothers at my house is so challenging to talk with. He's a pre-law major, and he loves to debate and win arguments. No matter what somebody talks about, this guy just listens long enough to mount a counterattack. He doesn't care about understanding others, just about beating them. I've quit talking when he's around.

Question: Based on what Eric says above, what form of nonlistening do you think his fraternity brother tends to engage in?

Literal Listening

literal listening Listening only to the content level of meaning and ignoring the relational level of meaning.

The final form of nonlistening is **literal listening,** which is listening only to the content level of meaning and ignoring the relationship level of meaning. Literal listeners get the information in a message, but they miss the feelings and relationship dimension.

In summary, nonlistening comes in many forms, including pseudolistening, ambushing speakers, monopolizing the stage, responding defensively, attending selectively, and listening literally. Being aware of forms of nonlistening enables you to exercise control over how you listen and thus how fully and mindfully you participate in communication with others.

Guidelines for Effective Listening

Effective listening is an active process that is tailored to specific purposes. Informational listening, critical listening, and relational listening entail different listening styles and behaviors. We'll discuss guidelines to improve effectiveness of each type of listening.

Informational and Critical Listening

Much of the time, we listen to gain information. We listen for information in classes, in professional meetings, when important news stories are reported, and when we need guidance on everything from medical treatment to driving directions. In all of these cases, the goal of **informational listening** is to gain and understand information.

informational listening Listening to gain and understand information; tends to focus on the content level of meaning.

Closely related to informational listening is **critical listening**, in which we listen to form opinions and to evaluate people and ideas. Critical listening requires us to analyze and evaluate information and the people who express it. We decide whether a speaker is credible and ethical by judging the thoroughness of a presentation, the

critical listening Attending to communication to analyze and evaluate the content of communication or the person speaking.

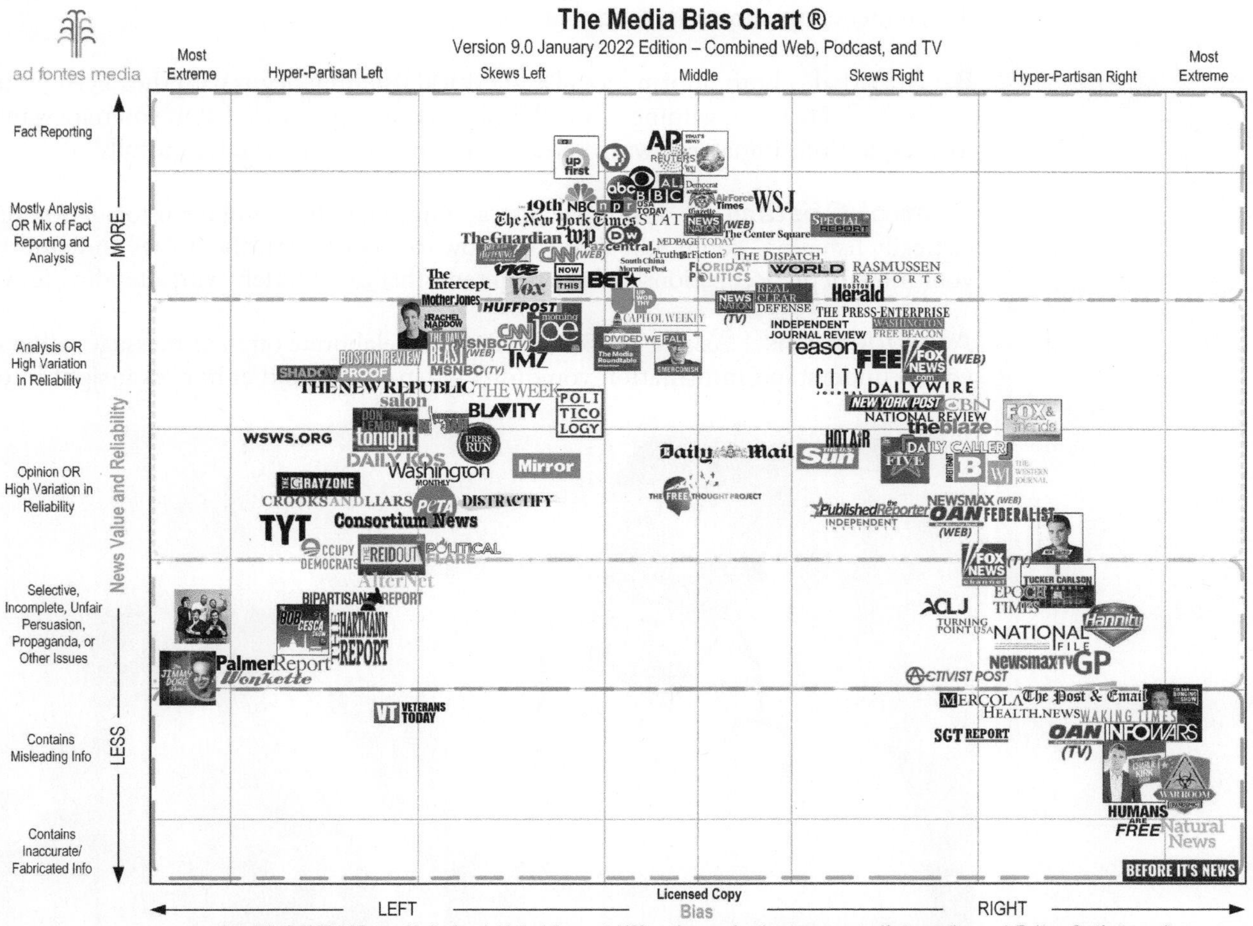

The Media Bias Chart is a great way to check whether a source is politically biased and how reliable it tends to be. Covering websites, TV and video, and podcast and audio sources, the interactive online version is very comprehensive. Take a look at some sources in the lower right and lower left quadrants of the chart. See if you can recognize any of them. Did you realize they were considered inaccurate sources? Then, look at some of the sources at the top center of the chart. Have you referred to them before? What do you find they have in common, and how do they differ from the sources in the lower corners?

accuracy of evidence, and the carefulness of reasoning. In Chapter 13, we discuss ways to evaluate evidence.

There is so much misinformation online that we need to take extra care to exercise critical listening when communicating digitally. Anyone can post anything online, so accuracy is not guaranteed. While engaged in social listening, you might ask yourself:

- What qualifies this person to have an informed stance on this issue?
- Does this person have any vested interest or any ties to others who have stakes in the issue?
- What is this person's track record of accuracy?
- Does this person seem to be relying on a biased source?

Another way to keep your critical thinking sharp is to check other sources of information on the same issue to see if there is a consistent opinion. Be sure to check if those sources have known biases, as well. Consistency doesn't necessarily equal right, but by at least checking what you read online, you can be a more savvy digital media consumer and social listener.

Be Mindful Both informational and critical listening begin with the decision to be mindful. Focus on gaining as much information as you can. Later, you may want to ask questions if material wasn't clear even though you listened mindfully.

Control Obstacles Minimize distractions when listening for information or critically listening. You might shut a window to block out traffic noises and empty your mind of preoccupations and prejudgments that can interfere with attending fully.

Ask Questions Asking speakers to clarify or elaborate on their messages allows you to understand information you didn't grasp at first and enhances insight into

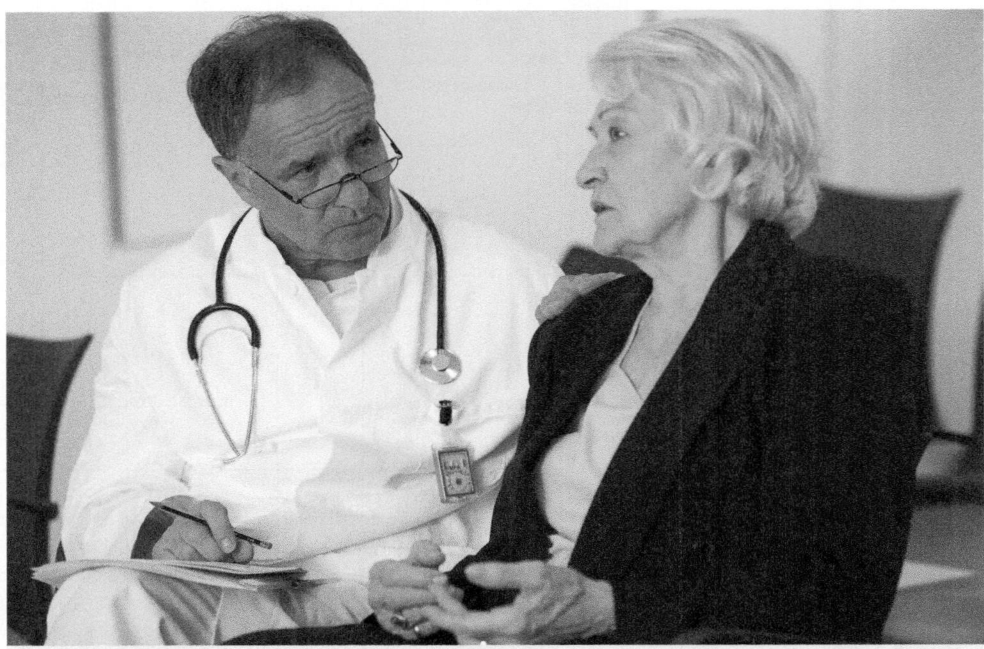

Listening to discriminate is vital when doctors communicate with patients.
Fancy/Veer/Corbis/Fancy/Jupiter Images

Communication Highlight

Between a Rock and a Hard Place

Most of us have had the experience of being frustrated by a speaker who used specialized language that we couldn't understand. That experience is common for bilingual and multilingual people in the United States whose primary language is not English, as they may have never been taught common idioms in their English language classes (Anjarini & Hatmanto, 2021).

According to communication scholar Wen-Shu Lee (1994, 2000), phrases that often defy understanding for those who grew up speaking a language other than English include *miss the boat* (Where is the boat? I don't see a boat.), *kick the bucket* (Who's kicking what bucket?), *chew the fat* (Why would you want to chew fat?), *between a rock and a hard place* (Why is someone in such a position?), and *hit the road* (Why would anybody hit a road?).

Go to the online resources for this chapter to learn more about English slang and bilingual and multilingual people who are learning the English language.

content that you did comprehend. Questions also compliment speakers because they indicate that you are interested and want to know more.

- When listening critically, it's appropriate to ask probing questions of speakers: "What is the source of your statistics on the rate of unemployment?"
- "Have you talked with anyone who holds a point of view contrary to yours?"

For those people who speak English as a second language, it's especially important and appropriate to ask questions about terminology they don't understand, particularly colloquial terms (Lee, 1994, 2000). Sensitive communicators avoid or explain idioms when speaking with people whose primary language is different from theirs. If speakers don't offer explanations, listeners should request them.

Use Aids to Recall To understand and remember important information, we can apply the principles of perception we discussed in Chapter 2. For instance, we tend to notice and recall stimuli that are repeated. To use this principle to increase recall, repeat important ideas to yourself immediately after hearing them.

Another way to increase retention is to use mnemonic (pronounced "nemonic," rhymes with *demonic*) devices, which are memory aids that create patterns for what you've heard. You probably already do this in studying. For instance, KIM is a mnemonic to remember that Kim (K) from Iowa (I) is going into medicine (M).

Organize Information Organizing information increases retention. For example, suppose a friend tells you he is confused about long-range goals, doesn't know what he can do with a math major, wants to locate in the Midwest, wonders whether graduate school is necessary, likes small towns, needs some internships to try out different options, and wants a family eventually. You could regroup this stream of concerns into two categories: academic information (careers for math majors, graduate school, internship opportunities) and lifestyle preferences (Midwest, small town, family). Remembering those two categories allows you to retain the essence of your friend's concerns, even if you forget many of the specifics.

Relational Listening

relational listening Listening to support another person or to understand another person's feelings and perceptions; focuses on the relational level of meaning as much as on the content level of meaning.

In some listening situations, we're as concerned or even more concerned with the relational level of meaning than the content level. We engage in **relational listening** when we listen to a friend's worries, counsel a coworker, or talk with a parent about health concerns. Whenever supporting a person and maintaining a relationship are key goals, we should engage in relational listening, which requires active involvement with the other person.

Be Mindful The first requirement for effective relational listening is to be mindful. You'll recall that this was also the first step in informational and critical listening. When we're interested in relational meanings, however, a different kind of mindfulness is needed. Instead of focusing our minds on information, we need to concentrate on understanding feelings. Thus, mindful relational listening calls on us to pay attention to subtle clues to feelings and perceptions.

Suspend Judgment When listening to provide support, it's important to avoid highly judgmental responses. When we judge what another says, we move away from that person and their feelings. To curb evaluative tendencies, ask whether you really need to pass judgment in the present moment.

Only if someone asks for our judgment should we offer it when we are listening to support. Even if our opinion is sought, we should express it in a way that doesn't devalue others. Sometimes people excuse strongly judgmental comments by saying, "You asked me to be honest" or "I mean this as constructive criticism." Too often, however, the judgments are not constructive and are harsher than candor requires.

José My best friend makes it so easy for me to tell whatever is on my mind. She never puts me down or makes me feel stupid or weird. Sometimes I ask her what she thinks, and she has this way of telling me without making me feel wrong if I think differently. What it boils down to is respect. She respects me and herself, so she doesn't have to prove anything by acting better than me.

Understand the Other Person's Perspective One of the most important principles for effective relational listening is to grasp the other person's perspective. This means we have to step outside of our own point of view, at least long enough to understand how another person sees things. Active listening conveys effort to understand, which, in turn increases the other person's satisfaction with interaction (Weger, Minei, & Robinson, 2014).

paraphrasing A method of clarifying others' meaning by restating their communication using different terminology.

minimal encouragers Communication that, by expressing interest in hearing more, gently invites another person to elaborate.

Paraphrasing is an active listening technique to clarify another's meaning or needs by reflecting our interpretations of the speaker's communication back to them. For example, a friend might confide, "I'm really scared my kid brother is messing around with drugs." We could paraphrase this way: "It sounds as if you think your brother may be experimenting with drugs." This paraphrase allows us to clarify whether the friend has any evidence of the brother's drug involvement. **Minimal encouragers** are responses that express interest in hearing more and invite another person to elaborate. They indicate that we are listening, following, and interested. Examples of minimal encouragers are "Tell me more," "Really?" "Go on," and "Then what happened?" We can also use nonverbal minimal encouragers, such as a raised eyebrow to show we're involved, a nod to indicate we understand, or widened eyes to indicate we're fascinated. Keep in mind that these are *minimal* encouragers intended to prompt, rather than interfere with, the flow of another's talk.

To enhance understanding of what another feels or wants from us we can ask questions. For instance, we might ask, "How do you feel about that?" or "Do you want to talk about how to handle the situation, or do you just want to air the issues?" Asking directly signals that we really want to help and allows others to tell us how we can best do that.

Express Support Central to relational listening is communicating support. This doesn't necessarily require you to agree with another's perspective or ideas, but you should communicate support for the person. The following conversation between a father and son illustrates how we can support a person even if we don't agree another.

Son: Dad, I'm changing my major from business to drama.

Father: Oh.

Son: Yeah, I've wanted to do it for some time, but I kept holding back because acting isn't as safe as accounting.

Father: That's true.

Son: But I've decided to do it anyway.

Father: Frankly, that worries me. Starving actors are a dime a dozen. You wouldn't have any economic security.

Son: I know acting isn't as secure as business, but it's what I really want to do.

Father: Why does acting matter so much to you.

Son: It's the most creative, totally fulfilling thing I've ever done. Business doesn't do that for me. I feel like I have to give this a try, or I'll always wonder if I could have made it.

Father: Couldn't you finish your business degree and get a job and act on the side?

Son: No. I've got to give acting a full shot—give it everything I have, to see if I can make it.

Father: Well, I still have reservations, but I guess I can understand having to try something that matters this much to you. I'm just concerned that you'll lose years of your life to something that doesn't work out.

Son: Well, I'm kinda concerned about that too, but I'm more worried about wasting years of my life in a career that I don't like.

Father: I wouldn't make the choice you're making, but I respect your decision.

Communication & Careers

An Addition to Legal Training

What does it take to be an effective attorney? According to Neil Hamilton (2011–2012), listening is critical. Hamilton reports that attorneys who listen actively to clients are more effective for several reasons. First, the attorneys get more information. Second, active listening encourages clients to give fuller accounts of events and to provide more details. Third, actively listening enhances attorney–client relationships by building trust and respect. Hamilton encourages law schools to include listening in their curricula. Specifically, he advocates reflecting and paraphrasing as key skills.

This dialogue illustrates several principles of effective relational listening:

1. The father's first two comments are minimal encouragers that invite his son to elaborate thoughts and feelings.
2. The father encourages his son to explain how he feels.
3. Later, the father suggests a compromise solution. When his son rejects that, the father respects the son's position.
4. The father makes his own position clear, but he separates his personal stance from his respect for his son's right to make his own choices.

Sometimes it's difficult to listen openly and nonjudgmentally, particularly if we don't agree with the person speaking, as in the example. However, if your goal is to support another person, then sensitive, responsive involvement without evaluation is critical.

Other Purposes of Listening

Listening for information to evaluate critically and listening to support others are two major listening purposes. In addition, we will briefly discuss other listening goals.

Listening for Pleasure Sometimes we listen for pleasure, as when we attend concerts, listen to podcasts or audiobooks, or enjoy conversation with witty, funny people. When we listen for pleasure, we don't need to concentrate on organizing and remembering as much as when we listen for information, although retention is important if you want to be able to tell a joke to someone else later. Yet listening for pleasure does require mindfulness, hearing, and interpretation.

Listening to Discriminate In some situations, we listen to make fine discriminations in sounds to draw valid conclusions and act appropriately in response. For example, doctors and nurses listen to discriminate when they use stethoscopes to

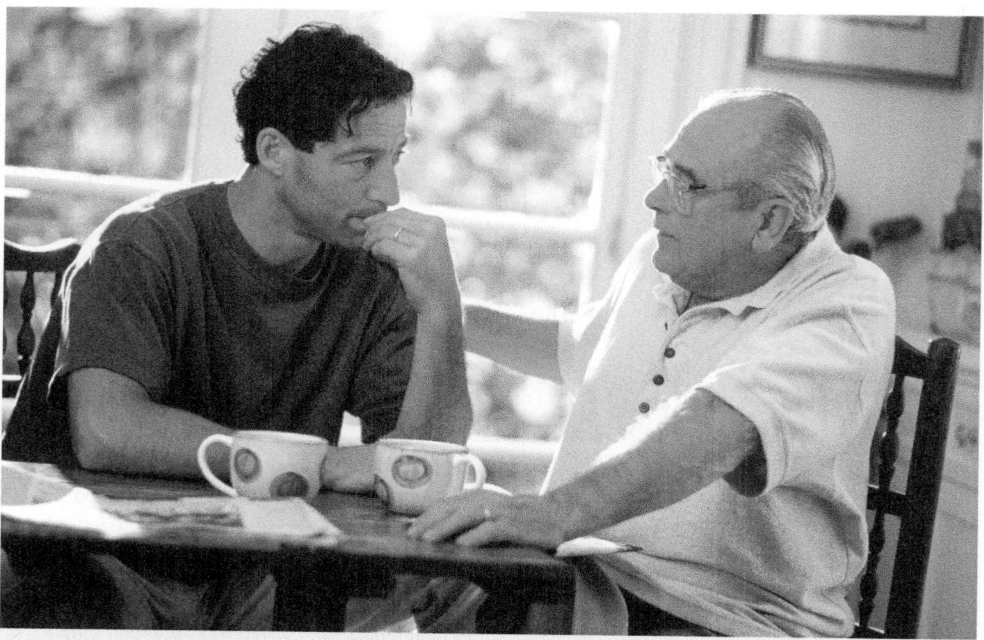

Mindful listening is one of the greatest gifts we can give to another.
Daniel Bosler/Stone/Getty Images

diagnose heart functioning or lung congestion. Parents listen to discriminate among a baby's cries for attention, food, or a diaper change. Voice teachers listen to discriminate when coaching their students on adjustments to their singing technique. Skilled mechanics can distinguish between engine sounds that most people cannot detect.

Chapter Summary

According to Zeno of Citium, an ancient philosopher, "We have been given two ears but a single mouth, in order that we may listen more and talk less." Thousands of years later, we can still learn from his comment. Listening is a major and vital part of communication, yet too often we don't consider it as important as talking. In this chapter, we've explored the complex and demanding process of listening.

We began by distinguishing between hearing—physically receiving messages—and listening. The former is a straightforward physiological process that doesn't take effort on our part. Listening, in contrast, is a complicated and active process involving being mindful, hearing, selecting and organizing, interpreting, responding, and remembering. Listening well takes commitment and skill.

To understand what interferes with effective listening, we discussed obstacles in situations and messages and obstacles in us. Listening is hindered by message overload, complexity of material, and external noise in communication contexts. In addition, listening can be hampered by our preoccupations and prejudgments, lack of effort, and failure to recognize differences in listening styles. These obstacles to listening give rise to various types of nonlistening, including pseudolistening, monopolizing, selective listening, defensive listening, ambushing, and literal listening. Each of these forms of nonlistening signals that we aren't fully present in interaction.

We identified ways that principles of effectively listening pertain to digital communication. To conclude the chapter, we identified guidelines for different listening goals. Informational listening and critical listening require us to adopt a mindful attitude and to think critically, organize and evaluate information, clarify understanding by asking questions, and develop aids to retention of complex material. Relational listening also requires mindfulness, but it calls for other, distinct listening skills. Suspending judgment, paraphrasing, giving minimal encouragers, and expressing support enhance the effectiveness of relational listening.

Experiencing Communication in Our Lives

Case Study: Family Hour

Apply what you've learned in this chapter by analyzing the following case study, using the accompanying questions as a guide.

Over spring break, 20-year-old Josh visits his father. He wants to convince his family to support him in joining a fraternity that has given him a bid and decided he should have the conversation in person, rather than as part of their ongoing text message thread. On his second day home, Josh decides to bring it up. His dad is seated on the couch, reading the news online. Josh sits down and opens the conversation.

Josh: Well, something pretty interesting has happened at school this semester.

Dad: Oh, did you find a girlfriend? That's great. I was about your age when your mother and I started dating, and it was the best part of college. She was so pretty —the most gorgeous thing I'd ever seen. Before long, we got serious. Yep, it was about when I was 20, like you are now.

Josh: Well, no, I haven't found a girlfriend, but I did get a bid from Sigma Chi.

Dad: Sigma Chi. What is that—a fraternity?

Josh: Yeah, it's probably the coolest fraternity on campus. I attended some rush parties this semester—mainly out of curiosity, just to see what they were like.

Dad: **Oh, no**—why? I told you to stay away from fraternities! They cost a lot of money, and they're a huge distraction.

Josh: Well, I know you told me to stay away from fraternities, but I did check a few out. I could work part-time to help pay the membership fee and monthly dues. Besides, it's not that much more expensive when you figure I'd be eating at the house, and . . .

Dad: Do you realize how much it costs just for you to go to that private college? I'm paying almost $50,000 a year! You have no idea how lucky you are to be going to the school you wanted to go to, with me paying your way, when there's a great state college around the corner.

Josh: But we could work it out so that a fraternity wouldn't cost you anything. Like I said, I . . .

Dad: If you want to take a job, fine. I could use some help paying your tuition and fees. But you're not taking a job just so you can belong to a party house.

Josh: I thought they were just party houses too, until I attended rush. Now, I went to several houses that were that way, but Sigma Chi isn't. I really liked the brothers at Sigma Chi. They're interesting and friendly and fun, so I was thrilled when . . .

Dad: I don't want to hear about it. You're not joining a fraternity. I told you what happened when I was in college. Right after I joined one, my grades dropped from As and Bs to Cs and Ds. When you live in a fraternity house, you can't study like you can in your dorm room or the library. There's no need for you to repeat my mistake.

Josh: But, Dad, I'm not you. Joining a fraternity wouldn't necessarily mean that my grades . . .

Dad: What do you mean, you're not me? You think I wasn't a good student before I joined the fraternity? You think you're so smart you can party all the time and still get good grades? I thought that too, and was I ever wrong! There was always music blaring and girls in the house and video games—anything but studying. I wasn't stupid. It's just not an atmosphere that encourages academic work.

Josh: I'd like to give it a try. I really like these guys, and I think I can handle being in Sigma Chi and still . . .

Dad: Well, you think wrong!

Questions for Analysis and Discussion

1. What forms of ineffective listening are evident in this dialogue?
2. If you could advise Josh's father on listening effectively, what would you tell him to do differently?
3. Would you offer any advice to Josh on how he could listen to his father more effectively?

Key Concepts

ambushing
critical listening
defensive listening
hearing
informational listening
listening
literal listening
mansplaining
mindfulness
minimal encouragers
monopolizing
paraphrasing
pseudolistening
relational listening
selective listening
social listening

For Further Reflection and Discussion

1. To improve your listening skills, observe people who are experts at effective listening. Watch a television program that features interviews—Sunday morning news shows, for example. Select one interview to observe, and answer the following questions about it:
    - How does the interviewer phrase questions to encourage the interviewee to talk? Are questions open or closed, biased or unbiased?
    - How is the interviewer seated in relation to the interviewee—how close, at what angle?
    - Does the interviewer paraphrase the interviewee's responses?
    - Does the interviewer make minimal responses?
    - How, if at all, does the interviewer show that they understand and respect the interviewee's perspective?
    - How, if at all, does the interviewer demonstrate attentiveness?
2. Apply the principles we've discussed to enhance memory.
    - The next time you meet someone, repeat their name to yourself three times after you are introduced.
    - Invent mnemonics to create patterns that help you remember basic information in a message.
    - Organize ideas into categories. To remember the main ideas of this chapter, you might use major subheadings to form categories: listening process, obstacles to listening, and listening goals. The mnemonic LOG (i.e., listening, obstacles, goals) could help you remember those topics.
3. What different ethical responsibilities accompany listening for information and listening relationally?
4. Who is your prototype of an excellent listener? Describe what the person does that makes them effective. Do the person's listening behaviors fit with the guidelines offered in this chapter?
5. American Public Media developed a radio program called "The Story," which presents interviews with regular people who have interesting stories to tell about their lives. "The interviewer uses excellent listening skills to bring the interviewees out and make their stories sing. Look up "The Story" and listen to one podcast episode of your choice. As you listen, pay particular attention to the interviewer: How do they demonstrate engagement with the interviewee? How do they encourage the interviewee to expand on points and to move along with the story?

Syda Productions/Shutterstock.com

A different language is a different vision of life.

Federico Fellini

The Verbal Dimension of Communication

To what extent do you think language influences your perceptions of reality?

Learning Objectives

After studying the topics in this chapter, you should be able to:

1. Explain the key principles of verbal communication.
2. Identify some of the ways in which language is symbolic.
3. Apply strategies from this chapter to improve your verbal communication and make it more effective.

Perhaps you are familiar with the story of Helen Keller. As an infant, she contracted an illness that caused her to become a Deaf-Blind person. As a small child experiencing the world around her, Helen reacted to stimuli in her immediate environment, but she did not show any ability to self-reflect, grasp meanings, or communicate with others.

This changed when Helen was the age of 7. With the guidance of her teacher Annie Sullivan, Helen quickly learned the manual alphabet: in just a few weeks, Helen could use her hands to spell words. At first, Helen didn't have a way to understand that her fingers' and Annie's fingers' actions were communicating meaning. So, to help Helen make the connection between movement and meaning, Annie helped Helen hold one hand under the spout of a water pump and spelled W-A-T-E-R into her other hand. Helen got it; she connected the actions of Annie's fingers to the cool liquid running over her hand. Annie and Helen had shared meaning.

After Helen understood how to communicate, she was unstoppable: She graduated with honors from Radcliffe, authored nearly a dozen books, met 12 U.S. presidents, learned to read and write four languages other than English, and lectured throughout the United States, Europe, and Asia.

symbol An arbitrary, ambiguous, and abstract representation of a phenomenon. Symbols are the basis of language, much nonverbal behavior, and human thought.

arbitrary Random; not determined by necessity. Symbols are arbitrary because there is no particular reason for any one symbol to stand for a certain referent.

In this chapter, we take a close look at language. We begin by defining symbols, which are the basis of language. Second, we explore principles of verbal communication. Next, we consider what language allows us to do. The final section of the chapter focuses on guidelines for effective use of language.

Learning to use language opened the human world of meaning for Helen Keller.
Library of Congress Prints and Photographs Division [LC-USZ62-69879]

Features of Symbols

Language consists of symbols. A symbol is a representation of a person, event, or other phenomenon. For instance, the word *house* is a symbol that stands for a type of building. *Direct message, influencer, follower,* and *friend request* are words we have coined to represent ways we use social media to communicate. The key to understanding symbols is to realize that they are usually arbitrary, ambiguous, and abstract ways of representing things.

Symbols Are Arbitrary

Symbols are **arbitrary**, which means they are not usually intrinsically connected to what they represent. For instance, the word *book* has no necessary or natural connection to what you are reading now. We could substitute a different word, as long as we agreed it would stand for what we now call a book. Certain words seem right because as a society we agree to use them in particular ways, but they have no natural correspondence to their referents.

Because language is arbitrary, we can create private communication codes. For example, most professions rely on buzzwords that are not understood by outsiders. Two primary tasks of military intelligence are to invent secret codes and to break the secret codes of others. Go to the book's online resources for this chapter to learn about code talkers in the military during World War II.

Because language is arbitrary, we can create new words and terms. Today, many people work remotely, out of *virtual offices,* a term nobody had heard 20 years ago. The word *friend* was a noun until people on social network websites began using it as a verb—rather than "following" or "connecting," one person *friends* another on some social media platforms. While some of the words we invented to describe social media interactions are variations on words and phrases that already existed—instant message, netiquette, cyberbullying, tweet—others are wholly new inventions. For instance, blog, virtual reality, and avatar are words we created to name experiences in computer-mediated communication. What additional terms can you think of that have been created to refer to interaction on social media?

Symbols Are Ambiguous

ambiguous Subject to more than one interpretation. Symbols are ambiguous because their meanings vary from person to person and context to context.

Symbols are also **ambiguous**, which means their meanings aren't fixed in an absolute way. The meanings of words vary based on the values and experiences of those who use them. *Government regulation* may mean positive assistance to citizens who are suffering from pollutants emitted by a chemical company. To owners of the chemical company, however, *government regulation* may mean being forced to adopt costly measures to reduce pollution. Although the words are the same, their meanings vary according to individuals' interests and experiences.

Although words don't mean exactly the same thing to everyone, many symbols have an agreed-on range of meanings within a culture. Thus, we all understand that *dog* means a four-footed creature, but each of us also has personal meanings for the word based on dogs we have known and our experiences with them. We've all experienced dynamic speakers, yet we may differ in our notions of what concrete behaviors would lead us to label a speaker *dynamic* (remember the abstraction ladder we discussed in Chapter 2).

The ambiguity of symbols explains why misunderstandings occur. Your supervisor tells you it's important to be "a team player," which you assume means you should cooperate with coworkers. However, your supervisor may mean that you are expected to initiate and participate in teams on the job. To minimize the likelihood of misunderstanding, we can offer clear, concrete translations of ambiguous words.

The ambiguity of language takes on a new dimension when we are communicating online. The meaning of words in tweets, texts, or emails may be more ambiguous than the meaning of words in face-to-face conversations; in fact, some experts argue that while people think others understand their messages about 90% of the time, they are actually misunderstood about 50% of the time (Jenkins, 2020). This is in part because digital media do not allow us to use the full range of nonverbal communication that often helps us understand one another. To counter this issue, more people are using images like emoji, digital stickers, and memes to add meaning and minimize ambiguity in online conversations—even in business environments, where they were once considered unprofessional (Jenkins, 2020).

Communication Highlight

Lost in Translation

Language doesn't always translate well across cultures. Consider these examples of failed marketing efforts as corporations tried to cross cultures, only to learn their product names or slogans mean something very different in other cultures.

- The liqueur "Irish Mist" was surprisingly unpopular in Germany. The reason: It was marketed as "Irischer Mist" in Germany, with a literal translation of "Irish Dung"—not very appetizing.
- When General Motors exported its Chevrolet Nova to South America, there were problems. In Spanish, *no va* means "does not go"—not a great advertisement for a car!

To avoid such cross-cultural blunders, many companies now hire consultants to develop names that will work for their products in other countries. In China, BMW is *Precious Horse*; Reebok shoes are *Quick Steps*; Coca-Cola is *Tasty Fun*; Marriott is *Wealthy Elites*; and Heineken is *Happiness Power* (Wines, 2011).

Symbols Are Abstract

Finally, symbols are **abstract**, which means not concrete or tangible. They stand for ideas, people, events, objects, feelings, and so forth, but they are not the things they represent. In Chapter 2, we discussed the abstraction ladder, whereby we move farther and farther away from concrete reality. The symbols we use vary in abstractness. *Managerial potential* is an abstract term. *Presentational skills* is less abstract. Even more concrete expressions are *experience in speaking to large groups and hosting webinars.*

abstract Removed from concrete reality. Symbols are abstract because they are inferences and generalizations derived from a total reality.

Adiva My resident assistant told us we must observe "quiet hours" from 7 to 10 each night so that people can study. But everyone on my hall plays music and talks during quiet hours. My adviser told me I needed to take courses in social diversity, so I took a class in oral traditions of Asian cultures. Then my adviser told me that is a non-Western civilization course, not one in social diversity.

Question: Adiva's experiences sound frustrating. How do you think *ambiguity* might play a role in the contradictions she is describing?

Because symbols are arbitrary, ambiguous, and abstract, they allow us to share complex ideas and feelings with others. At the same time, symbols have the potential to create misunderstandings. When we understand that symbols are ambiguous, arbitrary, and abstract, we can guard against their potential to hinder communication.

Review It!

Features of Symbols:

- Arbitrary
- Ambiguous
- Abstract

Principles of Verbal Communication

Three principles clarify how we use verbal communication and how it affects us.

Interpretation Creates Meaning

Because symbols are arbitrary, ambiguous, and abstract, their meanings aren't self-evident or absolute. Instead, we have to interpret the meaning of symbols.

If a work associate says, "Let's go to dinner after work," the comment could be an invitation to explore transforming the work relationship into a friendship or it might indicate that the person issuing the invitation is interested in a romantic relationship. Effective communicators are alert to possible misunderstandings, and they check perceptions with others to see whether meanings match.

Communication Is Rule Guided

communication rules Shared understandings of what communication means and what behaviors are appropriate in various situations.

Verbal communication is patterned by unspoken but broadly understood rules (Argyle & Henderson, 1984; Shimanoff, 1980). **Communication rules** are shared understandings of what communication means and what kinds of communication are and are not appropriate in various situations. For the most part, rules aren't explicitly taught. In the course of interacting with our families and others, we unconsciously absorb rules that guide how we communicate and how we interpret others' communication.

regulative rules Communication rules that regulate interaction by specifying when, how, where, and with whom to talk about certain things.

Two kinds of rules guide communication (Cronen, Pearce, & Snavely, 1979; Pearce, Cronen, & Conklin, 1979). **Regulative rules** specify when, how, where, and with whom to talk about certain things. For instance, we follow regulative rules for turn taking in conversation. In formal contexts, we usually know not to interrupt when someone else is speaking, but in more informal settings, interruptions may be appropriate. Talking during formal speeches is appropriate in some contexts, as in traditional Black churches and public meetings. Regulative rules also define when, where, and with whom it's appropriate or inappropriate to communicate in particular ways. It is generally not appropriate to tell somber stories at celebratory events and, conversely, it is generally inappropriate to laugh and tell jokes at funerals (but it may be okay at wakes). Some couples have the rule that it's okay to kiss in private but not in public. On the job, there are often unwritten regulative rules that executives may interrupt subordinates but that subordinates may not interrupt executives.

Review It!

Types of Communication Rules:

- Regulative
- Constitutive

These rules apply to digital communication, as well. What regulative rules have evolved to govern when, where, and with whom it is appropriate to communicate online and digitally? Are there people you do not text, but instead call or email? Are there people you do not email but always text? Do you follow different rules for sharing personal information online and in face-to-face conversations?

Jude I can talk to Sam about politics all night long. Usually, we agree, but we also disagree on some issues and we enjoy arguing. I can't talk with Travis about politics. He totally disagrees with most of what I believe and he shuts down because he hates conflict. On the other hand, I can get into really deep discussions with Travis about religious stuff, and Sam has no interest in that.

Question: What kinds of communication rules seem to apply to Jude's conversations with Sam? with Travis?

constitutive rules Communication rules that define what communication means by specifying how certain communicative acts are to be counted.

Constitutive rules tell us how to count certain kinds of communication. We learn that paying attention counts as showing respect, hugging counts as affection, and raising the middle finger counts as an insult. Social interactions tend to follow rules that are widely shared in a specific society. We follow constitutive rules when using digital media, too. Think about the norms in your digital social circles: What counts as a timely reply to a text message? What would be interpreted as rude? On different social media platforms, certain types of engagement are likely to count

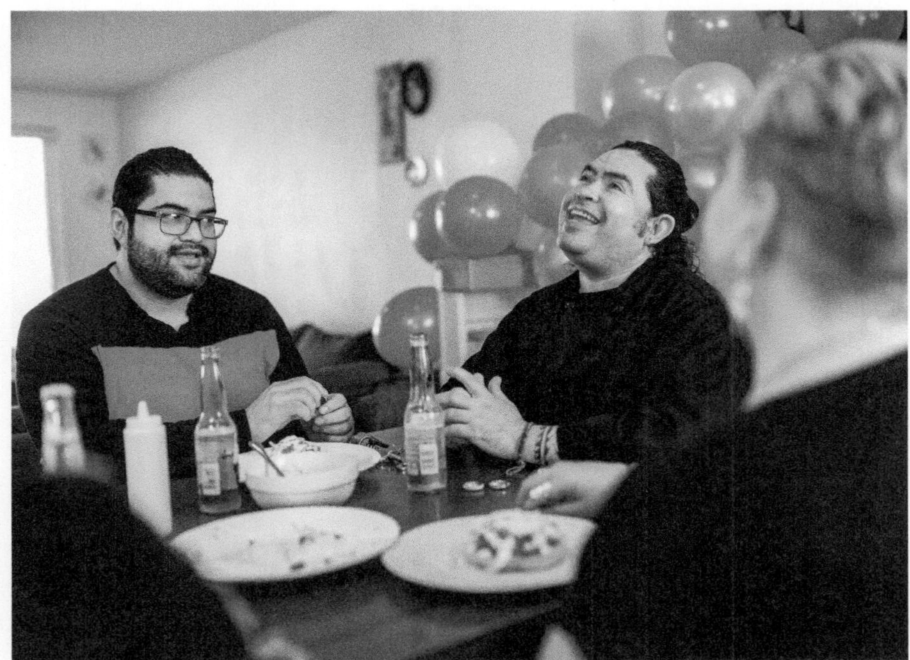

What regulative and constitutive rules govern mealtime conversation in your family?
iStock.com/Fotografia Inc.

as supportive, while others are not—with rules matching the context. So for example, using a laughing emoji or "laugh react" in response to a story that was meant to be humorous is supportive; the same response to a post by someone you disagree with would be understood as an insult.

Interaction between intimates also follows rules, but these may not be shared by the culture as a whole. Intimate partners negotiate private rules to guide how they communicate and what certain things mean. Couples craft personal rules that specify how to argue, express love, make decisions, and show support.

We may not realize that rules exist until one is broken and we realize that we had an expectation. Becoming aware of communication rules empowers you to consciously create ones that promote healthy interaction and relationships.

Punctuation Affects Meaning

In formal styles of writing, we use periods to define where ideas stop and start. Similarly, in communication, **punctuation** is the mental mark of the beginnings and endings of particular interactions (Watzlawick, Beavin, & Jackson, 1967). For example, when a teacher steps to the front of a classroom, we perceive that class is beginning. When the CEO sits down at a conference table, we perceive the beginning of a meeting. When a speaker says, "Thank you for your attention" and folds notes, we regard that as the end of the formal speech.

punctuation Defining the beginning and ending of interaction or interaction episodes.

When we don't agree on punctuation, problems may arise. A common instance of conflicting punctuation is the demand–withdraw pattern illustrated in Figure 5.1 (Bergner & Bergner, 1990; Caughlin & Vangelisti, 2000; Wegner, 2005). This occurs when one person tries to express closeness and the other strives to maintain autonomy by avoiding interaction. The more one partner pushes for closeness, the more the other partner withdraws. Each partner punctuates the beginning

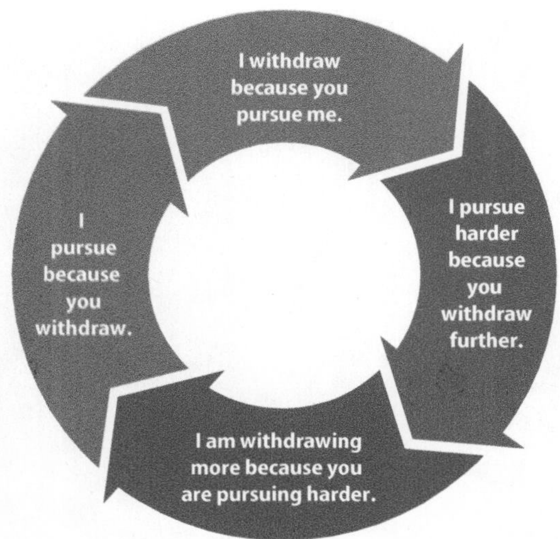

Figure 5.1
The Demand–Withdraw Pattern

of the interaction with the other's behavior. Thus, the demander thinks, "I pursue because you withdraw," and the withdrawer thinks, "I withdraw because you pursue."

Effective communicators realize that people don't always punctuate the same way. When they punctuate differently, they ascribe different meanings interaction. To break out of destructive cycles such as demand–withdraw, partners need to discuss how each of them is punctuating the experience. This reminds us of the importance of perspective taking.

Steven My parents say I am irresponsible if I don't tell them about something I do. So then they probe me and call more often to check up on me. I hate that kind of intrusion, so I don't return their calls and I sidestep questions. That makes them call more and ask more questions. That makes me clam up more. And we just keep going in circles.

Question: Steven's comment illustrates the demand–withdraw pattern. How do you think perspective-taking between him and his parents might improve their interpersonal communication?

Symbolic Abilities

Because we use symbols, we live in a world of ideas and meanings. Instead of just reacting to others and our environments, we think about them and sometimes transform them. In much the same way, we don't simply accept ourselves as we are but continuously work to change and grow. Philosophers of language have identified five ways symbolic capacities affect our lives (Cassirer, 1944; Langer, 1953, 1979). As we discuss each, we'll consider how to realize the constructive power of symbols and minimize the problems they can generate.

Symbols Define

We use symbols to define experiences, people, relationships, feelings, and thoughts. As we saw in Chapter 2, the definitions we give to phenomena shape what they mean to us. When we label people, we focus attention on particular aspects of them, and we necessarily obscure other aspects of who they are. We might define a person as an environmentalist, a teacher, a foodie, and a Republican. Each way of classifying the person directs our attention to certain, and not other, aspects of identity. We might discuss wilderness legislation with the environmentalist, talk about testing with the teacher, swap recipes with the foodie, and discuss politics or not, depending on our own political stance, with the Republican. We tend to interact with people according to how we define and classify them.

Totalizing is using a single label to represent the totality of a person. We fixate on one symbol to define someone and fail to recognize many other aspects of who they are. Totalizing also occurs when we dismiss people by saying, "He's a liberal," "They're old," "She's Pakistani," "They're queer," "She's preppy," "She's a housekeeper," or "He's a jock." When we totalize others, we negate most of who they are by spotlighting a single aspect of their identity.

totalizing Responding to people as if one aspect of them were the sum total of who they are.

Furthermore, when we totalize others and negate complex aspects of their identity, we risk causing or perpetuating social harm by marginalizing them. **Marginalization** systematically prevents certain groups and individuals from fully engaging in society, such as social, economic, and political life (Alakhunova et al., 2015; Causadias & Umaña-Taylor, 2018). Marginalization is a process that can happen when people with power in society totalize those who have less power. These power imbalances can be related to race, age, gender, ethnicity, socioeconomic status, ability, or religion, to name a few. Those who have been subjected to marginalization are said to be *marginalized.*

Marginalization A condition and process preventing individuals and groups from equal participation in wider society, including social, economic, and political life.

Note that marginalization is context-dependent. Different groups can be marginalized at different times, in different societies, by different processes. For example, the marginalization of Muslims increased dramatically after the terrorist attacks of September 11, 2001 (Causadias & Umaña-Taylor, 2018), with Muslims across various societies experiencing Islamophobia in different ways. For example, Switzerland held a referendum to ban construction of minarets, or towers for mosques, while in the U.S., Muslims were significantly more likely than any other major religion to report having personally experienced religious or racial discrimination (Gallup, 2011). Likewise, some groups, such as people with a history of incarceration and felony, face marginalization across cultures (Alakhunova et al., 2015). For example, in both Bangladesh and Washington, D.C., those who have a history of incarceration and felons are often reduced to the category of "convicted felon," and then denied the equal access to resources and opportunities such as employment, promotions, voting, and decision-making that others in the same societies enjoy (Alakhunova et al., 2015).

What these examples have in common is the totalizing of people within a certain group or groups. Reducing them to a specific, narrow, totalized identity led to their exclusion and/or perpetuates their disempowerment.

Nanya I'm Indian, and that's all a lot of people here see in me. They see that my skin is dark and I wear a sari, and they put me in the category "foreigner" or, if they are observant, "Indian." They mark me off as different, foreign, not like them, and they can't see anything else about me. How would they feel if I categorized them as "Americans" and didn't see their individual qualities?

Question: Nanya's experience is not a rare one. In the U.S., some white people have a tendency to totalize people of color and people from other marginalized backgrounds. Can you think of any communication strategies people can use to go beyond obvious and totalizing symbols to form a deeper understanding of people who differ from them?

Wedding bands symbolize commitment.
iStock.com/Orbon Alija

Symbols influence how we think and feel about experiences and people. For example, some romantic couples define differences as positive forces that energize a relationship, while others define differences as problems or barriers to closeness (Wood, Dendy, Dordek, Germany, & Varallo, 1994). Partners who label differences as constructive may approach disagreements with more curiosity and a growth mindset, while partners who label differences as problems may tend to deny differences or avoid talking about them.

How we think about relationships directly affects what happens in them, including how we communicate with one another. Negative beliefs can interfere with our relationships, while beliefs about our own strengths can prompt us to be more curious and positive—helping us to develop stronger, more loving relationships (Seligman, 2012).

Abby About 3 years ago, my husband and I were seriously considering divorce. We decided to try marital counseling first, and that saved our marriage. The counselor helped us see that we noticed problems, aggravations, and faults in each other and didn't see all of the good qualities in each other and our relationship. Now we have a "warts-and-all" philosophy, which means we accept each other the way we are, instead of looking for perfection. Changing how we think about our marriage really has changed what it is for us.

As Abby's commentary indicates, our definitions of relationships can create self-fulfilling prophecies. Once we select a label for relationships or other phenomena, we tend to see what our label names and to overlook what it doesn't. This suggests an ethical principle for using and interpreting language: We should consider what the language that we and others use includes and excludes.

Symbols Evaluate

Symbols are not neutral. They are laden with values. We tend to describe people we like with language that accents their good qualities and downplays their flaws. The reverse is generally true of descriptions of people we don't like. My friend is *casual;* someone I don't like is *sloppy.* Restaurants use language that is designed to heighten the attractiveness of menu items. "Tender lobster accented with drawn butter" sounds more appetizing than "crustacean murdered by being boiled alive and then drenched in saturated fat."

In recent years, we have become more sensitive to different ways of naming various racial and ethnic groups. For example, in describing descendants of the African diaspora within the U.S., the terms *African American* and *Black* are currently the most commonly used terms (Ridley-Merriweather et al., 2021). The word *Black*, capitalized, is preferred to *black*, without capitalization, as the capitalization is meant to signify identity (as a proper noun) rather than a color. But they are not fully interchangeable terms. *African American* is a term that applies to people born in the U.S. with African ancestry—typically, but not always, descendants of those who had been enslaved. In contrast, *Black* is not specific to U.S. nationality and therefore can be inclusive of more people. Whether people identify with one of these terms—or prefer another, like *African*, *Afro-Caribbean* or *Afro-Latino*—is a matter of individual choice. Various descendants of the African diaspora prefer one term over the other to describe their identity (Ridley-Merriweather et al., 2021).

Meanwhile, the word *Hispanic* emphasizes the Spanish language spoken in the home countries, whereas *Latino*, *Latina*, and *Latinx* are terms that focus on the geographic origins of Latin American men, women, and people (gender-inclusive), respectively. Like *African-American* and *Black*, *Hispanic* and *Latino/a/x* are not truly interchangeable. First, "Hispanic" encompasses only people descended from countries where Spanish was spoken, while "Latino," "Latina," and "Latinx" includes groups from Latin America where languages other than Spanish are spoken. Secondly, "Latinx" is popular for its strengths in raising awareness of gender as a nonbinary concept; but some are concerned that affixing an "x" ending onto Spanish—which is an Anglo, rather than Latin, linguistic practice—implies that Latino/a culture is somehow problematic. Because of these complexities, different people of Latin-American and/or Hispanic descent prefer to describe themselves using different terms.

Ultimately, an ethical guideline for using language is to try to learn and respect individuals' preferences for describing their identities. Approaching people from different ethnic groups with cultural humility and asking how they prefer to be described is a great way of building cultural competency.

Loaded language consists of words that strongly slant perceptions and thus meanings. For example, Americans belonging to different political parties tend to use different language to disparage one another's political views. Sonnad (2014) reports that conservatives are likely to use the term "elitist" to disparage people with liberal social and political values—for example, calling them *liberal elitists.* At the same time, liberal commentators are more likely to insult people with conservative

loaded language An extreme form of evaluative language that relies on words that strongly slant perceptions and hence meanings.

social and political values with the term "extremist"—for example, *right-wing extremists.* Loaded language also fosters negative views of older people. According to the AARP, terms such as *over the hill, blue-hairs, little old lady,* and *geriatric* are ageist, and therefore should not be used; they even advise against *elderly* and *senior citizen* (Duarte & Albo, 2018). The Associated Press agrees: Its style guide now calls for journalists to use phrases like *older adult* and *older person,* rather than terms like *senior citizen, seniors,* and the elderly (Parker, 2021). In 2014, the U.S. Patent and Trademark Office canceled the Washington Redskins' trademark on the name *redskins* because the term has been described by Native Americans as disrespectful (A Victory for Tolerance, 2014).

Symbols Organize Perceptions

We use symbols to organize our perceptions. As we saw in Chapter 2, we rely on cognitive schemata to classify and evaluate experiences. How we organize experiences affects what they mean to us. For example, your prototype of a good friend affects how you judge particular friends. When we place someone in the category of friend, the category influences how we interpret that person's communication. An insult is likely to be viewed as teasing if made by someone we define as a friend but a call to battle if made by someone we classify as an enemy. The words don't change, but their meaning varies, depending on how we classify the person uttering them.

Because symbols organize thought, they allow us to think about abstract concepts such as professionalism, democracy, morality, and community. Thinking abstractly relieves us of having to consider every specific object and experience individually.

Our capacity to abstract can also distort thinking. A primary way this occurs is in stereotyping—thinking in broad generalizations about a whole class of people or experiences. Examples of stereotypes are "Sorority women are fake," "Ph.D.s are smart," and "Democrats tax and spend." Notice that stereotypes can be positive or negative.

Stereotypes can discourage us from recognizing important differences among the phenomena we lump together. Thus, we have an ethical responsibility to stay alert to differences among the things and people that we place in a single category.

Communication Highlight

Language Shapes Our Realities

Language shapes our perceptions in ways that reflect a culture's values and experiences (Whorf, 1956). In one part of Australia, people speak Guugu Yimithirr, a language that does not include the terms *right* and *left.* In Guugu Yimithirr, special locations are described in relation to a compass. Thus, a person speaking this language might ask to have the pepper passed north (Monastersky, 2002). People recall colors more clearly if their language provides distinct terms, so English speakers do not remember shades of blue (light blue, dark blue) as precisely as Russian speakers who have different words for light blue (*goluboy*) and dark blue (*sinly*) (Gentner & Boroditsky, 2009).

Symbols Allow Hypothetical Thought

Who was your best friend when you were 5 years old? What would you do if you won the lottery? To answer these questions, you must think hypothetically, which means thinking about experiences and ideas that are not part of your concrete, present situation. Because we can think hypothetically, we can plan, dream, remember, fantasize, set goals, and weigh alternative courses of action.

Hypothetical thought is possible because we use symbols. When we symbolize, we name ideas so that we can hold them in our minds and reflect on them. We can contemplate things that currently have no real existence. For example, you've invested many hours in studying because you imagine having a college degree. The degree is not real now, nor is the self that you will become once you have the degree. Yet the idea is sufficiently real to motivate you to work hard for many years.

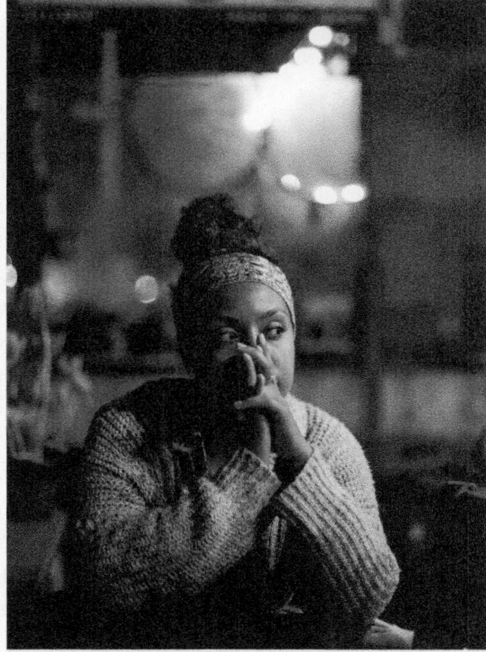

Self-reflection allows us to manage the image we project to others.
Kevin Turcios/Unsplash.com

Close relationships rely on ideas of history and future. One of the strongest glues for intimacy is a history of shared experiences (Wood, 2006a). Knowing that they have weathered rough times in the past helps partners get through current trials. Shared experiences with digital media can also help with relationship development, as seen in studies with children (Wernholm, 2019) and romantic partners (Greenberg & Neustaedter, 2013) alike. Belief in a future also sustains intimacy. We interact with people we don't expect to see again differently than people who are continuing parts of our lives. Talking about the future also enhances intimacy because it suggests that more lies ahead.

hypothetical thought Cognitive awareness of experiences and ideas that are not part of the concrete, present situation.

Symbols Allow Self-Reflection

Just as we use symbols to reflect on what goes on outside of us, we also use them to reflect on ourselves. In an argument, you may want to insult a coworker who

Communication Highlight

Body Image

"I'm so fat." "I hate my hips." "Why can't I get my stomach flat?" Sound familiar? Most women engage in negative talk about their bodies (Engeln, 2015)—but doing so is more harmful than many people realize. People who engage in negative body talk are more likely to feel ashamed of their bodies or parts of them and to develop eating disorders, and they're not likely to make different diet and exercise choices (Arroyo & Harwood, 2012; Engeln, 2015).

Instead, negative body talk reinforces people's judgments about larger bodies. It also influences the self-images of the people around them, and it contributes to eating disorders, shame, isolation, and avoidance of medical care. It's also of a piece with racism, as systemic racism is inextricably interwoven with fatphobia and calls for practitioners and the public to fight against obesity (Aaron & Stanford, 2021; MacNeill, 2021).

It's time to change the conversation to focus on how harmful body-shaming is instead and raise awareness that negative body talk reflects implicit and explicit biases, including fatphobia.

has criticized you, but you censor that impulse. You remind yourself that it's impolite to put others down and that doing so might create future problems with that coworker.

The ability to self-reflect allows us to think about who we want to be and set goals for becoming the self we desire. We can feel shame, pride, and regret for our actions—emotions that are possible because we self-reflect. We can control what we do in the present by imagining how we might later feel about our actions.

Self-reflection also allows us to manage our image, or the identity we present to others. Because we reflect on ourselves from social perspectives, we are able to consider how we appear in others' eyes. Our ability to manage how we appear sometimes is called *facework* because it involves controlling the face we present to others. When talking with teachers, you may consciously present yourself as a respectful, engaged student. When communicating with someone you'd like to date, you may choose to be more attentive and social than you are in other circumstances. In work situations, you may do facework to create an image of yourself as responsible, ambitious, and dependable. Continuously, we adjust how we present ourselves so that we sculpt our image to fit particular situations and people.

Review It!

Symbolic Abilities:

- Definition
- Evaluation
- Organization
- Hypothetical Thought
- Self-reflection

Summing up, we use symbols to define, evaluate, and organize experiences, think hypothetically, and self-reflect. Each of these abilities helps us create meaning in our lives.

Guidelines for Effective Verbal Communication

We've explored what symbols are and how they may be used differently in distinct social communities. Building on these understandings, we can now consider ways to improve the effectiveness of our verbal communication.

Engage in Dual Perspective

dual perspective The ability to understand another person's perspective, beliefs, thoughts, or feelings.

The single most important guideline for effective verbal communication is to engage in **dual perspective**. Dual perspective involves taking another person's point of view into account as you communicate. For instance, effective public speakers take listeners' values into consideration when planning and presenting speeches. The same is true of friends who communicate well: They take each other's perspective into account.

We don't need to abandon our own perspectives to recognize those of others. In fact, it would be just as unethical to stifle your own views as to dismiss those of others. *Dual perspective*, as the term implies, consists of two perspectives. It entails understanding both our own and another's point of view and acknowledging each when we communicate. For example, you and your supervisor may disagree about a performance review. It's important that you understand why your supervisor assigns the ratings they do, even if you don't share their perceptions. By understanding the supervisor's perceptions and ratings, you enhance your ability to have a good working relationship and to perform effectively on the job.

Own Your Feelings and Thoughts

We sometimes use language that obscures our responsibility for how we feel and what we think. For instance, people say, "You made me feel inadequate about my job performance," or "You hurt me," as if what they feel is caused by someone else. On a more subtle level, we sometimes blame others for our responses to what they say.

"You're too demanding" really means that you don't like what someone else wants or expects. The sense of feeling pressured by another's expectations is in you.

Our feelings and thoughts result from how we interpret others' communication, not from their communication itself. Others sometimes exert a great deal of influence on how we feel and how we see ourselves. Yet they do not directly cause our feelings. Although how we interpret what others say may lead us to feel certain ways, we can't hold them directly responsible for our feelings. In relationships with manipulative or hurtful people, you may find it useful either to communicate in ways that don't enable the other and that do preserve your integrity or to leave the relationship before it jeopardizes your own well-being.

Effective communicators take responsibility for themselves by using language that owns their thoughts and feelings. They own their feelings and do not blame others for what happens in themselves. To take responsibility for your own feelings, rely on *I*-language instead of *you*-language. Table 5.1 gives examples of the difference.

In working with inmates who have violent histories, one of the key skills we teach is using *I*-language. At the outset, the inmates say things such as, "She made me hit her by acting so nasty." Through instruction, exercises, and practice, they learn to change their *you*-language to *I*-language, saying, "I hit her because I didn't like how she was acting." The inmates say that learning *I*-language is empowering because it helps them see that they have more control over their actions than they had realized.

There are two differences between *I*-language and *you*-language. First, *I*-statements own responsibility, whereas *you*-statements project it onto another person. *You*-language is likely to arouse defensiveness, which doesn't facilitate healthy communication. Second, *I*-statements offer more description than *you*-statements. *You*-statements tend to be abstract accusations, which is one reason they're ineffective in promoting change. *I*-statements, on the other hand, provide concrete descriptions of behaviors and feelings without directly blaming another person for how we feel.

Some people feel awkward when they first start using *I*-language. This is natural because most of us are accustomed to using *you*-language. With commitment and practice, however, you can learn to communicate using *I*-language. Once you feel comfortable using it, you will find that *I*-language has many advantages. It is less likely than *you*-language to make others defensive, so *I*-language opens the doors for dialogue.

Table 5.1 ***You*-Language and *I*-Language**

You-Language	*I*-Language
You hurt me.	I feel hurt when you ignore what I say.
You make me feel small.	I feel small when you tell me that I'm selfish.
My boss intimidates me.	When my boss criticizes my work, I feel intimidated.
You're really domineering.	When you shout at me, I feel dominated.
The speaker made me feel dumb.	I felt uninformed when the speaker discussed such complex information.
You humiliated me.	I felt humiliated when you mentioned my problems in front of our friends.

I-language is also more honest. We deceive ourselves when we say, "You made me feel . . . " because others don't control how we feel. Finally, *I*-language is more empowering than *you*-language. When we say, "You hurt me," or "You made me feel bad," we give control of our emotions to others. This reduces our personal sense of being a moral free agent and, by extension, our motivation to change what is happening. Using *I*-language allows us to own our feelings while also explaining to others how we interpret their behaviors.

Roth I never realized how often I use you-language. I'm always saying my boyfriend makes me feel happy or my father makes me feel like a failure. What I'm beginning to see is that they really don't control my feelings. I do.

Respect What Others Say About Their Feelings and Ideas

Has anyone ever said to you, "You shouldn't feel that way"? If so, you know how infuriating it can be to be told that your feelings aren't valid, appropriate, or acceptable. It's equally destructive to be told our thoughts are wrong. When someone says, "How can you think something so stupid?" we feel devalued. Even if you don't feel or think what someone else does, you can still respect another person's perspective.

We also disrespect others when we speak for them instead of letting them speak for themselves. In Chapter 2, we learned about mind reading, and it is relevant to speaking for others. As we have seen, our distinct experiences and ways of interpreting life make each of us unique. We seldom, if ever, completely grasp what another person feels or thinks. Although it is supportive to engage in dual perspective, it isn't supportive to presume that we fully understand someone else's feelings or thoughts, especially when they differ from us in important ways. It's particularly important not to assume we understand people from other cultures or social communities.

Respecting how others express their thoughts and feelings is a cornerstone of effective communication. We also grow when we open ourselves to perspectives, feelings, and thoughts that differ from our own.

Communication & Careers

Corporatespeak

It's not new that any profession has some language unique to it, but the jargon in the business world sometimes baffles new hires. What would you think if your supervisor asked to schedule a bilateral with you? What if you were asked if you have enough bandwidth to take on a project and to prepare some decks for it? Welcome to Corporatespeak 2015 (Katzman, 2015).

A bilateral is a one-on-one meeting. Bandwidth is time. Decks are PowerPoint slides.

Strive for Accuracy and Clarity

Because symbols are arbitrary, abstract, and ambiguous, the potential for misunderstanding always exists. Although we cannot entirely eliminate misunderstandings, we can minimize them.

Be Aware of Levels of Abstraction Misunderstandings are most likely when language is very abstract. For instance, suppose a professor says, "Your papers should demonstrate a sophisticated conceptual grasp of the material and its pragmatic implications." Would you know how to write a paper to satisfy the professor? You might not, because the language is very abstract and unclear. Here's a more concrete description: "Your papers should include definitions of the concepts and specific examples that show how they apply in real life." With this less abstract statement, you would have a better idea of what the professor expected.

Abstract language is particularly likely to lead to misunderstandings when people talk about how they want one another to change. Concrete language and specific examples help people share understandings of which behaviors are unwelcome and which ones are wanted. For example, "I want you to be more responsible about your job" does not explain what would count as being more responsible. Is it arriving on time, taking on extra assignments, or something else? It isn't clear what the speaker wants unless more concrete descriptions are supplied. Likewise, "I want to be closer" could mean the speaker wants to spend more time together, talk about the relationship, do things together, or anything else. Vague abstractions lend themselves to misunderstanding.

"Well, then, if 'commandments' seems too harsh to me, and 'guidelines' seems too wishy-washy to you, how about 'the 10 Policy Statements'?"

Qualify Language Another way to increase the clarity of communication is to qualify language. Two types of language should be qualified. First, we should qualify generalizations so we don't mislead ourselves or others. "Politicians are crooked" is a false statement because it overgeneralizes. A more accurate statement would be, "A number of politicians have been shown to have engaged in illegal activities."

We should also qualify language when describing and evaluating people. **Static evaluation** consists of assessments that suggest that something is unchanging or frozen in time. These are particularly troublesome when applied to people: "Lauren is selfish," "Carson is irresponsible," or "Dylan is generous." Whenever we use the word *is,* we suggest that something is inherent and fixed. In reality, we aren't static but continuously changing. A person who is selfish at one time may not be at another. A person who is irresponsible on one occasion may be responsible in other situations.

static evaluation Assessments that suggest something is unchanging or static. "Mike is impatient" is a static evaluation.

Indexing is a technique developed by early communication scholars that allows us to note that our statements reflect only specific times and circumstances (Korzybski, 1948). To index, we would say "Ann$_{\text{June 6, 1997}}$ acted selfishly," "Don$_{\text{on the task committee}}$ was irresponsible," Bob$_{\text{in college}}$ was generous." See how indexing ties description to a specific time and circumstance? Mental indexing reminds us that we and others are able to change in remarkable ways.

indexing A technique of noting that statements reflect specific times and circumstances and may not apply to other times or circumstances.

Ryan I had a couple of accidents right after I got my driver's license. Most teenagers do, right? But to hear my father, you'd think I am a bad driver today. Those accidents were 5 years ago, and I haven't even had a ticket since then. But he still talks about "Reckless Ryan."

Question: By calling Ryan "Reckless Ryan" 5 years after those driving accidents, Ryan's father is making a static evaluation, How do you think generalizing Ryan in this way might impact their relationship? What communication strategy might Ryan's father try using to make his evaluation of Ryan more fair?

We've considered four guidelines for effective verbal communication. Engaging in dual perspective is the first principle and a foundation for all others. A second guideline is to take responsibility for our own feelings and thoughts by using *I*-language. Third, we should respect others as the experts on what they feel and think and not speak for them or presume we know what they think and feel. The fourth principle is to strive for clarity by choosing appropriate degrees of abstraction, qualifying generalizations, and indexing evaluations, particularly ones applied to people.

Chapter Summary

In this chapter, we've discussed the world of words and meaning, which make up the uniquely human universe of symbol users. Because symbols are arbitrary, ambiguous, and abstract, they have no inherent meanings. Instead, we actively construct meaning by interpreting symbols based on perspectives gleaned through interaction with others and our personal experiences. We also punctuate to create meaning in communication.

We use symbols to define, evaluate, and organize our experiences. In addition, we use symbols to think hypothetically so we can consider alternatives and inhabit all three dimensions of time. Finally, symbols allow us to self-reflect so we can monitor our own behaviors.

Digital media rely on symbols just as face-to-face communication does. We noted that there are different types of ambiguity in language used in texts, emails, and social media than in communication between people who are physically together. In other respects, symbols perform similarly wherever they occur: whether face-to-face or online, regulative and constitutive rules guide communication, and in both new words are continually being created.

Because symbols are abstract, arbitrary, and ambiguous, misunderstandings can occur between communicators. We can reduce the likelihood of misunderstandings by being sensitive to levels of abstraction. In addition, we should engage in dual perspective, own our thoughts and feelings, respect what others say about how they think and feel, and monitor abstractness, generalizations, and static evaluations. In Chapter 6, we will continue our discussion of the world of human communication by exploring the fascinating realm of nonverbal behavior.

Experiencing Communication in Our Lives

Case Study: The Roommates

Apply what you've learned in this chapter by analyzing the following case study, using the accompanying questions as a guide. These questions and a video of the case study are also available online for *Communication in Our Lives*.

Bernadette and Celia were assigned to be roommates a month ago when the school year began. Initially, both were pleased with the match because they discovered commonalities in their interests and backgrounds. They are both sophomores from small towns, they have similar tastes in music and television programs, and they both like to stay up late and sleep in.

Lately, however, Brianna has been irritated by Celia's housekeeping or lack of it. Celia leaves her clothes lying all over the room. If they cook in, Celia often leaves the pans and dishes for hours, and then it's usually Brianna who cleans them. Brianna feels she has to talk to Celia about this problem, but she hasn't figured out how or when to talk. When Celia gets in from classes, Brianna is sitting and reading a textbook on her bed.

Celia: Hey Bri, how's it going?

Celia drops her book bag in the middle of the floor, flops on the bed, and kicks her shoes off on the floor. As Brianna watches, she feels her frustration peaking and decides now is the time to talk to Celia about the problem.

Brianna: You shouldn't do that. You make me nuts the way you just throw your stuff all over the room.

Celia: I don't "throw my stuff all over the room." I just took off my shoes and put my books down, like I do every day.

Brianna: No, you didn't. You dropped your bag right in the middle of the room, and you kicked your shoes and left them in a mess where they landed. And you're right—that is what you do every day.

Celia: There's nothing wrong with wanting to be comfortable in my own room.

Brianna: Comfortable is one thing. But you're so messy. Your mess makes me really miserable.

Celia: Since when? This is the first I've heard about it.

Brianna: Since we started rooming together, but I didn't want to say anything about how angry you make me. I just can't stand it any more. You shouldn't be so messy.

Celia: Sounds to me like you've got a problem—you, not me.

Brianna: Well it's you and your mess that are my problem. Do you have to be so sloppy?

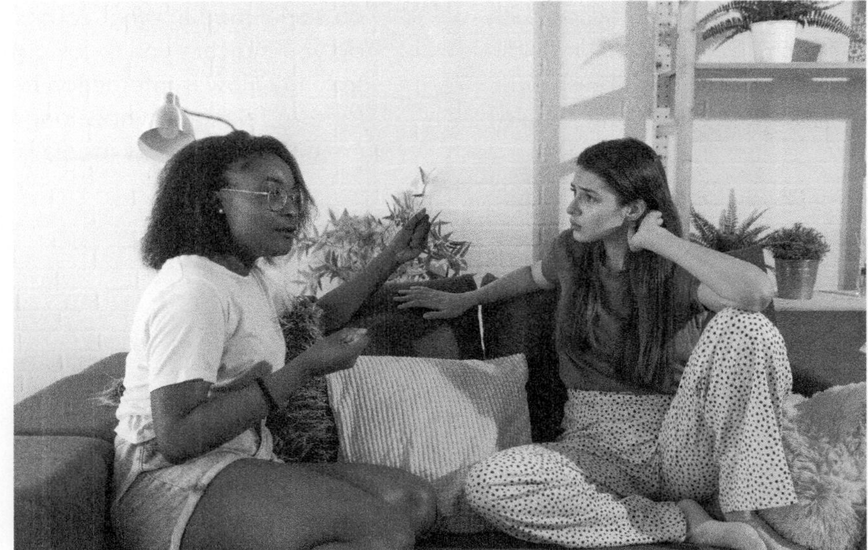
iStock.com/Srdjanns74

Questions for Analysis and Discussion

1. Identify examples of *you*-language in this conversation. How would you change it to *I*-language?
2. Identify examples of loaded language and ambiguous language.
3. Do you agree with Celia that the problem is Brianna's, not hers?
4. Do Celia and Brianna seem to engage in dual perspective to understand each other?

Key Concepts

abstract
ambiguous
arbitrary
communication rules
constitutive rules
dual perspective
hypothetical thought
indexing
loaded language
marginalization
punctuation
regulative rules
static evaluation
symbol
totalizing

For Further Reflection and Discussion

1. Pay attention to *I*- and *you*-language in your own communication and that of others. What happens when you switch a *you*-statement to an *I*-statement? Does it change how you feel or what happens in interaction?
2. What is a good term for describing someone with whom you have a serious romantic relationship? *Boyfriend* and *girlfriend* no longer work for many people. Do you prefer *significant other, partner, special friend*, or another term? Why?
3. What ethical responsibilities should accompany the right to free speech? Do you think individuals have an unqualified right to say whatever they want or are there limits to what people should be allowed to say?
4. Articulate the ethical basis for the third guideline presented in this chapter: Respect what others say about their feelings and ideas. Why might it be ethical to do so and unethical not to do so?
5. Identify a stereotype you use, and consider ten people to whom you might apply it. Identify differences between the people. At first, this may be difficult because stereotypes gloss over differences. What do you discover as you look for individual variations in the people you lumped together under a single symbol?
6. Identify communication rules for conversations on social media. What counts as joking (how do you indicate you're joking)? What counts as trolling? How is interaction regulated with rules for turn-taking and how long typical comments are on various social media sites?

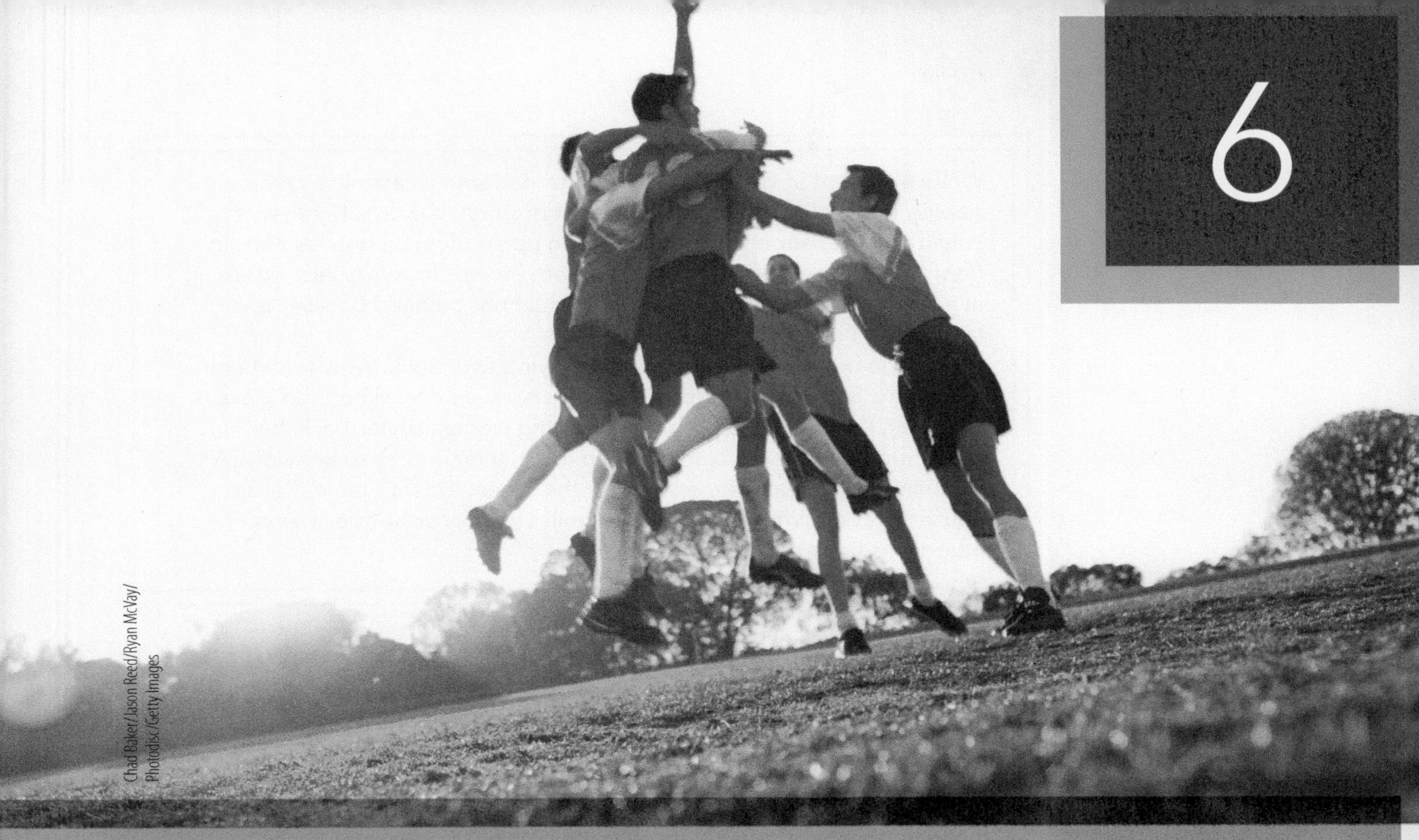
Chad Baker/Jason Reed/Ryan McVay/Photodisc/Getty Images

6

What you do speaks so loud that I cannot hear whata you say.

Ralph Waldo Emerson

The Nonverbal Dimension of Communication

Learning Objectives

After studying the topics in this chapter, you should be able to:

1. Explain the principles of nonverbal communication.
2. Explain the types of nonverbal communication.
3. Apply chapter guidelines to improve your nonverbal communication.

How well can you recognize others' feelings based on their nonverbal communication?

While a student at Yale, Kenta Koga interned with a Japanese company, hoping that would lead to a permanent position. It didn't. Kenta was criticized by his supervisors for speaking up and for crossing his arms in front of senior colleagues. A student from Brown University, also interning in a Japanese company, was told she could not be hired because she laughed too much (Tabuchi, 2012).

Kenzie notices another student studying two tables away from her in the library. Something about her catches Kenzie's eye. When she looks up at her, Kenzie smiles warmly. The young woman smiles back, her eye contact lingering a bit more than usual, then returns to her work. A few minutes later, as Kenzie walks by the other student's table, Kenzie pauses to compliment her hair. She smiles warmly as Kenzie speaks, then introduces herself.

These examples illustrate the power of nonverbal communication. In the first case, the students interning in Japanese companies were perceived as being rude because they violated nonverbal norms of the host country. In the library scene, we see a pattern of successful nonverbal communication between two women who are interested in one another. Kenzie follows gendered communication norms for lesbian flirting by paying attention to subtle body language cues: indirectly signaling her interest with gaze and compliment, and waiting to see if she responds in a positive way (Taimi, 2022).

Ethnicity, gender, sexual orientation, and socioeconomic class are identities that we create and sustain by performing them day in and day out (Butler, 2004; Milani, 2019). In this sense, nonverbal communication, like language, is a primary way in which we announce who we are. The intricate system of nonverbal communication helps us establish identity, negotiate relationships, and create environments.

For many years, it has been a widely held belief that nonverbal behaviors account for 65–93% of the total meaning of communication (Birdwhistell, 1970; Hickson, Stacks, & Moore, 2003). Although scholars argue that the 93% statistic is an overstatement stemming from misunderstood research results (Burgoon, 1985; Lapakko, 2007), researchers agree: Nonverbal communication significantly impacts how we are understood. This is even true online, as messages that include relevant emoji (for example) can be easier to understand than those without (Daniel & Camp, 2020). Nonverbal communication's breadth is a reason for this: It includes everything from dress and eye contact to body posture and vocal inflection.

In this chapter, we explore the fascinating realm of nonverbal interaction. We will identify principles of nonverbal communication and types of nonverbal behavior, with attention to relationships between nonverbal communication and digital media, and discuss guidelines to improve the effectiveness of our nonverbal communication.

Principles of Nonverbal Communication

nonverbal communication All forms of communication other than words themselves; includes inflection and other vocal qualities as well as several other behaviors.

Nonverbal communication is all aspects of communication other than words themselves. It includes how we utter words (i.e., inflection, volume), features of environments that affect communication (i.e., temperature, lighting), and objects that influence personal images and interaction patterns (i.e., dress, jewelry). Five key points highlight the nature and power of nonverbal communication.

Similar to and Different from Verbal Communication

Nonverbal communication and verbal communication are similar in some ways and different in others.

Similarities Like verbal communication, nonverbal behavior is symbolic, which means it is arbitrary, ambiguous, and abstract. Thus, we can't be sure what a smile or a gesture means, and we can't guarantee that others understand the meanings we intend to express with our own nonverbal behaviors. Second, like verbal communication, our nonverbal behavior and our interpretations of others' nonverbal behaviors are guided by constitutive and regulative rules.

A third similarity between the two communication systems is that both are culture bound. Our nonverbal communication reflects and reproduces values and norms of the particular culture and social communities to which we belong (Knapp, Hall, & Hogan, 2013; Orbe & Harris, 2015; Samovar, Porter, McDaniel, & Roy, 2015). For instance, dress considered appropriate for women varies across cultures: Some women in the United States wear miniskirts; women in some other countries wear headscarves. Dress also reflects organizational identities: Many professionals wear business suits or dresses; carpenters usually wear jeans; medical professionals typically wear white lab coats; and military personnel wear uniforms.

Review It!

Similarities to Verbal:

- Symbolic
- Rule-Guided
- Culture Bound
- Intentional or Unintentional

Last, both verbal and nonverbal communication may be either intentional or unintentional. For instance, in a job interview we are highly conscious of our dress and posture as well as the words we use. At other times, our verbal and nonverbal communication may be unintentional. If an interviewer asks you a difficult question, your facial expression may reveal that you are caught off guard, or you may accidentally speak ungrammatically.

Differences There are also differences between the two systems of communication. First, nonverbal communication is perceived as more honest. If verbal and nonverbal behaviors are inconsistent, most people trust the nonverbal behavior. There is little evidence that nonverbal behavior actually is more trustworthy than verbal communication; after all, we often control it quite deliberately. Nonetheless, it tends to be *perceived* as more trustworthy (Epley, 2014).

Second, unlike verbal communication, nonverbal communication is multichanneled. Verbal communication usually occurs within a single channel; oral verbal communication is received through hearing, and written verbal communication and sign language are received through sight. In contrast, nonverbal communication may be seen, felt, heard, smelled, and tasted. We often receive nonverbal communication simultaneously through two or more channels, as when we feel a hug while hearing a whispered "I love you."

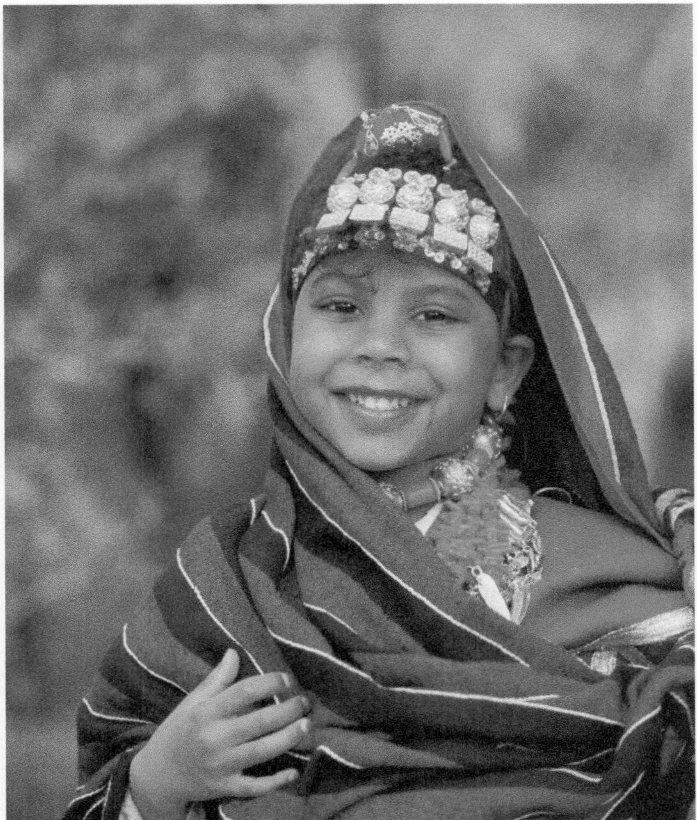

Different cultures prescribe different styles of dress.
Frans Lemmens/The Image Bank/Getty Images

Review It!

Differences from Verbal:

- Perceived as More Honest
- Multichanneled
- Continuous

Finally, nonverbal communication is more continuous than verbal communication. We begin speaking at one moment and stop speaking at another moment. In contrast, nonverbal communication tends to flow continually. Before we speak, our facial expressions and posture express our feelings; as we speak, our body movements and appearance communicate; and after we speak, our posture changes, perhaps relaxing.

Supplements or Replaces Verbal Communication

Nonverbal behaviors interact with verbal communication in five ways. First, nonverbal behaviors repeat verbal messages. For example, you might say "yes" while nodding your head.

Second, nonverbal behaviors may highlight verbal communication, as when you use inflection to emphasize certain words ("This is the *most* serious consequence of the policy that I oppose"). Third, nonverbal behaviors may complement or add to words. Public speakers often emphasize verbal statements with forceful gestures and increases in volume and inflection. Fourth, nonverbal behaviors may contradict verbal messages, as when a group member says, "Nothing's wrong" in a hostile tone of voice. Finally, we sometimes substitute nonverbal behaviors for verbal ones. For instance, you might roll your eyes to indicate that you are exasperated by something.

Because nonverbal communication is such a helpful companion to verbal communication, we have developed ways to communicate nonverbally when using social media, email, and text messages. Words alone don't tell us whether the person who wrote them is serious, sarcastic, or playful, which prompted the invention of text-based emoticons and abbreviations, such as:

;) = smile + wink to symbolize playfulness
<3 = heart
LOL = laughing out loud

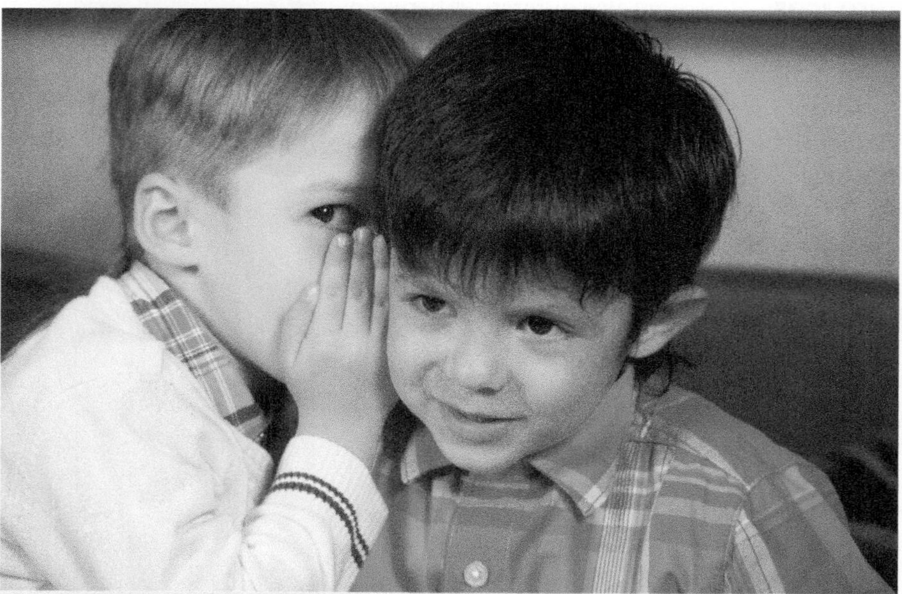

Based on nonverbal cues, what can you infer about these two children's relationship?
ArtWell/Shutterstock.com

Since then, developers have created other ways that we can add nonverbal content to digital media, such as emoji, digital stickers, and animated gifs. Many of these don't need translating when shared between users who have different languages. People also enjoy interspersing their messages with other items, such as memes, to lend further meaning to their digital text.

Regulates Interaction

You generally know when a professor welcomes discussion from students and when someone expects you to speak. But how do you know? There are no explicit, verbal cues to tell us when to speak and when to keep silent. Instead, conversations usually are regulated nonverbally (Guerrero & Floyd, 2006). We use our eyes and body posture to indicate that we want to enter conversations. We invite people to speak by looking directly at them, often after asking a question, even in group settings (Auer, 2017; Knapp & Hall, 2006; Weiss, 2018).

Related to this, some people find videoconference meetings to be more fatiguing than face-to-face meetings. When looking at groups of people separated into individual on-screen squares, it is hard to pick up on coworkers' nonverbal cues: through the monitor, everyone appears to be looking at everybody else (Foster School of Business, 2021).

Communication Highlight

Cross-Cultural Nonverbal Clashes

Cross-cultural misunderstandings aren't limited to verbal communication, according to Siu Wa Tang, chair of the Department of Psychiatry at the University of California at Irvine (Emmons, 1998). When Tang and a colleague visited pharmaceutical plants in Changchun, China, Tang was well accepted, but his colleague was not. The Chinese took an immediate and strong dislike to the colleague. Tang says the problem was facial expressions. His United States colleague used facial expressions that Americans would interpret as showing honesty and directness but which the Chinese people interpreted as aggressive and rude.

Based on this experience, Tang conducted experiments to test the universality of facial expressions. He found that a few basic feelings and expressions were understood across cultures. Happiness and sadness, for example, were nonverbally expressed in similar ways. However, other facial expressions did not translate so well. Nine out of 10 Americans interpreted a photograph of a face as showing fear, yet 6 of 10 Japanese identified the same photograph as expressing surprise or sadness. A photo identified by 9 of 10 Americans as showing anger was interpreted by 75% of Japanese as expressing disgust or contempt. Another source of cross-cultural nonverbal misunderstandings is eye contact. Americans generally consider it polite to look another person in the eye when conversing, but Japanese look at each other's cheeks; to look another in the eyes is perceived as very aggressive.

Cross-cultural communication clashes can also happen in the workplace, between members of various cultures within the United States, or in global workgroups—which have become more common since the widespread adoption of group video conferencing apps in workplaces during the Covid-19 pandemic (Richter, 2021). For example, while team members from the United States and Australia may be comfortable sharing their unfiltered ideas, those from countries that are more hierarchical, such as Japan, may only voice their ideas after their more senior colleagues have had a chance to do so. Meanwhile, in brainstorming sessions, people from some countries such as Brazil may see overlapping conversations full of interruptions as engaging, while others may find this communication style difficult and feel cut out of the conversation, not engaged or included (Toegel & Barsoux, 2016).

Darcy I know one guy who dominates every conversation. I'd never noticed this until we studied how nonverbal behaviors regulate turn taking. This guy won't look at others when he's talking. He looks out into space, or sometimes he gives you a hard stare, but he never looks at anyone like he's saying, "Okay, your turn now."

Establishes Relationship-Level Meanings

In Chapter 1, we noted that there are two levels of meaning in communication. To review: The content level of meaning concerns actual information or literal meaning; the relationship level of meaning defines communicators' identities and the relationship between them. Nonverbal communication is often more powerful than verbal language in conveying relationship-level meanings (Manusov & Patterson, 2006).

Nonverbal communication is used to convey three dimensions of relationship-level meanings: *responsiveness, liking*, and *power* (Mehrabian, 1981). Yet how we convey relationship meanings and what specific nonverbal behaviors mean depends on the communication rules we've learned in our particular cultures and social communities.

Responsiveness We use eye contact, facial expressions, and body posture to indicate interest in others, as Kenzie did in one of the examples that opened this chapter. We signal friendliness by laughing. But as in the example with the interns in Japanese companies, laughter doesn't mean the same thing in all cultures.

Maryam Americans do more than one thing at a time. In Nepal, when we talk with someone, we are with that person. We do not also write on paper or have the television on. We talk with the person. It is hard for me to accept the custom of giving only some attention to each other in conversation.

Question: Think about how you typically interact with friends and family. How often are you doing something else at the same time, like watching television or using apps on your phone? In what circumstances do you give them your undivided attention?

As Maryam's observation indicates, different cultures teach members distinct rules for showing responsiveness.

Liking A second dimension of relationship-level meaning is liking. In Western societies, smiles and friendly touching usually indicate positive feelings, whereas frowns and belligerent postures express antagonism. Have you ever noticed how often political candidates shake hands, slap backs, and otherwise touch people whose votes they want? Similarly, in work settings, people who like one another often sit together, exchange eye contact, and smile at one another.

Power The third aspect of relationship-level meanings is power, or control. We use nonverbal behaviors to assert dominance, express deference, and negotiate status and influence. Powerful people, such as bosses, touch those with less power, such as secretaries, more than those with less power touch those with more power (Hall, Coats, & Smith-LeBeau, 2004). In general, men assume more space and use greater volume and more forceful gestures than women—and these gendered patterns begin as early as preschool age (Charafeddine et al., 2020; Moujahid et al., 2022; Yu & Ngan, 2019).

Ramona In my home, my father sits at the head of the table, and he has his chair in the family room and his workroom. My mother does not have her chair anywhere in the house, and she has no room of her own either.

Question: What does the example Ramona offers tell us about gendered power dynamics in her household? What do the spaces her father occupies likely signal to the family and to visitors about his status relative to others in their home?

The connection between power and space is evident in the fact that CEOs usually have spacious offices, entry-level and mid-level professionals have smaller offices, and secretaries often have minuscule workstations, even though secretaries often store and manage more material than those higher in the organizational chain of command. Regulative communication rules also tacitly specify that people with status or power have the right to enter the space of people with less power, but the converse is not true. Space also reflects power differences in families. Adults usually have more space than children; like Ramona's father, men more often than women have their own rooms and sit at the head of the table. Men are also more likely than women to move into others' space, as the young woman in the library moved to Kenzie's table in the example at the beginning of this chapter.

Note that the dimensions of nonverbal communication we're discussing in this chapter are important in digital media and new technology, as well. For example, designers of artificial intelligence (AI), virtual reality, and robotics use these principles to help their creations interact as realistically and engagingly with people as possible (Hoppe et al., 2020; Yu & Ngan, 2019). Understanding what makes nonverbal communication effective is extremely valuable in fields such as human-computer interaction and machine learning, where communication experts can find many interesting research and career opportunities.

Also of interest is the research that suggests women tend to find videoconference meetings, like those on Zoom, more fatiguing than men. Women experience more scrutiny or surveillance of their appearances and engagement than men do in society, which is directly related to gendered power dynamics. Because of this, women learn to self-surveil from an early age and tend to be more attuned to physical or digital "mirrors" in social situations than men are. Women's self-surveillance may therefore contribute to their higher reported levels of "Zoom fatigue": they experience more anxiety and stress than men do from constantly seeing themselves on screen during these digitally mediated social interactions (Fauville et al., 2021). While research has not yet been published on Zoom fatigue in relation to people of other identities that face high scrutiny, like BIPOC, LGBTQIA+, disabled, and larger-bodied people, it is possible that some people from these communities have similar experiences.

Review It!

Dimensions of Relationship-Level Meaning:

- Responsiveness
- Liking
- Power

Reflects Cultural Values

As noted above, nonverbal communication reflects rules of specific cultures and social communities (Liu, 2016; Mehrabian, 2017/1972). This implies that most nonverbal behavior isn't instinctual but learned in the process of socialization.

Have you ever seen a bumper sticker or t-shirt that says, "If you can read this, you're too close"? That slogan proclaims North Americans' fierce territoriality. We value our private spaces, and we resent—and sometimes fight—anyone who trespasses on what we consider our turf. We want private homes with rooms for each person and large lots. On the job, a reserved parking space and a private office with a door mark status; employees with lower status often park in satellite lots and share offices or have workstations without doors.

In cultures where individuality is less valued, people are less territorial. For instance, Brazilians routinely stand close together in shops, buses, and elevators, and when they bump into each other, they don't apologize or draw back. Similarly, in countries such as Hong Kong with a dense population and a lack of affordable housing, people live and work in very close quarters (Chan & Wong, 2021). Studies have indicated that because people there are used to this, territoriality is uncommon (Chan, 1999)—although some newer studies suggest the matter may be more complex, with greater levels of territoriality than previously believed (La Grange & Yau, 2019). Meanwhile, in some cultures—Italy, for example—dramatic nonverbal displays of emotion are typical, but other cultures consider more reserved displays of emotion appropriate (Matsumoto, Franklin, Choi, Rogers, & Tatani, 2002).

What nonverbal cues to power relations do you perceive in this photo?
Jonatan Fernstrom/Jupiter images

Sucheng In the United States, each person has so much room. Every individual has a separate room in which to sleep and sometimes another separate room in which to work. Also, I see that each family here lives in a separate house. People have much less space in China. Families live together, with sons bringing their families into their parents' home and all sharing the same space. At first when I came here it felt strange to have so much space, but now I sometimes feel very crowded when I go home.

Question: With the costs of housing in the United States constantly rising, record numbers of American families have been living in intergenerational households (Cohn & Passel, 2018). Perhaps yours is one of them. Based on what you've learned so far in this chapter, how do you think these changes might shift cultural norms within communities where multigenerational living is common?

Patterns of eye contact also reflect cultural values. In the United States, frankness and assertion are valued, so meeting another's eyes is considered appropriate and a demonstration of personal honesty. Yet, as we've noted, in many Asian and northern European countries, direct eye contact is considered abrasive and disrespectful (Axtell, 2007; Samovar et al., 2015). On the other hand, in Brazil, eye contact often is so intense that people from the United States consider it rude staring.

This has interesting implications for digitally mediated interactions, such as videoconference meetings. One study notes that when people look at coworkers on screen, our proximity to our respective cameras creates the illusion that we are gazing at one another from a close distance, and directly, rather than in a side view like at a conference table. This means that in meetings on Zoom and similar applications, we are interacting with coworkers, acquaintances, and strangers in a proximity and frontal manner that is normally reserved for close relationships—which can contribute to people's feelings of videoconferencing fatigue (Bailenson, 2021).

Greeting behaviors also vary across cultures. In the United States and many other Western countries, the handshake is the most common way to greet. Arab men are more likely to kiss each other on both cheeks as a form of greeting. Embraces are typical greetings in Mexico. Bowing is the standard form of greeting in some Asian cultures (Samovar et al., 2015).

In sum, we've noted five features of the nonverbal communication system. First, there are similarities and differences between nonverbal and verbal communication. Second, nonverbal behavior can supplement or replace verbal communication. Third, nonverbal behaviors regulate interaction. Fourth, nonverbal communication is often especially powerful in establishing and expressing relational meanings. Fifth, nonverbal behaviors reflect cultural values and are learned, not instinctive. We're now ready to explore the many types of behavior in the intricate nonverbal communication system.

Types of Nonverbal Communication

In this section, we will consider nine forms of nonverbal behavior, noticing how we use each to communicate.

Communication & Careers

Police Trained in Cultural Sensitivity to Nonverbal Communication

Part of training to become police officers in New York is studying a manual titled "Policing in a Multicultural Society." The manual was developed because officers who are unaware of cultural differences in nonverbal behaviors were misinterpreting behaviors of some people who had immigrated to the United States (Goldstein, 2013). The manual includes the following:

1. Immigrants from rural Mexico are socialized to avoid direct eye contact. This should not be interpreted as deceitfulness.
2. Immigrants from Puerto Rico often engage in eye-checking with others. This should not be interpreted as sending signals not to speak honestly.
3. African immigrants often shake hands with a light touch of palms instead of a firm grip. This is not an indicator of shiftiness.
4. Arab immigrants may get out of their cars when stopped by police. This is a sign of courtesy. Do not interpret this as aggression.
5. Arab immigrants tend to speak loudly. This should not be interpreted as shouting or belligerence.

Kinesics

kinesics Body position and body motions, including those of the face.

Kinesics is body position and body motions, including those of the face. Our bodies express a great deal about how we see ourselves. A speaker who stands erect and is relaxed announces self-confidence, whereas someone who slouches and shuffles may seem unsure of themselves.

How we position ourselves relative to others may express our feelings toward them. On work teams, friends and allies often sit together, and competitors typically maintain distance. Americans often cross their legs, but this is perceived as offensive in Ghana and Turkey (Samovar et al., 2017).

Our faces are intricate messengers. Our eyes can shoot daggers of anger, issue challenges, express skepticism, or radiate love. With our faces, we can indicate disapproval (scowls), doubt (raised eyebrows), love (eye gazes), and challenge (stares). The face is particularly powerful in conveying responsiveness and liking (Guéguen & De Gail, 2003). For example, a pedestrian's smile has the power to prompt approaching drivers' to drive more carefully (Guéguen et al., 2016). This knowledge is driving developments in diverse new fields, such as healthcare robots in areas such as reception and therapeutic care (Johanson et al., 2021; Kim et al., 2021; Sutherland et al., 2019).

Our eyes communicate some of the most important and complex messages about how we feel. If you watch infants, you'll notice that they focus on others' eyes. As adults, we often look at eyes to judge emotions, honesty, interest, and self-confidence. Among Westerners, eye contact tends to increase feelings of closeness.

Haptics

haptics Nonverbal communication that involves physical touch.

Haptics is physical touch. Touch is the first of our senses to develop, and touching and being touched are essential to a healthy life (Farroni et al., 2022).

Touch conveys emotions.
Crystal Kirk/Shutterstock.com

Touching also communicates power and status. Cultural views of women as more touchable than men are reflected in gendered patterns. Women tend to touch others to show liking and intimacy, whereas men more typically rely on touch to assert power and control (Wood, 2010).

Yvette When I was pregnant, total strangers would walk up to me and touch my belly. It was amazing—and disturbing. They seemed to think they had a right to touch me or that the baby wasn't me, so they could touch him. Amazing!

Question: Many pregnant women who experience this dynamic feel disturbed by it, like Yvette does, as they regard it as an invasion of their personal space. What do you think might be some of the implicit messages communicated to a pregnant woman when strangers reach out and touch her belly? What does it convey about her status and rights to autonomy, as an "expectant mother," in relation to others?

Physical Appearance

Western culture places an extremely high value on **physical appearance**. For this reason, most of us notice how others look, and we form initial evaluations based on their appearance. Although our initial judgments may be inaccurate, they can affect our decisions about friendships, dating, and hiring. In fact, economist Daniel Hamermesh (2011) reports that people who are above average in attractiveness are likely to make 3–4% more than people who are below average in attractiveness. That could add up to well over $200,000 over the course of a career.

physical appearance Physical features of people and the values attached to those features; a type of nonverbal communication.

Cultures stipulate ideals for physical form. In the United States, these ideals are communicated consistently through visual media, including television, movies, commercials, and social media, which tend to most favorably depict people who fit within a relatively narrow range features, including body type, hair color and texture, facial proportions, and more—an issue I detail in my book, *The Princess Problem* (Hains, 2014). Currently, cultural ideals in the West emphasize thinness in women and muscularity in men (Davies-Popelka, 2015; Kimmel, 2013; Spar, 2013). In an effort to meet these ideals, some men engage in extreme body building or use steroids, and some women diet excessively and develop eating disorders. (Go to the book's online resources for this chapter to visit the National Eating Disorders Association's website to learn about eating disorders and ways to help people who have them.) While it is easy to see that cultural ideals such as these are gendered, it is less easy to see that they are also racialized.

To be specific, many Western beauty ideals celebrate *White* beauty ideals, and uphold stereotypically White features as more attractive than those of other races and ethnicities—a legacy, perhaps, of European colonialism (Donnella, 2019), during which colonizers subjugated the people whose lands they colonized, treating them as less human or less than human. During this time, in the eighteenth century, racial theorists such as the German author Johann Friedrich Blumenbach defined White or Caucasian beauty as inherently superior to that of all other races (Painter, 2010)—and as beauty and goodness were considered to be associated with one another, this idea was used to suggest that White people were indeed better than others, and to justify their harmful actions towards those they believed to be inferior. For centuries since, this damaging idea has supported the racist notion of White supremacy—and it is still shaping how people see themselves today.

Among the Western cultural standards for appearance that are rooted in White beauty ideals are ideas about nose shape (a smaller, straight nose) and eyelid shape (rounder, with a double rather than single eyelid). It is telling, then, that nose reshaping and eyelid surgery are now the most common type of cosmetic surgery among men and women alike (American Society of Plastic Surgeons, 2021). Behind these top-two procedures, in order of popularity, the most popular surgeries for men are cheek implants, liposuction, and ear surgery; for women, face lift, breast augmentation, and liposuction (American Society of Plastic Surgeons, 2021).

The United States also has the highest demand, globally, for less-invasive treatments, many of which are meant to make the patient look more youthful. This reflects ageism's role in Western beauty ideals. The most popular minimally invasive procedure for United States men and women in 2020 was botulinum toxin type A, more commonly known as Botox or called by other brand names. Next most common among men, in order of popularity, are laser skin resurfacing, laser hair removal, soft tissue fillers, and microdermabrasion; for women, soft tissue fillers, chemical peel, laser skin resurfacing, and laser hair removal (American Society of Plastic Surgeons, 2021).

Experts note that such procedures' popularity has increased as they have become more socially acceptable, and they predict the market for such services in North America to reach $46.07 billion by 2028 (Globe Newswire, 2021).

Western beauty ideals extend beyond Western cultures, though, and influence the industrial beauty complex beyond the United States. This makes sense when we consider that the United States does significant business in exporting media, like movies and television shows, to other countries, which circulates Western cultural values beyond our national boundaries. Video-based social media can easily circulate from the United States around the world, as well. In this way, traditional and digital media have helped to spread and uphold White beauty ideals globally. They have contributed to ideas of attractiveness as linked to stereotypically White features and lighter skin (a concept called "colorism," as it's about skin tone rather than race) in not just the United States, but also many other countries (Choi & Reddy-Best, 2021; Perry, Stevens-Watkins, & Oser, 2013). These ideas have helped to drive the popularity of treatments such as skin lightening creams—which can be very harmful to the skin (Pollock et al., 2021)—and cosmetic surgery in a range of nations (Edmonds & Leem, 2021).

Also to meet cultural appearance standards—but driven by a desire to better communicate their identities to the world around them—trans people and gender-nonconforming people sometimes have gender-affirming surgery (also called gender confirmation surgery). The American Society of Plastic Surgeons (2022) notes that the goal of such procedures is "to give transgender individuals the physical appearance and functional abilities of the gender they know themselves to be," with popular procedures including facial feminization surgery, transfeminine top surgery, transfeminine bottom surgery, facial masculinization surgery, transmasculine top surgery, and transmasculine bottom surgery. Trans people may elect to have any combination of these procedures, or none at all; each person's journey is individual.

Cass I found out how much appearance matters when I was in an auto accident. It messed up my face so that I had scars all over one side and on my forehead. All of a sudden, nobody was asking me out. All these guys who had been so crazy about me before the accident lost interest. Some of my girlfriends seemed uneasy about being seen with me. When I first had the wreck, I was so glad to be alive that I didn't even think about plastic surgery. After a couple of months of seeing how others treated me, however, I had the surgery.

Artifacts

Artifacts are personal objects with which we announce our identities and personalize our environments. We craft our image by how we dress, the jewelry we wear, and the objects we carry and use. George W. Bush insisted on formal dress—coat and tie—at all times in the Oval Office (Stolberg, 2009). But Barack Obama sometimes took off his jacket while working in the Oval Office, and he often skipped the tie on weekends. Go to the book's online resources for this chapter to learn more about norms for professional dressing.

artifacts Personal objects we use to announce our identities and personalize our environments.

We also use artifacts to define settings and personal territories. At annual meetings of companies, the CEO usually speaks from a podium that bears the company logo. In much the same manner, we claim our private spaces by filling them with photos of family members and other objects that matter to us and reflect our experiences and values. Lovers of art adorn their homes with paintings and sculptures. Religious families display pictures of holy scenes and the *Bible*, the *Qur'an*, the *Vedas*, the *Koran*, or another sacred text.

Naomi I've moved a lot since coming to college—dorm, apartment, another apartment, and another apartment. I never feel a place is home until I put the photograph of my grandmother holding me on my dresser. Then it's home.

Question: Think about your own personal artifacts that you use as decorations and how they communicate something about your identity. If you were to move to a new space, which artifacts would you prioritize to decorate your new space? Which are most important to you—and why?

Artifacts can express personal identity. Approximately 26% of Americans in the 18- to 29-year age range have at least one tattoo, and 38% of people ages 30–39 (Zuckerman, 2020). Tattoos are now more common among people with higher education levels than among those with lower education levels (32% vs. 26%), including 30% of college graduates. But many people who get tattoos later want to get rid of them: Since 2011, tattoo removal services have increased by about 32%, and experts say tattoo removal rates will continue to increase (Zuckerman, 2020).

We also use artifacts to express ethnic and religious identity. Kwanzaa is an African American holiday tradition that celebrates the centrality of home, family, and community. The kinara is a branched candleholder that holds seven candles, one of which is lit during each day of Kwanzaa. The Jewish holiday, Hanukkah, features the menorah that holds candles while Seder features an elaborate meal in which each item represents a part of Jewish history. The Christian tradition includes Christmas trees and Nativity scenes.

Proxemics

proxemics A type of nonverbal communication that includes space and how we use it.

Proxemics is space and how we use it. Every culture has norms for using space and for how close people should be to one another (Samovar et al., 2015). In a classic study, Edward Hall (1966) found that in the United States, we interact with social acquaintances from a distance of 4 to 12 feet but are comfortable with 18 inches or less between us and close friends or romantic partners. In some cultures greater or lesser distances are considered comfortable.

Space also signals status; greater space is assumed by those of higher status. The prerogative of entering someone else's personal space is also linked to power; those with greater power are most likely to trespass into others' territory.

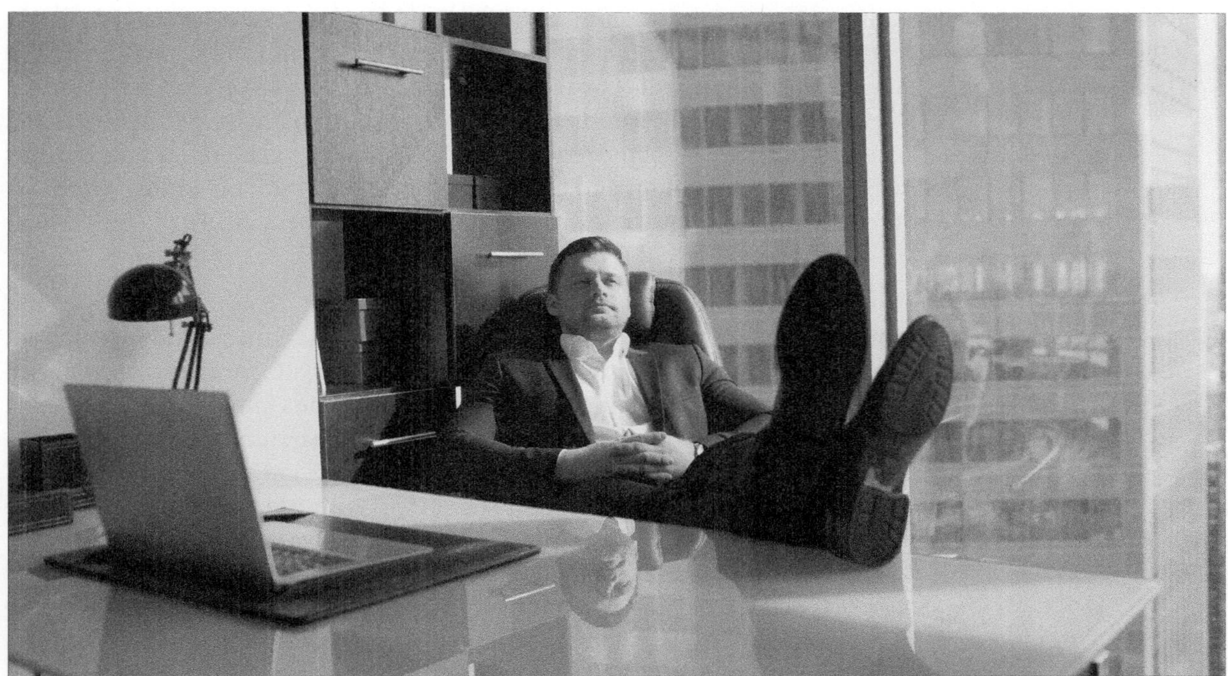

What does this executive's space convey about his power and openness to others?
Brad Perks Lightscapes/Alamy Stock Photo

How space is arranged also tells us something about the expected form of interaction in the space. Formal businesses may have private offices with doors and little common space. In contrast, more casual businesses are likely to have fewer doors and more common space to encourage interaction between employees. Families that enjoy interaction tend to arrange furniture to invite conversation and eye contact.

Environmental Factors

Environmental factors are elements of settings that affect how we feel and act. For instance, we respond to architecture, colors, room design, temperature, sounds, smells, and lighting. Rooms with comfortable chairs invite relaxation, whereas rooms with stiff chairs prompt formality. Dimly lit rooms can enhance romantic feelings, although dark rooms can be depressing.

environmental factors Elements of settings that affect how we feel and act. Environmental factors are a type of nonverbal communication.

Restaurants use environmental features to control how long people linger over meals. For example, low lights, comfortable chairs or booths, and soft music often are part of the environment in upscale restaurants where patrons tend to linger.

Casinos go a step further and exploit their environments to encourage gamblers to stay longer and spend more money. Casino designers carefully consider color schemes, layout, temperature, and fragrance in the air—and often have few clocks and windows, in hopes that people will lose track of time (Freundlich, 2021). Neuropsychologists note that casinos' design encourages players to make riskier choices, such as betting more (Clark et al., 2013).

In comparison to these environments, fast-food eateries have hard plastic booths and bright lights, which encourage diners to eat and move on. To make a profit, inexpensive restaurants have to get people in and out as quickly as possible.

A New Jersey hospital recently redesigned rooms to increase natural light and otherwise create more attractive environments. Patients in the redesigned rooms asked for 30% less medication and rated food better than patients in the unremodeled rooms even though the food was the same (Kimmelman, 2014).

Chronemics

chronemics A type of nonverbal communication concerned with how we perceive and use time to define identities and interaction.

Chronemics is how we perceive and use time to define identities and interaction. Important people with high status can keep others waiting. Conversely, people with low status are expected to be punctual. For example, in the United States and China alike, it's considered appropriate for a person with less bargaining power in a situation to arrive to an appointment early, as a way to show enthusiasm, respect, and sincerity towards the more powerful party (Lin, 2005). It is standard practice to have to wait, sometimes a long while, to see a doctor, even if you have an appointment. This carries the message that the doctor's time is more valuable than ours. Subordinates are expected to report punctually to meetings, but bosses are allowed to be tardy. Professors can be late to class, and students are expected to wait, but students sometimes are reprimanded if they arrive after a class begins.

On the other hand, professors who reply quickly to their students' emails—regardless of what they write—are seen as more competent and caring by their students (Tatum et al., 2017), which may make a difference in their course evaluations. Perceptions are similar of doctors and other people in positions of authority who are careful with their time. This shows that even though cultural norms make it acceptable for people of higher status to keep others waiting, there are benefits to working to be responsive and punctual. In other words, it's not a power that should be abused.

Chronemics express cultural attitudes toward time. In Western societies, time is valuable, so speed is highly valued (Calero, 2005; Honoré, 2005). Thus, we replace our computers and cell phones as soon as faster models hit the market. We often try to do several things at once to get more done. Many other cultures have far more relaxed attitudes toward time and punctuality. In many South American countries, it's not impolite to come late to meetings or classes, and it's not assumed that people will leave at the scheduled ending time. Whether time is treated casually, or closely watched and measured out, reflects larger cultural attitudes toward living.

Communication Highlight

Environmental Racism

According to Robert Cox, former president of the Sierra Club, the term *environmental racism* arose to describe a pattern whereby toxic waste dumps and hazardous industrial plants are located in low-income neighborhoods and communities of color (Cox, 2016). The pattern is clear: The space of marginalized and poor people can be invaded and contaminated, but the territory of more affluent citizens cannot be. Go to the book's online resources for this chapter to learn more about environmental racism (also called *environmental justice*). This site provides information on the Environmental Protection Agency's strategies for preventing environmental racism.

The amount of time we spend with different people reflects our priorities. A manager spends more time with a new employee who seems to have executive potential than with one who seems less impressive. A speaker spends more time responding to a question from a high-status member of the audience than to a person of lower status. We spend more time with people we like than with those we don't like.

Paralanguage

Paralanguage is vocal communication that does not involve words. It includes sounds, such as murmurs and gasps, and vocal qualities, such as volume, rhythm, pitch, and inflection. Our voices are versatile instruments that tell others how to interpret us and what we say. Vocal cues signal others to interpret what we say as a joke, threat, statement of fact, question, and so forth. Vocal cues also express irritation. Effective public speakers know how to modulate inflection, volume, and rhythm to enhance their verbal messages.

paralanguage Vocal communication that does not include actual words; for example, sounds, vocal qualities, accents, and inflection.

We use our voices to communicate feelings. Whispering, for instance, often signals secrecy, and shouting conveys anger. Depending on the context, sighing may communicate empathy, boredom, or contentment. Research indicates that tone of voice is a powerful clue to feelings between marital partners. Negative vocal tones are among the most important symbols of marital dissatisfaction (Gottman, 1994b). Negative intonation may also signal dissatisfaction or disapproval in work settings. The reverse is also true: A warm voice conveys liking, and a playful lilt suggests friendliness.

Communication Highlight

Sounding Like a Leader

Running for elected office is a challenge. How can a candidate convince others that they will be a good leader? Voice lessons are among the tools at their disposal. Studies indicate that people prefer leaders who have lower voices—a pattern that holds true across gender (Klofstad et al., 2012). While voice pitch doesn't make a person a more effective leader, it does make them more electable (Klofstad & Anderson, 2018). This carries over to other fields, too. In business, people whose voices are deeper are more competitive for leadership positions (Mayew et al., 2013).

This makes it easy to understand, then, why British Prime Minister Margaret Thatcher sought out vocal coaching early in her political career. After contending with sexist remarks that characterized her natural speaking voice as shrill, she learned how to both lower her voice and speak in a more measured cadence (Picard, 2020). Newscaster Carole Simpson did the same after being told by a boss that "women's voices are shrill and not authoritative enough" (Bennett, 2019). And when biotech company Theranos was deemed to be fraudulent, with no real product on offer, endless speculation began as to whether its deep-voiced founder Elizabeth Holmes had deliberately lowered her voice (Cunningham, 2022)—the implication being that perhaps a falsely lowered voice was part of her efforts to defraud investors and fool the public.

Question: To this day, various vocal coaches offer training to help people sound more authoritative—more like leaders (Genard, 2020). What stereotypes do you think shape widespread ideas about how leaders and authority figures should sound? How do you think these stereotypes are harmful to various people, even beyond the spheres of business and politics?

We use our voices to communicate how we see ourselves and wish to be seen by others. For instance, we use a firm, confident voice in job interviews or when explaining why we deserve a raise. We also know how to make ourselves sound apologetic, seductive, or angry when it suits us. People who speak at a slow-to-moderate rate are perceived as having greater control over interaction than people who speak rapidly (Tusing & Dillard, 2000), and people who speak loudly and take longer turns-at-talk are perceived as more dominant (Burgoon et al., 2021).

Rayna When I first moved to the United States, I didn't understand many words and idioms. I did not understand that "A bird in the hand is worth two in the bush" meant it is smart to hold on to what is sure. I did not understand that "hang a right" meant to turn right. So when I did not understand, I would ask people to explain. Most times they would say the very same thing over, just louder and more slowly, like I was deaf or stupid. I felt like saying to them in a very loud, slow voice, "I am Indian, not stupid. You are stupid."

We use paralanguage to perform class and gender. Our pronunciation of words, our accents, and the complexity of our sentences perform our social class. To perform masculinity, men use strong volume, low pitch, and limited inflection, all of which conform to cultural prescriptions for men to be assertive and emotionally controlled. To perform femininity, women tend to use higher pitch, softer volume, and more inflection. Because these gendered performances make a significant difference in how others perceive our gender, some transgender and gender-diverse people seek support from voice teachers. Through gender-affirming voice lessons, these teachers coach people to explore new ways of using their voices to meet societal expectations and reflect their identities (American Speech-Language-Hearing Association, n.d.).

Silence

silence The lack of verbal communication or paralanguage. Silence is a type of nonverbal communication that can express powerful messages.

A final type of nonverbal behavior is **silence**, which can communicate powerful messages. The assertion "I'm not speaking to you" actually speaks volumes. We use silence to communicate different meanings. For instance, silence indicates contentment when intimates are so comfortable they don't need to talk. Silence can also communicate awkwardness, as you know if you've ever had trouble keeping conversation going with a new acquaintance. We feel pressured to fill the void.

Silence can also disconfirm others. In some families, children are disciplined by being ignored. No matter what the child says or does, parents refuse to acknowledge their existence. In later life, the silencing strategy may also surface. You know how disconfirming silence can be if you've ever said hello to someone and gotten no reply. Even if the other person didn't deliberately ignore you, you felt slighted. In some military academies, such as West Point, silencing is a recognized method of stripping a cadet of personhood if they are perceived as having broken the academy code. Whistle-blowers and union-busters are often shunned by peers. Similarly, the Catholic Church excommunicates people who violate its canons.

The complex system of nonverbal communication includes kinesics, haptics, physical appearance, artifacts, proxemics, environmental features, chronemics, paralanguage, and silence. We use these nonverbal behaviors to announce our identities and to communicate how we feel about relationships with others.

Review It!

Types of Nonverbal Communication:

- Kinesics
- Haptics
- Physical Appearance
- Artifacts
- Proxemics
- Environmental Factors
- Chronemics
- Paralanguage
- Silence

Guidelines for Improving Nonverbal Communication

Nonverbal communication, like its verbal cousin, can be misinterpreted. You can reduce the likelihood of misunderstandings in nonverbal communication by following two guidelines.

Monitor Your Nonverbal Communication

The monitoring skills we have stressed in other chapters are also important for competent nonverbal communication. Think about the ways we use nonverbal behaviors to announce our identities. Are you projecting the image you desire? Do your facial and body movements represent how you see yourself and how you want others to perceive you? Do people ever tell you that you seem uninterested when they are talking to you? If so, you can monitor your nonverbal actions and modify them to more clearly communicate involvement and interest. You can also set up your spaces to invite the kind of interaction you prefer.

Interpret Others' Nonverbal Communication Tentatively

In this chapter, we've discussed findings about the meanings people tend to attach to nonverbal behaviors. It's important to realize that these are only generalizations about how we interpret nonverbal communication. We cannot state what any particular behavior means to specific people in a particular context. For instance, we've said that people who like each other tend to be physically closer when interacting. However, sometimes people prefer autonomy and want personal space. In addition, someone may maintain distance because she or he has a cold and doesn't want a partner to catch it. Also, the generalizations we've discussed may not apply to people from non-Western cultures. Ethical communicators qualify their interpretations of nonverbal behavior by considering personal and contextual considerations.

Personal Qualifications Nonverbal patterns that accurately describe most people may not apply to particular individuals. Although eye contact generally indicates responsiveness, some people close their eyes to concentrate when listening. In such cases, it would be inaccurate to conclude that a person who doesn't look at us isn't listening. Similarly, people who cross their arms and condense into a tight posture may be expressing hostility or lack of interest in interaction. However, the same behaviors might mean a person is cold. Most people use less inflection, fewer gestures, and a slack posture when they're not really interested in what they're talking about. However, fatigue can result in the same behaviors.

To avoid misinterpreting others' nonverbal communication, you can check perceptions and use *I*-language, not *you*-language, which we discussed in Chapter 5. You can check perceptions to find out whether the way you interpret another's nonverbal behavior is what that other person means: "I sense that you're not really involved in this conversation; is that how you feel?" In addition, you can rely on *I*-language. *You*-language might lead us to inaccurately say of someone who doesn't look at us, "You're communicating lack of interest." A more responsible statement would use *I*-language to say, "When you don't look at me, I feel you're not interested in what I'm saying." Using *I*-language reminds us to take responsibility for our judgments and feelings. In addition, it reduces the likelihood that we will make others defensive by inaccurately interpreting their nonverbal behavior.

Contextual Qualifications Like the meaning of verbal communication, the significance of nonverbal behaviors depends on the contexts in which they occur. Most people are more at ease on their own turf than on someone else's, so we tend to be more friendly and outgoing in our homes than in business meetings and public spaces. We also dress according to context. When I am on campus or in business meetings, I dress professionally, but at home, I usually wear jeans or running clothes.

In addition to our immediate settings, nonverbal communication reflects cultures. We are likely to misinterpret people from other cultures if we impose the norms and rules of our culture on them. An Arab who stands practically on top of others to talk with them is not being rude, according to their culture's standards, although Westerners might interpret them as such.

Eleni I have been misinterpreted very much in this country. In my first semester here, a professor told me he wanted me to be more assertive and to speak up in class. I could not do that, I told him. He said I should put myself forward, but I have been brought up not to do that. In Taiwan, that is very rude and ugly, and we are taught not to speak up to teachers. Now that I have been here for 3 years, I sometimes speak in classes, but I am still quieter than Americans. I know my professors think I am not so smart because I am quiet, but that is the teaching of my country.

Question: Reading about Eleni's experience makes me think about the importance of cultural humility. How might Eleni's professor have approached her differently about her level of participation in class?

Even within a single culture, different social communities have distinct rules for nonverbal behavior. A man who doesn't make "listening noises" may be listening intently according to the rules of masculine speech communities. Similarly, when women nod and make listening noises while another is talking, men may misperceive them as agreeing. According to the rules typically learned in feminine social communities, ongoing feedback is a way of signaling interest, not necessarily agreement. We should adopt dual perspective when interpreting others, especially when they belong to cultures or communities that are different from ours.

Chapter Summary

In this chapter, we've explored the world beyond words. We learned that there are similarities and differences between nonverbal communication and verbal communication. Next, we noted that nonverbal communication supplements or replaces verbal messages, regulates interaction, reflects and establishes relationship-level meanings, and expresses cultural membership.

We discussed nine types of nonverbal communication: kinesics, haptics, physical appearance, artifacts, proxemics, environmental features, chronemics, paralanguage, and silence. Each form of nonverbal communication reflects cultural understandings and values and also expresses our personal identities and feelings toward others. We then considered how nonverbal communication operates in the realm of digital communication.

Because nonverbal communication, like verbal communication, is symbolic, it has no inherent, universal meaning. Instead, we construct meaning as we notice, organize, and interpret nonverbal behaviors.

Key Concepts

artifacts
chronemics
environmental factors
haptics
kinesics
nonverbal communication
paralanguage
physical appearance
proxemics
silence

For Further Reflection and Discussion

1. Attend a gathering of people who belong to a social community different from yours. Observe nonverbal behaviors of the people there: How do they greet one another, how much eye contact accompanies interaction, and how close to one another do people stand and sit?
2. Visit restaurants near your campus. Describe the kinds of seats, lighting, music (if any), and distance between tables. Do you find any connections between nonverbal patterns and expensiveness of restaurants?
3. Describe the spatial arrangements in the home of your family of origin. Was there a room in which family members interacted a good deal? How was furniture arranged in that room? Who had separate space and personal chairs in your family? What do the nonverbal patterns reflect about your family's communication style?
4. What ethical issues are entailed in interpreting others' nonverbal communication? What would be ethical and unethical interpretations?
5. What do nonverbal behaviors say about how intimate people are? To find out, observe (a) a couple who you know are very close, (b) a clerk and a shopper in a store, and (c) a teacher and student who are talking. How closely do the people sit or stand to each other? How do their postures differ? What facial expressions and eye contact do they use in each situation?

We love because it's the only true adventure.

Nikki Giovanni

Communication in Personal Relationships

Learning Objectives

After studying the topics in this chapter, you should be able to:

1. Explain the three dialectics in relationships.
2. Explain how communication patterns shift as a relationship begins, grows, endures, declines, and ends.
3. Apply this chapter's guidelines to improve your ability to build and maintain healthy relationships.

What is the single most important quality you look for in a close friend?

Robin Dunbar (2012) studies the science of human love. As much as Dunbar tries to reduce love to scientific principles, he admits he can't explain why we yearn for the people we love or why thinking of a beloved makes us happy. Dunbar is one of the latest in a long line of scholars who have tried and failed to unravel the mysteries of human love and longing. Although science can't fully explain personal relationships, it has produced much useful knowledge about them.

In this chapter, we focus on communication in two special types of personal relationships: friendships and romantic relationships. To launch the discussion, we'll define personal relationships. Next, we'll consider how communication guides the development of friendships and romances over time. Third, we will discuss some of the ways that digital communication affects personal relationships. Finally, we'll identify guidelines that should help you meet the challenges to personal relationships in our era.

Defining Personal Relationships

Personal relationships are unique commitments between irreplaceable individuals who are influenced by rules, relational dialectics, and surrounding contexts. We'll discuss each part of this definition.

personal relationship A relationship defined by uniqueness, rules, relational dialectics, and commitment and affected by contexts. Personal relationships, unlike social ones, are irreplaceable.

Uniqueness

Most of our relationships are social, not personal. In social relationships, participants adhere to social roles rather than interacting as unique individuals. For instance, you might exchange class notes with a classmate, play racquetball each week with a neighbor, and talk about politics with a coworker. In each case, the other person could be replaced by someone else taking the same role. The value of social relationships lies more in what participants do than in who they are because a variety of people could fulfill the same functions.

In personal relationships, however, the particular people—who they are and what they think, feel, and do—define the connection. When one person in a personal relationship leaves the relationship or dies, that relationship ends. We may later have other intimates, but a new romantic partner or best friend will not replace a former one.

Commitment

passion Intensely positive feelings and desires for another person. Passion is based on the rewards of involvement and is not equivalent to commitment.

commitment A decision to remain with a relationship. One of three dimensions of enduring romantic relationships, commitment has more impact on relational continuity than does love alone.

For most of us, passion springs to mind when we think about intimacy. **Passion** involves intensely positive feelings and desires for another person. The emotional high of being in love or discovering a new friend stems from passion. It's why we fall "head over heels." Despite its excitement, passion isn't the primary building block of long-lasting personal relationships.

Passion is a feeling based on the rewards of involvement with a person. **Commitment**, in contrast, is a decision to remain in a relationship in spite of troubles, disappointments, sporadic boredom, and lulls in passion. Communication

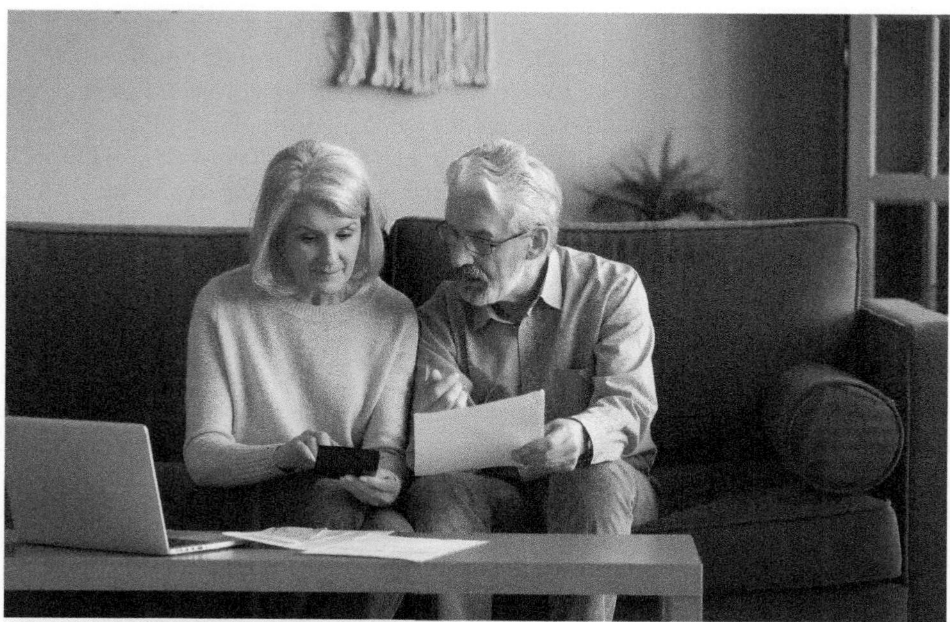

Which dialectic has been most challenging in one of your long-term relationships?
fizkes/Shutterstock.com

helps with commitment: Partners who are clearer about their identity *as a couple* are more committed to one another than those who are less clear (Emery et al., 2021). The hallmark of commitment is the intention to share the future. Committed partners are unlikely to bail out if the going gets rough. Instead, they weather bad times (Badiou, 2012), working to resolve conflicts and keep their commitment to one another (Emery et al., 2020). This is true of same-sex and cross-sex relationships alike (Rotosky & Riggle, 2019). In fact, studies indicate that same-sex relationships often have an asset in their problem-solving skill set: more flexibility in gender roles, which leads to greater relationship stability (Rotosky & Riggle, 2019).

investments Something put into a relationship that cannot be recovered should the relationship end. Investments, more than rewards and love, increase commitment.

Commitment grows out of **investments**, or what we put into relationships that we could not retrieve if the relationship were to end. When we care about another person, we invest material things, such as money and possessions. We also invest time: Building a relationship requires both parties to spend a good amount of time together—about 40 to 60 hours to become casual friends, and perhaps 100 to 200 hours to become close friends (Hall, 2018). Even more important, we invest energy, trust, and feelings. In doing this, we invest *ourselves.* For good or ill, the more we invest in a relationship, the more difficult it is to end it (Eastwick et al., 2018).

Relationship Rules

rules Patterned ways of behaving and interpreting behavior; all relationships develop rules.

All relationships have **rules** that guide how partners interact. Relationship rules define what is expected, what is not allowed, and when and how to do various things. As you may recall from Chapter 5, two kinds of rules guide our communication. *Constitutive rules* define the meaning of various types of communication in personal relationships. For instance, women friends often count listening to problems as demonstrating care, whereas men often count doing things together as showing care (Metts, 2006; Wood, 2005). Couples work out constitutive rules to define what counts as loyalty, support, rudeness, love, joking, and so forth.

Regulative rules influence interaction by specifying when and with whom to engage in various kinds of communication. Some friends have a regulative rule that says it's okay to criticize each other in private but not okay to do so in front of others. Some romantic partners limit physical displays of affection to private settings.

Affected by Contexts

Personal relationships are not isolated from the social world. Friendships and romances are affected by social circles, family units, social media norms, and society as a whole. For instance, families may approve or disapprove of our choices of intimates or friends. Our social circles have norms of the appropriateness of activities such as recreation, community service, and religious engagement.

Kaya I had never drunk much until I started going out with Steve. He was 10 years older than me. We usually spent time with his friends, who were also older and in business. All of them drank—not like a whole lot or anything, but several drinks a night. Pretty soon, I was doing that too—it was just part of the relationship with Steve.

Question: Many people find their tastes and interests are influenced by the people they spend a lot of time with. Can you think of an example of how a friend or social circle changed your own interests?

Changes in society and social norms accompany changes in the forms that relationships take. Western society has increasing numbers of single parent families, gay and trans families, and blended families. Whereas in the 1970s, only 0.2% of the United States population cohabited, or lived together outside of marriage, today, about 15% of all people ages 18 to 34 do so (Gurrentz, 2018), and 19% of new marriages are between people of different races—most commonly between one White and one Hispanic spouse (Parker & Barroso, 2021).

Further, 67% of mothers in the United States are in the paid labor force, and about 41% of all families in the United States have a woman who is the primary or exclusive breadwinner (Glynn, 2021). Looking at these data with an intersectional lens reveals that this varies by race and ethnicity: For example, more than 68% of Black mothers were their families' primary or exclusive breadwinners, while only 37% of White mothers were (Glynn, 2021). It also varies by socioeconomics: Mothers are most likely to be the exclusive breadwinner in low-income families, and the rate of mothers as sole earners declines steadily as the family's overall income increase (Glynn, 2021)—a fact that may be related to the gender wage gap, among other factors.

The growing number of dual-career couples is revising traditional expectations about how much each partner participates in earning income, homemaking, and child care (Choose Your Parents, 2014; Coontz, 2014; Miller, 2014; Pedulla & Thébaud, 2015) and how much organizations are supposed to accommodate working parents (Wood & Dow, 2010; Wood & Fixmer-Oraiz, 2017). In all of these ways, our social circles and the larger society as well are contexts that influence the relationships we form and how we communicate within them.

Social media have also expanded our possible friends and romantic partners. Before digital media existed, our choices of friends and romantic partners were largely limited to the people we encountered face to face. Today, 9% of Americans say that they're currently using dating apps, while 28% say they have used them in the past. Interestingly, generation gaps accentuate dating app usage: Among millennials, 17% report using a dating app, whereas only 3% of baby boomers do (YouGov America, 2021).

Relational Dialectics

relational dialectics
Opposing forces or tensions that are normal parts of all relationships. Three relational dialectics are autonomy/connectedness, novelty/predictability, and openness/closedness.

A final feature of personal relationships is **relational dialectics**, which are opposing and continual tensions that are normal in personal relationships. Scholars have identified three relational dialectics (Baxter, 1990, 1993; Baxter & Montgomery, 1996; Erbert, 2000).

Autonomy/Connection In most close relationships, frequent friction arises from the contradictory impulses for autonomy and connection. Because we want to be deeply linked to intimates, we cherish sharing experiences, thoughts, and feelings. At the same time, we need independence, so we sometimes seek distance, even from the people we love most. Friends and romantic partners may vacation together and be with each other almost all the time for a week or more. Yet the intense closeness leads them to crave time apart once the vacation ends. Autonomy and closeness are natural human needs. The challenge is to preserve individuality while also creating intimacy.

Justin For a long time, I've been stressed about my feelings. Sometimes I can't get enough of Dylan, and then I feel crowded and don't want to see them at all. I never understood these switches, and I was afraid I was unstable or something. Now I see that I'm pretty normal after all.

Novelty/Predictability The second dialectic is the tension between wanting familiar routines and wanting novelty. Routine provides security and predictability in our lives. Friends often have standard times to get together, and they develop preferred interaction routines (Braithwaite & Kellas, 2006; Jones et al., 2015; Thurnell-Read, 2021). Romantic couples develop preferred times and places for going out, and they establish patterns for interacting. Families have rituals to mark holidays (Bruess, 2015; Bruess & Hoefs, 2006). Yet too much routine is boring, so friends occasionally explore a new restaurant, romantic couples periodically do something spontaneous, and families change established rituals.

Openness/Closedness The third dialectic is the tension between desires for openness and privacy. We want to share our inner selves with our intimates, yet there are times when we don't feel like sharing and topics that we don't want to talk about. All of us need some privacy, and our partners need to respect that (Petronio & Caughlin, 2006).

Managing Dialectics Leslie Baxter (1990) identifies four ways intimates deal with dialectical tensions. One response, **neutralization**, negotiates a compromise in which each dialectical need is met to an extent but neither is fully satisfied. A couple might agree to be somewhat open but not intensely so. The **separation** response favors one need in a dialectic and ignores the other. For example, friends might agree to make novelty a priority and suppress their needs for routine. Separation also occurs when partners cycle between dialectical poles to favor each pole alternately. For example, friends may get together on weekends and have little contact during the week.

A third way to manage dialectics is **segmentation**: assigning each need to certain spheres, issues, activities, or times. For instance, friends might be open about many topics but not discuss politics or religion.

Review It!

Relational Dialectics:

- Autonomy/Connection
- Novelty/Predictability
- Openness/Closedness

neutralization One of four responses to relational dialectics; involves balancing or finding a compromise between two dialectical poles.

separation One of four responses to relational dialectics, in which friends or romantic partners assign one pole of a dialectic to certain spheres of activities or topics and the contradictory dialectical pole to distinct spheres of activities or topics.

Marianne Bart and I used to be spontaneous all the time. There was always room for something unexpected and unplanned. That changed when we had the twins last year. Now our home life is totally regulated, planned to the last nanosecond. If we get off schedule in getting the boys dressed and fed in the morning, then we're late getting to day care, which means we have to talk with the supervisor there, and then we're late getting to work. We try to have some spontaneity times when Bart's folks take the boys for a weekend, but it's a lot harder now that the boys are in our life.

Question: Many people find that their friendships and romantic relationships change after becoming parents. Maybe you are a parent yourself. If so, do you recall any changes in your friendship groups after you became a new parent? Or, if not, do you recall experiencing a change in your relationship with a friend or family member after they became a new parent?

The final method of dealing with dialectics is **reframing**. This complex strategy redefines apparently contradictory needs as not really in opposition. In a study of romantic partners (Wood, Dendy, Dordek, Germany, & Varallo, 1994), some couples said their autonomy enhanced closeness. Knowing they were separate in some ways allowed them to feel safer being connected. These partners transcended the apparent tension between autonomy and closeness to define the needs as mutually enhancing.

Research suggests that the least satisfying way to manage dialectical tension is separation in which only one need is fulfilled (Baxter, 1990). Separation is unsatisfying because repressing any natural human impulse diminishes us. The challenge is to find ways to honor and satisfy the variety of needs that humans have. Understanding that dialectics are natural and constructive allows us to accept and grow from the tensions they generate.

segmentation One of four responses to relational dialectics. Segmentation responses meet one dialectical need while ignoring or not satisfying the contradictory dialectical need.

reframing One of four responses to relational dialectics. The reframing response transcends the apparent contradiction between two dialectical poles and reinterprets them as not in tension.

Novelty provides vitality to relationships.
Sept commercial/Unsplash.com

The Evolutionary Course of Personal Relationships

Each relationship develops in unique ways. Yet there are commonalities in how personal relationships tend to progress. We'll explore typical patterns for the evolution of friendships and romances.

Friendships

Although friendships sometimes blaze to life quickly, usually they unfold through fairly predictable stages (Rawlins, 1981, 1994). We meet a new person at work, in class, on an athletic team, in a club, or online. During initial face-to-face encounters, we rely on standard social rules and roles, and we tend to be careful about what we disclose. In the early stage of online relationships, people often venture into more personal, self-disclosing communication than they would at a similar stage of face-to-face acquaintance.

Josh I met Stan online. We were both in the same chat room, and it was like we were on the same wavelength, so we started messaging each other privately. After a couple of months, it was like I knew Stan better than any of my close friends here, and he knew me, too—inside and out. It seemed safer or easier to open up online than in person. Maybe that's why we got so close so fast.

Question: Self-disclosures can sometimes feel easier online. Why do you think this might be? Have you ever had an experience like Josh's?

If both people are interested, they communicate to learn whether they have shared interests and whether they enjoy interacting. The perception of shared interests is often very important during the initial stage of developing a friendship (Campbell et al., 2018). For many people, attraction is more important at the same stage in a romantic relationship (Campbell et al., 2018), but this does vary: For those that identify as asexual, shared interests are usually the place of connection, even in intimate relationships; and for those who identify as demisexual, an emotional connection needs to happen before attraction forms (Cleveland Clinic, 2022).

In general, meeting a person repeatedly, in casual situations, helps us learn what we have in common and develop friendships. This is why we are more likely to make close friends at certain times and contexts in life: through education, in the workplace, through one's children, and in one's own neighborhood (Thomas, 2019)—when more frequent casual encounters are likely. Note that we are more likely to make racially diverse friendships in certain settings: through work, neighborhood, and our children—especially in early to mid-life (Thomas, 2019)—settings where casual contact can reveal shared interests quickly.

As people discover shared interests, they generally spend more time together and are more relaxed. To signal that we're interested in being friends, we could introduce a more personal topic. People who have gotten to know each other online may arrange a face-to-face meeting. As people interact more personally, they begin to form a foundation for friendship.

At some point, people begin to think of themselves as friends. When this happens, social norms and roles become less important, and friends begin to work out their own private ways of relating. Some settle into patterns of getting together for specific things (e.g., watching games, discussing books, exercising, shopping).

When friends feel established in each other's lives, friendship stabilizes and transcends perceived differences. As trust and knowledge of each other expand, friends become more deeply woven into each other's life. Stabilized friendships may continue indefinitely.

While some friendships last for years or even lifetimes, not all do. Sometimes friends drift apart because each is pulled in a different direction by personal or career demands (Grayling, 2013). In other cases, friendships deteriorate because they've become boring. Breaking relationship rules can also end friendships. Telling a friend's secrets to a third person or being dishonest may violate the rules of the friendship. Even when serious violations occur between friends, relationships can sometimes be repaired, if both friends are committed to rebuilding trust and talking openly about their feelings and needs.

Review It!

Features of Personal Relationships:

- Uniqueness
- Committed
- Guided by Rules
- Affected by Contexts
- Influenced by Relational Dialectics

When friendships deteriorate, communication changes in predictable ways. The most obvious changes are reductions in frequency and intimacy of communication. In some cases, defensiveness and uncertainty rise, causing people to be more guarded and less open.

Romantic Relationships

Like friendships, romances also have a typical—but not a universal—evolutionary path. For most of us, romance progresses through the stages of escalation, navigation, and deterioration.

Escalation Before a romantic relationship begins, there are individuals who have particular needs, goals, experiences, and qualities that affect what they want in others and relationships. Individuals have learned constitutive and regulative communication rules that affect how we interact with others and how we interpret their communication.

Romantic relationships usually start with predictable social interaction. The meaning of early communication is found on the relational level of meaning, not the content level. The content level of meaning of "Do you like jazz?" is unimportant. But on the relationship level of meaning, the comment says "I'm available and possibly interested. Are you?"

A feeling of mutual attraction is very important in the initial stage of a romantic relationship—more salient, at this stage, than shared interests are (Campbell et al., 2018). That said, some people have strict criteria for relationship partners, and social media can be very useful to establish commonalities. For example, within your existing social circles, you might have trouble finding partners who are under 35 years old, Indian, and not interested in having children. However, you can specify those criteria on a dating site and find people who meet them (Ansari, 2015).

Out of all the people we meet, we are attracted romantically to only a few. The three greatest influences on initial attraction are self-concept, proximity, and similarity. Our self-concept affects our choices of candidates for romance. Sexual orientation, for example, is a primary influence on our consideration of potential romantic partners.

In addition to self-concept, proximity influences initial attraction. We can interact only with people we meet, whether in person or virtually. Consequently, the places in which we live, work, and socialize, as well as online communities in which we participate, constrain the possibilities for relationships. Some contexts, such as college campuses, promote meeting potential romantic partners, whereas other contexts are less conducive to meeting and dating. Also, digital media have some downsides in this regard: Ironically, because dating sites provide us so many potential matches, we may feel dissatisfied with very good options, believing that ever-better matches are always out there (Ansari with Klinenberg, 2015).

Similarity is also important in romantic relationships. In the realm of romance, "birds of a feather flock together" seems truer than "opposites attract" (Samp & Palevitz, 2009). In a study of opposite-sex couples, Leikas et al. (2019) found that this was most true of political values, with relationships between two politically conservative partners the most common type. In contrast, personality traits are less likely to be shared by couples (Leikas et al., 2019), though couples may come to share certain personality traits the longer they stay together (Lampis et al., 2017). Most of us are attracted to people whose values, attitudes, and lifestyles are similar to ours and to people who are about as physically attractive as we are.

If early interaction increases attraction, then we may increase the amount and intimacy of interaction. During this phase, partners spend more and more time together, and they rely less on external events such as concerts or parties. Instead, they immerse themselves in the budding relationship and may feel they can't be together enough. Additional and more personal disclosures are exchanged, and partners increasingly learn how the other feels and thinks. As caring develops, physical desirability increases—in other words, as people get to know and like each other, they perceive each other as more physically attractive (Tierney, 2015). Compared to face-to-face relationships, online relationships tend to form more rapidly and tend to involve greater idealization in which partners have overly positive perceptions of one another.

At some point, partners consider whether they want the relationship to be permanent or at least extended. For most of America's history, a great majority of citizens have married. This is no longer the case. In 1950, only 4 million Americans lived alone (Ansari, 2015); in early 2021, 37 million did—a full 15% of adults over the age of 18 (Census Bureau, 2021). In 1960, 72% of American adults were married whereas only 53% were in 2019 (Edwards, 2015; Fry and Parker, 2021). Between 1996 and 2019, cohabitation in the United States more than quintupled, rising from 2.9 million to 17 million couples (Angier, 2013; Gurrentz, 2019).

Partners who do want to stay together may cohabit or marry. Either way, they will work through any problems and obstacles to long-term viability. Couples may need to work out differences in religions and conflicts in locations and career goals. In same-sex relationships, partners often have to resolve differences about openness regarding their sexual orientations and acceptance by families, and even the workplace: An inclusive environment makes a big difference in LGBT employees' feelings of job satisfaction (Hur, 2020), but not all workplaces are inclusive. Discrimination against gender-diverse individuals is an ongoing problem in many workplaces (Hur, 2020). This has consequences for the employees' personal lives beyond work, with researchers finding that in same-gender relationships, partners are more likely to feel relationship dissatisfaction if the couple's relationship is not "out" across all contexts (Akers et al., 2021).

Kyle When Todd and I got together, I knew he was the one for me—the man I wanted to spend the rest of my life with. But we had a huge problem. He is totally out, and I'm not. If I came out at my job, I'd be off the fast track immediately, and I'd probably be fired. It was a huge issue between us because he wanted me to be as out as he is—like to take him with me to the holiday parties at my company. I can't do that. It's still a real tension between us.

As you might expect, during this phase of romance, communication often involves negotiation and even conflict. Issues that aren't problems in a dating relationship may have to be resolved to allow a long-term future. Some couples find they cannot resolve problems. It is entirely possible to love a person with whom we don't want to share our life.

Commitment is a decision to stay with a relationship permanently. This decision transforms a romantic relationship from one based on past and present experiences and feelings into one with a future.

Navigation In long-term relationships, the longest span of time is navigation, which is the ongoing process of communicating to sustain intimacy in the face of changes in oneself, one's partner, the relationship, and surrounding contexts. Couples continuously work through new issues, revisit old ones, and accommodate changes in their individual and joint lives. To use an automotive analogy, navigating involves both preventive maintenance and periodic repairs (Galvin & Braithwaite, 2015; Stafford, 2009). Navigating communication aims to keep intimacy satisfying and healthy and to deal with problems and tensions. Couples who talk issues through and make decisions thoughtfully have higher quality relationships than couples who are less communicative (Parker-Pope, 2014). The later years in very long-term marriages can be the happiest, in part because couples have learned to focus on what matters and not to sweat the small stuff. Other research (Parker-Pope, 2009b) confirms the finding that many couples find the "empty nest years" the happiest in their marriages because there are fewer stresses and more couple time.

relational culture A private world of rules, understandings, and patterns of acting and interpreting that partners create to give meaning to their relationship; the nucleus of intimacy.

The nucleus of intimacy is **relational culture**, a private world of rules, understandings, meanings, and patterns of interacting that partners create for their relationship (Wood, 1982). Relational culture includes how couples manage relational dialectics. Relational culture also includes communication rules, usually unspoken, about how to express anger, love, sexual interest, and so forth. Especially important in navigation is small talk, through which partners weave together the fabric of their history and their current lives, experiences, and dreams.

Not all intimately bonded relationships endure. Nearly half of first marriages end within 20 years (Tobbe, 2012). As of 2021, 54% of men and 61% of women between ages 60 and 69 have been divorced. This is a higher rate than in the general 20+ adult population, where 34% of women and 33% of men have divorced (Gurrentz and Mayola-Garcia, 2021). Tensions within a relationship, as well as pressures and problems in surrounding contexts, may contribute to declines in intimacy.

Deterioration Deterioration often begins when one or both partners reflect and sometimes brood about dissatisfaction with the relationship. It's easy for this to become a self-fulfilling prophecy: As gloomy thoughts snowball and awareness of positive features of the relationship ebbs, partners may talk themselves into the failure of their relationship.

There are some general sex and gender differences in what generates dissatisfaction (Barstead, Bouchard, & Shih, 2013; Burchell & Ward, 2011; Duck & Wood, 2006). For women, unhappiness most often arises when communication declines in quality or quantity. Men are more likely to be dissatisfied by specific behaviors or the lack of valued behaviors or by having domestic responsibilities that they feel aren't a man's job. Because many women are socialized to be sensitive to interpersonal nuances, they are generally more likely than men to notice tensions and early symptoms of relationship problems.

If unchecked, dissatisfaction tends to lead to the breakdown of established patterns, understandings, and rules that have been part of the relationship. Partners may stop talking after dinner, no longer bother to call when they are running late, and in other ways depart from rules and patterns that have defined their relational culture. As the relational culture weakens, dissatisfaction mounts.

Communication Highlight

The Four Horsemen of the Apocalypse

Psychologist John Gottman has spent more than 20 years studying marriages and counseling couples (Gottman, 1994a, 1994b, 1999; Gottman & Silver, 1994). He concludes that there is no difference in the amount of conflict between happily married couples and couples who divorce or have unhappy marriages.

Healthy and unhealthy marriages do differ in two important respects. First, partners who are unhappy together and who often divorce tend to engage in what Gottman calls "corrosive communication patterns." Gottman views these destructive communication practices as "the four horsemen of the apocalypse":

complaint and criticism
defensiveness and denial of responsibility
expressions of contempt
stonewalling

These "four horsemen of the apocalypse" foster negative feelings: anger, fear, sadness, and dissatisfaction. Often these destructive communication patterns are evident in extensive nagging, which can profoundly sour marriages, according to Dr. Howard Markman, who directs the Center of Marital and Family Studies (Bernstein, 2012).

Gottman thinks the most corrosive is **stonewalling**, or refusing to discuss issues that are causing tension in a relationship. Stonewalling blocks the possibility of resolving conflicts. In addition, on the relationship level of meaning it communicates that the problems aren't worth dealing with.

The second major difference between marriages that succeed and those that fail is not bad moments but a predominance of good moments. Happy couples have as many conflicts and tensions as unhappy ones, but they have more enjoyable times together. Says Gottman, a positive balance is everything.

stonewalling Refusal to discuss issues that are creating tension in a relationship. Stonewalling is especially corrosive in relationships because it blocks the possibility of resolving conflicts.

Conflict, which is normal in all enduring relationships, may escalate when a relationship is deteriorating. In addition, partners may feel less motivated to manage conflict constructively, so it can become increasingly hurtful and unproductive, which may accelerate relational decline. The communication highlight on this page identifies key aspects of conflict that can kill relationships.

Whether a relationship survives at this juncture depends on how committed partners are, whether they perceive attractive alternatives to the relationship, and whether they have the communication skills to work through problems constructively.

If partners lack commitment or the communication skills they need to restore intimacy, they often begin to tell others about problems in the relationship and to seek support from others. Friends and family members can provide support by being available and by listening. Although self-serving explanations of breakups are common, they aren't necessarily constructive. We have an ethical responsibility to monitor communication during this period so that we don't say things we'll later regret.

When an important relationship ends, each partner works individually to make sense of what it meant, why it failed, and how it affected them. Typically, partners mourn the failure to realize that which once seemed possible. Yet mourning and sadness may be accompanied by other, more positive outcomes from breakups. People report that breaking up gives them new insights into themselves, improved family relationships, and gave them more clear ideas about future partners (Tashiro & Frazier, 2003).

Luke I'd been with Maggie for nearly a year when our relationship ended. Things had been a little rough, but I thought that was natural in long-distance relationships. I found out it was over when I saw her status update on social media!

Guidelines for Maintaining Healthy Personal Relationships

We'll consider ways to deal with four common challenges that friends and romantic partners face.

Manage Distance

One of the greatest problems for long-distance commitments is inability to share small talk face to face and to engage in daily routines. Unlimited calling plans are a great way to stay in touch about the day-to-day stuff in your lives.

A second common problem for long-distance relationships is unrealistic expectations for time together. Because long-distance friends and partners have so little time together physically, they may feel that there should be no conflict and that they should be with each other during the time they are together. Yet this is an unrealistic expectation. Conflict and needs for autonomy are natural in all relationships. They may be even more pronounced in long-distance relationships because friends and partners are used to living alone and have established independent rhythms that may not mesh well.

The good news is that these problems don't necessarily sabotage long-distance romance. Many people maintain satisfying commitments despite geographic separation. Go to the book's online resources for this chapter to learn more about long-distance relationships and ways to connect with people who are in them.

Create Equitable Romantic Relationships

On the job, we expect equity: to be treated the same as other employees at our level. If we are asked to do more work than our peers, we can appeal to a manager or supervisor. In romantic relationships, however, there is no supervisor to ensure equity. Researchers report that the happiest dating and married couples believe both partners invest equally (DeMaris, 2007; Pedulla & Thébaud, 2015). When we think we are investing more than our partner is, we tend to be resentful. When it seems our partner is investing more than we are, we may feel guilty (Guerrero, La Valley, & Farinelli, 2008). That said, motive matters: If we feel they are investing more for partner-focused reasons, we are more likely to feel gratitude than when their investments seem to be motivated by their own self-interest (Visserman et al., 2018).

Traditionally, women were assigned care of the home and family because men were more likely to be the primary or only wage earners. That is no longer true. Today, 57.4% of women in the United States participate in the workforce (Bureau of Labor Statistics Reports, 2021), and many women in heterosexual partnerships earn more money than their male partners (Adams, 2014; Ream, 2012). Furthermore, in some areas, the gender wage gap may be closing: As of 2022, women ages 20 to 29 earned as much or more than their male counterparts in 22 of 250 United States metropolitan areas, including New York City and Washington, D.C. (Pew Research Center, 2022). Unfortunately, divisions of family and home responsibilities inadequately reflect women's employment status. Though women outnumber men in the paid workforce, women still do nearly twice as much housework and childcare in comparison to their male counterparts (Smith & Johnson, 2020).

Gay and lesbian couples report a greater desire for shared power and decision-making than do heterosexual couples (Hunter, 2012), though this varies, of course: For example, in their study of lesbian couples, Rothblum et al. (2018) found that if one partner identifies as femme, the relationship is likely to be characterized by heteronormative attitudes, including a less equitable division of household (with more work for the femme partner). Note that this finding has complexity, though, as those who identify as femme are often both self-aware and subversive: Femme identity is a celebration and refiguration of femininity, as Donish (2017) so thoughtfully explains—one that can be empowering for some queer people and alienating for others.

In any case, although few partners demand moment-to-moment equality, most of us want our relationships to be equitable over time (Wood, 2011). Equity has multiple dimensions. We may evaluate the fairness of financial, emotional, physical, and other contributions to a relationship. One area that strongly affects satisfaction of spouses and cohabiting partners is equity in housework and child care. Inequitable division of domestic obligations fuels dissatisfaction and resentment, both of which harm intimacy (Alberts, Tracy, & Trethewey, 2011; Coontz, 2013, 2014).

As a rule, women assume **psychological responsibility** for relationships, which involves remembering, planning, and coordinating domestic activities (Hochschild with Machung, 2003). Parents may take turns driving children to the doctor, but often the mother remembers when check-ups are needed, makes appointments, and reminds the father to take the child. Both partners may sign birthday cards, but women typically remember birthdays and buy cards and gifts. Successful long-term relationships in our era require partners to communicate collaboratively to design equitable divisions of responsibility.

psychological responsibility The responsibility for remembering, planning, and coordinating domestic work and child care. In general, women assume the psychological responsibility for child care and housework even if both partners share in the actual tasks.

Molly It really isn't fair when both spouses work outside of the home but only one of them takes care of the home and kids. For years, that was how Sean's and my marriage worked, no matter how much I tried to talk with him about a more fair arrangement. Finally, I had just had it, so I quit doing everything. Groceries didn't get bought, laundry piled up and he didn't have clean shirts, he didn't remember his mother's birthday (and for the first time ever, I didn't remind him), and bills didn't get paid. After a while, he suggested we talk about a system we could both live with.

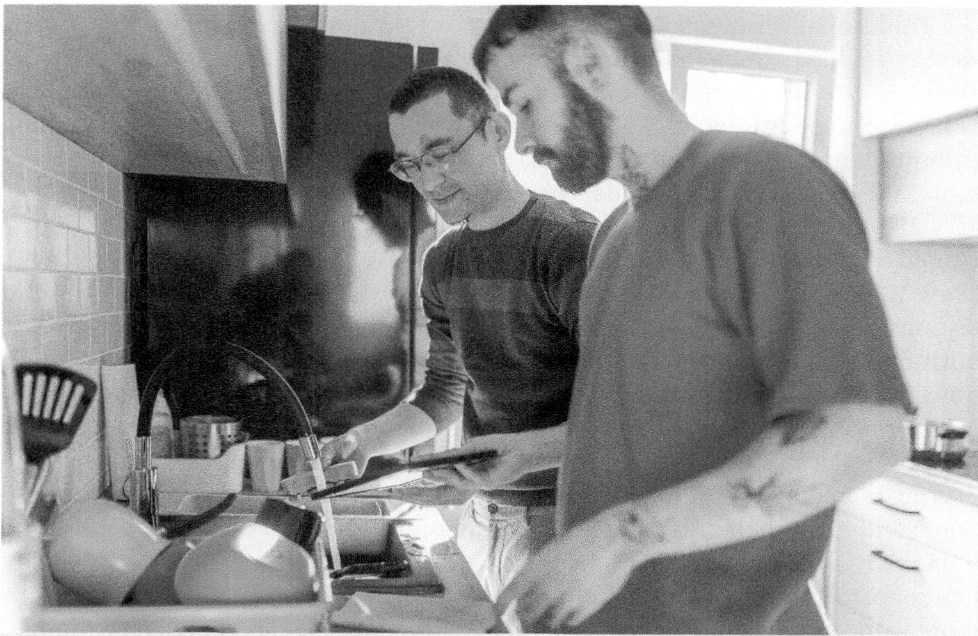

Equitable participation in domestic responsibilities enhances partners' satisfaction.
iStock.com/Zoranm

Resist Violence and Abuse Between Intimates

Intimate partner violence is experienced and perpetrated by both sexes; by gay people, lesbian people, straight people, and transgender people; and by members of all races and economic classes. Those most commonly harmed by intimate partner violence are women ages 20 to 24, women in the lowest household income brackets, and Black and Native American women (National Organization for Women, 2022). Within the LGBTQIA+ community, Black people are most likely to be harmed by physical intimate partner violence—and significantly more lesbian and bisexual women, and bisexual men, have experienced intimate partner rape and physical violence than have their straight counterparts (DC Volunteer Lawyers Project, 2021). Oklahoma, Kentucky, Missouri, and Nevada have the highest rates of intimate partner violence; North Dakota, Rhode Island, Virginia, and New York, the least (World Population Review, 2022).

In the United States, 25% of women have been violently attacked by husbands or boyfriends; more than 50% of the perpetrators of female homicide in the United States were a current or former male intimate partner (Centers for Disease Control and Prevention, Oct. 2021). In addition to causing serious physical and emotional injuries, intimate partner violence causes financial hardships including job loss for many women, with between 20 and 61% of women who are abused by an intimate partner losing their jobs for abuse-related reasons (National Coalition Against Domestic Violence, 2017).

Children suffer, too: Witnessing intimate partner violence can cause serious long-term mental and physical health problems for children, heightens their risk of being harmed by child abuse, and may increase the chance that they themselves will be violent in future relationships (Office on Women's Health, 2019). In approximately 30 to 60% of families in which either intimate partner violence or child abuse occurs, the other does, too (Mattison, 2021).

Of about 81,000 women and girls killed around the world in 2020, intimate partners or family members perpetrated about 58% of these cases. Also, worldwide, at least 26% of girls and women aged 15 and older have been victims of intimate partner violence—and in low- and lower-middle-income regions and countries, such as those where resources are scarce and women's educational opportunities more limited, these rates are even higher (UN Women, 2022). Violence is high not only in marriages but also in dating and cohabiting relationships, with women in cohabiting relationships experiencing physical violence from their domestic partner more than twice as often as their married peers (Wong et al., 2016). In addition to physical abuse, verbal, sexual, and emotional brutality poison altogether too many relationships.

A rising form of intimate partner violence is stalking, which is repeated, intrusive behavior that is uninvited and unwanted, that seems obsessive, and that makes the target afraid or concerned for their safety. Stalking is particularly easy on campuses because it isn't difficult to learn others' routines. Social networking sites give stalkers more ways to learn about (potential) victims' habits and patterns (Spitzberg & Cupach, 2014). Cyberstalking is a related concern: Former partners may monitor their exes' online communication, interfere with their communication with other people, and harass them through methods such as defamation, doxing, online impersonation, revenge porn, and unsolicited pornography (2021). About 40% of people in the United States now report having been harassed online, often over politics; about 11% report experiencing sustained harassment and/or cyberstalking (Vogels, 2021). While stalking is illegal in all 50 states, cyberstalking laws are newer and vary more.

Intimate partner violence tends to follow a predictable cycle: Tension mounts in the abuser, the abuser explodes by being violent, the abuser then is remorseful and loving, the victim feels loved and reassured that the relationship is working, and then tension mounts anew and the cycle begins again. Too often, people don't leave abusive relationships because they feel trapped by economic pressures or by relatives and clergy who counsel them to stay (Foley, 2006; Jacobson & Gottman, 1998). Without intervention, the cycle of violence is unlikely to stop. Abusive relationships are unhealthy for everyone involved. They violate the trust that is a foundation of intimacy, and they jeopardize the comfort, health, and sometimes the lives of victims of violence.

Review It!

Stages in Cycle of Violence

- Tension
- Explosion
- Remorse
- Honeymoon

Communication is related to intimate partner violence in two ways. Most obviously, patterns of communication between couples and the intrapersonal communication of abusers can fuel tendencies toward violence. Some partners deliberately annoy and taunt each other. Also, the language abusers use to describe physical assaults on partners includes denial, trivializing the harm, and blaming the partner or circumstances for "making me do it" (notice this is a form of *you-language).* These intrapersonal communication patterns allow abusers to deny their offenses, justify violence, and cast responsibility outside themselves. When these patterns are calculated to cause the abused to doubt their own judgments and reality, it is known as **gaslighting**—an insidious form of abuse most common in romantic relationships, but which occurs in other relationships, as well (Gordon, 2022).

gaslighting Abusive, covert manipulation that misleads the target about their own experiences, causing them to question their own judgments, undermining their perceptions of reality.

Cyberstalking

What to Do If You Are Cyberstalked

It can be hard to prove you are being cyberstalked. Taking steps to protect yourself while keeping records of your experiences is very important. Here are suggestions based on recommendations from the organization Domestic Shelters, which specializes in helping people experiencing domestic violence (Kippert, 2021), as well as from my own work in this area (Hains, 2020).

1. **Don't reply.** A common saying on social media is "Don't feed the trolls," because engaging with harassers excites them and prompts them to continue the behavior. This advice applies to cyberstalking, as well.
2. **If you feel you're in danger, call 911**, especially if the cyberstalker is making threats against you or your household.
3. **Log every cyberstalking incident**. Keep records of what happens, when. Keep a folder with screenshots with time and date stamps and other information you feel is relevant.
4. **After logging their activity, report and block the stalker from sending you further messages via social media or your phone**. If they switch to a new profile, log that activity and then report and block that account, as well. They may be blocked from the social media app entirely based on your reports.
5. **Lock down your information on social media**. Keep personal information and details about locations where you spend your time off of the publicly visible sections of your social media profiles. Make sure your publicly searchable online resume, if you have one, doesn't contain your home address or phone number, either.
6. **Opt out of personal broker directories**. Personal broker directories (like Spokeo and Whitepages) publish people's personal details, including birthdate, home address, phone number, family members' names (and their contact information). Search for your name on these sites and request an immediate removal of your personal data through each site's opt-out page. Most sites will remove the information instantly. This will make it harder for cyberstalkers to intrude into your offline life.
7. **Change all your passwords and make sure your new passwords are secure**. Use two-step authentication wherever you can—email, social media accounts, and so on. Also, check whether your cell phone carrier requires a pin to change your account details. (It should.)
8. **File for an Order of Protection**. How to do so will vary by state, but your local domestic violence association should be able to direct you to the right method in your jurisdiction.

Violence is highly unlikely to stop on its own. The cycle shown in Figure 7.1 is self-perpetuating. Further, violence that begins in the home may precede violent crime outside of the home. As two people who work with intimate partner violence phrase it, "Women and children are target practice, and the home is the training ground for men's later actions" (Shifman & Tillet, 2015, p. A21).

Violent relationships are not the victims' fault. If you know or suspect that someone you care about is a victim of abuse, don't ignore the situation, and don't assume it's none of your business. It is an act of friendship to notice and offer to help. Note that it is important for those seeking to help a victim of abuse to broach

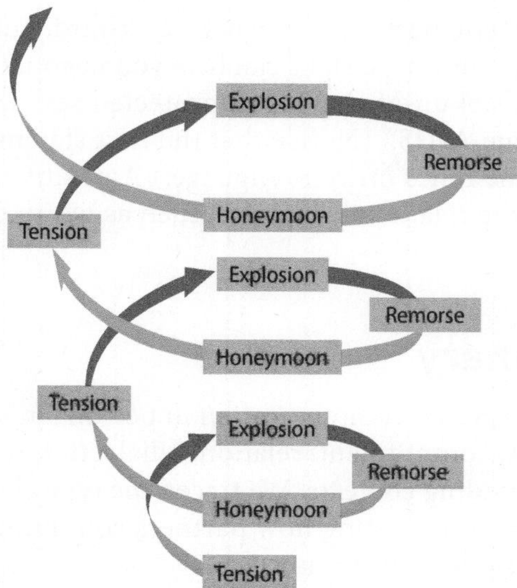

Figure 7.1
The Cycle of Abuse

the topic in private. Email, or other communication forms that might be monitored by the abuser, could cause potential risk or harm. A truly private conversation in an unmonitored channel or setting—in person, if possible—is best. Victims of violence must make the ultimate decision about what to do, but the support and concern of friends can help them.

Negotiate Safer Sex

In our era, sexual activities pose serious, even deadly, threats to people of all sexual orientations. Since the beginning of the HIV/AIDS epidemic in 1981, more than 700,000 Americans have died from HIV-related illness, and 1.2 million currently live with an HIV diagnosis (KFF, 2021). Meanwhile, nearly 68 million Americans—1 in 5 people—have a sexually transmitted infection (STI) on any given day (Centers for Disease Control and Prevention, Jan. 2021). Nearly 20 million new cases are diagnosed each year, more than half among people ages 15 to 24 (Office of Disease Prevention and Health Promotion, 2020). Because STDs often have no symptoms, they are often undiagnosed and untreated. The long-term effects of untreated STDs can be severe: infertility, blindness, liver cancer, increased vulnerability to HIV, and death.

Despite the real dangers of unsafe sex, many people find it awkward to ask partners direct questions (i.e., "Have you been tested for HIV?" "Are you having sex with anyone else?") or to make direct requests to partners (i.e., "I want you to wear a condom," "I would like you to be tested for STDs before we have sex"). It can be difficult to talk explicitly about sex and the dangers of STDs. However, it is far more difficult to live with a disease or the knowledge that you have infected someone else.

A second reason some people don't practice safer sex is that they hold erroneous and dangerous misperceptions. Among these are the assumptions that you are safe if you and your partner are monogamous, the belief that you can recognize "the kind of person" who might have an STD, and the idea that planning for sex destroys the spontaneity. These are dangerous, false beliefs that can put you and your partners at grave risk. Another reason people sometimes fail to practice safer sex is that their rational thought and control are debilitated by alcohol and other drugs.

Discussing and practicing safer sex may be awkward, but there is no sensible alternative. Good communication skills can help you negotiate safer sex. It is more constructive to say, "I feel unsafe having unprotected sex" than "Without a condom, you could give me AIDS." (Notice that the first statement uses *I*-language, whereas the second one relies on *you*-language.) A positive communication climate is fostered by using relational language, such as *we, us,* and *our relationship,* to talk about sex.

Chapter Summary

In this chapter, we've explored communication in personal relationships, which are defined by uniqueness, commitment, relational dialectics, relationship rules, and interaction with surrounding contexts. We traced the typical evolutionary paths of friendships and romances by noting how partners communicate as relationships develop, stabilize, and sometimes decline.

In the final section of the chapter, we considered four challenges that friends and romantic partners face. The communication principles and skills we have discussed in this and previous chapters help us meet the challenges of sustaining intimacy across geographic distance, creating equitable relationships, resisting violence, and negotiating safer sex. Good communication skills enable us to meet these challenges so that our relationships survive and thrive over time.

Experiencing Communication in Our Lives

Case Study: Growing Together

Apply what you've learned in this chapter by analyzing the following case study, using the accompanying questions as a guide.

Evan and Arden are preparing dinner together. Arden has just finished a certificate program at college and shared the possibility of continuing coursework in the fall for a bachelor's degree in engineering.

Evan: If you're keeping your project management job, why would you need a bachelor's in engineering? You're not an engineer.

Arden: Not now anyway. But I think I might like to be one.

Evan: Oh. When did this happen?

Arden: Since taking these classes. I didn't realize how interesting it is! Sometimes I get really bored at my job and I think about trying something else.

Evan: So our life is boring now?

Arden: Whoa, I didn't say that. I just said my *job* can be boring.

Evan: Mine can too – do you think I enjoy updating charts all day? That's how jobs are. But *I* still want to see you at night.

Arden: But, my getting another degree isn't about *us*.

Evan: How is this not about *us* if you're deciding to spend four nights a week in classes? I'll never see you. And how would we afford all those classes, anyway? It's not like your job will pay for any of this.

Arden: No, it won't. The money will be an issue to discuss. But I'm pretty sure I can get some grants. And we can definitely figure out how to make more time for us – maybe do more lunches together during the week? Our jobs aren't that far apart.

Evan: I'm just confused. I thought we liked our life the way it is. Now it seems like you want to be someone else. Is this... not enough for you anymore?

Arden: Hey, I love our life. I guess this was a lot for me to throw at you. I just wanted to tell you what I was thinking; we can keep talking about it, and I won't do anything without you. And I certainly don't want to be someone new. Maybe just someone with a new career. Ok?

Evan: Ok. I guess there are ways to make this work if it's what you really want. I just hope you won't think less of me when you have a college degree and I don't.

Arden: Never! You're better at your job than anyone with a college degree could ever be. I respect that.

Questions for Analysis and Discussion

1. What love styles do you think Evan and Arden have? What cues in dialogue lead you to identify each person's love style?
2. Based on the dialogue, how would you judge Evan and Arden's levels of commitment to the relationship?
3. If Arden decides to pursue college classes in the fall, what suggestions for maintaining contact in long-distance relationships might be applied to this couple?

Key Concepts

commitment
gaslighting
investments
neutralization
passion
personal relationship
psychological responsibility
reframing
relational culture
relational dialectics
rules
segmentation
separation
stonewalling

For Further Reflection and Discussion

1. Think about the distinction between passion and commitment in personal relationships. Describe relationships in which commitment is present but passion is not. Describe relationships in which passion exists but not commitment. What can you conclude about the values of each?
2. Does a person who wants to end a serious romantic relationship have an ethical responsibility to talk with their partner about why they are no longer interested in maintaining the relationship? Under what conditions are we ethically obligated to help a partner through a breakup?
3. Apply the idea of investments and commitments to an employment context. Think about the jobs that you have had in your life. Which ones did you invest most heavily in? Were you more committed to those jobs than ones in which you invested less?
4. Talk with someone who was raised in a culture different from the one in which you were raised. Ask them what they consider the most important qualities in a friend and in a romantic partner. Reflect on similarities and differences in their answers and the answers you would give.

8

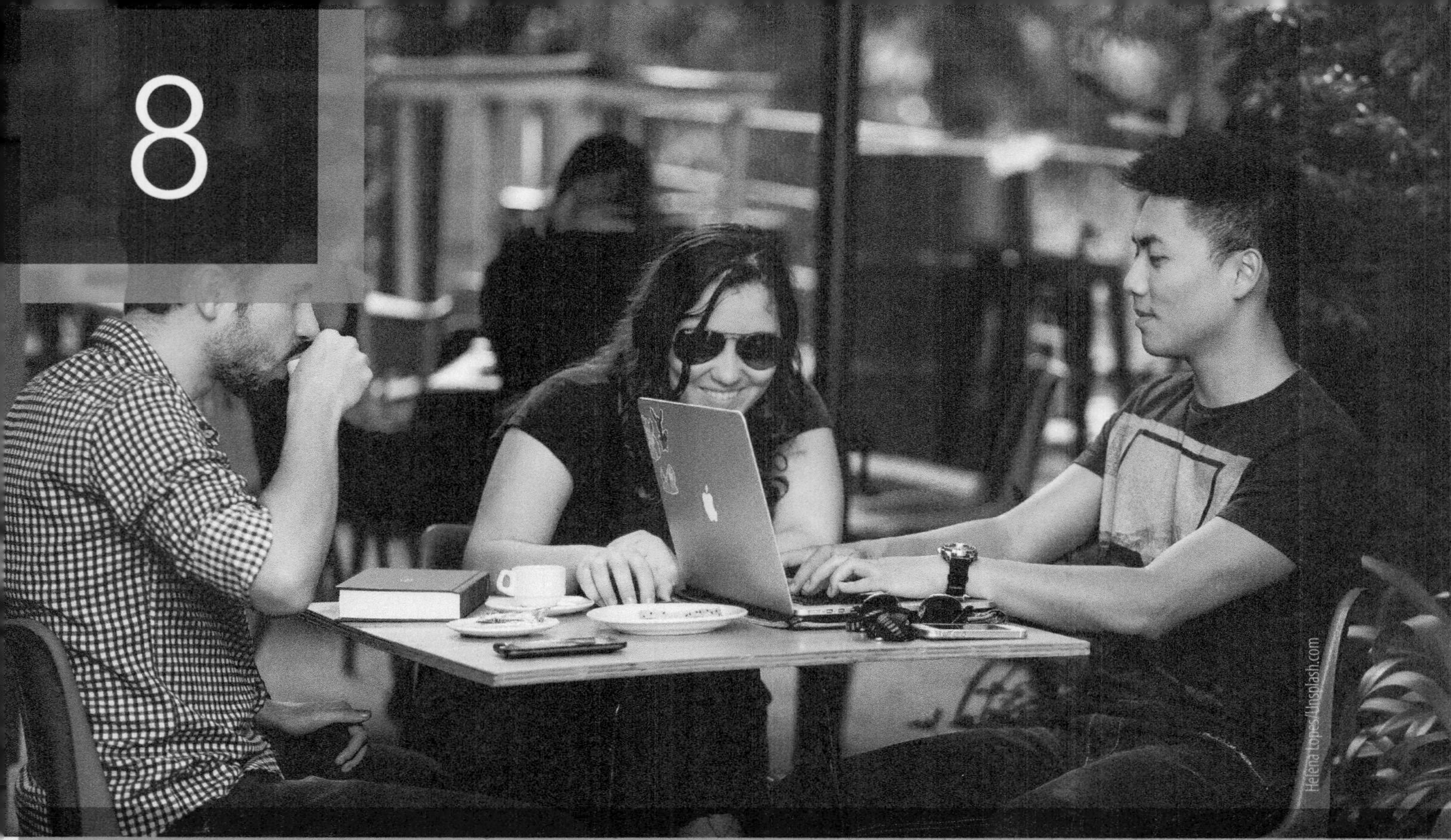

Never doubt that a small group of thoughtful committed citizens can change the world; indeed, it's the only thing that ever has.

Margaret Mead

Communication in Groups and Teams

Learning Objectives

After studying the topics in this chapter, you should be able to:

1. Apply the definition of a small group to a situation to determine whether it constitutes a group.
2. Explain how group dynamics affect small group communication.
3. Explain the role of accountability in small group dynamics and communication.
4. Define *virtual group* in the context of human communication and identify at least three strategies to maximize performance of virtual groups.
5. Explain the characteristics of healthy groups and apply chapter guidelines to improve your interactions in small groups.

How many groups do you currently belong to?

- "Teams take too much time to decide anything."
- "Working in groups increases creativity."
- "Groups suppress individuality."
- "Teams make better decisions than individuals."

You probably agree more with some of these statements than others. Actually, there's some truth to each statement. Groups generally do take more time to reach decisions than individuals, yet decisions informed by group discussion can be superior to those made by one person. Although group interaction stimulates creativity, it may also suppress individual opinions.

Communication is a major influence on whether groups and teams are productive and enjoyable or inefficient and unpleasant. Communication in groups and teams calls for many of the skills and understandings that we've discussed in previous chapters. For example, constructive group communication requires that members express themselves clearly, check perceptions, practice cultural humility, and listen mindfully. This chapter will increase your understanding of how groups work and enhance your ability to participate in and lead groups and teams effectively.

The chapter opens by defining groups and teams and identifying potential weaknesses and strengths of collective work. We then examine features of small groups. The third section of the chapter focuses on virtual group communication. In the final section, we discuss guidelines for effective participation and leadership.

Understanding Groups and Teams

Pick up any newspaper or browse social media and you will read announcements and advertisements for social groups, volunteer service committees, personal support groups, health teams, focus groups sought by companies trying out new products, and political action coalitions.

The tendency toward group work is especially pronounced in the workplace (Barge, 2009; Beebe & Masterson, 2011; Rothwell, 2015). Whether you are an attorney working with a litigation team, a medical technician who participates in a health delivery team, or a middle manager on a team assigned to find ways to increase productivity, working with others probably will be part of your career.

So, what are groups and teams? Are six people standing together on a street corner waiting to cross the street a group? Are five people studying independently in a library a group? Are four students standing in line to buy books a group? The answer is *no* in each case. These are collections of individuals, but they are not groups.

For a group to exist, there must be interaction and interdependence between individuals, a common goal, and shared rules of conduct. Thus, we can define a **group** as three or more people who interact over time, depend on one another, and follow some shared rules of conduct to reach a common goal. To be a group, members must perceive themselves as interdependent—as somehow needing one another (Adams & Galanes, 2011; Harris & Sherblom, 2010).

group Three or more people who interact over time, are interdependent, and follow shared rules of conduct to reach a common goal. The team is one type of group.

Communication & Careers

Teamwork in Health Care

For many years, it was common for people to believe that doctors' medical expertise mattered more than any other skill. But today, medical schools and health care organizations have been recognizing teamwork's importance among practitioners, and the difference it makes in patient outcomes. When doctors disregard the expertise of nurses and other team members, for example, they can undermine effective teamwork and cause medical errors, with dire consequences (Nagourney, 2006). To change this, teamwork skill development is becoming more common in medical schools and in professional development opportunities for established practitioners. Due to the complex, interdisciplinary nature of many medical cases, teamwork is becoming increasingly recognized as a best practice in health care, and medical students and practitioners are now receiving more support in developing their collaborative skills (Iqbal, 2020).

team A special kind of group characterized by different and complementary resources of members and a strong sense of collective identity. All teams are groups, but not all groups are teams.

A **team** is a special kind of group that is characterized by different and complementary resources of members and a strong sense of collective identity. Like all groups, teams involve interaction, interdependence, shared rules, and common goals. Yet a team is distinct in two respects. First, teams consist of people with diverse skills and experience. Whereas group members may have similar backgrounds and abilities, a team consists of people who have different resources. Second, members of teams tend to support one another well and develop a strong sense of collective identity (Dalcher, 2018).

Because groups consist of individuals who are interdependent and who interact over time, groups develop rules that members understand and follow. You'll recall from previous chapters that constitutive rules state what counts as what. For example, in some groups, disagreement counts as a positive sign of involvement, whereas other groups regard disagreement as negative. Regulative rules regulate how, when, and with whom we interact. For instance, a group might have regulative rules stipulating that members don't interrupt each other and that it's okay to be a few minutes late but more than 10 minutes is a sign of disregard for other group members. Groups generate rules over time in the process of interacting and figuring out what works for them.

Groups also have shared goals. People form groups to accomplish political goals, establish social programs, protest zoning decisions, and improve the well-being

Mieko When I first came here to go to school, I felt very alone. I met some other students from Japan, and we formed a group to help us feel at home in the United States. For the first year, that group was most important to me and the others because we felt uprooted. The second year, it was good but not so important because we'd all started finding ways to fit in here, and we felt more at home. When we met the first time of the third year, we decided not to be a group anymore. The reason we wanted a group no longer existed.

Question: What do you understand was the reason Mieko's group stopped existing? Do you think the group was successful in achieving its goal?

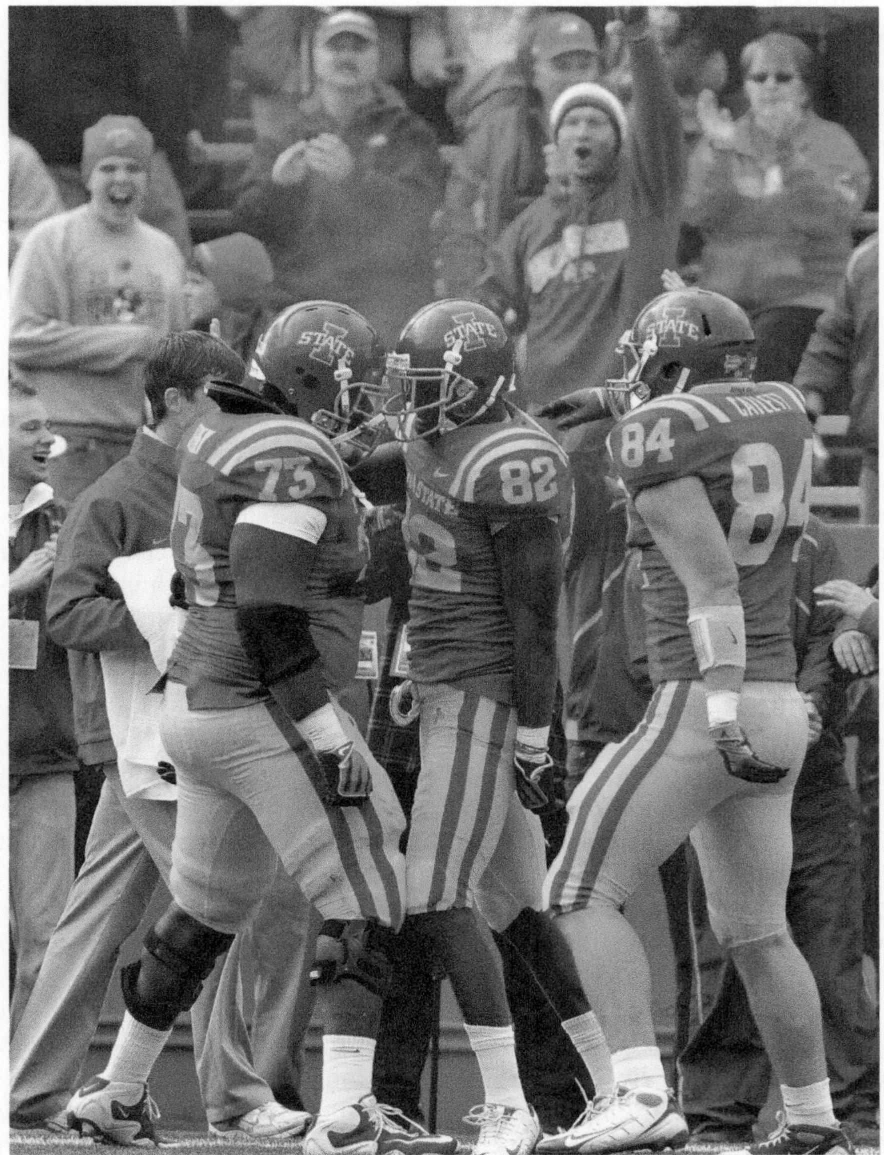

Interaction between team members often heightens commitment to collective goals.
David K Purdy/Getty Images Sport/Getty Images

of historically marginalized groups. Workers form teams to protect their benefits, develop and market products, evaluate and refine company programs, and improve productivity. Other groups form around goals such as promoting personal growth (therapy groups), sharing a life (families), socializing (singles clubs), having fun and fitting in (peer groups), or participating in sports (intramural teams). As Mieko explains in her commentary, without a common goal, a group doesn't exist. Groups end if the common objective has been achieved or if it ceases to matter to members. To better understand small groups, we'll now consider their potential values and limits, features that affect participation, and the influence of culture on group communication.

Potential Limitations and Strengths of Groups

Researchers have compared individual and group decision making. As you might expect, the research identifies both potential weaknesses and potential strengths of groups.

Potential Limitations of Groups

Significant disadvantages of group discussion are the time needed for the group process; the possibility of inadequate diversity and inclusion; and the potential for pressure to conform. All three can interfere with high-quality work from groups. A fourth potential problem is reduced individual responsibility.

Time From your own experience, you know that groups take longer to decide something than individuals. Operating solo, an individual can think through ideas efficiently and choose the one they consider best. In group discussion, however, all members must have an opportunity to voice their ideas and to respond to the ideas others put forward. In addition, groups need time to deliberate about alternative courses of action. Thus, group discussion probably is not a wise choice for routine policy making or emergency tasks. When creativity and thoroughness are important, however, the values of groups may outweigh the disadvantage of time.

Lack of Diversity and Inclusion People from specific backgrounds (such as women, Black people, disabled people, and LGBTQ+ people) have historically been marginalized or excluded from various arenas and groups. If an organization assigns only one person from such a background to join a specific group, and they are outnumbered by people from a historically advantaged background, that person is at risk of **tokenization** and being assigned an unfair **burden of representation** during group discussions. This is a stressful experience for many, and it can also make it harder for them to make contributions to the group on points they would rather speak to, if the group is continuously seeking their perspective as a representative of people who share a specific background.

To avoid such inequities and foster better team environments, good leaders will ensure their organizations are practicing **inclusivity** by placing a critical mass of people from historically disadvantaged backgrounds within each group or team: not just one, but, say, three or more (Sherrer, 2018). Good leaders will also actively practice and encourage their team members to practice cultural humility, which (as discussed in Chapter 1) means being open-minded and respectful about cultural differences, willing to learn, and aware of one's own cultural biases.

Tokenization Hiring or including a person from a historically marginalized group for the appearance of diversity, in a way that is not truly inclusive.

Burden of representation When only one person from a historically marginalized group is part of a team, that person may feel pressed to speak for *all* members of that group.

Inclusivity Ensuring all people, regardless of background, feel welcome within a group, with equal access to opportunities and resources and without experiencing tokenization in the process.

Conformity Pressures Groups also have the potential to suppress individuals and encourage conformity. This can happen in two ways. First, conformity pressure may exist when a majority of members has an opinion different from that of a minority of members or a single member. It's hard to hold out for your perspective when most of your peers have a different one.

Second, conformity pressures may arise when one member is extremely charismatic, powerful, or prestigious. Even if that person is all alone in a point of view, they may have sufficient status to sway others. Sometimes a high-status member doesn't intend to influence others and may not overtly exert pressure.

In effective groups, all members understand and resist conformity pressures. They realize that a high-status member isn't necessarily smarter than others, that the majority is sometimes wrong, and that the minority, even a minority of one, is sometimes right.

Lance I used to belong to a creative writing group where all of us helped each other improve our writing. We were all equally vocal, and we had a lot of good discussions and even disagreements when the group first started. But then one member of the group got a story of hers accepted by a big magazine, and all of a sudden we thought of her as a better writer than any of us. She didn't act any different, but we saw her as more accomplished, so when she said something, everybody listened and nobody disagreed. It was like a wet blanket on our creativity because her opinion just carried too much weight once she got published.

Question: Lance's anecdote is a good example of a high-status member influencing the group without realizing it. Based on what you've learned so far, what are some ways you think the group members could have resisted the conformity pressure they experienced in this situation?

Reduced Individual Responsibility A third potential disadvantage of group work is the possibility of **social loafing**, which exists when members of a group exert less effort than they would if they worked alone (Zhu & Wang, 2018). If an individual is charged with a task and the task doesn't get done, the individual can be held accountable. When a group is charged with a task, however, members may have less of a sense of accountability for the end product.

social loafing Exists when members of a group exert less effort than they would if they worked alone.

Potential Strengths of Groups

Groups also have noteworthy advantages. In comparison to individuals, groups generally have greater resources, are more thorough and more creative, and generate greater commitment to decisions.

Greater Resources A group obviously exceeds any individual member in the number of ideas, perspectives, experiences, and expertise it can bring to bear on solving a problem. On a team, one member may know the technical aspects of a product, while another understands market psychology, and a third has expertise in cost analysis, and so forth (Fujishin, 2014).

Review It!

Potential Limitations of Groups:

- Time
- Lack of Diversity and Inclusion
- Conformity Pressures
- Reduced Individual Responsibility

Greater Thoroughness Groups also tend to be more thorough than individuals, probably because members act as a check-and-balance system for each other (Rothwell, 2015). The parts of an issue one member doesn't understand, another person does; the details of a plan that bore one person interest another; and the holes in a proposal that one member overlooks are recognized by others. The greater thoroughness of groups isn't simply the result of more people. The discussion process promotes more critical and more careful analysis because members propel each other's thinking. It also isn't the result of more smart people. Studies indicate that social sensitivity may have a greater influence on groups' effectiveness in problem-solving: the ability to cooperate well matters more (Woolley et al., 2010). **Synergy** is a special kind of collaborative vitality that enhances the efforts, talents, and strengths of individual members (Lippold, 2021; Rothwell, 2015).

Synergy Collaborative vitality that enhances the efforts, talents, and strengths of individual members.

Greater Creativity The third value of groups is that they are generally more creative than individuals. Any individual eventually runs out of new ideas, but groups seem to have almost infinite generative ability. As members talk, they build on each other's ideas, refine proposals, discover new possibilities in each other's comments, and so forth. Often, the result is a greater number of ideas and more creative final solutions.

Laura The first time I heard about brainstorming was on my job, when the supervisor said all of us in my department were to meet and brainstorm ways to cut costs for the company. I thought it was silly to take time to discuss cost saving when each person could just submit suggestions individually. But I was wrong. When my group started, each of us had one or two ideas—only that many. But the six of us came up with more than 25 ideas after we'd talked for an hour.

Question: Laura describes a cost-cutting brainstorming session that generated many new ideas. Why do you think this collective work resulted in more ideas than might have been generated individually? Have you ever experienced something like this in your own life?

Communication Highlight

Einstein's Mistakes

That's the title of a book by Hans Ohanian (2009). As brilliant as Albert Einstein may have been, he didn't make his great discoveries alone. He is most famous for $E = mc^2$, the equation expressing the law of relativity. However, his proof of the law contained a number of mathematical errors. Another physicist, Max Von Laue, worked out a complete and correct proof, at which point $E = mc^2$ was on scientifically solid ground.

There is also evidence that Einstein's wife, Mileva Marić—a physicist and mathematician—collaborated significantly with Einstein, and that he did not credit her for her contributions to his work (Gagnon, 2016). This kind of appropriation of their wives' expertise and labor is now known to have been widespread among male scholars and writers in the early 20th century, raising awareness of how often women's invisible labor has been involved in men's professional achievements and accolades (Mazanec, 2017).

The myth of the individual genius is popular in Western societies, in part because they place high value on individualism. However, great innovations, discoveries, and inventions usually result from alternating between the in-depth explorations of individual work and the idea exchanges that characterize group work (Bernstein & Shore, 2018). Although the norms of our society dictate that one person is most likely to get the credit—the raise, the patent, or the Nobel Prize—it takes many to do the work.

Review It!

Potential Strengths of Groups:

- Resources
- Thoroughness
- Creativity
- Commitment

Greater Commitment Finally, an important strength of groups is their potential to generate stronger commitment to decisions. The greater commitment fostered by group discussion arises from two sources. First, participation in the decision-making process enhances commitment to decisions, which is especially important if members are to be involved in implementing the decision. Second, because groups have greater resources than an individual decision maker, their decisions are more likely to take into account the perspectives of various people whose cooperation is needed to implement a decision. This is critical because a decision can be sabotaged if the people it affects dislike it or believe their perspectives weren't considered.

Greater resources, thoroughness, creativity, and commitment to group goals are powerful values of group decision making. To realize these values, however, members must be aware of the trade-off of time needed for group discussion and must resist pressures to conform, or to induce others to conform, without critical thought.

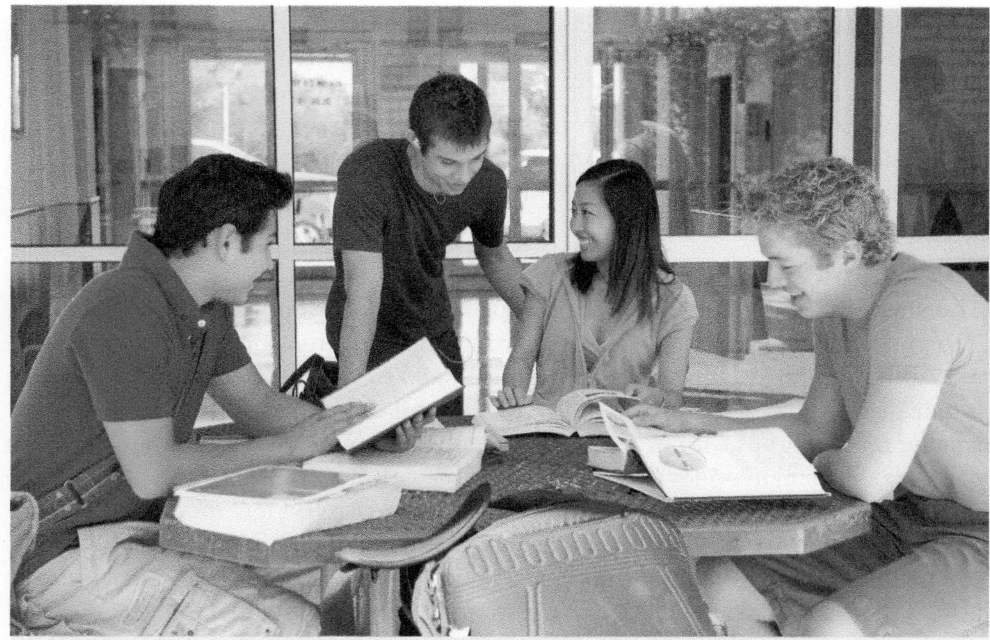

How does communication in groups affect members' commitment to group decisions?
Yellow Dog Productions/Photodisc/Getty Images

Features of Small Groups

The group strengths we've identified are realized only if members participate effectively. Thus, we need to know what influences communication in small groups. We'll consider five features of small groups that directly affect participation.

Cohesion

Cohesion is the degree of closeness, esprit de corps, and group identity. In highly cohesive groups, members consider themselves to be linked tightly together and unified in their goals. This increases members' satisfaction with the group and, in turn, their productivity (Forsyth, 2009).

cohesion Closeness among members of a group; esprit de corps.

Communication can enhance cohesion in three ways. First, communication that emphasizes the group or team and the common objectives of all members builds cohesion. Second, cohesion is fostered by communication that highlights similarities between members. A third way to enhance cohesion is by talking in ways that allow all members to feel valued and part of the group.

Cohesion and participation influence each other reciprocally. Cohesion is promoted when all members participate. At the same time, because cohesion generates a feeling of identity and involvement, once established, it fosters participation. Encouraging all members to be involved and attending responsively to everyone's contributions generally foster cohesion and continued participation.

Although cohesion is important for effective group communication, too much cohesion can cause problems. When members are extremely close, they may be less critical of each other's ideas and less willing to engage in the analysis and arguments necessary for the best outcomes. When groups are too cohesive, they may engage in

groupthink The cessation of critical, independent thought on the part of a group's members about ideas generated by the group.

groupthink, a process in which members cease to think critically and independently about ideas generated by the group. Groupthink can be harmful; for example, when it occurs in health care settings, it may impede effective patient care (DiPierro et al., 2021; Cleary et al., 2019). Members perceive their group so positively that they share the illusion that it cannot make bad decisions. Consequently, they are less careful in evaluating ideas, which can result in inferior group outcomes.

Group Size

The sheer number of people in a group affects the amount of communication. The greater the number of people in a group, the fewer the contributions any individual may make. Because participation is linked to satisfaction and commitment, larger groups may generate less satisfaction and commitment to decisions than smaller ones. Groups with nine or more members may form cliques and may be less cohesive than smaller ones (Benenson, Gordon, & Roy, 2000).

Groups can be too small as well as too large. With too few members, a group has limited resources, which eliminates one of the primary advantages of groups. Also, in very small groups, members may be unwilling to disagree or criticize each other's ideas because alienating one person in a three- or four-person group would dramatically diminish the group. Five to seven members seems to be the ideal size for a small group meeting (Gomez, 2017).

Molly The worst group I was ever in had three members. We were supposed to have five, but two dropped out after the first meeting, so there were three of us to come up with proposals for artistic programs for the campus. Nobody would say anything against anybody else's ideas, even if we thought they were bad. For myself, I know I held back from criticizing a lot of times because I didn't want to offend either of the other two. We came up with some really bad ideas because we were so small we couldn't risk arguing.

Question: The dynamic Molly describes is common in small groups. Aside from inviting new members to join their group, what do you think the small group of three could have done to encourage the kind of open critique necessary to come up with better ideas?

Power Structure

power The ability to influence others; a feature of small groups that affects participation.

power over The ability to help or harm others. Power over others usually is communicated in ways that highlight the status and influence of the person using the power.

power to The ability to empower others to reach their goals. People who use power to help others generally do not highlight their own status and influence.

Power structure is a third feature that influences participation in small groups. **Power** is the ability to influence others (Rothwell, 2015; Young et al., 2001). There are different kinds of power, or ways of influencing others.

Power over is the ability to help or harm others. This form of power usually is expressed in ways that highlight the status and visibility of the person wielding influence. A group leader might exert positive *power over* a member by providing mentoring, positive reports to superiors, and visibility in the group. A leader could also exert negative *power over* a member by withholding these benefits, assigning unpleasant tasks, and responding negatively to the member's communication during group meetings.

Power to is the ability to empower others to reach their goals. *Power to* is expressed in creating opportunities for others, recognizing achievements and facilitating others in accomplishing their goals (Conrad & Poole, 2012). Group members use *power to* foster a win–win group climate in which each member's success is seen as advancing collective work.

Stanley The different kinds of power we discussed make me think of my high school. The principal came over the intercom to make announcements or lecture us on improper behaviors and threaten us about what was going to happen if we misbehaved. The teachers were the ones with power to. Most of them worked to empower us. They were the ones who gave us encouragement and praise. They were the ones who helped us believe in ourselves and reach our goals.

The power structure of a group refers to the distribution of power among various members. If all members of a group have equal power, the group has a *distributed power structure.* On the other hand, if one or more members have greater power than others, the group has a *hierarchical power structure.* In some cases, hierarchy takes the form of one person who is more powerful than all others, who are equal in power to each other. In other cases, hierarchy may be more complicated, with more than two levels of power. A leader might have the greatest power, three others might have power equal to each other's but less than the leader's, and two other members might have little power.

How is power related to participation? First, members with high power tend to be the centers of group communication: They talk more, and others talk more to them. **Social climbing** is the attempt to increase personal status in a group by winning the approval of high-status members. If social climbing doesn't work to increase the status of the climber, they may become a marginal participant in the group. In addition, members with a great deal of power often have greater influence on group decisions. Not surprisingly, high-power members tend to find group discussion more satisfying than members with less power (Young et al., 2001). This makes sense because those with power get to participate more and get their way more often.

social climbing The attempt to increase personal status in a group by winning the approval of high-status members.

Communication Highlight

Five Bases of Power

What is power? How does a person get it? There is more than one answer to each of these questions because there are different sources of power (Arnold & Feldman, 1986).

Reward power	The ability to give people things they value, such as attention, approval, public praise, promotions, and raises
Coercive power	The ability to punish others through demotions, firing, and undesirable assignments
Legitimate power	The organizational role, such as manager, supervisor, or CEO, that results in others' compliance
Expert power	Influence derived from expert knowledge or experience
Referent power	Influence based on an individual's likeability, personal charisma and personality

Power not only influences communication but also is influenced by communication. In other words, how members communicate can affect the power they acquire. People who demonstrate expertise in the group's task and who help build group cohesion tend to acquire power quickly.

Interaction Patterns

Another important influence on participation is the group's interaction patterns. Some groups are centralized so that most or all communication is funneled through one or two people (Figure 8.1). Other groups have decentralized patterns, in which communication is more balanced and thus more satisfying to everyone. As you might suspect, the power of individual members and the power structure of the group often affect interaction patterns. If one or two members have greater power than others, a centralized pattern of interaction is likely to emerge. Decentralized patterns are more typical when members have relatively equal power.

Group Norms

norms Informal rules that guide how members of a group or culture think, feel, act, and interact. Norms define what is normal or appropriate in various situations.

A final small-group feature that affects communication is **norms.** Norms are standardized guidelines that regulate how members act and how they interact with each other. Our definition of a small group, in fact, emphasizes that individuals must share understandings about their conduct. Like rules in relationships, a group's norms define what is allowed, what is not allowed, and what kind of participation is rewarded.

Group norms regulate all aspects of a group's life, from the trivial to the critical. Fairly inconsequential norms may regulate whether members take breaks and eat during meetings. More substantive norms govern how carefully members prepare

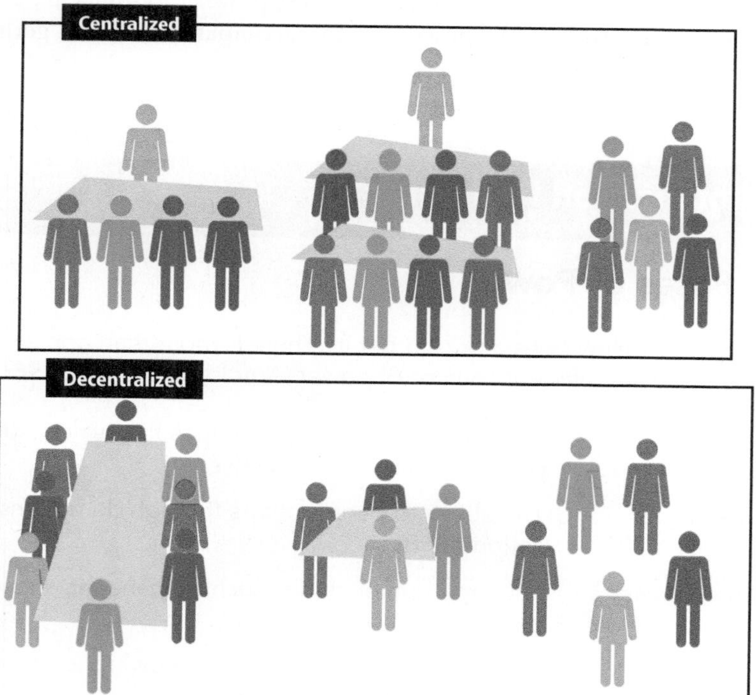

Figure 8.1
Group Interaction Patterns

for meetings, how critically they analyze ideas, how well they listen to one another, and how they deal with differences and conflict.

Norms grow directly out of interaction. For example, at a group's initial meeting, one person might dismiss another's idea as dumb, and several members might not pay attention when others are speaking. If this continues for long, a norm of disrespect will develop. On the other hand, when one member says an idea is dumb, another person might counter by saying, "I don't think so. I think we ought to consider the point." If others then do consider the idea, a norm of respectful communication may develop.

Because norms become entrenched, it's important to pay attention to them from the outset of a group's existence. By noticing patterns and tendencies, you can exert influence over the norms that take hold in groups.

Review It!

Features of Groups that Affect Communication:

- Cohesion
- Size
- Power Structure
- Interaction Patterns
- Norms

Virtual Group Communication

Whereas physical copresence was once required for groups and teams to exist and work together, that is no longer the case. Today, many groups may operate remotely, relying on virtual conferences. In fact, as the available technology has improved and workplace norms have changed, virtual employment has increased by 91% over the past decade (Norwich University Online, 2020). The Covid-19 pandemic accelerated this shift, with the percentage of people working remotely jumping from 3.4% at the beginning of 2020 to 43% in the first week of April 2020 (Norwich University Online, 2020).

Even not accounting for the unique challenges of the pandemic, it's easy to understand why virtual teams and remote employment have soared in popularity over time. When employees work from home, the employer is spared the cost of leasing and maintaining office space and equipment. They can also eliminate the expense of flights for members who live in different locations and they save members' time by not requiring packing and travel.

Virtual groups have unique strengths and challenges. Think about your own experiences in virtual group meetings. How can you tell when it is a good time for you to speak? How does this differ from your experiences with speaking during in-person meetings?
Chris Montgomery/Unsplash.com

Yet, virtual teams also pose challenges. To be effective, virtual teams must adapt to the computer-mediated communication (CMC) environment in which they operate. In other words, effective leadership and participation in virtual teams requires adjustments from face-to-face style, and there is some evidence that as more businesses shifted to remote operations, team cohesion may have become lowered as a result of lack of face-to-face contact (Norwich University Online, 2020).

The two greatest challenges for virtual teams are limited nonverbal cues and constraints on building relationships and group climate (Virtual Team Challenges, n.d.). Many of the nonverbal cues we take for granted in face-to-face interaction are absent or limited in virtual groups. How do members know when it's their turn to speak? How do they know how others interpret their ideas? How do they know whether others are listening? Missing also are some of the informal interactions that build relationships among members of face-to-face groups. There is no water cooler where people get comfortable with each other through casual conversations. The literal pat on the back or smile that build report may not be possible in virtual groups.

Those who have studied best practices in virtual groups recommend various strategies for meeting the key challenges of virtual groups and fostering their resiliency (Kilcullen et al., 2021; Kirkman & Stoverink, 2021), including the following:

1. Set group norms, including agreed-upon guidelines for how collaboration, decision-making, and responding to requests will occur.
2. Build team confidence by establishing clear goals and a shared vision for the group.
3. Select a team leader who communicates frequently and individually with team members. They should work to reinforce organizational norms; be engaging during conversations; and be disciplined about responding to calls and emails in a timely fashion, showing a high level of care and concern for the team members' and the team's best interest.
4. Create and use support systems like team building activities and delivering and receiving feedback in a way that ensures the virtual work environment is psychologically safe, emphasizing inclusivity and accessibility and encouraging perspective-taking among group members.
5. Communicate frequently and clearly and encourage pro-diversity beliefs. Use technology to increase everyone's opportunities to contribute and discuss mistakes constructively.
6. Be flexible with work schedules and adaptable to changing conditions, such as work-life conflicts. Cross-train team members on each other's roles and responsibilities and inspire individuals to stretch beyond what they know themselves to be capable of, developing new strengths and building confidence.

Guidelines for Communicating in Groups and Teams

To realize the strengths of group work and avoid its potential weaknesses, members must participate constructively, provide leadership, and manage conflict so that it benefits the group and its outcomes.

Participate Constructively

Because communication is the heart of all groups, the ways members communicate are extremely important to the effectiveness of group process. There are four kinds of communication in groups (Table 8.1). The first three—*task communication, procedural communication,* and *climate communication*—are constructive because they foster good group processes and outcomes. The fourth kind of communication is *egocentric,* or *dysfunctional, communication.* It tends to detract from group cohesion and effective decision making.

Table 8.1 Types of Communication in Groups

Task Communication	Climate Communication
Initiates ideas Seeks information Gives information Elaborates ideas Evaluates and offers critical analysis	Establishes and maintains healthy climate Energizes group process Harmonizes ideas Recognizes others Reconciles conflicts Builds enthusiasm for group
Procedural Communication	**Egocentric Communication**
Establishes agenda Provides orientation Curbs digressions Guides participation Coordinates ideas Summarizes others' contributions Records group progress	Aggresses toward others Blocks ideas Seeks personal recognition (brags) Dominates interaction Pleads for special interests Confesses, self-discloses, and seeks personal help unrelated to the group's focus Disrupts tasks Devalues others Trivializes group and its work

Task Communication **Task communication** focuses on the problems, issues, or information before a group. It provides ideas and information, ensures members' understanding, and uses reasoning to evaluate ideas and information. Task contributions may initiate ideas, respond to others' ideas, or provide critical evaluation of information before the group. Task contributions also include asking for ideas and evaluation from others. Task comments emphasize the content of a group's work.

task communication One of three constructive forms of participation in group decision making; focuses on giving and analyzing information and ideas.

Procedural Communication If you've ever participated in a disorganized group, you understand the importance of **procedural communication**, which helps a group get organized and stay on track. Procedural contributions establish an agenda, coordinate the comments of different members, and record group progress. In addition, procedural contributions may curb digressions and tangents, summarize progress, and regulate participation so that everyone has opportunities to speak and nobody dominates.

procedural communication One of three constructive ways of participating in group decision making. Procedural communication orders ideas and coordinates the contributions of members.

Climate Communication A group is more than a task unit. It also includes people who are involved in a relationship that can be more or less pleasant and open. **Climate communication** focuses on creating and maintaining a supportive climate that encourages members to contribute cooperatively and evaluate ideas critically (Fujishin, 2014). Climate comments emphasize a group's strengths and progress, encourage cooperative interaction, recognize others' contributions, reconcile conflicts, and build enthusiasm for the group and its work.

climate communication One of three constructive forms of participation in group decision making. Climate communication focuses on creating and sustaining an open, engaged atmosphere for discussion.

Egocentric Communication The final kind of group communication is not recommended but does sometimes occur in groups. **Egocentric communication,** or dysfunctional communication, is used to block others or to call attention to

egocentric communication An unconstructive form of group contribution that blocks others or calls attention to oneself.

oneself. It detracts from group progress because it is self-centered rather than group centered. Examples of egocentric talk are devaluing another member's ideas, trivializing the group's efforts, aggressing toward other members, bragging about one's own accomplishments, dominating, disrupting group work, and pleading for special causes that aren't in a group's interest. Another form of egocentric communication is making cynical remarks that undermine group cohesion and enthusiasm.

Task, procedural, and climate communication work together to foster productive, organized, and comfortable group discussion. Egocentric communication, on the other hand, can sabotage a group's climate and hinder its progress. Communicating clearly that egocentric behavior will not be tolerated in your group fosters norms for effective interaction.

Figure 8.2 provides an excerpt from a group discussion will give you concrete examples of each type of group communication. Each comment is coded as one of the four types of communication we have identified. This excerpt includes all four kinds of communication that we've discussed. Notice how skillfully Ana communicates to defuse tension between Xavier and Brianna before it disrupts the group. You might also notice that Connor provides the primary procedural leadership for the group, and Bob is effective in interjecting humor.

In effective group discussion, communication meets the task, procedural, and climate demands of teamwork and avoids egocentrism that detracts from group progress and cohesion. By understanding how varied types of communication affect collective work, you can decide when to use each type of communication in your own participation in groups. Although you may not be proficient in all three valuable kinds of group communication right now, with commitment and practice you can develop the skill.

Review It!

Types of Group Communication

- Task
- Procedural
- Climate
- Egocentric

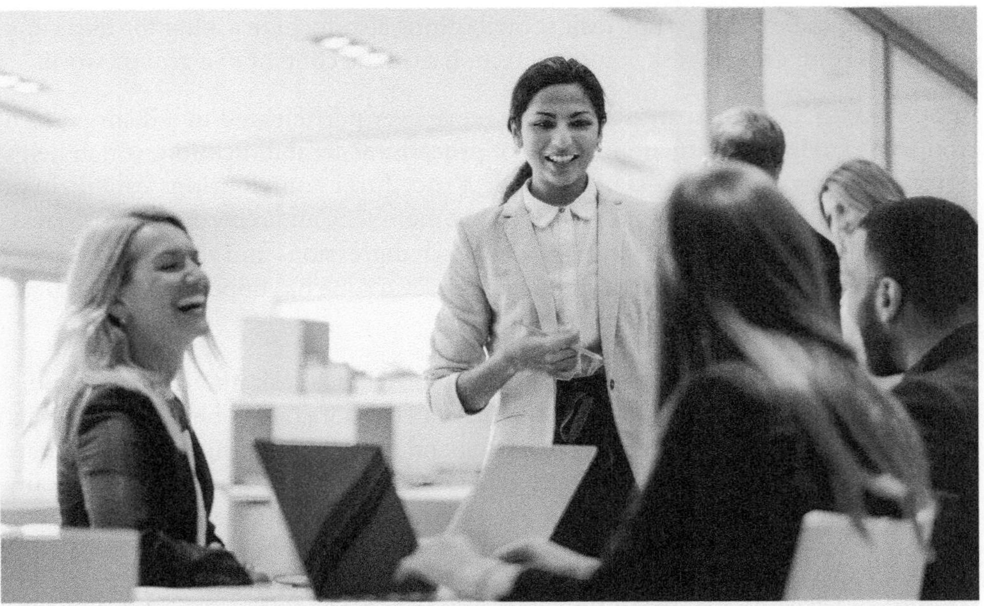

Effective teams have good climate communication, along with task and procedural communication.
gremlin/E+/Getty Images

CONNOR: We might start by discussing what we see as the goal of this group. (procedural)
BRIANNA: That's a good idea. (climate)
XAVIER: I think our goal is to come up with a better meal plan for students on campus. (task)
CONNOR: What do you mean by "better"? Do you mean cheaper or more varied or more tasteful? (task)
ANA: I think we need to consider all three. (task)
CONNOR: Well, we probably do care about all three, but maybe we should talk about one at a time so that we can keep our discussion focused. (procedural)
XAVIER: Okay, I vote we focus first on taste—like it would be good if there were some taste to the food on campus! (task and climate [humor])
BRIANNA: Do you mean taste itself or quality of food, which might also consider nutrition? (task)
XAVIER: Pure taste! When I'm hungry, I don't think about what's good for me, just what tastes good. (task)
BRIANNA: Well, maybe that's a reason why we might want the food service to think about nutrition—because we don't. (task)
XAVIER: If you're into healthy food, that's your problem. I don't think nutrition is something that's important in the food service on campus. (task; possibly also egocentric if his tone toward Brianna was snide)
CONNOR: Let's do this: Let's talk first about what we would like in terms of taste itself. (procedural) Before we meet next time, it might be a good idea for one of us to talk with the manager of the cafeteria to see whether they have to meet any nutritional guidelines in what they serve. (task)
ANA: I'll volunteer to do that. (task)
CONNOR: Great. Thanks, Ana. (climate)
XAVIER: I'll volunteer to do taste testing! (climate [humor])
BRIANNA: With how quickly you inhale food, you'd better not. (egocentric)
XAVIER: Yeah, like you have a right to criticize me. (egocentric)
ANA: Look, none of us is here to criticize anyone else. We're here because we want to improve the food service on campus. (climate) We've decided we want to focus first on taste (procedural), so who has an idea of how we go about studying that? (task)

Figure 8.2
Excerpt of Group Communication

Provide Leadership

All groups need leadership. However, leadership is not necessarily one individual. Instead, leadership is a set of behaviors that helps a group maintain a good climate and accomplish tasks in an organized way. Sometimes one member provides guidance on task and procedures, and another member focuses on building a healthy group climate by recognizing and responding to members' ideas and feelings (Covey, 2012) as well as by encouraging cohesion. It's also not uncommon for different people to provide leadership at different times in a group's life. The person who guides the group at the outset may not be the one who advances the group's work in later phases. Even when an official leader exists, other members may contribute much of the communication that provides the overall leadership of a group.

Leadership is maintaining set of communication functions that establishes a good working climate, organizes group processes, and ensures that discussion is substantive. Whether a group has one or multiple leaders, the primary responsibilities of leaders are to organize discussion, to ensure sound research and reasoning, to promote norms for mindful listening and clear verbal and nonverbal communication,

leadership Set of communicative functions that assists groups in accomplishing tasks efficiently, staying organized, and maintaining a good climate.

to create a productive climate, to build group morale, and to discourage egocentric communication that detracts from group efforts. Krystal's commentary provides an example of effective shared leadership.

Krystal The most effective group I've ever been in had three leaders. I was the person who understood our task best, so I contributed the most to critical thinking about the issues. But Belinda was the one who kept us organized. She really knew how to see tangents and get us off of them, and she knew when it was time to move on from one stage of work to the next. She also pulled ideas together to coordinate our thinking. Kevin was the climate leader. He could always tell a joke if things got tense, and he was the best person I ever saw for recognizing others' contributions. I couldn't point to any one leader in that group, but we sure did have good leadership.

Question: Having multiple leaders within a group can be a great way to draw upon different people's leadership strengths. What do you think are the conditions necessary for multiple leaders to emerge within a single group? What would it take to help make this kind of diffusion of leadership responsibilities in a future group of your own?

In sum, whether provided by one member or several, effective leadership involves communication that advances a group's task, organizes deliberations, builds group morale, controls disruptions, and fosters a constructive climate.

Manage Conflict Constructively

Conflict is natural in groups and it can be productive. Conflict stimulates thinking, helps members consider diverse perspectives and avoid groupthink, and enlarges members' understanding of issues involved in making decisions and generating ideas (Rothwell, 2015). To achieve these goals, however, conflict must be managed skillfully. Although many of us may not enjoy conflict, we can nonetheless recognize its value—even its necessity—for effective group work.

Disruptive Conflict Effective members promote conflict that is constructive for the group's tasks and climate and discourage conflict that disrupts healthy discussion. Conflict is disruptive when it interferes with effective work and a healthy communication climate. Typically, disruptive conflict is marked by egocentric communication that is competitive as members vie with each other to wield influence and get their way. Accompanying the competitive tone of communication is a self-interested focus in which members talk about only their own ideas, solutions, and points of view. The competitive and self-centered communication in disruptive conflict fosters diminished cohesion and a win–lose orientation to conflict.

Group climate deteriorates during disruptive conflict. Members may feel unsafe volunteering ideas because others might harshly evaluate or scorn them. Personal attacks may occur as members criticize one another's motives or attack one another personally. Recall the discussion in Chapter 7 about communication that fosters defensiveness; we saw that defensive climates are promoted by communication that expresses evaluation, superiority, control orientation, neutrality, certainty, and closed-mindedness. Just as these forms of communication undermine healthy

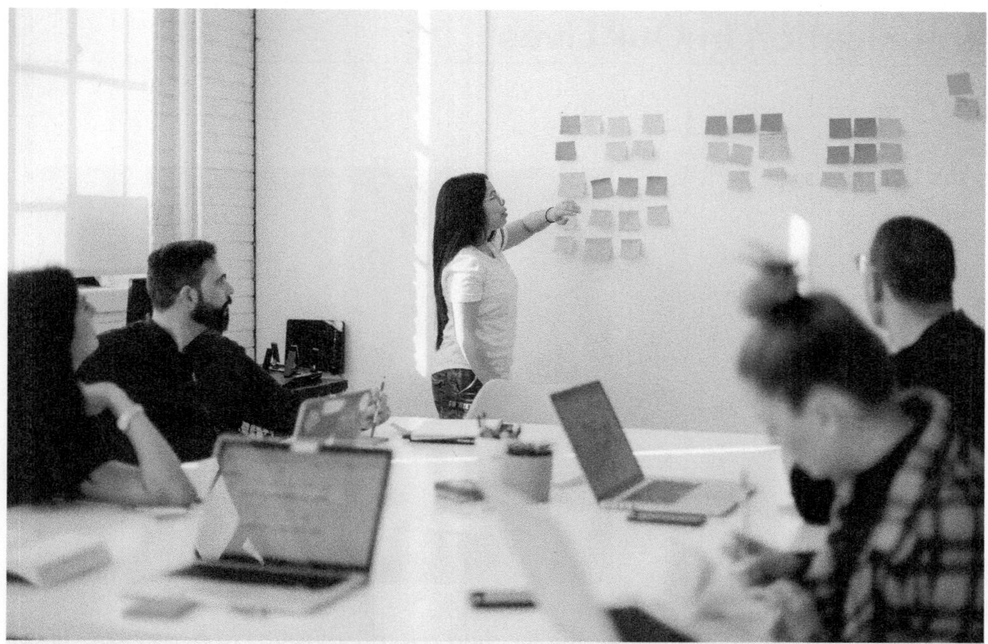

Effective leadership encourages all members to participate constructively.
Jason Goodman/Unsplash.com

climates in personal relationships, they also interfere with group climate and productivity (Fujishin, 2014).

Constructive Conflict Constructive conflict occurs when members understand that disagreements are natural and can help them achieve their shared goals. Communication that expresses respect for diverse opinions reflects this attitude. Members also emphasize shared interests and goals. The cooperative focus of communication encourages a win–win orientation. Discussion is open and supportive of differences, and disagreements focus on issues, not personalities.

To encourage constructive conflict, communication should demonstrate openness to different ideas, willingness to alter opinions when good reasons exist, and respect for the integrity of other members and the perspectives they express. Also, keep in mind that conflict grows out of the entire system of group communication. Thus, constructive conflict is most likely to occur when members have established a supportive, open climate of communication. Group climate is built throughout the life of a group, beginning with the first meeting. It is important to communicate in ways that build a strong climate from the start so that it is already established when conflict arises.

Chapter Summary

In this chapter, we've considered what small groups are and how they operate. We identified potential weaknesses and strengths of groups and discussed features of groups that affect group process. We then considered how to maximize the potential of digital communication in group contexts. Guidelines for group work are to participate effectively, provide leadership, and manage conflict.

Experiencing Communication in Our Lives

Case Study: The Class Gift

Apply what you've learned in this chapter by analyzing the following case study, using the accompanying questions as a guide.

Andy, Erika, Camilla, Finley, and Jenn are in charge of deciding what their graduating class will give to their university as the class gift. This is the second meeting of their group.

Finley *(looking around at the other members)*: Hi, everyone—it's good to see you all again.

Camilla: We are definitely the best group on campus!

Andy: We're looking fine, for sure.

Finley *(glances at watch)*: Okay, all of you fine-looking people *(smiles at Andy)*, it's 10 minutes after. Has anyone heard from Jenn?

Erika, Camilla, and Andy shake their heads and shrug.

Finley: Okay, well, let's get started and hope she joins us in a couple of minutes. I want to get rolling on this project!

Erika: Hear, hear! I'm really psyched about doing this. Our class is really lit, and I want us to come up with a gift that's as lit as we are.

Andy: It would have to *on fire*! *(The four laugh).*

Finley: Okay, then what can we do for our class gift? Anybody have a suggestion?

Camilla: When we met last week, one idea we all kind of liked was giving a sculpture— you know, for the main quad, where everyone would see it.

Andy: Yeah, I agree; that's the best idea we came up with.

Camilla: The image I have is a sculpture of a student studying—like maybe reading a book.

Erika: Hold on. Studying is *not* lit.

Andy: Definitely not. I know--maybe we could have a sculpture of players on our basketball team?

Erika: Oh, please, that's even worse.

Jenn walks in and pulls a chair into the circle with the others. Erika and Finley smile at her as she joins them. Camilla gives her a quick hug.

Andy: Hey, Jenn. Glad you made it.

Jenn: Sorry I'm late. I was meeting with a study group for my Literature essay exam tomorrow.

Camilla *(smiling mischievously)*: I rest my case. Jenn was studying—and her subject was *LIT*!

Erika *(groaning at the pun)*: Are you making Dad jokes again?

Finley: Wait a minute, let's give Camilla's idea a chance. A sculpture. I kind of like the idea of a sculpture.

Jenn: That would be unique. I don't think any other class has given a sculpture.

Erika: I'm not against a sculpture. I just don't think a student studying is the most exciting thing. Is it really "us"?

Finley: Maybe not the most exciting, but it really gets at what being a student is all about.

Andy: Fair. I mean, the sculpture should celebrate this school and its values.

Finley: What about you, Erika? Is this idea working for you yet?

Erika: Personally, I don't love it. But the most important thing is that we come up with something we can all support, and you all seem to like this idea.

Camilla: I don't think any of us is settled on the idea yet. Maybe we could come up with a different kind of sculpture that we'd *all* love. Does anyone have a different idea for the sculpture?

Erika, Finley, and Andy shrug no.

Jenn: How about a sculpture of a student in regalia—as if the student is graduating? Isn't that the goal of being here?

Erika: That's interesting—instead of symbolizing studying to get to the goal, we could symbolize achieving it.

Andy: I don't know. Those regalia are pretty weird looking, and students only wear them one day. Students might not identify with that as much as a sculpture of a student in everyday clothes. This isn't Hogwarts.

Jenn *(laughing)*: Good point.... You could be right.

Camilla: Yeah, but we do identify with the *goal* that the regalia symbolize. I don't know that students wouldn't identify with a sculpture of a student wearing the regalia.

Finley: I think they might.

Erika: I'm not convinced.

Camilla: We're just speculating and stating our own opinions. Let's do some research to find out what students think. Why don't we do a couple of sketches—one of a student studying and one of a student in regalia—and do a survey asking students which they like better?

Jenn: Good idea, but can we keep brainstorming first? We might come up with more sculpture ideas to include if we talk longer.

Questions for Analysis and Discussion

1. Apply material from this chapter to analyze the features of this small group.
2. How effective is the climate communication in this group?

Key Concepts

burden of representation
climate communication
cohesion
egocentric communication
group
groupthink
inclusivity
leadership
norms
power
power over
power to
procedural communication
social climbing
social loafing
synergy
task communication
team
tokenization

For Further Reflection and Discussion

1. Test the claim that groups tend to be more creative than individuals. Ask five students individually to write down all the ways they can think of to improve a popular social media platform. When they have run out of ideas, ask them to form a group and generate as many improvements for the platform as they can. Did the individuals or the group produce more ideas?
2. Interview a professional in the field you hope to enter after college. Ask them to identify the different work groups and teams they have been part of in the past year. How many of the types of groups and teams described in this chapter do your interviewee name?
3. What ethical responsibilities accompany having power in a group? What are ethical and unethical uses of power in group and team situations?
4. Observe a group discussion on your campus or in your community. Record members' contributions by classifying them as task, climate, procedural, or egocentric. Does the communication you observe explain the effectiveness or ineffectiveness of the group?
5. **Workplace.** Interview a professional in the field you hope to enter after college. Ask them to identify how various groups and teams discussed in this chapter are used on the job. If you are already employed in a career, reflect on your experiences with groups on the job.
6. **Engagement.** This chapter points out that groups exist within cultural contexts that affect how they operate. Talk with classmates or other students who were raised in a culture that is different from your own. Ask them what values of their culture are reflected in the ways groups operate.

9

> Find a job you like and you add five days to every week.
>
> **H. Jackson Brown, Jr.**

Communication in Organizations

Learning Objectives

After studying the topics in this chapter, you should be able to:

1. Explain the influence of company culture on organizational communication.
2. Describe various types of organizational communication.
3. Draw on personal experience to provide examples of organizational communication, such as rites, rituals, stories, and structures.
4. Evaluate the advantages and disadvantages of digital technology on organizational communication.
5. Explain the role and effects of online surveillance in organizational communication.
6. Apply chapter guidelines to improve your effectiveness when communicating in and with organizations, despite common barriers.

Should employers monitor employees' use of digital media during work hours?

A patient dies after what should have been routine surgery—one of the approximately 100,000 deaths that result from preventable medical errors in United States hospitals each year (Rodziewicz, Houseman, & Kipskind, 2022). As soon as the patient is pronounced dead, the blame game begins. The doctor in charge of the case claims the nurse was not monitoring vital signs. The nurse insists that they noted drops in the patient's blood pressure on the chart, but the doctor didn't pay attention. The doctor says the nurse should have directly mentioned the drop, not just made a note on the chart. The nurse replies that the doctor has previously responded angrily and defensively to being informed about patient information that's also on the chart. Both the nurse and the doctor seem more interested in defending themselves than figuring out what went wrong. That's almost inevitable in a culture of blame.

When assigning blame is a priority, staff may hide errors rather than report them, rather than talk honestly about what—not who—is the problem (Rodziewicz, Houseman, & Kipskind, 2022). Within institutions, a culture of blame functions to shield organizations from criticism and punitive action, scapegoating individual practitioners for systemic issues (Kellman, 2022). These issues need to be addressed to improve patient care and reduce risks, and health care organizations can do so by cultivating a culture of safety (Sim et al., 2022). A safety culture exists when management and employees share a strong commitment to ensuring the safety of the work environment and to making safety of patients and employees paramount. In a safety culture, employees at all ranks feel free to report errors and near misses without fear of being reprimanded or punished. Open communication increases awareness of challenges to safety and enables teamwork in overcoming them.

To assess their culture, many hospitals routinely survey staff, asking them to rate their organization's emphasis on teamwork, openness in communicating about errors, and freedom to question actions and decisions, including those of staff with higher authority. Hospitals can use these survey data to encourage more open communication. Many hospital leaders prioritize strengthening their institutions' safety culture, which studies show leads to better patient care and cost savings alike (Sim et al., 2022).

Communication is central to cultivating a safety culture—or any other kind of organizational culture. It is communication—upward, downward, lateral, internal, and external—that defines an organization's identity, guides its actions, and specifies members' roles and responsibilities.

Communication in organizations is the topic of this chapter. In the first section, we identify key features of organizational communication. Next, we discuss the overall culture of the organization, which establishes the context for communication among members of the organization. In the third section of the chapter, we consider the impact of digital media's increasing presence in organizational contexts. Finally, we discuss three guidelines for communicating in organizations in our era.

Key Features of Organizations

Much of what you've learned in previous chapters applies to communication in organizations. For instance, effective communication on the job requires listening, verbal and nonverbal competence, appreciation of cultural differences, and the ability to work well on teams. To build on what you've already learned, we'll discuss three features of organizations: structure, communication networks, and links to external environments.

Structure

structure In an organization, the set of procedures, relationships, and practices that provides predictability for members so that they understand roles, procedures, and expectations and so that work gets done.

Structure orders activity in organizations. It is a set of procedures, relationships, and practices that provides predictability for members of an organization so that they understand roles, procedures, and expectations related to doing work.

Most modern organizations rely on a hierarchical structure, which assigns different levels of power and status to different members and specifies who is to communicate with whom about what. Rigidly hierarchical organizations have strict rules about following the chain of command. In more loosely structured organizations, members may communicate more openly with their own peers and with peers of their supervisors.

Communication Networks

communication networks Formal and informal links between members of organizations.

A second characteristic of organizational communication is that it occurs in **communication networks**, which are formal and informal links between people (Modaff, Butler, & DeWine, 2011). In most organizations, people belong to multiple networks. For example, faculty belong to social networks that include colleagues; task networks consisting of people with whom they discuss teaching, research, and

Virtual networks are essential in professional life.
AntonioDiaz/Shutterstock.com

departmental and university issues; and ad hoc networks that arise to respond to specific crises or issues. Overlaps among networks to which we belong ensure that faculty will interact with many people in a university.

In addition to physical networks, virtual networks are common in most professions (Kurtzberg, 2014; Rothwell, 2015). Virtual networks are essential for employees who work remotely. In 2019, an estimated 8.9 million or 5.7% of working Americans engaged in remote employment (American Community Survey). After the start of the Covid-19 pandemic, this number jumped to 48.7 million, or 35% of the workforce. A 2021 survey found that about 83% of employees who can work from home hoped to continue doing so at least one day a week, while 54% hoped to continue to working from home most of the time or full-time (Coate, 2021). Due to changes in workplace culture and work-life balance many people experienced during the Covid-19 pandemic, analysts expect that about 22% of the workforce will work remotely by 2025 (Apollo Technical, 2022). Laptops, phones, high-speed Internet, and various applications make this kind of work possible. As we noted in Chapter 8, although virtual workplaces pose challenges, the benefits are substantial.

Links to External Environments

Like other communication systems, organizations are embedded in contexts that affect how they work and whether they succeed or fail (Siebold, Hollingshead, & Yoon, 2013). In other words, an organization's operation cannot be understood simply by looking only within the organization. We must also grasp how it is related to and affected by the larger environment.

The Covid-19 pandemic is a good case study in how much context matters. The broader context of the pandemic had many consequences for organizations and businesses. For example:

- At the start of the pandemic, when little was known about the Coronavirus and no vaccine existed to prevent or mitigate it, shutdowns became commonplace as public health officials attempted to contain the virus's spread by asking people to stay home.
- As customers stayed home, businesses lost income and could not pay their bills. Many received Covid relief funds, but many businesses struggled and closed anyway. A brief recession occurred, in which the economy declined significantly for about two months (Center on Budget and Policy, 2020).
- As businesses cut payrolls to try to remain solvent, and those that could not closed their operations, tens of millions of people lost their jobs—especially in low-wage industries (National Bureau of Economic Research, 2021).
- As day cares and schools shut down, a child care crisis emerged. Due to widespread gender disparities in households, mothers were disproportionately burdened with child care duties, losing their jobs as a result (Miller, 2021).
- Inequalities stemming from structural racism resulted in disproportionately severe employment and economic impacts among Black people, Latino people, and other people of color (National Bureau of Economic Research, 2021).
- As businesses struggled and demanded more of employees, workers felt disrespected and underpaid, given the risks of the pandemic and how much harder it had made their home lives. The "Great Resignation" took place: People quit

their jobs at a rate higher than at any point in the previous two decades (Parker & Horowitz, 2022).

- Labor force and supply chain issues made it hard for businesses that stayed open to acquire the equipment, materials, and goods they needed to meet their obligations to clients and customers (Allianz Trade, 2021).
- By late 2020, analysts feared the supply chain would suffer from widespread insolvency taking the form of a domino effect, in which one company after another left invoices unpaid and customers unserved (Allianz Trade, 2021).
- States intervened to prevent an insolvency domino effect. They gave unprecedented amounts of aid to businesses across the market (Allianz Trade, 2021) while also providing more forms of aid to individuals and families struggling with unemployment, food insecurity, an inability to keep up with bills, and more (National Bureau of Economic Research, 2021).

Although internal factors may have contributed to particular businesses' troubles, many organizations suffered or survived because of factors outside their organizational boundaries. When external conditions are good, and when aid and support are available, even mediocre companies can survive. When external conditions are bad, and safety nets are few, many good companies can be hurt or driven out of business alongside the bad.

Either way, there are implications for individual people and families. It's important to bear in mind that those implications are often inequitable, tangled together with structural and systemic problems like racism, ableism, gender bias, socioeconomic disparities, and so on.

Question: Disabled, chronically ill, and immunocompromised people had requested communication networks, access, and remote work options for decades prior to the pandemic. What does their implementation when the general populace needed them, followed by their removal from many workplaces when the general populace did not, reveal about ableism, marginalization, and exclusion in our culture?

Review It!

Features of Organizations:

- Structure
- Communication Networks
- Links to External Environment

Organizational Culture

organizational culture Ways of thinking, acting, and understanding work that are shared by members of an organization and that reflect an organization's distinct identity.

Organizational culture consists of ways of thinking, acting, and understanding work that are shared by members of an organization and that reflect an organization's distinct identity.

Similarly to how ethnic cultures consist of meanings shared by members of the ethnic groups, organizational cultures consist of meanings shared by members of organizations. As new members of ethnic cultures are socialized into preexisting meanings and traditions, so too are new members of organizations socialized into preexisting meanings and traditions (Argyris, 2012; Eisenberg, Goodall, & Trethewey, 2013; Miller, 2014). And paralleling how a culture's way of life continues even though particular people leave or die, an organization's culture persists despite turnover.

The relationship between communication and organizational culture is reciprocal: Communication between members of an organization creates, sustains, and sometimes alters the culture. At the same time, organizational culture influences patterns of communication. Four kinds of communication that are particularly important in developing, expressing, and sustaining organizational culture are vocabularies, stories, rites and rituals, and structures.

Communication & Careers

Caution: Work May Be Hazardous to Your Health

What makes jobs stressful? Big issues such as harassment and incompetent leadership are surely stressful, but the biggest stressor may be the continuous stream of uncivil, rude behavior from bosses and coworkers. Georgetown University's McDonough School of Business Professor Christine Porath (2015) identifies common rude behaviors that take a daily toll on employees:

- Interruptions
- Walking away from a conversation
- Answering calls in the middle of meetings
- Taking credit for wins but blaming others for losses
- Not saying please and thank you
- Swearing
- Putting others down

But many employees who complain about the above rude behaviors admit to engaging in some pretty uncivil actions themselves:

- Ignoring invitations
- Not listening
- Emailing/texting during meetings
- Belittling others nonverbally
- Not saying please and thank you

Often, power dynamics are at play in uncivil actions, with sexism, ableism, racism, ageism, and other forms of discriminatory behavior taking the form of microaggressions and outright hostility.

The costs of incivility are significant. Intermittent stressors such as the above behaviors compromise the immune system and can lead to serious health conditions including ulcers and heart problems. In addition, uncivil work environments are linked to missing information and reduced cognitive processing.

Vocabularies

Similarly to how the language of an ethnic culture reflects and expresses its history, norms, values, and identity, the *vocabulary* of an organization reflects and expresses its history, norms, values, and identity.

Hierarchical Language Many organizations and professions have vocabularies that distinguish levels of status among members. The military, for example, relies on language that continually acknowledges rank (i.e., *Yes, sir*, *chain of command*), which reflects the close ties between rank, power, and privilege. Salutes, as well as stripes and medals on uniforms, are part of the nonverbal vocabulary that emphasizes rank and honors.

"I've never actually seen a corporate ladder before."

Unequal terms of address also communicate rank. For instance, the CEO may use first names ("Good morning, Bob") when speaking to employees. Unless given permission to use the CEO's first name, however, lower status members of an organization typically use *Mr.*, *Ms.*, *Sir*, or *Ma'am* to address the CEO. Colleges and universities use titles to designate faculty members' rank and status: instructor, assistant professor, associate professor, full professor, and distinguished (or chaired) professor. Faculty generally use students' first names, whereas students tend to use titles to address their teachers: Dr. Armstrong or Professor Armstrong, for example.

Masculine Language Because organizations historically have been run by White, cisgendered men, it's not surprising that many organizations have developed and continue to use language more related to such men's interests and experiences than to those of other people (Kirkland, 2015; Moseson et al., 2020; Zaidman, 2020). Consider the number of phrases in the working world that are taken from stereotypically masculine pursuits such as sports (i.e., home run, ballpark estimate, touchdown, take a big swing, develop a game plan, be a team player, take a time out, the starting lineup) and military life (i.e., battle plan, mount a campaign, plan of attack, under fire, get the big guns, defensive move, offensive strike), or from male sexual parts and activities (i.e., an arrogant person is *cocky*; you can *hit* on a person, *shaft* someone, or *stick it to* them; bold professionals have *balls or big dick energy*).

Less prevalent in most organizations is language that reflects other peoples' interests and experiences: feminine language (i.e., put something on the back burner, percolate an idea, stir the pot, give birth to a plan, nurse an idea along) and nonbinary and trans-inclusive language (i.e., "Hey, everyone" instead of "Hey, guys") (Moseson et al., 2020; Zaidman, 2020). Meanwhile, Black masculine

Communication Highlight

Language in Left Field

The prevalence of sports-related terms in United States business culture can pose challenges for international business conversations. Consider these foul balls that only Americans understood (Jones, 2007):

While at a global leadership meeting in Italy, William Mitchell, CEO of Arrow Electronics, wanted to change the agenda, so he said, "I'm calling an audible."

At a meeting with Indian executives, Alan Guarino, CEO of Cornell International, tried to change a contractual clause by demanding "a jump-ball scenario."

AFLAC CEO Dan Amos baffled Japanese executives when he told them that using the AFLAC duck for ads in Japan would be a "slam dunk."

language is often excluded entirely from the workplace, dismissed by White people as unprofessional and ungrammatical (i.e., terms of Black masculine endearment and support such as "homie" and "brotha," or the use of *be* for present tense, as in "I be the head nurse") (Kirkland, 2015).

In consequence, people from minoritized groups routinely **code-switch**—changing their patterns of speech and mannerisms in complex ways—to fit in with the predominantly White, male, heterosexual workplace culture. Unfortunately, code-switching can be burdensome and exhausting to engage in. As a form of invisible labor (which is generally unnoticed by heterosexual, cisgendered, White people), it disproportionately impacts marginalized people (Ekemezie, 2021; Holden, 2019). Whether intentional or not, language that reflects traditionally White, cisgendered masculine experiences and interests can bind men together while excluding women, LGBTQIA+ people, BIPOC people, and others.

code-switching Switching between different styles of speech, mannerisms, and behaviors to fit within different contexts and social settings. Code-switching can also refer more specifically to when a person of color changes their self-presentation to make those around them more comfortable, particularly in predominantly white settings where the person's race or ethnicity is at risk of being negatively stereotyped.

Similarly, many organizations in the United States reflect White and Christian values and experiences more than those of other ethnic and religious groups—and many White and Christian people are unaware of these unearned advantages they enjoy (Gray, 2019; Kivel, 2019; Todd et al., 2020). For instance, most portraits are of White people, usually males; official holidays generally include Christmas but not Kwanzaa or Hanukkah; public and private buildings, stores, and workplaces are more likely to close on Sunday, rather than the Muslim and Jewish Sabbaths on Friday and Saturday (Kivel, 2019). Even the yearly calendar used for official purposes is calculated approximately from the birth of Jesus. Though such biases are invisible to people of these backgrounds, they nonetheless make organizations feel unwelcoming to others (Kivel, 2019; Miller, 2015a).

Communication & Careers

Gender Bias in Job Postings

- Opening for manager who is aggressive and ready to tackle mission critical.
- Opening for manager who has passion for learning and building partnerships.

Do you perceive any bias in these two job postings? According to tech companies that make software used in hiring, they reflect binary assumptions about gender: The first post is likely to attract mainly males and the second is likely to attract primarily females. Why? Because their language entails subtle biases that signal stereotypical gender preferences. One of these tech companies has identified more than 25,000 phrases that indicate gender bias. Job posts that include references to aggressiveness, sports, and military nearly always signal that the jobs are intended for men, rather than other genders (Miller, 2015a).

Interestingly, although some job posts feature inclusivity statements—or a note that the employer values diversity and inclusion in hiring and employment—researchers have found such statements are unlikely to make ads more appealing to people whose gender identity is not reflected in the main job description (Kanij et al., 2022). The gender biases in the ad copy send a stronger message than boilerplate inclusivity language does. This highlights the importance of being truly thoughtful about equity and inclusion and keeping the full spectrum of gender in mind when creating job descriptions (Zavaletta, 2022).

Stories

Scholars of organizational culture recognize that humans are storytellers by nature. In professional life, the stories we tell do some real work in establishing and sustaining organizational cultures. In a classic study, Michael Pacanowski and Nick O'Donnell-Trujillo (1983) identified three kinds of stories within the organizational context.

Corporate Stories Corporate stories convey the values, style, and history of an organization. Just as families have favorite stories about their histories and identities that they retell often, organizations have favorite stories that reflect their collective visions of themselves (Mumby, 2006a; Pacanowski & O'Donnell-Trujillo, 1983).

One important function of corporate stories is to socialize new members into the culture of an organization. Newcomers learn about the history and identity of an organization by listening to stories of its leaders as well as its trials and triumphs. For example, both Facebook and Google are known for their informal style and workplace perks. Veteran employees regale new employees with tales about the companies' founders. These stories socialize new employees into the cultures of the companies.

When retold among members of an organization, stories foster feelings of connection and vitalize organizational culture. As long-term members of organizations rehash pivotal events—crises, successes, and takeovers—in the organization's history, they cement bonds among them and their identification with the organization.

Jed I sing with the Gospel Choir, and we have a good following in the Southeast. When I first joined the group, the other members talked to me. In our conversations, what I heard again and again was the idea that we exist to make music for God and about God, not to glorify ourselves. One of the choir members told me about a singer who had gotten on a personal ego trip because of all the bookings we were getting, and he started thinking he was more important than the music. That guy didn't last long with the group.

Question: Jed's commentary provides an example of how stories express and reinforce organizational culture. Have you ever heard a cautionary tale in a workplace or organization about someone who was perceived as a bad fit for the group? What assumptions did it reveal?

Personal Stories Members of organizations also tell stories about themselves. Personal stories are accounts that announce how people regard themselves and how they want to be perceived by others (Cockburn-Wootten & Zorn, 2006). For example, if Sabra perceives herself as a team player, she could simply tell new employees "I am a person who believes in teamwork." On the other hand, she could define her image by telling a story: "When I first started working at this clinic, most folks were operating in isolation, and I thought a lot more could be accomplished if we collaborated. Let me tell you something I did to make that happen. After I'd been on staff for 3 months, I was assigned to work up a plan for downsizing our billing department. Instead of just developing a plan on my own, I talked with other managers, and then I met with people in accounting to get their ideas. The plan we came up with reflected all of our input." This narrative gives a concrete, coherent account of how Sabra regards herself and wants others to perceive her.

Review It!

Organizational Stories:

- Corporate
- Personal
- Collegial

Collegial Stories The third type of organizational story is accounts of other members of the organization. When I first became a faculty member, a senior colleague took me out to lunch and told me anecdotes about people in the department and the university. At the time, I thought he was simply sharing some interesting stories. Later, however, I realized he had told me who the players were so that I could navigate my new context.

Collegial stories told by coworkers tell us what to expect from whom. "If you need help getting around the CEO, Jane's the one to turn to. A year ago, I couldn't finish a report by deadline, so Jane rearranged his calendar so he thought the report wasn't due for another week." "Roberts is a real stickler for rules. Once when I took an extra 20 minutes on my lunch break, he reamed me out." Whether positive or negative, collegial stories assert identities for others in an organization. They are part of the informal network that teaches new workers how to get along with others in the organization.

Rites and Rituals

Rites and rituals are verbal and nonverbal practices that express and reproduce organizational cultures. They do so by providing standardized ways of expressing organizational values and identity.

Rites **Rites** are dramatic, planned sets of activities that bring together aspects of an organization's culture in a single event. Harrison Trice and Janice Beyer (1984) identified six kinds of organizational rites. Rites of passage are used to mark membership in different levels or parts of organizations. For example, a retirement is often symbolized by a lunch or dinner, acknowledging the retiring employee's contributions. A desk plaque with a new employee's name and title is a rite that acknowledges a change in identity. *Rites of integration* affirm and enhance the sense of community in an organization. Examples are holiday parties, annual picnics, and retreats.

rites Dramatic, planned sets of activities that bring together aspects of an organization's culture in a single event.

Organizational cultures also include rites that blame or praise people. Demotions and firings are blaming rites. The counterpart is enhancement rites, which praise individuals and teams that embody the organization's goals and self-image. Campuses bestow awards on faculty who are especially gifted teachers and chaired professorships on outstanding scholars. Many sales companies give awards for productivity (i.e., most sales of the month, quarter, or year). Audrey describes an enhancement rite in her sorority.

Audrey In my sorority, we recognize sisters who make the dean's list each semester by putting a rose on their dinner plates. That way everyone realizes who has done well academically, and we can also remind ourselves that scholarship is one of the qualities we all aspire to.

Renewal rites aim to help organizations manage change. Training workshops serve this purpose, as do meetings at which new leaders are introduced and their visions are explained. Organizations also develop conflict resolution rites to deal with differences and discord. Examples are HR counseling, grievance, arbitration, collective bargaining, mediation, executive fiat, and ignoring or denying problems.

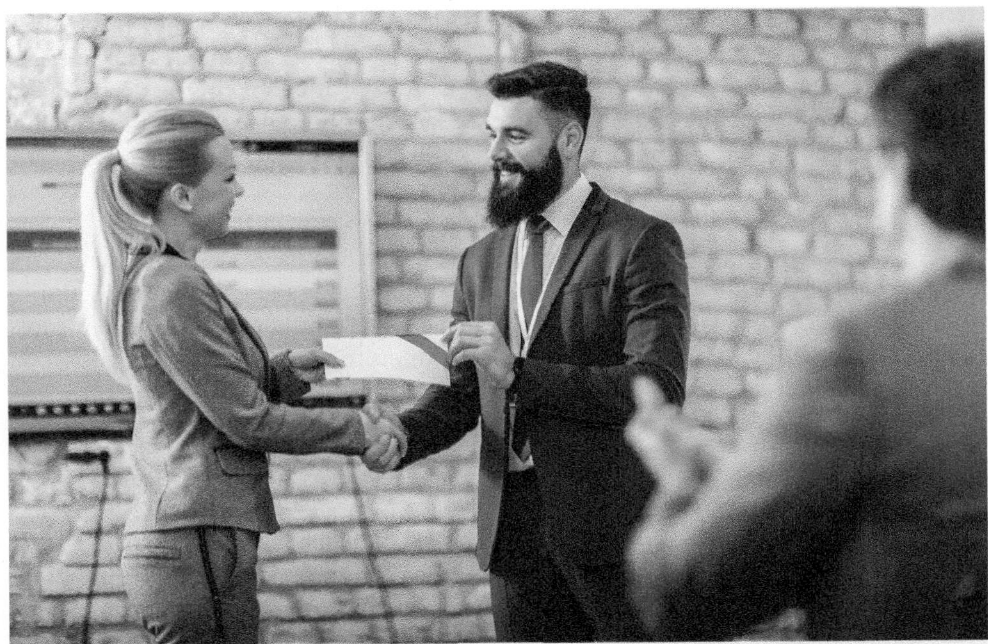

Organizational rites often honor those who exemplify what an organization stands for.
Michaeljung/Shutterstock.com

rituals Forms of communication that occur regularly and that members of an organization perceive as a familiar and routine part of organizational life.

Rituals **Rituals** are the forms of communication that occur regularly and that members of an organization perceive as familiar and routine parts of organizational life. Rituals differ from rites in that rituals don't necessarily bring together a number of aspects of organizational ideology into a single event. Rather, rituals are repeated communication performances that communicate a particular value or role definition.

Organizations have personal, task, and social rituals. *Personal rituals* are routine behaviors that individuals use to express their organizational identities. In their study of organizational cultures, Pacanowski and O'Donnell-Trujillo (1983) noted that Lou Polito, the owner of a car company, opened all the company's mail every day. Whenever possible, Polito hand-delivered mail to the divisions of his company to communicate his openness and his involvement with the day-to-day business.

Social rituals are standardized performances that affirm relationships between members of organizations (Mokros, 2006; Mumby, 2006a). Some organizations have a company dining room to encourage socializing among employees. In the United Kingdom and Japan, many businesses have afternoon tea breaks. Many employees develop griping rituals in which the purpose is to complain about problems, not to solve them. Sharon provides an example of an office griping ritual.

Sharon Where I work, we have this ritual of spending the first half-hour or so at work every Monday complaining about what we have to get done that week. Even if we don't have a rough week ahead, we go through the motions of moaning and groaning. It's kind of like a bonding ceremony for us.

Task rituals are repeated activities that help members of an organization perform their jobs. Common task rituals are forms and procedures that members of organizations are expected to use to do various things. These forms and procedures standardize task performance in a manner consistent with the organization's view of itself and how it operates. For example, physicians are trained to follow a routine upon meeting a patient, known as Five-Step Patient-Centered Interviewing:

1. Set the stage for the interview (30 to 60 seconds)
2. Elicit chief concern and set an agenda (1 to 2 minutes)
3. Begin with non-focusing skills that help the patients express themselves (30 to 60 seconds)
4. Use focusing skills to learn three things, symptom story, personal context, and emotional context (3–10 minutes)
5. Transition from patient-centered to clinician-centered phase (30–60 seconds)

These steps help doctor elicit important information to serve their patients' health care needs in an equitable way, in which the patient and doctor are partners in the decision-making process (American College of Obstetricians and Gynecologists, 2014/2016).

Structures

Organizational cultures are also represented through structural aspects of organizational life. As the term implies, structures organize relationships and interaction between members of an organization. We'll consider four structures that express and uphold organizational culture: roles, rules, policies, and communication networks.

Roles **Roles** are responsibilities and behaviors that are expected of people because of their specific positions in an organization. Most organizations formally define roles in job descriptions:

roles The collection of responsibilities and behaviors associated with and expected of a specific position in an organization.

> *Training coordinator*: Responsible for assessing needs and providing training to Northwest branches of the firm; supervises staff of 25 professional trainers; coordinates with director of human relations.

A role is not tied to any particular person. Rather, it is a set of functions and responsibilities that could be performed by any number of people who have particular talents, experiences, and other relevant qualifications. If one person quits or is fired, another can be found as a replacement. Regardless of who is in the role, the organization will continue with its structure intact. The different roles in an organization are a system, which means they are interrelated and interacting. Each role is connected to other roles within the system. Organizational charts portray who is responsible to whom and clarify the hierarchy of power among roles in the organization.

Rules Rules, which we discussed in Chapter 5, are patterned ways of interacting. Rules are present in organizational contexts just as they are in other settings of interaction. As in other contexts, organizational rules may be formal (in the contract or organizational chart) or informal (norms for interaction).

Within organizations, constitutive rules specify what various kinds of communication mean. Socializing with colleagues after work may count as showing team spirit. Participating in training sessions and dressing like upper management may communicate ambition.

Regulative rules specify when, where, and with whom communication occurs. Organizational charts formalize regulative rules by showing who reports to whom. Other regulative rules may specify that problems should not be discussed with people outside the organization and that personal communication with people outside the organization is (or is not) permitted during working hours. Lyle's commentary points out what counted as violating the chain of command in his company.

Lyle I found out the hard way that a company I worked for was dead serious about the organizational chart. I had a problem with a coworker, so I talked with a guy in another department I was friends with. Somehow my supervisor found out, and he was furious that I had "gone outside of the chain of command" instead of coming straight to him.

Question: Why might a company prefer for employees to follow the chain of command when problems between coworkers arise? What type of office culture is encouraged by this type of regulative rule?

policies Formal statements of organizational practices. An organization's policies reflect and uphold the overall culture of the organization.

Policies **Policies** are formal statements of practices that reflect and uphold the overall culture of an organization. Most organizations codify policies governing such aspects of work life as hiring, promotion, benefits, grievances, and medical leave. The content of policies in these areas differs among organizations in ways that reflect the distinct cultures of diverse work environments.

Organizational policies also reflect the larger society within which organizations are embedded. For example, as public awareness of sexual harassment has increased, most organizations have developed formal policies that prohibit sexual harassment and detail the procedure for making complaints.

Communication Networks As we noted previously in this chapter, communication networks link members of an organization together through formal and informal forms of interaction and relationship. These networks play key roles in expressing and reinforcing the culture of an organization.

Job descriptions and organizational charts, which specify who is supposed to communicate with whom about what, are formal networks. They define lines of upward communication (i.e., subordinates to superiors: providing feedback, reporting results), downward communication (i.e., superiors to subordinates: giving orders, evaluating job performance, establishing policies), and horizontal communication (i.e., peer to peer: coordinating between departments).

The informal communication network is more difficult to describe because it is neither formally defined nor based on fixed organizational roles. Friendships, alliances, car pools, and adjoining work spaces can create informal networks through which a great deal of information flows. Most professionals have others within their organization with whom they regularly check perceptions and past whom they run certain ideas.

Communication outside the formal channels of an organization is sometimes called the *grapevine*, a term that suggests its free-flowing quality. Grapevine activity can occur in many ways. It may be face to face, during casual conversation during break time or just before or after work. It may also occur outside of work using digital communication, such as social media, text messages, and/or email discussion threads shared by colleagues using their private (non-work) email accounts. Grapevine communication, although continual in organizational life, tends to be especially active during periods of change. This makes sense because we engage in communication to reduce our uncertainty and discomfort with change. New information (like a fresh rumor or an effort to unionize) activates the grapevine.

Review It!

Organizational Structures:

- Roles
- Rules
- Policies
- Networks

Digital Media and Organizational Communication

Technologies have revolutionized how organizations operate. Let's discuss six attributes of the digital workplace.

First, digital media can increase productivity and efficiency. We count on email and messaging apps to keep us informed, expect material we need to come to us in virtual formats, and rely on personal and shared drives for record-keeping. Much of the information we need—from company reports to research—is available online, saving our time in tracking it down. These and other time savers mean that digital media can boost productivity, keeping team members connected, engaged, and productive.

Second, technologies increase organizational flexibility. The quality of today's laptops, smart phones, intranet, and wi-fi have helped many companies shift some or all of their operations to remote work, saving on office space and equipment costs. Virtual meeting technology allows people to have business meetings from separate locations, saving travel time and making scheduling easier. Even in offices that are primarily face to face, digital technologies are a boon to employees who experience temporary mobility limitations from surgery or accidents, as they may be able to meet all of their job requirements without leaving their homes. Similarly, if a child is ill, a nanny is sick, or a day care center closes, employees may be able to stay home as caregiver while still doing their work, minimizing the use of their sick time benefits.

Third, digital media enlarge the range of professional contacts. LinkedIn began as a tool to link entrepreneurs and has expanded to help professionals network, job-seek, and recruit in many fields. Active job-seekers may survey job opportunities posted on these sites.

Fourth, digital media increase an organization's marketing reach and strength. Organizations use social media to gather information about potential or actual customers and clients, listen and respond to stakeholders, create demand for products, and build and reward loyalty. Touching thousands of people costs almost nothing and is instant; Facebook is constantly urging me to pay small sums, like $5, to boost posts and reach thousands more people. (I don't, but for those looking to grow their audiences, the low cost and ease of use is appealing!) That's quite a change from a couple of decades ago, when businesses had to send letters via mail or pay operators to make calls, which took significant time and money.

But digital media in the workplace can present challenges, too. Social media and online shopping can be powerful distractions from work, interfering with our productivity, job performance, and success. Also, many employers consider it unethical for employees to engage in personal communication while on the clock. As the Communication Highlight on this page indicates, many employers use sophisticated systems to track and surveil employees' use of digital media—even remotely.

The final impact we will note is related to the prior one: Employers want to benefit from the fact that employees are wired and may send messages after working hours, interfering with employees' work-life balance. But when a workplace culture involves excessive workloads and a lot of after-hours work, employees can experience prolonged stress and feel their workplace is toxic—which some analysts suggest was a driving factor for the Great Resignation associated with the Covid-19 pandemic (Oyster Team, 2022).

Guidelines for Effective Communication in Organizations

We'll discuss two guidelines that are particularly relevant to organizational communication in our era.

Balance Investments in Work and the Rest of Your Life

None of us is only a career person. We are also parents and citizens and people who have responsibilities and passions outside of the workplace. Each of us needs to balance our investments in our work and in other aspects of life, including family, recreation, civic engagements, and community involvement.

Communication Highlight

Keeping Track of Employees

A majority of today's employers monitor their employees. According to one study, more than two-thirds of employers surveil remote employees, using software to track their performance and/or online activity, and 90% report tracking how much time employees spend on work vs. non-work activities during the work day. This can have dire consequences: 73% of employers reported using stored recordings of staff calls and emails when conducting employee performance reviews, and 46% have fired workers based on information they gathered while surveilling their remote work (Express VPN, 2021). Here are a few facts to keep in mind:

- In most cases, employers have the right to monitor employees' computer screens while they are working and to examine what is stored in their hard drives and other storage spaces.
- Employers have the right to monitor employees' Internet usage, including email.
- In most cases, employers have the right to monitor employees' phone calls and to obtain records of calls made. Personal calls are an exception; employers are supposed to cease monitoring if they realize a call is personal.
- In most cases, employers have the right to videotape employees. Videotaping is not allowed in bathrooms, locker rooms, cafeterias, and other places where courts have ruled it would be intrusive (Workplace Fairness, 2022).

Many workplaces do not make it easy to have a life outside of work, especially given the high amounts of housing and student loan debt many employees must pay. In a survey of people who work outside of their homes, 48% of women and 39% of men said the demands of work interfered with their personal lives too often (June, 2012). Some employees even put off child bearing because of work demands: Almost 40% of women and 27% of men said they had done this (June, 2012).

The United States is the only Western country and one of only three countries in the world that do not provide paid family leave to all workers. Of 185 countries in the U.N.'s most recent study, 182 offer some level of financial support to new mothers on maternity leave. The three that do not are Oman, Papua New Guinea, and the United States (Rowe-Finkbeiner, 2014; Zarocostas, 2014). Further, at least 70 countries provide paid leave to fathers (Coontz, 2013; Weber, 2013; Zarocostas, 2014). In addition to institutional barriers, social norms can also constrain efforts to balance work and life. Some men subscribe to traditional views of masculinity and are unwilling to let family responsibilities affect their careers, which often means a female partner's career suffers from her commitment to family. Men who would like to take family leave often do not because they fear that doing so would reduce their status at work (Miller, 2015b; Parker & Wang, 2013; Weber, 2013).

Organizations with the best chance of thriving in the future will adapt to the realities of contemporary workers and their families (Buzzanell & Kirby, 2013; Williams, 2013). Recognizing this, many organizations are becoming more flexible and generous in supporting employees' nonwork commitments. Doing so reduces turnover and increases employees' commitment to organizations.

Manage Personal Relationships on the Job

A second challenge of organizational life involves relationships that are simultaneously personal and professional. You will probably be involved in a number of such relationships during your life. Although management has traditionally discouraged personal relationships, particularly romantic ones, between employees, they develop anyway. The goal, then, is to understand these relationships and manage them effectively.

Friendships between coworkers or supervisors and subordinates often enhance job commitment and satisfaction (Allen, 2006; Mokros, 2006; Mumby, 2006a). Yet workplace friendships also have drawbacks. On-the-job friendships may involve tension between the role expectations for friends and for colleagues. A supervisor may have difficulty rendering a fair evaluation of a subordinate who is also a friend. The supervisor might err by overrating the subordinate friend's strengths or might try to compensate for personal affection by being especially harsh in judging the subordinate friend. Also, workplace friendships that deteriorate may create stress and job dissatisfaction (Sias, Heath, Perry, Silva, & Fix, 2004).

Have you ever had a personal relationship with a coworker?
Stockbyte/Getty Images

Darcy It's hard for me now that my best friend has been promoted over me. Part of it is envy, because I wanted the promotion too. But the hardest part is that I resent her power over me. When Billie gives me an assignment, I feel like as my friend she shouldn't dump extra work on me. But I also know that as the boss she has to give extra work to all of us sometimes. It just doesn't feel right for my best friend to tell me what to do and evaluate my work.

Question: Friendships in the workplace can be sources of pleasure, but they can also be problematic. What do you think are some of the other drawbacks of on-the-job friendships? What has your experience with workplace friendships been like?

Romantic relationships between people who work together are also increasingly common. Most women and men work outside the home, sometimes spending more hours on the job than in the home. In Chapter 8, we learned that proximity is a key influence on the formation of romantic relationships. It's no surprise, then, that people who interact almost daily sometimes find themselves attracted to each other. Workplace romances involve many of the same tensions that operate in friendships between supervisors and subordinates. In addition, romantic relationships are likely to arouse coworkers' resentment (Chory & Hoke, 2019). Romantic breakups also tend to be more dramatic than breakups between friends.

Gene Once, I got involved with a coworker where I was working. We were assigned to the same team and really hit it off, and one thing led to another, and we were dating. I guess it affected our work some, since we spent a lot of time talking and stuff in the office. But the real problem came when we broke up. It's impossible to avoid seeing your "ex" when you work together in a small office, and everyone else acted like they were walking on eggshells around us. When my "ex" finally quit, you could just feel tension drain out of everyone else in our office.

Question: Some researchers, including Chory and Hoke (2019), note a tendency towards work-life *blending*, rather than *balance*, among younger generations of employees—integrating all facets of one's life, rather than separating them. Besides the issues with dating at work that Gene mentions, what other challenges might you associate with work-life blending? What strengths?

It's unrealistic to assume that we can avoid personal relationships with people on the job. The challenge is to manage those relationships so that the workplace doesn't interfere with the personal bond, and the intimacy doesn't jeopardize professionalism. Friends and romantic partners may need to adjust their expectations and styles of interacting so that personal and work roles do not conflict. It's also advisable to make sure that on-the-job communication doesn't reflect favoritism and privileges that could cause resentment in coworkers. It's important to invest extra effort to maintain an open communication climate with other coworkers.

Chapter Summary

The culture of an organization is created, sustained, and altered in the process of communication between members of an organization. As they talk, interact, develop policies, and participate in the formal and informal networks, they continuously weave the fabric of their individual roles and collective life. We also discussed the role of digital media in organizational life.

Organizations, like other contexts of communication, involve a number of challenges. To meet those challenges, we discussed two guidelines. One is to find ways to balance commitments to work and other spheres of your life. A second guideline is to manage personal relationships in the workplace so that professionalism and intimacy do not conflict. The communication skills we've discussed throughout this book will help you navigate the tensions and challenges of close relationships on the job.

Experiencing Communication in Our Lives

Case Study: Liam Misses the Banquet

Apply what you've learned in this chapter by analyzing the following case study, using the accompanying questions as a guide.

Liam recently began working at a new job. Although he's been in his new job only for 5 weeks, he likes it a lot, and he's excited about his future trajectory there. But last week, a problem arose. Along with all other employees, Liam was invited to the annual company gala on Friday night. At the gala, everyone socializes, and management gives awards to employees for outstanding performance. Liam's son was in a dance recital the night of the gala, so he chose to attend the recital. The banquet invitation had stated only, "Hope to see you there" and contained no RSVP, so Liam didn't mention to anyone that he couldn't attend. When he arrived at work the next Monday morning, however, he discovered he should have rearranged his plans to attend or, at the very least, should have told his supervisor why he would not be at the event. Some coworkers who had been around a few years took him aside and mentioned that top management regards the annual banquet as a "command performance" that signifies company unity and loyalty. Later in the day, Liam had the following exchange with his manager.

Liam's Manager: I was surprised you skipped the gala last Saturday. I had really thought you were committed to our company.

Liam: Sorry—we had a family event that was scheduled months ago.

Liam's Manager: Well, I wish you had rescheduled. We notice who is with us and who isn't.

Questions for Analysis and Discussion

1. How does the concept of constitutive rules, which we first discussed in Chapter 5, help explain the misunderstanding between Liam and his manager?
2. How might Liam use the informal network in his organization to learn the normative practices of the company and the meanings they have to others in the company?
3. How do the ambiguity and abstraction inherent in language explain the misunderstanding between Liam and his manager?
4. How would you suggest that Liam repair the damage done by his absence from the company gala? What might he say to his manager? How could he use *I*-language, indexing, and dual perspective to guide his communication?
5. Do you think the gala is a ritual? Why or why not?

Key Concepts

code switch
communication networks
organizational culture
policies
rites
rituals
roles
structure

For Further Reflection and Discussion

1. Think about a group to which you belong. It may be a work group or a social group, such as a fraternity or interest club. Describe some common rites and rituals in your group. What do these rites and rituals communicate about the group's culture?
2. One of the best ways to learn about social and organizational trends that are reshaping the world of work is to subscribe to online magazines with high-quality content that's relevant to your interests. Entrepreneur.com discusses emerging trends and resources for entrepreneurs. The Nonprofit Times offers in-depth coverage of interest to nonprofit executives.
3. How can organizational rites and rituals normalize discrimination against particular groups? Identify examples of organizational rites and rituals that encourage or allow unequal treatment based on factors such as race, gender, sex, ethnicity, sexual orientation, ability, socioeconomic class, and family caregiver status. How can such rites and rituals be replaced with new ones that are more ethical and inclusive?

> Preservation of one's own culture does not require contempt or disrespect for other cultures.
>
> **César Chavez**

Communication and Culture

Learning Objectives

After studying the topics in this chapter, you should be able to:

1. Define *culture* in communication.
2. Explain the role of cultural differences in communication, with attention to the five dimensions of culture.
3. Explain the relationships among multiple social communities that coexist within a single culture.
4. Explain strategies to improve communication between cultures and social communities.

To what extent is your identity individual and to what extent is it based on groups you belong to?

Our era is one of global connectivity. More than ever in history, people from different cultures interact, work together, and live side by side. Further, events in one part of the world reverberate around the globe. When Nepal was devastated by earthquakes in 2015, people all over the world sympathized and offered support. When Greece was on the brink of economic collapse in 2012 and again in 2015, financial markets around the world quavered.

The most culturally diverse nation that exists, the United States becomes home to more immigrants every year than any other nation (Budiman, 2020). To participate effectively in the United States and to be part of the global society, we need to understand and adapt to the communication to people of varied cultural backgrounds. The competitive and direct style of negotiation customary among Westerners may offend Korean business people (Kim & Meyers, 2012). Friendly touches that are comfortable to most United States citizens may be perceived as rude and intrusive by Germans or suggestive by Ugandans (Muwanguzi & Musambira, 2013). In some cultures, direct eye contact is interpreted as honesty, whereas in other cultures it is interpreted as disrespect.

In this chapter, we explore relationships between communication and culture. First, we'll define culture and discuss the intricate ways it is entwined with communication. Then, we'll focus on guidelines for increasing the effectiveness of communication between people of different cultures.

Understanding Culture

culture Beliefs, understandings, practices, and ways of interpreting experience that are shared by a number of people.

Although the word **culture** is part of our everyday vocabulary, it's difficult to define. Culture is part of everything we think, do, feel, and believe, yet we can't point to a thing that is culture. Most simply defined, culture is a way of life. It is a system of ideas, values, beliefs, structures, and practices that is communicated by one generation to the next and that sustains a particular way of life. To understand cultures more fully, we now consider four key premises about them.

Cultures Are Systems

The first premise about cultures is that they are systems. A culture is not a random collection of ideas, beliefs, values, and customs; rather, it is a coherent system of understandings, traditions, values, communication practices, and ways of living. As anthropologist Edward T. Hall noted years ago, "You touch a culture in one place and everything else is affected" (1977, p. 14).

Culture is one of the most important systems within which communication occurs. We are not born knowing how close to stand to others, how to express disagreement politely, or how much personal information to reveal to friends, in person or online. We learn our culture's rules for these behaviors as we interact with others. For each of us, our culture directly shapes how we communicate, teaching us how much eye contact is polite, and whether argument and conflict are desirable in groups, personal relationships, or social media, and how much disclosure is appropriate.

You'll recall from our previous discussion of systems that the parts of a system interact and affect one another. Because cultures are systems, aspects of a culture are interrelated and work together to create a whole. For example, one of the major changes in Western society was the Industrial Revolution. Before the mid-1800s, most families lived and worked together in one place. In agricultural regions, adults and children worked together to plant, tend, harvest, and store crops and to take care of livestock. In cities, family businesses were common. This preindustrial way of life promoted cooperative relationships and family togetherness. The invention of fuel-powered machines led to mass production in factories, where workers spent 8 or more hours each day. In turn, this activated competition among workers to produce and earn more, and on-the-job communication became more competitive and individualistic. In a time of strictly delineated gender roles, as men were hired for industrial jobs, women assumed primary responsibilities in the home, and men's roles in family life diminished. Thus, a change in work life produced reverberations throughout the culture—and those reverberations continue to persist: At the onset of the Covid-19 pandemic, when many people began working from home, men's adherence to these gendered roles despite being physically present in the household took many people aback: Study after study found that among heterosexual couples in which both partners worked from home, men left women to do the brunt of household labor and child care—an ongoing inequity with disparate impacts on women's careers and mental health (Johnston et al, 2020; Wazir, 2021).

Communication & Careers

What's Your CQ?

You're familiar with IQ and maybe even EQ (emotional intelligence), but do you know about CQ? CQ is **cultural intelligence**, which includes motivational, cognitive, and behavioral abilities to understand and adapt to a range of contexts, people, and patterns of interaction (Livermore, 2015). CQ has four components:

- *Drive*—extent of motivation for and confidence in interacting with people from other cultures.
- *Knowledge*—extent of understanding of religion, values, norms, and languages in other cultures.
- *Strategy*—ability to predict how interaction should unfold in unfamiliar cultural settings, yet to be open to changing plans if necessary.
- *Action*—capacity to adapt behavior to particular situations by drawing on a broad repertoire of behaviors.

CQ is required for leadership in an era when Coca-Cola sells more beverages in Japan than in the United States, negotiations typically involve people from different cultures, and organizations increasingly have production facilities in multiple countries. The ability to recognize, respect, and adapt to varying norms of doing business and diverse patterns of thought and action is critical to professional success in international organizations.

Go to the book's online resources for this chapter to learn more about CQ and the tests for measuring it.

The technological revolution that began in the 1970s and continues today has also had multiple and interrelated repercussions in cultural life. Social media and smartphones allow people to form and maintain relationships over great distances and to stay in nearly constant touch with friends and family members. Video conferencing and other apps make it possible for many people to work at home. New technologies change how, where, and with whom we communicate, just as they change the boundaries we use to define work and personal life. Because cultures are holistic systems, no change is ever isolated from the overall system.

Cultures Vary on Five Dimensions

Geert Hofstede (1991, 2001; Hofstede et al., 2010), a Dutch anthropologist and social psychologist, provided insight into defining features of cultures. Before becoming a faculty member, Hofstede trained managers and supervised personnel research at IBM. In that job, Hofstede surveyed more than 100,000 IBM employees in countries all over the world. He noticed that there were clear differences among IBM employees in different cultures. Intrigued by his findings, Hofstede left IBM to study cultural differences. His program of research identified five key dimensions that vary among cultures.

individualism/collectivism One of five dimensions of variation among cultures, this refers to the extent to which members of a culture understand themselves as part of and connected to their families, groups, and cultures.

Individualism/Collectivism The first dimension on which Hofstede found cultures vary is **individualism/collectivism**, which refers to the extent to which members of a culture understand themselves as part of and connected to their families, groups, and cultures. In cultures high in collectivism (e.g., Pakistan, China), people's identity is deeply tied to their groups, families, and clans (Luhrmann, 2014; Neuliep, 2014). In cultures high in individualism (e.g., United States, Australia), people tend to think of themselves as individuals who act relatively independently.

Communication scholar Stella Ting-Toomey has studied cultural differences in what she calls face, which includes individual and cultural facets of identity. For instance, individual facets of your identity include your major or profession and your achievements, whereas cultural facets of your identity include your membership in your family, your work and social networks, and your location in a specific collective society. Ting-Toomey and Dorjee (2019) report that in collectivist cultures, group identity is more important than individual identity, or face. In individualist cultures, individual identity is more important than group identity.

uncertainty avoidance One of five dimensions of variation among cultures, this refers to the extent to which people try to avoid ambiguity and vagueness.

Uncertainty Avoidance The second dimension of cultural variation is **uncertainty avoidance**, which refers to the extent to which people try to avoid ambiguity and vagueness. In some cultures (e.g., Poland, South Korea), people like to have everything spelled out very explicitly in order to avoid misunderstandings. Yet, in other cultures (e.g., Hong Kong, Sweden), uncertainty is more tolerated and expectations are more flexible.

power distance One of five dimensions of variation among cultures, Hofstede used this term to refer to the size of the gap between people with high and low power and the extent to which that gap is regarded as normal.

Power Distance The third dimension of cultural variation that Hofstede described is **power distance**, which refers to the size of the gap between people with high and low power and the extent to which that gap is regarded as normal. In some cultures (e.g., India, China), the distance between high and low power is great and is often inherited. Significant power differences that are passed on in families cultivate a society in which people respect the powerful, and there is low expectation of movement between classes, castes, or levels. In cultures where power distance is small (e.g., New Zealand, Norway), people tend to assume that those in power have earned it, rather than simply gaining power by virtue of being in powerful families.

Cultural differences in power relations may lead to misunderstandings. A Ugandan immigrant to the United States interpreted the relatively casual and egalitarian relationships between professors and students as rudeness by the students. The immigrant commented that, "The students drink, eat in class, talk back to professors . . . all this is unacceptable behavior in Uganda. No wonder Americans are losing their jobs to outsourcing because they are not respectful" (Muwanguzi & Musambira, 2013, n.d.).

Masculinity/Femininity The fourth dimension of cultural variation Hofstede posited is **masculinity/femininity** (Laigo, 2020). As in reality gender exists on a continuum, this gender binary can be understood as a problematic reflection of Western biases (Morgenroth et al., 2020). Nevertheless, this dimension refers to the extent to which a culture values aggressiveness, competitiveness, looking out for yourself, and dominating others and nature (considered masculine orientations, in alignment with stereotypes about masculinity) versus gentleness, cooperation, and taking care of others and living in harmony with the natural world (considered feminine orientations, aligned with stereotypes about femininity). In cultures that are considered higher in femininity (e.g., the Netherlands, Norway), men and women are understood to be more gentle, cooperative, and caring. In cultures that are considered higher in masculinity (e.g., Japan, Germany), however, men are understood to be more aggressive and competitive. In highly masculine cultures, women may also be considered competitive and assertive, but generally they are less so than men.

masculinity/femininity One of five dimensions of variation among cultures; Hofstede used this to refer to the extent to which a culture values aggressiveness, competitiveness, looking out for yourself, and dominating others and nature (considered masculine orientations) versus gentleness, cooperation, and taking care of others and living in harmony with the natural world (considered feminine orientations).

Long-Term/Short-Term Orientation The final dimension was not included in Hofstede's original work, but he added it later when it became clear to him that cultures varied how long-term their orientations are. **Long-term/short-term orientation** refers to the extent to which members of a culture think about and long term (history and future) versus short term (present). Long-term planning, thrift, and industriousness and respect for elders and ancestors are valued in cultures with a long-term orientation (e.g., Japan, Korea). In contrast, living for the moment, not saving for a rainy day, and not having as much respect for elders and ancestors are more likely to be found in cultures with a short-term orientation (e.g., Australia, Germany). The long-term end of the continuum is associated with what are sometimes called Confucian values, although cultures not historically connected with this influence can also have a long-term orientation. This value is not just about future—it is also about respect for one's ancestors and plans and hopes for those who follow.

long-term/short-term orientation One of Hofstede's five dimensions of variation among cultures, this refers to the extent to which members of a culture think about and long term (history and future) versus short term (present).

Review It!

Dimensions of Cultural Variation:

- Individualism/Collectivism
- Uncertainty Avoidance
- Power Distance
- Masculinity/Femininity
- Long-Term/Short-Term Orientation

Cultures Are Dynamic

The third principle of cultures is that they are **dynamic**, which means they evolve and change over time. Scholars (Samovar et al., 2015, 2017) have identified four primary sources of change in cultural life. The first is *invention*, which is the creation of tools, ideas, and practices. The classic example of a tool is the wheel, which had far-reaching implications. Not only did its invention alter modes of transportation, but it is also the foundation of many machines and technologies. Other inventions that have changed cultural life are medical devices such as pacemakers, the computer, and the automobile.

dynamic Evolving and changing over time.

Cultures also invent ideas that alter social life. For example, the United States was founded on the concept of *democracy,* which influenced laws, rights, and responsibilities. Another concept that has changed Western life is environmental awareness. Information about our planet's fragility has infused cultural consciousness. Terms such as *environmental responsibility* and *environmental ethics* have entered our everyday vocabularies, reshaping how we understand our relationship with the environment.

A second source of cultural change is *diffusion*, which involves borrowing from other cultures. What we call English includes a number of words imported from many cultures: *brocade, touché,* and *yin and yang.* United States businesses adopt best practices from businesses in other countries just as those countries adopt best practices developed in the United States.

Review It!

Sources of Cultural Change:

- Invention
- Diffusion
- Calamity
- Communication

A third source of cultural change is *calamity,* which is adversity that brings about change in a culture. For example, war may devastate a country, destroying land and people alike. Cultural calamity may also involve disasters such as hurricanes, volcanic eruptions, and pandemics.

A fourth source of cultural change is *communication.* A primary way in which communication propels change is by naming things in ways that shape how we understand them. For instance, the terms *date rape* was coined in the late 1980s. Although historically, many women had been forced to have sex by men they were dating, there was previously no term that named what happened as a violent invasion and a criminal act (Wood, 1992). The term *acquaintance rape* also took hold in the 1980s, thanks to the pioneering book *I Never Called it Rape* by feminist journalist Robin Warshaw (1988); her book, supported by a major study by *Ms. Magazine*, noted that 73% of women who were sexually assaulted by a date or acquaintance didn't identify their experience as rape. Importantly, both terms have since expanded in their usage to encompass sexual victimization of those in the LGBTQIA+ community, as well, whose experiences were sometimes brushed off and not legally recognized as "rape" due to homophobia and other biases (Messinger & Koon-Mangin, 2019). Similarly, the term *sexual harassment* names a practice that has certainly always existed, but only in 1975 was labeled and given social reality, and is an ongoing problem (Durana et al., 2018; Wood, 1994c).

As a primary tool of social movements, communication impels significant changes in cultural life. In the 1950s and 1960s, the civil rights movement in the United States used communication to transform laws and views of Black people. Powerful leaders such as the Reverend Martin Luther King Jr., Shirley Chisholm, and Malcolm X raised pride in Black identity and heritage and inspired Black people to demand their rights in United States. Simultaneously, Black leaders used communication to persuade the non-Black citizens to rethink their attitudes and practices. More recently, the use of hashtag activism such as #BlackLivesMatter on social media has brought ongoing racism against Black people to the forefront of cultural conversations, again persuading non-Black people to rethink the reality of Black people's lived experiences in the United States (Jackson et al., 2020). Hashtag activism has similarly affected advocacy, organizing, and communication for other marginalized and oppressed groups, as well, including Asian people, LGBTQIA people, and women, with movements such as #StopAsianHate, #LoveIsLove, #OwnVoices, and #MeToo.

In addition to bringing about change directly, communication also accompanies other sources of cultural change. Inventions such as antibiotics had to be explained to medical practitioners and to a general public that believed infections were caused by fate and accident, not viruses and bacteria. Ideas and practices borrowed from other cultures similarly must be translated into the language and culture of a particular society. Cultural calamities, too, must be defined and explained: Did the volcano erupt because of pressure in the earth or because of the anger of the gods? Did we lose the war because we had a weak military or because our cause was wrong? The ways a culture defines and communicates about calamities establish what these events mean and imply for future social practices and social life.

Invention, diffusion, calamity, and community ensure that cultures are highly dynamic—always changing in subtle and not-so-subtle ways.

Multiple Social Communities Coexist Within a Single Culture

The fourth principle about cultures is that they may include multiple social communities, which are also called cocultures. When we speak of different cultures, we often think of geographically distinct regions. For instance, India, South America, Africa, and Europe are separate cultures. Yet geographic separation isn't what defines a culture. Instead, a culture exists when a distinct way of life shapes what a group of people believes, values, and does, as well as how they understand themselves. Even within a single country, there are numerous social communities with distinct ways of life.

Social communities, or cocultures, are groups of people who live within a dominant culture, yet also are members of another group that is not dominant in that culture. For example, immigrants may identify with both the culture to which they have moved and the culture of their homeland. Social communities are distinct from dominant culture although not necessarily opposed to or entirely outside of it. Since the colonial days, mainstream Western culture has reflected the values and experiences of Western, heterosexual, cisgendered, young and middle-aged, middle- and upper-class, able-bodied White men who are Christian, at least in heritage if not in actual practice.

social communities Groups of people who live within a dominant culture yet who also have common distinctive experiences and patterns of communicating.

Yet Western culture includes many groups that do not identify exclusively with the mainstream. LGBTQIA+ people experience difficulty in a society that includes many people who do not respect them. People who have disabilities encounter problems as they attempt to live and work in a society that is made for able-bodied people. Muslims in the United States grapple with a culture that doesn't accommodate or value their traditions.

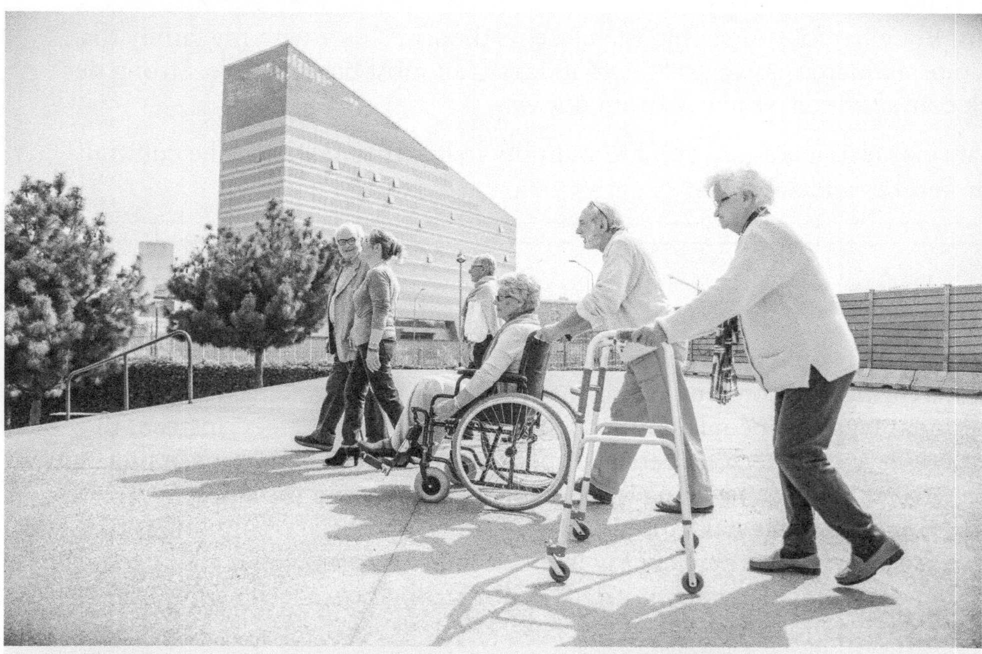

Members of some social communities may find it difficult to navigate mainstream culture.
oneinchpunch/Depositphotos.com

Mainstream ideology is evident in nonverbal communication. For example, Western culture often conveys the message that people with disabilities don't matter. Notice how many buildings have no ramps and how many public presentations don't include signers for people with impaired hearing. Most campus and business buildings feature portraits of White men, leaving people of color and women unrepresented.

Dimensions of cultural variation, which we discussed earlier in this chapter, apply to social communities. Collectivist cultures and social communities regard people as deeply connected to their families, groups, and communities. Thus, priority is given to harmony, group welfare, and interdependence (Jandt, 2012; Samovar et al., 2015, 2017). Collectivist cultures and social communities tend to rely on a **high-context communication style**, which is indirect and undetailed. Because it is assumed that people are deeply interconnected, people do not feel the need to spell everything out in explicit detail (Jandt, 2012).

high-context communication style The indirect and undetailed communication favored in collectivist cultures.

Individualistic cultures and social communities regard each person as distinct from others; individuality is more prominent than membership in groups, families, and so forth. Priority is given to personal freedom, independence, and individual rights. Members of individualist cultures and social communities generally use a **low-context communication style**, which is explicit, detailed, and precise. The emphasis on individuality means that communicators cannot presume others share their meanings and values (Jandt, 2012).

low-context communication style The direct, precise, and detailed communication favored in individualistic cultures.

Sabrina I get hassled by a lot of White girls on campus about being dependent on my family. They say i should grow up and leave the nest. They say i'm too close to my folks and my grandparents, aunts, uncles, and cousins. But what they mean by "too close" is that i'm closer with my family than most Whites are. It's a White standard they're using, and it doesn't fit most black people. Strong ties with family and the black community have always been our way.

Question: How might Sabrina's classmates use cultural humility to better understand the cultural differences between their families and Sabrina's?

When people from different cultures and social communities interact, their different ways of communicating may cause misunderstandings. For instance, traditional Japanese people don't touch or shake hands to greet. Instead, they bow to preserve each person's personal space, which is very important in that culture. In Greece, however, touching is part of being friendly and sociable.

Gender as a Social Community. Of the many social communities that exist, gender has received particularly intense study. A lot is known about gender as a social community, making it useful in illustrating how social communities shape members' communication.

A caveat: Research about gender as a social community has over-emphasized the experiences of White, heterosexual men and women (Brown & Greenfield, 2021). While newer research explores gender-nonconforming social communities, these studies are still lacking in other forms of intersectionality. While reading this section, please keep this limitation in mind.

It has long been understood that White, cisgendered women talk more expressively and are more likely to focus on feelings and relationships than White cisgendered men, who speak in more instrumental, competitive ways (Fixmer-Oraiz & Wood, 2019; Hancock & Rubin, 2014; Kimbrough et al., 2013; Paaßen et al., 2017; Rudman & Glick, 2021).

Such studies also find that women use social media more than men do, and in different ways: for example, to connect with others, give and receive support, follow influencers, and maintain relationships. In contrast, men more often use social media for technology and gaming products (Efosa et al., 2017; Kimbrough et al., 2013; Lokithasan, 2019; Tifferet, 2020). During the Covid-19 pandemic lockdowns, when other means of socializing with friends and families became unavailable, men and women both used social media more often (Brown & Greenfield, 2021; Snyder, 2020). Still, gendered communication differences persisted: Women were more likely to post about family relationships and health care, while men were more likely to post about sports cancellations and politics (Tsao et al., 2021).

Meanwhile, studies indicate that transgender people can quickly adapt their communication styles to reflect gendered language norms and conversational topics. Doing so helps them clearly present their gender identities to others (Murray, 2016; Van Borsel et al., 2014)—useful evidence that gender is socially constructed and performed, not immutable or fixed.

At the same time, researchers say that cisgendered men and women's language patterns are becoming less differentiated. They're expressing themselves in increasingly similar, less gendered ways than people from earlier generations tended to (Hancock & Rubin, 2014; Leaper & Ayres, 2007).

Communication styles can also vary significantly among people who identify with various gender-nonconforming communities, such as gay, lesbian, queer, or bisexual. They can choose to offer (or not offer) cues about their sexual orientation through their communication choices to people inside or outside those social communities (Fasioli, 2017). They can also adopt the culture and communication norms of subcommunities within these social communities. Straight people may not notice these patterns, but they can be clear markers of membership to others who share their group affinities (Hajek et al., 2005; Hajek, 2017).

Researchers have long held that cisgendered men and women tend to regard the primary basis of relationships differently from one another. For example, studies indicate that women more often build relationships by talking about feelings, personal issues, and daily life (e.g., Braithwaite & Kellas, 2006) while men are less emotionally intimate (e.g., Inman, 1996). However, newer studies with larger numbers of people from more stages of life report that across many different subgroups, men and women reported similarly supportive friendships (Gillespie et al., 2014), though men may be less likely than women to have close confidants (Campos-Castillo et al., 2020). Other studies do note, though, that with homophobia declining, more men are engaging in closer, "bromantic" friendships. Such relationships are emotionally intimate, expressive, and physically demonstrative (Robinson, Anderson, & White, 2018; Scoats & Robinson, 2019). This signals that men's social communities may be evolving, and that gender constructs can change over time.

Other Social Communities Gender isn't the only social community, and communication between men and women is not the only kind of interaction that may be plagued by misunderstandings. Research indicates that communication patterns vary between social classes. For example, working-class people tend to stay closer to and rely more on extended family than do middle- and upper-class Americans (Bui & Miller, 2015). Working-class men have tended to see physical strength and practical skills as more central to masculinity than middle- and upper-class men (Mumby, 2006a). But studies have found that in "hustle" culture—characterized by a lifestyle of overworking to pursue ever-higher income and career success—working-class and middle- to upper-class men alike valorize typical perceptions of masculinity, such as assertiveness, ambition, and strength (Berdahl et al., 2018).

Racial and ethnic social communities may also have distinct communication patterns. For example, research indicates that African Americans generally communicate more assertively than European Americans (Gonzalez, Houston, & Chen, 2011; Orbe & Harris, 2015). What some African Americans consider authentic, powerful exchanges may be perceived as antagonistic by people from different social communities. In general, African Americans also communicate more interactively than European Americans. This explains why some African Americans call out responses such as "Tell it," "That's right," and "Keep talking" during speeches, church sermons, and other public presentations. What many White people regard as interruptions, some African Americans perceive as constructive participation in communication and community.

Notice that in discussing social communities and their communication patterns, I use qualifying words. For instance, I note that *most* women behave in certain ways and that *in general* Black people *tend to* communicate more interactively than many White people. This is to remind us that not all members of a social community behave in the same way. Although generalizations are useful and informative, they should not mislead us into thinking that all members of any social community think, feel, and communicate alike. We engage in stereotyping and uncritical thinking when we fail to recognize differences between individual members of social groups.

Review It!

Premises About Cultures:

- They Are Systems
- They Vary Along Five Dimensions
- They Are Dynamic
- They May Include Multiple Social Communities

In this section, we have discussed four key premises about cultures. First, cultures are systemic. Second, there are five dimensions that distinguish cultures. Third, we noted that cultures are dynamic, continuously. Finally, we saw that multiple social communities with distinct norms, values, and practices may coexist within a single culture. With these understandings of culture in mind, let's now elaborate the connections between cultures and communication.

Communication's Relationship to Culture and Social Communities

As our discussion so far suggests, communication and culture influence each other. Culture is reflected in communication practices; at the same time, communication practices shape cultural life. We'll discuss two principles that illuminate the intimate relationship between communication and social communities and cultures.

Communication Expresses and Sustains Cultures

Patterns of communication reflect cultural values and perspectives. For example, many Asian languages include numerous words to describe specific relationships (grandmother's brother, father's uncle, youngest son, oldest daughter). This reflects the cultural emphasis on family relationships (Ferrante, 2009). There are fewer English words to describe precise kinship bonds.

The respect of many Asian cultures for older people is reflected in language. "I will be 60 tomorrow" is an Asian saying that means, "I am old enough to deserve respect." In contrast, Western cultures tend to prize youth and to have many positive words for youthfulness (*young in spirit, fresh*) and negative words for seniority (*has-been, outdated, old-fashioned, over the hill*) (Ferrante, 2009).

In the process of learning language, we also learn our culture's values. The importance that most Asian cultures attach to age is structured into Asian languages. For instance, the Korean language makes fine distinctions between different ages, and any remark to another person must acknowledge the other's age (Ferrante, 2009). Eastern cultures also tend to place greater emphasis on family and community than on individuals. If you are Korean, you introduce yourself as Lastname Firstname (for example, "Wood Julia") to communicate the greater value placed on familial than personal identity. Calendars reflect cultural traditions and values by designating significant days as holidays that should be recognized and honored. In the United States, the Fourth of July commemorates the United States independence from Britain; Eastern societies have a day each year to honor the older people. In this way, calendars tell us who is in the mainstream in a given society and who is not.

Understandings of family differ from culture to culture.
Pontino/Alamy Stock Photo

Communication Highlight

Proverbs Express Cultural Values

Here are examples of sayings that reflect the values of particular cultures (Gudykunst & Lee, 2002; Samovar et al., 2017).

- "It is the nail that sticks out that gets hammered down." This Japanese saying reflects the idea that a person should not stand out from others but instead should conform.
- "No need to know the person, only the family." This Chinese axiom reflects the belief that individuals are less important than families.
- "A zebra does not despise its stripes." Among the African Masai, this saying encourages acceptance of things and oneself as they are.

Go to the book's online resources for this chapter to learn proverbs in other countries such as Turkey and Palestine.

Rachael It is hard to be Jewish in a Christian society, especially in terms of holidays. For me, Rosh Hashanah and Yom Kippur are high holy days, but they are not holidays on the calendar. Some of my teachers give me grief for missing classes on holy days, and my friends don't accept that I can't go out on Saturday, which is our sacred day. At my job, they act like I'm being a slouch and skipping work because my holidays aren't their holidays. They get Christmas and New Year's Day off, but I celebrate Hanukkah and Rosh Hashanah. And I don't have to tell you why making Easter a national holiday offends Jewish people.

Question: What does the observation of Christmas—but not other religions' high holidays—as days off from work and school tell us about dominant United States values? In a country whose founding philosophy includes the separation of church and state, how is this inequality problematic, and what might schools and workplaces do about it?

We Learn Culture in the Process of Communicating

We learn a culture's views and patterns in the process of communicating. As we interact with others, we come to understand the beliefs, values, norms, and language of our culture. By observing how others communicate, we learn language *(dog)* and what it means (i.e., a pest, a pet, a work animal, or food to eat). This allows us to participate in a social world of shared meanings.

From the moment of birth, we begin to learn the beliefs, values, norms, and language of our society. We learn our culture's values in a variety of communication contexts. We learn to respect our elders, or not to, through observations: how others communicate with older people and what others say about elders. We learn what body shape is valued from media representations and how others talk about people of various physical proportions. By the time we are old enough to appreciate the idea that culture is learned, our beliefs, values, languages, and practices are already thoroughly woven into who we are and are almost invisible to us.

In today's world, digital technologies allow us access to and interaction among members of different cultures and social communities. Websites and social media

Both verbal and nonverbal communication reflect cultural teachings. Here, an elder and a young boy wear traditional yarmulkes and partake of unleavened bread and wine as part of Passover Seder.
Drazen Zigic/Shutterstock.com

provide us with information on any religion, sexual orientation, gender identity, race, or ethnicity, which can help us learn a great deal about cultures and social communities that we do might not otherwise have ready access to. Digital media can even help us join those communities, with studies suggesting that social media can function as important sites of informal learning about not only others, but ourselves—such as emerging LGBTQIA+ identity (Fox & Ralston, 2016).

In sum, we've discussed that communication is a primary way in which cultures are expressed and sustained and that communication is a primary way that each of us learns our culture's codes so that we can participate effectively in it.

Guidelines for Improving Communication Between Cultures and Social Communities

You have already encountered a number of people from cultures and social communities different than your own. In the years to come, you will continue to do so. Let's consider two principles for enhancing communication between members of different cultures and social communities.

Resist the Ethnocentric Bias

Most of us unreflectively use our home culture as the standard for judging other cultures. Some Japanese people may regard many European Americans as rude for maintaining direct eye contact, whereas some European Americans may perceive traditional Japanese people as evasive for averting their eyes (Jandt, 2012; Samovar et al., 2017). Many Westerners' habitual self-references may appear egocentric to some Korean people, and many Koreans' unassuming style may seem passive to

ethnocentrism The tendency to regard ourselves and our way of life as superior to other people and other ways of life.

cultural relativism The idea that cultures vary in how they think, act, and behave as well as in what they believe and value; not the same as moral relativism.

hate groups Collections of people that advocate and engage in hatred, aggression, or violence toward members of particular groups.

some Westerners. How we view others and their communication depends more on the perspective we use to interpret them than on what they say and do.

Ethnocentrism is the use of one's own culture and its practices as the standard for interpreting the values, beliefs, norms, and communication of other cultures. Literally, ethnocentrism means to put our own ethnicity (*ethno*) at the center (*centrism*) of the universe. Ethnocentrism fosters negative judgments of anything that differs from our own ways. In extreme form, ethnocentrism can lead one group of people to think it has the right to dominate and exploit other groups and to engage in genocide.

To reduce our tendencies to be ethnocentric, we should first remind ourselves that culture is learned. What is considered normal and right varies between cultures. In place of ethnocentrism, we can adopt the perspective of **cultural relativism**, which recognizes that cultures vary in how they think, act, and behave as well as in what they believe and value. Cultural relativism reminds us that something that appears odd or even wrong to us may seem natural and right from the point of view of a different culture. That awareness facilitates understanding among people of different cultures and cocultures.

Hate Groups

Avoiding Hate Groups and Misinformation

It's crucial to be on guard against **hate groups**, which are collections of people that advocate and engage in hatred, aggression, or violence toward members of a particular race, ethnicity, gender, sexual orientation, gender identity, religion, or any other selected segment of society. In 2021, there were 733 identified hate groups in the United States—down from 838 in 2020 and a peak of 1,021 in 2018 (Morrison, 2022). Hate groups stoke stereotypes, ethnocentrism, and violence. These groups specialize in degrading social communities and cultures that they dislike. They also encourage hateful attitudes and violence toward members of particular communities and cultures, regularly using violent rhetoric to demonize others and polarize the nation (Byman, 2021). They show up at peaceful protests to cause trouble, and they spread their propaganda online through various platforms in insidious ways, using subtler forms of misinformation to lure in young White males, especially, to join them. Studies suggest that they have, unfortunately, been very effective in using social media to promote their ideologies of hate, such as White supremacy and racial separatism (Hall, 2018).

In the United States, the FBI follows hate groups, and two organizations have taken the lead in monitoring online hate groups: The Anti-Defamation League and the Southern Poverty Law Center. CivilRights.org notes that we can all play a role in combatting hate speech online and stopping the spread of violent actions, as follows:

- Hold platforms accountable for hate speech. Report tweets, YouTube videos, Instagram posts, Facebook posts, and other speech that spreads hate to the platforms that are hosting it and demand action. If given the opportunity, be specific about what you find offensive and why.
- Raise awareness of the problem. Talk to your friends and family about why hate speech is not a problem just for the Internet, but our societies and culture at large.
- Support people who are targets of hate speech. Fight back against harmful messages in public places by publicly standing with victims and showing solidarity.
- Boost positive messages of tolerance. Part of modeling what we don't want to see is modeling what we do want to see.
- Notify organizations fighting hate about the worst instances you see. Tracking hate, where it's coming from, and who it's directed at is an important part of fighting it (CivilRights.org, 2017).

Recognize That Interacting with Diverse People Is a Process

We don't move suddenly from being unaware of how people in other cultures communicate to being totally comfortable and competent interacting with them. Dealing with diversity is a gradual process that takes time, experience with a variety of people, and a commitment to learning about a range of people and communication styles with cultural humility, as discussed in previous chapters. We will discuss five responses to diversity, ranging from rejection to complete acceptance.

Resistance A common response to diversity is **resistance**, which occurs when we attack the cultural practices of others or proclaim that our own cultural traditions are superior. Without education or reflection, many people deal with diversity by resisting the practices of cultures and social communities different from their own. Some people think their judgments reflect universal truths about what is normal and right. They aren't aware that they are imposing the arbitrary yardstick of their own particular social communities and culture and ignoring the yardsticks of other cultures and social communities.

resistance A response to cultural diversity in which the cultural practices of others are attacked or the superiority of one's own cultural traditions is proclaimed.

Brenda I overheard three of my classmates complaining about all of the mess and noise in the building where we have a class. They were saying what an inconvenience it is. The construction is to install an elevator in the building so that students like me, who are in wheelchairs, can take classes in classrooms on the second and third floor. I don't think my classmates are mean, but I do think they've never put themselves in my shoes—or my wheelchair! Every semester they pick classes according to what they want to take and when they want to take it. My first criterion is finding classes that I can get to—either first floor or in buildings that are wheelchair accessible.

Resistance may be expressed in many ways. It fuels racial slurs, anti-Semitic messages, and homophobic attitudes and actions. Resistance may also motivate members of a culture or social community to associate only with each other and to resist recognizing any commonalities with people from other cultures or social communities.

Members of a culture or social community may resist their own group practices in an effort to fit into the mainstream. **Assimilation** occurs when people give up their own ways and adopt those of the dominant culture. For many years, assimilation was the dominant response of immigrants who came to the United States. The idea of the United States as a "melting pot" encouraged newcomers to melt into the mainstream by abandoning anything that made them different from native-born Americans. More recently, Reverend Jesse Jackson used the metaphor of a family quilt, which portrays the United States as a country in which people's unique values and customs are visible, as are the individual squares in a quilt; at the same time, each group contributes to a larger whole, just as each square in a quilt contributes to its overall beauty.

assimilation The giving up of one's own culture's ways for those of another culture.

The practice of code-switching, which we discussed previously, is a form of assimilation. When a person preserves one's own cultural practices while among those who share the same background, but intentionally or unintentionally changes their speech, behavior, and/or appearance to blend into the dominant culture, they are performing the assimilation of cultural norms (Dickens & Chavez, 2018). Unfortunately, code-switching is an often mentally exhausting process, and when people feel compelled to code-switch or otherwise assimilate to be accepted into mainstream culture, this is a barrier to inclusivity (Hode, 2017).

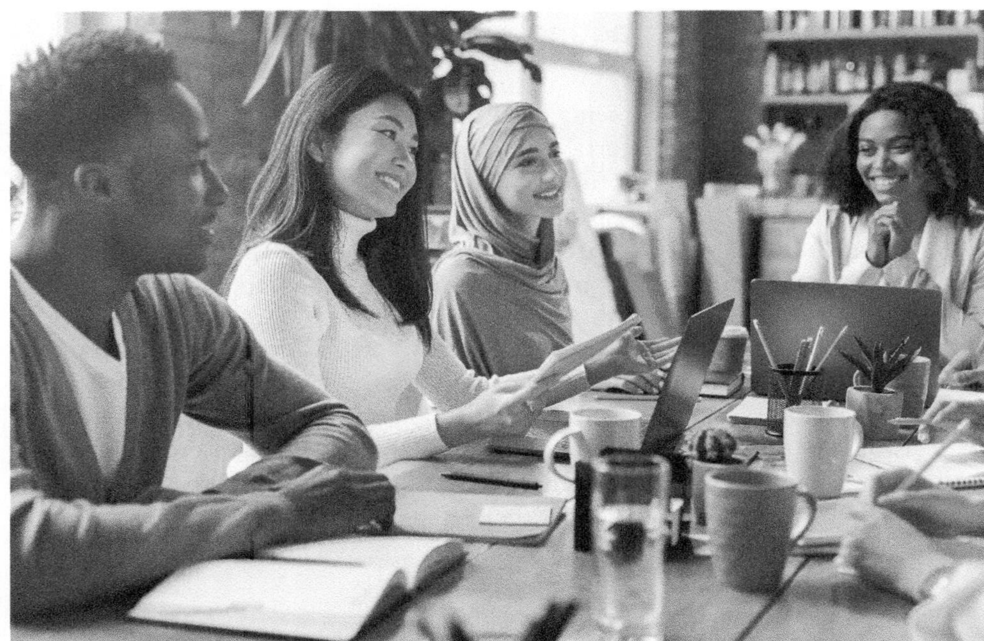

Interacting with those who differ from us enlarges our understanding of people and communication.
istock.com/Prostock-Studio

tolerance A response to diversity in which one endures differences even though one does not approve of or understand them.

Tolerance A second response to diversity is **tolerance**, enduring and striving to accept the differences we encounter even though we may not approve of or even understand them. Tolerance involves respecting others' rights to their own ways even though we perceive their ways are wrong, inferior, or offensive, as embodied by the phrase "Hate the sin, love the sinner"—often understood to be a form of microaggression (Lomash et al., 2018). Judgment still exists, but it's not actively imposed on others. Because judgment nevertheless exists, a position of tolerance can be harmful, threatening people's social identities and their psychological needs for belonging, esteem, control, and certainty (Verkuyten et al., 2020). This means that while the intent may be positive, the impact of being tolerated is often negative.

Caleb When I came out, some members of my family were really supportive, but others could do better. My aunt is barely tolerant, and loves to say disdainful things like, "Hate the sin, love the sinner." One day I saw a meme that said, "Turns out my friends who love to tell me they 'hate the sin, love the sinner' feel very attacked when I tell them I 'hate the belief, love the believer.'" So I used that line to respond to my aunt the last time she said "Hate the sin, love the sinner." Even though "belief" and "believer" are no way as loaded as "sin" and "sinner," she was furious!

Question: What does Caleb's story say about the shortcomings of "tolerance"? How might you explain, to a friend or family member, why claiming to love someone while detesting a central part of who they are isn't actually an inclusive practice?

Understanding A third response to diversity involves **understanding** that differences are rooted in cultural teachings and that no customs, traditions, or behaviors are intrinsically better than any others. This response grows out of cultural relativism and cultural humility, which we discussed previously. Rather than assuming that whatever differs from our ways is a deviation from a universally right standard (ours), we realize that diverse values, beliefs, norms, and communication styles are rooted in distinct cultural perspectives. A person who responds to diversity with understanding might notice that a Japanese person doesn't hold eye contact, but they wouldn't assume that the Japanese person was deceitful. Instead, they would try to learn what eye contact means in Japanese society to understand the behavior in its native cultural context. Curiosity, rather than judgment, dominates in this response to cultural diversity.

understanding A response to cultural diversity in which it is assumed that differences are rooted in cultural teachings and that no traditions, customs, and behaviors are intrinsically more valuable than others.

Respect Once we move beyond judgment and begin to understand the cultural basis for practices that diverge from our own, we may come to **respect** differences. We can appreciate different perspectives on the relationship of family and self, varied approaches to marriage, and various communication styles. We don't have to adopt others' ways, or coerce them into adopting ours, to respect one another. Respect allows us to acknowledge and value differences while remaining personally anchored primarily in our own cultural values and customs.

respect A response to cultural diversity in which one values customs, traditions, and values that differ from one's own.

Review It!

- Responses to Diversity:
- Resistance
- Tolerance
- Understanding
- Respect
- Participation

Participation A final response to diversity is **participation**, in which we incorporate some of the practices and values of other groups into our own lives. More than other responses, participation encourages us to develop new skills and perspectives and to nurture a civic culture that celebrates both differences and commonalities. Participation should be engaged in respectfully, avoiding the disrespectful, offensive, and/or stereotypical practices associated with **cultural appropriation**. Cultural appropriation is when a dominant group exploits traditions and characteristics of a group they have marginalized and/or oppressed, inappropriately and/or without acknowledgment, for their own profit or purposes (Jacobs, 2022). Regardless of the *intent*, cultural appropriation is not respectful, and its *impact* is similar to theft—mirroring the exploitative practices of Western colonialism.

Participation calls for us to be **multilingual**, which means we are able to speak and think in more than one language. Members of many social communities already are at least bilingual: Many Black people know how to operate in mainstream White society and in traditional Black communities (Orbe & Harris, 2015). Most women know how to communicate in both feminine and masculine ways, and they adapt their style to the people with whom they interact. Bilingualism is also practiced by many Asian American people, Hispanic people, lesbians, gay men, and members of other groups that are simultaneously part of a dominant culture and marginalized communities.

In the course of our lives, many of us move in and out of various responses as we interact with people from multiple cultures and social communities. Most of us will discover that our responses change over time.

participation A response to cultural diversity in which people incorporate some practices, customs, and traditions of other groups into their own lives.

cultural appropriation When a dominant group exploits the culture of a marginalized and/or oppressed group, taking for their own benefit elements of another culture.

multilingual Able to speak and think in more than one language.

Communication Highlight

Learning Bias

Racial bias is still a problem in America. According to a Pew Research Center study conducted in March of 2021, 80% of Black adults feel that Black people face a lot of racial discrimination in our society (Daniller, 2021). Only 38% of White participants, however, agreed with that statement.

What can explain the discrepancy between the views of Black and White people? One explanation is that most White people believe they are not racially biased but still hold implicit biases. That's the idea behind Project Implicit, a virtual lab managed by scholars at Harvard, the University of Virginia, and the University of Washington. After 6 years of testing people's biases, the findings of their landmark study were clear: 75% of Whites have an implicit pro-White/anti-Black bias. While some Black people also harbor implicit racial biases—some pro-Black and some pro-White—they found that Black people are the least likely of all races to have any racial bias (Blow, 2009).

Another question studied by scientists at Project Implicit is when racial prejudice starts. According to Mahzarin Banaji, a professor at Harvard, it starts at much earlier ages than most of us think. Banaji has devoted her career to studying hidden and often subtle biases and attitudes. According to Banaji's research, children as young as 3 years old have the same level of bias as adults (Fogg, 2008).

Chapter Summary

In this chapter, we've learned about the close connections between communication and cultures. Our communication reflects our culture's values and norms; at the same time, our communication sustains those values and norms and the perception that they are natural and right. We also discussed the importance of learning to communicate effectively in a multicultural society and ways in which digital media can assist us in learning about and interacting with people different from us. Moving beyond ethnocentric judgments based on our own culture allows us to understand, respect, and sometimes to participate in a diverse world and to enlarge ourselves in the process.

But differences between us are only part of the story. It would be a mistake to be so aware of differences that we overlook our commonalities. We all have feelings, dreams, ideas, hopes, fears, and values. Our common humanness transcends many of our differences.

Experiencing Communication in Our Lives

Case Study: The Job Interview

Apply what you've learned in this chapter by analyzing the following case study, using the accompanying questions as a guide.

Mei-ying Yung is a senior who has majored in computer programming. Mei-ying's aptitude for computer programming has earned her much attention at her college. She has developed and installed complex new programs to make advising more efficient and to reduce the frustration and errors in registration for courses. Although she has been in the United States for 6 years, in many ways Mei-ying reflects the Chinese culture into which she was born and in which she spent the first 15 years of her life. Today Mei-ying is interviewing for a position at New Thinking, a fast-growing tech company that specializes in developing programs tailored to the needs of individual companies. The interviewer, Barton Hingham, is a White, 32-year-old male from California, where New Thinking is based. As the scenario opens, Ms. Yung walks into the small room where Mr. Hingham is seated behind a desk. He rises to greet her and walks over with his hand stretched out to shake hers.

Hingham: Good morning, Ms. Yung. I've been looking forward to meeting you. Your résumé is most impressive.

Ms. Yung looks downward, smiles, and shakes Mr. Hingham's hand with an unusually weak grip. He gestures to a chair, and she sits down in it.

Hingham: I hope this interview will allow us to get to know each other a bit and decide whether there is a good fit between you and New Thinking. I'll be asking you some questions about your background and interests. And you should feel free to ask me any questions you have. Okay?

Yung: Yes.

Hingham: I see from your transcript that you majored in computer programming and did very well. I certainly didn't have this many As on my college transcript!

Yung: Thank you. I've been very fortunate to have good teachers.

Hingham: Tell me a little about your experience in writing original programs for business applications.

Yung: I don't have a lot of experience, but I have been grateful for the chance to help my college.

Hingham: Tell me about how you've helped the college. I see you designed a program for advising. Can you explain to me what you did to develop that program?

Yung: Not really so much. I could see that much of advising is based on rules, so I only needed to write those rules into a program so our advisors could help students more quickly.

Hingham: Perhaps you're being too modest. I've done enough programming myself to know how difficult it is to develop a program for something with as many details as advising. There are so many majors, each with different requirements and regulations. How did you program all of that variation?

Yung: I read the handbook on advising and the regulations on each major, and then I programmed decision trees into an advising template. It wasn't so hard.

istock.com/Tomwang112

Hingham: Well that's exactly the kind of project we do at New Thinking. People come to us with problems in their jobs, and we write programs to solve them. Does that sound like the kind of thing you would enjoy doing?

Yung: Yes, I very much enjoy solving problems to help others.

Hingham: What was your favorite course during college?

Yung: They were all very valuable. I enjoyed them all.

Hingham: Did you have one course in which you did especially well?

Yung: (*blushing, looking down*) No, I wouldn't say that. I tried to do well in all my courses.

Later, Barton Hingham and Molly Cannett, another interviewer for New Thinking, are discussing the day's interviews over dinner. Like Barton, Molly is White and in her early 30s, and also a California native.

Cannett: Did you find any good prospects today?

Hingham: Not really. I thought I was going to be bowled over by this one woman who has done some incredibly intricate programming on her own while in college. But she showed no confidence or initiative in the interview. It was like the transcript and the person were totally different.

Cannett: Hmmm, that's odd. Usually when we see someone who looks that good on paper, the interview is just a formality.

Hingham: Yeah, but I guess the formality is more important than we realized—her interview was so terrible, I still don't know what to make of it.

Questions for Analysis and Discussion

1. How does Mei-ying Yung's communication reflect her socialization in Chinese culture?
2. What could enhance Barton Hingham's ability to communicate effectively with people who were raised in non-Western cultures?

Key Concepts

assimilation
cultural appropriation
cultural intelligence
cultural relativism
culture
dynamic
ethnocentrism
hate groups
high-context communication style
individualism/collectivism
long-term/short-term orientation
low-context communication style
masculinity/femininity
multilingual
participation
power distance
resistance
respect
social communities
tolerance
uncertainty avoidance
understanding

For Further Reflection and Discussion

1. Some scholars claim that there are many distinct social communities in the United States. Examples are deaf people, people with disabilities, and people 65 years and older. Do you agree that these groups qualify as distinct social communities? What is needed for a group to be considered a specific and distinctive social community?
2. Are the different styles of communication typical of distinct social communities evident in online interaction? For instance, do you notice patterned differences between messages written by women and men? If you notice differences, are they consistent with the generalizations about gendered social communities that we discussed in this chapter?
3. Think critically about how you do and do not fit generalizations about your racial or ethnic group. Identify three ways in which you reflect what is generally true of your group. Identify three ways in which you personally diverge from generalizations about your group. Extend this exercise by thinking critically about how people in racial or ethnic groups other than your own do and do not fit generalizations about their group.
4. Reflect on the different responses to diversity that we discussed in the last section of this chapter. What ethical values do you perceive in each response?
5. This chapter encourages people to resist the ethnocentric bias, but doesn't offer a specific plan or set of guidelines for reaching that ethical goal. Based on what you've learned in Chapters 1–9, as well as your life experiences, what can you suggest as concrete steps people can take to resist or at least reduce the tendency to judge other cultures by the norms and values of their culture of origin?

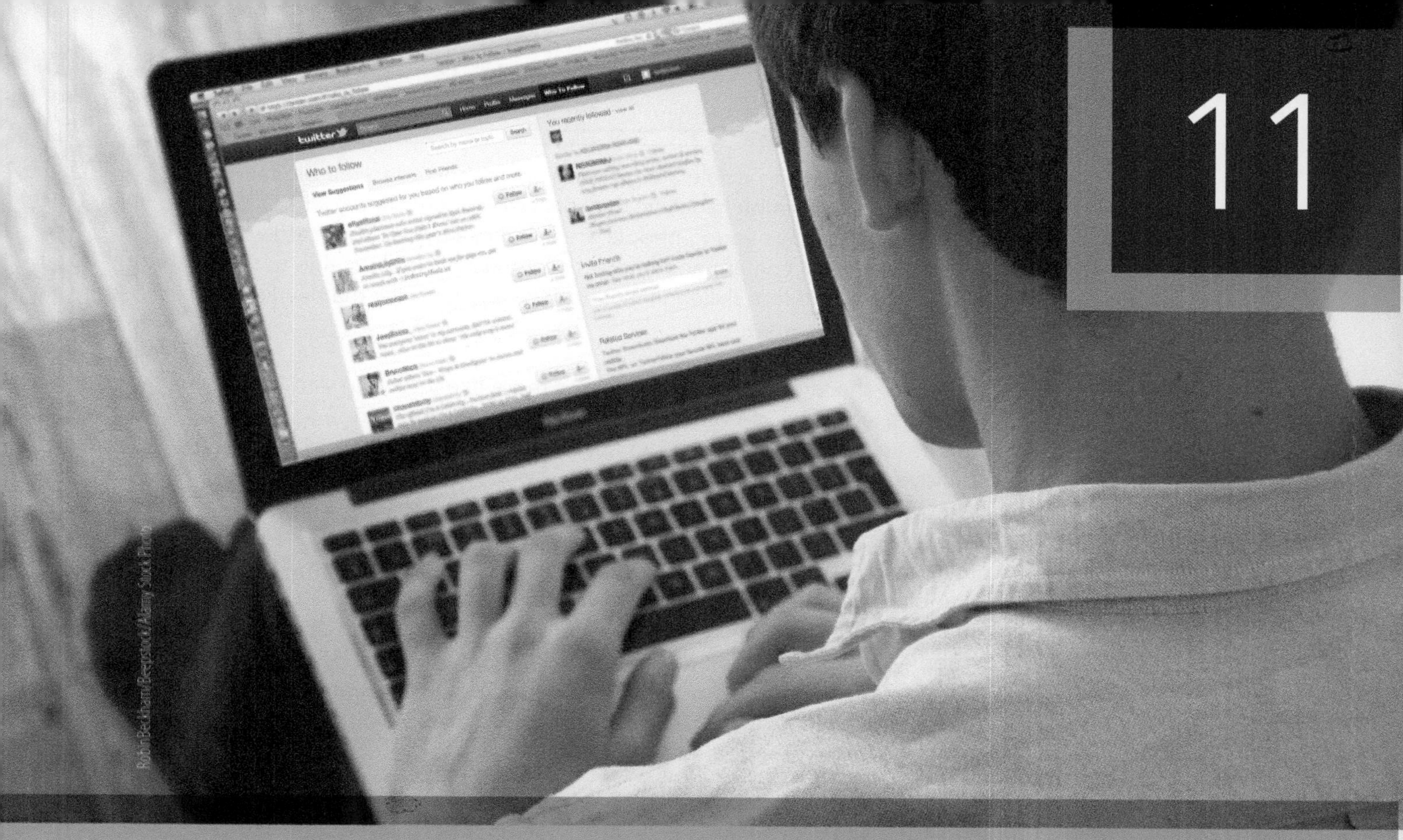

11

Media and Media Literacy

> Television and the Internet are the most powerful socializing and enculturating forces in society.
>
> **Arthur Asa Berger**

Learning Objectives

After studying the topics in this chapter, you should be able to:

1. Explain three key ways in which social media differ from traditional mass media.
2. Explain the functions of mediated communication in our lives.
3. Provide examples of media acting as gatekeepers and discuss the effects on public opinion.
4. Apply chapter guidelines to improve your critical media literacy skills.

In an average day, how much time do you spend using digital media?

- Because young people are growing up connected to the digital world, they will be nimble, analytic thinkers who connect easily with others.
- Because today's young people are living in a hyperconnected world, full of digital content and interactions, they will be less able to think in depth and less skilled in face-to-face relationships than earlier generations were.

Which of these two predictions seems more likely to you? Are our ever-present, always-on devices making us smarter, more engaging, and more socially skilled or just the reverse? Whichever prediction you believe, you're in good company.

When the Pew Research Center polled people who are Internet experts, 55% said they believed that being electronically connected would make today's youth more capable than their predecessors of managing complex tasks and relating to others. On the other hand, 40% of the Internet experts believed that the extensive connectedness of young people would undermine their abilities for deep thinking and making meaningful relationships with others (Gregory, 2012). Despite their different overall predictions, the experts did agree on one issue: Either you control your engagement with media, or the media will control you.

The goal of this chapter is to increase your understanding of the media you use so that you can be an empowered, media-literate person. In this media-saturated and media-engaged era, we benefit from thinking carefully about how our intense engagement with media affects our lives. How do we use media to develop and negotiate identity, participate in relationships, and form opinions and perspectives, and participate in civic life? These are questions we'll consider in this chapter. We begin by defining and distinguishing between mass media and social media, despite the ever-blurring boundary between them. Next, we explore how mass media and social media affect our lives. The last part of this chapter focuses on media literacy, a critical skill for living in today's world.

The Nature and Scope of Media

Media is a broad term that includes both mass media and social media. In this section, we define and distinguish between mass media and social media.

Mass Media

mass media Channels of mass communication, such as television and radio.

Mass media are electronic or mechanical channels of delivering one-to-many communication—in other words, they are means of transmitting messages to large audiences. Mass media broadcast messages to large groups of people who generally are not in direct contact with the sources of the messages. Mass media include television, newspapers, magazines, radios, books, and so forth. Television programs attract millions of viewers; advertisements on television and online reach millions of people each week; newspapers, apps, and web sites provide news updates to vast numbers of people. Each of these media reaches a mass audience.

Social Media

Social media are the means of connecting and interacting actively. Social media include various networking platforms like Facebook and Twitter, video sites like YouTube and TikTok, and image-based sites like Instagram, Pinterest, and Snapchat. Social media allow us to interact actively, collaborate, and participate in self-organizing, fluid communities. Social media are seamlessly integrated into our routines and identities (Dijck, 2013; Luttrell, 2014; Styer, 2012; Turkle, 2011).

social media Apps and sites that allow people and organizations to create, and share photos, videos, and information for personal, social, political, and professional reasons.

The key differences between mass media and social media are how they are *distributed*; how they are *produced*; the *flow of power* associated with them; the nature of their *content*; and the type of *consumer/producer relationship* they have, as Australian communication scholar Terry Flew clearly articulated in *Communication, Politics and Culture* (2009). My updated version of his delineation is as follows:

- **Distribution**: Mass media are distributed at a large scale, to a mass audience; social media content can be shared with a much smaller audience.
- **Production**: Mass media have complex divisions of labor, with many employees involved in creating any given media text, such as a TV show or movie; social media content can be created by individuals quickly and easily, using smartphones, apps, and other digital technologies.
- **Power**: Mass media have a one-way flow of information, from producers to viewers; on social media, there is a two-way flow, with everyone able not just to view, but also to produce.
- **Content**: Mass media strive to appeal to as broad an audience as possible, to earn as much revenue as possible on any given text, due to financial imperatives. Social media users can make content with broad appeal to build a following and pursue monetization, but overall social media content is not targeting a truly mass audience. Social media audiences are much more segmented than mass media audiences.
- **Producer/consumer relationship**: Mass media producers have impersonal and anonymous relationships with viewers that they regard as target audiences. Social media content is more likely to be produced by individual users who are known to their audiences, and with whom they may have more personal relationships. In fact, many social media users post content specifically for friends and family already known to them.

The boundaries between mass media and social media sometimes blur; the most popular social media influencers now garner massive audiences and millions in earnings, and mass media corporations increasingly use social media in their mix. But while mass media corporations can participate on social media like the rest of us, the reverse is not true: Your aunt can't just decide to upload her cute animal videos to network television for prime-time viewing, no matter how much her family and friends enjoy seeing them on social media.

Rich Before I became a full-time student here, I took three asynchronous online courses. It was great to be able to do the classes at home when I could make time. But the content of the class was only part of the experience. What I really loved was talking with other students in the same classes. Some of us set up a group chat so we could talk even when we weren't on the online course. I really loved the interaction with other students.

Question: What have your experiences with online classes been like? Do they appeal to you? Do they create access for you? Why or why not?

The lines between social and mass media are not always clear cut, however. For instance, if you send a video to a friend individually on SnapChat and then post it to a broader audience on TikTok or YouTube, is the video personal communication, mass communication, or both? It is more appropriate to think of media as a continuum that ranges from clearly interpersonal, on one end, to clearly mass, on the other end, with a lot of mediated communication between those two ends (Figure 11.1).

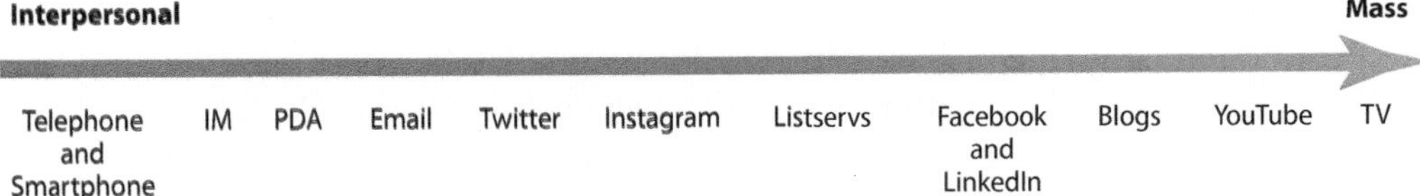

Figure 11.1
The Media Continuum

Understanding the Media's Role in Our Lives

In this section, let's explore our relationship with media. We'll consider the media's potential to shape our individual worldviews and our society, and how much agency we as audience members have in relation to the industry's power.

Understanding the Media

Researchers have spent many decades studying the media. Their insights about media institutions, our expanding media choices, and new forms of connectivity are useful. They can help professionals and activists promote social causes, products, and services. They can also help students better understand the media's power—and what we can do to resist it when needed.

The Media Shape Our Attitudes and Behaviors We are all part of society. Each of us is socialized, or taught about social norms, throughout life. These lessons influence our self-identities, and they come from many people and social institutions: parents, peers, education, the legal system, religious institutions, and media (Hanan et al., 2021; Ohme and de Vreese, 2020). Over time, our socialization continues, and we adopt new ideas and adapt to new social contexts.

The media can influence these changes, but they generally don't *tell* us how to behave or what to believe. Instead, the socializing function of the media—their role in shaping attitudes and behaviors—happens indirectly, through storytelling.

For example, the U.S. legalized gay marriage in 2015. Just beforehand, between 2003 and 2013, popular opinion about it shifted dramatically (Pew Research Center, 2013). Some scholars believe increasing popular, positive media portrayals of gay men (Reilly, 2020) and lesbians (Armstrong et al., 2020)—like *Queer Eye for the Straight Guy* and *The Ellen DeGeneres Show*—helped more people support gay marriage.

Growing Support for Same-Sex Marriage

Allowing gays and lesbians to marry legally

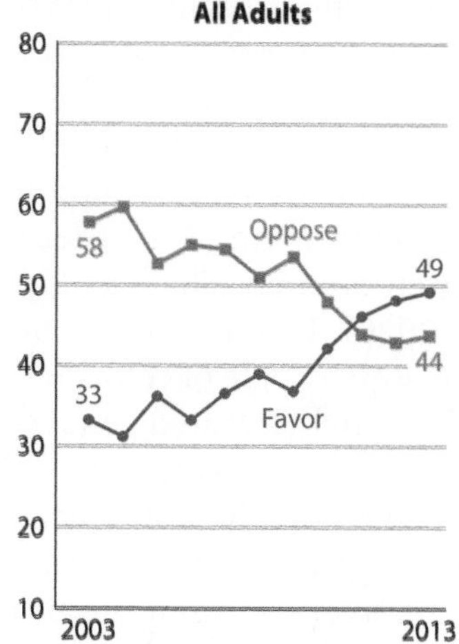

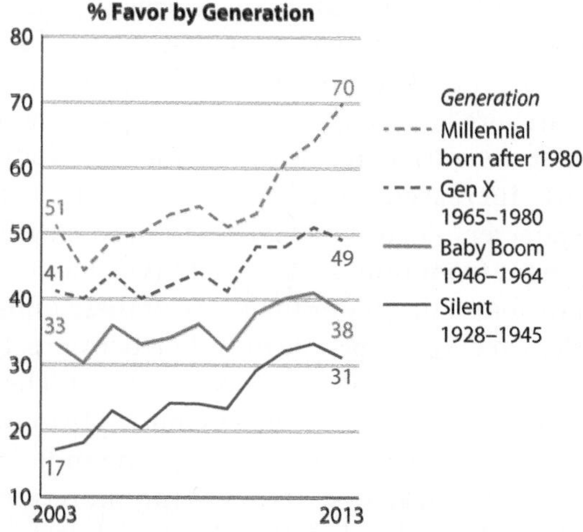

Some scholars believe that positive media portrayals of gay men and lesbians contributed to the dramatic rise in support for gay marriage that occurred from 2003 to 2013, prior to its legalization in 2015. Can you recall the media bringing a new issue to your attention, or changing your thinking on a social cause or controversy? If so, what do you remember about that?

Source: pewresearch.org/politics/2013/03/20/growing-support-for-gay-marriage-changed-minds-and-changing-demographics/

On-screen stories can shape our beliefs about social issues and causes. For example, studies suggest social media has influenced people's ideas about body positivity. This is because influencers and other individuals present alternative images to the unusually thin female body ideal most common on screen, in advertisements, and in girls' and women's magazines (Cohen et al., 2020).

Media Representation Matters Many researchers agree that media representation—how media depict people of various social categories and identities—is influential. The media show overrepresented groups in greater percentages than they exist in the general population; underrepresented groups, disproportionately less. Specifically, the media's most overrepresented group is White, middle- and upper-class, able-bodied, cisgendered men. About 57.8% of the U.S. population identifies as White (Bahrampour & Mellnik, 2021), and about 49.2% as male (U.S. Census Bureau, 2019). When the media show them in greater percentages than these on screen, they're overrepresented.

Sensvector/Shutterstock.com

Common in the media, many people share memes on social media. Have you ever encountered a meme that made you rethink a common perspective?

The media have simultaneously underrepresented people from other backgrounds, featuring them less often and in narrower types of stories and roles (Edström, 2018; Mastro, 2017; Sui & Paul, 2016). This has been gradually improving, though; for example, you might have noticed more diversity in newer *Star Wars* films than the franchise's earlier offerings (Harrison, 2019).

Researchers have studied how often various media types represent different people. A recent study of the movie industry found that women's representation has greatly increased, possibly to the point of equality with men: 50% of lead movie characters in 2018 and 2019's top-grossing films were women. That's a huge improvement from only 23% in 2007 (Geena Davis…, 2020). Unfortunately, the same study found that fewer than 25% of these films' casts were people of color, and several depicted White people only. Furthermore, the films rarely featured gender-nonconforming people (Geena Davis…, 2020). These are serious shortcomings.

So, how do we explain the newfound parity for women, but not others? Women's representation likely increased because the industry realized that movies starring strong female characters were making more money, on average, than movies with male leads (Delbyck, 2018). Financial data like these can effect change. For this reason, new findings from the Geena Davis Institute and Movio (2020) seem promising: When a film features an actor of a certain race or ethnicity, more people who share that race or ethnicity come to see it in theaters. This could offset the problematic loss of White audience members, who can be less interested in films with higher percentages of non-White actors (Aumer et al., 2017; Weaver, 2011).

But why do media overrepresent White people (especially men) in the first place? The answer may have to do with audience preferences, but it may also relate to who's overrepresented off-screen, in positions of power.

Who Runs the Media? Collectively, media industries, institutions, and brands are worth an estimated $2 trillion globally—$720 billion in the U.S. alone (Guttman, 2021). Reflecting broader patterns in society (Lu et al., 2020; Voytko, 2021), upper-class, able-bodied, cisgendered White men are overrepresented in media industry leadership roles.

Patterns of Privilege

In media and entertainment:

- 60% of the 15 people who direct major news organizations are White men (Lu et al., 2020).
- 82% of the 17 highest-paid actors are men (Hall, 2021).
- 85% of the executives who run the music industry are White. One is a woman (Lu et al., 2020).
- 88% of the 25 people who run the top TV networks and Hollywood studios are White. Ten are women (Lu et al., 2020).
- 100% of the people who edit the 15 most-read magazines are White. Three are women (Lu et al., 2020).
- 100% of the 10 highest-paid athletes are men (McKimm, 2021).
- 100% of the 15 billionaires who own U.S. news media companies are men, the vast majority White (Vinton, 2016).

The Black Lives Matter movement has been driving nationwide diversity, equity, and inclusion efforts, though (Think Tank for Inclusion & Equity, 2021). Media industries have therefore been hiring more people from underrepresented communities. As Charlene Polite Corley, VP of Diverse Insights & Partnerships at Nielsen, has explained:

> "Our data shows broad appeal across audiences for inclusive content on TV. Not only are viewers turning to television with the expectation to have their own identity groups represented, the content we consume is also a way to explore cultural experiences different from our own. Expanding diverse representation on screen is one part of meeting that demand. Ensuring we can move beyond stereotypes or tropes for diverse talent also requires we continue to diversify who writes—and edits—the story."

Their goal is to bring more perspectives to the table. Unfortunately, diversifying media workplaces isn't enough: They need equity and inclusion training, too. For example, the Think Tank for Inclusion and Equity (2021) compared the experiences of TV writers from overrepresented (White, male) and underrepresented (BIPOC, women, LGBTQIA+, disabled, deaf, age 50+) communities. The researchers found that underrepresented writers:

- face significantly more discrimination or sexual harassment;
- are talked over nearly twice as often;
- are more likely to have an idea rejected that is later accepted when someone else pitches it; and
- are more likely to be punished (reprimanded, fired, and/or not asked back) after pushing back against problematic content or storylines.

This suggests bias and tokenization interfere with underrepresented writers' work, including their ability to improve TV representations and storylines. Industry leaders need to ensure everyone is treated equitably and all ideas are valued.

This raises a question: What can we, as audience members, do about this problem?

We Can and Do Make Choices about Media Use Despite media industries' tremendous power, we audience members also have agency: the ability to act independently and make free choices. We can apply our agency to our screen time and give our attention to media that reflect our values. We can even create and share our own media, circulating new ideas. Doing so is easier than ever, thanks to digital media tools and social media platforms available to nearly anyone with Internet access.

Uses and gratifications theory says we use media to fulfill our needs and desires (Camilleri & Falzon, 2021; Reinhard & Dervin, 2009; Vaterlaus & Winter, 2021). For example, if you are bored and want excitement, you might watch a feature-length action film or YouTube compilations of exciting stunts, sports, or pranks. In contrast, when stressed, you might watch comedy or humor, or scroll through cute animal pictures or funny memes.

uses and gratification theory The theory that people choose to attend to mass communication in order to fulfill personal needs and preferences.

Katie "Sometimes I don't know why I pick up my phone and scroll through social media. It's kind of a habit, I guess. It's nice to see what my friends and family are doing. I never thought of it this way before, but maybe social media just keeps me company and helps me feel like I belong, like I'm not alone."

Question: The last time you watched a feature-length film, TV show, or short video on your favorite social media platform, why did you choose it? Because the content mattered to you? To escape from problems and worries? Because it featured celebrities or influencers you like? Were you scrolling randomly while bored or had nothing better to do?

Likewise, many people use social media to relieve anxiety or loneliness and connect with others. But does it work? Some studies say yes (Sheldon et al., 2021; Yang et al., 2021), while others say social media can make us feel worse (Bettman et al., 2021; Charmaraman et al., 2021; Hunt et al., 2018) or have mixed results (Cauberghe et al., 2021; Hunt et al., 2021). This is important knowledge: If we notice social media isn't uplifting us, we can choose to change our social media habits—limiting our time or looking for more helpful content.

Theories about audiences' communicative agency (Ytre-Arne & Das, 2020) also offer useful insights. They suggest several ways we can put media to work:

- to participate in various cultures and communities (Cavalcante, 2018; Lammers et al., 2018; Waldron, 2018);
- for civic-political engagement (Campbell, 2018; Chen et al., 2012);
- for creative expression (Acar et al., 2019; Zhang et al., 2021); and
- to connect with others (Kumar & Epley, 2021).

Civic-political engagement includes talking back to media producers and brands and winning others to a cause. Strength in numbers can force corporations to make changes. For example, through hashtag activism, people engage in online activism, stamping it with a hashtag. Hashtags make their work easy to find and link their posts to a social movement. As Jackson et al. (2020) explain, this effects measurable change: Hashtags like #BlackLivesMatter, #MeToo, #NoBodyIsDisposable, #GirlsLikeUs, #TrayvonMartin, #Ferguson, and #CrimingWhileWhite have influenced media coverage, political debates, in-person protests, and even presidential agendas.

It's empowering to think about theories of media use that acknowledge our agency and collective power. But does the media industries' enormous power somehow limit our agency and empowerment? Unfortunately, the answer seems to be "yes." Let's examine why.

gatekeeper A person or group that decides which messages pass through the gates of media that control information flow to consumers.

The Media Constrain Our Choices Media institutions have always constrained viewers' agency. To explain this, let's begin with a classic media studies theory: Gatekeeping. A **gatekeeper** is a person or group that decides which messages will reach audience members.

Gatekeepers include:

- Reporters, who decide whose perspectives to present and whose to ignore.
- Film industry executives, who decide which movie ideas to greenlight and which to pass on, based on beliefs about what moviegoers (often imagined to be young White men and teenage boys) want.
- Social media moderators and algorithm programmers, who decide whether to flag misinformation as fake news, allow it without moderation, or ban it.
- Editors of news media, books, and magazines, who screen stories before publication and decide where to place and promote each story (cover, front page, back page, and whether to include it in email summaries or push notifications).
- Streaming platform and television network executives, who may order (or not order) a new season of a television show based on recent ratings, using proprietary metrics unavailable to the public.
- TV writers, who decide upon storylines for various characters with their writers room colleagues.
- Owners, executives, and producers, who filter information for radio and television programs and major, corporate-owned online/social media brands.
- Children's media industry executives, who use factors external to quality to inform their decisions on what to greenlight—for example, whether a property is "toyetic" enough to increase their profits through toy sales.
- Government agencies, which may pressure news media outlets not to broadcast certain information, citing for example public safety or national security.
- Influencers, who decide which sponsored content opportunities to accept, based on compensation offered and alignment with their personal brand image.
- Wikipedia editors, who decide which new entries—and which edits to existing entries—to keep or delete.
- Advertisers, who can exert influence over media content—for example, withdrawing advertising campaigns and funds in response to public outcry.

Gatekeepers' behind-the-scenes decisions shape our perceptions of what is (and is not) happening in the world and what is (and is not) important. As **agenda setting** theory explains, media industry professionals' decisions direct the public's attention to some and not other ideas, events, people, and perspectives (Grygiel, 2021; Vos & Russell, 2019; Welbers & Opgenhaffen, 2018).

agenda setting Mass media's ability to select and call to the public's attention ideas, events, and people.

For example, **cultivation theory** states that television promotes an inaccurate worldview, which viewers assume reflects real life. Local television news stations across the U.S. are biased towards reporting on violent crimes in nearby urban areas, stereotyping non-White, socioeconomically disadvantaged people who may live there. The more time audience members spend watching TV, the more likely they are to believe these areas and people are extremely dangerous (Alitavoli & Kaveh, 2018; Gerbner, 1990). In other words, through a cumulative process called **cultivation**, television shapes heavy viewers' beliefs about social reality. The result is prejudice and fear of victimization, which can mitigate people's altruistic, Good Samaritan tendencies (Shah et al., 2020)—especially, perhaps, among suburban White people who have little to no direct lived experience in diverse urban neighborhoods.

cultivation theory The theory that television promotes an inaccurate worldview that viewers nonetheless assume reflects real life.

cultivation The cumulative process by which television fosters beliefs about social reality.

Kelly I didn't think much about sex and violence in the media until my daughter was old enough to watch. When she was 4, I found her watching a popular TV-14 show that had a sex scene that felt practically pornographic. It just wasn't age-appropriate. What does seeing that do to the mind of a 4-year-old girl? We don't let her watch television now unless we can monitor what she sees, and we've added age restrictions to her profile on all our streaming apps.

Question: How might Kelly's concerns relate to the concepts of cultivation theory and cultivation?

Audience digitization also constrains our choices, in a much more individualized way. Audience digitization is the process by which digital media corporations use big data methods to individually track and harvest our information (Livingstone, 2019; Ytre-Arne & Das, 2020). Through data mining, corporations can identify deeply personal information about our lives—like knowing a teen is pregnant before she has told her family, raising reproductive rights concerns (Hill, 2012)—and program algorithms to gatekeep what content we encounter, based on these insights (Wallace, 2018).

The result is an asymmetric power differential between us and media corporations (Andrejevic, 2014). We know our business, and they know their business *and* our business, too.

There's no good way to opt out of digitization and still use social media, streaming services, online shopping sites, and credit cards—at least not without looking like a criminal and upsetting family members, as one journalist found (Vertesi, 2014). But if we know corporations are digitizing us, we can opt into as many privacy settings as possible, be careful what we share by text and messaging apps (which big data also tracks), use alternatives to texts that offer more security via end-to-end encryption, and pay attention to evidence of algorithms at work. For example, we can notice when social media sites channel us into **echo chambers**: spaces or feeds that deny us a multiplicity of diverse ideas (Cinelli et al., 2021; Wall Street Journal, 2016). Developing this kind of awareness is important, because echo chambers make us more likely to encounter rumors and misinformation (Choi et al., 2020) and mistake them for being accurate (Yang & Tian, 2021).

echo chambers Social media spaces designed, by people or by algorithms, to present only uniform ideas, rather than diverse, competing, or conflicting perspectives.

These facts make it clear: Everyone can benefit from developing and growing their critical media literacy skills.

Guidelines for Developing Critical Media Literacy Skills

media literacy The ability to understand the influence of mass media and to access, analyze, evaluate, and respond to mass media in informed, critical ways.

Because mass and social media pervade our lives, we need to be responsible and thoughtful about how we use them—and how they use us. This requires us to develop **media literacy**, which is the ability to understand the influence of mass media and to access, analyze, evaluate, create, and respond actively to mass media in informed, critical ways. Figure 11.2 shows the components of media literacy. Just as it takes effort to become literate in reading, writing, and oral communication, it

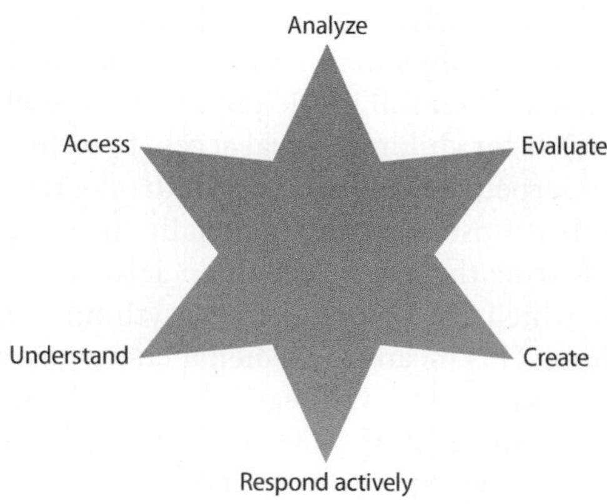

Figure 11.2
The Components of Media Literacy

takes effort to develop literacy in reading and creating media. How media literate you are depends on the extent to which you work to develop and apply critical skills.

Understand the Influence of Media

Media literacy begins with understanding the extent to which social and mass media influence us. Do they determine individual attitudes and social perspectives, or are they two of many influences on individual attitudes and social perspectives? The first view is both naive and overstated. It obscures the complex, multiple influences on how we think as individuals and how we organize social life. It also assumes that media are linear—that we passively receive whatever mass media's gatekeepers send us and that we don't exercise thought as we engage in communication via social media.

The second view represents a thoughtful, qualified assessment of the influence of media and our ability to exercise control over their effects. Media, individuals, and society interact in complex ways. We are not unthinking sponges that absorb whatever is poured on us. Instead, we can interact thoughtfully and critically with media to mediate how they affect our identities and what they encourage us to believe, think, feel, and do.

If we choose to interact thoughtfully with media to control their impact on us, then we embrace questions about access to media and deliberate choices of how to engage them.

Access to Media

Access is the capacity to own and use televisions, tablets, computers, smartphones, and so forth. You may be thinking that access is not an issue. After all, you probably have and regularly use four or more personal media as well as engaging with mass media. But not everyone does.

Democratic Access The term **digital divide** refers to the gap between people and communities with access to media, especially social media, and people and communities with less or no access.

digital divide The gap between people and communities with access to media, especially social media, and people and communities with less or no access.

Generally speaking, access to technologies is limited to individuals and groups that are already privileged by their social, professional, and economic status. In the short run, it can be expensive to provide access and training for people who cannot afford to purchase it for themselves. In the long run, however, it is far less costly than the problems of a society in which a small technology elite is privileged and many citizens are excluded from full participation. This is why many schools now provide laptops and tablets for children: equal access to technology through schools removes a barrier that perpetuates the inequity of the digital divide. Also, although some people assume that those who are financially insecure cannot afford smart phones, the opposite is true: those who are financially insecure cannot afford *not* to have smart phones, which are a pipeline to everything from social support networks to job applications. This means that when it comes to smart phones, the digital divide is not as obvious as it was in the early days of cell phones, when the digital world was less integrated into everyday life, and people with means were the most likely to have mobile phones when they were new.

One area in which the digital divide is more obvious than others is the smart home. People who can afford the newest technology have been the first to own multiple smart devices, which are connected to each other in ways that help manage their homes (e.g., a person can set an Alexa device to start their daily routine by ringing an alarm to wake them, turn on the lights around the home, and adjust the household thermostat). Because access to such technologies is based on wealth, **convergence**—the integration of mass media and digital technologies—can increase the divide between haves and have-nots. But if smart homes become as ubiquitous and necessary for day-to-day life as the smart phone has, we may see this digital divide lessen—while some other new technology, adopted first by those who can most easily afford it, becomes a site of differentiation between the haves and the have-nots.

convergence The integration of mass media and digital technologies.

Expose Yourself to a Range of Media Sources In addition to the issue of democratic access to mass communication, each of us faces a personal challenge in deciding what we attend to. Many people access only media that support the views they already hold. For instance, if you are conservative politically, you might visit politically conservative blogs and websites, follow conservative commentators on Twitter, and listen to conservative television programs. The problem with that is that you don't expose yourself to criticisms of conservative policies and stances, and you don't give yourself the opportunity to learn about more liberal policies and positions. The same is true if you are politically liberal—you cannot be fully informed if you engage only media that share your liberal leanings. To be truly informed about any issue, you must attend to multiple, and even conflicting, sources of information and perspective.

Analyze Media

When we are able to analyze something, we understand how it works. If you aren't aware of the grammatical structure and rules of a language, you can't write, read, or speak that language effectively. If you are unaware of the patterns that make up basketball, you will cannot easily understand what happens in a game. In the same way, if you don't understand patterns in media, you can't understand fully how the media work.

James Potter (2009) pointed out that most media use a few standard patterns repeatedly. Most stories, whether on television, movies, or advertisements, open with some problem or conflict that progresses until it climaxes in final dramatic scenes. Romance stories typically follow a pattern in which we meet a main character who has suffered a bad relationship or has not had a serious relationship. The romance pattern progresses through meeting Mr. or Ms. Right, encountering complications or problems, resolving the problems, and living happily ever after. And advertising often tells stories in which a problem of some kind is solved by a product or service, which serves the function of a hero in the narrative.

Just as media follow a few standard patterns for entertainment, they rely on basic patterns for presenting news. There are three distinct but related features by which media construct the news.

- Selecting what gets covered: Only a minute portion of human activity is reported in the news. Gatekeepers in the media decide which people and events are newsworthy. By presenting stories on these events and people, the media make them newsworthy.
- Choosing the hook: Reporters and journalists choose how to focus a story, or how to "hook" people into a story. In so doing, they direct people's attention to certain aspects of the story. For example, in a story about a politician accused of sexual misconduct, the focus could be the charges made, the politician's denial, or the increase in sexual misconduct by public figures.
- Choosing how to tell the story: In the aforementioned story, media might tell it in a way that fosters sympathy for the person who claims to have been the target of sexual misconduct (i.e., interviews with the victim, references to other victims of sexual misconduct); or media might tell it in a way that inclines people to be sympathetic toward the politician (i.e., shots of the politician with his or her family, interviews with colleagues who proclaim the politician's innocence). Each way of telling the story encourages people to think and feel distinctly about the story.

Critically Evaluate Media Messages

When interacting with mass communication, you should think critically to assess what is presented. Rather than accepting news accounts unquestioningly, you should be thoughtful and skeptical. It's important to ask questions such as these:

- Why is this story getting so much attention? Whose interests are served, and whose are muted?
- What is the source of the statistics and other forms of evidence? Are the sources current? Do the sources have any interest in taking a specific position? (e.g., tobacco companies have a vested interest in denying or minimizing the harms of smoking.)
- What's the hook for the story, and what alternative hooks might have been used?
- Are stories balanced so that a range of viewpoints are given voice? For example, in a report on environmental bills pending in Congress, do news reports include statements from the Sierra Club, industry leaders, environmental scientists, and so forth?

It's equally important to be critical in interpreting other kinds of mass communication, such as music, magazines, the news, and billboards. When listening to a piece of popular music, ask what view of society, relationships, and so forth it portrays, who and what it represents as normal, and what views of relationships it fosters. Raise the

puffery In advertising, superlative claims for a product that seem factual but are actually meaningless.

same questions about the images in magazines and on billboards. When considering an ad, ask whether it offers meaningful evidence or merely groundless claims for a product's superiority. Asking questions such as these allows you to be critical and careful in assessing what mass communication presents to you.

Communication Highlight

Puffery: The Very Best of Its Kind!

One of the most popular advertising strategies is **puffery**, superlative claims that seem factual but are actually meaningless. For instance, what does it mean to state that a particular juice has "the most natural flavor"? Most natural in comparison to what? Other juices? Other drink products? Who judged it to have the most natural flavor: The corporation that produces it? A random sample of juice drinkers? What does it mean to say a car is "the new benchmark"? Who decided this was the new benchmark? To what is this car being compared? It's not clear from the ad, which is only puffery.

Recently, researchers tested the advertising claims for dozens of fitness products such as sports drinks, oral supplements, footwear, and wrist bands. The researchers could not find valid scientific support for a single claim. In fact, the products that were carefully tested "appear to have no effect on strength, endurance, speed or reduced muscle fatigue" (Bakalar, 2012, p. D5). All of the claims are puffery. Media-literate people don't buy the claims or the products.

You should also keep a critical eye on claims that look or sound like facts. Tim Clydesdale (2009) found that claims and reports grounded in fact appear side by side with opinions those that have no basis. Communication professor Rayford Steele (2009) extended this thinking one step further. He argued that newer media tempt people to rely on peer opinion rather than expert authority. In the online world, everyone may state opinions, make claims, and so on. The problem is that not everyone is equally qualified, and not every opinion is equally well grounded. When we don't think critically about sources and their qualifications, we impede our ability to make reasoned judgments about which opinions really are supported and good.

The popular online encyclopedia, Wikipedia, illustrates both the advantages and drawbacks of open-source architecture on the Internet. The good news is that anyone can add, delete, or edit entries in Wikipedia. The bad news is that anyone can add, delete, or edit entries in Wikipedia! You or I can access Wikipedia and edit entries regardless of whether we have any expertise on those topics, and whether someone with expertise will notice and correct any errors we introduce depends on many factors. When anyone can contribute to a popular Internet source, we need to exercise more than usual critical thinking about what we find there.

Respond Actively

People may respond actively or passively to mass and social media. If we respond passively, we mindlessly consume messages and the values implicit in them. On the other hand, if we respond actively, we recognize that the worldviews presented in mass communication are not unvarnished truth but partial, subjective perspectives that serve the interests of some individuals and groups while disregarding or misrepresenting the interests of others. Responding actively to mass communication includes choosing consciously how and when to use it, questioning what is presented, and involving yourself in controversies about media, particularly the newer technological forms. Responding actively to social media requires us to use our devices deliberately, choosing when to text and when to talk face-to-face, when to be online and when not to.

Participate in Decision Making about Media Responding actively is not just looking out for ourselves personally. It also requires us to become involved in thinking about how media influence cultural life and how, if at all, media should be regulated. We've already discussed the escalation of violence in media and the digital divide. But there are other issues, particularly in the context of the Internet and the Web. What guidelines are reasonable? What guidelines infringe on freedom of speech and the press? We need to think carefully about what kinds of regulations we want and how to implement them.

Privacy is a key issue for those interested in regulation of social media. Many online advertisers rely on *cookies*, small electronic packets of information about users that the advertisers store in users' personal browsers. *Spyware* is a means by which a third party (neither you-the-user nor the website you are visiting) tracks your online activity and gains personal information about you. Because spyware is implanted on users' computers, it can monitor a range of online activities in which users engage. Should cookies, spyware, and similar tools be regulated? Should users have the right to control who monitors their online communication and with whom it is shared?

Much of the media, particularly social media, remains unregulated. We have an ethical responsibility to become involved in questions of whether regulations should be developed and, if so, who should develop and implement them.

Chapter Summary

In this chapter, we have examined mass and social media. We've explored ways in which these media influence our lives. They affect what we know and think about the world around us, and they affect how we think and act in our lives, both online and offline.

The second section of the chapter focused on developing media literacy so that we can be informed, critical, and ethical citizens in a media-saturated world. To be responsible participants in social life, we need to think critically about what is included—and what is made invisible—in mass and social media.

Media-literate people do not accept media messages unthinkingly. Instead, they analyze and evaluate the messages and respond actively by participating thoughtfully in considerations about the extent of regulation of media and the people who should exercise that regulation.

Perhaps a good way to end this chapter is by returning to the opening observation that media, both mass and social, are not inherently good or bad. Michael Rich (2012), a pediatrician who directs the Center on Media and Child Health, reminds us, "It's what we do with the tools that decides how they affect us and those around us" (p. D5).

Experiencing Communication in Our Lives

Case Study: Online Relationships

Apply what you've learned in this chapter by analyzing the following case study, using the accompanying questions as a guide.

Christina is visiting her family for holidays. One evening after dinner, her mother comes into her room, where Christina is typing at her computer. Her mother sits down, and the following conversation takes place.

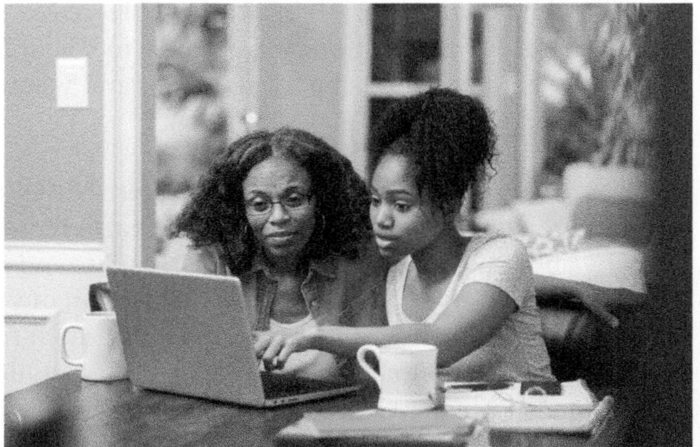
iStock.com/SDI Productions

Mom: Am I disturbing you?

Chris: No, I'm just signing off on email.

Mom: Emailing someone?

Chris: Just a guy.

Mom: Someone you've been seeing at school?

Chris: Not exactly.

Mom: (Laughs) Well, either you are seeing him or you're not, honey. Are you two dating?

Chris: Yeah, you could say we're dating.

Mom: (Laughs) What's he like?

Chris: He's funny and smart and easy to talk to. We're interested in the same things, and we share so many values. Brandon's just great. I've never met anyone like him.

Mom: When do I get to meet him?

Chris: Well, not until I do. (Laughs) We met online and haven't gotten together in person yet.

Mom: Online? You act as if you know him!

Chris: I *do* know him, Mom! We've talked a lot—we've told each other lots of stuff.

Mom: How do you know what he's told you is true? For all you know, he's a 50-year-old mass murderer!

Chris: You've been watching too many Netflix true crime documentaries. Brandon's 23, he's in college, and he comes from a family like ours.

Mom: How do you know that? He could be lying.

Chris: So? A guy I meet at school could lie, too.

Mom: Chris, you can't be serious about someone you haven't met.

Chris: I have met him, Mom, just not face to face. I know him better than lots of guys I've dated for months.

Mom: This makes me really nervous, honey. Please don't meet him by yourself.

Chris: Mom, you're making me feel sorry I told you how we met. This is why I didn't tell you about him before. Nothing I say is going to change your mind about dating online.

Mom: (Pauses) You're right. I'm not giving him—or you—a chance. Let's start over. Tell me what you like about him.

Chris: Well, he's thoughtful.

Mom: Thoughtful? How so?

Chris: If I say something one day, he'll come back to it a day or so later, and I can tell he's thought about it, like he's really interested in what I say.

Mom: So he really pays attention to what you say?

Chris: Exactly. So many guys I've dated don't. They never return to things I've said. And when I come back to things he's said with ideas I've thought about, he really listens.

Mom: Like he values what you think and say?

Chris: Exactly! I really appreciate that about him.

Questions for Analysis and Discussion

1. Identify examples of ineffective and effective listening on the part of Chris's mother.
2. What do you perceive as the key obstacle to listening for Chris's mom during the early part of this conversation?
3. Identify specific listening skills that Chris's mother uses once she chooses to listen mindfully.
4. Is Chris's mother being unethical by not continuing to state her concerns about Chris's safety?

Key Concepts

agenda setting
convergence
cultivation
cultivation theory
digital divide
echo chambers
gatekeeper
mass media
media literacy
puffery
social media
uses and gratification theory

For Further Reflection and Discussion

1. Would it be ethical to exercise control over the violence presented in media? Do you think viewers, especially children, are harmed by the prevalence of violence in media? If you think there should be some controls, what groups or individuals would you trust to exercise them?
2. Susan Crawford is a legal scholar with particular expertise on Internet law and issues of privacy, intellectual property, and advertising. Her blog gives her opinions on a range of legal issues entailed by cyberspace. Go to the book's online resources for this chapter to read her blog.
3. In this chapter, you have learned about some of the ways that gatekeepers shape understanding, perspectives, and attitudes. Apply what you've learned by identifying ways that I, as the author of this chapter, shaped the information presented to you.
   - *Gatekeeping*: Whose points of view do I emphasize in discussing mass communication and media literacy? Are there other involved groups that I neglect or ignore?
   - *Agenda setting*: Which aspects of mass communication did I call to your attention? Which aspects of mass communication did I not emphasize or name?
4. Watch 2 hours of commercial television, either prime-time on a network or from a major streaming service. Pay attention to the dominant ideology that is represented and normalized in the programming. Who are the good and bad characters? Which personal qualities are represented as admirable, and which are represented as objectionable? Who are the victims and victors, the heroes and villains? What goals and values are endorsed?
5. Communication technologies have vastly increased our ability to learn about and participate in cultures other than our own. Identify an issue that interests you—the election and voting process, a human rights issue, education—and use digital media to learn about that issue in the context of a specific culture other than your own.
6. Consider the parts of your identity that help make who you are. This could encompass race, gender, disability, sexual orientation, body size, age, and so on. It also could include other attributes, like religion, relationships (e.g., parent, child, spouse, etc.), the region you live in, your accent, immigrant status, the housing you live in, who lives in your home, being vegetarian, being a veteran, even the pet(s) you own. How often do you see people who share these characteristics in the media? When you do, are they treated well, or somehow diminished? What about people from other groups—how does their treatment compare to the treatment of people more like you?

Pojoslaw/Shutterstock.com

There are three things to aim at in public speaking: first, to get into your subject, then to get your subject into yourself, and finally, to get your subject into the heart of your audience.

Alexander Gregg

Planning Public Speaking

Learning Objectives

After studying the topics in this chapter, you should be able to:

1. Prepare for a public speech using strategies for audience analysis, topic selection, and information sourcing.
2. List the three general speaking purposes.
3. Explain the difference between a speech's general purpose and its specific purpose.
4. Analyze the audience for a speech using demographic and subject-related data.

How many speeches have you given in the past 5 years?

- Hank is a commercial artist at a public relations firm. On Thursday, Hank's supervisor asks him to prepare a 10-minute presentation for a client whose million-dollar account the firm hopes to get.
- Bonnie's first performance review is scheduled for next week. She knows her supervisor always asks employees he reviews what they think they have brought to the company, and she wants to have a smart, confident answer.
- Juan is the best man at his friend's wedding. He knows it is traditional for the best man to give a toast to the newly married couple, and he wants his remarks to be really meaningful.
- At the first meeting of class, the professor asks each person to "say a few words" to introduce himself or herself. Brittany wants to make a good impression on her peers with her self-introduction.
- Haven, an aspiring influencer whose followers enjoy their photographs, is asked by an established influencer to join them in a live video. Haven doesn't have a lot of experience appearing on video-based platforms, and wants to be engaging so that they have a good chance of gaining new followers.

Although these people aren't professional speakers, each of them is called on to speak. Competence in public speaking increases your chances of advancing professionally. In addition, you expand your impact in social situations and your ability to have a voice in community and civic affairs. Expressing ideas is so basic to a democratic society that it is the very first amendment to the United States Constitution.

The role of speaking in professional life is more obvious in some occupations than in others. If you plan to be an attorney, a politician, a salesperson, or an educator, it's easy to understand that speaking in public, whether face-to-face or in virtual contexts, will be a routine part of your life. The importance of public speaking is less obvious, yet also present, in other careers. In fact, you're likely to find that speaking to small and large groups is part of everyday life in the workplace, such as giving a report, presenting an idea to coworkers, making a proposal to a client, informing a patient about a procedure, or explaining a play to teammates. The ability to present ideas effectively in public situations will also enhance your influence in civic, social, and political contexts. You'll have opportunities to voice your ideas at zoning meetings, political events, and school boards. Although some people may have more experience and perhaps more aptitude for public speaking than others, everyone can learn to make effective presentations. As we will discuss, many of the skills we've discussed in the previous chapters are relevant to effective public communication, whether in-person or in synchronous online settings.

This chapter and the four that follow lead you through the process of planning, developing, and presenting informative and persuasive speeches. In this chapter, we'll first note similarities between public speaking and other kinds of communication we've studied. Next, we'll discuss foundations of effective public speaking: selecting and limiting topics, defining a general purpose and a specific purpose, and developing a thesis statement. The third section of the chapter emphasizes adapting speeches to particular speaking occasions and to particular audience members' orientations to topics and speakers. The final section of the chapter identifies ways that digital media can assist you in planning a speech.

The next four chapters build on material presented in this one. Chapter 13 identifies types of support for public speeches and discusses methods of conducting research. In Chapter 14, we'll learn about ways to organize and present public speeches, and we'll discuss ways to increase your confidence as a public speaker. Chapter 15 focuses on informative public speeches, and Chapter 16 focuses on persuasive public speeches. After reading these five chapters, you should be able to plan, develop, and present an effective speech.

Public Speaking Is Enlarged Conversation

Years ago, James Winans (1938), a distinguished professor of communication, remarked that effective public speaking is really enlarged conversation. Winans meant that the skills of successful public speaking are not so different from those we use in everyday conversations.

Public communication is also like conversation in a second way. It occurs naturally in everyday life. Public speaking is not just giving a long speech in front of a crowd. More often, it is speaking for 5 or even 2 minutes to fewer than 20 people. It happens in meetings, hallways, and receptions. It happens at retreats and workshops. It happens on virtual conferencing platforms and live social media streams. It happens in boardrooms and ballrooms.

Effective public communication uses and builds on skills and principles we've discussed in the previous chapters. Whether we are talking with a couple of friends or speaking to an audience of 500, we need to consider audience members'

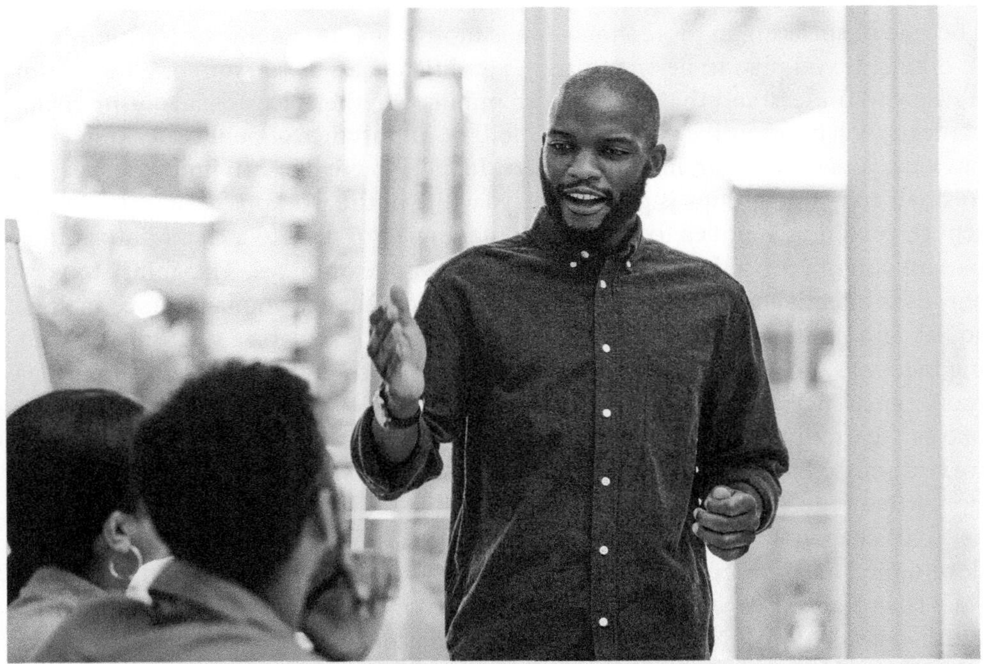

Does this speaker appear to be effective?
Billy Hustace/Photographer's Choice/Getty Images

perspectives, adapt to the situation, express our ideas clearly, organize what we say so that others can follow our thinking, explain and support our ideas, and be personally engaging. In public speaking, as in everyday conversation, these are the skills of effective communication.

Chloe I had a great history teacher last year. We met twice a week in a synchronous online class for 75 minutes, so I was prepared for serious boredom. But it never seemed like he was "lecturing" at us through the screen. It was more like he was talking with us—telling interesting stories and asking what we thought about stuff. The 75 minutes just flew by every time.

Choose and Refine a Topic

When people think of public speaking, they often focus on the delivery. However, 90% of a speech happens before it is delivered. The choices you make in planning your speech are the foundation of your effectiveness.

A well-crafted speech begins with a thoughtfully selected topic, a clear purpose, and a concise thesis statement that audience members grasp quickly and retain.

Choose Your Topic

The first step in preparing a public speech is to select a topic. Often the topic is selected for you. For instance, your supervisor might ask you to brief a team on some issue or to give a report on a training program you attended. In other cases, you will prepare remarks for an occasion that constrains what you should say. For example, if you are asked to present an award, the occasion demands that you talk about what the award means and the accomplishments of the recipient.

For the class you are taking, you may have the opportunity to select your own topic. If you don't already have a topic in mind, you might consult newspapers, social media, data-backed sites like the Pew Research Center, and online news websites. Go to the book's online resources for this chapter to visit online websites.

Select a Topic That Matters to You When you care about your topic, you already know something about it. In addition, personal interest in the subject will make your delivery more engaging and more dynamic. Maybe you have strong beliefs about the death penalty, abortion care, funding of college athletics,

Communication Highlight

The First Amendment: Freedom of Religion, Speech, and Press

"Congress shall make no law respecting an establishment of religion, or prohibiting the free exercise thereof; or abridging the freedom of speech, or of the press; or the right of people peaceably to assemble, and to petition the Government for a redress of grievances."

—Amendment I, The Constitution of the United States

or environmental responsibility. In cases where your topic is assigned to you—for instance, your supervisor might tell you to make a report—then your challenge is to find something in the topic with which you can connect personally.

Select a Topic Appropriate to the Speaking Occasion You should also consider the expectations, demands, and constraints of particular speaking situations (Ferguson, 2008). Some contexts virtually dictate speech topics. For example, a rally for a political candidate demands speeches that praise the candidate and a ceremony honoring a person requires speakers to pay tribute to the person.

Pat When we had our Phi Beta Kappa induction last spring, we had a very well-known scholar give the speech. He began by talking about how great our basketball team is and how we may win the championship this year. He talked about the team for about 5 minutes before he said anything else. It's not like I'm against sports or anything. I mean, I go to games and I think our team is way cool. But Phi Beta Kappa is the highest academic honor society on campus. It didn't seem the right situation to be leading a rally for the team.

Question: The speaker Pat recalls may have thought he was expressing shared enthusiasm about the university basketball team, but not all honor society inductees shared that enthusiasm. How might the speaker have mentioned his passion for the team without being perceived by attendees like Pat as going overboard?

Physical setting is also part of the speaking occasion. For in-person speeches, you know what your classroom is like and the time of day you will speak, which can inform decisions such as what background color to use for slides. (In low light, use a dark background color; in a small room with lights on, use a lighter background.) For virtual talks, you can choose in advance where you'll speak from and check the background noise and light levels at that time of day. Check in advance that you will be heard clearly and clearly lit on screen, adjusting your location and lighting as needed.

In other speaking situations, familiarize yourself with the physical setting ahead of time as best you can. Is the room in which you will speak large or small? Is it well lit or dim? Are chairs comfortable or not? Will you present your speech at 10 a.m., after a heavy lunch, or in the evening? Will audience members have sat through a long day of meetings and speeches? If you cannot investigate the answers to these questions yourself, ask an organizer for information on the space and the attendees' schedules that day, as each of these factors influences audience members' ability to pay attention.

If you are not able to become familiar with the speaking context ahead of time, try to check the room the day of your talk. You might be able to control some possible hindrances, such as temperature or seating arrangement. If undesirable aspects of the setting are beyond your control (i.e., uncomfortable seating, speaking after the audience has had a big meal), do your best to compensate for them. A dynamic and engaging delivery can do much to surmount audience members' lethargy or discomfort.

Sometimes, you won't know the physical setting even an hour in advance or won't be able to control it. In that case, adapt as best you can on the spot. Once, my partner, Robbie, was asked to give a keynote speech after dinner at a meeting of the Student Sierra Club. In the past, he had given many keynote speeches at Sierra Club meetings. Based on past events, Robbie assumed that the dinner would be in a banquet room and that people would be dressed somewhat formally. He prepared a 30-minute speech, which he planned to deliver from a speaking podium. He dressed in a good suit and tie. When he got to the meeting, he discovered that the dinner was a cookout—certainly appropriate for a Sierra Club group, but not what he was expecting!

Robbie quickly adapted his appearance by taking off his jacket and tie and rolling up his shirtsleeves. He then adapted the content of his speech and his delivery to the informal speaking situation in which he found himself. He decided to eliminate some of the quotations from environmental leaders because the light from the campfire would not be sufficient for him to read the quotations from note cards, and he didn't want to risk misquoting sources. And he adapted his planned, forceful, podium delivery to a more conversational, storytelling style. Robbie would have been ineffective had he not adapted to the physical setting.

One important note: It's best not to complain to the audience if the setting isn't what you were expecting. You want the audience to be comfortable and feel confident in you as a speaker, and to start on a positive note. I've seen speakers complain about the setting not being expected and express nervousness or discomfort. More often than not, such commentary is off-putting, starting the entire talk on a negative note. In these circumstances, I always advise my students to remember that a speech is a type of performance. In other words: "Fake it till you make it!"

Select a Topic Appropriate to Your Audience Effective speakers also select topics that will appeal to the needs, interests, and situations of their audience. A speech is not primarily a chance to showcase yourself by showing how smart, clever, funny, or knowledgeable you are. Rather, it is first and foremost a chance to affect others—that's the reason for speaking. And if you want to affect others, you begin thinking about them in the first stages of planning a speech.

In selecting a topic or thinking about one assigned to you, ask how the topic is or can be relevant to your audience, what knowledge they have, and what experiences and concerns they are likely to share with you. Later in this chapter, we'll discuss in depth how you can take these factors into consideration.

Communication Highlight

Connecting Yourself with Your Topic

One of the most powerful ways for speakers to enhance impact is to show personal involvement with their topics. At their acceptance speeches at Academy Awards ceremonies, speakers often demonstrate this in a compelling way. When Karen Rupert Toliver and Matthew A. Cherry won the Best Animated Short Film award in 2020 for their seven-minute animation *Hair Love*, both connected the film to their lived experiences and broader issues impacting Black people's everyday lives. Toliver—the first Black woman to receive an award in this category—spoke to the importance of on-screen representation, saying, "In cartoons, that's how we first see our movies, and that's how we shape our lives and how we see the world." Cherry then used his speech to amplify the need for legislation prohibiting discrimination based on hairstyle and hair texture, noting, "There's a very important issue that's out there, the CROWN Act, and if we can help get this passed in all 50 states, we can help stories like Deandre Arnold's to stop from happening" (Betáková, 2022), Arnold, who had recently made headlines after his Texas high school suspended him for the length of his dreadlocks, was also Cherry's guest at the Oscars, demonstrating the depth of the filmmakers' commitment to their short's topic.

Review It!

Choose a Topic That:

- Matters to You
- Is Appropriate to the Occasion
- Is Appropriate to the Audience
- Is Narrowed

mind map A holistic record of information on a topic. Mind mapping is a method that can be used to narrow speech topics or to keep track of information gathered during research.

Narrow Your Topic Effective speakers limit their speeches to a manageable focus (McGuire, 1989). If you're interested in the general topic of health care reform, you might narrow that to reducing the costs of drugs or increasing preventive medicine (wellness). You can't cover the broad topic of health care reform in a single speech, but you can cover a particular aspect of it.

Another way to narrow your speaking purpose is to use a *mind map* (Jaffe, 2016). A **mind map** is a holistic record of information on a topic, which many visual thinkers prefer to an outline. You create a mind map by free-associating ideas in relation to a broad area of interest. For example, perhaps you want to speak on the general topic of the environment. To narrow that broad topic to a manageable focus for a single speech, you could brainstorm issues related to the topic. Figure 12.1 shows many specific issues that might occur to someone who creates a mind map on the topic of environment. If you would like to use a software program to map your ideas, go to the book's online resources for this chapter.

Define Your General and Specific Purposes in Speaking

The second step in designing an effective speech is to define your purpose for speaking. This involves two steps. First, decide on your general purpose. Second, refine your general purpose into a specific purpose.

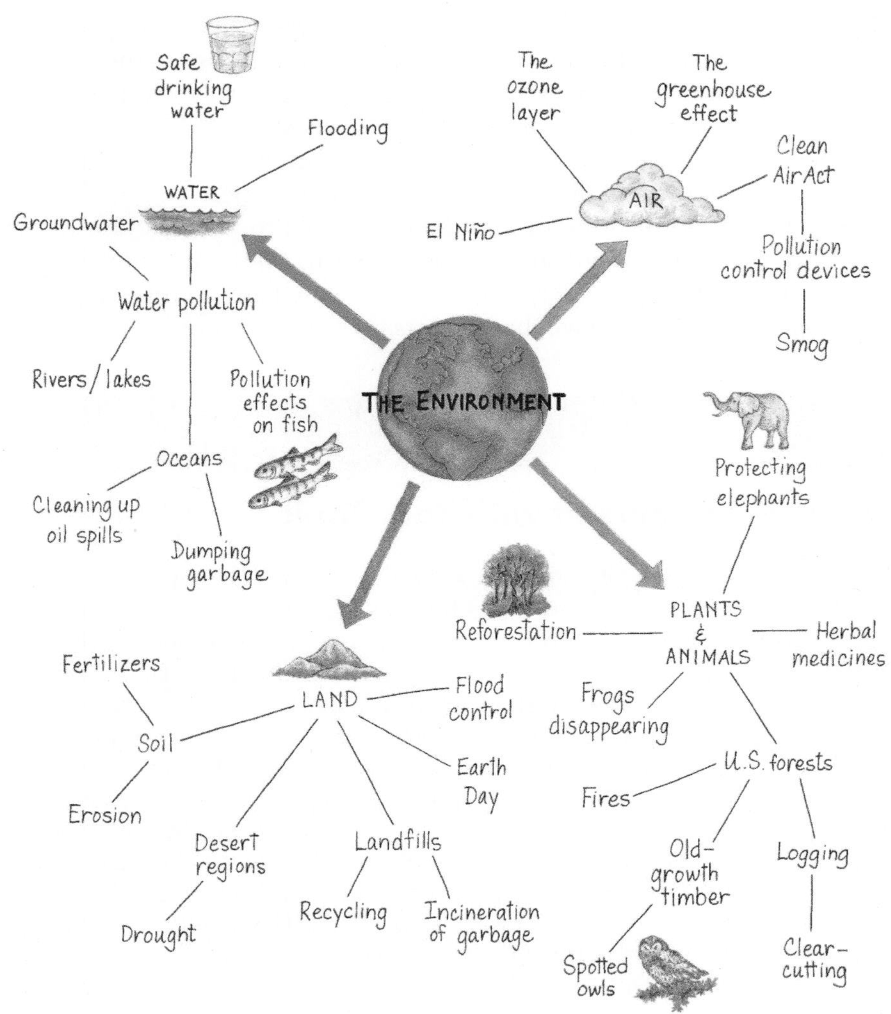

Figure 12.1
A Mind Map

General Purposes of Speaking Traditionally, three general speaking purposes have been recognized: informing, persuading, and entertaining (Table 12.1). You probably realize that these purposes often overlap. For example, informative speeches routinely include humor or stories that aim to keep the audience interested. Speeches intended to inform may also persuade people to adopt new beliefs, attitudes, or actions. Although speeches often involve more than one general purpose, usually one purpose is primary.

Speeches to inform have the primary goal of increasing audience members' understanding, awareness, or knowledge about some topic. When you speak to inform, your goal is to tell the audience something they don't already know.

speech to inform A speech, the primary goal of which is to increase audience members' understanding, awareness, or knowledge of some topic.

Consider several purposes for informative speaking:

- to teach audience members how to do something
- to correct audience members' misconceptions
- to make audience members aware of a problem
- to describe a new procedure or policy

Speeches to persuade aim to change or reinforce people's attitudes, beliefs, or behaviors or to motivate people to act. Persuasive goals are to influence attitudes, change practices, alter beliefs, and to motivate action. Rather than an entertainer or teacher, the persuasive speaker is an advocate who argues for a cause, issue, policy, attitude, or action. To persuade, a speech must do more than provide information, although information typically is part of persuasive speaking as well. Persuasive purposes include the following:

speech to persuade A speech, the primary goal of which is to change audience members' attitudes, beliefs, or behaviors or to motivate them to action.

- To convince audience members to do something they are not currently doing
- To convince audience members to stop doing something they are currently doing
- To motivate audience members to support a specific policy, law, or candidate

Table 12.1 **Speaking Purpose**

General Purposes		
To Inform	**To Persuade**	**To Entertain**
Speaking to define, instruct, explain, clarify, demonstrate, teach, or train	Speaking to influence attitudes, beliefs, or actions; to convince, motivate to action, inspire, or sell	Speaking to create interest, amusement, warm feelings; to celebrate, remember, or acknowledge others or events; to create or fortify ties between people
Specific Purposes		
To help listeners understand the balloting procedure used in the 2000 presidential elections in Florida	To persuade listeners to sign a petition demanding new voting systems for all districts in the United States	To have listeners laugh at my jokes in the after-dinner speech at the retreat

- To convince audience members to buy a product
- To inspire audience members to give time or money to a worthy cause

Review It!

Three General Purposes of Speaking:

- To Inform
- To Persuade
- To Entertain

speech to entertain A speech, the primary goal of which is to amuse, interest, or engage the audience.

specific purpose A behavioral objective or observable response that a speaker specifies as a gauge of effectiveness; reinforces a speaker's more general speaking goals.

In **speeches to entertain**, the primary objective is to interest, amuse, or please audience members. You might think that speeches to entertain are presented only by accomplished comics and performers. Actually, in the course of our lives, many of us will be involved in speaking to entertain. You might be asked to give an after-dinner speech, to present a toast at a friend's wedding, or to make remarks at a retirement party for a colleague. In each case, the primary goal is to entertain, although the speech might include information about the occasion, the couple being married, or the colleague who is retiring. You might also talk live or upload a video in which you are speaking to social media, for entertainment purposes or to blend information and entertainment, given the medium and why people use it.

Even when your primary purpose in speaking is not to entertain, you'll want to interest audience members whom you intend to inform or persuade. If you want to include some entertainment in your speech, it's a good idea to test your jokes or amusing comments in advance. Don't assume that others will find humor in something you think is funny, and don't rely exclusively on close friends' judgment; after all, friends often think alike and have similar senses of humor.

Humor isn't the only means of entertaining. We also entertain by telling stories to share experiences, build community, pass on history, and teach lessons. Storytelling is prominent in cultures that emphasize oral, more than written, communication. In some countries and in some social communities in the United States, individual and collective histories are kept alive through storytelling (Einhorn, 2000; Fitch, 2000; Schram & Schwartz, 2000). Storytelling is prominent in many religions, in which beliefs and practices are conveyed across the generations through writing and oral traditions alike. Storytelling also has the power to give a voice to people who are marginalized or oppressed, and generations of teaching through story have helped storytelling serve as a vehicle for social justice and change (Janesick, 2019).

Storytelling is a powerful way to pass on history and strengthen community bonds. It plays a central role in oral cultures.
Mark Richards/PhotoEdit

Specific Purposes of Speaking Once you have decided on your general speaking purpose, you will want to define a **specific purpose**, which is a behavioral objective or observable response that will indicate that you achieved your communication goal. Here are some examples of specific speaking purposes:

- I want 25% of audience members to sign up to donate blood.
- I want a majority of audience members to be able to give correct answers to questions about how HIV is and is not spread.
- I want audience members to know this candidate's stand on free trade.
- I want viewers of this live stream to share it with others and grow my social media following.

Develop a Thesis Statement

Once you have selected and narrowed your speaking topic and defined your general and specific purpose, you're ready to develop

Communication & Careers

The Elevator Speech

- You hop on an elevator and press the button for the 12th floor. The door closes and another passenger says to you, "I've seen you in this building before. Where do you work?"
- You are at a community fund-raiser dinner. As the salads are served, the person seated to your right asks, "What do you do?"
- You are on a flight to a conference. As the plane takes off, your seatmate says, "Hi, I'm Sam" and waits for you to say something.

The "elevator speech" is how you present yourself in 30 seconds to 2 minutes—the time it takes an elevator to travel several flights in an elevator. Think of it as your oral business card. It's essential for effective networking, so savvy professionals spend time preparing whip smart elevator speeches.

the thesis statement for your speech. A **thesis statement** is the main idea of an entire speech. It should capture the heart of your speech in a short, precise sentence that audience members can remember easily (Table 12.2).

thesis statement The main idea of an entire speech. It should capture the key message in a concise sentence that audience members can remember easily.

A good thesis statement is one that audience members grasp at the beginning of your talk and remember after you have finished. They may forget the specific details and evidence you present, but you want them to remember the main idea.

In sum, the first steps in planning a public speech are to select and narrow a topic, define your general and specific speaking purposes, and develop a clear, concise thesis statement (Table 12.3). Now we're ready to consider the key process of

Table 12.2 **Sample Thesis Statements**

Ineffective	Effective
Think twice before you decide you're for gun control.	Gun control jeopardizes individuals' rights and safety.
Vegetarianism is a way of life.	Vegetarian diets are healthful and delicious.
Big business should get breaks.	Tax breaks for businesses are good for the economy.

Table 12.3 **Steps in Planning Public Speaking**

Step	Example
1. Identify the broad topic.	Education
2. Narrow the topic.	Continuing education
3. Define a general purpose.	To persuade
4. Determine a specific purpose.	To motivate listeners to take courses after graduating from college
5. Develop a thesis statement.	"Taking courses after you graduate can enrich your personal life and your professional success."

adapting your speaking goals, content, and delivery to specific audience members and speaking contexts.

Analyze Your Audience

A student named Jake gave a persuasive speech to convince audience members to support affirmative action, meaning policies to eliminate unlawful discrimination against job applicants and make hiring practices more equitable. His ideas were well organized, and his delivery was dynamic. The only problem was that he didn't explain exactly what it does and does not involve, and his audience had little background on affirmative action. Some had even heard mistruths about it, wrongly believing that affirmative action discriminates against white people. Jake mistakenly assumed his audience members understood how affirmative action works, and he focused on its positive effects. They weren't persuaded because he failed to give them information they needed, such as dispelling myths about it or concrete examples of action policies. This example also illustrates the point that speeches often combine more than one speaking purpose; in this case, giving information was essential to Jake's primary goal of persuasion.

Another student named Christie spoke passionately about vegetarianism. She provided dramatic evidence of the cruelty animals suffer as they are raised and slaughtered. When we polled the audience after her speech, only 2 of 30 had been persuaded to consider vegetarianism. Why was Christie ineffective? Because she didn't recognize and address their beliefs that vegetarians eat bland food. Christie might have persuaded them by sharing descriptions about how delicious vegetarian meals are, but she didn't think to do so—and they weren't about to consider a diet that they thought was unappetizing.

Christie and Jake made the mistake of not adapting to their audiences. In all forms of communication—whether advertising, public relations, political campaigning, or public speaking—tailoring your message to your intended audience is crucial. While preparing a speech, speakers need to investigate what their audience already knows and believes, as well as what reservations they might have about a topic (Coopman & Lull, 2013; Griffin, 2015). To paraphrase the advice of the ancient Greek rhetorician Aristotle, "The fool persuades me with their reasons, the wise person with my own." That is, effective speakers work with audience members' reasons, values, knowledge, and concerns.

Demographic Audience Analysis

demographic audience analysis A form of audience analysis that seeks information about the general features of a group of audience members.

Demographic audience analysis identifies general features common to a group of audience members. Demographic characteristics include age, sex, gender, ability, sexual orientation, religion, cultural heritage, race and ethnicity, occupation, political allegiances, income, and educational level. Demographic information is useful in two ways.

First, demographic information can help you adapt your speech to your audience. For example, if you know their age or age range, you know what experiences are likely to be part of their history. You could assume that 40-year-olds know a fair amount about 9/11 but that 20-year-olds might not. You can assume that people in their 50s remember the Gulf War, but younger people do not. In speaking situations with audience members of different ages, either restrict your references to the ones that will be familiar to people of all ages or explain any references that might not be understood by some of them.

Age is also linked to persuadability. In general, as people age, they are less likely to change their attitudes, perhaps because they've held their attitudes longer than younger people or because they've acquired knowledge that supports their attitudes (Meyers, 1993). Thus, it's generally reasonable to expect to move older audience members less than younger ones toward new beliefs, attitudes, or actions.

Other demographic information can also guide speakers in preparing presentations that will interest and involve particular audience members. Because we live in a diverse society, effective speakers must be careful not to use examples that exclude some groups. For instance, the use of generic male language (*chairman*, the pronoun *he* to refer to a doctor) and binary language to discuss gender (referring to "men and women" as though this encompasses all adult people) is not inclusive. Similarly, referring to the winter break from school as "the Christmas holiday" ignores audience members who are not Christian.

Speakers also use demographic information to make inferences about their audience's likely beliefs, values, and attitudes. For example, assume you plan to give a speech on the general topic of health care reform. If your audience's average age is 68 years, they are likely to be more interested in options for long-term care of older adults than in methods of birth control. Those with an average age of 21 years, on the other hand, would be likely to perceive birth control as more immediately relevant than ensuring reasonable options for long-term care. Skilled politicians do this quite well while campaigning for office, highlighting different elements of their political platforms as they speak with different groups of constituents.

Knowing something about the general characteristics of an audience may also suggest what type of evidence and which authorities will be effective. Statistics bore many people, especially if presented in a dull manner, but they might be interesting to an audience of economists or mathematicians. A quotation from Bernie Sanders or Alexandria Ocasio-Cortez is more likely to be effective with a liberal audience than with a conservative one. Citing Justice Sonja Sotomayor might impress a group of social workers more than citing Brett Kavanaugh would. Speakers may also draw on demographic information to create connections with their audiences. Politicians create points of identification with voters in diverse regions. In the South, a candidate might tell stories about growing up in a Southern town; in New England, the candidate might reminisce about college years at Harvard; in the Midwest, the candidate might speak about friends and family who live there. It is unethical for a speaker to disguise or distort their background, ideas, or positions to build common ground their audience. However, understanding the demographic characteristics of an audience helps a speaker decide which aspects of their life and interests to emphasize in particular situations.

Lamont A big filmmaker came to talk to our class, and I figured he was in a world totally different from ours. I mean, the man makes multimillion-dollar movies and knows all the big stars. But he started his talk by telling us about when he was in college, and he talked about his favorite classes, about a bar he went to on Fridays, and about the special friends he'd made at college. I felt like he understood what my life is about, like he wasn't so different from me after all.

Question: The filmmaker showed communication acumen in how he addressed Lamont's class. Think about the other types of groups a filmmaker might address. How might he have changed his talk's introduction to connect with other audiences?

Situational Audience Analysis

situational audience analysis A method of audience analysis that seeks information about specific audience members that relates directly to a topic, speaker, and occasion.

A second method of audience analysis is **situational audience analysis**, which seeks information about audience members that relates directly to the speaker's topic and purpose. Situational audience analysis allows a speaker to discover what audience members already know and believe about a topic, speaker, and occasion so that the speaker can adapt to their audience.

Audience Members' Orientation Toward the Topic Speakers want to begin by piquing audience members' interest. How does the topic affect their lives? Why should they care about what you have to say? Emma, a student of mine, began an informative speech about breast cancer this way: "Think about 8 women who matter to you. According to statistics, 1 of those 8 women will develop breast cancer."

You also want to analyze audience members' knowledge about your topic so that you can adapt appropriately. What do they already know about the topic? How much information (or misinformation) do they have? Once you have assessed your audience members' knowledge about your topic, you can decide how much information to provide.

Finally, in assessing your audience members' orientation toward your topic, you want to know what attitudes they hold. If they already favor something you are proposing, you don't need to persuade them to adopt a positive attitude. Instead, you may want to move them to action—to motivate them to act on what they already favor. On the other hand, if your audience members are against or indifferent to something you are proposing, your persuasive goal is to convince them to consider your point of view.

Audience Members' Orientation Toward the Speaker Audience members' perceptions of a speaker shape how they respond to the message. Do the audience members already know who you are? Do they respect your expertise on the topic? Do audience members believe you care about what is good for them? If not, you need to give audience members reasons to trust your expertise and to believe that you are interested in their welfare.

If you are not an expert on a topic, you will want to demonstrate to audience members that you know what you are talking about. Describe your experiences with the topic. Include research that shows you are knowledgeable. Because a speaker's credibility is critical to effectiveness, we'll return to this topic when we discuss using evidence (Chapter 13), building a strong introduction to a speech (Chapter 14), and increasing credibility (Chapter 16).

Audience Members' Orientation Toward the Speaking Occasion Politicians and corporations can afford to conduct sophisticated polls to discover what people know, want, think, and believe. How do ordinary people engage in situational audience analysis? You may gather information about audience members through conversations, interviews, or surveys. You might conduct a survey to learn about your classmates' knowledge of and attitudes toward your thesis statement. The results of your survey should give you sufficient insight into the opinions of students on your campus to enable you to adapt your presentation to the students in your class. You can even pose questions at the beginning of any speech, asking audience members to raise their hands, stand up, or say "yes!" if they have experience with your topic, and adjust your remarks accordingly.

Demographic and situational audience analysis provides you with direct knowledge of audience members and information from which you can draw additional inferences. Taking your audience into consideration allows you to build a speech that is adapted to your particular audience and thus likely to have impact.

Review It!

Types of Audience Analysis:

- Demographic
- Situational

Chapter Summary

In this chapter, we considered the first steps in designing effective presentations. Planning includes selecting and limiting your topic, defining your general and specific purposes, and developing a clear thesis statement. In addition, designing an effective presentation requires consideration of audience members. Effective speakers take into account what audience members know, believe, value, think, and feel about the topic, speaker, and occasion. When a speaker adapts to audience members, they are likely to be more receptive to the speaker's ideas. Online search engines and databases can help you research topics, but exercise critical thinking about information you find online.

In the next chapter, we'll discuss ways to conduct research and use research in public speaking. Building good arguments increases a speaker's credibility and enhances the power of ideas presented. Before proceeding to Chapter 13, complete the checklist to make sure you've done the preliminary work to create a strong foundation for your speech.

Checklist for Planning a Public Speech

My speech topic is ______________________________

____

My general purpose is ______________________________

____

My specific purpose is ______________________________

____

My thesis statement is ______________________________

____

1. I know the following demographic information about the people who will attend my speech:

   Age: ______________________________

   Education: ______________________________

   Political position: ______________________________

   Gender ratio: ______________________________

   Ethnicities: ______________________________

   Other: ______________________________

2. I know the following information about my particular audience members:

Audience members' interest in my topic: ________

____

Audience members' knowledge about my topic: ______________________________

____

Audience members' personal experience with my topic: ______________________________

____

Audience members' beliefs about my topic: _____

____

Audience members' attitudes toward my thesis: ______________________________

____

Audience members' expectations of the speaking occasion: ______________________________

____

Audience members' orientation toward me as a speaker: ______________________________

____

Experiencing Communication in Our Lives

Case Study: A Model Speech of Introduction

Apply what you've learned in this chapter by analyzing the following case study, using the accompanying questions as a guide.

Dan's assignment was to present a speech of introduction in which he introduces his classmates to Dr. Evelyn Horton. Dr. Horton is a doctor who specializes in family medicine, the profession that Dan hopes to enter.

"If you don't listen to your patients, you'll never be able to provide them with good medical care." That was the first thing Dr. Evelyn Horton said to me when I asked her what kinds of communication are essential to her work. Last Monday, I interviewed her because I hope one day to be a doctor. I want to introduce you to Dr. Horton and to describe the role of communication in her work as a doctor. I'll focus on the importance of two communication skills that Dr. Horton emphasized: listening and building a supportive, trusting relationship.

The first communication skill that Dr. Horton emphasized is listening. She told me that one of the reasons she wanted to become a doctor is that she had encountered too many doctors who didn't listen to her when she was a patient. "How can a doctor treat you if they don't listen to you?" asked Dr. Horton. Dr. Horton isn't alone in feeling that many doctors don't listen. The Journal of the American Medical Association reported last year that patients' biggest dissatisfaction with doctors is that they don't listen.

I asked Dr. Horton to explain what was involved in effective listening. She said, and I quote, "To be a good listener, I have to let my patients know I really want to hear what's going on with them. I have to give them permission to tell me how they are feeling and if anything is bothering them." Some of the ways that Dr. Horton does this are to repeat what patients tell her so that they will elaborate, and to keep eye contact with them when they are speaking.

So focusing on patients and encouraging them to talk openly with her are the keys to effective listening in Dr. Horton's practice. The second communication skill that Dr. Horton emphasized is building a supportive, trusting relationship with her patients. She told me about one of her patients who

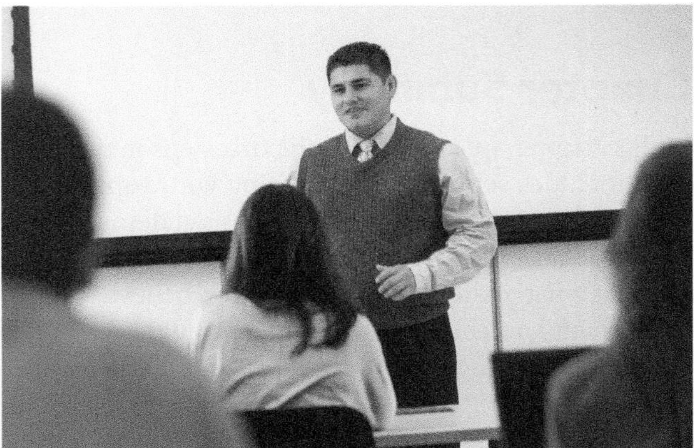

had an eating disorder. Dr. Horton suspected the problem, but she couldn't do much to treat it until her patient, a 19-year-old woman, was willing to admit she had a problem.

How did Dr. Horton gain the patient's trust? She told me that she showed the patient she wasn't going to judge her—that it was okay to say anything, and it would be confidential. When the patient made a small disclosure about being afraid of gaining weight, Dr. Horton recalled, and I quote, "I told her many women have that fear, and there are healthy ways to control weight." Later, the patient told her that sometimes she skipped meals. Dr. Horton responded, and again I quote her, "That's an understandable thing to do when you're afraid of gaining weight, but there are healthier ways to maintain a good weight." As Dr. Horton responded without judgment to the patient, the young woman gradually opened up and told Dr. Horton about her excessive dieting and exercise. Together, they worked out a better, healthier approach to managing her eating disorder.

Being nonjudgmental, then, is a key to building a trusting doctor–patient relationship. Now you've met Dr. Evelyn Horton, a doctor who knows the importance of communication to her work. For her, listening and building a supportive, trusting relationship with patients are the keys to being a good doctor. Let me close with one last statement Dr. Horton made. She told me, "To treat people, you have to communicate well with them."

Questions for Analysis and Discussion

1. Does Dan's speech give you a sense of who Dr. Horton is?
2. Did Dan's introduction catch your attention and give you a road map of what he would cover in his speech?
3. How did Dan move you from one part of his speech to the next?
4. How did quotes and examples from Dr. Horton add to the speech?
5. Was Dan's conclusion effective?
6. Which model of communication presented in Chapter 1 best describes Dr. Horton's communication with patients?

Key Concepts

demographic audience analysis
mind map
situational audience analysis
specific purpose
speech to entertain
speech to inform
speech to persuade
thesis statement

Sharpen Your Skill

1. **Selecting and Narrowing Your Topic**

   Identify three broad topics or areas that you care about.

   Topic 1: ______________________

   Topic 2: ______________________

   Topic 3: ______________________

   Now list three subtopics for each one. The subtopics should be narrow enough to be covered well in a short speech.

   Topic 1: 1. ______________________
   2. ______________________
   3. ______________________

   Topic 2: 1. ______________________
   2. ______________________
   3. ______________________

   Topic 3: 1. ______________________
   2. ______________________
   3. ______________________

   Select one of the nine subtopics for your upcoming speech.

2. **Defining Your Purpose and Thesis Statement**

   Write out the general purpose of your speech.

   I want my speech to ______________________

   ____

   Define the specific purpose of your speech by specifying the observable response that will indicate you have succeeded:

   At the end of my speech, I want audience members to ______________________

   ____

   Does your specific purpose require you to meet subordinate goals, such as including information in a persuasive speech?

   To achieve my specific purpose I need to [entertain, inform, and/or persuade]. ______________________

   ____

For Further Reflection and Discussion

1. Think about one presentation that you recently attended—perhaps a lecture in a class or a speech at a campus event. To what extent did the speaker seem to take the audience into consideration? Identify specific factors that affect your perception of the speaker's knowledge of you and other audience members. Did this make a difference in the speaker's effectiveness?
2. In this chapter, we discussed the importance of adapting to particular audience members. What ethical considerations apply to the process of adapting speeches to particular audience members? Is it ethical for a speaker not to disclose certain experiences with a topic? Is it ethical for a speaker to leave out evidence that is contrary to their speaking goal?
3. Check two databases for sources on a topic that interests you. Track down two sources from each database to read in detail.
4. Go to the book's online resources for this chapter to review commonly believed myths about public speaking.

Researching and Developing Support for Public Speeches

> Handle them carefully, for words have more power than atom bombs.
>
> **Pearl Strachan**

Learning Objectives

After studying the topics in this chapter, you should be able to:

1. Explain the difference between primary and secondary research sources.
2. Explain the difference between peer-reviewed and non-peer-reviewed sources used for speeches.
3. List ways to conduct primary and secondary research.
4. Explain the value of seeking information from multiple cultural perspectives when gathering information.
5. List five kinds of evidence used by effective public speakers.
6. Properly cite sources for a public speech.

What type of evidence do you find most compelling?

- Guns kill too many people.
- Guns killed 45,222 Americans in 2021 alone.
- Guns have killed more Americans since 1981 than have died in all of the wars America has ever fought.

Which of the aforementioned statements do you find most interesting and most persuasive (Crawford and Lutz, 2019; Department of Veteran Affairs, 2021; National Safety Council, 2022)? If you are like the most people, the third statement is most compelling. The first statement is a weak generalization. The second gives a concrete number that is stunning, but the statistic is not related to anything. The third statement offers a comparison that puts gun deaths in a broader perspective. This illustrates the difference that strong evidence can make in a speech. It also shows that evidence is not only a matter of facts and statistics, but also of a speaker's imagination and effort to make it meaningful.

A speaker's success is tied directly to whether their audience understands, believes, and accepts what they say. In this chapter, you will learn how to conduct research and weave it into your speech so that audience members understand and believe in you and your message. You will also learn how digital media can assist you in conducting research for your speech. Throughout the process of researching and building support for a speech, it's important to conduct research and select evidence adapted to particular audience members.

Conducting Primary and Secondary Research

secondary research Research using already existing sources that you compile from various publications.

primary research Research that you collect yourself, such as interviewing or surveying people.

Research is essential to a sound informative or persuasive speech. We'll discuss four types of research: online research and library research—known as **secondary research**—and interviews and surveys, known as **primary research**.

Secondary Research

When you conduct secondary research, you find and make use of data other people have gathered for various reports and publications. Secondary research is a great starting point for any speech.

Online Research

Online research is often the first step in researching a topic. They are fast and convenient and they often provide lots of material. However, the material's quality is not assured. It may be highly credible or may be junk. Most newspapers have fact checkers who check all information in articles before they go to press. In contrast, the accuracy of information posted on the Internet is not assured. People who create or contribute to websites may not have evidence for their claims. They may have vested interests in particular viewpoints. Information you find online should be verified. Look into the credibility of the site you are using, and if referring to Wikipedia, don't quote the Wikipedia article itself. Instead, look at the references that the Wikipedia editors are using, and visit those resources to read and quote them directly.

Library Research

Libraries have a wealth of information that can help you develop and support the ideas in your speech. Begin your research by seeking help from your library's reference librarian or subject area specialist relevant to your topic. Check your library website to identify these librarians and to learn whether they have drop-in hours or, if not, how to make an appointment to receive support in person, by phone, or through video conferencing. Be prepared to describe your speech topic to your librarian, and ask for suggestions on relevant sources of information.

The librarian will probably direct you to the online catalogue, which lists holdings by author, title, and subject. The online catalogue will help you find reference works that can provide background information on people whom you cite in your speech. The catalogue will also let you search newspapers and scholarly databases for very current information on your topic (see Figure 13.1).

While doing library research, be sure to look for **peer-reviewed research**, meaning scholarly research that has been carefully scrutinized by other experts in the field prior to publication. Because it has been carefully scrutinized in this way, peer-reviewed publications are considered the most trustworthy type of secondary source.

peer-reviewed research
Scholarly research that has been carefully scrutinized by other experts in the field as a condition of publication.

Bear in mind that some, but not all, research that you will find via library databases has been peer-reviewed. Many databases have a box you can check to filter to "Peer Reviewed Journals" only, and using this will greatly increase the odds that your search results are scholarly in nature.

You will be able to tell if an article is peer-reviewed by considering the following:

- Was it published in a newspaper or magazine? If so, it is not peer-reviewed.
- Is it labeled "conference paper" or "presentation"? If so, it may have been peer-reviewed for acceptance for the authors to present at a conference, but this is highly variable; some conferences only review abstracts, not entire papers. Use these sources with caution.

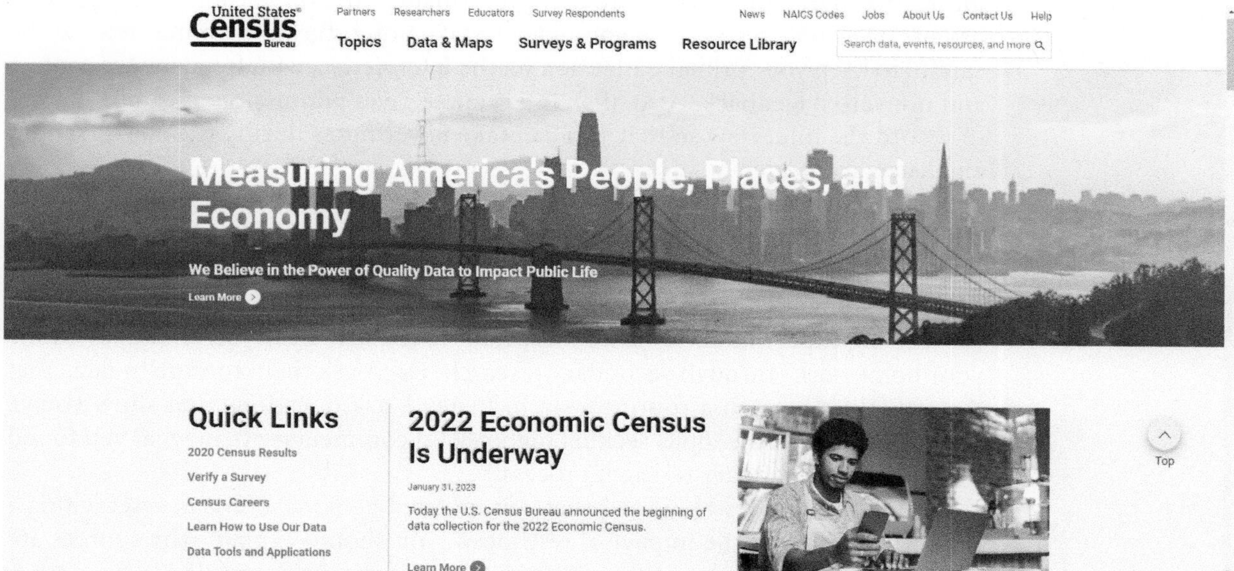

Figure 13.1
Online Research Includes Websites, such as the United States Census Bureau, which Provides Information on Demographics and Many Facets of American Life

- Was it published in a scholarly journal? If you're not sure, look up the publication title online. Find the website and see if it's a journal. Then see:
  - Is it marked "Commentary" or "Review"? If so, it is not peer-reviewed; it is an opinion piece or a review of a book or other publication.
  - Is it lengthy and featuring many citations, including a robust reference list? If so, it is most likely peer-reviewed! Check the journal website to see if it's a peer-reviewed publication (perhaps under a heading like "instructions for authors") to be sure.

Primary Research

Primary research is a great way to learn more about a topic and answer questions that were unanswered by your secondary research. If you do secondary research first (even though it may sound funny for *secondary* research to happen *first*), you will ask better, more insightful questions during the primary research process.

Interviews

Interviews allow you to gather information, to check the accuracy of ideas you have, and to understand the perspective of people who are experts or who have special experience with your topic.

You need to plan ahead for interviews. When you call or email to request an interview, identify yourself, explain the purpose of the interview, and state the approximate length of time you expect the interview to take. If the interviewee is in your local area, discuss whether they prefer to meet in person or via video conferencing, and check whether they have any interpretation or other access needs you should prepare for. If the interview will be conducted virtually, agree upon which platform you'll use and set the meeting up in advance. Also prepare a list of questions in advance to ensure that you don't forget important questions.

In addition to questions you prepare, you'll want to invite interviewees to initiate ideas. As experts, they may be aware of information and dimensions of a topic that haven't occurred to you. It's a good idea to take notes during the interview, but be careful to keep your primary attention on the interviewee, with frequent eye contact and nonverbal feedback. Also, if an interviewee gives permission, it can be helpful to record the interview so that you can take fewer notes during the conversation, and listen again later.

If the interviewee mentions sources they've read or published that are directly relevant to your project, make a note of these and try to access them directly. You might also ask if it's possible for them to send you copies or links to these sources if you cannot find them yourself.

During expert interviews, it's important to make it clear you've already "done your homework" through secondary research. Don't ask them to explain facts that are available through a routine search. Instead, ask questions that show you've already read upon the topic, seeking higher-level commentary than what you found through your secondary research process.

Quoting interviewees shows that you invested personal effort in researching a topic. To maximize the impact of testimony, you should explain why sources are qualified as experts. You may credit your sources in several ways:

"After 10 years in the position of chief of campus police, Chris Brenner says, . . ."

"In an interview I conducted with Chris Brenner, longtime chief of campus police, he told me that. . ."

"To find out about crime on our campus, I interviewed the chief of campus police. According to Chief Brenner, . . ."

Cole It was really effective when Joel told us he had interviewed police officers to find out their views about drivers who use cell phones. He had lots of good information from other sources, but what really impressed me was that he took time to talk with police officers himself. I felt like that showed he cared enough to really learn about his topic in a personal way.

Question: Why do you think mentioning your speech's sources makes a difference to your audience?

Surveys

Survey research involves asking a number of people about their opinions, views, values, actions, or beliefs. You can create and print simple surveys to hand out to people in person, or you can use software like SurveyMonkey to create online surveys that are more complex. These are advantageous because they can include screening questions at the beginning to make sure those who respond have the required background, and they can also include "skip logic," where the next screen a person sees depends on their answers to the question they are answering (skipping over other questions that don't apply to them).

survey research Research that involves asking a number of people about their opinions, preferences, actions, or beliefs.

Surveys are useful in two situations. First, sometimes there's no published research on something important to your speech. Yumiko, a student taking his first speaking course, was concerned that many of his peers at the university had misperceptions about Japanese people and their traditions. He decided to use his speech as an opportunity to correct misperceptions. After 2 weeks of research, he was discouraged because he couldn't find any studies of United States college students' views of Japanese people. We developed a short questionnaire on views of Japanese people that he handed out to 100 students on campus. This gave Yumiko some information about local students' perceptions (Table 13.1).

Second, sometimes you can directly survey your audience. Although this isn't always feasible, when possible, a survey helps you find out what audience members know. Based on what you learn, you can include information they don't have and avoid boring them by telling them what they already know. Surveys of audiences also allow you to discover what personal experience they have pertinent to your topic. Attitudes based on direct experience are more difficult to change (Wu & Shaffer, 1988).

Audience surveys can also help you learn what attitudes they hold. At a minimum, you'll want to know whether your audience members agree or disagree with your position and how strong their attitudes are. If you want to argue for easing immigration restrictions, and your audience members are strongly against that, then you might choose to limit your persuasive goal to reducing the strength of their resistance to making immigration easier. On the other hand, if they already agree with your position, you might try to move them toward action by asking them to write letters to senators or to vote for candidates who share their attitudes. What you can achieve in a given speech depends to a large extent on the starting beliefs and knowledge of your audience (Wu & Shaffer, 1988).

Seeking Diverse Perspectives in Your Research

In the research process, you can strengthen your speech by seeking information from multiple cultural perspectives. We tend to approach any topic we discuss with the bias of our own experiences. When in the research process we can learn about experiences that differ from our own, and integrate these into our speeches, we demonstrate that we are knowledgeable, credible, and inclusive of audience members whose backgrounds differ from our own.

Review It!

Types of Research:

- Primary
- Secondary
- Online
- Library
- Interviews
- Surveys

Table 13.1 Guidelines for Constructing Surveys

The following guidelines will help you construct a survey that will provide you with solid information.

1. Respondents should be chosen to reflect the population (or larger group) whose opinions you seek to understand. (Students may reflect students' opinions. However, students generally would not reflect homeowners' opinions.)
2. Respondents should be qualified to answer the questions. (Only people who are informed about inflation and living expenses have the information to answer this question: "How much should the cost-of-living adjustment be for Social Security recipients?")
3. Questions should be worded to avoid bias. ("You favor gun control, don't you?" is a leading question that biases respondents toward answering affirmatively. The question "Do you favor gun control?" is not biased. You will get different responses if you ask people if they favor "helping the poor" and if they favor "welfare.")
4. Each question should focus on only one issue. ("Do you favor Medicare and Medicaid?" asks respondents' opinions on two distinct issues. This question should be split into two separate questions.)
5. Questions should allow for all possible responses. (It would not be accurate to ask respondents whether they are Democrats or Republicans because those two responses don't include other possible choices, such as Libertarians and Independents.)
6. Questions should rely on language that will be clear to respondents. (For years, the United States Bureau of the Census asked people whether they worked "full time," which the bureau defined as 35 hours a week or more. However, many respondents interpreted "full time" to mean 40 hours a week or more. The bureau revised the wording of the question to remove the ambiguity.)
7. Avoid negative language in survey items; it tends to be confusing. (Respondents are likely to misunderstand the question "Do you agree or disagree that the United States should not have socialized medicine?" The question is clearer when phrased this way: "Do you agree or disagree that the United States should have socialized medicine?")

Now that we have discussed ways to conduct research, we're ready to consider specific forms of support, or evidence.

Mia After the Supreme Court overturned *Roe v. Wade*, I drafted a speech arguing that the decision was wrong, and why abortion care matters. But when some classmates who agreed with the decision read it as part of my class's peer review process, they said it didn't feel like I understood their perspectives. I realized that in my speech, I hadn't acknowledged why some people support the SCOTUS decision, so I did more research on Conservative views. I made sure to acknowledge those perspectives, and then I rebutted the misinformation in a respectful way. It definitely made the speech stronger than it had been when it was fully focused on why I disagreed with the decision.

Question: Why do you think acknowledging other people's perspectives can strengthen a speech? How does doing so influence audience members' receptiveness to a speaker?

Using Evidence to Support Ideas

Evidence is material used to support claims a speaker makes. Evidence serves a number of important functions in speeches. First, it can be used to make ideas clearer, more compelling, and more interesting. Second, evidence fortifies a speaker's opinions. Finally, evidence heightens a speaker's credibility. Speakers who use good evidence show that they are informed and prepared.

evidence Material used to support claims. Types of evidence are statistics, examples, comparisons, and quotations. Visual aids may be used to represent evidence graphically.

> **Martel** We had a guest speaker in my econ class. He quoted Nobel Prize–winning economists and the findings of a report that was just done and hasn't even been published yet. All of us felt he was highly informed and credible.

Five forms of support are widely recognized. Before including any form of evidence in a speech, the speaker should check the accuracy of the material and the credibility of the source. When presenting evidence to audiences, speakers have an ethical responsibility to give credit to the source (an oral footnote).

Statistics

Statistics are numbers that summarize many individual cases or demonstrate relationships between phenomena. Including statistics can enhance speaker credibility (Crossen, 1997). For example, a speaker could demonstrate the prevalence of injuries caused by drivers who are under the influence of alcohol by stating, "According to the American Automobile Association, one in four people injured in traffic accidents is the victim of a driver who had been drinking." Statistics can also be used to document connections between two or more things. For instance, a speaker could say, "According to the Highway Patrol, you are 50% more likely to have an accident if you drink before driving."

statistics A form of evidence that uses numbers to summarize a great many individual cases or to demonstrate relationships between phenomena.

Statistics aren't boring, but they can be poorly presented. Effective speakers translate statistics into information that is meaningful to the audience (see Table 13.2). To describe a million people experiencing homelessness in terms their audience would immediately understand, a student speaker said, "That's 50 times the number

Cartoon by Signe Wilkinson. Reprinted by permission of Cartoonists & Writers Syndicate/cartoonweb.com

Table 13.2 Guidelines for Using Statistics Effectively

Used unimaginatively, statistics are likely to bore listeners. To avoid this fate when you are speaking, follow these guidelines for using statistics effectively.

- Limit the number of statistics you use in a speech. A few well-chosen numbers mixed with other kinds of support can be dramatic and persuasive, whereas a laundry list of statistics can be monotonous and ineffective.
- Round off numbers so that listeners can understand and retain them. We're more likely to remember that "approximately a million Americans are homeless" than that "987,422 Americans are homeless."
- Select statistics that are timely. Occasionally, an old statistic is still useful. For example, the number of people who died in the Great Plague is not likely to change over the years. In most cases, however, the most accurate statistics are recent. Remember that statistics are a numerical picture of something at a specific time. But things change, and speakers should get new snapshots when they do.
- Make statistics interesting to listeners by translating statistics into familiar and relevant information.

of students on our campus." Here's how another student speaker translated the statistic that one in four college-age women will be raped in her lifetime: "Of the seventeen women students in this room today, four will probably be raped sometime during their lives."

Examples

examples Forms of evidence; single instances that make a point, dramatize an idea, or personalize information. The three types of examples are undetailed, detailed, and hypothetical.

Examples are single instances used to make a point, dramatize an idea, or personalize information. There are three types of examples that have different uses for speakers.

Undetailed Examples When speakers want to make a point quickly, undetailed examples are useful. These are brief references that quickly recount specific instances of something. One student opened a speech on the costs of textbooks by saying, "Remember standing in the long lines at the bookstore and paying for more than your tuition at the start of this term?" His audience immediately identified with the topic of the speech.

Detailed Examples Detailed examples provide more elaborate information than undetailed ones, so they are valuable when audience members aren't familiar with an idea. A student included this detailed example in her speech on environmental justice:

> Most of you haven't lived near a toxic waste dump, so you may not understand what's involved. In one community, the incidence of cancer is 130% higher than in the country as a whole. The skin on one man's hands was eaten away when he touched the outside of a canister that stored toxic waste. His skin literally dissolved when it came in contact with the toxin.

Detailed examples create vivid pictures that can be moving and memorable. However, because they take time to present, they should be used sparingly.

Stories or anecdotes are a type of detailed example. Presidents routinely include stories in their speeches to personalize their ideas and create identification with their audiences. Religions rely on stories—parables in Christianity, *teichos* in Buddhism—to teach values and persuade people to follow them. Attorneys rely on stories to persuade judges and jurors, taking all the known facts in a case and weaving them together in a way that makes sense and supports their clients' accounts of events. The attorneys with whom I consult tell me that the key challenge in trial court is to create a story that covers all the facts and is more believable than the story created by the opposing counsel.

Speakers often tell a story to personalize abstract issues. To help a middle-class audience understand the personal meaning of poverty, a student told this story about a woman he interviewed to prepare his speech:

> To start her day, Annie pours half a glass of milk and mixes it half and half with water so that the quart she buys each week will last. If she finds day-old bread on sale at the market, she has toast, but she can't afford margarine. Annie coughs harshly and wishes this throat infection would pass. She can't afford to go to a doctor. Even if she could, the cost of drugs is beyond her budget. She shivers, thinking that winter is coming. That means long days in the malls so that she can be in heated places. It's hard on her and the kids, but the cost of heat is more than she can pay. Annie is only 28 years old, just a few years older than we are, but she looks well into her forties. Like you, Annie grew up expecting a pretty good life, but then her husband left her. He doesn't pay child support, and she can't afford a detective to trace him. Her children, both under 4, are too young to be left alone, so she can't work.

The story about Annie puts a human face on poverty. A story that has depth takes time, so speakers have to consider whether the point they want to make justifies the time a story will take.

Communication Highlight

The Typical American Family

John F. Kennedy was a powerful public speaker. He wove many kinds of support into his speeches to strengthen his credibility and increase the impact of his ideas.

On May 19, 1962, President John F. Kennedy used the following hypothetical example in his speech at the rally for the National Council of Senior Citizens at Madison Square Garden.

Let's consider the case of a typical American family—a family which might be found in any part of the United States. The husband has worked hard all of his life, and now he has retired. He might have been a clerk or a salesman or worked in a factory. He always insisted on paying his own way. This man, like most Americans, wants to care for himself. He has raised his own family, educated his children, and he and his wife are drawing Social Security now. Then his wife gets sick, not just for a week, but for a very long time. First the savings go. Next, he mortgages his home. Finally, he goes to his children, who are themselves heavily burdened. Then their savings begin to go. What is he to do now? Here is a typical American who has nowhere to turn, so he finally will have to sign a petition saying he's broke and needs welfare assistance.

Diamond Images/Getty Images

Review It!

Types of Examples:

- Undetailed
- Detailed
- Hypothetical

Hypothetical Examples Sometimes a speaker has no real example that adequately makes a point. In such cases, a speaker can create a hypothetical example, which is not factual but can add clarity and depth to a speech. To be effective, hypothetical examples must be realistic illustrations of what you want to exemplify. Hypothetical examples often are used to portray average cases rather than to represent a single person or event. If you use a hypothetical example, you have an ethical responsibility to inform your audience that it is not a factual example.

Comparisons

comparisons Forms of evidence that use associations between two things that are similar in some important way.

similes Direct comparisons that typically use the words like or as to link two things.

metaphors Implicit comparisons of two different things that have something in common, often using one word in place of another to communicate their likeness.

quotations Forms of evidence that use exact citations of statements made by others. Also called testimony.

Comparisons are associations between two things that are similar in some important way or ways. **Similes** are explicit comparisons that typically use the words *like* or *as* to link two things: "A teacher is like a guide." "Service is like paying dues for membership in a community." **Metaphors** are implicit comparisons that suggest likeness between two things that have something in common: "A teacher is a guide," "Service is the dues you pay for belonging to a community."

Quotations

Quotations, or testimony, are statements made by others. If someone has stated a point in an especially effective manner, then you may want to quote that person's words. Quotations may also be used to substantiate ideas. Using an expert's testimony may be persuasive to an audience, but only if they respect the expert who is quoted. Thus, it's important to provide "oral footnotes" in which you identify the name, position, and qualifications of anyone you quote, as well as the date of the quoted statement. For example, in a speech advocating tougher laws for driving under the influence, you might say, "Speaking in 2016, our senior state senator, Ben Adams, observed that if we had enacted the proposed law 3 years ago, 23 people killed by drunk drivers would be alive today."

Whenever you quote another person, you are ethically obligated to give credit to that person, just as you credit the sources of all forms of evidence. This can be done by changing your tone of voice after stating an authority's name, or by saying, "John Smith stated that. . . ." It is also acceptable to say "quote" at the beginning of

Communication Highlight

I Have a Dream

In 1963, Reverend Martin Luther King Jr. delivered his moving speech, "I Have a Dream" to more than 200,000 people gathered on the National Mall in front of the Lincoln Memorial. In it, he compared the unfulfilled promises of the United States to African American citizens to an unpaid check. He said that the nation's founders had guaranteed rights to citizens and that those rights were a check for which payment was due. Comparing promises due to all citizens to a check was a compelling metaphor.

Go to the online resources for this chapter to search for more information about Martin Luther King Jr.'s "I Have a Dream" speech.

AP Images/Anonymous

a quotation and "end quote" at the end of it, although this method of citing sources becomes boring if it is used repeatedly in a speech.

Effective and ethical quotations meet three criteria. First, as we've already noted, sources should be people whom audience members know and respect or whom they will respect once you identify the source's credentials (Cooper & Lull, 2013; Olson & Cal, 1984). Michael Phelps is an awesome athlete. However, his swimming skill has no relevance to Subway sandwiches, which he endorses in ads. Subway is counting on the **halo effect**, the tendency to assume that an expert in one area is also an expert in other areas. Although some people may fall prey to the halo effect, discerning people will not. Ethical speakers rely on authorities who are qualified, and they identify authorities' qualifications.

halo effect The tendency to assume that an expert in one area is also an expert in other unrelated areas.

Ethical quotations must also meet the criterion of accuracy. For instance, you should respect the context in which comments are made. It is unethical to take a statement out of context to make it better support your ideas. Also, it's unethical to alter a direct quotation by adding or deleting words. Sometimes, writers omit words and indicate the omission with ellipses: "Noted authority William West stated that 'there is no greater priority . . . than our children.'" In oral presentations, however, it is difficult to indicate omitted words smoothly. When using quotations, speakers have an ethical responsibility to be accurate and fair in representing others and their ideas.

Finally, quotations should come from unbiased sources. It's hardly convincing when scientists paid by the tobacco industry tell us cigarettes don't cause cancer. Likewise, thoughtful audience members may not believe the CEO of a coal mining company who states that mining causes no environmental damage. Whether or not the statement is true, they are likely to think the CEO has a vested interest that makes them less than trustworthy.

Visual Aids

visual aids Presentation of evidence by such visual means as charts, graphs, photographs, and physical objects to reinforce ideas presented verbally or to provide information.

Visual aids are unlike the other types of evidence we have discussed. They do not prove claims with data. They do, however, clarify claims and make them accessible and memorable, which supports an overall presentation. **Visual aids** are

Is this speaker using his visual aid effectively?
Tashi-Delek/E+/Getty Images

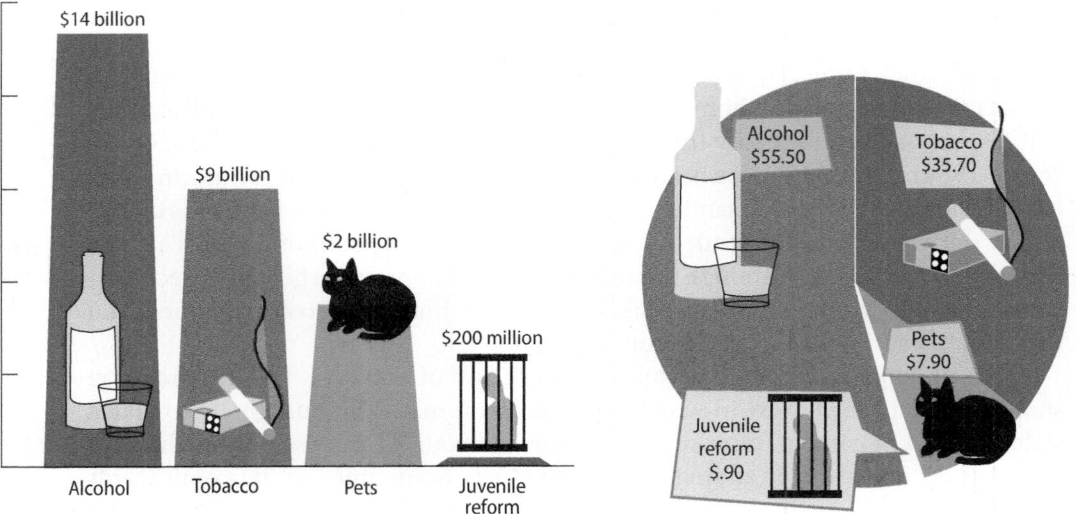

Figure 13.2
Bar Graphs Dramatize Statistics

Figure 13.3
Pie Charts Clarify Proportions

charts, graphs, photographs, slides, and physical objects. Visual aids can increase understanding and retention of ideas presented in a speech (Hamilton, 2015). Visual aids also tend to increase interest in a presentation because they add variety to the message (Hamilton, 2015).

Visual aids can be used either to reinforce ideas presented verbally or to provide information. For example, Figure 13.2 is a bar graph that could effectively strengthen statistics on juvenile reform. Pie charts can forcefully emphasize contrasts and proportions (Figure 13.3). You can also use technologies to create visual aids. You may want to use part of a film or create a video to dramatize a point in your speech. A student speaker showed parts of the Disney film *Pocahontas* to support her claim that the main character was different from the historical figure.

Diagrams or models help speakers explain complex concepts and unfamiliar topics. Especially in speeches of demonstration, a model or physical diagram can be useful. Photographs can reinforce verbal messages, or they can be messages in their own right. To fortify her argument that development is eroding coastal land, a student showed enlarged pictures of an island community before development, when healthy sand dunes existed, and after development, when the dunes had eroded.

Handouts—printouts, pamphlets, brochures, stickers, postcards, and so on—are also useful visual aids. Because handouts can be kept by attendees, they are particularly valuable when a speaker wants information to remain with their audience. After a speech encouraging students to vote for a bill currently under consideration by the state legislature, a student gave every attendee a handout with the names, addresses, and phone numbers of their representatives. This was effective because it avoided breaking up a speech to pass out paper and audience members reading the handout while the speaker was talking.

Guidelines for Using Visual Aids For visual aids to be effective, they should be large enough and clear enough to be seen clearly by all audience members. As obvious as this advice is, speakers routinely violate it by showing slides and physical objects that can be seen clearly only by those close to the speaker, or that are too small for viewers watching on a smaller-sized screen such as a phone.

Secondly, visuals should be simple and uncluttered. Visuals with a great deal of information are more likely to confuse than clarify. Especially if you are presenting a series of slides, simplicity is important. You can create effective slides by following the guidelines in Table 13.3.

Thirdly, accessibility matters. For example, if you show a slide with images on them, don't assume all audience members will be able to see them. Describe the

Table 13.3 **Guidelines for Using Slides in a Speech**

To create effective slides, including PowerPoint presentations for speeches, follow these guidelines:

1. Each slide should focus on a single concept or point and key information to support that concept or point (phrases or keywords generally are preferable to whole sentences or lengthy text).
2. Fonts should be large enough to be read by listeners at the back of the speaking room. Generally, main points should appear in 36-point type, supporting ideas should appear in 24- or 28-point type, and text should appear in type no smaller than 18 points.
3. Typefaces should be clean and clear. Avoid script styles, *overuse of italics,* or TRENDY TYPEFACES. They are distracting and can detract from clarity.
4. Mix uppercase and lowercase lettering. ALL CAPITAL LETTERS CAN BE HARD TO READ.
5. Use art to provide visual relief from text and enhance interest. If using a computerized presentation program, consider using clip art or pictures imported from the Web.
6. Use one design consistently. Computerized programs such as PowerPoint have design templates. Stick with one design to provide visual continuity and transitions.
7. Select a color scheme that is visually strong but not overpowering. Especially if you are showing a series of slides, avoid glaring colors that can tire listeners. Occasionally, you may violate this guideline to adapt to your particular listeners. For instance, if you are speaking at the banquet of a company whose logo is teal and White, you might want a teal and White color scheme.
8. Use special effects sparingly. It may be effective to have text zoom in from the right with a blaring sound on one slide, but it would be tiring and ineffective for text to zoom in on slide after slide.
9. Use visual highlighting sparingly. It can be effective to **boldface** or highlight one particularly important idea. However, the impact of visual highlighting is lost when it is overdone.
10. Give credit to those who created material you use. Acknowledge authors of quotations or other material. You should also get permission to use any materials that are not in the public domain.
11. Don't sacrifice content for flashy visuals. Visual aids, including computerized ones, should enhance your content, not substitute for it.
12. Make slides bright enough that you do not have to darken the room fully.

images so that those who are blind or have impaired vision can follow your presentation. Likewise, if you show a video as part of your presentation, make sure it has captions for spoken words and descriptions for other audio content, like music. That way, those who are unable to hear the content can follow along, too. To learn more about how you can ensure equal access to your presentation, read the guide "Equal Access: Universal Design of Your Presentation" by Sheryl Burgstahler, Ph.D., available freely online.

Many visual aids are verbal texts—main ideas of a speech, major points in a policy, or steps to action. When visual texts are used, certain guidelines apply. As a general rule, a visual text should have no more than six lines of words, should use phrases more than sentences, and should use a simple typeface. A good basic rule is to use visual aids to highlight key information and ideas, not to summarize all content.

Third, visual aids should be safe and nondistracting. Some visual aids are not appropriate for use in any circumstances. For example, a real, functional firearm is dangerous. In addition to the fact that "there's no such thing as an unloaded gun," firearms may frighten and distract people from following the speech. Other visual aids that are risky and should be avoided include live animals, illegal substances, and chemicals that could react with one another. It's also unwise to use visual aids that might seriously upset or disgust others. The purpose of visuals

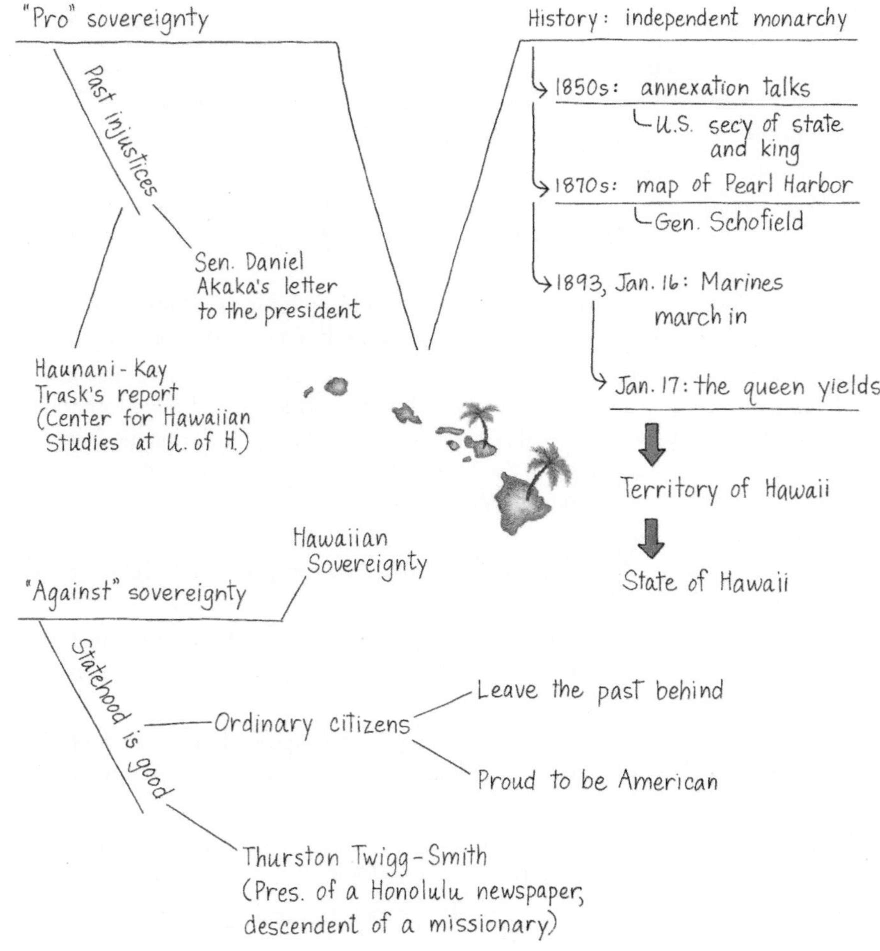

Figure 13.4
Mind Map of Evidence
Source: Jaffe, C. (2007). Public Speaking: Concepts and Skills for a Diverse Society, Fifth Edition, Belmont, CA: Wadsworth.

is to enhance your speech, not to be so sensational that they take attention away from your ideas.

Although visual aids can be effective, it's possible to have too much of a good thing. As a rough guideline for deciding how many visuals to use in a speech, Cheryl Hamilton (2015) suggests this formula:

$$\frac{\text{Length of speech}}{2} + 1 = \text{Maximum number of visuals}$$

If you are preparing a 10-minute speech, you should include no more than six visual aids ($10/2 + 1 = 6$). Note that each slide in a series of slides counts as one visual aid.

There are also some guidelines for using visual aids effectively. First, remove or cover visual aids before and after you use them. A visual aid that's strong enough to be effective will distract attention from what you are saying if it is left in view when not in use. Also, maintain visual contact with your audience when using visual aids. Novice speakers often make the mistake of facing their charts or pictures when discussing them. This breaks the connection between speaker and audience.

It's a good idea to keep an ongoing record of evidence you discover during the research process. There are two ways to do this. The traditional method is to write out each piece of evidence and save the file. In Chapter 12, we discussed mind maps as a way to narrow the focus of a broad topic. The same method can also help you record information. To construct a mind map for your speech, begin by writing the subject of your presentation in the center of a blank page. Then, draw a line from the center to each piece of evidence that you discover as you conduct your research. Once you have a complete record of information you've gathered, you can decide which evidence to include in your presentation. Figure 13.4 shows a mind map record of information for a speech on Hawaiian sovereignty.

Whereas evidence such as statistics, examples, and quotations can provide strong logical support, visual aids and analogies often are more powerful in adding clarity, interest, and emotional appeal to a speech. All forms of evidence, when carefully chosen and ethically used, tend to increase the credibility audience members confer on a speaker and the extent to which they retain the speaker's ideas (Table 13.4).

Table 13.4 **Testing Evidence**

Five questions help speakers test whether evidence is ethical and effective. Each question addresses a specific criterion for assessing the worth of evidence:

1. Is there enough evidence to support a claim? (sufficiency)
2. Is the evidence accurately presented—quotations are verbatim, nothing is taken out of context? (accuracy)
3. Does the evidence relate directly to the claim it is intended to support? (relevance)
4. Is the evidence appropriately timely—are statistics, quotations, examples, and comparisons current or appropriate for the time discussed? (timeliness)
5. Is the evidence free of biases such as vested interest? (impartiality)

Communication Highlight

Evaluating Online Sources for Speeches

Material found online is not necessarily trustworthy. Anyone can set up a website, and anyone can make claims on the Internet. Because Internet content is unregulated, you should be especially critical while evaluating it. To assess information found on the Internet, begin by applying the five standard tests for evidence summarized in Table 13.4. In addition, ask the following questions:

1. Can you verify the material independently (by checking another source or consulting an expert)?
2. Does the source have the experience, position, or other credentials to be an authority?
3. Does the source have any vested interest in making the claim or presenting the alleged information?
4. Does the source acknowledge other sources, including ones that advance different points of view?

If you decide the online material is sound, you should cite it in your bibliography as well as your text, using the following format:

Hulme, M., & Peters, S. (2001). *Me, my phone, and I: The role of the mobile phone*. Workshop: Mobile communications: Understanding users, adoption, and design, Seattle WA.

Go to the book's online resources for this chapter to find basic principles for evaluating material found online, as well as links to multiple websites that discuss the credibility of online sources.

Chapter Summary

The process of researching a speech includes interviewing experts who can expand your insight into the subject, searching online for relevant material, scouting libraries for evidence, and conducting surveys to find out about others' beliefs, practices, and knowledge relevant to your topic. It isn't unusual for speakers to revise the focus of a speech in the course of conducting research. This is appropriate when information you discover modifies or alters your knowledge or even your position.

Research for a speech provides speakers with different kinds of evidence that they can use to clarify, dramatize, and energize a speech. The five types of support we discussed are statistics, examples, comparisons, quotations, and visual aids. Each of these is effective when used thoughtfully and ethically and when adapted to the interests, knowledge, attitudes, experiences, and access needs of audience members.

Now that you've gone through the phases of planning, researching, and finding support for speeches, we're ready to consider the final steps in designing effective presentations. Chapter 14 explains how to organize and present public speeches. Before you move on to Chapter 14, take a moment to fill in this chapter's checklist for researching and supporting your speech.

Checklist for Researching and Supporting a Public Speech

1. I conducted the following research:
   A. Review of my personal experience showed that ______________________________
   ____
   B. I interviewed (name/title): ______________________________
   ____
   (name/title): ______________________________
   (name/title): ______________________________
   C. I checked these three indexes: ______________________________
   ____
   D. I checked these three online sources: ______________________________
   ____
   E. I surveyed on the following issues: ______________________________
   ____
2. I found the following key evidence for my speech:
   A. Statistics: ______________________________
   B. Authorities I will quote: ______________________________
   C. Examples: ______________________________
   D. Comparisons: ______________________________
   E. Visual aids: ______________________________
3. I have all the information to identify my sources appropriately and to explain why they are qualified and relevant to the ideas I will present.

Experiencing Communication in Our Lives

Case Study: Understanding Hurricanes

Apply what you've learned in this chapter by analyzing the following case study, using the accompanying questions as a guide.

Think about a time you've been absolutely terrified—whether it was by a person, event, or situation, and all you wanted to do was go home and be with your family and friends.

Now imagine the feeling you might have if you were that afraid, but you had no idea if your home would even be there when you arrived. This is the reality for many people living on the coastlines of the United States. Hurricanes affect the lives of those living in their direct paths, but they can also affect the entire country.

I have lived about 45 minutes from the Gulf Coast of Texas my entire life and have seen and experienced the destruction caused by hurricanes first hand, especially in the past decade. (Slide 1: Picture of hurricane that hit my hometown.) This is a picture of my hometown when a hurricane hit it.

Today, I'd like to speak with you about the way hurricanes work, the ways they affect our whole country and, most importantly, the toll they have on the people who live in their direct paths.

Karlsson/Heimsmyndir/Getty Images

To begin, let's discuss how hurricanes form and the varying degrees of intensity of them so we can be better informed when we watch news broadcasts and read newspaper reports about them.

Several basic conditions must be present for a hurricane to form. According to Discovery

Communications, hurricanes form "when an area of warm low-pressure air rises and cool, high pressure seizes the opportunity to move in underneath it." This causes a center to develop. This center may eventually turn into what is considered a hurricane. The warm and moist air from the ocean rises up into these pressure zones and begins to form storms. As this happens, the storm continues to draw up more warm moist air and a heat transfer occurs because of the cool air being heated causing the air to rise again. "The exchange of heat creates a pattern of wind that circulates around a center," (the eye of the storm), "like water going down a drain." The "rising air reinforces the air that is already" being pulled up from the surface of the ocean, "so the circulation and speeds of the wind increase."

Classifications of these types of storms help determine their intensity so we can prepare properly for them. Winds that are less than 38 miles per hour are considered tropical depressions. Tropical storms have winds that range from 39 to 73 miles per hour. And lastly, hurricanes are storms with wind speeds of 74 miles per hour and higher.

When storms become classified as a hurricane, they become part of another classification system that is displayed by the Saffir–Simpson Hurricane Scale. Hurricanes are labeled as categories 1–5 based on their wind intensity level or speed. (Slide 2: Hurricane scale chart) Hurricane Ike was labeled differently at different places. (Slide 3: Map showing the different places Ike was labeled in the different categories)

Knowing how and where hurricanes occur help us determine how our daily lives, even here in Kentucky, may be affected when one hits.

A hurricane can affect more than just those living in its direct path and these effects can actually be seen across the country in terms of the environment and the economy.

Hurricanes affect wildlife in negative ways. According to *Business Insider*, hurricanes cause water temperature and salinity changes that can be catastrophic for marine life, and currents so strong that manatees are swept inland to canals and ponds or out into the open ocean. They can become disoriented and die if they are not rescued. (Slide 4: Manatee being rescued)

Hurricanes also affect the economy. Prices climb close to all-time highs when hurricanes hit. According to OPIS energy analysis global head Tom Kloza, quoted in the *New York Post* on June 24, 2022, gas prices skyrocket when major hurricanes hit, cautioning that they could reach "apocalyptic" heights during a hurricane season in the near future. Lucia Kassai reported, in an August 29, 2021, article in *Bloomberg News*, that Hurricane Ida caused 6 refineries, 7 platforms, 2 ports, and 1 pipeline in the Gulf region to shut down. Almost 12% of the entire United States refining capacity was affected as Ida made landfall on August 29, 2021, she reported. That's why even residents here in Lexington saw a dramatic spike in gas prices immediately following Ida's landfall.

Energy costs to heat and cool our homes also rise. When consumers have to pay more to heat and cool our homes, we also have less to spend eating out at restaurants. And we have less to spend on nonessentials at the mall. So, economically we all feel the ripple effect when hurricanes hit.

Hurricanes also hurt communities of color a lot more than White communities. In the *Harvard Political Review*, on October 13, 2020, Sofia Andrade explained that because of systemic inequalities, marginalized communities have less access to health care, insurance, safe evacuation resources, and storm-proof, modern infrastructures, which means hurricanes cost those communities a lot more than they should. She said, quote, "A 2019 study found that Black and Latinx residents in American counties that experienced $10 billion in damages from natural disasters like hurricanes between 1999 and 2013 lost an average of $27,000 and $29,000, respectively. White people in counties with similar losses due to natural disasters instead gained an average of $126,000" (Slide 5: Bar chart showing Black and Latinx average loss in red, below $0 line, and average gain among White people in green, above $0 line). These statistics can't be overlooked.

So, yes, we all feel the effects of hurricanes, but we should not overlook the dramatic ways in which people who live in the direct path of a hurricane are affected, and how within those paths, some people risk greater physical and financial harm than others.

When a hurricane hits, many of these people become homeless, at least for a while, and suffer emotionally and financially as they evacuate to places all over the country, including Kentucky!

People who go through hurricanes suffer extreme emotional effects. Evacuation is stressful because people have to pack up what they can and have no way of knowing if their home will still be standing or inhabitable when they return (Slides 5 and 6: Before and after pictures from Hurricane Nicholas).

Even returning home is emotionally taxing because returning home means rebuilding homes, neighborhoods, and even memories. Though we try to get back to a "normal" life, it can never really be the same as it once was. Instead, it's what Silicon Valley venture capitalist and investor, Roger McNamee, calls the "new normal" in his book, The New Normal: Great Opportunities in a Time of Great Risk.

Because they have to rebuild their homes and lives, people also go through financial difficulties. People battle with insurance companies about whether a home has wind or water damage as they seek financial assistance. Insurance companies will often claim that it is the one (wind or water) the homeowner is uninsured for.

Price gouging is another financial challenge hurricane victims face. When families and businesses begin the process of rebuilding, people come from outside areas to help with labor and materials and will charge exorbitant fees. An example of this is when my father needed people to help remove two trees from our home in September 2017 after Hurricane Harvey.

To close, I'd like to remind you that hurricanes affect victims who live in their direct path and the country as a whole. To understand some of these effects, we talked about how hurricanes work, how they affect our country and daily lives, the impacts they have on the lives of people who live through them, and how those impacts are unequal. Maybe knowing some of these facts will help each of us appreciate our homes, our families, and different communities' situations just a little bit more. (Handout: Hurricane tracking charts)

References

Andrade, S. (2020, Oct. 13). Hurricanes are not your great equalizer. *Harvard Political Review.* https://harvardpolitics.com/hurricanes-are-not-your-great-equalizer/

Anderson, D. (2019, Aug. 27). What happens to fish and other sea creatures underwater during a hurricane. *Business Insider.* https://www.businessinsider.com/what-happens-fish-dolphins-sea-animals-hurricane-2018-10

Associated Press. (2008, October 8). Windstorm costs insurers $550M. *Newark Advocate,* p. x.

Barrabi, T. (2022, June 24). Gas prices could reach 'apocalyptic' levels during hurricane season, oil expert warns. *New York Post.* https://nypost.com/2022/06/24/gas-prices-could-reach-apocalyptic-levels-during-hurricane-season-oil-expert/

Kassai, L. (2021, Aug. 29). U.S. Gulf oil producers, refiners shut as Ida comes ashore. *Bloomberg News.* https://www.bloomberg.com/news/articles/2021-08-29/u-s-gulf-oil-producers-refiners-shutting-as-ida-nears

Marshall, B., Freudenrich, C., & Lamb, R. How hurricanes work. Retrieved October 8, 2008, from http://www.howstuffworks.com/hurricanes.htm

McNamee, R. (2004). *The new normal: Great opportunities in a time of great risk.* New York: Penguin.

Questions for Analysis and Discussion

1. Identify the types of evidence that the speaker used to develop the point in this excerpt from a speech.
2. Was the evidence effective? Did it meet the five tests for evidence?
3. Was the evidence ethical?
4. In an early draft of this speech, the speaker did not include multiple cultural perspectives. Paragraph 13 and the last half of Paragraph 14 were added to do so. How did this addition strengthen the speech?

Key Concepts

comparisons
evidence
examples
halo effect
metaphors
peer-reviewed research
primary research
quotations
secondary research
similes
statistics
survey research
visual aids

Sharpen Your Skill

1. **Background on Experts**

   Research the credentials of three authorities you plan to cite in your speech. Below, write important information that contributes to their credibility.

   1. ______________ holds the following titles: ______________ and has the following experiences and qualifications: ______________
   2. ______________ holds the following titles: ______________ and has the following experiences and qualifications: ______________
   3. ______________ holds the following titles: ______________ and has the following experiences and qualifications: ______________

2. **Bringing Statistics Alive**

   Practice translating statistics into interesting and meaningful information. Here's an example.

   Statistic: Americans annually spend $14 billion on alcohol, $9 billion on tobacco, $2 billion on pets, and $200 million on juvenile reform.

   Translation: For every $1 spent on juvenile reform in the United States, $70 are spent on alcohol, $45 on tobacco, and $10 on pets.

   Statistic: Children under 10 watch television an average of 50 hours each week.

   Translation: ______________________________

   Statistic: The Stealth bomber program cost $40 billion and produced a total of 20 aircraft.

   Translation: ______________________________

   Statistic: The number of working poor, people who make $13,000 or less a year, rose from 12% of the workforce in 2000 to 18% in 2013.

   Translation: ______________________________

   Now, apply what you've learned to your own speech. Select three statistics you could use in your speech, and translate them into meaningful, interesting terms.

   Statistic 1: ______________________________

   can be translated this way ______________________________

   Statistic 2: ______________________________

   can be translated this way ______________________________

   Statistic 3: ______________________________

   can be translated this way ______________________________

For Further Reflection and Discussion

1. After you've interviewed two experts on your topic, reflect on what you learned. What did they explain, reveal, or show you that added to your knowledge of the topic?
2. How did the process of researching your speech affect your understandings, beliefs, and speaking goal? Explain what changed and why.

3. Use an online database through your college or university library to find current evidence to support your speech. Type in the keywords relevant to your topic. If you plan to speak on a health-related topic, use publications such as Consumer Health Database, Health and Medicine, Medline, or ScienceDirect. If you plan to speak on a public policy issue, check out databases such as Environmental Studies and Policy or Global Issues. If you plan to speak on media representation or the media industries, look up Communication and Mass Media Complete, or check out the research publications offered on the website of the Geena Davis Institute on Gender and Media.
4. Pay attention to evidence in a speech delivered in one of your classes, whether face to face or remote. Evaluate the effectiveness of evidence. Are visuals clear and uncluttered? Does the speaker explain the qualifications of sources cited, and are those sources adequately unbiased? What examples and comparisons are presented, and how effective are they? Evaluate the ethical quality of the evidence used. Did the speaker provide enough information for you to assess the expertise of any sources cited? Did the speaker show that the sources were not biased?
5. Experiment with PowerPoint or other software to create slide decks. Notice how different designs, colors, and special effects affect the clarity and impact of your slides.

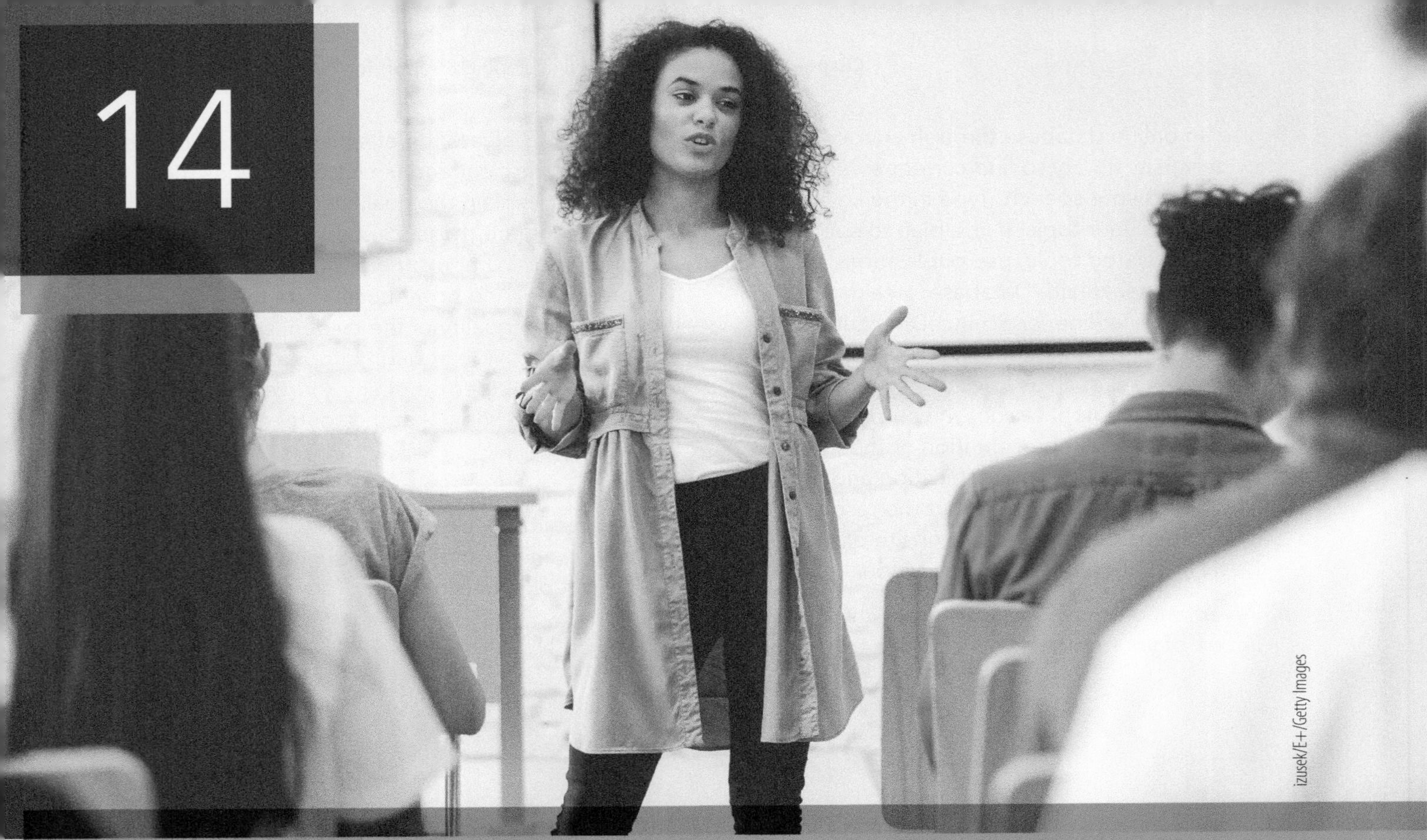

As long as there are human rights to be defended; as long as there are great interests to be guarded; as long as the welfare of nations is a matter for discussion, so long will public speaking have its place.

William Jennings Bryan

Organizing and Presenting Public Speeches

Learning Objectives

After studying the topics in this chapter, you should be able to:

1. Design the individual elements of an effective speech.
2. Explain the standard outline format and distinguish between working outlines, formal outlines, and key word outlines used in public speaking.
3. Analyze the verbal and nonverbal aspects of oral style and delivery.
4. Explain ways to capture audience members' attention.
5. Explain the four speech delivery methods: impromptu, extemporaneous, manuscript, and memorized.
6. Explain and use strategies to manage communication apprehension and public speaking anxiety.

What aspects of delivery are most important to you when you are listening to a speech?

- Millions of people have back problems in this country. It's hard to recover from back problems, particularly ruptures of discs. A lot of problems result from strains caused by lifting heavy objects. People could save themselves a lot of pain if they avoided doing things that hurt their backs. It's important to take care of your back because a disc rupture can immobilize you for up to 2 weeks. Another way discs rupture is from unhealthy everyday habits such as sitting too long in one position or not using chairs that provide good support.
- Millions of people in this country who suffer from back problems could save themselves a lot of pain by avoiding the two primary causes of back injury. One major cause is excessive strain, for example, from lifting heavy objects. A second cause is unhealthy everyday habits, such as sitting too long in one position. Avoiding strain and unhealthy habits can save weeks of recuperation.

Which of these paragraphs was easier for you to understand and follow? Which one made more sense to you? If you're like most people, the second paragraph seemed more logical and coherent. The content of the two paragraphs is the same. What differs is how they are organized. In the first paragraph, the speaker doesn't tell us that they are going to focus on two causes of back problems. Instead, the speaker wanders from discussing one cause (strain) of back problems, to noting the length of recuperation time, and then back to discussing a second cause (unhealthy habits) of back problems.

In contrast, in the second paragraph the speaker tells us that there are two primary causes of back problems, so we're prepared at the outset to learn about two categories. The speaker next explains both causes, and only then does the speaker discuss the recuperation time we're in for if we don't take care of our backs. The organization of the second paragraph makes it easier to follow and retain the information presented.

This chapter guides you through the process of organizing your speech and practicing your delivery. In the pages that follow, we'll consider alternative ways to organize ideas, styles of delivery, and ways to practice effectively. We will also discuss ways that digital media can assist you in organizing and presenting speeches.

Organizing Speeches

Organization increases speaking effectiveness for several reasons. First, people like structure, and they expect ideas to come to them in an orderly way. Second, audience members can understand and remember content that is well organized because they grasp connections between ideas. Third, audience members find an organized speech more persuasive than a disorganized one. Finally, good organization enhances a speaker's credibility because it reflects well on a speaker's preparation and respect for the audience.

Organizing an effective speech is not the same as organizing a good paper, although the two forms of communication benefit by some similar structural principles. Effective organization for oral communication differs from organization for written communication in three key ways:

1. Oral communication requires more explicit organization.
2. Oral communication benefits from greater redundancy within the message.
3. Oral communication should rely on less complex sentence structures.

Unlike readers, audience members can't refer back to a previous passage if they become confused or forget a previous point. To increase audience members' comprehension and retention, speakers should use simple sentences, provide signposts to highlight organization, and repeat key ideas (Woolfolk, 1987). Consistent with the need for redundancy in oral communication, good speeches follow the form of telling the audience what you're going to tell them, presenting your message, then reminding them of your main points. This translates into preparing an introduction, a body, and a conclusion for an oral presentation.

Effective organization begins with a good outline. We'll discuss different kinds of outlines and how each can help speakers organize their ideas. Next, we'll focus on organizing the body of a speech because that is the substance of a presentation. Finally, we'll discuss how to build an introduction and a conclusion and how to weave in transitions to move the audience from one point to another.

Review It!

Oral Communication:

- Requires Explicit Organization
- Benefits from Redundancy
- Relies Less on Complex Sentences

Outlining Speeches

An outline helps you organize your ideas and make sure that you have enough evidence to support your claims. An outline also provides you with a safety net in case you forget what you intend to say or are interrupted by a question or a disturbing noise. There are three kinds of outlines: working, formal, and key word.

working outline A sketch of main ideas and their relationships; used by and intended only for the speaker.

The Working Outline

Speakers usually begin organizing their ideas by creating a **working outline** to give themselves a basic map of the speech. The working outline is just for the speaker; it is their sketch of the speech. In it, the speaker usually jots down main ideas to see how they fit together. Once the ideas are laid out in a basic structure, the speaker can tell where more evidence is needed, where ideas don't seem well connected, and so forth. Working outlines usually evolve through multiple drafts as speakers see ways to improve their speeches. Because working outlines aren't meant for others' eyes, they often include abbreviations and shorthand that make sense only to the speaker.

formal outline A complete outline of a speech, including the parts of a speech, main points, supporting material, transitions, and citations for sources.

The Formal Outline

A **formal outline** includes all main points and subpoints, supporting materials, and transitions, along with a bibliography of sources. It should not be the whole speech unless you are giving a manuscript speech, which we will discuss later in this chapter.

An effective formal outline has main headings for the introduction, body, and conclusion. Under each main point are subpoints, references to support each subpoint, and abbreviated transitions. If your speech includes quotations, statistics, or other evidence that must be presented with absolute accuracy, you should write the evidence in full, either in your outline, on separate index cards, or on a digital tablet you will use when speaking. Your written evidence should include the source and date of the evidence so that you can provide oral footnotes to audience members. Full references should be listed as your bibliography, or **Works Cited**. Table 14.1 presents guidelines for constructing formal outlines. Figure 14.1 shows a sample formal outline prepared by a student on the topic of inequities in heterosexual marriages, in which wives do a disproportionate amount of housework and caregiving, while their husbands do not.

works cited A list of sources used in preparing a speech.

Review It!

Three Kinds of Outlines:

- Working
- Formal
- Key Word

Table 14.1 **Principles for Preparing a Formal Outline**

1. Use full sentences for each point.
2. Each point or subpoint in a speech should have only one idea.
3. Use standard symbols and indentation for outlines.
   I. Roman numerals are used for main points.
      A. Capital letters are used for subpoints that support main points.
         1. Arabic numbers are used for material that supports subpoints.
            a. Lowercase letters are used for material that amplifies supporting material.
4. A point, subpoint, or supporting material should never stand alone. If you have a point I, you must have a point II (and possibly III). If you have a subpoint A, there must be a subpoint B (and possibly C). Outlines show how ideas are developed and related. If there is only one subpoint, you don't need to outline it—it's the main point.
5. Strive for parallelism when wording main points and subpoints. This adds to the coherence of a speech and makes it easier for listeners to follow. Here's an example of parallel wording of main and subpoints in a speech:
   I. Poor advising diminishes students' academic experiences.
      A. Students lose out by taking courses that don't interest them.
      B. Students lose out by missing courses that would interest them.
   II. Poor advising delays students' graduation.
      A. Some students have to return for a fifth year to graduate.
      B. Some students have to take extension courses to graduate.
      C. Some students have to attend summer school to graduate.
6. Include all references in your outline. These should be written as full citations according to the guidelines of a standard style manual, such as those published by the Modern Language Association (MLA) or the American Psychological Association (APA), or *The Chicago Manual of Style*. Your instructor may specify the style guidelines that you should follow.
7. Cite sources using accepted style guidelines for research reports. Three widely used systems for citing sources in papers and speech outlines are APA, MLA, and Council of Biology Editors (CBE). You can learn how to cite your sources using each set of guidelines by visiting these websites:

   APA: http://owl.english.purdue.edu/handouts/research/r_apa.html

   MLA: http://library.osu.edu/sites/guides/mlagd.php

   CBE: http://library.osu.edu/sites/guides/cbegd.html

Figure 14.1
A Formal Outline

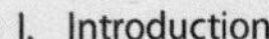

I. Introduction
   A. **Attention:** Would you vote for a system in which half of us work only one job, the other half of us work two jobs, and everyone gets equal rewards? No? Well that's the system that most families in this country have today.
   B. **Thesis statement:** Women's double shift in the paid labor force and the home has negative effects on them personally and on marriages.
   C. **Preview:** In the next few minutes, I will show that the majority of married women work two jobs: one in the paid labor market and one when they get home. I will then trace the harmful effects of this inequitable division of labor.

II. Body
   A. The majority of married women today work two jobs: one in the paid labor market and a second one when they get home each day.
      1. Most families today have two wage earners.
         a. Only 17% of contemporary families have one earner.
         b. As married women have taken on full-time jobs outside of the home over the past three decades, husbands of working wives have increased the amount of housework and child care they do from 20% to 30%.
      2. Working wives do more "homework" than working husbands.
         a. Research shows that husbands tend to do the less routine chores while wives do most of the daily chores.

(continued)

key word outline An abbreviated speaking outline that includes only key words for each point in a speech. The key words trigger the speaker's memory of the full point.

The Key Word Outline Some speakers prefer a less detailed formal outline, called a **key word outline**. As the term implies, a key word outline includes only key words for each point. The speaker uses words that will jog her or his memory of each idea in the speech. Figure 14.2 shows a key word outline for a student speech.

Organizing the Body of a Speech

The body of a speech develops and supports the central idea, or thesis statement, by organizing it into several points that are distinct yet related. In short speeches of 5–10 minutes, no more than three points can be developed well, and two are often adequate. In longer speeches of 11–20 minutes, more points can be developed.

We'll discuss seven organizational patterns. As we discuss each pattern, you'll have the opportunity to think about how you might use it in your speech. In Chapter 16, we'll discuss one additional pattern that can be especially effective for persuasive speaking.

b. Husbands' reasons for not doing more work in the home are that they are tired after work, they don't feel men should do many home chores, and their wives don't expect them to help out more.

3. Working wives tend to do more homemaking and child care chores, regardless of which spouse earns more in the job outside the home.
   a. Consider Jeremy and Nancy. She earns 65% of the family's income, and she does 80% of the child care and home chores.
   b. Sociologist Arlie Hochschild found that 2 out of 10 husbands in two-worker families do 50% of the work involved in homemaking and child care.

Transition: Now that we've seen what the double shift is, let's consider its effects.

B. The double shift harms women's health and creates marital stress.
   1. The double shift harms women's physical and psychological health.
      a. Research shows that women who work outside of the home and do most of the homemaking and child care suffer sleep deprivation, reduced immunity to infections, and increased susceptibility to illnesses.
      b. A recent study by the American Medical Association found that working women who do the majority of "homework" are more stressed, depressed, and anxious.
   2. The double shift also erodes marital satisfaction.
      a. Women resent husbands who don't contribute a fair share to home life.

(continued)

Figure 14.1
A Formal Outline
(Continued)

The Temporal Pattern Temporal patterns (also called time and chronological patterns) organize ideas on the basis of temporal relationships. Audience members find it easy to follow a time pattern because we often think in terms of temporal order: what follows what, what comes first, and what comes next.

Time patterns are useful for describing processes that take place over time, explaining historical events, and tracing sequences of action. Time patterns are also effective for presentations that create suspense and build to a climax. One student speaker led his audience through the detective work of pharmaceutical research to develop a new drug for treating mood disorders.

Thesis: Our campus has changed over time.
Main Point 1: Our school was founded in 1895 as a private academy for young men.
Main Point 2: In 1928, the school was reorganized as a public university.
Main Point 3: In 1960, the school began admitting women as well as men.

The Spatial Pattern Spatial patterns organize ideas according to physical relationships. This structure is especially appropriate for speeches that describe or

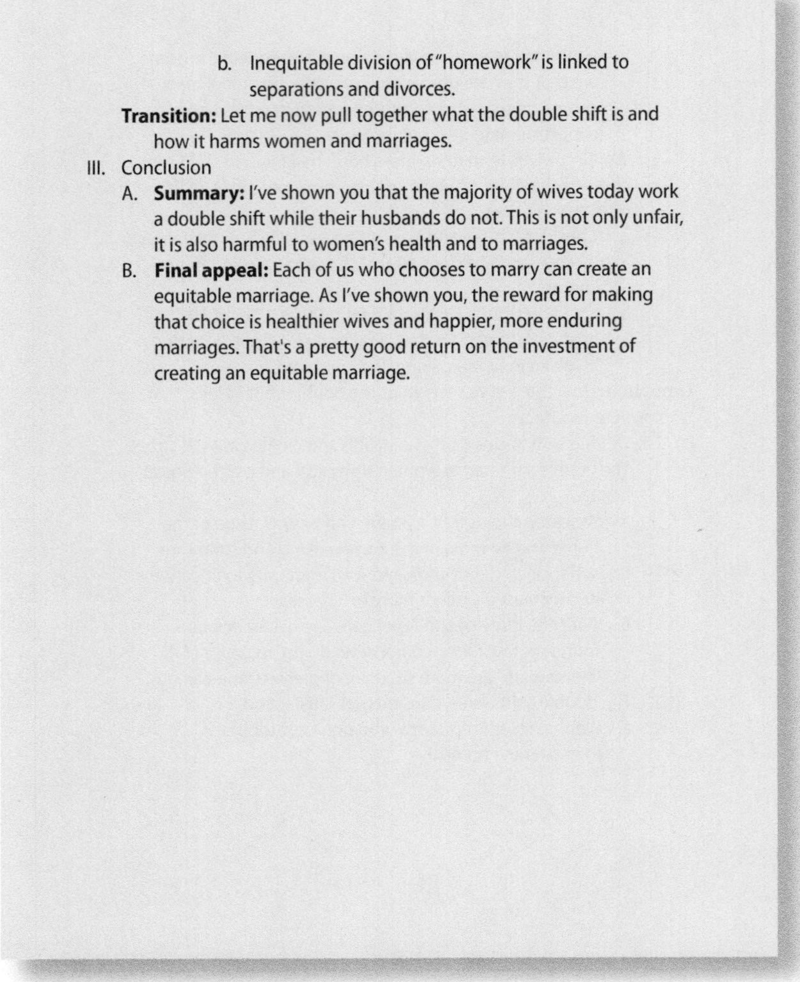
b. Inequitable division of "homework" is linked to separations and divorces.

Transition: Let me now pull together what the double shift is and how it harms women and marriages.

III. Conclusion

A. **Summary:** I've shown you that the majority of wives today work a double shift while their husbands do not. This is not only unfair, it is also harmful to women's health and to marriages.

B. **Final appeal:** Each of us who chooses to marry can create an equitable marriage. As I've shown you, the reward for making that choice is healthier wives and happier, more enduring marriages. That's a pretty good return on the investment of creating an equitable marriage.

Figure 14.1
A Formal Outline
(Continued)

explain layouts, geographic relationships, or connections between objects or parts of a system.

Spatial patterns can be used to structure both informative and persuasive speeches. Student speakers have successfully used spatial patterns to inform their audience about the relationships between components of nuclear reactors and the four levels of forest vegetation. In persuasive speeches, students have relied on spatial patterns to argue that urban sprawl is increasing in the United States and that global climate change will have devastating effects throughout the world.

Thesis: Our campus includes spaces for learning, socializing, and living.
Main Point 1: At the center of our campus are the classroom buildings.
Main Point 2: Surrounding the classroom buildings are places for students to eat and socialize.
Main Point 3: The south part of campus consists of dormitories and apartments for students with families.

The Topical Pattern Topical patterns order a presentation into several categories, classes, or areas of discussion. The classification pattern is appropriate when

I. Introduction
  A. Half work one, half work two
  B. Effects—personal, on marriage
  C. Majority of married women; effects of inequity
II. Body
  A. Majority of married women—two jobs
    1. Two wage earners standard
      a. 17% single wage earner
      b. 10% increase in husbands' contribution
    2. 20% husbands assume half
    3. Pattern varies
      a. Class
        i. Jacob and Ina
        ii. John and Jennifer
      b. Education
    4. Women's double shift not tied to salary
      a. Jeremy and Nancy
      b. Hochschild study (see card 1)
  B. Effects
    1. Physical and psychological
      a. Sleep, illness, infection
      b. Stress unhappiness
    2. Marital satisfaction erodes
      a. Resentment
        i. Marion
        ii. Study (see card 2)
      b. Marital stability
        i. Divorce statistics (see card 3)
        ii. Therapist quote (see card 4)
III. Conclusion
  A. Unfair + health harms + marital stability and satisfaction
  B. Your choice—return on investment

Figure 14.2
A Key Word Outline

your topic breaks down into two or three areas that aren't related temporally, spatially, causally, or otherwise. Although topical patterns don't have the organic power of structures that highlight relationships, they can effectively order points in a speech.

Topical patterns are appropriate for informative speeches on the three branches of government, the social and academic activities funded by student fees, and the contributions of students, faculty, and staff to campus life.

Topical patterns can also be effective for persuasive speeches. In a speech urging students to vote for a candidate, one student focused on the candidate's personal integrity, experience in public service, and commitment to the community. Another student designed a persuasive speech that extolled the benefits of student fees.

Thesis: Student fees fund extracurricular, intellectual, and artistic activities on campus.

Main Point 1: Fully 40% of student fees is devoted to extracurricular organizations.

Main Point 2: Another 30% of student fees pays for lectures by distinguished speakers.

Main Point 3: The final 30% of fees supports concerts and art exhibits.

The Star Pattern The star pattern is a variation on the topical structure (Jaffe, 2016). A standard topical organization has two or three points that a speaker covers in the same order and to the same extent each time the speech is given. With a star pattern, however, a speaker might start with different points and give more or less attention to specific points when speaking to different audiences.

One of the more common uses of the star pattern is in political speeches. Most candidates for office have a standard stump speech that includes their key positions and proposals. The order in which a candidate presents points and the extent to which each point is developed vary from audience to audience. For example, a candidate's platform might include strong support for the environment, enhancing the fiscal security of the United States, and ensuring adequate care for older adults. When the candidate speaks to environmental activists, they would lead with the stand on the environment and elaborate it in detail. When the candidate speaks to citizens aged 65 and older, the speaker would begin by emphasizing their commitment to the older citizens' health and to strengthening Medicare and Medicaid. When the candidate speaks to young and middle-aged audiences, the first point would be ensuring the fiscal security of the United States so young people aren't strapped with debt. Using the star pattern, the candidate could adapt the order of points and the emphasis placed on each one. It would not be ethical to misrepresent positions to suit different audiences, but it is both ethical and effective to adapt the order and emphasis on points.

Similarly, a star pattern can be used to describe the ways in which different groups contribute to campus life, and the order of points could vary for audiences of students, staff, and faculty.

Thesis: Our campus reflects contributions of administrators, faculty, students, and staff.

Main Point 1: Administrators are in charge of planning and coordinating all aspects of campus life.

Main Point 2: Faculty take the lead in charting the academic character of college life.

Main Point 3: Students are the primary designers of extracurricular life on campus.

Main Point 4: Staff make sure that the initiatives of administrators, faculty, and students are implemented consistently.

Emma I'm an orientation counselor, and I think I've been using the star pattern to talk to new students, but I didn't know you called it that. With each new group, I have to tell them about the campus and town and school policies and so forth. With first-year students, I start off by talking about school policies because not knowing them can get the kids in trouble. With junior transfers, I get to that last and just spend a little time on it. With out-of-state students, I spend more time talking about the town and even the region—how the South is, which some of them don't understand. I pretty much cover everything with each group, but how I do it varies a lot, depending on who is in the group.

The Comparative Pattern As the term suggests, comparative patterns compare two or more objects, people, situations, events, or other phenomena. This structure is also called *comparison/contrast* and *analogical organization.* It encourages the audience to be aware of similarities or differences between two or more things or to understand a new idea, process, or event in terms of one with which they're already familiar.

Mayumi I selected comparative organization for my informative speech about American and Japanese marriages because I wanted the class to understand how people from my country think differently about marriage than Americans do. I divided my speech into courtship, division of household work, and meaning of divorce to show some different tendencies between American and Japanese cultures in each area.

Question: Why do you think a comparative organization can be helpful in introducing audience members to a different culture?

Students giving persuasive speeches have used the comparative pattern to argue that media literacy is as important as oral and written literacy and that undergraduate education is different from career preparation. In each case, the comparative structure invites the audience to perceive how two or more phenomena are alike or different.

Thesis: Health maintenance organizations are inferior to private medical practices.
Main Point 1: Health maintenance organizations provide less individualized patient care than private practices do.
Main Point 2: Health maintenance organizations are less likely than private practices to authorize important diagnostic tests.
Main Point 3: Health maintenance organizations place less emphasis on preventive care than private medical practices do.

Medical professionals frequently present information to patients.
National Cancer Institute/Unsplash.com

The Problem–Solution Pattern This pattern divides a topic into two major areas: a problem and a solution. Usually, a speaker begins by describing a problem and its severity and then proposes a solution. Occasionally, this sequence is inverted when a speaker begins by discussing a solution and then explains the problem it solves.

The problem–solution pattern is effective for persuasive speeches because it lends itself naturally to advocating policies, answers, and actions. Students have used this pattern effectively to persuade others that many people who are severely ill or dying (problem) could be helped if more people were organ donors (solution), and that the overcrowding of jails and the backlog of court cases (problems) could be decreased if all victimless crimes were made misdemeanors (solution).

The power of this pattern derives from the sequential involvement it invites from the audience. If they accept a speaker's description of a problem and believe the problem is important or urgent, they hunger for a solution. The speaker, who presents a solution that addresses the problem they've already acknowledged, has a good chance of convincing audience members to endorse the recommended proposal.

Thesis: Victimless crimes should be reclassified as misdemeanors.
Main Point 1: Currently, courts across the nation are overwhelmed by cases in which there is no victim.
Main Point 2: Reclassifying victimless crimes as misdemeanors would dramatically ease the burden on our courts.

Although most often used for persuasive speeches, the problem–solution structure can be used for informative presentations with thesis statements, such as "The new vendors you've seen in the cafeteria (solution) are in response to student complaints about lack of variety in food options (problem)."

The Cause–Effect and Effect–Cause Patterns This pattern is used to argue a direct relationship between two things: a cause and an effect. In some instances, speakers want to inform people that a situation, policy, or practice (effect) results from certain previous choices or events (causes). In other cases, speakers argue that a specific action (cause) will lead to an effect. Cause–effect and effect–cause patterns are appropriate for both informative and persuasive speeches.

It is extremely difficult to prove unequivocal causation, however. Research may show that two things (for example, smoking and lung cancer) are closely related, but it cannot conclusively prove that smoking directly and unvaryingly causes lung cancer. Thus, speakers using this pattern generally demonstrate relationships, or correlations, between two things, and this is often persuasive to the audience.

Thesis: Raising the minimum wage would be bad for our economy.
Main Point 1: Raising the minimum wage would reduce worker productivity.
Main Point 2: Raising the minimum wage would lead to greater unemployment.
Main Point 3: Raising the minimum wage would increase the costs of what we buy.

The seven patterns we've discussed represent different ways to organize public presentations. To structure your speech effectively, you should consider how each of the eight patterns might shape the content and impact of your presentation.

Review It!

Organizational Patterns:

- Temporal
- Spatial
- Topical
- Star
- Comparative
- Problem–Solution
- Cause–Effect

Designing the Introduction

The introduction to a speech is the first thing audience members hear. A good introduction accomplishes four goals: (a) It captures the audience's attention; (b) it presents a clear thesis statement; (c) it enhances the speaker's credibility; and (d) it previews how the speech will be developed. That's a lot to accomplish in a short time, so careful thought is required to design a strong introduction.

Capture Audience Members' Attention The first objective of an introduction is to gain audience members' attention (Verderber, Sellnow, & Verderber, 2015). There are many ways to gain audience members' attention and interest. You might begin with a dramatic piece of evidence, such as a stirring quotation, a striking visual aid, or a startling statistic or example. Each of these forms of evidence can capture audience members' interest and make them want to hear more.

You may also open with a question that invites the audience to become involved with the topic. "Do you know the biggest cause of death among college students?" "Would you like to know how to double your chances of getting a job offer?" Questions engage the audience personally at the outset of a speech.

There are other ways to capture audience members' attention. For example, speakers sometimes refer to current events or experiences of audience members that are related to the topic of a speech. A student who spoke on homelessness immediately after fall break opened this way: "If you're like me, you went home over the break and enjoyed good food, a clean bed, and a warm, comfortable house—all the comforts that a home provides. But not everyone has those comforts."

Another effective way to capture your audience's attention is to provide them with direct experience, which is a highly effective foundation for persuasion (Baron & Berne, 1994). For example, in a speech advocating a low-fat diet, a speaker began

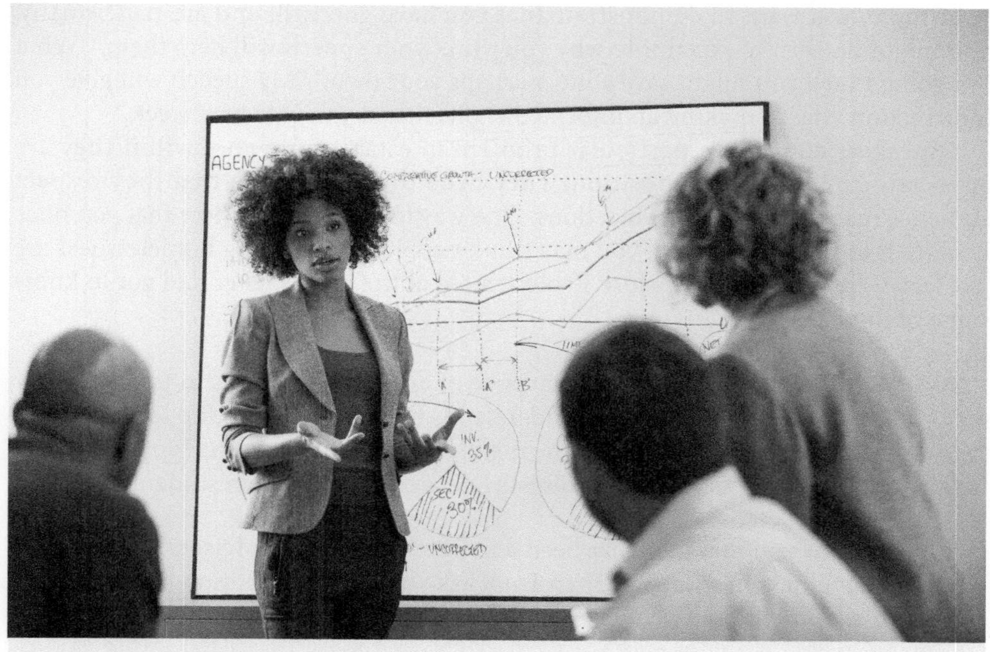

Does this speaker seem engaging?
Image Source RF/Cadalpe/Getty Images

the presentation by passing out low-fat cookies he had baked, giving all the audience members an immediate experience with delicious and healthful food.

When appropriate to the speaking situation, humor can also be an effective way to open a speech—but only if it succeeds in amusing the audience. Thus, it's a good idea to try jokes out on people who are similar to your audience.

Present a Clear Thesis Statement The second function of an introduction is to state the main message of your speech, which is the thesis statement we discussed in Chapter 12. Your thesis should be a short, clear sentence that directly states the overall theme of your presentation.

- "I will describe problems with advising on our campus and ask your help in solving them."
- "I will inform you of your legal rights when interviewing for a job."
- "I will show you that the death penalty is ineffective and discriminatory."

Build Credibility The third function of an introduction is to establish a speaker's credibility. Audience members regard a speaker as credible if they seem qualified to speak on a topic, shows goodwill toward them, and demonstrates dynamism.

To show that they are qualified to speak on a topic, speakers may mention their personal experience: "I am a hemophiliac." Speakers may also explain how they gained expertise on their topics. "For the past 2 years, I have volunteered at the homeless shelter here in town." If you do not have personal experience with a topic, let the audience know that you have gained knowledge in other ways. "I interviewed 10 people who work with abused children."

In addition to letting your audience know that you are qualified to speak on your topic, you want to demonstrate that you have goodwill and are trustworthy. You might do this by explaining why you think your speech will help them. "What I'm going to tell you might save a life, perhaps your own." "My speech will give you information vital to making an informed choice when you vote next week."

Speakers confront a particular problem in establishing goodwill if they are advocating an unpopular position. They need to demonstrate that they respect audience members' possible objections. One way to do this is to show that you once held their attitudes. "Some of you may think people experiencing homelessness are just lazy. I thought so, too, before I volunteered at the local shelter and got to know some of them."

Preview the Body The final purpose of an introduction is to preview your major points so that your audience understands how you will develop ideas and can follow you. The preview announces the main points of your speech. Typically, a preview enumerates or lists the main points. Here are examples from student speeches:

- "I will show you that there has been a marked decrease in advisers' accessibility and helpfulness to students. Then I will ask you to sign a petition that asks our provost to hire more advisers and provide ongoing training to them."
- "To convince you that the death penalty should be abolished, I will first provide evidence that it is not effective as a deterrent to crime. Second, I will demonstrate that the death penalty discriminates against marginalized communities."

Communication Highlight

Gaining Audience Members' Attention

Here are examples of ways in which students have captured audiences' initial attention:

Question to create suspense: "Have you ever wondered what life would be like if there were no deadly diseases?"

Startling evidence: "Nearly two-thirds of people over 60 who are poor are women."

Personal involvement: "Many of you have to work extra hours to make the money to buy your textbooks so that the student store can make its 35% profit—that's right, 35% profit just for selling you a book."

Inviting participation: "Imagine that you could design the undergraduate curriculum at this university. What would you recommend for all students who attend?"

Quotation: "Mahatma Gandhi said, 'You must be the change that you wish to see in the world.'"

Dramatic example: "My brother Jim and I grew up together, and we were best friends. He taught me to play basketball; I gave him advice on girls he was dating; we went to California together one summer. Jim would be 22 today if he had not been killed last summer by a drunk driver."

Craft the Conclusion

The next step in organizing a speech is to craft a conclusion. An effective conclusion summarizes content and provides a memorable final thought (Griffin, 2015). As you may realize, these two functions are similar to the attention and preview in introductions. In repeating key ideas and leaving the audience with a compelling final thought, a speaker provides psychological closure on the speech. Like introductions, conclusions are short. Thus, you have to accomplish the two objectives of a conclusion very concisely.

To summarize the content of your speech, it's effective to restate your thesis and each major point. Here are examples from student speeches:

- "Today I've identified two key problems with advising: an insufficient number of advisers and inadequate training of advisers. Both of these problems can be solved if you will join me in urging our president to increase the number of advisers and the training they get."
- "My speech has informed you of your legal rights in interviews and what you can do if an interviewer violates them."
- "I've shown you that the death penalty doesn't prevent crime and that it discriminates against marginalized communities."

After reviewing main points, a conclusion should offer the audience a final idea, ideally something particularly memorable or strong or an ending that returns to the opening idea to provide satisfying closure. In a speech on environmental activism, the speaker began with "'One earth, one chance' is the Sierra Club motto" and ended with "We have one chance to keep our one earth. Let's not throw it away." This was effective because the ending returned to the opening words but gave them a slightly different twist. A student who argued that the death penalty should be abolished ended the speech with this statement: "We need to kill the death penalty before it kills anyone else." A third example, again from a student speaker, is this memorable closing: "I've given you logical reasons to be a blood donor, but let me close with something more personal: I am alive today because there was blood available for a massive transfusion when I had my automobile accident. Any one of us could need blood tomorrow." Effective conclusions are short and focused. They highlight central ideas one last time and offer the audience a powerful or compelling concluding thought.

Build in Transitions

transitions Words and sentences that connect ideas and main points in a speech so that audience members can follow a speaker.

The final organizational issue is **transitions**—words and sentences that connect ideas and main points in a speech so that audience members can follow a speaker. Transitions signal that you are through talking about one idea and are ready move to the next one. Effective transitions are like signposts. They say where you have been and where you are heading (Coopman & Lull, 2015).

Transitions may be words, phrases, or entire sentences. Within the development of a single point, it's effective to use transitional words or phrases such as *therefore, and so, for this reason, as this evidence suggests,* and *consequently*. To make transitions from one point to another in a speech, phrases can be used to signal audience members that you are starting to discuss a new idea:

- "My second point is . . ."
- "Now that we have seen how many people immigrate to the United States, let's consider what they bring to us."
- "In addition to the point I just discussed, we need to think about . . ."

To move from one to another of the three major parts of a speech (i.e., introduction, body, and conclusion), you can signal your audience with statements that summarize what you've said in one part and point the way to the next. For example, here is an internal summary and a transition between the body of a speech and the conclusion:

"I've now explained in some detail why we need stronger educational and health programs for new immigrants. Let me close by reminding you of what's at stake."

Transitions also may be nonverbal. For example, you might hold up one, two, and three fingers to reinforce your movement from the first to the second to the third main point in the body of your speech. Changes in vocal intensity, eye contact, and inflection can effectively mark movement from one idea to the next. For instance, you could conclude the final point of the body of your speech with strong volume and then drop the volume to begin the conclusion. Silence is also effective in marking transitions. A pause after the introduction signals to the audience that a speaker is going to a new place. Visual aids also help the audience move with a speaker.

Transitions are vital to effective speaking. If the introduction, body, and conclusion are the bones of a speech, the transitions are the sinews that hold the bones together.

Presenting Public Speeches

We turn now to the final aspect of public speaking: presenting, or delivering, your speech. We'll first discuss building your speaking confidence. We then describe oral style, pointing out how it differs from written style. Then, we'll consider alternative styles of delivery.

Building Speaking Confidence

Speaking confidence enhances effectiveness. Yet there are very few people who don't sometimes feel apprehensive about public speaking (Richmond & McCroskey, 1992). If you are among the 95% of Americans who have some speaking anxiety (Richmond & McCroskey, 1995a), you are in good company. As you prepare to present your speech, it's important for you to understand **communication apprehension**, which is anxiety associated with speaking.

communication apprehension Anxiety associated with real or anticipated communication encounters. Communication apprehension is common and can be constructive.

The first thing to understand is that a degree of anxiety is natural and helpful to speakers. It stimulates our bodies to produce adrenaline and extra blood sugar, which increase energy so that we are more dynamic.

Although a degree of anxiety about speaking is natural, too much can interfere with effectiveness. Anxiety strong enough to hinder our ability to interact with others is communication apprehension.

Causes of Communication Apprehension

There are two types of communication apprehension: situational and chronic. For many of us, certain situations spark anxiety. For instance, if you are scheduled to speak to a group that is known to be hostile to you or your ideas, anxiety is to be expected.

Communication & Careers

I'd Rather Skip the Tournament Than Talk to the Press

Alex Grimm/Getty Image sport/Getty Images

Many professions call for occasional public speaking, and that's especially true for celebrities including sports stars—many of whom unfortunately report that press conferences exacerbate their anxiety surrounding public speaking. For example, pro tennis star Naomi Osaka quit the French Open in 2021, shocking the sports world, given her global second-place ranking in the sport. In explaining her anxiety, she cited "huge waves of anxiety before I speak to the world's media" that have led to "long bouts of depression" (iNews, 2021). Public speaking coach Vanessa Cuddeford notes that women and Black people can experience more fear of publicly speaking before the media, stating that many Black women athletes are rightfully concerned that the press will portray them as "the angry Black woman"—a terrible stereotype that can harm their careers (iNews, 2021). Cuddeford helps clients navigate these issues, but also calls on the press to change the nature of their coverage (iNews, 2021).

Meanwhile, the personal histories of athletes such as golf legend Annika Sorenstam show that communication apprehension can be successfully managed, even in high-pressure situations: As a teen, Sorenstam was so apprehensive of public speaking that she often deliberately played to win second place, to avoid giving the winner's speech. She credits her dad for noticing this and advocating for second- and third-place tournament winners to also speak. As a result, she developed a confident speaking style, for which she is grateful: "This tactic forced me to face my fear and was exceptionally beneficial to me in the long run," she says (Golfscape, 2019).

Five situational factors may generate apprehension. First, we tend to be more anxious when communicating with people who are unfamiliar to us or whom we perceive as different from us. Apprehension is also likely to be present in new or unfamiliar situations, such as your first job interview. A third situational cause of apprehension is being in the spotlight. When we are the center of attention, we tend to feel self-conscious and anxious that we might embarrass ourselves. Fourth, we may feel apprehensive when we're being evaluated.

A final situational reason for apprehension is a past failure or failures in a particular speaking situation. For example, my doctor called me one day to ask me to coach her for a speech she had to give to a medical society. Eleanor had last given a public speech 8 years earlier in medical school. Just before the speech, her first patient had died, and she was badly shaken. As a result, she was disorganized, flustered, and generally ineffective. That single incident, which followed a history of successful speaking, was so traumatic that Eleanor developed acute speaking anxiety.

Communication apprehension is more difficult to manage when it is chronic. Rather than feeling anxious in specific situations, which is often appropriate, some people are generally apprehensive about communicating. People who have chronic communication anxiety learn to fear communication, just as some of us learn to fear heights or water (Beatty, Plax, & Kearney, 1985; DeFleur & Ball-Rokeach, 1989).

Managing Communication Apprehension

There are ways to manage communication apprehension. First, remember that some anxiety is natural and often helpful in speaking. Second, use positive self-talk, which we discussed in Chapter 3. Tell yourself, "I can do this." "My anxiety is going to keep me on my toes." Also challenge negative, self-defeating thoughts. If you find yourself thinking "I'm going to forget what I want to say and everyone will think I'm incompetent," challenge that by saying, "I will have my notes so I can remind myself of anything I forget. Everyone in the audience has forgotten at times, so they're not going to think anything of it if I refer to my notes." It's a good idea to speak aloud when engaging in self-talk. Hearing yourself reinforces the message.

positive visualization A technique of reducing speaking anxiety; a person visualizes herself or himself communicating effectively in progressively challenging speaking situations.

A third way to reduce communication apprehension is to engage in **positive visualization**, which aims to reduce anxiety by guiding apprehensive speakers through imagined positive speaking experiences (Hamilton, 2015). In professional life, managers are coached to visualize successful negotiations and meetings. In the world of sports, athletes are taught to imagine playing well, and those who engage in positive visualization improve as much as athletes who physically practice their sport. Go to the book's online resources for this chapter to read about positive visualization and other ways of reducing speaking anxiety.

Review It!

Managing Speaking Anxiety:

- Remember It's Natural and Helpful
- Use Positive Self-Talk
- Engage in Positive Visualization

If your communication apprehension is not responsive to these suggestions and if it interferes with your ability to express your ideas, ask your instructor to direct you to professionals who can work with you.

Oral Style

oral style The visual, vocal, and verbal aspects of the delivery of a public speech.

Oral style refers to speakers' visual, vocal, and verbal communication with audience members. *Oral style includes everything from* gestures and movement during a presentation to their sentence structures, volume, inflection, and speaking rate.

A common mistake of speakers, both new and experienced, is to use written style rather than oral style. But a speech is not a spoken essay. There are three primary qualities of effective oral communication (Wilson & Arnold, 1974). First, it is usually more informal than written communication. Thus, speakers use contractions and sentence fragments that would be inappropriate in a formal written document. The informal character of oral style also means it's appropriate for speakers to use colloquial words in informal speaking contexts. However, speakers shouldn't use slang or jargon that might offend any audience member or that might not be understood by some people.

Second, effective oral style tends to be more personal than written style. It's generally effective for speakers to include personal stories and personal pronouns, referring to themselves as "I" rather than "the speaker." In addition, speakers should sustain eye contact with audience members and show that they are approachable. Third, effective oral style tends to be more immediate and more active than written style. This is important because audiences for speeches must understand ideas immediately as they are spoken, whereas readers can take time to comprehend ideas. In oral presentations, simple sentences ("I have three points") and compound sentences ("I want to describe the current system of selling textbooks, and then I will propose a less costly alternative") are more appropriate than complex sentences ("There are many reasons to preserve the Arctic National Wildlife Refuge, some of which have to do with endangered species and others with the preservation of wilderness environment, yet our current Congress is not protecting this treasure").

Immediacy also involves moving quickly instead of gradually to develop ideas. Rhetorical questions, interjections, and redundancy also enhance the immediacy of a speech.

Review It!

Qualities of Oral Style:

- Informal
- Personal
- Immediate

Styles of Delivery

The style of delivery that's effective at a political rally is different from the style appropriate for an attorney's closing speech in a trial; a toast at a wedding requires a style different from that required for testimony before Congress. There are four presentational styles.

Impromptu Style **Impromptu speaking** involves little preparation. Speakers speak off the cuff, organizing ideas as they talk and working with evidence that is already familiar to them. You use an impromptu style when you make a comment in a class, answer a question you hadn't anticipated in an interview, or respond to a request to share your ideas on a topic. There is no time to prepare or rehearse, so you have to think on your feet.

impromptu speaking Public speaking that involves little preparation. Speakers think on their feet as they talk about ideas and positions with which they are familiar.

Impromptu speaking is appropriate when you know a topic well enough to organize and support your ideas without a lot of advance preparation. For instance, the president of a company could speak off the cuff about the company's philosophy, goals, and recent activities. Impromptu speaking is not an effective style when speakers are not highly familiar with topics and at ease in speaking in public.

Extemporaneous Style Probably the most common presentational style today, **extemporaneous speaking** relies on preparation and practice, but actual words aren't memorized. Extemporaneous speaking (also called *extemp*) requires speakers to do research, organize ideas, select supporting evidence, prepare visual aids, outline the speech, and practice delivery. Yet the speech itself is not written out in full. Instead, speakers speak from notes or an outline.

extemporaneous speaking A presentational style that includes preparation and practice but not memorization of words and nonverbal behaviors.

Effective extemporaneous speaking requires a fine balance between too little and too much practice. Not rehearsing enough may result in stumbling, forgetting key ideas, and not being at ease with the topic. On the other hand, too much practice tends to result in a speech that sounds canned. Extemporaneous speaking involves a conversational and interactive manner that is generally effective with the audience.

manuscript speaking A presentational style that involves speaking from the complete manuscript of a speech.

Manuscript Style As the term suggests, **manuscript speaking** involves speaking from the complete manuscript of a speech. After planning, researching, organizing, and outlining a presentation, a speaker then writes the complete word-for-word text and practices the presentation using that text (available in a large font printed out on paper on the screen of a tablet) or, in some highly formal settings, transferred to a teleprompter. One clear advantage of this style is that it provides security to speakers. Even if a speaker gets confused when standing before an audience, they can rely on the full text. A second advantage of manuscript speaking is that it ensures precise content, which is important in official ceremonies, diplomatic agreements, and formal press statements and legal proceedings.

There are also disadvantages to manuscript speaking. First, writing a speech in its entirety often results in written, rather than oral, style. A second hazard of manuscript speaking is the tendency to read the speech. It's difficult to be animated and visually engaged with your audience when reading a manuscript, so if you have the occasion to use this style, be sure to practice making your delivery dynamic.

> **Brad** Most of my professors are pretty good. They talk with us in classes, and they seem to be really involved in interacting with students. But I've had several professors who read their notes—like, I mean, every day. They'd just come in, open a file, and start reading. I had one professor who almost never looked at us. It didn't feel like a person was communicating with us. I'd rather have read his notes on my own.

TED talks feature speakers who have memorized their speeches and present them from a stage with one screen or more, but no podium. Question: What do you notice about this speaker's body language? How do you think the lack of a podium between her and the audience might influence the audience's perceptions of her as a speaker?
Lawrence Sumulong/Getty Images

Memorized Style The final presentational style is **memorized speaking**, which carries the manuscript style one step further. After going through all the stages of manuscript speaking (i.e., preparing, researching, organizing, outlining, writing out the full text, and practicing), a speaker commits the entire speech to memory and speaks from a manuscript that is in their head. The advantages of this style are the same as those for manuscript speaking: An exact text exists, so everything is prepared in advance and the speaker has security. This is the style used for TED talks, which are committed to memory and extensively rehearsed prior to presentation.

memorized speaking
A presentational style in which a speech is memorized word for word in advance.

There are serious disadvantages to memorizing. Because memorized speaking is based on a full written speech, the presentation may reflect written rather than oral style. In addition, memorized speaking is risky because a speaker has no safety net in case of memory lapses. Speakers who forget a word or phrase may become rattled and unable to complete the presentation. Memorized style also can limit effective delivery. It is difficult for a speaker to sound spontaneous when they have memorized an entire speech. Because the speaker is preoccupied with remembering the speech, they can't interact fully with their audience. These drawbacks of memorized speaking explain why it isn't widely used or recommended outside of the TED talk format.

Knowing the benefits and liabilities of each presentational style provides you with alternatives. For most speaking occasions, extemporaneous style is effective because it combines good preparation and practice with spontaneity. Go to the book's online resources for this chapter for additional tips for effective delivery.

Review It!

Styles of Delivery:

- Impromptu
- Extemporaneous
- Manuscript
- Memorized

Today, many people rely on tablets or smart phones instead of note cards when speaking.
AFP/Getty Images

Practice

For all styles, practice is important. As impromptu speeches are by definition unrehearsed, the best way to practice is by delivering different impromptu speeches when the opportunity arrives. For all the other types of speeches, practicing allows you to refine your ability to apply the guidelines in Table 14.2. Ideally, you should begin practicing your speech several days before you plan to deliver it. During practice, you should rely on the notes or outline in the same format you will use when you actually deliver the speech (paper or digital). This ensures that you will be familiar with your material. You should also practice with visual aids and any other materials you plan to use in your speech so that you are comfortable working with them.

Table 14.2 Guidelines for Effective Delivery

1. Adapt your appearance to your listeners and their expectations.
2. Adapt your appearance to the speaking situation. Formal dress is likely to be appropriate for a speech to executives that is given in an office or board room. However, if that same speech were given at a company retreat by the ocean, casual dress would be more appropriate.
3. Use gestures to enhance impact. Gestures can reinforce ideas and complement verbal messages.
4. Adopt a confident posture. Stand erect, with your shoulders back and your feet slightly apart for optimum balance.
5. Use confident, dynamic body movement to communicate your enthusiasm and confidence. Walk to the speaking podium (or wherever you will speak) with assurance: head up, arms comfortably at your side, at a pace that is neither hurried nor halting. As you speak, move away from the podium to highlight key ideas or to provide verbal transitions from one point to the next.
6. Maintain good eye contact with listeners. Try to vary your visual zone so that you look at some listeners at one moment and then move your gaze to a different segment of listeners.
7. Use volume that is strong but not overpowering. The appropriate volume will vary, depending on the size of your audience. You also need to adapt your volume to the environment. If a noisy air conditioner is running, you'll need to increase your volume to be heard. Be careful not to let your volume drop off at the end of sentences, a common problem for beginning speakers.
8. Use your voice to enhance your message. Pitch, rate, volume, and articulation are vocal qualities that allow you to add emphasis to important ideas. As you practice your speech, decide which words and phrases you want to emphasize.
9. Use pauses for effect. It is often effective to pause for a second or two after stating an important point or presenting a dramatic example or statistic.
10. Do not let accent interfere with clarity. For everyone but professional broadcasters, regional accents are acceptable. However, your speaking must be understandable to listeners.
11. Articulate clearly. Speakers lose credibility when they mispronounce words or when they add or delete syllables. Common instances of added syllables are *cohabitate* for *cohabit, orientated* for *oriented, preventative* for *preventive,* and *irregardless* for *regardless.*

There are many ways to practice a speech. Usually, speakers prefer to practice alone initially so that they gain some confidence and comfort. You may find it helpful to practice in front of a mirror to see how you look and to keep your eyes focused away from the outline. Practicing before a mirror is especially helpful in experimenting with different nonverbal behaviors that can enhance your presentational impact. Unless your goal is to memorize your speech, take breaks between practices so that you don't wind up memorizing the speech inadvertently.

It is also helpful to make a video of yourself practicing so that you can see and hear yourself and make decisions about how to refine your delivery. Students who watch videos of themselves practicing can often immediately spot areas for improvement and may find it easier to make refinements. Some things to watch for in the video: Are you keeping eye contact, rather than looking at your notes too much? Are you enunciating clearly, rather than mumbling or speaking so quickly that your words elide? Are you varying your pitch and rate of speech, and not speaking in a monotonous way? Are you standing in a confident manner and not fidgeting or shifting your weight a lot?

When you've rehearsed enough to feel comfortable with the speech, it's time to practice in front of others. Ask friends to listen, and invite their feedback on ways you can refine your presentation. If there are particular things you'd like them to watch or listen for, let them know in advance. If your speech will be delivered remotely, set up a video conference and ask friends to listen in the same format, in conditions as similar to your planned presentation (given in the same environment, at the same time of day, and with the same lighting) as possible. Practice until you know your material well but haven't memorized it (unless that's your goal)—then stop! Rehearsing too much is just as inadvisable as not practicing enough. You want to preserve the spontaneity that is important in oral style.

Chapter Summary

In this chapter, we focused on ways to organize and present public speeches. We first discussed the importance of speaking confidence and ways to build it. Next, we identified different types of outlines that assist speakers in organizing material. Third, we considered seven patterns for organizing speeches and explored how each pattern affects the residual message of a presentation. Which organizational structure is best depends on a variety of factors, including the topic, your speaking goal, and the audience with whom you will communicate. Finally, the fourth section of the chapter examined the advantages and disadvantages of different styles of delivery. public speeches.

To make sure that you've thought through all important aspects of organizing, outlining, and delivery, review the checklist at the end of this chapter. Then you'll be ready to proceed to Chapter 15, in which we analyze the full text of a student speech to see how organization, evidence, and other facets of public speaking work in an actual presentation.

Checklist for Organizing and Presenting a Speech

Complete this checklist to help you organize your next speech.

In addition, you can use Outline Builder to help you organize your speech.

1. How could you structure your speech using each of the organizational patterns we discussed? Write out a thesis statement for each pattern.
   A. temporal: ____________________
   B. spatial: ____________________
   C. topical: ____________________
   D. star: ____________________
   E. comparative: ____________________
   F. problem–solution: ____________________
   G. cause–effect: ____________________
   H. effect–cause:____________________
2. Which pattern have you decided to use?
   A. List the two or three main points into which you've divided your topic:____________________, : ____________________, and :____________________.
3. Describe the three parts of your introduction:
   A. I will gain attention by :____________________
   ____
   B. My thesis statement is ____________________
   ____
   C. My preview is ____________________
   ____
4. Describe the transitions you've developed to move audience members from idea to idea in your speech.
   A. My transition from introduction to the body of the speech is ____________________
   ____
   ____
   B. My transitions between major points in the body are ____________________
   ____
   ____
   C. My transition from the body to the conclusion of the speech is ____________________
   ____
   ____
5. Describe the two parts of your conclusion:
   A. Restatement of thesis and major points: ____________________
   B. Concluding emphasis: ____________________
6. The delivery style I will use is ____________________ because ____________________
7. I've practiced my speech
   A. on my own
   B. in front of others
   C. in front of a mirror
   D. in the room where I will deliver it
   E. on video

Experiencing Communication in Our Lives

Case Study: Analyzing Delivery: Speech of Self-Introduction

Apply what you've learned in this chapter by analyzing the following case study, using the accompanying questions as a guide.

Every year since I've remembered, we've gone back to Iowa and spent a week of that summer just being with my dad's parents, my grandparents. And each year, as I grew, I grew closer and closer to my grandfather. And it got to the point where I no longer just knew him as a relative but I knew him as a human being. Sitting outside on his porch one day, right before he died, he told me about his life. We were talking about what he had done, being in the Korean war, being a dentist, being a community leader, all the things he had ever achieved in his life—and it all sounded so perfect. I said, "Grandfather, what do you regret most in your life?" He said, "Adam, I regret not seeing more sunsets."

istock.com/insta_photos

A couple months later, he passed on, and I realized that I didn't enjoy every single minute with him as much as I could've, and I didn't have the time with him that I thought that I had. So I look at my wall now, and I see the quotes on it and see the stories on it and the pictures on it and I realize that everyone I've come into contact with, everyone I've ever met, everything I've done, has all contributed to shaping the person that I am.

Questions for Analysis and Discussion

1. Was the speaker dynamic—excited about the topic?
2. Was the speaker's language clear, immediate, and vivid?
3. Did the speaker use nonverbal communication to enhance effectiveness?
4. What style of speaking did the speaker use? Was this an appropriate choice for this speech, this occasion, and the particular audience members?

Key Concepts

communication apprehension
extemporaneous speaking
formal outline
impromptu speaking
key word outline
manuscript speaking
memorized speaking
oral style
positive visualization
transitions
working outline
works cited

Sharpen Your Skill

1. **Designing Your Introduction**

   Apply the principles we've discussed to develop an introduction to a speech you plan to give. Using the following outline, fill in full sentences for each element of your introduction.

   I. Introduction

   A. Attention: ______________________

   B. Thesis: ______________________

C. Credibility: ______________________________

D. Preview: ______________________________

2. Rehearsing Your Speech

You'll need three 20-minute periods at different times to complete this activity.

a. After you have prepared the outline that you will use when you present your speech, find a quiet place where you will not be disturbed. Present the speech as you intend to deliver it to your class. If your speech will be in person, as you rehearse, practice looking at different parts of the room as you will later engage in eye contact with classmates. If your speech will be delivered remotely, using video conferencing software, practice looking directly at the camera of the device you will be using—not your own image or other parts of the screen—so that you give your audience members the appearance of making eye contact with them as they watch you on screen.

b. Wait at least a few hours after your first practice to do the second one. If your speech will be in person, this time, practice in the same room, but stand in front of a mirror; ideally it should be a full-length mirror so that you can see yourself as audience members will see you. If your speech will be online, this time, do watch yourself on screen, rather than practicing looking at the camera. Give your speech as you plan to deliver it to your classmates. As you speak, notice your posture and nonverbal communication. Are you using effective hand gestures, facial expressions, and changes in body posture and position?

c. Wait at least a few hours after your second practice to do the third one. Invite several friends or classmates to join you in this practice session so that you have an audience.

- If your speech will be in person, go to your classroom or another classroom that is set up similarly to yours, and ask your friends to meet you there. Sit down in the room as you would sit in your class. Imagine the teacher announcing that it is your turn to speak. Get up from your seat, go to the podium or front of the classroom, and present your speech as you plan to deliver it to your classmates. Practice looking at different areas of the room or at your friends as you will later engage in eye contact with classmates. You can use a phone or laptop to record a video of this third rehearsal and then analyze your presentation as well as feedback from anyone you invited to be your audience.
- Or, if your speech will be delivered virtually, set up a video conference in conditions as similar to your planned presentation (given in the same environment, at the same time of day, and with the same lighting) as possible. Use video conferencing software that allows you to make and save a recording of the meeting. Send your friends an invitation link, and when they join you, practice your speech. Look directly at the camera of the device you will be using. Analyze the video of your presentation as well as feedback from your invited audience to make a final round of improvements.

For Further Reflection and Discussion

1. Does a speaker have an ethical responsibility to organize a speech well, or is organization strictly a strategic matter—something to help a speaker have impact? Does careful organization reflect ethical issues, such as respect for the audience?
2. Attend a public presentation and keep notes on how the speaker organizes the speech. What is the overall pattern of the presentation? Did the speaker make a wise choice? Identify transitions in the speech, and evaluate their effectiveness. Do the introduction and conclusion serve the appropriate speaking goals?
3. Give a 1- to 2-minute impromptu speech on your favorite activity. Next, spend 2 days preparing an extemporaneous speech on the same topic. How do the two speeches differ in quality and effectiveness?

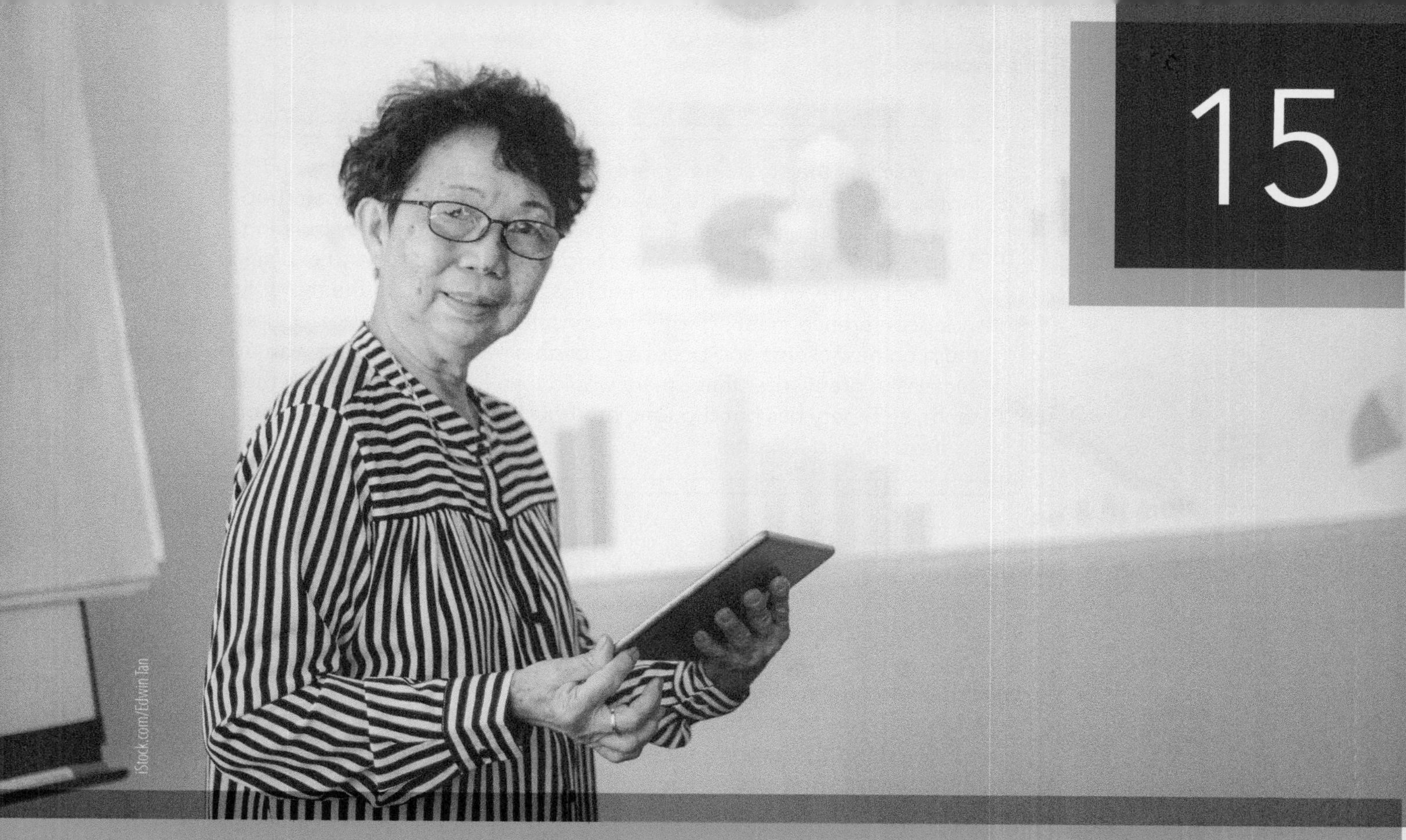

iStock.com/Edwin Tan

Informative Speaking

> Information is the currency of democracy.
>
> **Thomas Jefferson**

Learning Objectives

After studying the topics in this chapter, you should be able to:

1. Define informative speaking and explain four ways in which it differs from persuasive speaking.
2. List eight guidelines for effective informative public speeches.
3. Identify five ethical considerations speakers face when evaluating information to use as supporting material.
4. Organize an informative speech using an informative speech outline.

How common is informative speaking in everyday life?

Emery savors the steaming coffee as they pull up the calendar on their laptop and reviews the day's to-do list. Since launching their start-up fundraising consulting firm, Emery has been incredibly busy building a team. At 9 o'clock, Emery is meeting with their assistant to explain a new procedure for managing client files. At 10 o'clock is the monthly videoconference meeting with the consultancy's advisory board, updating them on new clients and possible growth areas. Lunch will be with a highly successful grantwriter that Emery would love to persuade to join their team, so Emery has put thought into how best to describe their company, its mission, and its culture.

Like many professionals, Emery does a lot of informational speaking. They have to be able to describe changing practices, explain procedures, and inform people about issues. To live and work effectively in today's world, we need to share information—in the workplace, in social situations, and in community and civic contexts. Skill at informative speaking is critical if you want to be effective personally, professionally, and socially. Go to the book's online resources for this chapter to learn more about the importance of informational speaking in professional life.

Building on what you've learned in Chapters 12–14, this chapter will guide you through the process of developing and presenting an informative speech. The process we discuss can also be used to develop short informational presentations, such as some of those on Emery's calendar. We will first highlight the importance of informative speaking in everyday life and note how it differs from persuasive speaking, which we will cover in Chapter 16. Then, we'll discuss guidelines for effective informative speaking. At the end of the chapter, you'll find a sample informative speech.

The Nature of Informative Speaking

informative speech
A presentation that aims to increase listeners' knowledge, understanding, or abilities.

An **informative speech** aims to increase listeners' knowledge, understanding, or abilities. Competence in informative speaking is important if you plan to coach sports, be part of neighborhood and civic groups, succeed in your profession, or teach anything to anyone (Hamilton, 2015; Morreale, Osborn, & Pearson, 2000).

Informative Speaking in Everyday Life

It's likely that you'll give a number of informative speeches in your life. Some will be short; some will be longer. Some will be formal; others will be informal. All of them will have the goal of conveying information to others. Consider these examples of everyday informative speaking:

- Explaining a medical procedure to a patient.
- Informing your neighbors about a mutual aid program that's improved the feeling of community and well-being in other towns.
- Briefing stakeholders on the new strategic plan your firm is implementing.

- Describing a new offensive strategy to the Little League team you coach.
- Telling a civic group about traditions in your culture.
- Reporting to your coworkers on what you learned at a conference so that they understand new developments in your field.

Comparing Informative and Persuasive Speaking

Informative speaking and persuasive speaking differ, yet they also have much in common. Both require forethought about listeners and the occasion, research, organization, supporting material, and delivery. There are also overlaps between informative and persuasive goals. For example, in an informative speech, you are trying to persuade listeners to attend to what you say and to care about learning. In persuasive speeches, you often need to inform listeners about certain issues to influence their values, attitudes, or behaviors.

Four differences between informative and persuasive speaking are particularly important.

The Controversial Nature of the Purpose The purposes of informative speeches tend to be less controversial than the purposes of persuasive speeches. Something is controversial when it can be debated or argued—in other words, when not everyone is likely to agree. Typically, informative presentations aim to give listeners new information: to teach, explain, or describe a person, object, event, process, or relationship. Persuasive speeches, on the other hand, often aim to change listeners' attitudes, beliefs, or behaviors.

Obviously, information can have persuasive impact, so it can be controversial. Yet the degree to which a purpose is controversial is much greater in persuasive speeches. An informative speech might have the specific purpose of describing the historical conditions that led to establishment of affirmative action policies. A persuasive speech on the same topic might have the specific purpose of persuading listeners to support or oppose affirmative action policies. Clearly, the latter purpose is more controversial than the former.

The Response Sought Related to their differing purposes are the responses informative and persuasive speeches seek from listeners. In the affirmative action example, the speaker giving an informative speech wants listeners to understand

Communication & Careers

Informative Speaking on the Job

What does skill in informative speaking have to do with career success? A lot. People who can present ideas clearly tend to be noticed and promoted. A 2015 article in *United States News & World Report* pointed out that good informative speaking skills are not just for presentations in front of large crowds. They are also critical to presenting ideas in team meetings and informing colleagues and board members of new policies, products, and issues. In other words, speaking skill is part of everyday work situations (Yeager, 2015).

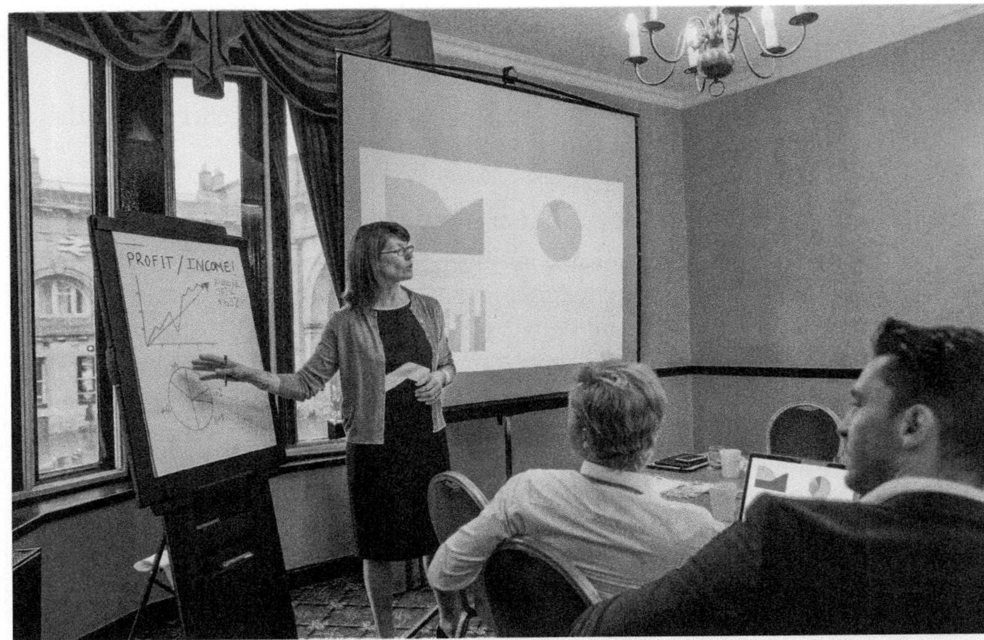

Most professionals today engage in informative speaking.
iStock.com/DGLimages

certain historical conditions. The speaker giving a persuasive speech wants listeners to believe that affirmative action is right or wrong, justified or not justified, or beneficial or harmful. The persuasive speaker might even want to persuade listeners to take specific actions to oppose or support affirmative action at local, regional, or national levels. In seeking to change listeners in some way, persuasive speeches seek a more powerful response: change rather than acceptance of new information.

The Evidence Needed Because persuasive speeches tend to be more controversial and seek to convince listeners to change in some way, they generally need stronger supporting material than informative speeches do. This does not mean that informative speeches don't need proof; they do. However, an effective persuasive speech generally must include more supporting material. Why? Because listeners expect more evidence when they are asked to think, feel, or act differently than when they are asked only to understand something. Listeners will want convincing evidence not only that discrimination exists and is wrong but also that affirmative action policies are an effective response to the problem.

In persuasive speeches, speakers also have a responsibility to anticipate and address listeners' reservations. Doing this effectively requires evidence. Perhaps, in researching public opinions on affirmative action, you learn that the most common objection is based on the assumption that it lowers standards for admission to schools and professions. To persuade listeners to support affirmative action, you should present evidence that shows that standards have not declined in institutions that follow affirmative action policies.

Vince Last week, I went to hear a speaker on capital punishment. He was trying to convince us that we should abolish it, but I wasn't convinced. What he mainly did was to inform us that there are cases where innocent people are convicted or even put to death. But he never showed us—or me, anyway—that abolishing capital punishment is the answer. Why can't we just reform it, like, require absolute proof of guilt before someone can be sentenced to die? And what about all the people who really are guilty of horrible things, like school killings or the Oklahoma bombing? Shouldn't they be sentenced to death? He never talked about that.

Question: What might the speaker have done before his talk in order to anticipate and address Vince's perspective as an audience member?

Credibility Needed Credibility is important to any speaker's effectiveness. As with evidence, however, the credibility a speaker needs varies with the speaking purpose. In general, a speaker who attempts to change people needs more credibility than a speaker who seeks only to inform them. Because credibility is so important in persuasive speaking, we will discuss it in depth in Chapter 16.

Review It!

Differences Between Informative and Persuasive Speeches:

- Controversialness
- Response Sought
- Evidence Needed
- Credibility Needed

Guidelines for Effective Informative Speaking

Eight guidelines are particularly important for informative speeches.

Provide Listeners with a Clear Thesis Statement

When giving an informative presentation, the speaker should state a simple, clear thesis that tells listeners what the speech will provide or do. The thesis should motivate listeners by alerting them that the information to come will be useful to them. As you'll recall from previous chapters, a good thesis is clear and direct: "At the end of my talk, you will understand the different support tactics and results of three well-regarded mutual aid programs in our county." Upon hearing this thesis, listeners know exactly what the speaker plans to give them and what they should get out of listening.

Connect with Listeners' Values and Experiences

As with all communication, informative speeches should build connections with listeners. For instance, in a speech with the specific purpose of describing mutual aid programs, a speaker might open by saying, "I know we share a concern for the well-being of our neighborhood and a desire to support one another in small ways, like picking up medications for people who are homebound, or supporting those experiencing food insecurity. What I want to do is describe the three well-regarded mutual aid programs in our county that have built community, increased allyship, and empowered people, so that we can make an informed choice about what is right for our community." This opening establishes a common ground between the speaker and listeners by noting that they "share a concern" and by using *we* language: "our neighborhood," "we can make," "our community."

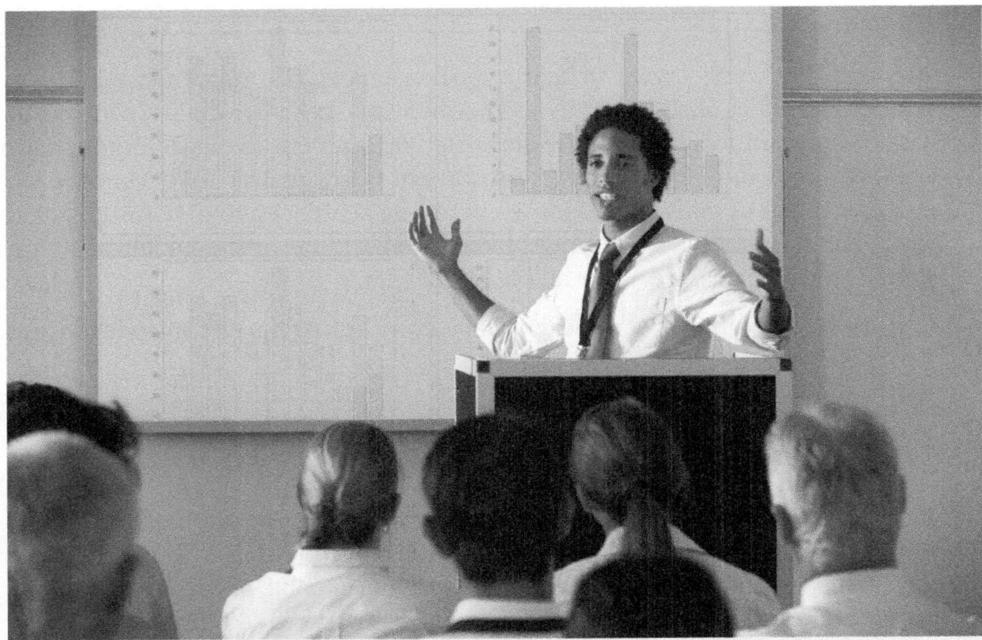

What are your impressions of this speaker?
iStockphoto.com/Cathy Yeulet

Motivate Listeners to Want Information

For an informative speech to be effective, listeners must be motivated to want what the speaker offers. In some cases, listeners are motivated for their own reasons. People who attend cardiopulmonary resuscitation (CPR) class want to learn how to perform CPR. They are already motivated.

In other cases, the speaker may need to motivate people to want information. For example, a supervisor may need to fuel employees' hunger for information on a new procedure the company wants them to follow. In this situation, the supervisor might say, "I know we all get tired of learning new procedures, but the one I'm going to explain today will make your jobs easier and increase your productivity." This statement motivates employees to listen, especially if their pay is based on their productivity.

Sarah I went to the placement office the other day for a workshop on interviewing. I wasn't really interested, but I thought I should go, so I was just kind of there but not really paying attention. Then the facilitator got us started. The first thing she said was that students who attend these workshops tended to get more and better job offers than students who don't. That definitely got my attention! From then on, I was listening very carefully and taking lots of notes.

Build Credibility with Listeners

As we've noted, for a speaker to be effective, listeners must perceive them as credible. When giving an informative speech, you should demonstrate that you have some expertise relevant to your topic. You may show you have personal experience

("I took a CPR course"). You may also demonstrate to listeners that you have gained information in other ways ("To prepare to talk to you today, I spoke with emergency department doctors about people whose lives were saved by CPR").

You'll also want to show listeners that you care about them or that the information you are offering will help them in some way. You might say, "This information may enable you to save a life one day."

Adapt to Diverse Listeners

You should speak in ways that include and respect diverse experiences, values, and viewpoints. People who have experienced a medical crisis and who would benefit from community support have had a different experience from those who have been fortunate enough to have not had a medical crisis. Citizens who were raised in highly communal cultures are likely to be more inclined toward communal efforts to protect a neighborhood than are people who were raised in highly individualistic cultures. Families without children may have different security concerns from families with children, especially young ones.

Dimitri I am looking for a new car, so I went to a dealership. I was looking at a model that Consumer Reports said has the highest safety rating. Then the salesman came over and started talking about the car I was looking at. His pitch was that it was cheap and fuel efficient. I asked him a couple of questions about safety issues, which are my primary concerns with cars, and he just brushed them back and kept telling me how economical it was. He lost that sale.

Question: Which of the organizational patterns for speeches detailed in Chapter 14 might the salesperson have used to increase his chances of winning Dimitri as a customer?

Organize So Listeners Can Follow Easily

In Chapter 4, we learned that listening is hard work. A speaker should make it easy for listeners to take in information. Applying the principles we discussed in Chapter 14, this means that you should structure your speech clearly. As we learned, your introduction should capture listeners' attention ("Would you like to increase your paycheck by 10%?"), provide a clear thesis ("I'm going to explain a new procedure that will increase your efficiency and income"), and preview what will be covered ("I will demonstrate a new method of sorting and routing stock and show how much faster and more accurate it is than the method we've been using").

Transitions should be woven throughout the speech to assist listeners in following the flow of ideas. The conclusion should summarize key points ("I've shown you how to increase your paycheck") and end with a strong idea or punch ("In this case, what's good for the company is also good for you").

The body of an informative speech should also be organized clearly (see Table 15.1). Temporal and spatial patterns can be effective for speeches that aim to demonstrate, describe, explain, or teach ("In my speech, I will describe how interviews progress from opening stage to substance and closing stage"). Topical patterns are commonly used for reports and briefings that address several areas of a topic ("I will summarize developments in our sales and marketing divisions").

Table 15.1 Organizing Informative Speeches

Specific Purpose	Thesis	Organizational Patterns
Listeners will learn how to recognize differences between poisonous and nonpoisonous plants.	I will teach you how to tell which plants are safe to eat.	Comparison/contrast
Team members will know management's response to our strategic plan.	I will summarize the feedback from management on our goals and implementation strategies.	Topical
To teach friends how I make crème brûlée.	I am going to take you through the steps involved in making a perfect crème brûlée.	Temporal
Employees will understand the reasons for a new procedure for sorting and routing stock.	I want to explain how the new procedure we're going to start using solves problems that have frustrated us for years.	Problem–solution

When introducing new or alternative ideas or procedures, the comparative pattern can be effective ("The new method of sorting and routing stock differs from our current method in two key ways").

Although they are less commonly used in informative presentations, problem–solution and cause–effect or effect–cause patterns can be good choices. For instance, an informative speech might explain how a new procedure for sorting and routing stock solves a problem. The same topic might be organized using a cause–effect pattern to show that the new procedure (cause) will increase productivity (effect).

Outline Builder accessed through MindTap, includes extensive prompts and a clear framework for organizing and developing speeches that incorporate a variety of informative strategies.

Design Your Speech to Enhance Learning and Retention

Much of the information we need to do our jobs and live our lives is not particularly interesting. This poses a challenge for you when you give an informative speech. The informative speaker is responsible for making material interesting to listeners. In addition, information can be complex and difficult to grasp, particularly in oral presentations. This creates a second challenge for informative speakers: You must do all you can to increase the clarity of the information. Five strategies can help you make your information interesting and clear.

Limit the Information You Present By the time you are ready to give an informative speech, you know a great deal about the topic. It's your job to sort through all your knowledge to choose wisely the two or three points you want to make. You may think five points are important. If you try to present all five, however, you risk having listeners remember none or the less important ones.

If you must cover more than two or three points to inform listeners fully, then you have two choices. You may give multiple informative talks, separated by time to allow listeners to absorb and apply the information you've provided before they get more. A second option is to rely on other principles of increasing clarity and interest that we discuss later in this chapter.

Move from Familiar to Unfamiliar It's normal to feel uneasy when you are asked to understand new information or learn a new process or skill. Speakers can reduce this anxiety by starting with what is familiar to listeners and moving to what is new. For instance, the supervisor in our example might open an informative speech by saying, "All of you know the sorting and routing procedure we've used for years. The new procedure extends what you already know. What you've done in the past is to sort incoming stock into three piles. From now on, you'll be sorting it into four. It's the same process—just one more pile." Upon hearing this, listeners realize that skills they already have will transfer to the new procedure.

Repeat Important Ideas Repetition increases retention (Jaffe, 2016). Have you ever been introduced to someone and not been able to remember the person's name 5 minutes later? That's because you heard it only once. The introduction probably was like this: "Pat, I'd like you to meet Leigh." If the person doing the introduction had wanted to help you remember Leigh's name, it would have been better to say this: "Pat, I'd like you to meet Leigh. Leigh and I go way back; we met in our sophomore year. We got together when Leigh and I were trying out for the chorus, and Leigh got a place when I didn't." In that short introduction, Leigh's name was mentioned four times. You'll probably remember it. You're more likely to remember something you hear four times than something you hear only once.

The same principle applies to informative speaking. As an illustration, let's return to our supervisor. It's important that employees retain the new classifications into which they will be sorting stock, so these bear repeating: "In the past you've sorted stock into new, returns, and used. As most of you know, the stock we've been putting in the return pile has really been of two types: stock that was missing something and stock that was defective. Now we're breaking returns into two separate piles: ones with missing parts and ones that are defective. So we have missings and defects. The missing pile is for stock that is missing a part. We can fix these items by adding the missing part. The defect pile is for stock that has something wrong with it. So missings and defects are the new piles we want to use." The repeated references to *missings* and *defects* increase listeners' ability to retain the new classifications for stock.

Highlight Key Material Do you become more attentive in class when a teacher says, "This next point is really important" or "You're likely to see this on the test"? Probably you do. That's what the teacher intends. They are highlighting key material to get your attention. In this example, the teacher highlighted by framing. "This material is important" is a frame that calls your attention to important material.

"This material is important."

MATERIAL

There are other ways to highlight key material. You might say something direct, such as, "Listen up. This is important." Or you might say, "I hope you'll really tune in to this next point." You could also say, "If you remember only one thing from my talk, it should be this: . . ." All of these statements give verbal clues to listeners that you are presenting especially important material.

You can also provide nonverbal clues to highlight key material. Raising volume or changing inflection tends to capture interest, so listeners are likely to listen more carefully when a speaker alters volume or inflection. Gestures can also emphasize the importance of key ideas. You can change your position—move from behind a podium to in front of it, move from sitting to standing—to draw listeners' attention.

Rely on Multiple Communication Channels If a speaker says, "Red berries often are poisonous," you might get the point. You'd be more likely to retain it if the speaker made that statement and also showed you pictures of red berries or gave you red berries. When we use multiple channels to communicate, we increase the likelihood that listeners will retain new information.

When you're presenting a lot of information or complex information during an in-person talk, handouts can greatly increase listeners' retention and ability to use new information. Listeners both hear the talk and see the notes summarizing key points. Visual aids, whether in person or on a digital platform, can also highlight information. The supervisor in our example might develop a visual aid to show the two new classifications that grow out of the one former one (Figure 15.1). Showing this while also talking about the two new classifications lets listeners learn and retain through two senses: seeing and hearing. The visual aid would be especially effective if the two new classifications stood out visually. They might be larger or a different color font.

Involve Listeners

Have you ever been a passenger when someone else was driving and later been unsure how to get back to where the two of you went? If you drive yourself, there's a greater likelihood that you'll learn how to get to the place. This common experience reminds us that we learn best when we do something ourselves rather than just hear or see someone else do it. There are many ways to involve listeners in informative speeches. We'll highlight four of the most effective (see Table 15.2).

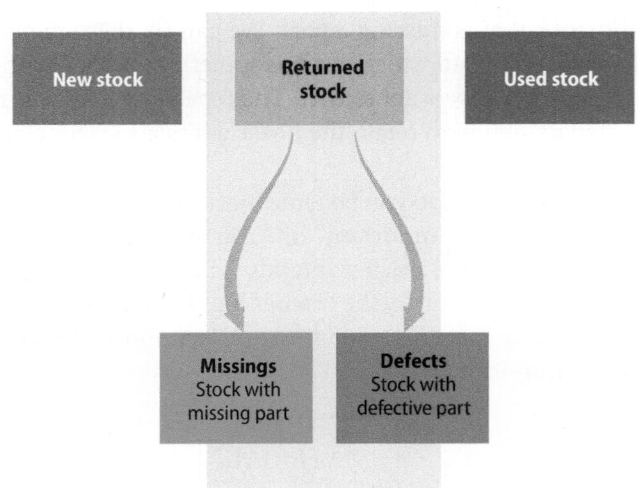

Figure 15.1
A Visual Aid to Illustrate a New Procedure

Table 15.2 **Generating a Sense of Listener Participation**

Specific Informative Purpose: To Teach Listeners How to Recognize Poisonous Plants	
Method	**Example**
Direct participation	I want each of you to smell the berries I'm handing out.
Rhetorical question	If you were stranded on a camping trip, would you know how to survive?
Poll listeners	How many of you have ever pulled a ripe berry off a bush and wondered if it was safe to eat?
Refer to specific listeners	Jane, remember when you watched Tom Hanks in *Castaway* and wondered how he knew what was safe to eat on the island?

Call for Participation You might give sticks to Boy Scouts and so they can rub them together as you demonstrate how to do this to start a fire (but only if fire codes allow this and if you can control possible danger). You might let people try a new procedure at a demonstration stand you set up. You might bring plants that are poisonous and nonpoisonous so that listeners can see, smell, and touch them as you describe how they differ.

Ask Rhetorical Questions You can also involve listeners by asking rhetorical questions. These are questions that a speaker doesn't actually expect listeners to answer. By asking them, however, a speaker invites listeners' mental participation: They are likely to answer rhetorical questions silently in their heads. "How many of you have ever wished you had an extra $100?" "What would you do if you made 20% more each week? Would you take a vacation, buy a new car, or pay some bills?"

Poll Listeners Another way to involve listeners is to poll them to find out what they think, feel, or want or what experiences they have had. "How many of you have ever not been able to drive after a medical procedure and worried how you'd run your errands and get to your follow-up appointments?" "How many of you would like to earn $100 more a week?" Speakers can ask for audible responses ("If you have had this experience, say yes") or a show of hands ("Let me see the hands of everyone who has had this experience").

Refer to Specific Listeners You may also speak directly to or about particular members of your audience. Ethically, you must be careful not to speak to or about others in ways that could embarrass them or reveal information they consider private. Speaking to or about specific listeners generates a sense of participation and community. "Shondra and Maeve, we were so concerned when we heard about your family's unexpected medical bills." "Just the other day, I overheard Elijah talking about what he'd do if he won the lottery. Well, Elijah, I've got good news for you: You may not win the lottery, but you can get more money."

Review It!

Guidelines for Informative Speaking:

- Clear Thesis
- Connect with Listeners
- Motivate Listeners
- Build Credibility
- Adapt to Diverse Listeners
- Organize
- Enhance Learning and Retention
- Involve Listeners

Use Effective and Ethical Supporting Materials

To be effective in informing listeners, speeches must include supporting material that is both effective and ethical. Effective supporting materials add interest, force, and clarity to a speech. Ethical supporting materials present accurate information fairly and without distortion (Lehman & DuFrene, 1999).

Returning to our previous example, the supervisor might take the average employee's salary and show how much it should go up using the new procedure. The speaker might develop a visual aid to show how that increase would multiply over a period of time (Figure 15.2).

To be ethical, supporting material should meet the criteria we discussed in Chapter 13 (see Table 13.4). To review, supporting material should be:

- Sufficient to achieve the speaking purpose, such as teaching or describing (sufficiency).
- Accurate, correct and complete, with sources cited, presented in its original context (accuracy).
- Relevant to the topic and claims made (relevance).
- Timely, usually current or in some cases historically situated (timeliness).
- Free of biases, such as vested interests (impartiality).

Using these criteria, it would be ethical for the speaker to tell employees that their wages should increase an average of 20% only if the speaker had adequate data to support that claim (the criterion of accuracy). If only 25% of employees who have used the new procedure increase their productivity, it would not be ethical to state that they could expect to increase their wages because only one in four could reasonably expect

Figure 15.2
A Visual Aid to Motivate Employees

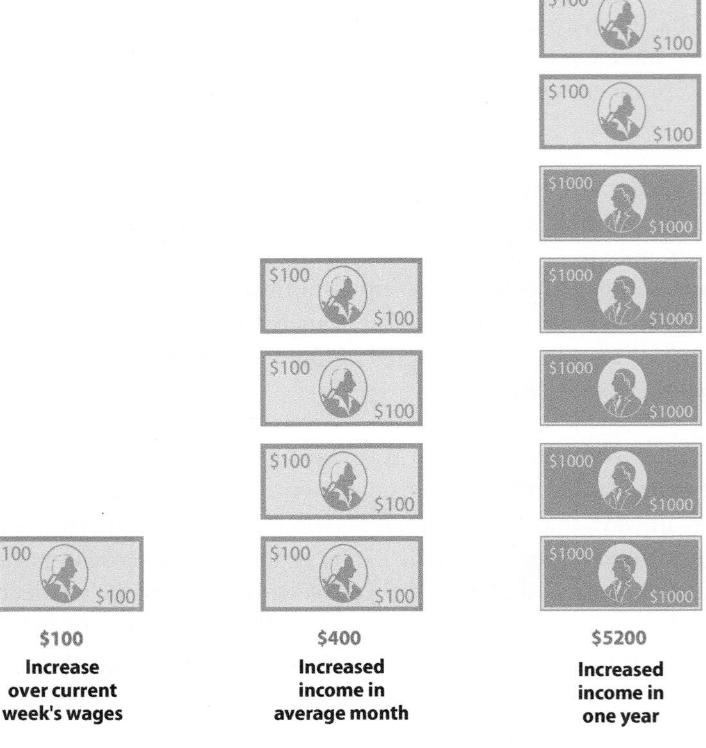

that. If most employees do increase their productivity by 20% but only after 4–6 months of adjusting to the new procedure, the speaker would be ethically obligated to inform them of the time lag (the criterion of timeliness). If employees who use the new procedure at other plants have different working conditions and tools, the change in their productivity might not generalize to the listeners in this case (the criterion of relevance).

Chapter Summary

In this chapter, we described the many types of informative speeches and noted how informative speaking differs from persuasive speaking. We then highlighted eight guidelines for effective informative speaking. Because these guidelines are at the heart of the impact of your informative presentations, we summarize them here:

1. Provide listeners with a clear thesis statement.
2. Connect with listeners' values and experiences.
3. Motivate listeners to want information.
4. Build credibility with listeners.
5. Adapt to diverse listeners.
6. Organize so listeners can follow easily.
7. Design your speech to enhance learning and retention.
8. Involve listeners.

In following these eight guidelines, speakers should use effective and ethical supporting materials to develop their ideas.

Informative Speech Outline

General Purpose: ______

Specific Purpose: ______

Introduction

I. Attention device ______

II. Motivation for listening ______

III. Thesis statement ______

IV. Preview of speech ______

Body

I. First main point ______

A. Supporting material ______

B. Supporting material (You may have only two main points) ______

C. Transition ______

II. Second main point (You may have more than two kinds of supporting materials for main points) ______

A. Supporting material ______

B. Supporting material ______

C. Transition ______

Transition to conclusion ______

Conclusion

I. Summary of main points ___

II. Strong closing statement ___

References ___

Evaluation Form for Informative Speeches

Speaker's Name: ___ Date: ___

Speech Topic: ___

1. Did the speaker capture listeners' initial attention? ___
2. Did the speaker motivate listeners to want information? ___
3. Did the speaker state a clear thesis? ___
4. Did the speaker preview the body of the speech? ___
5. Was the speech structured clearly and appropriately? ___
6. Were strong transitions provided between parts of the speech and main points in the body of the speech? ___
7. Did the speaker provide effective supporting material? ___
8. Did the speaker use ethical supporting material? ___
9. Did the speaker involve listeners directly by polling them, asking rhetorical questions, or speaking to or about particular listeners? ___
10. Did the speaker use strategies to enhance listeners' learning and retention? ___
11. Did the speaker connect the topic to listeners' experiences and values? ___
12. Did the conclusion summarize main points of the speech? ___
13. Did the speech end on a strong note? ___

Experiencing Communication in Our Lives

Case Study: Informative Speech, Camp Leadertown

I would not be the person I am today if it was not for Camp Leadertown. You're probably wondering what I'm talking about. What can so dramatically change someone's life?

As its name suggests, Camp Leadertown is a summer leadership camp. Now there are thousands of summer leadership camps all around the world. You have science camps, young life camps, all kinds of camps—camps that change our lives in positive ways.

The summer before my junior year, I attended Camp Leadertown. After camp I was never the same. So what exactly is Leadertown? What is its history and what goes on at camp that's so powerful? Today I'll discuss these three things with you.

According to its website, Camp Leadertown is a youth development program that focuses on diversity awareness, social justice, and personal empowerment. Its mission is to be a catalyst and facilitator for social change. This camp brings together people from different backgrounds and different cultures.

The Camp Leadertown organization has several types of programs, I attended their weeklong camp. It's filled with activities geared toward understanding diversity and inclusion through a great deal of educational activities that have emotional impact. Since it was founded in 1965, Camp Leadertown's goal has been to bring together a group of diverse young youth from a variety of different backgrounds.

During camp, leaders work with affinity groups, meaning groups of students that share a background. Then, through conversations within and across affinity groups, campers learn best practices like cultural humility. The campers become empowered to understand each other, and learn from each other—and this process completely changed my perspective, making be a better person and ally than I could have been without it.

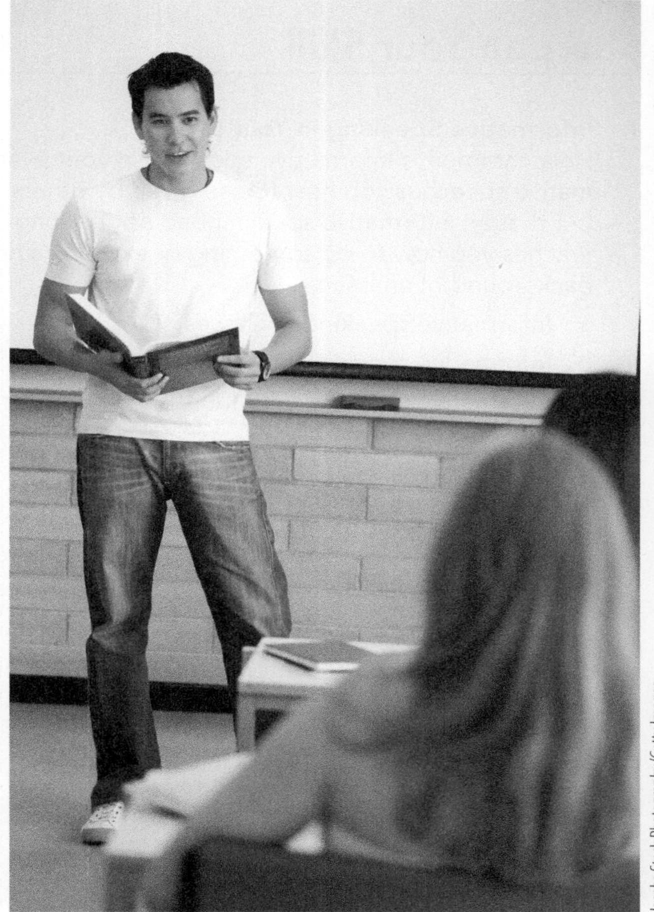

Jacobs Stock Photography/Getty Images

I hope you have learned a thing or two about this great organization. I hope Camp Leadertown will be around for years to come, helping our youth understand diversity, advocate for equity and inclusion, and understand each other. Camp Leadertown has great power: to change the world one person at a time.

Questions for Analysis and Discussion

1. Did the beginning of the Leadertown speech effectively capture your attention?
2. Did the preview forecast coverage adequately?
3. Did effective and ethical evidence support the main ideas?
4. Were there good transitions between main points?
5. Did the conclusion summarize main points in the speech?

Key Concepts

informative speech

Sharpen Your Skill

1. **Informative Speaking in Your Life**
   How common is informative speaking in your everyday life? For the next week, keep a record of the informative speeches you hear (those given by others), grouped into the five categories listed here. Remember that an informative speech need not be long—it may be just a couple of minutes in which someone teaches you how to do something or explains a new procedure, describes a rule or policy, or tells you the background of an issue.
   a. Informative speaking in classes
   b. Informative speaking on the job
   c. Informative speaking with friends
   d. Informative speaking on social media streams
   e. Other informative speaking

2. **Organizing Your Informative Speech**
   Apply the principles of effective organization as you develop your informative speech. Provide the following information for your speech:

   Introduction

   To capture listeners' attention and motivate them to listen, I will ________________

   My thesis statement is ________________

   To establish my initial credibility, I will ________________

   To preview my speech, I will say ________________

   My transition from the introduction to the body is ________________

   Body

   My organizational pattern is ________________

   To provide transitions from one main point to the next, I will say

   A. Points one to two: ________________

   B. Points two to three: ________________

   C. Point three to conclusion: ________________

   My transition from body to conclusion is

   Conclusion

   I will summarize the key points in my speech by saying ________________

   I will close with this strong statement: ________________

For Further Reflection and Discussion

1. Attend an informative speech. Identify the thesis and the organizational pattern. Evaluate the ethical and strategic quality of the speaker's evidence.
2. Go to the online resources for this chapter to find quotations that are relevant to your speech.
3. TED Talks offer many examples of informative speeches that employ different delivery styles, with the tagline "Ideas worth spreading." Go to Ted.com to find speeches on topics that interest you.

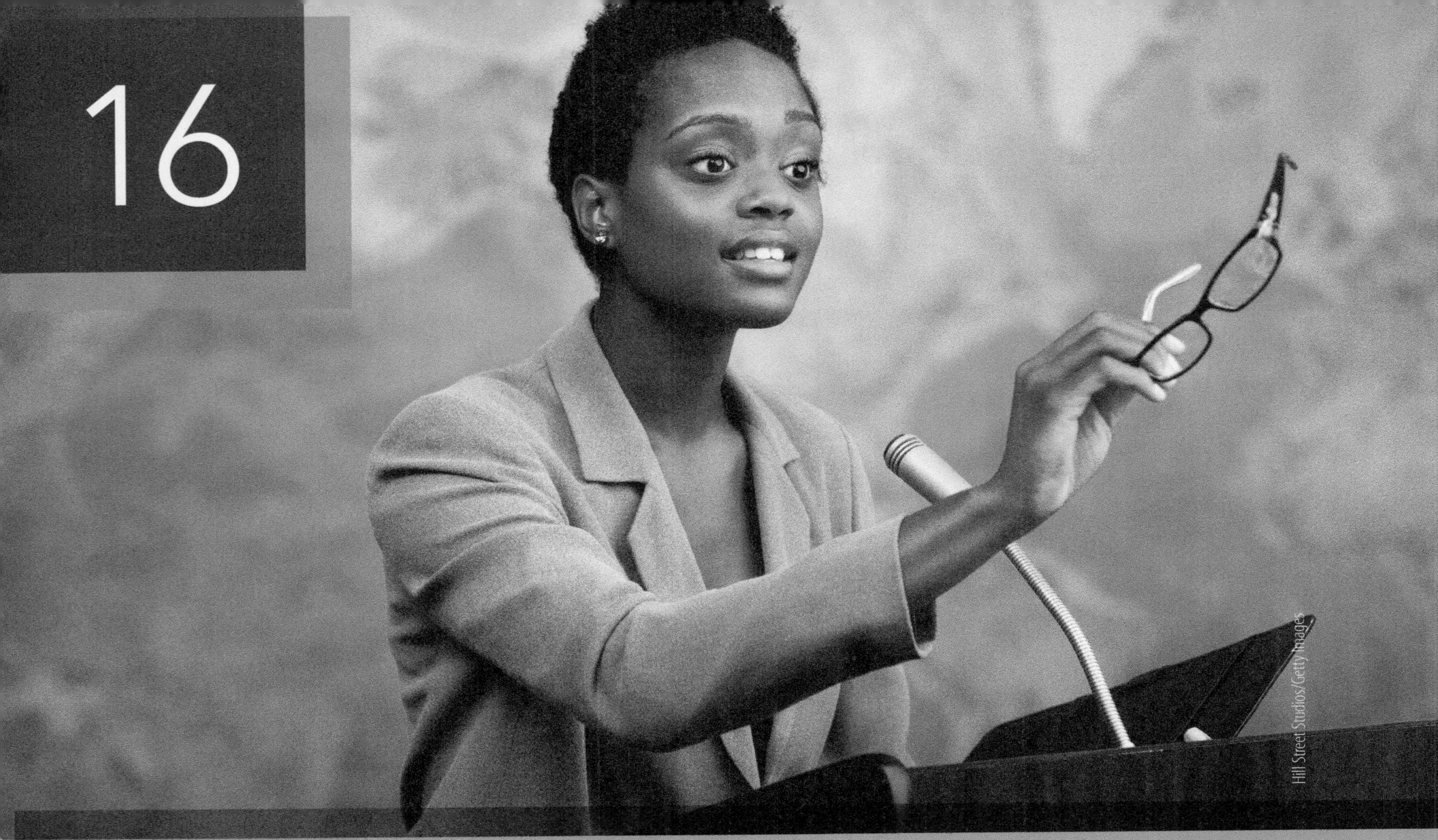

Whatever words we utter should be chosen with care for people will hear them and be influenced by them for good or ill.

Buddha

What leads you to perceive a speaker as credible?

Persuasive Speaking

Learning Objectives

After studying the topics in this chapter, you should be able to:

1. Define persuasive speaking and explain why persuasion is transactional, artistic, and gradual.
2. Summarize the nature of each of the three pillars of persuasion: ethos, pathos, and logos.
3. Define and provide an example for each of the three types of credibility: terminal, initial, and derived.
4. Organize persuasive speeches for persuasive impact
5. Recognize and avoid fallacious reasoning

- You want to persuade a patient to be more consciously engaged with their decisions around nutrition and movement.
- You are a finalist for a key position and have 3 minutes to explain why you should be selected.
- You want to convince the town council not to build a commercial center on the edge of your neighborhood.

Although most of us won't give persuasive speeches regularly, nearly all of us will find ourselves speaking persuasively at times. For instance, your manager might want you to persuade a potential client that your firm can provide the best service. In other cases, your values and commitments will compel you to speak in an effort to persuade others to ideas or actions that you think are right or desirable.

Building on the knowledge you've gained from the previous chapters, this chapter begins by defining persuasive speaking. Second, we discuss three pillars of persuasion and ways to build your credibility as a speaker. Next, we'll identify organizational patterns that are particularly effective for persuasive speeches. We close the chapter with guidelines for effective persuasive speaking.

Understanding Persuasive Speaking

Persuasive speeches aim to change others by prompting them to think, feel, believe, or act differently. You may want to alter the strength of others' attitudes for or against particular issues. You may want to convince others to use seat belts, vote for a candidate, or volunteer for community service. In each case, your goal is persuasive: You aim to change the people with whom you speak.

persuasive speech
A presentation that aims to change audience members by prompting them to think, feel, or act differently.

In thinking about persuasive speaking, it's important to keep three points in mind. First, like all other communication, persuasive speaking involves multiple communicators. The transactional model of communication we discussed in Chapter 1 is as relevant to persuasive speaking as it is to other kinds of communication. Effective persuasion is not something speakers do to audience members. Instead, it is engagement between a speaker and audience. Although the speaker may be in the spotlight, the audience are part of effective persuasive speaking, from planning to delivery. Speakers should consider audience members' experiences, expectations, values, and attitudes as they plan, research, and present speeches. Speakers should also attend to audience members' feedback during speeches.

Second, remember that persuasion is not coercion or force. The great rhetorical scholar Aristotle distinguished between what he called inartistic proofs and artistic proofs. An inartistic proof is a method of persuasion that is not created, controlled, or supplied by the speaker; or, according to some interpretations, that involves a threat of force. For instance, if someone signed a contract to provide ongoing services to your new workplace before you joined the company, they would be bound to continue doing so. You don't need to persuade them to continue providing services under a valid contract: you'd just need to enforce the contract. Likewise, if you hold a gun to someone's head and demand their money, you may get their money (and jail time, too). But in threatening that person, you haven't been artistic, and you haven't engaged in persuasion. Persuasion involves using reasons and words to motivate, not pre-existing documents like contracts or threat of force. Persuasion relies on artistic, not inartistic, proofs.

Third, persuasive impact usually is gradual and incremental. Although people's positions occasionally change abruptly, usually we move gradually toward new ideas, attitudes, and actions. When we hear a persuasive speech, we compare its message with our experience and knowledge. If the speaker offers strong arguments, good evidence, and coherent organization, we may shift our attitudes or behaviors to some degree. If we later encounter additional persuasion, we may shift our attitudes further.

Communication Highlight

The Persuasive Campaign for Designated Drivers

Have you ever been a designated driver? Have you ever been driven home by a designated driver? Today, most of us are familiar with the idea of a designated driver, but that wasn't always the case. In 1988, the Harvard School of Public Health launched the Harvard Alcohol Project, an intensive persuasive campaign to diffuse the concept of designated driver through American society. A pioneering venture, the Harvard Alcohol Project was the first time that a health organization partnered with mass media communication specialists (Harvard T. H, Chan School of Public Health, 2017).

The campaign began when Harvard convinced writers for top-rated television programs and major Hollywood studios to weave references to "designated driver" into characters' dialogue, making them part of story lines. This was designed to influence viewers' perceptions of appropriate behavior and to model the specific behaviors of asking for and serving as a designated driver.

Simultaneous with the introduction of the term into prime-time television shows, Harvard asked ABC, CBS, and NBC to air public service announcements encouraging the use of designated drivers. This was another first: the first time the three major networks simultaneously aired a public service campaign's messages. These networks collectively donated more than $100 million in free airtime each year.

By 1991, the term *designated driver* was added to *Merriam-Webster's Collegiate Dictionary,* signaling its widespread usage. Also in 1991, a Roper poll showed that 9 of 10 respondents in the United States knew about the designated driver program and rated it favorably.

When Harvard launched the campaign in 1988, annual fatalities attributed to drivers under the influence of alcohol were 23,626. By 1994, annual fatalities were 16,580, a decline of 30% in 6 years. Polling data suggests the Designated Driver Campaign contributed to this decrease (Koh & Yatsko, 2017).

This success paved the way for the United States Centers for Disease Control and Prevention to establish a steady presence in Hollywood, creating a Health & Society program that expertly consulted on and influenced health-related storylines in almost 900 TV episodes from 2009 to 2015 (Koh & Yatsko, 2017). The Harvard T. H. Chan School of Public Health credits several factors with the campaign's success in persuading the public to change their social drinking behaviors, including:

- its focus on a narrow and specific message—on a single component of the drunk driving problem that could make a difference;
- its call for only a modest, incremental behavior change—taking turns among friends as a designated driver, rather than asking for long-term behavior changes;
- its empowering message—with the tagline, "The Designated Driver is the Life of the Party"; and
- how easily the message could be communicated, by adding just a couple lines of dialogue into a script.

Communication & Careers

Sell Your Products, Sell Yourself

Forbes magazine published the results of a poll on the requirements for professional success. Seventy percent of business leaders who were polled said the ability to present ideas was critical to career advancement. The ability to speak effectively allows professionals to inspire others, sell products and services, attract funding, and—in general—sell oneself as a leader (Gallo, 2014).

Because persuasion tends to happen gradually and incrementally, speakers should understand the attitudes and behaviors of audience members and adapt their persuasive goals accordingly. For example, assume you believe that the Electoral College should be abandoned and you want to persuade others to your point of view. How would an effective persuasive speech differ if you knew in advance that audience members strongly favor the current Electoral College system or if you knew that they already have reservations about it?

In the first case, it would be unrealistic and ineffective to try to persuade audience members to support abolition of the Electoral College. A more realistic speaking purpose would be to persuade them that there are some disadvantages to the current electoral system. In this instance, you would be effective if you could reduce the strength of their position favoring the Electoral College. Because the second group already has reservations, you can build on those and lead them closer to supporting abolition of the Electoral College.

Review It!

Persuasion:

- Is Transactional
- Uses Artistic Proofs
- Is Usually Incremental

Presenting ideas persuasively is a critical skill for professional advancement.
wavebreakmedia/Shutterstock.com

The Three Pillars of Persuasion

Teachers in ancient Greece and Rome recognized three pillars of persuasion, which are also called three forms of artistic proof, or reasons people are persuaded: These are *ethos*, *pathos*, and *logos* (Kennedy, 1991). Although these three forms of proof are also important in other kinds of speaking, they assume special prominence when we engage in persuasion (Figure 16.1).

Ethos

ethos The perceived personal character of the speaker.

Ethos refers to the perceived personal character of the speaker. We are more likely to believe the words of people whom we perceive as having strong, good character. We tend to attribute high ethos to people if we perceive that:

- they have integrity
- they can be trusted
- they have goodwill toward us
- they know what they are talking about
- they are committed to the topic (show enthusiasm, dynamism)

Carl Last year, I had a teacher who didn't know anything about the subject. She made a lot of really vague statements, and when we tried to pin her down on specifics, she would blow off hot air—saying nothing at all. Nobody in the class thought she had any credibility.

Question: Sometimes, when people don't know the answer to a question, they don't acknowledge it, afraid they'll lose credibility—but dodging and trying to hide a gap in knowledge itself can do real harm to credibility, as in the case of Carl's teacher. What might be some good ways to show trustworthiness and goodwill when faced with a question that can't be answered in the moment?

Figure 16.1
The Three Pillars of Persuasion

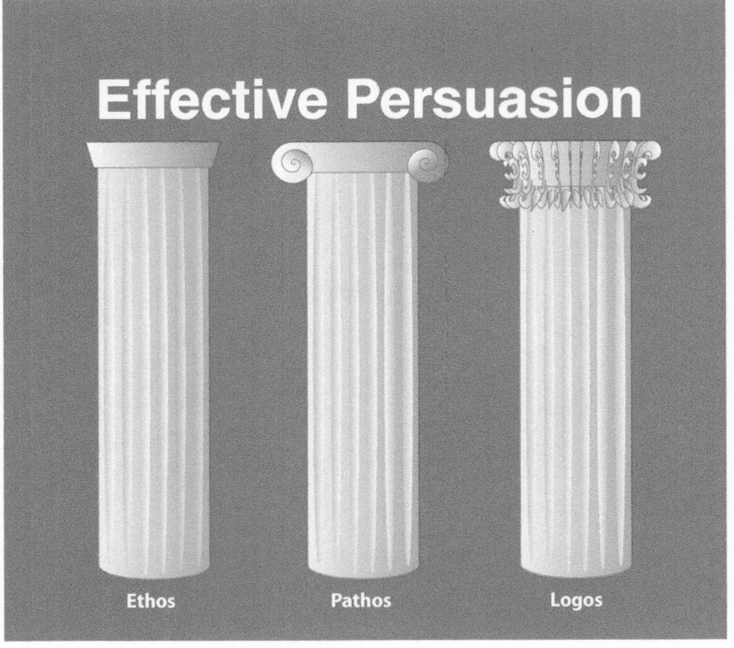

Table 16.1 Demonstrating Ethos

Dimensions of Ethos	Ways to Demonstrate
Goodwill	Identify common ground between you and listeners.
	Show respect for listeners' attitudes and experiences.
	Show that what you're saying will benefit them.
Expertise	Provide strong support for your claims.
	Document sources of support.
	Address concerns about or objections to your position.
	Demonstrate personal knowledge of the topic.
Trustworthiness	Use supporting materials ethically.
	Address other points of view fairly.
	Demonstrate that you care about your listeners.
Dynamism	Use appropriate volume and vocal emphasis.
	Assume a confident posture.
	Use gestures and kinesics to enhance forcefulness.
	Be energetic in presentation.

Because ethos is critical to persuasive impact, you should do what you can to demonstrate to your audience that you are of good character. Table 16.1 identifies specific ways that you can influence audience members' perceptions of your ethos.

Pathos

Pathos refers to emotional reasons for attitudes, beliefs, or actions. We are influenced by appeals to our passions, fears, love, compassion, and so forth. Emotional proofs address the more subjective reasons for our beliefs in people, ideas, causes, and courses of action.

pathos Emotional proofs for claims.

In preparing your persuasive presentation, develop ways to help your audience not just to understand your ideas but also to feel a certain way about them. You may want them to feel outraged about an injustice, compelled to help others, or afraid of a policy or possibility. Appealing to feelings such as these may enhance the persuasive impact of your speech. Table 16.2 shows particular ways to enhance pathos.

As Melanie notes, appeals to emotions are powerful—and dangerous. They can easily alienate audience members instead of involving them. Fear and guilt are uncomfortable emotions, so speakers should be cautious in arousing them. You may want your audience to fear what will happen if they don't do what you advocate, but you don't want them to be so overwhelmed by fear that they quit listening to you. Also, fear appeals can decrease a speaker's ethos if audience members are skeptical of the claimed dangers.

Generally, it's more effective to encourage your audience to do something they will feel good about (e.g., send money to help starving children overseas) than to berate them for what they are or aren't doing (e.g., living well themselves while others starve).

Melanie Last night, I saw an ad on television that asked viewers to help children who were starving in other countries. At first, I paid attention, but it just went over the top. The pictures were so heartbreaking that I just couldn't watch. I felt disgusted and guilty and mainly, what I really felt was turned off.

Question: Think back to the kinds of research we discussed in Chapter 13. What kind of research might have helped the advertisement's creators refine their advertisement to make it more effective before airing it?

logos Rational or logical proofs.

Review It!

Forms of Reasoning:

- Inductive
- Deductive

inductive reasoning A form of reasoning that begins with specific instances and forms general conclusions based on them.

Logos

The third reason for belief is **logos**, which is rational or logical proof. In persuasive speeches, logical proofs are arguments, reasoning, and evidence to support claims.

Forms of Reasoning Most reasoning can be classified as one or the other of two basic forms. **Inductive reasoning** begins with specific examples and uses them to draw a general conclusion (Faigley & Selzer, 2000). Suppose you want to present a speech arguing that climate change is damaging our environment. To reason inductively, you would start by citing specific places where global climate change has demonstrable impact, making the environment inhospitable to various plant and animal species in each case. Then you would advance the general conclusion that global climate change threatens life on our planet.

Table 16.2 Enhancing Pathos

Ways to Enhance Pathos in Persuasive Speaking	Example
Personalize the issue, problem, or topic.	Include detailed examples. Tell stories that give listeners a sense of being in situations, experiencing problems. Translate statistics to make them interesting and personal.
Appeal to listeners' needs and values.	Show how your position satisfies listeners' needs, is consistent with their values. Use examples familiar to listeners to tie your ideas to their values and experiences. Show listeners how doing or believing what you advocate helps them live up to their values. Include quotations from people whom listeners respect.
Bring material alive.	Use visual aids to give listeners a vivid, graphic understanding of your topic. Use striking quotes from people involved with your topic. Use active, concrete language to paint verbal pictures.

Deductive reasoning begins with a broad claim that audience members accept. Following this, the speaker then offers a specific claim that audience members also accept. The conclusion follows from the general claim combined with the specific claim. Reasoning deductively, you would start by stating a commonly accepted claim (i.e., "Climate change is having a negative impact on the world") and then advance a specific claim (i.e., "Our region is part of the world"). From these two claims, it naturally follows that "Climate change is having negative impact on our region" (your conclusion).

deductive reasoning A form of reasoning in which a general premise followed by a specific claim establishes a conclusion.

The Toulmin Model Another way to think about reasoning was originated by philosopher Stephen Toulmin (1958; Toulmin, Rieke, & Janik, 1984). Toulmin said that logical reasoning consists of three primary components: claims, grounds for the claims, and warrants that connect the claims to the grounds for them. In addition to these three basic parts of logical reasoning, Toulmin's model includes qualifiers and rebuttals. Figure 16.2 shows the **Toulmin model of reasoning**.

The first component of Toulmin's model is the **claim**, which is an assertion. For instance, you might advance this claim: "The death penalty does not deter crime."

To give persuasive impact to a claim, you need to provide some *grounds* for believing it. **Grounds** are evidence or data that support the claim. For example, you might cite statistics showing that crime did not diminish when some states enacted the death penalty or that crime did not rise when other states repealed the death penalty.

Consider a second example. You assert, or claim, that global climate change is harming the planet. Grounds, or evidence, to support that claim might include statistics to document the occurrence of global climate change, detailed examples of people whose lives have been negatively affected by changes in the earth's temperature, the testimony of credible scientists, and photos that show changes over time. All these kinds of evidence support your claim that global climate change harms the planet.

Toulmin model of reasoning A representation of effective reasoning that includes five components: claim, grounds (evidence), warrant (link between grounds and claim), qualifier, and rebuttal.

claim An assertion. A claim advanced in speaking requires grounds (evidence) and warrants (links between evidence and claims).

grounds Evidence that supports claims in a speech.

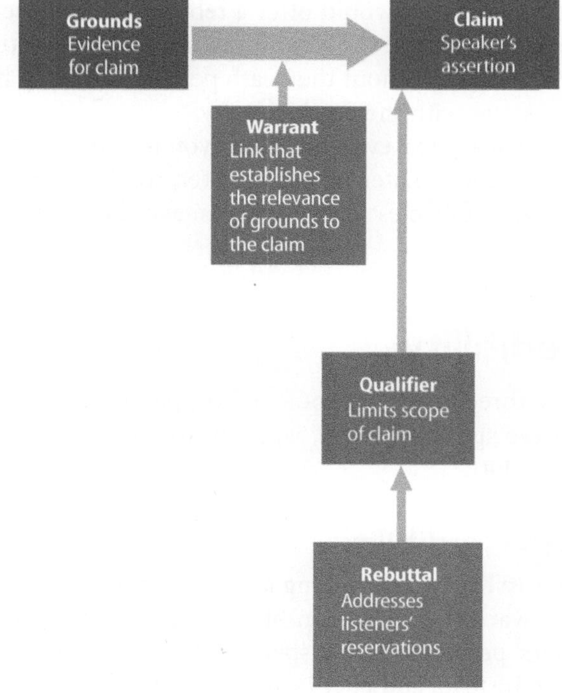

Figure 16.2
The Toulmin Model of Reasoning

warrant A justification for grounds (evidence) and claims in persuasive speaking.

Review It!

Elements of Toulmin Model:

- Claim
- Grounds
- Warrant
- Qualifier
- Rebuttal

Review It!

Forms of Proof:

- Ethos
- Pathos
- Logos

qualifier A word or phrase that limits the scope of a claim. Common qualifiers are ***most***, ***usually***, and ***in general***.

rebuttal A response to audience members' reservations about a claim made by a speaker.

Grounds are necessary to support claims. However, they aren't sufficient; the grounds must be justified. That justification is a **warrant**—an explanation of the relevance of the grounds to the claim. You've probably heard the word *warrant* in connection with law enforcement. If a police officer wants to search the home of Pat Brown, the officer must obtain a search warrant from a judge. The officer shows the judge evidence suggesting that Brown has engaged in criminal activity. If the judge agrees that the evidence links Brown to criminal activity, a search warrant is issued. However, if the judge thinks the evidence is insufficient to link Brown to criminal activity, a warrant is not issued. Warrants operate the same way in persuasive speaking. If your audience members perceive your evidence as relevant to and supportive of the claim, they're likely to believe your claim.

Let's return to the example of a speech against the death penalty. To support your claim that the death penalty does not deter crime, you provide statistics showing that crime rates did not increase when certain states repealed the death penalty. If the statistics were compiled by the Department of Justice, your audience members may perceive them as justifying the claim. On the other hand, if the statistics were compiled by an organization that opposes the death penalty, your audience members might perceive the source of the evidence as biased and therefore untrustworthy. In that case, audience members might decide that there was no warrant to justify linking the evidence to the claim.

A **qualifier** is a word or phrase that limits the scope of your claim. "Everyone can be rehabilitated" is a very broad claim—so broad that it is difficult to support. A more qualified claim would be qualified: "Some people who commit crimes can be rehabilitated." Finally, Toulmin's model includes **rebuttal**, which anticipates and addresses reservations that audience members are likely to have about claims. Speakers demonstrate respect for audience members by acknowledging and addressing their reservations.

In our example, the speaker might realize that audience members could say to themselves, "The death penalty may not deter all crimes, but it deters serious crimes like homicide." If the speaker has reason to think audience members may resist the claim on this basis, the speaker would offer a rebuttal to the reservation. It would be effective for the speaker to cite the *New York Times* 2012 investigative report that shows that since 1976, states without the death penalty have had homicide rates no higher than those of states with the death penalty.

Careful reasoning and good evidence allow you to offer logical appeals that are sound, effective, and ethical. Later in this chapter, we'll discuss some of the most common kinds of logical fallacies so that you can avoid them when you make persuasive presentations.

Building Credibility

We've noted that the three forms of proof—ethos, pathos, and logos—are the bases of effective persuasive speaking. Now, we want to consider more closely the key issue of speaker credibility.

Understanding Credibility

credibility The perception that a person is informed and trustworthy. Audiences confer it, or refuse to confer it, on speakers.

A speaker earns **credibility** by convincing audience members that they have integrity and goodwill toward them and can be trusted. Notice that credibility is tied to audience members' perceptions of a speaker. This means that credibility doesn't reside in the speaker. Instead, audiences confer or withhold it.

Soyana The greatest teacher I ever had taught a class in government policies and practices. Before coming to campus, he had been an adviser to three presidents. He had held a lot of different offices in government, so what he was teaching us was backed up by personal experience. Everything he said had so much more weight than what I hear from professors who've never had any practical experience.

Credibility arises from the three pillars of persuasion: ethos, pathos, and logos. Audiences are likely to find speakers credible if they demonstrate their personal integrity, establish emotional meaning for their topics, and present ideas logically and with good evidence.

Types of Credibility

Credibility is not static; it can change in the course of communication (Figure 16.3). Have you ever attended a public speech by someone you respected greatly and found the presentation disappointing? Did you think less of the speaker after the speech than before it? Have you ever gone to a presentation without knowing much about the speaker and found it so impressive that you changed an attitude or behavior? If so, then you know that credibility can increase or decrease as a result of a speech.

Developing Credibility

Initial Credibility Some speakers have high **initial credibility**, which is the expertise and trustworthiness recognized by audience members before a presentation begins. Initial credibility is based on titles, positions, experiences, or

initial credibility The expertise and trustworthiness that audience members attribute to a speaker before a presentation begins. Initial credibility is based on the speaker's titles, positions, experiences, or achievements known to audience members before they hear the speech.

Communication Highlight

Goodwill and Credibility

More than 2,000 years ago, the Greek rhetorician Aristotle wrote that a speaker's credibility depended on audience members' perceptions of the speaker's intelligence, character, and goodwill. Since Aristotle's time, research has established empirical support for strong links between credibility and perceived intelligence and character. But what about goodwill?

In a 1999 investigation, Jim McCroskey and Jason Teven found that perceived goodwill is positively linked to perceptions of likableness and believability. In other words, when audience members think a speaker cares about them and has ethical intentions toward them, they are likely to trust and like the speaker. The practical implication of this study is that speakers who want to be judged credible should establish goodwill toward audience members.

According to McCroskey and Teven (1999), goodwill tends to be established in three ways: showing understanding of audience members' ideas, feelings, and needs; demonstrating empathy, or identification, with their feelings; and being responsive to them while speaking.

Unfortunately, it can be easy to forget about goodwill's importance. In fact, Hunt and Wald (2020) argue that goodwill has become a "lost" aspect of credibility, and suggest researchers designing projects to study credibility should consider goodwill's role more often. This is helpful advice not just for scholars, but for any of us wishing to establish credibility with an audience.

Figure 16.3
Developing Credibility

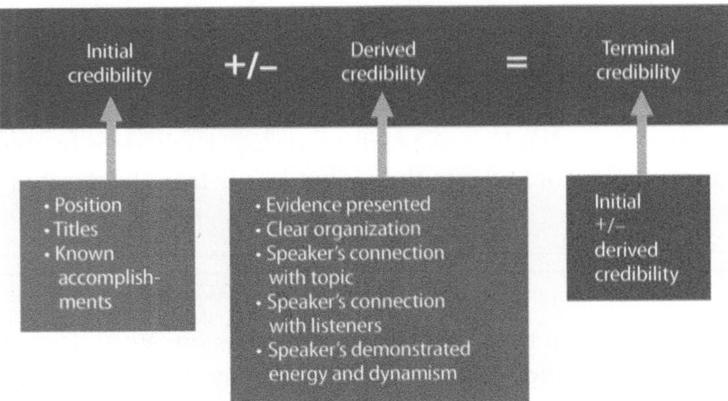

achievements that are known to audience members before they hear a speech. For example, most audience members would grant the Secretary of State high credibility on foreign affairs.

derived credibility The expertise and trustworthiness that audience members attribute to a speaker as a result of how the speaker communicates during a presentation.

Derived Credibility In addition to initial credibility, speakers may also gain **derived credibility**, which is the expertise and trustworthiness that audience members confer on speakers as a result of how speakers communicate during presentations. Speakers earn derived credibility by demonstrating care for audience members, by organizing ideas clearly and logically, by including convincing and emotionally compelling evidence, and by speaking dynamically. Speakers who are not well known tend not to have high initial credibility, so they must derive credibility from the quality of their presentations.

Effective speakers increase credibility in the course of presenting a speech.
Hero Images/Getty Images

Terminal Credibility The credibility of speaker at the end of a presentation is **terminal credibility**. It is the cumulative expertise, goodwill, and trustworthiness audience members attribute to a speaker—a combination of initial and derived credibility. Terminal credibility may be greater or less than initial credibility, depending on how effectively a speaker has communicated.

Review It!

Types of Credibility:

- Initial
- Derived
- Terminal

terminal credibility The cumulative expertise and trustworthiness audience members attribute to a speaker as a result of the speaker's initial and derived credibility; may be greater or less than initial credibility, depending on how effectively a speaker communicates.

Enhancing Credibility

As you plan, develop, and present a persuasive speech, you should aim to earn credibility. Below are ways to establish initial credibility and build derived and terminal credibility:

- State your qualifications for speaking on this topic: experiences you have had, research you have conducted.
- Show audience members that you care about them; make the speech relevant to their welfare.
- Appeal to audience members' emotions, but don't alienate or overwhelm them with excessively dramatic appeals.
- Use effective, ethical supporting materials.
- Communicate both verbally and nonverbally that you care about the topic and are involved with it.

Organizing Speeches for Persuasive Impact

In Chapter 14, we discussed ways to organize speeches. The principles you learned in that chapter apply to persuasive speaking:

- Your introduction should capture audience members' attention, provide a clear thesis statement, establish your credibility, and preview your speech.
- Your conclusion should summarize main points and end with a strong closing statement.
- You should provide internal summaries of main points.
- You should provide smooth transitions between the parts of your speech.
- The body of your speech should be organized to reinforce your thesis and show audience members how your ideas cohere.

To build on these general principles for organizing speeches, we want to focus on special organizational concerns relevant to persuasive speaking. We will discuss two topics: the motivated sequence pattern, which is particularly well adapted to persuasive goals, and the relative merits of one-sided and two-sided presentations.

The Motivated Sequence Pattern

Any of the organizational patterns that we discussed in Chapter 14 can be used to structure persuasive speeches. Table 16.3 shows how each of the seven patterns we discussed could support a persuasive thesis.

Table 16.3 Organizing for Persuasion

Lloyd Bennett works for a public relations firm that wants to convince Casual Cruise Lines to become a client. Lloyd could use any of the eight basic organizational patterns to structure his speech to persuade the cruise line to hire his firm.

Pattern	Thesis and Main Points
Time	Our firm can move Casual Cruise Lines into the future. I. Originally, Casual Cruise Lines attracted customers whose average age was 58 years. II. In recent years, that customer base has shrunk. III. To thrive in the years ahead, Casual Cruise Lines needs to appeal to younger customers.
Spatial	Our proposal focuses on redesigning the space on cruise ships to appeal to the 30- to 45-year-old market. I. In the staterooms, we propose replacing the conventional seafaring motif with abstract, modernistic art. II. In the public area of the lower deck, we propose replacing the current coffee shops with sushi and espresso bars and adding fitness rooms. III. On the upper deck, we propose building hot tubs beside the pool.
Topical	Our firm has the most experience advertising cruise lines and the most innovative staff. I. Our firm has increased revenues for three other cruise lines. II. Our firm has won more awards for innovation and creativity than the other firms Casual Cruise Lines is considering for this account.
Star	Let's consider how younger customers might be attracted if we revamped ship décor, activities, and cuisine. I. Younger customers like modern décor. II. Younger customers want youthful activities. III. Younger customers want trendy food.
Comparative	Casual Cruise Lines needs to adapt to younger customers whose needs and interests differ from those of older customers. I. We recommend 3-, 5-, and 7-day cruises because, although older people have the time for extended cruises, 30- to 45-year-olds can usually spare only a week or less at a time. II. Casual Cruise Lines should get rid of bingo and shuffleboard and add dancing and nightclubs, which are favorite leisure activities of 30- to 45-year-olds. III. We recommend adding 24-hour espresso bars and onboard fitness rooms to meet the preferences of 30- to 45-year-olds.
Problem–solution	We have a solution to Casual Cruise Lines' inability to attract younger customers. I. Casual Cruise Lines hasn't been able to get a substantial share of the lucrative 30- to 45-year-old market. II. Our advertising campaign specifically targets this market.

(Continued)

Table 16.3 **Organizing for Persuasion *(Continued)***

Cause–effect	The advertising campaign we propose will attract young, affluent customers by appealing to their interests and lifestyles. I. Our proposal's emphasis on luxury features of the cruise caters to this market's appreciation of extravagance. II. Our proposal to feature adults-only cruises caters to this market's demonstrated preferences. III. Our proposal to offer 2-day to 4-day cruises meets this market's interest in long weekend getaways.

In addition to the patterns we have already discussed, there is an eighth structure that can be highly effective in persuasive speaking: the **motivated sequence pattern** (Monroe, 1935). It has proven quite effective in diverse communication situations (Haugen & Lucas, 2019; Hummadi et al., 2019; Parviz, 2019). The primary reason for the effectiveness of the motivated sequence pattern is that it follows a natural pattern of human thought by gaining audience members' attention, demonstrating a need, offering a solution, and then helping them visualize and act on the solution. This pattern progressively increases audience members' motivation and personal involvement with a problem and its solution. The motivated sequence pattern includes five sequential steps.

motivated sequence pattern A pattern for organizing persuasive speeches that consists of five steps: attention, need, satisfaction, visualization, and action.

In the first step, audience members' attention is drawn to the subject. Here, a speaker makes a dramatic opening statement (e.g., "Imagine this campus under water"), shows the personal relevance of the topic (e.g., "The town we live in is only above sea level because there is so much ice in the Arctic"), or otherwise captures audience members' attention.

The second step establishes need with evidence and reasoning that a real and serious problem exists (e.g., "Human activity that is heating the earth's atmosphere is causing the Arctic ice caps to melt"). Next is the satisfaction step, in which a speaker recommends a solution (e.g., "Strong environmental regulations of fossil fuels, such as coal, oil, and natural gas, can reverse climate change and protect our town from sea level rise"). The fourth step, visualization, increases audience members' commitment to the solution identified in the satisfaction step by helping them imagine the results that would follow from adopting the recommended solution (e.g., "You will be able to continue enjoying our beautiful coastal region as long as you'd like, and so will your children and grandchildren. Moreover, we'll all have peace of mind").

Outline Builder includes extensive prompts and a clear framework for organizing and developing speeches that incorporate a variety of persuasive strategies.

Finally, speakers move to the action step, which involves a direct appeal for concrete action on the part of audience members (e.g., "Refuse to buy cars that aren't hybrid or electric," "Support the city-wide initiative for converting all public transit busses to electric vehicles," "Sign this petition that I am sending to our senators in Washington, D.C."). The action step calls on audience members to take action to bring about the solution the speaker helped them visualize.

Velma I've heard a lot of speeches on discrimination, but the most effective I ever heard was Cindy's in class last week. Other speeches I've heard focused on the idea that discrimination is wrong, but that's something I already believe, so they weren't helpful. Cindy, on the other hand, told me how to do something about discrimination. She showed me how I could act on what I believe.

Velma's commentary explains why the motivated sequence pattern is especially suited to persuasive speaking: It goes beyond identifying a problem and recommending a solution. In addition, it intensifies audience members' desire for a solution by helping them visualize what it would mean and gains their active commitment to being part of the solution. When audience members become personally involved with an idea and with taking action, they are more enduringly committed. Go to the book's online resources for this chapter to read tips and see a sample speech using the motivated sequence patterns.

Review It!

Steps in Motivated Sequence:

- Attention
- Need
- Satisfaction
- Visualization
- Action

One-Sided and Two-Sided Presentations

Perhaps you are wondering whether it's more effective to present only your own point of view or both sides of an issue in a persuasive speech. Research tells us that it depends on the particular audience a speaker addresses, which reminds us again that audience analysis and adaptation are critical to effective public speaking. Specifically, deciding whether to present one or both sides of an issue depend on the particular audience members' expectations, attitudes, and knowledge.

Audience Members' Expectations As we've noted before, effective speakers always try to learn what audience members expect so they don't fail to meet expectations. In educational settings, audience members are likely to expect speakers to discuss more than one side of an issue (Lasch, 1990). On the other hand, at campaign rallies, candidates are generally expected to present only their own views. Expectations may also be shaped by prespeech publicity. Imagine that you decide to attend a speech after seeing a flyer for a presentation on the pros and cons of requiring students to purchase meal plans. You might be irritated if the speaker presented only the pros or only the cons of the proposed requirement.

Audience Members' Attitudes It makes a difference whether audience members are likely to be favorably disposed toward your ideas (Griffin, 2015). If they already favor your position, you may not need to discuss alternative positions in depth. However, if audience members favor a position different from yours, then it's essential to acknowledge and deal with their views. If your audience members oppose what you propose, it's unlikely that you will persuade them to abandon their position and adopt yours. With an audience hostile to your views, it's more reasonable to try to lessen their hostility to your ideas or to diminish the strength of their commitment to their present position (Trenholm, 1991).

Failure to consider audience members' opposing ideas diminishes a speaker's credibility because audience members may assume that the speaker either is uninformed about another side or is informed but trying to manipulate them by not discussing it. Either assumption lessens credibility. Speakers have an ethical responsibility to give respectful consideration to audience members' ideas and positions. Doing so encourages reciprocal respect from audience members for the ideas you present.

Audience Members' Knowledge What an audience already knows or believes about a topic should influence decisions on whether to present one or more sides of an issue. Audience members who are well informed about a topic are likely to be aware of more than one side, so your credibility will be enhanced if you include all sides in your presentation (Jackson & Allen, 1990). Also, highly educated audience members tend to realize that most issues have more than one side, so they may be suspicious of speakers who present only one point of view.

In some instances, speakers know that later on audience members will be exposed to *counterarguments*—arguments that oppose those of a speaker. In such cases, it's advisable to inoculate audience members. **Inoculation** in persuasion is similar to inoculation in medicine. Vaccines give us limited exposure to diseases so that we won't contract them later. Similarly, persuasive inoculation "immunizes" audience members in advance against opposing ideas and arguments they may encounter in the future. If audience members later hear the other side, they have some resistance to arguments that oppose your position (Kiesler & Kiesler, 1971). For example, in political campaigns, candidates often make statements such as this: "Now, my opponent will tell you that we don't need to raise taxes, but I want to show you why that's wrong." By identifying and rebutting the opposing candidate's ideas in advance, the speaker inoculates audience members against an opponent's ideas (Allen et al., 1990).

inoculation "Immunization" of audience members to opposing ideas and arguments that they may later encounter.

But, a caveat: Recent studies show that some people who have very strongly held beliefs may react to evidence that they're wrong by doubling down, becoming even more certain about their position—sometimes known as the backfire effect (Nyhan, 2021; Swire-Thompson et al., 2022). To address this paradox, the World Health Organization (2017) offers guidance: In public speaking situations, consider your target audience to be the general public—not those who are deeply biased against your position. Focus on those whose minds you might be able to change, correcting misinformation not just by labeling it as "false," but by 1) explaining why it's false and 2) providing an alternative. This structure addresses your target audience's need for *explanations* of why those opposed to you are incorrect (p. 15).

There is no quick and easy formula for deciding whether to present one-sided or two-sided discussions of a topic. Like most aspects of public speaking, this decision involves judgment on the speaker's part. That judgment should be informed by ethical considerations of what audience members have a right to know and what content is necessary to represent the issues fairly. In addition, judgments of whether to present more than one side should take into account audience members' expectations, attitudes, and knowledge and the likelihood that audience members have been or will be exposed to opposing arguments.

Guidelines for Effective Persuasive Speeches

In this chapter, we've already discussed some guidelines for effective persuasive speaking. For instance, we discussed the importance of developing a speech that includes the three pillars of persuasion: ethos, pathos, and logos. We also emphasized the importance of speaker credibility, and we identified specific ways to build yours when you speak. We extended our previous discussion of organizing speeches to discuss the motivated sequence pattern and the merits of presenting one or two sides of arguments. In addition to these guidelines, three other principles are important for effective persuasive speaking.

Create Common Ground with Audience Members

In any communication context, common ground is important. That general principle has heightened importance in persuasive speaking. A persuasive speaker tries to move audience members to a point of view or action. It makes sense that they will be more likely to move with the speaker if they perceive some common ground with them. In other words, speakers seek to create with audience members a sense of **identification**, which is a recognition of commonalities (Burke, 1950). Audience members may think, "If we share all of these values and concerns, then maybe I should rethink my position on this one issue we disagree on."

identification The recognition and enlargement of common ground between communicators.

Effective persuasive speakers seek out similarities between themselves and their audience members and bring those similarities into audience members' awareness. A few years ago, a student of mine wanted to persuade his audience members that fraternities are positive influences on their members' lives. From polling students on campus, Steve knew that many held negative stereotypes of "frat men." He reasoned that most of his audience members, who did not belong to Greek groups, would be likely to view him both negatively and as different from them. This is how he established common ground in opening his speech:

> You've probably heard a lot of stories about wild fraternity parties and "frat men" who spend most of their time drinking, partying, and harassing pledges. I confess, I've done all of that as a brother in Delta Sigma Phi. I've also spent every Sunday for the last semester volunteering in the Big Brother Program that helps economically marginalized kids in the city. And I've built friendships with brothers that will last my entire life. Like many of you, I felt a little lost when I first came to this campus. I wanted to find a place where I belonged at college. Like you, I want to know people and be involved with projects that help me grow as a person. For me, being in a fraternity has done that.

This is an effective opening. Steve began by showing his audience that he realized some of them might hold some negative views of fraternity men. He went further and acknowledged that he personally fit some of those stereotypes. But then Steve challenged the adequacy of the stereotypes by offering some information that didn't fit with them. Having recognized and challenged stereotypes his audience members were likely to hold, Steve then began to create common ground. Most people in his audience could remember feeling lost when they first came to college. Most of them could identify with wanting to belong and to grow as people. Steve's opening successfully identified similarities between himself and themselves, so they were open to considering his argument that fraternities are valuable.

Adapt to Audience Members

A good persuasive speech is not designed for just anyone. Instead, it is adapted to specific audience members' knowledge, attitudes, motives, experiences, values, and expectations. As a speaker, your job is to apply what you learn about your audience members as you develop and present your speech.

Avoid Fallacious Reasoning

fallacy An error in reasoning.

A **fallacy** is an error in reasoning. Fallacies present false, or flawed, logic, which renders them ineffective with educated or thoughtful audiences. To be effective and ethical, you should avoid using fallacies in your speeches. To be a critical audience members, you should be able to recognize fallacies used by others. We'll discuss eight of the most common fallacies in reasoning.

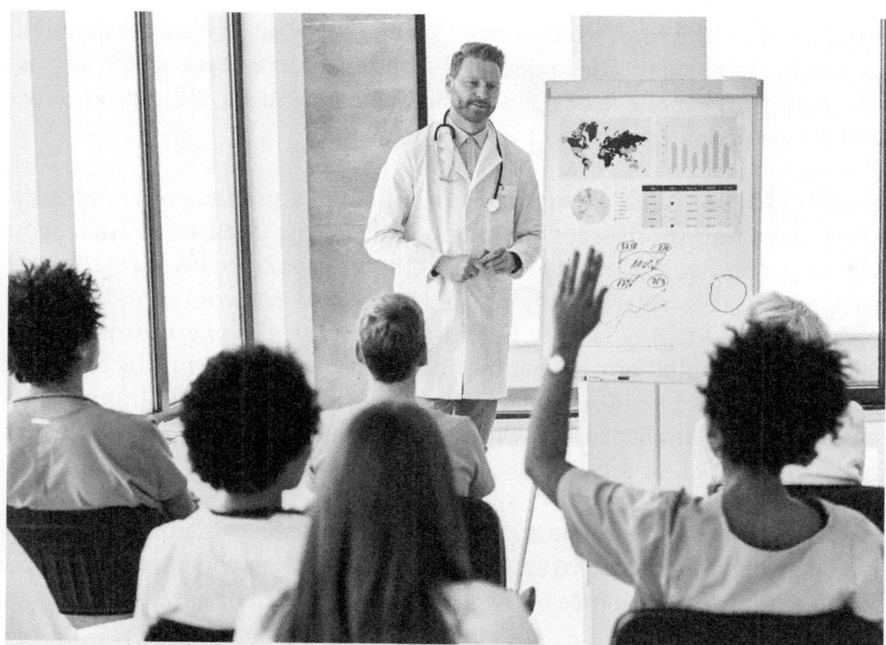

Ethical speakers do not engage in fallacious reasoning.
Cultura Creative/Alamy Stock Photo

Ad Hominem Arguments In Latin, the word *ad* means "to," and *hominem* means "human being." Thus, ***ad hominem* arguments** are ones that go to the person instead of the idea. It is not ethical to argue for your point of view by attacking the integrity of someone who has taken a stand opposing yours.

***ad hominem* arguments**
Arguments that attack the integrity of the person instead of the person's ideas.

"You can't trust what George Boxwood says about the importance of a strong military. After all, he never served a day in the military." Although it may be true that Boxwood didn't serve in the military, that doesn't necessarily discredit his argument about the importance of a strong military. Boxwood may have researched the topic vigorously, interviewed military personnel, and studied historical effects of strong and weak military forces. Boxwood's own service—or lack thereof—is not directly relevant to the quality of his argument for a strong military. Unethical speakers sometimes try to undercut people whose positions oppose their own by attacking the people, not the arguments. Critical audience members recognize this fallacy and distrust speakers who engage in it.

Post Hoc, Ergo Propter Hoc ***Post hoc, ergo propter hoc*** is a Latin phrase meaning "after this, therefore because of this." Sometimes when one thing follows another, we mistakenly think the first thing caused the second. Unethical speakers sometimes try to persuade us to think that a coincidental sequence is causal. For instance, the United States economy faltered and verged on recession after George W. Bush became president. Does that mean Bush and his administration caused the economic slowdown? Not necessarily. To support the claim that Bush caused the economic slowdown, a speaker would need to demonstrate that policies implemented by Bush hurt the economy.

post hoc, ergo propter hoc
Latin phrase meaning "After this, therefore because of this." The fallacy of suggesting or assuming that because event B follows event A, event A has therefore caused event B.

The Bandwagon Appeal When I was a child, I often tried to persuade my parents that I should be allowed to do something because all of my friends were doing it. Invariably, my parents rejected that reason and replied, "If all of your

bandwagon appeal The fallacious argument that because many people believe or act in a certain way, everyone should.

slippery slope The fallacy of suggesting or assuming that once a certain step is taken, other steps will inevitably follow that will lead to some unacceptable consequence.

friends jumped off the roof, would you?" At the time, that answer exasperated me. But my parents were right. They rejected the **bandwagon appeal**, which argues that because most people believe or act a particular way, you should too. Widely held attitudes are not necessarily correct, as Galileo proved.

Slippery Slope The **slippery slope** fallacy claims that once we take the first step, more and more steps inevitably will follow until some unacceptable consequence results. For example, an unethical speaker who wanted to argue against a proposal to restrict logging in a protected environmental area might state, "Restricting logging is only the first step. Next, the environmentalists are likely to want to prohibit any timber cutting. Pretty soon, we won't be able to build homes or furniture." The idea that we won't have lumber to build homes and furniture is extreme. It has little to do with the question of whether we should restrict logging in one particular area.

hasty generalization A broad claim based on too few examples or insufficient evidence.

Hasty Generalization A **hasty generalization** is a broad claim based on insufficient evidence. It is unethical to assert a broad claim when you have only anecdotal or isolated evidence or instances. Consider two examples of hasty generalizations based on inadequate data:

- Three congressional representatives have had affairs. Therefore, members of Congress are adulterers.
- An environmental group illegally blocked loggers and workers at a nuclear plant. Therefore, environmentalists are radicals who take the law into their own hands.

In each case, the conclusion is based on limited evidence. In each case, the conclusion is hasty and fallacious.

Red Herring Argument Years ago, fox hunters sometimes dragged a dead herring across the trail of a fox to see whether the dogs would be diverted (Gass, 1999). They were trying to train the dogs not to let the smell of the herring deflect them from hunting the fox. Speakers who try to deflect audience members from relevant issues engage in **red herring arguments**. They say something that is irrelevant to their topic or that doesn't really respond to an audience member's question. The point is to divert the audience member from something the speaker can't or doesn't want to address.

red herring argument An argument that is irrelevant to the topic; an attempt to divert attention from something the arguer can't or doesn't want to address.

Either–Or Logic What is wrong with the following statement: "Either abolish fraternities on our campus or accept the fact that this is a party school where drinking is more important than learning." The fallacy in this statement is that it implies there are only two options: either get rid of fraternities altogether or allow partying to eclipse academics. Are there no other alternatives? In most instances, **either–or logic** is simplistic and fallacious.

either–or logic The fallacy of suggesting or assuming that only two options or courses of action exist when in fact there may be more.

halo effect The tendency to assume that an expert in one area is also an expert in other unrelated areas.

Reliance on the Halo Effect The **halo effect** occurs when we generalize a person's authority or expertise in a particular area to other areas that are irrelevant to the person's experience and knowledge. It is fallacious to think that because a person is knowledgeable on particular topics, they are knowledgeable on all topics. When you see a celebrity endorse a product, ask yourself: Is this person an expert on products they are urging us to buy and use?

Table 16.4 Fallacies in Reasoning

Ad hominem attack	You can't believe what Jane Smith says about voting because she doesn't vote.
Post hoc, ergo propter hoc	The new flextime policy is ineffective because more people have been late getting to work since it went into effect.
Bandwagon appeal	You should be in favor of the new campus meal plan because most students are.
Slippery slope	If we allow students to play a role in decisions about hiring and tenure of faculty, pretty soon students will be running the whole school.
Hasty generalization	People should not be allowed to own Rottweilers because there have been three instances of Rottweilers attacking children.
Either–or	Tenure should be either abolished or kept exactly as it is.
Red herring argument	People who own Rottweilers should own cats instead. Let me tell you why cats are ideal pets.
Reliance on the halo effect	World-famous actor Richard Connery says that we should not restrict people's right to own firearms.

To be effective and ethical, persuasive speakers should avoid fallacies in reasoning (Table 16.4). Likewise, effective critical audience members should be able to detect fallacies in reasoning and to resist being persuaded by them.

Chapter Summary

This chapter focused on persuasive speaking. After noting the many situations in which persuasive speaking occurs, we identified ethos, pathos, and logos and the cornerstones of effective persuasion, and we highlighted ways in which speakers can incorporate each into presentations. Extending this, we discussed credibility, which is especially important in persuasive speaking. We identified three types of credibility—initial, derived, and terminal—and discussed ways in which speakers can build their credibility during the process of planning, developing, and presenting persuasive speeches. The next section of the chapter reviewed general organizational principles and highlighted organizational concerns that are particularly relevant to persuasive speaking.

We introduced the motivated sequence pattern, which can be powerful in moving audience members to accept and act on persuasive appeals. We also discussed the merits of one-sided and two-sided presentations, and we identified criteria for choosing the one that will be most effective in particular situations and with particular audience members.

The last section of the chapter provided guidelines for persuasive speaking. The first is to build common ground between a speaker and an audience members. The second is to adapt to particular audience members by tailoring a persuasive speech to their expectations, knowledge, experiences, motives, values, and attitudes. The third is to avoid fallacies in reasoning, which are usually ineffective and always unethical.

Experiencing Communication in Our Lives

Case Study: Persuasive Speech, No Child Left Behind: Addressing the School Dropout Rate Among Latinos

Apply what you've learned in this chapter by analyzing the following case study, using the accompanying questions as a guide.

Dana gave this speech in an introductory public speaking class. The assignment was to give a 4- to 6-minute speech, with a minimum of four sources cited. Students were also asked to create a preparation outline that included a Works Cited section.

I'll begin with a story from the *Santa Fe New Mexican* newspaper about a young woman named Mabel Arellanes. After becoming pregnant and dropping out of school at the age of 16 years, Mabel has reenrolled in high school and is now the junior class president. Although her dynamic change in attitude toward education has led her to the hope of becoming a lawyer, Mabel's story is not representative of the current trends among other Latinx people. I have been conducting extensive research on trends in the socioeconomic status, graduation rates, and the Latinx population in the United States. Today, I will discuss the problem of the Latinx dropout rate from high school and college, as well as provide a solution for addressing this intensifying issue. Let me begin by discussing the problem.

The Latinx dropout rate in secondary schools and colleges must be addressed. Why? Because the dropout rate is simply excessive and reflects structural inequities that we need to address. Statistics and first-hand accounts attest to this fact. According to *My Future NC*, Latinx students dropped out of high school in North Carolina at the highest rate of all races and ethnicities during the 2020–2021 school year, with only 81% graduating. This is six percentage points behind the statewide graduation rate of 87%. Gamaliel Fuentes, who dropped out of school at the age of 15 years, said, "We have no money; that's why I dropped out of school. [My father] asked me [to stay in school], but I decided. Now, if I could go back in time, I would stay still in school." The tendency for Latinx students to drop out is triggered by their disadvantaged socioeconomic status and structural challenges that hinder family support. The *Hispanic Outlook in Higher Education* has explained that students coming from families of lower socioeconomic status are less likely to succeed in college because high schools do not prepare them well. In addition, Latinx families expect their teens and young adults to contribute to

Lisa5201/Getty Images

the family's economic needs, and work schedules often conflict with studies.

Next, I will discuss the importance of addressing the Latinx dropout rate. Addressing the dropout rate will keep Latinos from remaining at a generally low economic status. It is no secret that income is heavily dependent on education level. According to the *Daily Evergreen* newspaper, a person with a bachelor's degree is likely to earn almost one million dollars more over their course of their lifetime than someone with no college education. While the National Center for Education Statistics found that people who identified as Hispanic earned 14.9% of bachelor's degrees awarded in the 2018–2019 academic year, the United States Census Bureau found that Latinos made up 18.3% of the national population in the same period. Ultimately, all who hold the belief that our country is the "land of opportunity" are affected by the Latinx dropout rate. Again, referencing the findings of the United States Census Bureau, in 2019, more than one-fifth of Hispanics under age 18 lived below the poverty line—almost three times the rate of White children. Even worse, experts believe the official poverty rate actually understates poverty among Latinx families. Also, Statistia.com notes that the average income among Latinx workers was $36,712 in 2019—more than $10,000 less than the national average, and more than $12,000 less than the average White salary of $49,140 in the same period, These figures show that financial inequities in the United States are far from exemplifying opportunity for Latinos.

What will happen if the problem is not solved? According to Pew Research, the percentage of Latinx people in our population is still climbing, increasing by 23% in the past decade, whereas the overall population has only grown by 7%. Therefore, ignoring this issue will lead to greater disparities for Latinx families. As I proceed to discuss the solutions for this problem, are you beginning to sense the urgency of this situation?

To solve the problem of a high dropout rate, we must fund cultural competency programs for teachers to help Latinx students and others from marginalized backgrounds succeed in education. I say this because programs that educate teachers about Latinx cultures and beliefs and that help Latinx students succeed in education will have the most direct impact on the dropout rate. Properly educated teachers will become aware of how they are able to meet the needs of diverse students. For example, the *Santa Fe New Mexican* reported on the success of a program called AVID, which boasts a 95% college entrance rate among its Latino students. This solution, which can be implemented at the national, state, and local levels, is dependent on increased funding and the efforts of educators with experience in Latinx culture. Increased funding will help reform educational budgets for Latinx communities and fund college success programs like AVID. This solution also requires the collective efforts of highly knowledgeable professionals with experience in education and in Latino culture who can train other educators.

Given proper attention and execution, the plan to address the Latinx dropout rate will help the dropout rate begin to fall and will instill pride in the Latinx community. Although it may take at least a decade before results are fully apparent, perhaps even a generation, ideally the plan will result in an increase in Latinx students earning bachelor's, master's, and doctoral degrees. The sense of accomplishment gained by furthering education will instill an overall sense of pride in the United States Latinx community, and as increased earnings raise Latinx families' incomes, they will be able to direct more resources towards supporting their children's educations, like families from more privileged backgrounds already do.

In summary, today I have discussed the problem of high dropout rate among Latinx students, and I have discussed a possible solution for addressing the issue. Hopefully, you can clearly see that the high Latino dropout rate is an issue of great concern, one that requires prompt and thorough attention.

Questions for Analysis and Discussion

1. Did Dana provide a strong introduction with an attention device, a clear thesis, and a clear preview?
2. Are the sources of evidence credible? Why or why not? Is there any reason to suspect that the sources are biased?
3. What other kinds of evidence might Dana have used to strengthen the persuasive impact of her message?
4. Did Dana's speech reflect awareness of ethos, pathos, and logos?
5. How did Dana adapt the message to audience members who were 19- to 24-year-old college students? Can you think of additional ways she might have adapted this message to these particular audience members? How might she have adapted it to a class with more students of nontraditional college age, over the age of 24?

Key Concepts

***ad hominem* arguments**
bandwagon appeal
claim
credibility
deductive reasoning
derived credibility
either–or logic
ethos
fallacy
grounds
halo effect
hasty generalization
identification
inductive reasoning
initial credibility
inoculation
logos
motivated sequence pattern
pathos
persuasive speech
post hoc, ergo propter hoc

qualifier
rebuttal
red herring argument
slippery slope
terminal credibility
Toulmin model of reasoning
warrant

Sharpen Your Skill

1. Using the Motivated Sequence Pattern

Think about how you might organize a speech using the motivated sequence pattern. Write a thesis and five main points for a motivated sequence appeal.

Thesis ______________________________

1. Attention: ______________________________
2. Need: ______________________________
3. Satisfaction: ______________________________
4. Visualization: ______________________________
5. Action: ______________________________

2. Deciding Whether to Present One or Two Sides

Apply what you have learned to decide whether you should present one or two sides in your persuasive speech.

1. Are your audience members likely to expect to hear more than one side of the issue?
   - A. How much education do they have? ______________________________
   - B. Has there been any prespeech publicity? ______________________________
   - C. Is there any reason to think that audience members do or do not care about hearing both sides? ______________________________
2. What are your audience members' attitudes toward your topic?
   - A. Do they have a position on the topic? If so, is it the same as yours?
     ____
   - B. How strongly do audience members hold their opinions on the topic?
     ____
3. What level of knowledge about the topic do your audience members have?
   ____
   - A. Do they know about more than one side of the issues?
     ____
   - B. How much information about the topic have they already gained?
     ____
4. Are your audience members likely to hear counterarguments after your speech?
   ____

For Further Reflection and Discussion

1. Reread this chapter's discussion of one-sided and two-sided persuasive speeches. When is it ethical to present only one side of a topic? When is it unethical? In answering this question, remember that ethical considerations are not necessarily the same as strategic ones. A speaker who uses unethical arguments or evidence might be effective in convincing audience members to think or do something.
2. Go to the book's online resources for this chapter to see and hear famous speeches.
3. Go to the book's online resources for this chapter to read an article on the importance of skill in persuasive speaking for top-level positions in business.
4. Apply the principles of persuasive speaking to prepare a 1-minute "elevator speech," which we mentioned in Chapter 12.
5. Ted Talks offer many examples of persuasive speeches that employ different delivery styles. Go to www.Ted.com to find speeches on topics that interest you.

Closing: Pulling Ideas Together

Communication is an intricate tapestry woven from the threads of self, others, perceptions, relationships, contexts, culture, climate, listening, and verbal and nonverbal messages. Each thread has its own distinct character, and yet each thread is also woven into the complex, ever-changing tapestry of human communication. We've taken time to discuss each thread in its own right and then explored how it blends with other threads in particular communication situations.

Sometimes a particular thread stands out boldly, as individual threads sometimes do in woven fabric. For instance, the thread of delivery is quite prominent in public speaking, and the thread of listening is less visible. Yet to be effective, speakers must understand and adapt to their listeners because listeners decide how credible a speaker is and how effective public communication can be. Similarly, in personal relationships the thread of climate stands out as particularly important. Yet, the climate we create through our communication is also important in organizational communication and small group work. Thus, even when threads of communication are muted in particular contexts of interaction, they are present and important.

At other times, an individual thread blends so completely with other threads that we don't perceive it as separate from the overall pattern of the tapestry.

Organization, for example, is present in interaction between friends as they decide what to talk about and how to sequence the topics. Yet in friends' conversation, the thread of organization is subdued, and other threads, such as sensitive listening, stand out. Similarly, the thread of delivery is subtle in casual conversations, yet our communication with friends is affected by how we articulate our ideas—by vocal force, volume, pace, and other aspects of delivery. The many threads that make up the tapestry of communication vary in intensity and prominence from one point in the tapestry to another, yet all are part of the whole.

To conclude our study of the communication tapestry, let's review what we've discussed and what it means for us. The overall goal of this book is to increase your insight into the ways in which communication is an integral part of our everyday lives.

We launched our journey in Chapter 1, which described the range of human communication and the modern academic field that bears its name. Chapter 2 allowed us to delve into the complicated process of perception so that we could understand how perception, thought, and communication interact. We learned that we seldom, if ever, perceive the full, raw reality around us. Instead, we perceive selectively, noticing only some things and overlooking others. The labels we use to name, classify, and evaluate our perceptions reverberate in our consciousness to shape what we perceive and what it means to us. In fact, most of the time, how we think, feel, and act are based less on objective realities in the external world than on how we label our selective perceptions of it. This is normal, yet it can cause us trouble if we forget that we are responding to our labels, not to the world itself. In Chapter 3, we explored the profound ways in which communication shapes personal identity and, in turn, the ways in which our identities shape how we communicate.

Chapters 4–6 focused on primary forms of communication: listening, verbal communication, and nonverbal behavior. As we considered each topic, we examined ways to improve our personal effectiveness as communicators. Particularly important to our understanding of these topics is the realization that people differ in their styles of listening and their verbal and nonverbal communication. Awareness of these differences helps us understand others on their terms. The principles and skills we discussed in these chapters should serve you well throughout your life as you seek to interact effectively and sensitively with others in personal, social, and professional contexts.

The second part of the book extended the first six chapters by weaving basic communication concepts and skills into contexts of interaction. In Chapter 7, we explored interpersonal communication in general and as it occurs in friendships and romantic relationships. The intimate bonds that grace our lives are communicative achievements because we create and sustain them largely through interaction and the meanings we assign to it. Communication is the lifeblood of intimacy. In dramatic forms, such as declarations of love and disclosure of secrets, and in everyday small talk, it is communication that continually breathes life and meaning into our relationships with others.

We moved to quite a different context in Chapter 8, which examined communication in small groups. There, we learned what types of communication facilitate and hinder effective group discussion and what communication responsibilities accompany effective membership and leadership. We also studied the standard agenda for problem solving, which gives participants an effective method of organizing group discussion.

damircudic/E+/Getty Images

Communication skills are a foundation for effectiveness in personal, professional, and social life.

Chapter 9 focused on organizational communication, with particular emphasis on how interaction among members of an organization creates an overall culture for the organization. The elaborate and fascinating relationships between culture and communication were the focus of Chapter 10. There, we unmasked the subtle ways in which communication creates and sustains the beliefs, values, and practices that define cultures and social communities. Equally important, we saw that cultures shape the forms and content of communication by telling us what is and is not important and what are appropriate and inappropriate ways of interacting with others. Understanding differences between cultures and social communities allows us to appreciate the distinct character of each one and to enlarge our own repertoire of communication skills. In Chapter 11, we explored mass communication and social media, which permeate our lives. Here, we focused on ways to develop critical skills that enhance your media literacy.

Part III of this book concentrated on public speaking. From the early stages of planning presentations, to researching and developing evidence, and finally to organizing, outlining, and practicing, public speaking involves skills that most of us already have and use in other communication situations. As is true for all interactions, good public speaking centers on others; the values, interests, knowledge, and beliefs of listeners guide what speakers can and cannot wisely say and how they develop and present their ideas. Effective public speaking, like effective everyday conversation, is a genuine interaction between people in which the views and values of all participants should be taken into account.

Throughout *Communication in Our Lives,* we've discussed that people differ in their communication and in the meanings they attach to words and actions. The cornucopia of cultures and social communities in our world gives rise to a fascinating range of communication styles. No single way of communicating is inherently superior to any other; the differences result from diverse cultural heritages and practices, each of which deserves respect and inclusion.

Learning not to impose our own communication patterns and our culture's judgments on others but instead approaching them with cultural humility allows us to enlarge and enrich who we are individually and collectively. Curiosity, appreciation, and openness to unfamiliar ways of communicating are vital to a healthy pluralistic society in which each of us preserves our own distinct identity while remaining part of and engaged with a larger whole.

If you have learned these principles and skills of human communication, then you have the foundation to be effective in personal, professional, and social settings. If you are committed to practicing and continually enlarging the principles and skills introduced in this book, then you can look forward to a life of personal growth, meaningful relationships, professional success, and social impact. What is more, you are on the threshold of a life filled with joy.

Glossary

A

abstract Removed from concrete reality. Symbols are abstract because they are inferences and generalizations derived from a total reality.

***ad hominem* argument** Argument that attacks the integrity of the person instead of the person's ideas.

agenda setting Mass media's ability to select and call to the public's attention ideas, events, and people.

ambiguous Subject to more than one interpretation. Symbols are ambiguous because their meanings vary from person to person and context to context.

ambushing Listening carefully in order to attack a speaker.

arbitrary Random; not determined by necessity. Symbols are arbitrary because there is no particular reason for any one symbol to stand for a certain referent.

artifacts Personal objects we use to announce our identities and personalize our environments.

assimilation The giving up of one's own culture's ways for those of another culture.

attachment style Any of several patterns of attachment that result from particular parenting styles that teach children who they are, who others are, and how to approach relationships.

attribution A causal account that explains why a thing happened or why someone acted a certain way.

B

bandwagon appeal The fallacious argument that because many people believe or act in a certain way, everyone should.

burden of representation When only one person from a historically marginalized group is part of a team, that person may feel pressed to speak for *all* members of that group.

C

chronemics A type of nonverbal communication concerned with how we perceive and use time to define identities and interaction.

claim An assertion. A claim advanced in speaking requires grounds (evidence) and warrants (links between evidence and claims).

climate communication One of three constructive forms of participation in group decision making. Climate communication focuses on creating and sustaining an open, engaged atmosphere for discussion.

code-switching Switching between different styles of speech, mannerisms, and behaviors to fit within different contexts and social settings. Code-switching can also refer more specifically to when a person of color changes their self-presentation to make those around them more comfortable, particularly in predominantly white settings where the person's race or ethnicity is at risk of being negatively stereotyped.

cognitive complexity The number of constructs used, how abstract they are, and how elaborately they interact to create perceptions.

cohesion Closeness among members of a group; esprit de corps.

commitment A decision to remain with a relationship. One of three dimensions of enduring romantic relationships, commitment has more impact on relational continuity than does love alone. It is also an advanced stage in the process of escalation in romantic relationships.

communication A systemic process in which people interact with and through symbols to create and interpret meanings.

communication apprehension Anxiety associated with real or anticipated communication encounters. Communication apprehension is common and can be constructive.

communication network A set of formal and informal links between members of organizations.

communication rules Shared understandings of what communication means and what behaviors are appropriate in various situations.

comparison A form of evidence that uses associations between two things that are similar in some important way.

constitutive rules Communication rules that define what communication means by specifying how certain communicative acts are to be counted.

constructivism The theory that we organize and interpret experience by applying cognitive structures, called *schemata.*

content level of meaning One of the two levels of meaning in communication. The content level of meaning is the literal, or denotative, information in a message.

convergence The integration of mass media, computers, and telecommunications.

credibility The perception that a person is informed and trustworthy. Listeners confer it, or refuse to confer it, on speakers.

critical listening Attending to communication to analyze and evaluate the content of communication or the person speaking.

critical thinking Examining ideas reflectively and carefully to decide what you should believe, think, or do.

cultivation The cumulative process by which television fosters beliefs about social reality.

cultivation theory The theory that television promotes an inaccurate worldview that viewers nonetheless assume reflects real life.

cultural appropriation When a dominant group exploits the culture of a marginalized and/or oppressed group, taking for their own benefit elements of another culture.

cultural competency Being interculturally proficient, able to communicate effectively and appropriately with people of other cultural backgrounds.

cultural globalization The circulation of media (including film, television, the Internet, and social media) and commodities around the globe, accompanied by ideas and values—a process mainly driven by industrialized Western cultures.

cultural humility Being open-minded about cultural differences, approaching others in a humble and respectful manner with a willingness to learn and an awareness of one's own cultural biases.

cultural intelligence Motivational, cognitive, and behavioral abilities to understand and adapt to a range of contexts, people, and patterns of interaction.

cultural relativism The idea that cultures vary in how they think, act, and behave as well as in what they believe and value; not the same as moral relativism.

culture Beliefs, understandings, practices, and ways of interpreting experience that are shared by a number of people.

D

***de jure* segregation** A complex system of laws and government policies that cause White and Black people to live in separate communities.

deductive reasoning A form of reasoning in which a general premise followed by a specific claim establishes a conclusion.

defensive listening Perceiving personal attacks, criticisms, or hostility in communication when no offense is intended.

demographic audience analysis A form of audience analysis that seeks information about the general features of a group of listeners.

derived credibility The expertise and trustworthiness that listeners attribute to a speaker as a result of how the speaker communicates during a presentation.

digital divide The gap between people and communities with access to media, especially social media, and people and communities with less or no access.

direct definition Communication that explicitly tells us who we are by specifically labeling us and reacting to our behaviors. Direct definition usually occurs first in families and then in interaction with peers and others.

dual perspective The ability to understand another person's perspective, beliefs, thoughts, or feelings.

dynamic Evolving and changing over time.

E

echo chambers Social media spaces designed, by people or by algorithms, to present only uniform ideas, rather than diverse, competing, or conflicting perspectives.

ego boundaries A person's internal sense of where they stop and the rest of the world begins.

egocentric communication An unconstructive form of group contribution that blocks others or calls attention to oneself.

either–or logic The fallacy of suggesting or assuming that only two options or courses of action exist when in fact there may be more.

empathy The ability to feel with another person or to feel what that person feels in a given situation.

environmental factors Elements of settings that affect how we feel and act. Environmental factors are a type of nonverbal communication.

ethnocentrism The tendency to regard ourselves and our way of life as superior to other people and other ways of life.

ethos The perceived personal character of the speaker.

evidence Material used to support claims. Types of evidence are statistics, examples, comparisons, and quotations. Visual aids may be used to represent evidence graphically.

example A form of evidence; a single instance that makes a point, dramatizes an idea, or personalizes information. The four types of examples are undetailed, detailed, hypothetical, and anecdotal.

extemporaneous speaking A presentational style that includes preparation and practice but not memorization of words and nonverbal behaviors.

F

fallacy An error in reasoning.

feedback Response to a message; may be verbal, nonverbal, or both. In communication theory, the concept of feedback appeared first in interactive models of communication.

formal outline A complete outline of a speech, including the parts of a speech, main points, supporting material, transitions, and citations for sources.

G

gaslighting Abusive, covert manipulation that misleads the target about their own experiences, causing them to question their own judgments, undermining their perceptions of reality.

gatekeeper A person or group that decides which messages pass through the gates of media that control information flow to consumers.

gender binary Categorizing gender into two opposite forms: masculine and feminine, aligned with the male and female sexes.

gender continuum Gender as an open-ended concept that can vary and include a person's gender identity, gender expression, conformity to gender roles, and anatomical or biological characteristics.

gender-nonconforming A person who does not conform to the gendered social norms and stereotypes associated with their sex.

grounds Evidence that supports claims in a speech.

group Three or more people who interact over time, are interdependent, and follow shared rules of conduct to reach a common goal. The team is one type of group.

groupthink The cessation of critical, independent thought on the part of a group's members about ideas generated by the group.

H

halo effect The tendency to assume that an expert in one area is also an expert in other unrelated areas.

haptics Nonverbal communication that involves physical touch.

hashtag activism When activists communicate on social media using hashtags to help direct attention to social justice matters.

hate groups Collections of people that advocate and engage in hatred, aggression, or violence toward members of particular groups.

hasty generalization A broad claim based on too few examples or insufficient evidence.

hearing The physiological activity that occurs when sound waves hit our eardrums. Unlike listening, hearing is a passive process.

high-context communication style The indirect and undetailed communication favored in collectivist cultures.

hypothetical thought Cognitive awareness of experiences and ideas that are not part of the concrete, present situation.

I

identification The recognition and enlargement of common ground between communicators.

identity script A guide to action based on rules for living and identity. Initially communicated in families, identity scripts define our roles, how we are to play them, and basic elements in the plot of our lives.

impromptu speaking Public speaking that involves little preparation. Speakers think on their feet as they talk about ideas and positions with which they are familiar.

inclusivity Ensuring all people, regardless of background, feel welcome within a group, with equal access to opportunities and resources and without experiencing tokenization in the process.

indexing A technique of noting that statements reflect specific times and circumstances and may not apply to other times or circumstances.

individualism/collectivism One of five dimensions of variation among cultures, this refers to the extent to which members of a culture understand themselves as part of, and connected to, their families, groups, and cultures.

inductive reasoning A form of reasoning that begins with specific instances and forms general conclusions based on them.

informational listening Listening to gain and understand information; tends to focus on the content level of meaning.

informative speech A presentation that aims to increase listeners' knowledge, understanding, or abilities.

initial credibility The expertise and trustworthiness that listeners attribute to a speaker before a presentation begins. Initial credibility is based on the speaker's titles, positions, experiences, or achievements known to listeners before they hear the speech.

inoculation "Immunization" of listeners to opposing ideas and arguments that they may later encounter.

interpersonal communication Communication between people, usually in close relationships such as friendship and romance.

interpretation The subjective process of evaluating and explaining perceptions.

intersectionality The idea that identity categories such as race, sex, sexual orientation, gender, size, ability, and socioeconomic class overlap, which can compound inequalities.

investment Something put into a relationship that cannot be recovered should the relationship end. Investments, more than rewards and love, increase commitment.

K

key word outline An abbreviated speaking outline that includes only key words for each point in a speech. The key words trigger the speaker's memory of the full point.

kinesics Body position and body motions, including those of the face.

L

leadership A set of functions that assists groups in accomplishing tasks efficiently and well while maintaining a good climate.

listening A complex process that consists of being mindful, physically receiving messages, selecting and organizing information, interpreting, responding, and remembering.

literal listening Listening only to the content level of meaning and ignoring the relational level of meaning.

loaded language An extreme form of evaluative language that relies on words that strongly slant perceptions and hence meanings.

logos Rational or logical proofs.

long-term/short-term orientation One of five dimensions of variation among cultures, this refers to the extent to which members of a culture think about long term (history and future) versus short term (present).

low-context communication style The direct, precise, and detailed communication favored in individualistic cultures.

M

mansplaining A slang term combining the words "man" and "explaining," used to criticize a communication style in which men fail to listen to people of other genders to discern what they already know before speaking.

manuscript speaking A presentational style that involves speaking from the complete manuscript of a speech.

marginalization A condition and process preventing individuals and groups from equal participation in wider society, including social, economic, and political life.

masculinity/femininity One of five dimensions of variation among cultures, this refers to the extent to which a culture values aggressiveness, competitiveness, looking out for yourself, and dominating others and nature (considered masculine orientations) versus gentleness, cooperation, and taking care of others and living in harmony with the natural world (considered feminine orientations).

mass media Channels of mass communication, such as television and radio.

media literacy The ability to understand the influence of mass media and to access, analyze, evaluate, and respond to mass media in informed, critical ways.

memorized speaking A presentational style in which a speech is memorized word for word in advance.

metaphor An implicit comparison of two different things that have something in common.

mindfulness Being fully present in the moment; the first step of listening and the foundation of all other steps.

mind map A holistic record of information on a topic. Mind mapping is a method that can be used to narrow speech topics or to keep track of information gathered during research.

mind reading Assuming that we understand what another person thinks or how another person perceives something.

minimal encouragers Communication that, by expressing interest in hearing more, gently invites another person to elaborate.

monopolizing Continually focusing communication on oneself instead of on the person who is talking.

motivated sequence pattern A pattern for organizing persuasive speeches that consists of five steps: attention, need, satisfaction, visualization, and action.

multilingual Able to speak and think in more than one language.

N

neutralization One of the four responses to relational dialectics; involves balancing or finding a compromise between two dialectical poles.

noise Anything that has potential to interfere with intended communication.

nonverbal communication All forms of communication other than words themselves; includes inflection and other vocal qualities as well as several other behaviors.

norm An informal rule that guides how members of a group or culture think, feel, act, and interact. Norms define what is normal or appropriate in various situations.

O

oral style The visual, vocal, and verbal aspects of the delivery of a public speech.

organizational culture Ways of thinking, acting, and understanding work that are shared by members of an organization and that reflect an organization's distinct identity.

P

paralanguage Vocal communication that does not include actual words; for example, sounds, vocal qualities, accents, and inflection.

paraphrasing A method of clarifying others' meaning by restating their communication.

participation A response to cultural diversity in which people incorporate some practices, customs, and traditions of other groups into their own lives.

particular others One source of social perspectives that people use to define themselves and guide how they think, act, and feel. The perspectives of particular others are the viewpoints of people who are significant to the self.

passion Intensely positive feelings and desires for another person. Passion is based on the rewards of involvement and is not equivalent to commitment.

pathos Emotional proofs for claims.

peer-reviewed research Scholarly research that has been carefully scrutinized by other experts in the field as a condition of publication.

perception The process of actively selecting, organizing, and interpreting people, objects, events, situations, and activities.

personal construct A bipolar mental yardstick that allows us to measure people and situations along specific dimensions of judgment.

personal relationship A relationship defined by uniqueness, rules, relational dialectics, and commitment and affected by contexts. Personal relationships, unlike social ones, are irreplaceable.

person-centered perception The ability to perceive another as a unique and distinct individual apart from social roles and generalizations.

perspective of the generalized other Viewpoint based on the rules, roles, and attitudes endorsed by the whole social community in which we live.

persuasive speech A presentation that aims to change listeners by prompting them to think, feel, or act differently.

physical appearance Physical features of people and the values attached to those features; a type of nonverbal communication.

policy A formal statement of an organizational practice. An organization's policies reflect and uphold the overall culture of the organization.

positive visualization A technique of reducing speaking anxiety; a person visualizes themselves communicating effectively in progressively challenging speaking situations.

post hoc, ergo propter hoc Latin phrase meaning "After this, therefore because of this." The fallacy of suggesting or assuming that because event B follows event A, event A has therefore caused event B.

power The ability to influence others; a feature of small groups that affects participation.

power distance One of the five dimensions of variation among cultures, this refers to the size of the gap between people with high and low power and the extent to which that gap is regarded as normal.

power over The ability to help or harm others. Power over others usually is communicated in ways that highlight the status and influence of the person using the power.

power to The ability to empower others to reach their goals. People who use power to help others generally do not highlight their own status and influence.

primary research Research that you collect yourself, such as interviewing or surveying people.

privilege Unearned advantages and opportunities experienced by people who share a racial or gender identity perceived as being at the top of the social hierarchy.

procedural communication One of three constructive ways of participating in group decision making. Procedural communication orders ideas and coordinates the contributions of members.

process Something that is ongoing and continuously in motion, the beginnings and endings of which are difficult to identify. Communication is a process.

prototype A knowledge structure that defines the clearest or most representative example of some category.

proxemics A type of nonverbal communication that includes space and how we use it.

pseudolistening Pretending to listen.

psychological responsibility The responsibility for remembering, planning, and coordinating domestic work and child care. In general, women assume the psychological responsibility for child care and housework even if both partners share in the actual tasks.

puffery In advertising, superlative claims for a product that seem factual but are actually meaningless.

punctuation Defining the beginning and ending of interaction or interaction episodes.

Q

qualifier A word or phrase that limits the scope of a claim. Common qualifiers are most, usually, and in general.

quotations A form of evidence that uses exact citations of statements made by others. Also called *testimony.*

R

rebuttal A response to listeners' reservations about a claim made by a speaker.

red herring argument An argument that is irrelevant to the topic; an attempt to divert attention from something the arguer can't or doesn't want to address.

reflected appraisal Our perceptions of others' views of us.

reframing One of four responses to relational dialectics. The reframing response transcends the apparent contradiction between two dialectical poles and reinterprets them as not in tension.

regulative rules Communication rules that regulate interaction by specifying when, how, where, and with whom to talk about certain things.

relational culture A private world of rules, understandings, and patterns of acting and interpreting that partners create to give meaning to their relationship; the nucleus of intimacy.

relational dialectics Opposing forces or tensions that are normal parts of all relationships. The three relational dialectics are autonomy/connectedness, novelty/predictability, and openness/closedness.

relational listening Listening to support another person or to understand another person's feelings and perceptions; focuses on the relational level of meaning as much as on the content level of meaning.

relationship level of meaning One of the two levels of meaning in communication; expresses the relationship between communicators.

resistance A response to cultural diversity in which the cultural practices of others are attacked or the superiority of one's own cultural traditions is proclaimed.

respect A response to cultural diversity in which one values others' customs, traditions, and values, even if one does not actively incorporate them into one's own life.

rite A dramatic, planned set of activities that brings together aspects of an organization's culture in a single event.

rituals A form of communication that occurs regularly and that members of an organization perceive as a familiar and routine part of organizational life.

role The collection of responsibilities and behaviors associated with and expected of a specific position in an organization.

rules Patterned ways of behaving and interpreting behavior; all relationships develop rules.

S

schemata (singular: *schema*) Cognitive structures we use to organize and interpret experiences. Four types of schemata are prototypes, personal constructs, stereotypes, and scripts.

script One of four cognitive schemata. A script defines an expected or appropriate sequence of action in a particular setting.

secondary research Research using already existing sources that you compile from various publications.

segmentation One of four responses to relational dialectics. Segmentation responses meet one dialectical need while ignoring or not satisfying the contradictory dialectical need.

selective listening Focusing on only selected parts of communication. We listen selectively when we screen out parts of a message that don't interest us or with which we disagree and also when we rivet attention on parts of communication that do interest us or with which we agree.

self A multidimensional process in which the individual forms and acts from social perspectives that arise and evolve in communication.

self-disclosure Revelation of information about ourselves that others are unlikely to discover on their own.

self-fulfilling prophecy An expectation or judgment of ourselves brought about by our own actions.

self-sabotage Self-talk that communicates that we're no good, we can't do something, we can't change, and so on. Undermines belief in ourselves and motivation to change and grow.

self-serving bias The tendency to attribute our positive actions and successes to stable, global, internal influences that we control and to attribute negative actions and failures to unstable, specific, external influences beyond our control.

separation One of four responses to relational dialectics, in which friends or romantic partners assign one pole of a dialectic to certain spheres of activities or topics and the contradictory dialectical pole to distinct spheres of activities or topics.

settler colonialism A form of colonization in which colonizers settle an area, replacing Indigenous people and taking their land and resources.

silence The lack of verbal communication or paralanguage. Silence is a type of nonverbal communication that can express powerful messages.

simile A direct comparison that typically uses the words *like* or *as* to link two things.

situational audience analysis A method of audience analysis that seeks information about specific listeners that relates directly to a topic, speaker, and occasion.

slippery slope The fallacy of suggesting or assuming that once a certain step is taken, other steps will inevitably follow that will lead to some unacceptable consequence.

social climbing The attempt to increase personal status in a group by winning the approval of high-status members.

social community A group of people who live within a dominant culture yet who also have common distinctive experiences and patterns of communicating.

social comparison Comparing ourselves with others to form judgments of our own talents, abilities, qualities, and so on.

social listening Actively attending to, observing, interpreting, and responding to auditory and visual digital content on social media.

social loafing Exists when members of a group exert less effort than they would if they worked alone.

social media Apps and sites that allow people and organizations to create, and share photos, videos, and information for personal, social, political, and professional reasons.

specific purpose A behavioral objective or observable response that a speaker specifies as a gauge of effectiveness; reinforces a speaker's more general speaking goals.

speech to entertain A speech the primary goal of which is to amuse, interest, or engage listeners.

speech to inform A speech the primary goal of which is to increase listeners' understanding, awareness, or knowledge of some topic.

speech to persuade A speech the primary goal of which is to change listeners' attitudes, beliefs, or behaviors or to motivate listeners to action.

standpoint theory The theory that a culture includes social groups that differently shape the knowledge, identities, and opportunities of members of those groups, which can lead to political consciousness.

static evaluation Assessments that suggest something is unchanging or static. "Bob is impatient" is a static evaluation.

statistics A form of evidence that uses numbers to summarize a great many individual cases or to demonstrate relationships between phenomena.

stonewalling Refusal to discuss issues that are creating tension in a relationship. Stonewalling is especially corrosive in relationships because it blocks the possibility of resolving conflicts.

stereotype A predictive generalization about people and situations.

structure In an organization, the set of procedures, relationships, and practices that provides predictability for members so that they understand roles, procedures, and expectations and so that work gets done.

survey research Research that involves asking a number of people about their opinions, preferences, actions, or beliefs relevant to a speaking topic.

symbol An arbitrary, ambiguous, and abstract representation of a phenomenon. Symbols are the basis of language, much nonverbal behavior, and human thought.

synergy Collaborative vitality that enhances the efforts, talents, and strengths of individual members.

system A group of interrelated elements that affect one another. Communication is systemic.

T

task communication One of the three constructive forms of participation in group decision making; focuses on giving and analyzing information and ideas.

team A special kind of group characterized by different and complementary resources of members and a strong sense of collective identity. All teams are groups, but not all groups are teams.

terminal credibility The cumulative expertise and trustworthiness listeners attribute to a speaker as a result of the speaker's initial and derived credibility; may be greater or less than initial credibility, depending on how effectively a speaker communicates.

thesis statement The main idea of an entire speech. It should capture the key message in a concise sentence that listeners can remember easily.

tokenization Hiring or including a person from a historically marginalized group for the appearance of diversity, in a way that is not truly inclusive.

tolerance A response to diversity in which one accepts differences even though one may not approve of or even understand them.

totalizing Responding to people as if one aspect of them were the sum total of who they are.

toulmin model of reasoning A representation of effective reasoning that includes five components: claim, grounds (evidence), warrant (link between grounds and claim), qualifier, and rebuttal.

transitions Words and sentences that connect ideas and main points in a speech so that listeners can follow a speaker.

U

uncertainty avoidance One of five dimensions of variation among cultures, this refers to the extent to which people try to avoid ambiguity and vagueness.

understanding A response to cultural diversity in which it is assumed that differences are rooted in cultural teachings and that no traditions, customs, and behaviors are intrinsically more valuable than others.

upward comparison The tendency to compare the self to people who exceed us in what they have or can do.

uses and gratification theory The theory that people choose to attend to mass communication in order to fulfill personal needs and preferences.

V

visual aids Presentation of evidence by visual means such as charts, graphs, photographs, and physical objects to reinforce ideas presented verbally or to provide information.

W

warrant A justification for grounds (evidence) and claims in persuasive speaking.

working outline A sketch of main ideas and their relationships; used by and intended only for the speaker.

works cited A list of sources used in preparing a speech.

References

Aaron, D. G., & Stanford, F. C. (2021). Is obesity a manifestation of systemic racism? A ten-point strategy for study and intervention. *Journal of Internal Medicine, 290*(2), 416–420. https://doi.org/10.1111/joim.13270

Acar, S., Neumayer, M., & Burnett, C. (2019). Social media use and creativity: Exploring the influences on ideational behavior and creative activity. *Journal of Creative Behavior, 55*(1), 39–52. https://doi.org/10.1002/jocb.432

Acker, J. (2013). Is capitalism gendered and racialized? In M. Andersen & P. H. Collins (Eds.), *Race, class, and gender: An anthology* (8th ed., pp. 125–133). Boston, MA: Cengage.

Adams, K., & Galanes, G. (2011). *Communicating in groups*. New York: McGraw-Hill.

Adams, S. (2014, April 21). How women breadwinners can save their relationships. *Forbes*. Retrieved from http://www.forbes.com/sites/susanadams/2014/04/21/how-women-breadwinners-can-save-their-relationships/

Adler, J. (2007, March 12). The great sorority purge. *Newsweek*, p. 47.

Adler, R., Hirsch, S., & Mordaunt, M. (Eds.). (2012). *Voice and communication therapy for the transgender/transsexual client: A comprehensive clinical guide* (2nd ed.). San Diego, CA: Plural Publications.

Adler, R., & Proctor, R., II. (2013). *Looking out, looking in* (14th ed.). Boston, MA: Cengage.

Afsahi, A. (2021). Gender difference in willingness and capacity for deliberation. *Social Politics: International Studies in Gender, State & Society, 28*(4), 1046–1072. https://doi.org/10.1093/sp/jxaa003

Akers, W. P., Cashwell, C., & Blake, S. D. (2021). Relationship satisfaction and outness: The impact of the closet on connection. *Sexual and Relationship Therapy*, 1–21.

Alakhunova, N., Diallo, O., Martin del Campo, I., & Tallarico, W. (2015). *Defining marginalization: An assessment tool.* A product of the partnership between four development professionals at the Elliot School of International Affairs & The Word Fair Trade Organization-Asia. George Washington University.

Alberts, J., Tracy, S., & Trethewey, A. (2011). An integrative theory of the division of domestic labor: Threshold level, social organizing and sense-making. *Journal of Family Communication, 11*, 21–28.

Alitavoli, R., & Kaveh, E. (2018). The U.S. media's effect on public's crime expectations: A cycle of cultivation and agenda-setting theory. *Societies, 8*(3), 58. https://doi.org/10.3390/soc8030058

Allen, B. J. (2006). Communicating race at WeighCo. In J. T. Wood & S. W. Duck (Eds.), *Composing relationships: Communication in everyday life* (pp. 146–155). Belmont, CA: Thomson Wadsworth.

Allen, M., Hale, J., Mongeau, P., Berkowitz-Stafford, S., Stafford, S., Shanahan, W., & Ray, C. (1990). Testing a model of message sidedness: Three replications. *Communication Monographs, 37*, 275–291.

Allianz Trade. (2021, February 22). *Insolvency risk: The Covid-19 domino effect explained*. https://www.allianz-trade.com/en_US/insights/understanding-insolvency-domino-effect.html

American College of Obstetricians and Gynecologists. (2014/2016). *Effective patient–physician communication*. Committee Opinion No. 587. https://www.acog.org/-/media/project/acog/acogorg/clinical/files/committee-opinion/articles/2014/02/effective-patient-physician-communication.pdf

American Community Survey. (n.d.). *Selected economic characteristics; 2019: ACS 1-year estimates data profiles.* United States Census Bureau. https://data.census.gov/cedsci/table?q=DP03&tid=ACSDP1Y2019.DP03

American Society of Plastic Surgeons. (2014). *Celebrating 15 years of trustworthy plastic surgery statistics.* Retrieved from http://www.surgery.org/media/news-releases/celebrating-15-years-of-trustworthy-plastic-surgery-statistics

American Society of Plastic Surgeons. (2021, April 27). 2020 Plastic surgery statistics report. *APS Connect*. https://www.plasticsurgery.org/news/plastic-surgery-statistics

American Society of Plastic Surgeons. (2022). Gender affirmation surgeries: Transgender-specific facial, top and bottom procedures. *APS Connect*. https://www.plasticsurgery.org/reconstructive-procedures/gender-affirmation-surgeries

American Speech-Language-Hearing Association. (n.d.). *Gender-affirming voice and communication change for transgender and gender-diverse people.* https://www.asha.org/public/speech/disorders/voice-and-communication-change-for-transgender-people/

Amodio, D., & Showers, C. (2006). "Similarity breeds liking" revisited: The moderating role of commitment. *Journal of Social and Personal Relationships, 22*, 817–836.

Andersen, M. L., & Collins, P. H. (Eds.). (2013). *Race, class, and gender: An anthology* (8th ed.). Belmont, CA: Wadsworth.

Anderson, D. (2020). U.S. high school students' social media use and political socialization. *Communication Today, 11*(2), 166–175.

Andrejevic, M. (2014). The big data divide. *International Journal of Communication, 8*, 1673–1689. https://ijoc.org/index.php/ijoc/article/view/2161

Angier, N. (2013, November 26). Families. *The New York Times*, pp. D1, D2–D3.

Anjarini, R. D., & Hatmanto, E. D. (2021, December). Challenges and strategies in understanding English idioms: English as a foreign language students' perception. In *International Conference on Sustainable Innovation Track Humanities Education and Social Sciences (ICSIHESS 2021)* (pp. 241–247). Atlantis Press.

Ansari, A. (2015, June 15). Love in an age of like. *Time*, pp. 40–46.

Ansari, A., & Klinenberg, E. (2015). *Modern romance.* New York: Penguin.

Apollo Technical. (2022, January 16). *Statistics on remote workers that will surprise you.* Apollo Technical Engineered Talent Solutions. https://www.apollotechnical.com/statistics-on-remote-workers/

Aratani, L. (2007, February 27). Teens aren't studying at 100%. *Raleigh News & Observer*, p. 4A.

Argyle, M., & Henderson, M. (1984). The rules of friendship. *Journal of Social and Personal Relationships, 1*, 211–237.

Argyris, C. (2012). *Organizational traps.* New York: Oxford University Press.

Arikewuyo, A. O., Lasisi, T. T., Abdulbaqi, S. S., Omosolo, A. I., & Arikewuyo, H. O. (2020). Evaluating the use of social media in escalating conflicts in romantic relationships. *Journal of Public Affairs*, 1–10. https://doi.org/10.1002/pa.2331

Armstrong, C. L., Hou, J., & McLeod, J. (2020). Is Ellen DeGeneres a "DeGenerate"? How TV's first out lesbian connects to public support for same-sex marriage. *Electronic News, 14*(1), 3–21. https://doi.org/10.1177/1931243120910483

Arroyo, A., & Harwood, J. (2012). Exploring the causes and consequences of engaging in fat talk. *Journal of Applied Communication Research, 40*, 167–187.

Ashline, L. (2021, May 22). What fat liberation means to me: It's not just about "all bodies." *National Association to Advance Fat Acceptance.* https://naafa.org/community-voices/fat-lib-means

Association of American Medical Colleges. (2022). *Core competencies for entering medical students.* https://www.aamc.org/services/admissions-lifecycle/competencies-entering-medical-students

Aubrey, J. S., Dajches, L., & Terán, L. (2021). Media as a source of sexual socialization for emerging adults. In E. M. Morgan & M. H. M. van Dulmen (Eds.), *Sexuality in emerging adulthood* (pp. 312–332). Oxford University Press.

Aumer, K., Blas, D., Huston, K., Mabuti, C., & Hsu, N. (2017). Assessing racial preferences in movies: The impact of mere-exposure and social identity theory. *Psychology, 8*(9), 1314–1325. https://doi.org/10.4236/psych.2017.89085

A Victory for Tolerance. (2014, June 21). *Raleigh News & Observer*, p. 9A.

Axtell, R. E. (2007). *Essential Do's and Taboos: The Complete Guide to International Business and Leisure Travel.* Wiley.

Azar, B. (2011). The limits of eyewitness testimony. *Monitor on Psychology, 40*(11). https://www.apa.org/monitor/2011/12/eyewitness

Bachen, C., & Illouz, E. (1996). Imagining romance: Young people's cultural models of romance and love. *Critical Studies in Mass Communication, 13*(4), 279–308. https://doi.org/10.1080/15295039609366983

Badiou, A. (2012). *In praise of love.* London: Serpent's Tail.

Bahrampour, T., & Mellnik, T. (2021, August 12). Census data shows widening diversity; number of White people falls for first time. *The Washington Post.* https://www.washingtonpost.com/dc-md-va/2021/08/12/census-data-race-ethnicity-neighborhoods/

Bailenson, J. N. (2021). Nonverbal overload: A theoretical argument for the causes of Zoom fatigue. *Technology, Mind, and Behavior, 2*(1). https://doi.org/10.1037/tmb0000030

Bailey, A. (1998, February 29). Daily bread. *Durham Herald-Sun*, p. C5.

Baird, J. (2014, April 7). Neither female nor male. *The New York Times*, p. A21.

Bakalar, N. (2012, July 24). Fitness products come mostly filled with fiction. *The New York Times*, p. D5.

Balaji, M., & Worawongs, T. (2010). The new Suzie Wong: Normative assumptions of white male and Asian female relationships. *Communication, Culture & Critique, 3*, 224–241.

Balcetis, E., & Dunning, D. (2010). Wishful seeing: Desirable objects are seen as closer. *Psychological Science, 21*, 147–152.

Baldwin, M., & Mussweiler, T. (2018). The culture of social comparison. *Proceedings of the National Academy of Sciences of the United States of America, 115*(39), 67–74. https://doi.org/10.1073/pnas.1721555115

Banse, R. (2004). Adult attachment and marital satisfaction: Evidence for dyadic configuration effects. *Journal of Social and Personal Relationships, 21*, 273–282.

Barash, S. (2006). *Tripping the prom queen*. New York: St. Martin's Griffin.

Barge, K. (2009). Social groups, workgroups, and teams. In W. F. Eadie (Ed.), *21st century communication: A reference handbook* (pp. 340–348). Thousand Oaks, CA: Sage.

Bargh, J. (1997). *The automaticity of everyday life*. Mahwah, NJ: Erlbaum.

Bargh, J. (1999, January 29). The most powerful manipulative messages are hiding in plain sight. *Chronicle of Higher Education*, p. B6.

Baron, N. (2010). *Always on: Language in an online and mobile world*. New York: Oxford University Press.

Baron, R. A., & Berne, D. (1994). *Social psychology* (7th ed.). Boston, MA: Allyn & Bacon.

Barroso, A. (2021). *For American couples, gender gaps in sharing household responsibilities persist amid pandemic*. Pew Research Center. https://www.pewresearch.org/fact-tank/2021/01/25/for-american-couples-gender-gaps-in-sharing-household-responsibilities-persist-amid-pandemic/

Barstead, M. G., Bouchard, L. C., & Shih, J. H. (2013). Understanding gender differences in co-rumination and confidant choice in young adults. *Journal of Social and Clinical Psychology, 32*, 791–808.

Bartlett, T. (2003, March 7). Take my chair (please). *Chronicle of Higher Education*, pp. A36–A38.

Baum, M. A., & Potter, P. B. (2019). Media, public opinion, and foreign policy in the age of social media. *Journal of Politics, 81*(2), 747–756. https://doi.org/10.1086/702233

Baxter, L. A. (1990). Dialectical contradictions in relational development. *Journal of Social and Personal Relationships, 7*, 69–88.

Baxter, L. A. (1993). The social side of personal relationships: A dialectical perspective. In S. Duck (Ed.), *Understanding relationship processes, Vol. 3: Social context and relationships* (pp. 139–165). Newbury Park, CA: Sage.

Baxter, L. A., & Montgomery, B. (1996). *Relating: Dialogues and dialectics*. New York: Guilford Press.

Beatty, M. J., Plax, T., & Kearney, P. (1985). Reinforcement vs. modeling theory in the development of communication apprehension: A retrospective analysis. *Communication Research Reports, 12*, 80–95.

Beck, J. (2021). How mindfulness impacts the way leaders connect with and develop followers. In S. K. Dhiman (Ed.), *The Routledge companion to mindfulness at work* (Chapter 8). Routledge.

Beebe, S., & Masterson, J. (2011). *Communication in small groups: Principles and practices*. New York: Allyn & Bacon.

Begley, S. (2009, February 16). Will the BlackBerry sink the presidency? *Newsweek*, pp. 36–39.

Beil, L. (2011, November 29). The certainty of memory has its day in court. *The New York Times*, pp. D1, D6.

Bellamy, L. (1996, December 18). Kwanzaa cultivates cultural and culinary connections. *Raleigh News & Observer*, pp. 1F, 9F.

Bendavid, N. (2013, October 31). Countries expand recognition for alternative "intersex" gender. *The Wall Street Journal*, p. A9.

Benenson, J., Gordon, A., & Roy, R. (2000). Children's evaluative appraisals in competition in tetrads versus dyads. *Small Group Research, 31*, 635–652.

Bennett, J. (2019, November 20). What do we hear when women speak? *The New York Times.*

Berdahl, J. L., Cooper, M., Glick, P., Livingston, R. W., & Williams, J. C. (2018). Work as a masculinity contest. *Journal of Social Issues*. https://repository.uchastings.edu/faculty_scholarship/1683/

Bergen, K., & Braithwaite, D. O. (2009). Identity as constituted in communication. In W. F. Eadie (Ed.), *21st century communication: A reference handbook* (pp. 166–173). Thousand Oaks, CA: Sage.

Bergner, R. M., & Bergner, L. L. (1990). Sexual misunderstanding: A descriptive and pragmatic formulation. *Psychotherapy, 27*, 464–467.

Berne, E. (1964). *Games people play*. New York: Grove Press.

Bernstein, E., & Shore, J. (2018, August 13). How intermittent breaks in interaction improve collective intelligence. *Proceedings of the National Academy of Sciences of the United States of America, 115*(35), 8743–8739. https://doi.org/10.1073/pnas.1802407115

Berrett, D. (2011, November 18). What spurs students to stay in college and learn? Good teaching and diversity. *Chronicle of Higher Education*, p. A27.

Berrett, D. (2012, February 3). "Adrift" in adulthood: Students who struggled in college find life harsher after graduation. *Chronicle of Higher Education*, p. A20.

Berry, L. (2014, May 21). "Ideal" body image differs by race. *Medscape Medical News*. Retrieved from http://www.medscape.com/viewarticle/825489

Bettmann, J. E., Anstadt, G., Casselman, B., & Ganesh, K. (2021). Young adult depression and anxiety linked to social media use: Assessment and treatment. *Clinical Social Work Journal, 49*, 368–379.

Birdwhistell, R. (1970). *Kinesics and context*. Philadelphia, PA: University of Pennsylvania Press.

Blair-Loy, M., Rogers, L. E., Glaser, D., Wong, Y. L. A., Abraham, D., & Cosman, P. C. (2017). Gender in engineering departments: Are there gender differences in interruptions of academic job talks? *Social Sciences, 6*(1), 29. https://doi.org/10.3390/socsci6010029

Blow, C. M. (2009, February 21). A nation of cowards? *The New York Times*, p. A17.

Bodey, K., & Wood, J. T. (2009). Grrrlpower: What counts as voice and who does the counting? *Southern Journal of Communication, 74*, 325–337.

Borchers, T. (2006). *Rhetorical theory: An introduction*. Belmont, CA: Thomson Wadsworth.

Bornstein, R., & Languirand, M. (2003). *Healthy dependency*. New York: Newmarket Press.

Bowlby, J. (1973). *Separation: Attachment and loss* (Vol. 2). New York: Basic Books.

Bowlby, J. (1988). *A secure base: Parent-child attachment and healthy human development*. New York: Basic Books.

Boyd, D., & Crawford, K. (2012). Critical questions for big data: Provocations for a cultural, technological, and scholarly phenomenon. *Information, Communication & Society, 15*(5), 662–679. https://doi.org/10.1080/1369118X.2012.678878

Brady, J. (2013, May 22). Some companies foster creativity, others fake it. *The Wall Street Journal*, p. A15.

Brady, M. (2015). *Understanding auditory learning: Integrating-listening K-12 classroom*. Retrieved from http://ltd.edc.org/understanding-auditory-learning-integrating-listening-k-12-classroom

Braithwaite, D., & Kellas, J. K. (2006). Shopping for and with friends: Everyday communication at the shopping mall. In J. T. Wood & S. W. Duck (Eds.), *Composing relationships: Communication in everyday life* (pp. 86–95). Belmont, CA: Thomson Wadsworth.

Brenning, K., Soenens, B., Braet, C., & Bosmans, G. (2011). An adaptation of the experiences in close relationships scale-revised for use with children and adolescents. *Journal of Personal and Social Relationships, 28*, 1048–1072.

Bridges, J. (2017). Gendering metapragmatics in online discourse: "Mansplaining man gonna mansplain..." *Discourse, Context & Media, 20*, 94–102. https://doi.org/10.1016/j.dcm.2017.09.010

Brody, J. (2015, July 14). Limit children's screen time, and your own. *The New York Times*, p. D7.

Brough, M., Literat, I., & Ikin, A. (2020). "Good social media?" Underrepresented youth perspectives on the ethical and equitable design of social media platforms. *Social Media and Society, 6*(2). https://doi.org/10.1177/2056305120928488

Brown, B. (2010). *The gifts of imperfection: Let go of who you think you're supposed to be and embrace who you are*. Hazelden Publishing.

Brown, B. (2012). *Daring greatly: How the courage to be vulnerable transforms the way we life, love, parent, and lead*. Avery Press.

Brown, G., & Greenfield, P. M. (2021). Staying connected during stay-at-home: Communication with family and friends and its association with well-being. *Human Behavior and Emerging Technologies, 3*(1), 147–156. https://doi.org/10.1002/hbe2.246

Bruess, C. (2015). Yard sales and yellow roses: Rituals in enduring relationships. In D. O. Braithwaite & J. T. Wood (Eds.), *Casing interpersonal communication* (2nd ed., pp. 111–116). Dubuque, IA: Kendall Hunt.

Bruess, C., & Hoefs, A. (2006). The cat puzzle recovered: Composing relationships through family ritual. In J. T. Wood & S. W. Duck (Eds.), *Composing relationships: Communication in everyday life* (pp. 65–75). Belmont, CA: Thomson Wadsworth.

Bryant, J., & Oliver, M. B. (Eds.). (2008). *Media effects* (3rd ed.). New York: Routledge.

Buber, M. (1970). *I and thou* (W. Kaufmann, Trans.). New York: Scribner.

Budiman, A. (2020, August 20). *Key findings about U.S. immigrants*. Pew Research Center. https://www.pewresearch.org/fact-tank/2020/08/20/key-findings-about-u-s-immigrants/

Buffett, J. (2022). Top skills employers look for in 2022. *Zety*.

Bui, Q., & Miller, C. (2015, December 23). The typical American lives only 18 miles from mom. *The New York Times*. https://www.nytimes.com/interactive/2015/12/24/upshot/24up-family.html

Burchell, J. L., & Ward, J. (2011). Sex drive, attachment style, relationship status and previous infidelity as predictors of sex differences in romantic jealousy. *Personality and Individual Differences, 51*, 657–661.

Bureau of Labor Statistics Reports. (2021 April). *Women in the labor force: A databook*. U.S. Bureau of Labor Statistics. Report 1092.

Burgoon, J. (1985). Nonverbal signals. In M. Knapp & G. Miller (Eds.), *Handbook of interpersonal communication* (pp. 344–390). Beverly Hills: Sage.

Burgoon, J. K., Wang, X., Chen, X., Pentland, S. J., & Dunbar, N. E. (2021). Nonverbal behaviors "speak" relational messages of dominance, trust, and exposure. *Frontiers in Psychology*, 12. https://doi.org/10.3389/fpsyg.2021.624177

Burke, K. (1950). *A rhetoric of motives*. Englewood Cliffs, NJ: Prentice Hall.

Burke, M., Cheng, J., & de Gant, B. (2020, April). Social comparison and Facebook: Feedback, positivity, and opportunities for comparison. In *Proceedings of the 2020 CHI conference on human factors in computing systems* (pp. 1–13). https://doi.org/10.1145/3313831.3376482

Burleson, B. R., & Rack, J. (2008). Constructivism theory. In L. A. Baxter & D. O. Braithwaite (Eds.), *Engaging theories in interpersonal communication: Multiple perspectives* (pp. 51–63). Thousand Oaks, CA: Sage.

Burney, M. (2012, March 15). Standing up to bullies. *Chronicle of Higher Education*, pp. 50–53.

Butler, S. M., & Sheriff, N. (2021). *How poor communication exacerbates health inequalities – And what to do about it*. Brookings. https://www.brookings.edu/research/how-poor-communication-exacerbates-health-inequities-and-what-to-do-about-it/

Buzzanell, P., & Kirby, E. (2013). Communicating work-life issues. In L. Putnam & D. Mumby (Eds.), *The SAGE handbook of organizational communication: Advances in theory, research and methods* (pp. 351–374). Thousand Oaks, CA: Sage.

Byman, D. L. (2021, April 9). *How hateful rhetoric connects to real-world violence*. Brookings. https://www.brookings.edu/blog/order-from-chaos/2021/04/09/how-hateful-rhetoric-connects-to-real-world-violence/

Calero, H. (2005). *The power of nonverbal communication: What you do is more important than what you say*. Los Angeles, CA: Silver Lake.

Camilleri, M. A., & Falzon, L. (2021). Understanding motivations to use online streaming services: Integrating the technology acceptance model (TAM) and the uses and gratifications theory (UGT). *Spanish Journal of Marketing, 25*(2), 216–236. https://doi.org/10.1108/SJME-04-2020-0074

Campbell, P. (2018). Occupy, Black Lives Matter, and suspended mediation. *Young: Nordic Journal of Youth Research, 26*(2), 145–160.

Campbell, P., Campbell, K., Nelson, J., Parker, M. L., & Johnston, S. (2018). Interpersonal chemistry in friendships and romantic relationships. *Interpersona: An International Journal on Personal Relationships, 12*(1), 34.

Campos-Castillo, C., Shuster, S. M., Groh, S. M., & Anthony, D. L. (2020). Warning: Hegemonic masculinity may not matter as much as you think for confidant patterns among older men. *Sex Roles, 83*, 609–621. https://doi.org/10.1007/s11199-020-01131-3

Candel, O.-S., & Turliuc, M. N. (2019). Insecure attachment and relationship satisfaction: A meta-analysis of actor and partner associations. *Personality and Individual Differences, 147*, 190–199. https://doi.org/10.1016/j.paid.2019.04.037

Carnegie, D. (1936). *How to win friends and influence people*. New York: Simon & Schuster.

Carr, N. (2011). *The shallows: What the Internet is doing to our brains*. New York: Norton.

Cassirer, E. (1944). *An essay on man*. New Haven, CT: Yale University Press.

Castleberry, J. (2019). Addressing the gender continuum: A concept analysis. *Journal of Transcultural Nursing, 30*(4), 403–409.

Cauberghe, V., Van Wesenbeeck, I., De Jans, S., Hudders, L., & Ponnet, K. (2021). How adolescents use social media to cope with feelings of loneliness and anxiety during COVID-19 lockdown. *Cyberpsychology, Behavior, and Social Networking, 24*(4), 250–257.

Caughlin, J., & Vangelisti, A. (2000). An individual difference explanation of why married couples engage in the demand/withdraw pattern of conflict. *Journal of Social and Personal Relationships, 17*, 523–551.

Causadias, J. M., & Umaña-Taylor, A. J. (2018). Reframing marginalization and youth development: Introduction to the special issue. *American Psychologist, 73*(6), 707.

Cavalcante, A. (2018). Tumbling into queer utopias and vortexes: Experiences of LGBTQ social media users on Tumblr. *Journal of Homosexuality, 66*(12), 1715–1735.

Census Bureau. (2021, November 29). *Census bureau releases new estimates on America's families and living arrangements*. United States Census Bureau. https://www.census.gov/newsroom/press-releases/2021/families-and-living-arrangements.html#:~:text=Men%20and%20women%20ages%2025,lived%20with%20an%20unmarried%20partner

Centers for Disease Control and Prevention. (2021, January 25). *CDC estimates 1 in 5 people in the U.S. have a sexually transmitted infection*. https://www.cdc.gov/media/releases/2021/p0125-sexualy-transmitted-infection.html#:~:text=It%20is%20estimated%20there%20were,aged%2015%20to24%20years%20old

Centers for Disease Control and Prevention. (2021, October 9). *Violence prevention: Intimate partner violence, fast facts*. https://www.cdc.gov/violenceprevention/intimatepartnerviolence/fastfact.html

Center on Budget and Policy Priorities. (2020, August 13). The COVID-19 economy's effects on food, housing, and employment hardships. *Covid Hardship Watch*. https://www.cbpp.org/sites/default/files/8-13-20pov.pdf

Chan, S. M., & Wong, H. (2021). Housing and subjective well-being in Hong Kong: A structural equation model. *Applied Research in Quality of Life, 17*, 1745–1766. https://doi.org/10.1007/s11482-021-10000-4

Chan, Y. (1999). Density, crowding, and factors intervening in their relationship: Evidence from a hyper-dense metropolis. *Social Indicators Research, 48*, 103–124.

Chang, K. (2015, March 3). New stage of progress in science. *The New York Times*, pp. D1, D5.

Charafeddine, R., Zambrana, I. M., Triniol, B., Mercier, H., Clément, F., Kaufmann, L., Reboul, A., et al. (2020). How preschoolers associate power with gender in male-female interactions: A cross-cultural investigation. *Sex Roles, 83*, 453–473. https://doi.org/10.1007/s11199-019-01116-x

Charmaraman, L., Richer, A. M., Liu, C., Lynch, A. D., & Moreno, M. A. (2021). Early adolescent social media–related body dissatisfaction: Associations with depressive symptoms, social anxiety, peers, and celebrities. *Journal of Developmental & Behavioral Pediatrics, 42*(5), 401–407. https://doi.org/10.1097/DBP.0000000000000911

Chen, H., Luo, S., Yue, G., Xu, D., & Zhaoyang, R. (2009). Do birds of a feather flock together in China? *Personal Relationships, 16*, 167–186.

Chen, P. (2012, June 5). The trouble with "doctor knows best." *Raleigh News & Observer*, p. D5.

Chew, S. L. (2018). Myth: Eyewitness testimony is the best kind of evidence. *Association for Psychological Science.* https://www.psychologicalscience.org/teaching/myth-eyewitness-testimony-is-the-best-kind-of-evidence.html

Chisler, J., & Barney, A. (2017). *Sizeism is a health hazard.* Paper presented at the 125th annual convention of the American Psychological Association, Washington, D.C. https://www.apa.org/news/press/releases/2017/08/sizeism-health.pdf

Choi, C. (2015, June 11). Taco Bell executives bone up on youth lingo. *Raleigh News & Observer*, p. 6A.

Choi, D., Chun, S., Oh, H., Han, J., & Kwon, T. (2020). Rumor propagation is amplified by echo chambers in social media. *Scientific Reports, 10*, 310. https://doi.org/10.1038/s41598-019-57272-3

Choi, E., & Reddy-Best, K. L. (2021). Southern Korean fashion media: Examining beauty ideals, race, and the prominence of whiteness between 2013 and 2017 in Céci magazine. 한국복식학회 | *International Journal of Costume and Fashion, 21*(2), 1–18. https://doi.org/10.7233/ijcf.2021.21.2.001

Choose Your Parents Wisely. (2014, July 26). *The Economist*, pp. 21–25.

Chory, R. M., & Hoke, H. G. G. (2019). Young love at work: Perceived workplace romance among millennial generation organizational members. *Journal of Psychology, 153*(6), 575–598.

Cinelli, M., Morales, G. D. F., Galeazzi, A., & Starnini, M. (2021). The echo chamber effect on social media. *Proceedings of the National Academy of Sciences of the United States of America.* https://doi.org/10.1073/pnas.2023301118

CivilRights.org. (2017, February 9). Online hate speech is pervasive. Here's how to start combating it. *The leadership conference education fund.* https://civilrights.org/edfund/resource/combat-online-hate-speech/

Clark, L., Averbeck, B., Payer, D., Sescousse, G., Winstanley, C. A., & Xue, G. (2013). Pathological choice: The neuroscience of gambling and gambling addiction. *Journal of Neuroscience*, 33(45), 17617–17623. https://doi.org/10.1523/JNEUROSCI.3231-13.2013

Cleary, M., Lees, R., & Sayers, J. (2019). Leadership, thought diversity, and the influence of groupthink. *Issues in Mental Health Nursing, 40*(8), 731–733. https://doi.org/10.1080/01612840.2019.1604050

Clydesdale, T. (2009, January 23). Wake up and smell the new epistemology. *Chronicle of Higher Education*, pp. B7–B9.

Coate, P. (2021, January 25). *Remote work before, during, and after the pandemic.* National Council on Compensation Insurance. https://www.ncci.com/SecureDocuments/QEB/QEB_Q4_2020_RemoteWork.html

Cockburn-Wootten, C., & Zorn, T. (2006). Cabbages and headache cures: Work stories within the family. In J. T. Wood & S. W. Duck (Eds.), *Composing relationships: Communication in everyday life* (pp. 137–145). Belmont, CA: Thomson Wadsworth.

Cohen, R., Newton-John, T., & Slater, A. (2020). The case for body positivity on social media: Perspectives on current advances and future directions. *Journal of Health Psychology, 26*(13), 2365–2373.

Cohn, D., & Passel, J. S. (2018). *A record 64 million Americans live in multigenerational households.* Pew Research Center.

Cole, T., & Leets, L. (1999). Attachment styles and intimate television viewing: Insecurely forming relationships in a parasocial way. *Journal of Social and Personal Relationships, 16*, 495–511.

Conrad, C., & Poole, M. (2012). *Strategic organizational communication in a global economy* (7th ed.). New York: Harcourt.

Cooley, C. H. (1912). *Human nature and the social order.* New York: Scribner.

Coontz, S. (2013). Gender equality. *The New York Times*, pp. 1, 6, 7.

Coontz, S. (2014, July 27). The new instability. *The New York Times*, pp. SR1, 7.

Coopman, S., & Lull, J. (2013). *Public speaking: The evolving art.* Belmont, CA: Wadsworth.

Coopman, S. J., & Lull, J. (2015). *Public speaking: The evolving art.* Cengage Learning.

Covey, S. (2012). *The 7 habits for managers.* Grand Haven, MI: Franklin Covey Brilliance Audio.

Cox, G., FireMoon, P., Anastario, M. P., Ricker, A., Escarcega-Growing Thunder, R., Baldwin, J. A., & Rink, E. (2021). Indigenous standpoint theory as a theoretical framework for decolonizing social science health research with American Indian communities. *AlterNative: An International Journal of Indigenous Peoples, 17*(4), 460–468.

Cox, J. R. (2016). Personal communication.

Cramwinckel, F. M., Scheepers, D. T., & van der Toorn, J. (2018). Interventions to reduce blatant and subtle sexual orientation- and gender identity prejudice (SOGIP): Current knowledge and future directions. *Social Issues and Policy Review, 12*, 183–217. https://doi.org/10.1111/sipr.12044

Crawford, N., & Lutz, C. (2019, November 3). *Human cost of post – 9/11 wars: Direct war deaths in major war zones.* Watson Institute International & Public Affairs, Brown University. https://watson.brown.edu/costsofwar/figures/2019/direct-war-death-toll-2001-801000

Crenshaw, K. (1989). Demarginalizing the intersection of race and sex: A Black feminist critique of antidiscrimination doctrine, feminist theory and antiracist politics. *University of Chicago Legal Forum, 1*(8), 139–167. https://chicagounbound.uchicago.edu/uclf/vol1989/iss1/8

Cronen, V. E., Pearce, W. B., & Snavely, L. (1979). A theory of rule-structure and types of episodes and a study of perceived enmeshment in undesired repetitive patterns ("URPs"). In D. Nimmo (Ed.), *Communication yearbook* (Vol. 3, pp. 225–240). New Brunswick, NJ: Transaction Books.

Cross, G. (2008). *Men to boys: The making of modern immaturity*. New York: Columbia University Press.

Crossen, C. (1997, July 10). Blah, blah, blah. *The Wall Street Journal*, pp. 1A, 6A.

Cunningham, K. (2022, March 3). What's behind the obsession over whether Elizabeth Holmes intentionally lowered her voice? *The Conversation*.

Cummings, M. (1993). Teaching the African American rhetoric course. In J. Ward (Ed.), *African American communication: An anthology in traditional and contemporary studies* (pp. 239–248). Dubuque, IA: Kendall/Hunt.

Dalcher, D. (2018). The wisdom of teams revisited: Teamwork, teaming and working for the common good. *PM World Journal, 7*(9), 1–13.

Daniel, T. A., & Camp, A. L. (2020). Emojis affect processing fluency on social media. *Psychology of Popular Media, 9*(2), 208–213. https://doi.org/10.1037/ppm0000219

Daniller, A. (2021, March 18). *Majorities of Americans see at least some discrimination against Black, Hispanic, and Asian people in the U.S.* Pew Research Center. https://www.pewresearch.org/fact-tank/2021/03/18/majorities-of-americans-see-at-least-some-discrimination-against-black-hispanic-and-asian-people-in-the-u-s/

Darics, E. (2017). E-leadership or "How to be boss in instant messaging?" The role of nonverbal communication. *International Journal of Business Communication, 57*(1), 3–29. https://doi.org/10.1177/2329488416685068

D'Arienzo, M. C., Boursier, V., & Griffiths, M. D. (2019). Addiction to social media and attachment styles: A systematic literature review. *International Journal of Mental Health and Addiction, 17*(4), 1094–1118. https://doi.org/10.1007/s11469-019-00082-5

Darling, A. L., & Dannels, D. P. (2003). Practicing engineers talk about the importance of talk: A report on the role of oral communication in the workplace, *Communication Education, 52*(1), 1–16, https://doi.org/10.1080/03634520302457

Davies-Popelka, W. (2015). Mirror, mirror on the wall: Weight, identity, and self-talk. In D. O. Braithwaite & J. T. Wood (Eds.), *Casing interpersonal communication* (2nd ed., pp. 25–32). Dubuque, IA: Kendall Hunt.

DC Volunteer Lawyers Project. (2021, June 28). *Domestic violence peaks more than ever for the LGBTQIA+ community*. https://www.dcvlp.org/domestic-violence-peaks-more-than-ever-for-the-lgbtqia-community/

Deal, T.E., & Kennedy, A.A. (1999). *The New Corporate Cultures: Revitalizing The Workplace After Downsizing, Mergers, And Reengineering*. London: Texere.

DeFleur, M. L., & Ball-Rokeach, S. (1989). *Theories of mass communication* (5th ed.). White Plains, NY: Longman.

Delia, J., Clark, R. A., & Switzer, D. (1974). Cognitive complexity and impression formation in informal social interaction. *Speech Monographs, 41*, 299–308.

DeMaris, A. (2007). The role of relationship inequity in marital disruption. *Journal of Social and Personal Relationships, 24*, 177–195.

Demircioğlu, Z. I., & Göncü Köse, A. (2021). Effects of attachment styles, dark triad, rejection sensitivity, and relationship satisfaction on social media addiction: A mediated model. *Current Psychology, 40*(1), 414–428. https://doi.org/10.1007/s12144-018-9956-x

Demographics. (2009, January 26). *Newsweek*, p. 70.

Department of Veteran Affairs. (2021, May). *America's wars*. Office of Public Affairs.

DeVito, J. (1994). *Human communication: The basic course* (6th ed.). New York: HarperCollins.

Dewey, C. (2014, January 17). How many of this year's Oscar nominees pass the Bechdel test? Not many. *Washington Post Blog*. Retrieved from http://www.washingtonpost.com/blogs/style-blog/wp/2014/01/17/howmany-of-this-years-oscar-nominees-pass-thebechdel-test-not-many/

Dickens, D. D., & Chavez, E. L. (2018). Navigating the workplace: The costs and benefits of shifting identities at work among early career U.S. Black women. *Sex Roles, 78*, 760–774. https://doi.org/10.1007/s11199-017-0844-x

Dickson, F. (1995). The best is yet to be: Research on long-lasting marriages. In J. T. Wood & S. W. Duck (Eds.), *Understanding relationship processes, Vol. 6: Understudied relationships: Off the beaten track* (pp. 22–50). Thousand Oaks, CA: Sage.

Dijck, J. (2013). *The culture of connectivity: A critical history of social media*. New York: Oxford University Press.

DiPierro, K., Lee, H., Pain, K. J., Durning, S., & Choi, J. J. (2021). Groupthink among health professional teams in patient care: A scoping review. *Medical Teacher, 44*(3), 309–318. https://doi.org/10.1080/0142159X.2021.1987404

Donish, C. (2017, December 4). Five queer people on what "femme" means to them. Vice. https://www.vice.com/en_us/article/d3x8m7/five-queer-people-on-what-femme-means-to-them

Donnella, L. (2019, February 6). Is beauty in the eye of the colonizer? *NPR Code Switch.* https://www.npr.org/sections/codeswitch/2019/02/06/685506578/is-beauty-in-the- eyes-of-the-colonize

Douglas, W. (2012, May 17). House Oks anti-domestic violence bill. *Raleigh News & Observer*, p. 3A.

Duarte, A., & Albo, M. (2018, February 2). Who you calling "young lady"? *AARP.*

Duck, S. W. (2006). The play, playfulness, and the players: Everyday interaction as improvised rehearsal of relationships. In J. T. Wood & S. W. Duck (Eds.), *Composing relationships: Communication in everyday life* (pp. 15–23). Belmont, CA: Thomson Wadsworth.

Duck, S. W., & McMahan, D. (2012). *Basics of communication* (2nd ed.). Thousand Oaks, CA: Sage.

Duck, S. W., & Wood, J. T. (2006). What goes up may come down: Gendered patterns in relational dissolution. In M. Fine & J. Harvey (Eds.), *The handbook of divorce and dissolution of romantic relationships* (pp. 169–187). Mahwah, NJ: Erlbaum.

Dunbar, R. (2012). *The science of love and betrayal.* London, UK: Faber & Faber.

Durana, A., Lenhart, A., Miller, R., Schulte, B., & Weingarten, E. (2018, September 26). Sexual harassment: A severe and pervasive problem. *Better Life Lab.* New America. https://www.newamerica.org/better-life-lab/reports/sexual-harassment-severe-and-pervasive-problem/introduction

Eastwick, P. W., Keneski, E., Morgan, T. A., McDonald, M. A., & Huang, S. (2018). What do short-term and long-term relationships look like? Building the relationship coordination and strategic timing (ReCAST) model. *Journal of Experimental Psychology: General, 147*, 747–781.

Edelman, B., & Larkin, I. (2014). Social comparisons and deception across workplace hierarchies: Field and experimental evidence. *Organizational Science, 26*, 78–98.

Edmonds, A., & Leem, S. O. (2021) Making faces racial: How plastic surgery enacts race in the US, Korea and Brazil. *Ethnic and Racial Studies, 44*(11), 1895–1913. https://doi.org/10.1080/01419870.2020.1791353

Edström, M. (2018). Visibility patterns of gendered ageism in the media buzz: A study of the representation of gender and age over three decades. *Feminist Media Studies, 18*(1), 77–93. https://doi.org/10.1080/14680777.2018.1409989

Edwards, H. (2015, August 3). The next social security crisis. *Time*, pp. 48–52.

Efosa, C., Mahesh S., Ogechi, A., & Nubi, A. (2017). The effects of gender on the adoption of social media: An empirical investigation. Twenty-third Americas Conference on Information Systems. Boston.

Ekemezie, C. (2021, January 21). *People of colour have always felt pressure to hide their personal identities in professional environments. Now, virtual work has complicated code-switching even more.* BBC.com. https://www.bbc.com/worklife/article/20210119-why-its-hard-for-people-of-colour-to-be-themselves-at-work

Einhorn, L. (2000). *The Native American oral tradition: Voices of the spirit and soul.* Westport, CT: Praeger.

Eisenberg, E., Goodall, H., & Trethewey, A. (2013). *Organizational communication: Balancing creativity and constraint.* Boston, MA: Bedford /St. Martin's.

Ellis, A. (1988). *How to stubbornly refuse to make yourself miserable about anything—Yes, anything.* New York: Lyle Stuart.

Emery, L. F., Gardner, W. L., Carswell, K. L., & Finkel, E. J. (2021). Who are "we"? Couple identity clarity and romantic relationship commitment. *Personality and Social Psychology Bulletin, 47*(1), 146–160. https://doi.org/10.1177/0146167220921717

Emmons, S. (1998, February 3). The look on his face: Yes, it was culture shock. *Raleigh News & Observer*, p. 5E.

Engeln, R. (2015, March 15). The problem with 'fat talk.' *The New York Times*, p. SR 12.

Epley, N. (2014). *Mindwise: How we understand what others think, believe, feel and want.* New York: Borzoi/Knopf.

Erbert, L. (2000). Conflict and dialectics: Perceptions of dialectical contradictions in marital conflict. *Journal of Social and Personal Relationships, 17*, 638–659.

ExpressVPN. (2021, December 1). *ExpressVPN survey reveals the extent of surveillance on the remote workforce.* ExpressVPN News. https://www.expressvpn.com/blog/expressvpn-survey-surveillance-on-the-remote-workforce/

Eytan, T., Benabio, J., Golla, V., Parikh, V., & Stein, S. (2011, Winter). Social media and the health system. *Permanente Journal, 15*, 71–74.

Facing History and Ourselves. (2014). "Culture and Identity: East and West." *The Nanjing Atrocities: Crimes of War.* https://www.facinghistory.org/nanjing-atrocities/identity/culture-and-identity-east-and-west

Faigley, L., & Selzer, J. (2000). *Good reasons.* Allyn & Bacon.

Farr, R. H., Simon, K. A., & Goldberg, A. E. (2020). Separation and divorce among LGBTQ-parent families. In A. E. Goldberg & K. R. Allen (Eds.), *LGBTQ-parent families* (pp. 337–348).

Farroni, T., Longa, L. D., & Valori, I. (2022). The self-regulatory affective touch: A speculative framework for the development of executive functioning. *Current Opinion in Behavioral Sciences, 43*, 167–173. https://doi.org/10.1016/j.cobeha.2021.10.007

Fasoli, F. (2017). Gay straight communication. In *Oxford Research Encyclopedia of Communication.* https://doi.org/10.1093/acrefore/9780190228613.013.469

Fauville, G., Luo, M., Queiroz, A. C. M., Bailenson, J. N., & Hancock, J. (2021). *Nonverbal mechanisms predict zoom fatigue and explain why women experience higher levels than men.* Available at SSRN. https://ssrn.com/abstract=3820035 or http://dx.doi.org/10.2139/ssrn.3820035

Fehr, B. (1993). How do I love thee: Let me consult my prototype. In S. W. Duck (Ed.), *Understanding relationship processes, Vol. 1: Individuals in relationships* (pp. 87–122). Newbury Park, CA: Sage.

Fehr, B., & Russell, J. A. (1991). Concept of love viewed from a prototype perspective. *Journal of Personality and Social Psychology, 60*, 425–438.

Ferguson, S. D. (2008). *Public speaking: Building competency in stages*. New York: Oxford University Press.

Ferrante, J. (2009). *Sociology: A global perspective* (7th ed.). Belmont, CA: Thomson Wadsworth.

Filson Moses, J. (2014). *Social identity in close relationships* [Doctoral dissertation, University of Minnesota]. ProQuest. https://www.proquest.com/openview/91f9b60e83c25f307c4756dcca0f26a8/

Fitch, N. (Ed.). (2000). *How sweet the sound: The spirit of African American history*. New York: Harcourt College.

Fixmer-Oraiz, N., & Wood, J. T. (2019). *Gendered lives: Communication, gender, and culture*. Cengage.

Flew, T. (2009). Democracy, participation and convergent media: Case studies in contemporary online news journalism in Australia. *Communication, Politics & Culture, 42*(2), 87–109.

Fogg, P. (2008, July 25). Thinking in black and white. *Chronicle of Higher Education*, p. B19.

Foley, M. (2006). Locating "difficulty": A multi-site model of intimate terrorism. In C. D. Kirkpatrick, S. W. Duck, & M. K. Foley (Eds.), *Relating difficulty: The processes of constructing and managing difficult interaction* (pp. 43–59). Mahwah, NJ: Erlbaum.

Ford Foundation. (1998, October 6). *Americans see many benefits to diversity in higher education, finds first ever national poll on topic*. Press release via Business Wire.

Forsyth, D. (2009). *Group dynamics* (5th ed.). Belmont, CA: Wadsworth Cengage.

Foster School of Business. (2021, January 24). *Work relationships are hard to build on Zoom—Unless you pick up on colleagues' nonverbal cues*. https://foster.uw.edu/research-brief/work-relationships-hard-build-zoom-unless-pick-colleagues-nonverbal-cues/

Fox, J., & Ralston, R. (2016). Queer identity online: Informal learning and teaching experiences of LGBTQ individuals on social media. *Computers in Human Behavior, 65*, 635–642. https://doi.org/10.1016/j.chb.2016.06.009

Fraley, R. C. (2019). Attachment in adulthood: Recent developments, emerging debates, and future directions. *Annual Review of Psychology, 70*, 401–422. https://doi.org/10.1146/annurev-psych-010418-102813

Francis, A. L., & Love, J. (2019). Listening effort: Are we measuring cognition or affect, or both? *Wiley Interdisciplinary Reviews, 11*(1), e1514. https://doi.org/10.1002/wcs.1514

Freeman, J. (2009). *The tyranny of e-mail*. New York: Simon & Schuster/Scribner.

Freundlich, K. (2021, February 24). *Casinos control much more than you think*. Morris Psychological Group.

Fry, R., & Parker, K. (2021 October 5). *Rising share of U.S. adults are living without a spouse or partner*. Pew Research Center. https://www.pewresearch.org/social-trends/2021/10/05/rising-share-of-u-s-adults-are-living-without-a-spouse-or-partner/

Fryberg, S. A., & Markus, H. R. (2003). On being American Indian: Current and possible selves. *Self and Identity, 2*, 325–344.

Fujishin, R. (2014). *Creating effective groups*. Summit, PA: Rowman & Littlefield.

Fwd.us. (2021, December 15). International students and graduates in the United States. https://www.fwd.us/news/international-students

Gagnon, P. (2016, December 19). The forgotten life of Einstein's wife. *Scientific American*. https://blogs.scientificamerican.com/guest-blog/the-forgotten-life-of-einsteins-first-wife/

Gallo, C. (2014, September 25). New survey: 70% say presentational skills are critical for career success. *Forbes*. http://www.forbes.com/sites/carminegallo/2014/09/25/new-survey-70-percent-say-presentation-skills-critical-for-career-success/

Gallup. (2011). *Islamophobia: Understanding Anti-Muslim sentiment in the West*. https://news.gallup.com/poll/157082/islamophobia-understanding-anti-muslim-sentiment-west.aspx

Galvin, K., Braithwaite, D., & Bylund, C. (2015). *Family communication: Cohesion and change*. Upper Saddle Ridge, NJ: Pearson.

García, I. (2020). Cultural insights for planners: Understanding the terms Hispanic, Latino, and Latinx. *Journal of the American Planning Association, 86*(4), 393–402.

Gass, R. (1999). *Fallacy list: SpCom 335. Advanced argumentation*. Fullerton, CA: California State University. Retrieved from http://commfaculty.fullerton.edu/rgass/fallacy31.htm

Gearhart, C. C., & Maben, S. K. (2021) Active and empathic listening in social media: What do stakeholders really expect? *International Journal of Listening, 35*(3), 166–187. https://doi.org/10.1080/10904018.2019.1602046

Genard, G. (2020, May 31). The voice of authority: How to sound like a leader. *Speak for Success!* https://www.genardmethod.com/blog/the-voice-of-authority-how-to-sound-like-a-leader

Gentner, D., & Boroditsky, L. (2009). Early acquisition of nouns and verbs: Evidence from the Navajo. In V. Gathercole (Ed.), *Routes to language* (pp. 5–86). New York: Taylor & Francis.

George, L. (1995, December 26). Holiday's traditions are being formed. *Raleigh News & Observer*, pp. C1, C3.

Georgetown University Center on Education and the Workforce. (2020). *Workplace basics: The competencies employers want*. https://cew.georgetown.edu/cew-reports/competencies/

Gerbner, G. (1990). Epilogue: Advancing on the path of righteousness (maybe). In N. Signorielli & M. Morgan (Eds.), *Cultivation analysis: New directions in media effects research* (pp. 250–261). Thousand Oaks, CA: Sage.

Gillespie, B. J., Lever, J., Frederick, D., & Royce, T. (2014). Close adult friendships, gender, and the life cycle. *Journal of Social and Personal Relationships, 32*(6), 709–736.

Globe Newswire. (2021, December 31). *North American non-invasive aesthetic treatment market forecast to reach USD 46.07 billion by 2028*. Globe Newswire: Research and Markets.

Glynn, S. (2021, March 29). *Breadwinning mothers are critical to families' economic security*. Center for American Progress. https://www.americanprogress.org/article/breadwinning-mothers-critical-familys-economic-security/

GMAC Research Team. (2020). *Employers still seek communication skills in new hires*. MBA.com.

Goldstein, J. (2013, June 11). A not-for-tourists guide to navigating a multicultural city (It's for the police). *The Wall Street Journal*, pp. A18, A19.

Goleman, D. (2007). *Social intelligence: The new science of human relationships*. New York: Bantam.

Goleman, D. (2011). *The brain and emotional intelligence*. Florence, MA: More than Sound.

Golfscape. (2019, August 6). Exclusive interview with golf legend Annika Sorenstam. *Futuri Visio: The Golfscape Blog*. https://golfscape.com/blog/exclusive-interview-annika-sorenstam/

Gomez, A. (2017, June 19). What is an ideal group size? *Clear Concept*. https://clearconceptinc.ca/what-is-an-ideal-group-size/

Gómez-López, M., Viejo, C., & Ortega-Ruiz, R. (2019). Well-being and romantic relationships: A systematic review in adolescence and emerging adulthood. *International Journal of Environmental Research and Public Health, 16*(13), 2415. http://dx.doi.org/10.3390/ijerph16132415

Gong, X., & Nikitin, J. (2021). "When i feel lonely, i'm not nice (and neither are you)": The short- and long-term relation between loneliness and reports of social behavior. *Cognition and Emotion, 5*, 1029–1038.

González, A., Houston, M., & Chen, V. (Eds.). (2012). *Our voices: Essays in culture, ethnicity, and communication*. New York: Oxford University Press.

Goo, S. K. (2015, February 19). *The skills Americans say kids need to succeed in life*. Pew Research Center. Retrieved from http://www.pewresearch.org/fact-tank/2015/02/19/skills-for-success/

Goranson, P. (2019). *Listening: Imperative for patient safety*. Global Listening Centre. https://www.globallisteningcentre.org/wp-content/uploads/2019/03/Listening-Patient-Safety.pdf

Gottman, J. (1993). The roles of conflict engagement, escalation, or avoidance in marital interaction: A longitudinal view of five types of couples. *Journal of Consulting and Clinical Psychology, 61*, 6–15.

Gottman, J. (1994a). *What predicts divorce? The relationship between marital processes and marital outcomes*. Hillsdale, NJ: Erlbaum.

Gottman, J. (1994b). Why marriages fail. *Family Therapy Newsletter*, pp. 41–48.

Gottman, J. (1999). *Seven principles for making marriages work*. New York: Crown.

Gottman, J. M., & Silver, N. (1994). *Why marriages succeed or fail: What you can learn from the breakthrough research to make your marriage last*. New York, Simon & Schuster.

Gordon, S. (2022, July 25). Ways to tell if someone is gaslighting you. *Verywell Mind*. Retrieved on August 17, 2022, from https://www.verywellmind.com/is-someone-gaslighting-you-4147470

Graham, G. R. (2018). *Poor communication leads to patient harm in intensive care units*. Gray Ritter Graham (GRGPC.com).

Gray, A. (2019, June 4). The bias of "professionalism" standards. *Stanford Social Innovation Review*. https://ssir.org/articles/entry/the_bias_of_professionalism_standards

Gray, M. J. (2013). *The relationship between gender identity and flirting style* [Master's thesis, Arkansas State University]. ProQuest.

Grayling, A. (2013). *Friendship*. New Haven, CT: Yale University Press.

Greenberg, S., & Neustaedter, C. (2013) Shared living, experiences, and intimacy over video chat in long distance relationships. In Neustaedter C., Harrison S., & Sellen A. (Eds.), *Connecting families*. London: Springer. https://doi.org/10.1007/978-1-4471-4192-1_3

Greene-Moton, E., & Minkler, M. (2019). Cultural competence or cultural humility? Moving beyond the debate. *Health Promotion Practice, 21*(1), 142–145. https://doi.org/10.1177/1524839919884912

Gregory, G., Healy, R., & Mazierkska, E. (2007). *The essential guide to careers in media and film*. Thousand Oaks, CA: Sage.

Gregory, T. (2012, March 5). Young adults in an age of "hyper-connectivity." *Raleigh News & Observer*, p. D1.

Griffin, C. (2015). *An invitation to public speaking* (5th ed.). Belmont, CA: Wadsworth.

Groopman, J. (2007). *How doctors think*. Boston, MA: Houghton Mifflin.

Grygiel, J., & Lysak, S. (2021). Police social media and broadcast news: An investigation into the impact of police use of Facebook on journalists' gatekeeping role. *Journalism Practice, 15*(7). https://doi.org/10.1080/17512786.2020.1759123

Gudykunst and Lee. (2002). Cross-Cultural Communication Theories. In D. Dankwa-Apawu (Ed.), *Eliminating Barriers to Cross-Cultural Communication though Curricular Interventions*, Ghana Institute of Journalism, Accra, p. 4.

Guéguen, N., & De Gail, M. (2003). The effect of smiling on helping behavior: Smiling and good Samaritan behavior. *Communication Reports, 16*, 133–140.

Guéguen, N., Eyssartier, C., & Meineri, S. (2016). A pedestrian's smile and drivers' behavior: When a smile increases careful driving. *Journal of Safety Research, 56*, 83–88.

Guerrero, L. (1996). Attachment style differences in intimacy and involvement: A test of the four-category model. *Communication Monographs, 63*, 269–292.

Guerrero, L., & Floyd, K. (2006). *Nonverbal communication in close relationships*. Mahwah, NJ: Erlbaum.

Guerrero, L., La Valley, A., & Farinelli, L. (2008). The experience and expression of anger, guilt, and sadness in marriage: An equity theory explanation. *Journal of Social and Personal Relationships, 25*, 699–724.

Gurrentz, B. (2018). *Cohabitation is down for young adults*. United States Census Bureau. https://www.census.gov/library/stories/2018/11/cohabitation-is-up-marriage-is-down-for-young-adults.html

Gurrentz, B. (2019, September 23). *Cohabiting partners older, more racially diverse, more educated, higher earners*. United States Census Bureau. https://www.census.gov/library/stories/2019/09/unmarried-partners-more-diverse-than-20-years-ago.html

Gurrentz, B., & Mayola-Garcia, Y. (2021, April 22). *Love and loss among older adults: Marriage, divorce, widowhood remain prevalent among older populations*. United States Census Bureau. https://www.census.gov/library/stories/2021/04/love-and-loss-among-older-adults.html

Gurung, L. (2020). Feminist standpoint theory: Conceptualization and utility. *Dhaulagiri Journal of Sociology and Anthropology, 14*, 106–115. https://doi.org/10.3126/dsaj.v14i0.27357

Guttman, A. (2021, September 17). Value of the global entertainment and media market from 2011 to 2024. https://www.statista.com/statistics/237749/value-of-the-global-entertainment-and-media-market/

Hains, R. C. (2014). *The princess problem: Guiding our girls through the princess-obsessed years*. Sourcebooks.

Hains, R. C. (2015, July 9). The problem with separate toys for girls and boys. *The Boston Globe*.

Hains, R. C. (2020). Being a female public intellectual in the age of social media: Navigating backlash, mansplainers, and trolls. In C. Carter Olson & T. Everbach (Eds.), *Testing tolerance and tough topics in the college classroom and on campus*. Volume sponsored by the Association for Educators in Journalism and Mass Communication. Rowman & Littlefield Publishers.

Hains, R. C., & Hunting, K. (2018). Gender and representation. In N. Jennings & S. Mazzarella (Eds.), *20 Questions about youth and the media* (2nd ed.). Peter Lang.

Hains, R. C., & Jennings, N. (Eds.). (2021). *The marketing of children's toys: Critical perspectives on children's consumer culture*. Palgrave.

Hajek, C. (2017). Gay male culture and intergroup communication. In *Oxford Research Encyclopedia of Communication*. https://doi.org/10.1093/acrefore/9780190228613.013.474

Hajek, C., Abrams, J. R., & Murachver, T. (2005). Female, straight, male, gay, and worlds betwixt and between: An intergroup approach to sexual and gender identities. In J. Harwood & H. Giles (Ed.), *Intergroup communication: Multiple perspectives*. Peter Lang.

Hall, E. T. (1966). *The hidden dimension*. New York: Anchor.

Hall, E. T. (1977). *Beyond culture*. New York: Doubleday.

Hall, J. A. (2018). How many hours does it take to make a friend? *Journal of Social and Personal Relationships, 36*(4), 1278–1296. https://doi.org/10.1177/0265407518761225

Hall, J. A., Coats, E., & Smith-LeBeau, L. (2004). Nonverbal behavior and the vertical dimension of social relations: A meta-analysis. *Psychological Bulletin, 131*, 898–924. [Cited in Knapp, M. L., & Hall, J. A. (2006). *Nonverbal communication in human interaction*. Belmont, CA: Thomson Wadsworth.]

Hall, J., Park, N., Song, H., & Cody, J. (2010). Strategic misrepresentation in online dating: The effects of gender, self-monitoring, and personality traits. *Journal of Social and Personal Relationships, 27*, 117–135.

Hall, L. (2017). *Race and online hate: Exploring the relationship between race and the likelihood of exposure to hate material online* [Unpublished doctoral dissertation]. Virginia Polytechnic Institute and State University.

Hall, N. (2021, August 22). 17 biggest movie star salaries of 2021 revealed. *Man of Many*. https://manofmany.com/entertainment/movies-tv/highest-paid-actors-2021

Hamachek, D. (1992). *Encounters with the self* (3rd ed.). Fort Worth, TX: Harcourt Brace Jovanovich.

Hamermesh, D. (2011). *Beauty pays: Why attractive people are more successful*. Princeton, NJ: Princeton University Press.

Hamilton, C. (2015). *Essentials of public speaking* (7th ed.). Belmont, CA: Wadsworth.

Hamilton, N. (2011–2012). Effectiveness requires listening: How to assess and improve listening skills. *Florida Coastal Law Review, 13*, 145–180.

Hancock, A. B., & Rubin, B. A. (2014). Influence of communication partner's gender on language. *Journal of Language and Social Psychology, 34*(1), 46–64. https://doi.org/10.1177/0261927X14533197

Haraway, D. (1988). Situated knowledges: The science question in feminism and the privilege of partial perspective. *Signs, 14*, 575–599.

Harding, S. (1991). *Whose science? Whose knowledge? Thinking from women's lives.* Ithaca, NY: Cornell University Press.

Hargie, O. (Ed.). (2018). *The handbook of communication skills.* Routledge.

Harmon, A. (2002). Talk, type, read e-mail: The trials of multitasking. In E. Bucy (Ed.), *Living in the information age* (pp. 79–81). Belmont, CA: Thomson Wadsworth.

Harris, T. E., & Sherblom, J. C. (2010). *Small group and team communication.* Boston, MA: Allyn & Bacon.

Harris, T. J. (1969). *I'm OK, you're OK.* New York: Harper & Row.

Harrison, R. (2019) Gender, race and representation in the Star Wars franchise: An introduction. *Media Education Journal, 65*(2), 16–19. http://eprints.gla.ac.uk/195627/

Harvard T. H. Chan School of Public Health. (2017). *Harvard alcohol project: Designated driver.* https://www.hsph.harvard.edu/chc/harvard-alcohol-project/

Haugen, J., & Lucas, K. (2019). Unify and present: Using Monroe's Motivated Sequence to teach team presentation skills. *Communication Teacher,* 33(2), 112–116. https://doi.org/10.1080/17404622.2018.1502886

Heider, F. (1958). *The psychology of interpersonal relations.* New York: Wiley.

Heine, S. J., & Hamamura, T. (2007). In search of East Asian self-enhancement. *Personality and Social Psychology Review, 11*, 1–24.

Heine, S. J., & Raineri, A. (2009). Self-improving motivations and culture: The case of Chileans. *Journal of Cross-Cultural Psychology, 40*, 158–163.

Helmrich, B. (August 10, 2015). Email etiquette 101: The do's and don'ts of professional emails. *Business News Daily.* Retrieved from http://www.businessnewsdaily.com/8262-email-etiquette-tips.html

Hendrick, C., & Hendrick, S. (1996). Gender and the experience of heterosexual love. In J. T. Wood (Ed.), *Gendered relationships* (pp. 131–148). Mountain View, CA: Mayfield.

Hendrick, S., & Hendrick, C. (2006). Measuring respect in close relationships. *Journal of Social and Personal Relationships, 23*, 881–899.

Hendrick, C., Hendrick, S., Foote, F. H., & Slapion-Foote, M. J. (1984). Do men and women love differently? *Journal of Social and Personal Relationships, 2*, 177–196.

Henrich, J., & Norenzayan, A. (2010). The weirdest people in the world? *Behavioral and Brain Sciences, 33*, 61–135.

Hermans, A., Muhammad, S., & Treur, J. (2021, March). How attachment to your primary caregiver influences your first adult relationship: An adaptive network model of attachment theory. In *Proceedings of the 21th International Conference on Computational Science, ICCS'21.* Springer Nature Switzerland AG.

Hesmondhalgh, D. (2007). *The cultural industries* (2nd ed.). Thousand Oaks, CA: Sage.

Hewes, D. (Ed.). (1995). *The cognitive bases of interpersonal perception.* Mahwah, NJ: Erlbaum.

Hickey, W. (2014, April 1). The dollar-and-cents case against Hollywood's exclusion of women. *Five Thirty Eight.* Retrieved from http://fivethirtyeight.com/features/the-dollar-andcents-case-against-hollywoods-exclusion-ofwomen/

Hill, K. (2012, February 16). How Target figured out a teen girl was pregnant before her father did. *Forbes.*

Hillis, K., Petit, M., & Jarrett, K. (2012). *Google and the culture of search.* New York: Routledge.

Hochschild, A., & Machung, A. (2003). *The second shift* (Rev. ed.). New York: Viking.

Hode, M. G. (2017, June 2017). *Is "professionalism" an obstacle to diversity & inclusion?* LinkedIn Pulse. https://www.linkedin.com/pulse/professionalism-obstacle-diversity-inclusion-goldstein-hode-phd/

Hoffman, J. (2010, June 28). Online bullies pull schools into the fray. *The New York Times,* pp. A13, A14, A15.

Hoffman, J. (2012, June 4). A warning to teenagers before they start dating. *The New York Times,* pp. A12, A13.

Hofstede, G. (1991). *Culture and organizations: Software of the mind.* New York: McGraw-Hill.

Hofstede, G. (2001). *Cultures' consequences: Comparing values, behaviors, institutions, and organizations across nations.* Thousand Oaks, CA: Sage.

Hofstede, G., Hofstede, G. J., & Minkov, M. (2010). *Cultures and organizations: Software of the mind* (3rd ed.). New York: McGraw-Hill.

Holden, M. (2019, August 12). The exhausting work of LGBTQ code-switching. *Vice.* https://www.vice.com/en/article/evj47w/the-exhausting-work-of-lgbtq-code-switching

Holt-Lunstad, J. (2020). Social isolation and health. *Health Affairs.* https://doi.org/10.1377/hpb20200622.253235

Holt-Lunstad, J., Smith, T. B., & Layton, J. B. (2010). Social relationships and mortality risk: A meta-analytic review. *PLoS Medicine, 7*, 1–20.

Honoré, C. (2005). *In praise of slowness*. San Francisco, CA: Harper.

Hoover, E. (2010, January 29). An immigrant learns 2 new languages. *Chronicle of Higher Education*, p. A22.

Hoppe, M., Rossmy, B., Neumann, D. P., Streuber, S., Schmidt, A., & Machulla, T. K. (2020, April). A human touch: Social touch increases the perceived human-likeness of agents in virtual reality. In *Proceedings of the 2020 CHI Conference on Human Factors in Computing Systems* (pp. 1–11). https://doi.org/10.1145/3313831.3376719

Houston, M., & Wood, J. T. (1996). Difficult dialogues, expanded horizons: Communicating across race and class. In J. T. Wood (Ed.), *Gendered relationships* (pp. 39–56). Mountain View, CA: Mayfield.

Hrabi, D. (2013, June 22–23). Nestle while you work. *The Wall Street Journal*, pp. D1, D8.

Huesmann, L. R., Moise-Titus, J., Podolski, C., & Eron, L. D. (2003). Longitudinal relations between children's exposure to TV violence and their aggressive and violent behavior in young adulthood: 1977–1992. *Developmental Psychology, 39*, 201–221.

Hummadi, A. S., Said, S. B. M., & Manan, A. B. A. (2019). Persuasive organizational patterns and rhetorical arguments in Donald Trump's policy speech on Jerusalem. *International Journal of Psychosocial Rehabilitation, 23*(2), 964–982. https://doi.org/10.37200/IJPR/V23I2/PR190343

Hunt, G., Marx, R., Lipson, C., & Young, J. (2018). No more FOMO: Limiting social media decreases loneliness and depression. *Journal of Social and Clinical Psychology, 37*(10), 751–768.

Hunt, K. P., & Wald, D. M. (2020). The role of scientific source credibility and goodwill in public skepticism toward GM foods. *Environmental Communication, 14*(7), 971–986. https://doi.org/10.1080/17524032.2020.1725086

Hunt, M., All, K., Burns, & Li, K. (2021). Too much of a good thing: Who we follow, what we do, and how much time we spend on social media affects well-being. *Journal of Social and Clinical Psychology, 40*(1). https://doi.org/10.1521/jscp.2021.40.1.46

Hunter, S. (2012). *Lesbian and gay couples: Lives, issues, and practice*. Chicago, IL: Lyceum Books, Inc.

Hur, H. (2020). The role of inclusive work environment practices in promoting LGBT employee job satisfaction and commitment. *Public Money & Management, 40*(6), 426–436.

Idemudia, E., Raisinghani, M., Adeola, O., & Achebo, N. (2017). The effects of gender on social media adoption: An empirical investigation. Proceedings of the 23rd Americans Conference on Information Systems, Boston, MA: *Social Computing, 15*.

iNews. (2021, June 2). Anxiety around public speaking is exacerbated for high-profile athletes. *iNews Lifestyle Essentials*. https://inews.co.uk/essentials/lifestyle/fear-public-speaking-high-profile-athletes-1030702

Inman, C. C. (1996). Friendships among men: Closeness in the doing. In J. T. Wood (Ed.), *Gendered relationships* (pp. 95–110). Mountain View, CA: Mayfield.

Innocence Project. (2018). *Eyewitness identification reform*. https://innocenceproject.org/eyewitness-identification-reform

Iqbal, M. (2020, April 13). Promoting collaborative and teamwork competency in medical students. *Harvard Macy Community Blog*. Harvard Macy Institute. https://harvardmacy.org/index.php/hmi/promoting-collaborative-and-teamwork

Irvine, M. (2012, June 4). Does texting ruin the art of conversation? *Raleigh News & Observer*, p. 3A.

Italie, L. (2014, July 31). Fashion industry, retailers face gender divide. *Raleigh News & Observer*, p. 8D.

Jackson, S., & Allen, J. (1990). *Meta-analysis of the effectiveness of one-sided and two-sided argumentation*. Paper presented at the International Communication Association, Montreal, Canada.

Jackson, S. J., Bailey, M., & Welles, B. F. (2020). *#HashtagActivism: Networks of race and gender justice*. MIT Press. https://doi.org/10.7551/mitpress/10858.001.0001

Jacobs, B. (2022, May 15). *What defines cultural appropriation?* BBC. https://www.bbc.com/culture/article/20220513-what-defines-cultural-appropriation

Jacobson, N. S., & Gottman, J. M. (1998). *When men batter women: New insights into ending abusive relationships*. United States: Simon & Schuster.

Jaffe, C. (2016). *Public speaking: Concepts and skills for a diverse society* (8th ed.). Belmont, CA: Wadsworth.

Jaffe, E. (2004). Peace in the Middle East may be impossible: Lee D. Ross on naïve realism and conflict resolution. *American Psychological Society Observer, 17*, 9–11.

Jandt, F. (2012). *An introduction to intercultural communication: Identities in a global community*. Thousand Oaks, CA: Sage.

Janesick, V. J. (2019). Life/ography as storytelling: Using letters, diaries, journals, and poetry to understand the work of female leaders. *Qualitative Inquiry, 25*(5), 492–499. https://doi.org/10.1177/1077800418817838

Jenkins, R. (2020, February, 27). 50 percent of emails and texts are misunderstood, but there's an easy way to change that. *Entrepreneur*. https://www.entrepreneur.com/article/346802

Jhally, S., & Katz, J. (2001, Winter). Big trouble, little pond. *UMass*, pp. 26–31. Retrieved from https://www.umass.edu/umassmag/archives/2001/winter2001/athens.html.

Johanson, D. L., Ahn, H. S., & Broadbent, E. (2021). Improving interactions with healthcare robots: A review of communication behaviors in social and healthcare contexts. *International Journal of Social Robotics, 13*, 1835–1850. https://doi.org/10.1007/s12369-020-00719-9

Johnston, R. M., Mohammed, A., & van der Linden, C. (2020). Evidence of exacerbated gender inequality in child care obligations in Canada and Australia during the COVID-19 pandemic. *Politics & Gender, 16*(4), 1131–1141. https://doi.org/10.1017/S1743923X20000574

Jones, D. (2007, March 30). Do foreign executives balk at sports jargon? *USA Today*, pp. 1B–2B.

Jones, H., Neal, S., Mohan, G., Connell, K., Cochrane, A., & Bennett, K. (2015). Urban multiculture and everyday encounters in semi-public, franchised cafe spaces. *The Sociological Review, 63*(3), 644–661.

Jones, N., Marks, R., Ramirez, R., & Rios-Vargas, M. (2021, August 12). *2020 census illuminates racial and ethnic composition of the country*. United States Census Bureau. https://www.census.gov/library/stories/2021/08/improved-race-ethnicity-measures-reveal-united-states-population-much-more-multiracial.html

Joshi, N. (2015, January 5). Doctor, shut up and listen. *The New York Times*, p. A15.

June, A. (2012, March 23). Work-life balance is out of reach for many scientists, and not just women. *Chronicle of Higher Education*, p. A29.

Kanij, T., Grundy, J., McIntosh, J., Sarma, A., & Aniruddha, G. (2022). A new approach towards ensuring gender inclusive SE job advertisements. 2022 IEEE/ACM 44th International Conference on Software Engineering: Software Engineering in Society (ICSE-SEIS), Pittsburgh, PA, pp. 1–11, https://doi.org/10.1145/3510458.3513016

Katzman, M. (2015, July 5). Baffled by buzzwords. *The New York Times*, p. BU7.

Kaufman, M., & Kimmel, M. (2011). *The guy's guide to feminism*. Berkeley, CA: Seal Press.

Keizer, G. (2010). *The unwanted sound of everything we want: A book about noise*. New York: Perseus-Public Affairs.

Kellerman, K. (2011, November). From communication professor to trial consultant. *Spectra*, pp. 11–15.

Kelley, H. H. (1967). Attribution theory in social psychology. In D. Levine (Ed.), *Nebraska symposium on motivation* (Vol. 15, pp. 192–238). Lincoln, NE: University of Nebraska Press.

Kellman, B. (2022, March 24). In nurses' trial, witness says hospital bears "heavy" responsibility for patient death. *Health News from NPR*. https://www.npr.org/sections/health-shots/2022/03/24/1088397359/in-nurses-trial-witness-says-hospital-bears-heavy-responsibility-for-patient-dea

Keltner, D., & Van Lange, P. A. (2018). It's the motive that counts: Perceived sacrifice motives and gratitude in romantic relationships. *Emotion, 18*(5), 625.

Kendall, D. (2011). *Framing class*. Lanham, MD: Rowman.

Kennedy, G. (Ed. & Trans.). (1991). *Aristotle on rhetoric*. London, UK: Oxford University Press.

KFF. (2021, June 7). The HIV/AIDS epidemic in the United States: The basics. https://www.kff.org/hivaids/fact-sheet/the-hivaids-epidemic-in-the-united-states-the-basics/

Khan, S. (2021, March 9). *Cultural humility vs. cultural competence – And why we need both*. Health City. https://healthcity.bmc.org/policy-and-industry/cultural-humility-vs-cultural-competence-providers-need-both

Kirkland, D. (2015). Black masculine language. In S. Lanehart (Ed.), *Oxford Handbook of African American Language*. Oxford University Press.

Kiesler, C. A., & Kiesler, S. B. (1971). Role of forewarning in persuasive communications. *Journal of Abnormal and Social Psychology, 18*, 210–221.

Kilbourne, J. (2010). *Killing us softly 4: Advertising's image of women* [Video]. Media Education Foundation.

Kilcullen, M., Feitosa, J., & Salas, E. (2021). Insights from the virtual team science: Rapid deployment during COVID-19. *The Journal of the Human Factors and Ergonomics Society*. https://doi.org/10.1177/0018720821991678

Kim, J., & Meyers, R. (2012). Cultural differences in conflict management styles in east and west organizations. *Journal of Intercultural Communication, 29*. Retrieved from http://www.immi.se/intercultural

Kim, S., Hirokawa, M., Matsuda, S., Funahashi, A., & Suzuki, K. (2021). Smiles as a signal of prosocial behaviors toward the robot in the therapeutic setting for children with autism spectrum disorder. *Frontiers in Robotics and AI, 8*, 599755. https://doi.org/10.3389/frobt.2021.599755

Kimbrough, A. M., Guadagno, R. E., Muscanell, N. L., & Dill, J. (2013). Gender differences in mediated communication: Women connect more than do men. *Computers in Human Behavior, 29*, 896–900.

Kimmel, M. (2008). *Guyland: The perilous world where boys become men*. New York: Macmillan.

Kimmel, M. (2013). *Angry white men*. New York: Nation.

Kimmel, M., & Messner, M. (2012). *Men's lives* (9th ed.). Upper Saddle Ridge, NJ: Pearson.

Kimmelman, M. (2014, August 22). In redesigned room, hospital patients may feel better already. *The New York Times*, pp. A1, A13.

Kippert, A. (2021, November 22). *A guide to cyberstalking: How to combat an abuser who's gone online to stalk and control a victim*. Domestic Shelters. https://www.domesticshelters.org/articles/ending-domestic-violence/a-guide-to-cyberstalking

Kivel, P. (2019). The everyday impact of Christian hegemony. In M. S. Kimmel & A. L. Ferber (Eds.). *Privilege: A reader*. Routledge. https://doi.org/10.4324/9780429494802

Kirkman, B. L., & Stoverink, A. C. (2021). Building resilient virtual teams. *Organizational Dynamics, 50*(1). https://doi.org/10.1016/j.orgdyn.2020.100825

Klofstad, C. A., & Anderson, R. C. (2018). Voice pitch predicts electability, but does not signal leadership ability. *Evolution and Human Behavior*. https://doi.org/10.1016/j.evolhumbehav.2018.02.007

Klofstad, C. A., Anderson, R. C., & Peters, S. (2012). Sounds like a winner: Voice pitch influences perception of leadership capacity in men and women. *Proceedings of the Royal Society B, 279*, 2698–2704. https://doi.org/10.1098/rspb.2012.0311

Knapp, M. L., & Hall, J. A. (2006). *Nonverbal communication in human interaction*. Belmont, CA: Thomson Wadsworth.

Knapp, M. L., Hall, J. A., & Hogan, T. (2013). *Nonverbal communication in human interaction*. Stamford, CT: Cengage.

Koc-Michalska, K., Schiffrin, A., Lopez, A., Bouilanne, S., & Bimber, B. (2019). From online political posting to mansplaining: The gender gap and social media in political discussion. *Social Science Computer Review, 39*(2), 197–210. https://doi.org/10.1177/0894439319870259

Koh, H., & Yatsko, P. (2017, February). Jay Winsten and the designated driver campaign. *Harvard Business School Case Study* (excerpt). https://www.hsph.harvard.edu/chc/2017/02/01/jay-winsten-and-the-designated-driver-campaign/

Kohlberg, L. (1958). *The development of modes of thinking and moral choice in the years 10 to 16* [Unpublished doctoral dissertation]. University of Chicago.

Kondo, M. (2014). *The life-changing magic of tidying up: The Japanese art of decluttering and organizing*. Random House.

Korkki, P. (2013, June 16). Business schools know how you think, but how do you feel? *The Wall Street Journal*, p. B1.

Korzybski, A. (1948). *Science and sanity* (4th ed.). Lakeville, CT: International Non-Aristotelian Library.

Krasnova, H., Wenninger, H., Widjaja, T., & Buxmann, P. (2013). *Envy on Facebook: A hidden threat to users' life satisfaction*. 11th International Conference on Wirtschaftsinformatik, Leipzig, Germany. Retrieved from https://karynemlira.com/wp-content/uploads/2013/01/Envy-on-Facebook_A-Hidden-Threat-to-Users%E2%80%99-Life.pdf

Kreps, G. L. (2010). *Health communication*. Thousand Oaks, CA: Sage.

Kumar, A., & Epley, N. (2021). It's surprisingly nice to hear you: Misunderstanding the impact of communication media can lead to suboptimal choices of how to connect with others. *Journal of Experimental Psychology: General, 150*(3), 595–607. https://doi.org/10.1037/xge0000962

Kurtzberg, T. (2014). *Virtual teams: Mastering communication and collaboration in the digital age*. Santa Barbara, CA: Praeger.

LaGrange & Yau, 2020 to La Grange & Yau, 2020 in chapter 6. Publicness vs. privateness: A study of public rental housing in Hong Kong. *Current Politics and Economics of Northern and Western Asia, 29*(2/3), 347–378.

Laigo, K. (2020, October 18). Masculine vs. feminine culture: Another layer of culture. *Women in Technology International*. https://witi.com/articles/1824/Masculine-vs.-Feminine-Culture:-Another-Layer-of-Culture/

Lammers, J. C., Magnifico, A. M., & Curwood, J. S. (2018). Literate identities in fan-based online affinity spaces. In K. A. Mills, A. Stornaiulo, A. Smith, & J. Z. Paynda (Eds.), *Handbook of writing, literacies, and education in digital cultures* (Chapter 14). Routledge.

Lampis, J., Cataudella, S., Busonera, A., & Carta, S. (2018). Personality similarity and romantic relationship adjustment during the couple life cycle. *The Family Journal, 26*(1), 31–39. https://doi.org/10.1177/1066480717741689

Landrum, R., & Harrold, R. (2003). What employers want from psychology graduates. *Teaching of Psychology, 30*, 131–133.

Langer, S. (1953). *Feeling and form: A theory of art*. New York: Scribner.

Langer, S. (1979). *Philosophy in a new key: A study in the symbolism of reason, rite, and art* (3rd ed.). Cambridge, MA: Harvard University Press.

Lapakko, D. (2007). Communication is 93% nonverbal: An urban legend proliferates. *Communication and Theater Association of Minnesota Journal, 34*(1), 7–19.

Larson, K. A. (2011). *Negotiating romantic and sexual relationships: Patterns and meanings of mediated interaction* [Doctoral dissertation, University of Kansas]. KU ScholarWorks.

Lasch, C. (1990, Spring). Journalism, publicity and the lost art of argument. *Gannett Center Journal*, 1–11.

Laswell, H. D. (1948). The structure and function of communication in society. In L. Bryson (Ed.), *The communication of ideas* (pp. 37–51). New York: Harper & Row.

Lawless, B. (2012). More than white: Locating an invisible class identity. In A. González, M. Houston, & V. Chen (Eds.), *Our voices: Essays in culture, ethnicity, and communication* (pp. 247–253). New York: Oxford University Press.

Lazo, A. (2014, January 28). California law gives new options to transgender students. *Wall Street Journal*, A4.

Leaper, C., & Ayres, M. M. (2007). A meta-analytic review of gender variations in adults' language use: Talkativeness, affiliative speech, and assertive speech. *Personality and Social Psychology Review, 11*, 328–362.

Leaper, N. (1999). How communicators lead at the best global companies. *Communication World, 16*, 33–36.

Lee, J. A. (1973). *The colours of love: An exploration of the ways of loving*. Don Mills, Ontario, Canada: New Press.

Lee, J. A. (1988). Love-styles. In R. J. Sternberg & M. L. Barnes (Eds.), *The psychology of love* (pp. 38–67). New Haven, CT: Yale University Press.

Lee, W. (1994). On not missing the boat: A processual method for intercultural understandings of idioms and lifeworld. *Journal of Applied Communication Research, 22*, 141–161.

Lee, W. (2000). That's Greek to me: Between a rock and a hard place in intercultural encounters. In L. Samovar & R. Porter (Eds.), *Intercultural communication: A reader* (9th ed., pp. 217–224). Belmont, CA: Wadsworth.

Lehman, C., & DuFrene, D. (1999). *Business communication* (12th ed.). Cincinnati, OH: South-Western.

Leikas, S., Ilmarinen, V. J., Verkasalo, M., Vartiainen, H. L., & Lönnqvist, J. E. (2018). Relationship satisfaction and similarity of personality traits, personal values, and attitudes. *Personality and Individual Differences, 123*, 191–198.

Lerner, B. (2015, February 24). Please stop making that noise. *The New York Times*, p. D4.

Leschizner, V., & Brett, G. (2021). Have schemas been good to think with? *Sociological Forum, 36*(1), 1207–1228. https://doi.org/10.1111/socf.12767

Levine, M. (2004, June 1). Tell the doc all your problems, but keep it to less than a minute. *The New York Times*, p. D6.

Levy, S. (2006, March 27). (Some) attention must be paid! *Newsweek*, p. 16.

Lin, L. (2005). Enhancing intercultural communication skills. *CSA Academic Perspective* (Vol. 1, pp. 44–46). http://citeseerx.ist.psu.edu/viewdoc/download?doi=10.1.1.502.1485&rep=rep1&type=pdf

Lippold, M. A. (2021). *The benefit of collaboration: Disentangling the sources of synergy in group judgments* [Doctoral dissertation, Georg-August University School of Science]. http://dx.doi.org/10.53846/goediss-45

Liu, M. (2016). Verbal communication styles and culture. In *Oxford Research Encyclopedia of Communication*. https://doi.org/10.1093/acrefore/9780190228613.013.162

Liu, P., He, J., & Li, A. (2019). Upward social comparison on social network sites and impulse buying: A moderated mediation model of negative affect and rumination. *Computers in Human Behavior, 96*, 133–140. https://doi.org/10.1016/j.chb.2019.02.003

Livermore, D. A. (2015) *Leading with cultural intelligence: The real secret to success* (2nd ed.). New York: AMACOM.

Livingstone, S. (2019). Audiences in an age of datafication: Critical questions for media research. *Television & New Media, 20*(2), 170–183. https://doi.org/10.1177/1527476418811118

Lokithasan, K., Simon, S., Jasmin, N. Z. B., & Othman, N. A. B. (2019). Male and female social media influencers: The impact of gender on emerging adults. *International Journal of Modern Trends in Social Sciences, 2*(9), 21–30.

Lomash, E. F., Brown, T. D., & Galupo, M. P. (2018). "A whole bunch of love the sinner hate the sin": LGBTQ microaggressions experienced in religious and spiritual context. *Journal of Homosexuality, 66*(10), 1495–1511. https://doi.org/10.1080/00918369.2018.1542204

Lowry, J. (2013, June 13). Hands-free devises not risk-free, study says. *Raleigh News & Observer*, p. 5A.

Lu, D., Huang, J., Seshagiri, A., Park, H., & Griggs, T. (2020, September 9). Faces of power: 80% are white, even as U.S. becomes more diverse. *The New York Times*. https://www.nytimes.com/interactive/2020/09/09/us/powerful-people-race-us.html

Lublin, J. S. (2010, July 6). The keys to unlocking your most successful career: Five simple but crucial lessons culled from many years of offering advice to workers, bosses and job seekers. *The Wall Street Journal*. Retrieved from http://www.wsj.com/articles/SB10001424052748704293604575343322516508414

Luhrmann, T. M. (2014, December 4). Wheat people vs. rice people. *The New York Times*, p. A29.

Luttrell, R. (2014). *Social media: How to engage, share, and connect*. Lanham, MD: Rowman & Littlefield.

Lutz-Zois, C., Bradley, A., Mihalik, J., & Moorman-Eavers, E. (2006). Perceived similarity and relationship success among dating couples: An idiographic approach. *Journal of Social and Personal Relationships, 23*, 865–880.

MacNeill, A. (2021, April 12). Racism and obesity are inextricably linked, says a Harvard doctor – And here's how she thinks that can change. *Boston.com*. https://www.boston.com/news/racial-justice/2021/04/12/racism-and-obesity-article-fatima-cody-stanford-daniel-aaron/

Madsen, S. R., Townsend, A., & Scribner, R. T. (2019). Strategies that male allies use to advance women in the workplace. *Journal of Men's Studies, 28*(3), 239–259. https://doi.org/10.1177/1060826519883239

Maes, C., & Vandenbosch, L. (2022). "I love my body; I love it all": Body positivity messages in youth-oriented television series. *Mass Communication and Society* (just-accepted). https://doi.org/10.1080/15205436.2022.2030756

Major, B., Schmidlin, A. M., & Williams, L. (1990). Gender patterns in social touch: The impact of setting and age. In C. Mayo & N. M. Henley (Eds.), *Gender and nonverbal behavior* (pp. 3–37). New York: Springer-Verlag.

Manusov, V., & Harvey, J. H. (2001). *Attribution, communication behavior, and close relationships*. Port Chester, NY: Cambridge University Press.

Manusov, V., & Patterson, M. L. (2006). *The Sage handbook of nonverbal communication*. Thousand Oaks, CA: Sage.

Manusov, V., & Spitzberg, B. (2008). Attribution theory. In L. A. Baxter & D. O. Braithwaite (Eds.), *Engaging theories in interpersonal communication: Multiple perspectives* (pp. 37–49). Thousand Oaks, CA: Sage.

Mastro, D. (2017). Race and ethnicity in US media content and effects. In *Oxford Research Encyclopedia of Communication.* https://oxfordre.com/communication/view/10.1093/acrefore/9780190228613.001.0001/acrefore-9780190228613-e-122

Matsumoto, D., Franklin, B., Choi, J., Rogers, D., & Tatani, H. (2002). Cultural influences on the expression and perception of emotion. In W. B. Gudykunst & B. Mody (Eds.), *The handbook of international and intercultural communication* (2nd ed., pp. 107–126). Thousand Oaks, CA: Sage.

Mattison, P. (2021, November 30). *Child abuse and domestic violence: Connections and common factors.* Prevent Child Abuse America. https://preventchildabuse.org/latest-activity/child-abuse-and-domestic-violence-connections-and-common-factors

Mayew, W. J., Parsons, C. A., & Venkatachalam, M. (2013). Voice pitch and the labor market success of male chief executive officers. *Evolution and Human Behavior, 34,* 243–248.

Mazanec, C. (2017, March 30). *#ThanksForTyping spotlights unnamed women in literary acknowledgments.* NPR. https://www.npr.org/2017/03/30/521931310/-thanksfortyping-spotlights-unnamed-women-in-literary-acknowledgements

McCombs, M., Ghanem, S., & Chernov, G. (2009). Agenda setting and framing. In W. F. Eadie (Ed.), *21st century communication: A reference handbook* (pp. 516–524). Thousand Oaks, CA: Sage.

McCoy, S. S., Dimler, L. M., Samuels, D. V., & Natsuaki, M. N. (2019). Adolescent susceptibility to deviant peer pressure: Does gender matter? *Adolescent Research Review, 4,* 59–71.

McCroskey, J., & Teven, J. (1999). Goodwill: A reexamination of the construct and its measurement. *Communication Monographs, 66,* 90–103.

McGuire, W. J. (1989). Theoretical foundations of campaigns. In R. E. Rice & C. K. Atkin (Eds.), *Public communication campaigns* (2nd ed., pp. 43–65). Newbury Park, CA: Sage.

McIntosh, P. (1989). *White privilege: Unpacking the invisible knapsack.* https://nationalseedproject.org/images/documents/Knapsack_plus_Notes-Peggy_McIntosh.pdf

McKimm, B. (2021, May 14). 10 highest-paid athletes for 2021. *Man of Many.* https://manofmany.com/entertainment/sport/highest-paid-athletes-2021

Mead, G. H. (1934). *Mind, self, and society.* Chicago, IL: University of Chicago Press.

Mehrabian, A. (2017/1972). *Nonverbal communication.* Routledge.

Mehrabian, A. (1981). *Silent messages: Implicit communication of emotion and attitudes* (2nd ed.). Belmont, CA: Wadsworth.

Mendelberg, T., Karpowitz, C. F., & Oliphant, J. B. (2014). Gender inequality in deliberation: Unpacking the black box of interaction. *Perspectives on Politics, 12*(1), 18–44. https://doi.org/10.1017/S1537592713003691

Messinger, A. M., & Koon-Magnin, S. (2019). Sexual violence in LGBTQ communities. In W. O'Donohue & P. Schewe (Eds.), *Handbook of sexual assault and sexual assault prevention.* Springer. https://doi.org/10.1007/978-3-030-23645-8_39

Metts, S. (2006a). Hanging out and doing lunch: Enacting friendship closeness. In J. T. Wood & S. W. Duck (Eds.), *Composing relationships: Communication in everyday life* (pp. 76–85). Belmont, CA: Thomson Wadsworth.

Metts, S. (2006b). Gendered communication in dating relationships. In B. Dow & J. T. Wood (Eds.), *Handbook of gender and communication research* (pp. 25–40). Thousand Oaks, CA: Sage.

Meyers, D. G. (1993). *Social psychology* (4th ed.). New York: McGraw-Hill.

Milani, T. (2019). Queer performativity. In K. Hall & R. Barrett (Eds.), *Language and sexuality.* Oxford University Press. https://doi.org/10.1093/oxfordhb/9780190212926.001.0001

Milbank, D. (2014, August 7). A welcome end to American whiteness. *Raleigh News & Observer,* p. 7A.

Milia, T. (2003). *Doctor, you're not listening.* Philadelphia, PA: Xlibris.

Miller, C. (2014). *Organizing communication: Approaches and processes* (8th ed.). Belmont, CA: Wadsworth/Cengage.

Miller, C. (2015a). Can an algorithm hire better than a human? *The New York Times,* p. SR 4.

Miller, C. (2015b, August 1). Millennial men aren't the dads of their hopes. *The New York Times,* pp. A1, A3.

Miller, C. (2021, May 17). The pandemic created a child care crisis. Mothers bore the burden. *The New York Times.* https://www.nytimes.com/interactive/2021/05/17/upshot/women-workforce-employment-covid.html

Mitchell, C., Dakhli, M., & Dinkha, J. (2015). Attachment styles and parasocial relationships: A collectivist society perspective. *Construction of Social Psychology: Advances in Psychology and Psychological Trends Series,* 105–121. https://doi.org/10.31235/osf.io/w5huy

Modaff, D., Butler, J., & DeWine, S. (2011). *Organizational communication: Foundations, challenges, and misunderstandings* (3rd ed.). Boston, MA: Allyn & Bacon.

Mokros, H. (2006). Composing relationships at work. In J. T. Wood & S. W. Duck (Eds.), *Composing relationships: Communication in everyday life* (pp. 175–185). Belmont, CA: Thomson Wadsworth.

Monastersky, R. (2002, March 29). Speak before you think. *Chronicle of Higher Education*, pp. A17–A18.

Monroe, A. H. (1935). *Principles and types of speech*. Glenview, IL: Scott, Foresman.

Morgenroth, T., Sendén, M. G., Lindqvist, A., Renström, E. A., Ryan, M. K., & Morton, T. A. (2021). Defending the sex/gender binary: The role of gender identification and need for closure. *Social Psychological and Personality Science, 12*(5), 731–740. https://doi.org/10.1177/1948550620937188

Morreale, S., Osborn, M., & Pearson, J. (2000). Why communication is important: A rationale for the centrality of the study of communication. *Journal of the Association for Communication Administration, 29*, 1–25.

Morrison, A. (2022, March 9). *Number of hate groups declined in 2021, but Proud Boys chapters surging, says SPLC*. PBS. https://www.pbs.org/newshour/nation/number-of-hate-groups-declined-in-2021-but-proud-boys-chapters-surging-says-splc

Morry, M. M., Kito, M., & Ortiz, L. (2010). The attraction–similarity model and dating couples: Projection, perceived similarity, and psychological benefits. *Personal Relationships, 18*(1), 125–143. https://doi.org/10.1111/j.1475-6811.2010.01293.x.

Moseson, H., Zazanis, N., Goldberg, E., Fix, L., Durden, M., Stoeffler, A., Hastings, J., et al. (2020). The imperative for transgender and gender nonbinary inclusion: Beyond women's health. *Obstetrics and Gynecology, 135*(5), 1059–1068. https://doi.org/10.1097/AOG.0000000000003816

Moujahid, M., Wilson, B., Hastie, H., & Lemon, O. (2022, March). Demonstration of a robot receptionist with multi-party situated interaction. In *Proceedings of the 2022 ACM/IEEE International Conference on Human-Robot Interaction* (pp. 1202–1203).

Muehlhoff, T. (2006). "He started it": Everyday communication in parenting. In J. T. Wood & S. W. Duck (Eds.), *Composing relationships: Communication in everyday life* (pp. 46–54). Belmont, CA: Thomson Wadsworth.

Mumby, D. K. (2006). Constructing working-class masculinity in the workplace. In J. T. Wood & S. W. Duck (Eds.), *Composing relationships: Communication in everyday life* (pp. 166–174). Belmont, CA: Thomson Wadsworth.

Murray, K. (2016). "I grew up knowing how to talk female": Transgender men's communicative changes in their post-transition lives. *Texas Linguistics Forum, 59*, 79–89.

Muwanguzi, S., & Musambira, G. (2013). Communication experiences of Ugandan immigrants during acculturation to the United States: A preliminary study. *Journal of Intercultural Communication, 31*. Retrieved from http://www.immi.se/intercultural/

Nagourney, E. (2006, May 9). Surgical teams found lacking, in teamwork. *The New York Times*, p. D6.

Nasie, M., Bar-Tal, D., Pliskin, R., Nahhas, E., & Halpern, E. (2014). Overcoming the barrier of narrative adherence in conflicts through awareness of the psychological bias of naive realism. *Personality and Social Psychology Bulletin 40*(11), 1543–1556. https://doi.org/10.1177/0146167214551153

Nass, C. (2012, May/June). The keyboard and the damage done. *Pacific Standard*, pp. 22–25.

National Bureau of Economic Research. (2021, July 19). *Determination of the April 2020 trough in US economic activity*. https://www.nber.org/news/business-cycle-dating-committee-announcement-july-19-2021

National Coalition Against Domestic Violence. (2017, April 12). *Quick guide: Economic and financial abuse*. https://ncadv.org/blog/posts/quick-guide-economic-and-financial-abuse

National Organization for Women. (2022). *Violence against women in the United States: Statistics*. https://now.org/resource/violence-against-women-in-the-united-states-statistic/

National Safety Council. (2022). *Injury facts; guns*. https://injuryfacts.nsc.org/home-and-community/safety-topics/guns/data-details/

Neitz, M. (2022). Feminist methodologies: Feminist standpoint analysis. In S. Engler & M. Strausberg (Eds.), *The Routledge handbook of research methods in the study of religion* (pp. 57–71). Routledge.

Neuliep, J. (2014). *Intercultural communication: A contextual approach*. Thousand Oaks, CA: Sage.

Newman, J. (2015, August 28). The perils of email auto-fill. *The New York Times*. Retrieved from http://mobile.nytimes.com/2015/08/30/fashion/the-perils-of-email-auto-fill.html?referrer=

Newsbeast. (2012, January 30). *Newsweek*, p. 12.

Nicotera, A., Clinkscales, M., & Walker, F. (2002). *Understanding organization through culture and structure*. Thousand Oaks, CA: Sage.

#NoBodyIsDisposable. (2020). About #NoBodyIsDisposable. https://nobodyisdisposable.org/about/

Norwich University Online. (2020, November 10). *4 challenges of virtual teams and how to address them*. Norwich University Online, Business Administration.

Nyhan, B. (2021, April 9). Why the backfire effect does not explain the durability of political misperceptions. *Proceedings of the National Academy of Sciences of the United States of America*. https://www.pnas.org/doi/full/10.1073/pnas.1912440117

Office of Disease Prevention and Health Promotion. (2020). *Healthy People 2030*. https://health.gov/healthypeople/about/workgroups/hiv-workgroup

Office on Women's Health. (2019, April 2). *Effects of domestic violence on children*. US Department of Health & Human Services. https://www.womenshealth.gov/relationships-and-safety/domestic-violence/effects-domestic-violence-children

Ohanian, H. (2009). *Einstein's mistakes*. New York: W.W. Norton.

Ohme, J., & de Vreese, C. (2020). Traditional and "New Media" Forms and Political Socialization. In J. Bulck (Ed.), *The International Encyclopedia of Media Psychology*, https://doi.org/10.1002/9781119011071.iemp0167

Olson, J. M., & Cal, A. V. (1984). Source credibility, attitudes, and the recall of past behaviors. *European Journal of Social Psychology, 14*, 203–210.

Opfer, C. (2011, November/December). Disappearing ink: The burgeoning business of tattoo removal. *Miller-McCune*, pp. 20–21.

Orbe, M., & Harris T. (2015). *Interracial communication: Theory into practice* (3rd ed.). Belmont, CA: Wadsworth.

Oyster Team. (2022, March 17). Key takeaways from our 2022 employee expectations report: Remote work, work-life balance, and culture are key. *Employee Expectations 2022 Report.* https://www.oysterhr.com/library/key-takeaways-from-our-2022-employee-expectations-report

Ostafichuk, P. M., & Sibley, J. (2019). Self-bias and gender-bias in student peer evaluation: An expanded study. *Proceedings of the Canadian Engineering Education Association*. https://doi.org/10.24908/pceea.vi0.13864.

Ozer, S., Meca, A., & Schwartz, S. J. (2019). Globalization and identity development among emerging adults from Ladakh. *Cultural Diversity and Ethnic Minority Psychology, 25*(4), 515–526. https://doi.org/10.1037/cdp0000261

Paaßen, B., Morgenroth, T., & Stratemeyer, N. (2017). What is a true gamer? The male gamer stereotype and the marginalization of women in video game culture. *Sex Roles, 76*, 421–435. https://doi.org/10.1007/s11199-016-0678-y

Pacanowsky, M., & O'Donnell-Trujillo, N. (1983). Organizational communication as cultural performance. *Communication Monographs, 30*, 126–147.

Painter, N. I. (2010). *The history of white people*. Norton.

Palumbo, D. B., Alsalman, O., De Ridder, D., Song, J. J., & Vanneste, S. (2018). Misophonia and potential underlying mechanisms: A perspective. *Frontiers in Psychology, 9*, 953.

Parker, K., & Barroso, A. (2021, February 15). *In Vice President Kamala Harris, we can see how America has changed*. Pew Research Center. https://www.pewresearch.org/fact-tank/2021/02/25/in-vice-president-kamala-harris-we-can-see-how-america-has-changed/

Parker, K., & Horowitz, J. M. (2022, March 9). *Majority of workers who quit a job in 2021 cite low pay, no opportunities for advancement, feeling disrespected.* Pew Research Center. https://www.pewresearch.org/fact-tank/2022/03/09/majority-of-workers-who-quit-a-job-in-2021-cite-low-pay-no-opportunities-for-advancement-feeling-disrespected/

Parker, K., & Rainie, L. (2020, April 13). Americans and lifetime learning in the knowledge age. *Pew Trusts: Trend Magazine*. https://www.pewtrusts.org/en/trend/archive/spring-2020/americans-and-lifetime-learning-in-the-knowledge-age

Parker, K., & Wang, W. (2013). Modern parenthood. Pew Research Center's Social & Demographic Trends Project, p. 14.

Parker, R. (2021). *AP style rules*. PR Newswire. https://mediablog.prnewswire.com/2020/09/09/ap-style-rules-correct-uses-for-race-related-terms-gender-neutral-words-and-election-lingo/

Parker-Pope, T. (2009a, January 13). A problem of the brain, not the hands: Group urges phone ban for drivers. *The New York Times*, p. D5.

Parker-Pope, T. (2009b, January 20). Your nest is empty? Enjoy each other. *The New York Times*, p. D5.

Parker-Pope, T. (2014, August 26). Marital bliss, one decision after another. *The New York Times*, pp. D1, D4.

Parviz, E. (2019). How to survive a zombie apocalypse: Using Monroe's Motivated Sequence to persuade in a public-speaking classroom, *Communication Teacher, 34*(1), 40–46. https://doi.org/10.1080/17404622.2019.1608370

Pearce, W. B., Cronen, V. E., & Conklin, F. (1979). On what to look at when analyzing communication: A hierarchical model of actors' meanings. *Communication, 4*, 195–220.

Pedulla, D., & Thébaud, S. (2015). Can we finish the revolution? Gender, work-family ideals, and institutional constraint. *American Sociological Review, 80*, 116–139.

Pekkala, K., & van Zoonen, W. (2022). Work-related social media use: The mediating role of social media communication self-efficacy. *European Management Journal, 40*(1), 67–76. https://doi.org/10.1016/j.emj.2021.03.004

Perlow, L. (2013). *Sleeping with your smartphone*. Boston, MA: Harvard Business Review Press.

Perry, B. L., Stevens-Watkins, D., & Oser, C. B. (2013). The moderating effect of skin color and ethnic identity affirmation on suicide risk among low-SES African American Women. *Race and Social Problems, 5*(1), 1–14.

Petronio, S., & Caughlin, J. (2006). Communication privacy management theory: Understanding families. In D. O. Braithwaite & L. A. Baxter (Eds.), *Engaging theories in family communication: Multiple perspectives* (pp. 35–49). Thousand Oaks, CA: Sage.

Pew Research Center. (2013). *Growing support for gay marriage: Changed minds and changing demographics*. https://www.pewresearch.org/politics/2013/03/20/about-the-survey-211/

Phillips, K. A., Ospina, N. S., & Montori, V. M. (2019). Physicians interrupting patients. *Journal of General Internal Medicine, 34*(10), 1695. https://doi.org/10.1007/s11606-019-05247-5

Piaget, J. (1932/1965). *The moral judgment of the child.* New York: Free Press.

Picard, C. (2020, November 26). *What Margaret Thatcher's voice really sounded like.* Yahoo. https://www.yahoo.com/lifestyle/margaret-thatchers-voice-really-sounded-000000564.html

Poell, T., & van Dijck, J. (2015). Data and agency. *Big Data & Society.* https://doi.org/10.1177/2053951715621569

Pollock, S., Taylor, S., Oyerinde, O., Nurmohamed, S., Dlova, N., Sarkar, R., Galadari, H., et al. (2021). The dark side of skin lightening: An international collaboration and review of a public health issue affecting dermatology. *International Journal of Women's Dermatology, 7*(2), 158–164. https://doi.org/10.1016/j.ijwd.2020.09.006

Pomputius, A. (2019). Can you hear me now? Social listening as a strategy for understanding user needs. *Medical Reference Services Quarterly, 38*(2), 181–186.

Porath, C. (2015, June 21). No time to be nice. *The New York Times*, pp. SR 1, 6, 7.

Potter, J. (2009). *Media literacy* (4th ed.). Thousand Oaks, CA: Sage.

Prang, A. (2021, October 24). Gender-neutral toys for children gain ground. *The Wall Street Journal.*

Prevalence of Domestic Violence. (2013, August). *The advocates for human rights.* Retrieved from http://www.stopvaw.org/prevalence_of_domestic_violence

Pulido, L. (2021). Geographies of race and ethnicity III: Settler colonialism and nonnative people of color. In A. Y. Ramos-Zayas & M. M. Rúa (Eds.), *Critical dialogues in Latinx studies: A reader* (pp. 51–63). New York University Press.

Qin, Y. S., & Linjuan, R. M. (2021) Why does listening matter inside the organization? The impact of internal listening on employee-organization relationships. *Journal of Public Relations Research, 33*(5), 365–386. https://doi.org/10.1080/1062726X.2022.2034631

Quenqua, D. (2014, August 3). Tell me, even if it hurts me. *The New York Times*, pp. SR 1, 8–9.

Ratanawongsa, N., Hailu, B., & Schillinger, D. (2021). Health communication as a mediator of health care disparities. In I. Dankwa-Mullan, E. Pérez-Stable, K. L. Gardner, X. Zhang, & A. M. Rosario (Eds.), *The science of health disparities research.* Wiley. https://doi.org/10.1002/9781119374855.ch20

Rawlins, W. K. (1981). *Friendship as a communicative achievement: A theory and an interpretive analysis of verbal reports* [Unpublished doctoral dissertation]. Temple University, Philadelphia, PA.

Rawlins, W. K. (1994). Being there and growing apart: Sustaining friendships during adulthood. In D. Canary & L. Stafford (Eds.), *Communication and relational maintenance* (pp. 275–294). New York: Academic Press.

Read, D. L., Clark, G. I., Rock, A. J., & Coventry, W. L. (2018). Adult attachment and social anxiety: The mediating role of emotion regulation strategies. *PLoS One, 13*(12), e0207514. https://doi.org/10.1371/journal.pone.0207514

Ream, Diane Show. (2012, June 25). *Aired on NPR 10–11 a.m.* EDS.

Reilly, C. (2020). Change in the blink of a queer eye: Exploring recent shifts in LGBTQ+ representation, agency, and intersectionality in pop culture. In S. L. Raye, S. Masta, S. T. Cook, & J. Burdick (Eds.), *Ideating pedagogy in troubled times: Approaches to identity, theory, teaching, and research* (pp. 213–231). Information Age Publishing.

Reinhard, C. D., & Dervin, B. J. (2009). Media uses and gratifications. In W. F. Eadie (Ed.), *21st century communication: A reference handbook* (pp. 506–515). Thousand Oaks, CA: Sage.

Rhodewalt, F. (Ed.). (2007). *Personality and social behavior.* Florence, KY: Psychology Press.

Rice, A. (2011, November 25). Bleary-eyed students can't stop texting, even to sleep, a researcher finds. *Chronicle of Higher Education*, p. A13.

Richmond, V. P., & McCroskey, J. C. (1992). *Communication: Apprehension, avoidance, and effectiveness* (3rd ed.). Scottsdale, AZ: Gorsuch Scarisbrick.

Richmond, V. P., & McCroskey, J. C. (1995a). *Communication: Apprehension, avoidance, and effectiveness.* Scottsdale, AZ: Gorsuch Scarisbrick.

Richmond, V. P., & McCroskey, J. C. (1995b). *Nonverbal communication in interpersonal relations* (3rd ed.). Boston, MA: Allyn & Bacon.

Richtel, M. (2011, December 15). As doctors use more devices, potential for distraction grows. *The New York Times*, pp. A1, A4.

Richtel, M. (2015). *A deadly wandering.* New York: William Morrow/HarperCollins.

Richter, F. (2021, September 1). Zoom retains pandemic gains as hybrid work is here to stay. *Statista.*

Ridley-Merriweather, K. E., Hoffmann-Longtin, K., & Owusu, R. K. (2021). Exploring how the terms "Black" and "African American" may shape health communication research. *Health Communication*, 1–7. https://doi.org/10.1080/10410236.2021.1993533

Risman, B. J. (2018). Gender as a social structure. In B. J. Risman, C. M. Froyum, & W. J. Scarboroudh (Eds.), *Handbook of the Sociology of Gender* (pp. 19–43). Springer.

Roberts, A. L., Rosario, M., Slopen, N., Calzo, J. P., & Austin, S. B. (2013). Childhood gender nonconformity, bullying victimization, and depressive symptoms across adolescence and early adulthood: An 11-year longitudinal study. *Journal of the American Academy of Child and Adolescent Psychiatry, 52*(2), 143–152. https://doi.org/10.1016/j.jaac.2012.11.006

Robinson, G. (2001, March 4). Sometimes a thank you is enough. *The New York Times*, pp. 16, 18.

Robinson, J. D. (2009). Media portrayals and representations. In W. F. Eadie (Ed.), *21st century communication: A reference handbook* (pp. 497–505). Thousand Oaks, CA: Sage.

Robinson, S., Anderson, E., & White A. (2018). The bromance: Undergraduate male friendships and the expansion of contemporary homosocial boundaries. *Sex Roles, 78*, 94–106. https://doi.org/10.1007/s11199-017-0768-5

Rodziewicz, T. L., Houseman, B., & Hipskind, J. E. (2022, January 4). *Medical error reduction and prevention*. National Library of Medicine. https://pubmed.ncbi.nlm.nih.gov/29763131/

Roncallo-Dow, S., & Arango-Forero, G. (2017). Apresentação das três dimensões da fragmentação da audiência. *Signo y Pensamiento, 36*(70). https://doi.org/10.11144/Javeriana.syp36-70.idaf

Ross, K. (2013). *Gendered media: Women, men, and identity politics*. Lanham, MD: Rowman & Littlefield.

Rothblum, E. D., Balsam, K. F., & Wickham, R. E. (2018). Butch, femme, and androgynous gender identities within female same-sex couples: An actor-partner analysis. *Psychology of Sexual Orientation and Gender Diversity, 5*(1), 72–81. https://doi.org/10.1037/sgd0000258

Rothenberg, P. (2006). *Race, class, and gender in the United States* (7th ed.). New York: Worth.

Rothstein, R. (2017). *The color of law: A forgotten history of how our government segregated America*. Liveright.

Rothwell, J. D. (2015). *In mixed company: Small group communication* (9th ed.). Belmont, CA: Wadsworth.

Rostosky, S. S., & Riggle, E. D. B. (2019). What makes same-sex relationships endure? In A. E. Goldbert & A. P. Romero (Eds.), *LGBTQ divorce and relationship dissolution: Psychological and legal perspectives and implications for practice* (pp. 49–69). Oxford University Press.

Rowe, A. C., & Carnelley, K. B. (2005). Preliminary support for the use of a hierarchical mapping technique to examine attachment networks. *Personal Relationships, 12*, 499–519.

Rowe-Finkbeiner, K. (2014, April 30). The motherhood penalty. *Politico Magazine*. http://www.politico.com/magazine/story/2014/04/the-motherhood-penalty-106173.html#.U6aurdJOXq4

Rudman, L. A., & Glick, P. (2010). *The social psychology of gender*. New York: Guilford Press.

Rudman, L. A., & Glick, P. (2021). *The social psychology of gender: How power and intimacy shape gender relations*. Guilford Press.

Rusli, E. (2013, June 12). When words just aren't enough some turn to flatulent bunnies. *The Wall Street Journal*, pp. A1, A14.

Salas, E., & Frush, K. (2012). *Improving patient safety through teamwork and team training*. New York: Oxford University Press.

Salerno, S. (2005). *Sham: How the self-help movement made America helpless*. New York: Three Rivers Press.

Samovar, L. A., Porter, R. E., & McDaniel, E. R. (2012). *Intercultural Communication: A reader*. Wadsworth Cengage Learning.

Samovar, L., Porter, R., McDaniel, E. R., & Roy, C. (Eds.). (2015). *Intercultural communication: A reader* (14th ed.). Belmont, CA: Wadsworth.

Samovar, L., Porter, R., McDaniel, E., & Roy, C. (2017). *Communication between cultures* (9th ed.). Boston, MA: Cengage.

Samp, J. A., & Palevitz, C. E. (2009). Dating and romantic partners. In W. F. Eadie (Ed.), *21st century communication: A reference handbook* (pp. 322–330). Thousand Oaks, CA: Sage.

Sawyer, K. (2008). *Group genius: The power of creative collaboration*. New York: Basic.

Schiavo, R. (2007). *Health communication: From theory to practice*. San Francisco, CA: Jossey-Bass.

Schmidt, J., & Uecker, D. (2007). Increasing understanding of routine/everyday interaction in relationships. *Communication Teacher, 21*, 111–116.

Scholz, M. (2005, June). A "simple" way to improve adherence. *RN, 68*, 82.

Schram, P., & Schwartz, H. (2000). *Stories within stories: From the Jewish oral tradition*. Leonia, NJ: Jason Aronson.

Schramm, W. (1955). *The process and effects of mass communication*. Urbana, IL: University of Illinois Press.

Schumpeter. (2011, December 31). *Economist*, p. 50.

Schüutz, A. (1999). It was your fault! Self-serving biases in autobiographical accounts of married couples. *Journal of Social and Personal Relationships, 16*(2), 193–208. https://doi.org/10.1177/0265407599162004

Schwab, H. (2014, October 9). 'Nude' improved. *Raleigh News & Observer*, pp. D1, 2.

Scoats, R., & Robinson, S. (2019). From stoicism to bromance: Millennial men's friendships. In R. Magrath, J. Cleland, & E. Anderson (Eds.), *The Palgrave handbook of masculinity and sport* (pp. 379–392). https://doi.org/10.1007/978-3-030-19799-5_21

Scott, J., & Leonhardt, D. (2013). Shadowy lines that still divide. In M. Andersen & P. H. Collins (Eds.), *Race, class, and gender: An anthology* (8th ed., pp. 117–124). Boston, MA: Cengage.

Segrin, C., Hanzal, A., & Domschke, T. (2009). Accuracy and bias in newlywed couples' perceptions of conflict styles and the association with marital satisfaction. *Communication Monographs, 76*, 207–233.

Seligman, M. E. P. (2002). *Authentic happiness*. New York: Free Press.

Seligman, M. E. P. (2012). *Flourish: A visionary new understanding of happiness and well-being. Authentic happiness*. Simon & Schuster.

Servaty-Seib, H., & Burleson, B. (2007). Bereaved adolescents' evaluations of the helpfulness of support-intended statements: Associations with person centeredness and demographic, personality, and contextual factors. *Journal of Social and Personal Relationships, 24*, 207–223.

Shah, Z., Chu, J., Ghani, U., Qaisar, S., & Hassan, Z. (2020). Media and altruistic behaviors: The mediating role of fear of victimization in cultivation theory perspective. *International Journal of Disaster Risk Reduction*. https://doi.org/10.1016/j.ijdrr.2019.101336

Shanahan, J., & Jones, V. (1999). Cultivation and social control. In D. Demers & K. Viswanath (Eds.), *Mass media, social control, and social change* (pp. 89–116). Ames, IA: Iowa State University Press.

Shannon, C., & Weaver, W. (1949). *The mathematical theory of communication*. Urbana, IL: University of Illinois Press.

Shattuck, T. R. (1980). *The forbidden experiment: The story of the wild boy of Aveyron*. New York: Farrar, Straus & Giroux.

Sheldon, P., Antony, M. G., & Ware, L. J. (2021). Baby Boomers' use of Facebook and Instagram: Uses and gratifications theory and contextual age indicators. *Heliyon, 7*(4). https://doi.org/10.1016/j.heliyon.2021.e06670

Shellenbarger, S. (2013, September 11). The biggest distraction in the office is sitting next to you. *The Wall Street Journal*, pp. D1, D3.

Sherrer, K. (2018, February 26). What is tokenism, and why does it matter in the workplace? *Vanderbilt Owen Graduate School of Management*. https://business.vanderbilt.edu/news/2018/02/26/tokenism-in-the-workplace/

Shifman, P., & Tillet, S. (2015, February 3). To stop violence, start at home. *The New York Times*, p. A21.

Shimanoff, S. B. (1980). *Communication rules: Theory and research*. Beverly Hills, CA: Sage.

Sias, P., Heath, R., Perry, T., Silva, D., & Fix, B. (2004). Narratives of workplace friendship deterioration. *Journal of Social and Personal Relationships, 21*, 321–340.

Siebold, D., Hollingshead, A., & Yoon, K. (2013). Embedded teams and embedding organizations. In L. Putnam & D. Mumby (Eds.), *The SAGE handbook of organizational communication: Advances in theory, research and methods* (pp. 327–350). Thousand Oaks, CA: Sage.

Sim, M. A., Ti, L. K., Mujumdar, S., Chew, S. T. H., Penanueva, D. J. B., Kumar, B. M., & Ang, S. B. L. (2022). Sustaining the gains: A 7-year follow-through of a hospital-wide patient safety improvement project on hospital-wide adverse event outcomes and patient safety culture. *Journal of Patient Safety, 18*(1), e189–e195. https://doi.org/10.1097/PTS.0000000000000725

Sim, M. A., Ti, L. K., Mujumdar, S., Skipper, A. Marks, L. D., Moore, T, J., & Dollahite, D. C. (2021). Black marriages matter: Wisdom and advice from happily married Black couples. *Family Relations, 70*(5), 1369–1383. https://doi.org/10.1111/fare.12565

Smith, K. E., & Johnson, W. (2020, May 4). Gender equity starts in the home. *Harvard Business Review*.

Smith, K. E., & Pollak, S. D. (2021). *Early life stress and perceived social isolation influence how children use value information to guide behavior*. Society for Research in Child Development. https://doi.org/10.1111/cdev.13727

Smith, R. (1998, December 1). *Civility without censorship: The ethics of the Internet cyberhate*. Speech delivered at the Simon Wiesenthal Center/Museum of Tolerance, Los Angeles, CA.

Smith, S., Choueiti, M., & Pieper, K. (2013). *Race/ethnicity in 500 popular films: Is the key to diversifying cinematic content held in the hand of the black director?* Retrieved from http://annenberg.usc.edu/sitecore/shell/Applications/~/media/PDFs/RaceEthnicity.ashx

Snyder, V. (2020, August 10). *What marketers need to know about people's social media patterns during the pandemic*. Busines.com.

Solnit, R. (2008/2012). Men explain things to me [updated with 2012 introduction]. *Guernica*. https://www.guernicamag.com/rebecca-solnit-men-explain-things-to-me/

Sonnad, N. (2014). *These are Americans' favorite insults, by political affiliation*. Quartz.

Spaeth, M. (1996, July 1). "Prop" up your speaking skills. *The Wall Street Journal*, p. A15.

Spar, D. (2013). *Wonder women: Sex, power and the quest for perfection*. New York: Sarah Crichton Books.

Spitzberg, B., & Cupach, W. (2014). *The dark side of relational pursuit* (2nd ed.). New York: Routledge.

Stafford, L. (2009). Spouses and other intimate partnerships. In W. F. Eadie (Ed.), *21st century communication: A reference handbook* (pp. 296–302). Thousand Oaks, CA: Sage.

Stapel, D. A., & Blanton, H. (Eds.). (2006). *Social comparison theories: Key readings*. Florence, KY: Psychology Press.

Stewart, M. C., & Arnold, C. L. (2017). Defining social listening: Recognizing an emerging dimension of listening. *International Journal of Listening, 32*(2), 85–100.

Stobbe, M. (2012, March 22). Move-in before marriage no longer predicts divorce. *Raleigh News & Observer*, p. 4A.

Stolberg, S. (2009, January 29). From the top, the White House unbuttons formal dress code. *The New York Times*, pp. A1, A14.

Stornaiuolo, A. Smith, & J. Z. Paynda (Eds.), *Handbook of writing, literacies, and education in digital cultures* (Chapter 14). Routledge.

Styer, J. (2012). *Talking back to Facebook*. New York: Scribner.

Sui, M., & Paul, N. (2016). Latino portrayals in local news media: Underrepresentation, negative stereotypes, and institutional predictors of coverage. *Journal of Intercultural Communication Research, 46*(3), 273–294. https://doi.org/10.1080/17475759.2017.1322124

Sun, Y., Lee, D. K., Xiao, X., Li, W., & Shu, W. (2021). Who endorses conspiracy theories? A moderated mediation model of Chinese and international social media use, media skepticism, need for cognition, and COVID-19 conspiracy theory endorsement in China. *Computers in Human Behavior, 120*. https://doi.org/10.1016/j.chb.2021.106760

Sutherland, C. J., Ahn, B. K., Brown, B., Lim, J., Johanson, D. L., Broadbent, E., MacDonald, B. A., et al. (2019). The doctor will see you now: Could a robot be a medical receptionist? *2019 International Conference on Robotics and Automation (ICRA)* (pp. 4310–4316). https://doi.org/10.1109/ICRA.2019.8794439

Swidler, A. (2001). *Talk of love: How culture matters*. Chicago, IL: University of Chicago Press.

Swire-Thompson, B., Miklaucic, N., Wihbey, J. P., Lazer, D., & DeGutis, J. (2022). The backfire effect after correcting misinformation is strongly associated with reliability. *Journal of Experimental Psychology: General, 151*(7), 1655–1665. https://doi.org/10.1037/xge0001131

Sypher, B., Bostrom, R., & Siebert, J. (1989). Listening, communication abilities, and success at work. *Journal of Business Communication, 26*, 293–303.

Tabuchi, H. (2012, May 30). Educated, but not fitting in. *The New York Times*, pp. B1, B2.

Taimi. (2022, February 16). 15 lesbian flirting tips that can turn you into a pro. *Taimi Blog*. https://taimi.com/blog/15-lesbian-flirting-tips-that-turn-you-into-a-pro

Tamilselvi, N., & Saranya, B. (2022). An experimental study on the role of social media on female body image among college students. *湖南大学学报(自然科学版)|Journal of Hunan University (Natural Sciences), 49*(1).

Tashiro, T., & Frazier, P. (2003). "I'll never be in a relationship like that again": Personal growth following romantic relationship breakups. *Personal Relationships, 10*, 113–128.

Tatum, N. T., Martin, J. C., & Kemper, B. (2017). Chronemics in instructor–student e-mail communication: An experimental examination of student evaluations of instructor response speeds. *Communication Research Reports, 35*(1), 33–41. https://doi.org/10.1080/08824096.2017.1361396

Tavernise, S., & Gebeloff, R. (2021, August 12). Census shows sharply growing numbers of Hispanic, Asian and multiracial Americans. *The New York Times*. https://www.nytimes.com/2021/08/12/us/us-census-population-growth-diversity.html

Tavris, C., & Aronson, E. (2007). *Mistakes were made (but not by me): Why we justify foolish beliefs, bad decisions, and hurtful acts*. New York: Harcourt.

The Geena Davis Institute on Gender in Media, & Movio. (2020). *I want to see me: Why diverse on-screen representation drives cinema audiences*. https://movio.co/i-want-to-see-me/

The Learning Network. (2022, January 13). What's going on in this graph? U.S. population diversity shift. *The New York Times*. https://www.nytimes.com/2022/01/13/learning/whats-going-on-in-this-graph-jan-19-2022.html

Think Tank for Inclusion & Equity. (2021). *Behind the scenes: The state of inclusion and equity in TV writing*. https://seejane.org/wp-content/uploads/ttie-behind-the-scenes-2021-report.pdf

Thomas, R. J. (2019). Sources of friendship and structurally induced homophily across the life course. *Sociological Perspectives, 62*(6), 822–843. https://doi.org/10.1177/0731121419828399

Thompson, F., & Grundgenett, D. (1999). Helping disadvantaged learners build effective learning skills. *Education, 120*, 130–135.

Thrun, S. (2011, December 6). Leave the driving to the car, and reap benefits in safety and mobility. *The New York Times*, p. D4.

Thurnell-Read, T. (2021). 'If they weren't in the pub, they probably wouldn't even know each other': Alcohol, sociability and pub based leisure. *International Journal of the Sociology of Leisure, 4*, 61–78. https://doi.org/10.1007/s41978-020-00068-x

Tierney, J. (2013, March 19). Good news beats bad on social networks. *The New York Times*, p. D3.

Tierney, J. (2015, June 30). Love at gradually evolving sight. *The New York Times*, p. D6.

Tifferet, S. (2020). Gender differences in social support on social network sites: A meta-analysis. *Cyberpsychology, behavior, and social networking, 23*(4), 199–209. https://doi.org/10.1089/cyber.2019.0516

Tilsley, A. (2010, July 2). New policies accommodate transgender students. *Chronicle of Higher Education*, pp. A19–A20.

Ting-Toomey, S., & Dorjee, T. (2019). *Communicating across cultures*. The Guilford Press.

Todd, N. R., Yi, J., Blevins, E. J., McConnell, E. A., Mekawi, Y., & Bergmann, B. A. B. (2020). Christian and political conservatism predict opposition to sexual and gender minority rights through support for Christian hegemony. *American Journal of Community Psychology, 66*(1–2), 24–38. https://doi.org/10.1002/ajcp.12420

Toegel, G., & Barsoux, J.-L. (2016, June 8). 3 situations where cross-cultural communication breaks down. *Harvard Business Review*.

Toulmin, S. (1958). *The uses of argument*. Cambridge, MA: Cambridge University Press.

Toulmin, S., Rieke, R., & Janik, A. (1984). *An introduction to reasoning* (2nd ed.). New York: Macmillan.

Trenholm, S. (1991). *Human communication theory* (2nd ed.). Englewood Cliffs, NJ: Prentice Hall.

Trice, H., & Beyer, J. (1984). Studying organizational cultures through rites and ceremonials. *Academy of Management Review, 9*, 653–669.

Tropp, L. R., & Wright, S. C. (2003). Evaluations and perceptions of self, in-group, and out-group: Comparisons between Mexican-American and European-American children. *Self and Identity, 2*, 203–221.

Tsai, F., & Reis, H. (2009). Perceptions by and of lonely people in social networks. *Personal Relationships, 16*, 221–238.

Tsao, S., Chen, H., Tisseverasinghe, T., Yang, Y., Li, L., & Butt, Z. A. (2021). What social media told us in the time of COVID-19: A scoping review. *The Lancet Digital Health, 3*(3), E175–E194. https://doi.org/10.1016/S2589-7500(20)30315-0

Tugend, A. (2011, July 2). Comparing yourself to others: It's not all bad. *The New York Times*, p. B6.

Turkle, S. (2011). *Alone together: Why we expect more of technology and less of each other*. New York: Basic.

Tusing, K., & Dillard, J. (2000). The sounds of dominance: Vocal precursors of perceived dominance during interpersonal influence. *Human Communication Research, 26*, 148–171.

United States Census Bureau. (2019). *Quick facts: United States*. https://www.census.gov/quickfacts/fact/table/US/LFE046219

U.N. Women. (2022, February). *Facts and figures: Ending violence against women*. https://www.unwomen.org/en/what-we-do/ending-violence-against-women/facts-and-figures

Van Borsel, J., Cayzeele, M., Heirman, E., & T'sojen, G. (2014). Conversational topics in transsexual persons. *Clinical Linguistics & Phonetics, 28*(6). https://doi.org/10.3109/02699206.2013.875594

Vaterlaus, J. M., & Winter, M. (2021). TikTok: An exploratory study of young adults' uses and gratifications. *The Social Science Journal*. https://doi.org/10.1080/03623319.2021.1969882

Verkuyten, M., Yogeeswaaran, K., & Adelman, L. (2020). The negative implications of being tolerated: Tolerance from the target's perspective. *Perspectives on Psychological Science, 15*(3), 544–561. https://doi.org/10.1177/1745691619897974

Vertesi, J. (2014). My experiment opting out of big data made me look like a criminal. *Time*. https://time.com/83200/privacy-internet-big-data-opt-out/

Vinton, K. (2016). These 15 billionaires own America's news companies. *Forbes*. https://www.forbes.com/sites/katevinton/2016/06/01/these-15-billionaires-own-americas-news-media-companies

Virtual Team Challenges. (n.d.). Retrieved from http://onlinemba.unc.edu/research-and-insights/developing-real-skills-for-virtual-teams/virtual-team-challenges

Visserman, M. L., Righetti, F., Impett, E. A., Keltner, D., & Van Lange, P. A. (2018). It's the motive that counts: Perceived sacrifice motives and gratitude in romantic relationships. *Emotion, 18*(5), 625.

Vitriol, J. A., Appleby, J., & Borgida, E. (2018). Racial bias increases false identification of Black suspects in simultaneous lineups. *Social Psychological and Personality Science, 10*(6), 722–734. https://doi.org/10.1177/1948550618784889

Voges, M. M., Giabbiconi, C-M., Schöne, B., Waldorf, M., Hartmann, A., & Vocks. S. (2019). Gender differences in body evaluation: Do many show more self-serving double standards than women? *Frontiers in Psychology, 12*. https://doi.org/10.3389/fpsyg.2019.00544

Vogels, E. A. (2021, January 13). *The state of online harassment*. Pew Research Center. https://www.pewresearch.org/internet/2021/01/13/the-state-of-online-harassment/

Vos, T. P., & Russell, F. (2018). "Jonahalism": Theorizing journalism's institutional relationships. Presented at the International Association for Media and Communication Research (IAMCR) conference, *Journalism Research and Education Division*, Eugene, Oregon, June 23.

Voytko, L. (2021, October 5). Women make up just 14% of The Forbes 400. But these 56 moguls are worth a collective $564 billion. *Forbes*. https://www.forbes.com/sites/lisettevoytko/2021/10/05/the-richest-women-in-america-2021-forbes-400/?sh=3352c6281b23

Vranjes, J., Brone, G., & Feyaerts, K. (2018). Dual feedback in interpreter-mediated interactions: On the role of gaze in the production of listener responses. *Journal of Pragmantics, 134*, 15–30. https://doi.org/10.1016/j.pragma.2018.06.002

Waldron, J. (2018). Online music communities and social media. In B. Bartleet & L. Higgins (Eds.), *The Oxford handbook of community music* (pp. 109–130). Oxford UP.

Walker, S. (2007). *Style and status: Selling beauty to African American women*. Lexington, KY: University of Kentucky Press.

Wallace, J. (2018). Modelling contemporary gatekeeping: The rise of individuals, algorithms and platforms in digital news dissemination. *Digital Journalism, 6*(3). https://doi.org/10.1080/21670811.2017.1343648

Wall Street Journal. (2016). *Blue feed, red feed: See liberal Facebook and conservative Facebook, side by side*. https://graphics.wsj.com/blue-feed-red-feed/

Warach, B., Josephs, L., & Gorman, S. (2019). Are cheaters sexual hypocrites? Sexual hypocrisy, the self-serving bias, and personality style. *Personality and Social Psychology Bulletin, 45*(4). https://doi.org/10.1177/0146167219833392

Warshaw, R. (1988). *I never called it rape: The "Ms." report on recognizing, fighting, and surviving date and acquaintance rape*. Harper & Row Publishers.

Watson, A. (2020, November 10). Film industry – Statistics and facts. *Statista*. https://www.statista.com/topics/964/film/

Watters, E. (2013, March/April). We aren't the world. *Pacific Standard*, pp. 46–53.

Watzlawick, P., Beavin, J., & Jackson, D. D. (1967). *Pragmatics of human communication*. New York: W. W. Norton.

Wazir, Z. (2021, June 28). *Gender gap in child care increases during pandemic*. U.S. News. https://www.usnews.com/news/best-countries/articles/2021-06-28/women-men-provided-unequal-child-care-during-pandemic

Weaver, A. J. (2011). The role of actors' race in white audiences' selective exposure to movies. *Journal of Communication, 61*(2), 369–385. https://doi.org/10.1111/j.1460-2466.2011.01544.x

Weber, L. (2013, June 13). Why dads don't take paternity leave. *The Wall Street Journal*, pp. B1, B7.

Webster, J. G., & Ksiazek, T. B. (2012). The dynamics of audience fragmentation: Public attention in an age of digital media. *Journal of Communication, 62*(1), 39–56. https://doi.org/10.1111/j.1460-2466.2011.01616.x

Weger, H., Bell, G. C., Minei, E., & Robinson, M. (2014). The relative effectiveness of active listening in initial interactions. *International Journal of Listening, 28*, 13–31.

Wegner, H., Jr. (2005). Disconfirming communication and self-verification in marriage: Associations among the demand/withdraw interaction pattern, feeling understood, and marital satisfaction. *Journal of Social and Personal Relationships, 22*, 19–31.

Weimann, G. (2000). *Communicating unreality: Modern media and the reconstruction of reality*. Newbury Park, CA: Sage.

Weiss, C. (2018). When gaze-selected next speakers do not take the turn. *Journal of Pragmatics, 133*, 28–44. https://doi.org/10.1016/j.pragma.2018.05.016

Welbers, K., & Opgenhaffen, M. (2018). Social media gatekeeping: An analysis of the gatekeeping influence of newspapers' public Facebook pages. *New Media and Society, 20*(12), 4728–4747. https://doi.org/10.1177/1461444818784302

Wen, L., & Kosowsky, J. (2013). *When doctors don't listen*. New York: St. Martin's/Thomas Dunne.

Wernholm, M. (2019). Children's shared experiences of participating in digital communities. *Nordic Journal of Digital Literacy, 13*(4), 38–55.

West, C., & Zimmerman, D. H. (1987). Doing gender. *Gender and Society, 1*, 125–151.

Whitman, T., White, R., O'Mara, K., & Goeke-Morey, M. (1999). Environmental aspects of infant health and illness. In T. Whitman & T. Merluzzi (Eds.), *Lifespan perspectives on health and illness* (pp. 105–124). Mahwah, NJ: Erlbaum.

Whorf, B. (1956). *Language, thought, and reality*. New York: MIT Press/Wiley.

Williams, G. (1995). *Life on the color line: The true story of a white boy who discovered he was black*. New York: Plume.

Williams, J. (2013, June 6). Pay gap deniers. *Huffington Post*. Retrieved from http://www.huffingtonpost.com/joan-williams/pay-gap-deniers_b_3391524.html

Williams, R. (1994). *The non-designer's design book: Design and typographic principles for the visual novice*. Berkeley, CA: Peachpit Press.

Wilson, J. F., & Arnold, C. C. (1974). *Public speaking as a liberal art* (4th ed.). Boston, MA: Allyn & Bacon.

Winans, J. A. (1938). *Speechmaking*. New York: Appleton-Century-Crofts.

Wines, M. (2011, November 12). Picking the pitch-perfect brand name in China. *The New York Times*, p. A4.

Wolvin, A. (2009). Listening, understanding and misunderstanding. In W. F. Eadie (Ed.), *21st century communication: A reference handbook* (pp. 137–146). Thousand Oaks, CA: Sage.

Wong, J. Y., Choi, A. W.-M., Fong, D. Y-T., Choi, E. P. H., Wong, J. K.-S., So, F. L., Lau, C.-L., et al. A comparison of intimate partner violence and associated physical injuries between cohabitating and married women: A 5-year medical chart review. *BMC Public Health, 16*, 1207.

Wood, J. T. (1982). Communication and relational culture: Bases for the study of human relationships. *Communication Quarterly, 30*, 75–84.

Wood, J. T. (1992). Telling our stories: Narratives as a basis for theorizing sexual harassment. *Journal of Applied Communication Research, 4*, 349–363.

Wood, J. T. (1994a). Engendered identities: Shaping voice and mind through gender. In D. Vocate (Ed.), *Intrapersonal communication: Different voices, different minds* (pp. 145–167). Hillsdale, NJ: Erlbaum.

Wood, J. T. (1994c). *Who cares? Women, care, and culture*. Carbondale, IL: Southern Illinois University Press.

Wood, J. T. (2005). Feminist standpoint theory and muted group theory: Commonalities and divergences. *Women & Language, 28*, 61–64.

Wood, J. T. (2006a). Chopping the carrots: Creating intimacy moment by moment. In J. T. Wood & S. W. Duck (Eds.), *Composing relationships: Communication in everyday life* (pp. 15–23). Belmont, CA: Thomson Wadsworth.

Wood, J. T. (2007a). *Gendered lives* (7th ed.). Belmont, CA: Wadsworth.

Wood, J. T. (2010a). *Interpersonal communication: Everyday encounters*. Boston, MA: Wadsworth-Cengage Learning.

Wood, J. T. (2010b). The can-do discourse and young women's anticipations of future. *Women & Language, 33*, 103–107.

Wood, J. T. (2011). Which ruler do we use? Theorizing the division of domestic labor. *Family Communication Journal, 11*, 39–49.

Wood, J. T., Dendy, L., Dordek, E., Germany, M., & Varallo, S. (1994). Dialectic of difference: A thematic analysis of intimates' meanings for differences. In K. Carter & M. Presnell (Eds.), *Interpretive approaches to interpersonal communication* (pp. 115–136). New York: State University of New York Press.

Wood, J. T., & Dow, B. (2010). The invisible politics of "choice" in the workplace. In S. Hayden & L. Hallstein (Eds.), *Contemplating maternity in an era of choice* (pp. 203–225). New York: Lexington.

Wood, J. T., & Duck, S. (2006). Introduction. In J. T. Wood & S. Ducks (Eds.), *Composing relationships: Communication in everyday life* (pp. 1–13). Belmont, CA: Thomson Wadsworth.

Wood, J. T., & Fixmer-Oraiz, N. (2017). *Gendered lives* (12th ed.). Boston, MA: Cengage.

Woolfolk, A. E. (1987). *Educational psychology*. Englewood Cliffs, NJ: Prentice Hall.

Woolley, A. W., Chabris, C. F., Pentland, A., Hashmi, N., & Malone, T. W. (2010). Evidence for a collective intelligence factor in the performance of human groups. *Science*. https://doi.org/10.1126/science.1193147

Workplace Fairness. (2022). *Surveillance at work*. Workplace Fairness. https://www.workplacefairness.org/workplace-surveillance#:~:text=Employers%20can%20legally%20monitor%20almost,use%20GPS%20tracking%2C%20and%20more

World Health Organization. (2017). *How to respond to vocal vaccine deniers in public*. https://www.euro.who.int/__data/assets/pdf_file/0005/315761/Vocal-vaccine-deniers-guidance-document.pdf

World Population Review. (2022). *Domestic violence by state 2022*. https://worldpopulationreview.com/state-rankings/domestic-violence-by-state

Wu, C., & Shaffer, D. R. (1988). Susceptibility to persuasive appeals as a function of source credibility and prior experience with attitude object. *Journal of Personal and Social Psychology, 52*, 677–688.

Yang, J., & Tian, Y. (2021). "Others are more vulnerable to fake news than I am": Third-person effect of COVID-19 fake news on social media users. *Computers in Human Behavior, 125*. https://doi.org/10.1016/j.chb.2021.106950

Yang, S., Huang, L., Zhang, Y., Zhang, P., & Zhao, Y. C. (2021). Unraveling the links between active and passive social media usage and seniors' loneliness: A field study in aging care communities. *Internet Research*. https://doi.org/10.1108/INTR-08-2020-0435

Yeager, M. (June, 2015). How to use public speaking skills at work. *U.S. News & World Report*. Retrieved from http://money.usnews.com/money/blogs/outside-voices-careers/2015/06/25/how-to-use-public-speaking-skills-at-work

Yen, H. (2012, May 17). Minority birthrate now surpasses whites in US, Census shows. *Huffington Post*. Retrieved from http://www.huffingtonpost.com/2012/05/17/minorities-birth-rate-now-surpass-whites-in-us-census_n_1523230.html

Yoshimura, C. G., & Galvin, K. (2017). General systems theory: A compelling view of family life. In D. O. Braithwaite & L. A. Baxter (Eds.), *Engaging theories in family communication: Multiple perspectives* (pp. 164–174). Thousand Oaks, CA: Sage.

Young, S., Wood, J., Phillips, G., & Pedersen, D. (2001). *Group discussion* (3rd ed.). Prospect Heights, IL: Waveland.

Ytre-Arne, B., & Das, R. (2020). Audiences' communicative agency in a datafied age: Interpretative, relational and increasingly prospective. *Communication Theory, 31*, 1–19. https://doi.org/10.1093/ct/qtaa018

Yu, C.-E., & Ngan, H. F. B. (2019). The power of head tilts: Gender and cultural differences of perceived human vs human-like robot smile in service. *Tourism Review*, 74(3), 428–442. https://doi.org/10.1108/TR-07-2018-0097

Zaidman, N. (2020). The incorporation of self-spirituality into Western organizations: A gender-based critique. *Organization, 27*(6). https://doi.org/10.1177/1350508419876068

Zarocostas, J. (2014, May 14). U.S. alone in not paying maternity leave. *Raleigh News & Observer*, p. 3A.

Zavaletta, V., Allen, B. J., & Parikh, A. K. (2022). Re-defining gender diversity through an equitable and inclusive lens. *Pediatric Radiology*, 52(9), 1743–1748. https://doi.org/10.1007/s00247-022-05332-8

Zhang, J., Zhang, M., Liu, Y., Lyu, R., & Cui, R. (2021). Research on the integration of media literacy innovative concept and entrepreneurship education and digital dynamic creative expression talents. *Frontiers in Psychology*. https://doi.org/10.1002/jocb.432

Zhang, Q. (2010). Asian Americans beyond the model minority stereotype: The nerdy and the left out. *Journal of International and Intercultural Communication, 3*, 20–37.

Zhu, M., & Wang, H. (2018). A literature review of social loafing and teams with group development. *SSRN*. http://dx.doi.org/10.2139/ssrn.3176383

Zuckerberg, R. (2013). *Dot complicated*. New York: HarperCollins.

Zuckerman, A. (2020). *38 tattoo statistics: 2020/2021 industry, trends & demographics*. CompareCamp. https://comparecamp.com/tattoo-statistics/

Index

Note: Page numbers followed by *f* indicate figures or photos and those followed by *t* indicate tables.

D

M

N

Q

R

V

W

Y

Z